DIPLOMACY IN THE MIDDLE EAST

DIPLOMACY IN THE MIDDLE EAST

The International Relations of
Regional and Outside Powers

Edited by

L. Carl Brown

I.B. TAURIS

LONDON · NEW YORK

Reprinted in 2006 by I.B.Tauris & Co Ltd
New edition published in 2004
6 Salem Road, London W2 4BU
175 Fifth Avenue, New York NY 10010
www.ibtauris.com

In the United States of America and Canada distributed by Palgrave Macmillan, a division of St Martin's Press
175 Fifth Avenue, New York NY 10010

First published in 2001 by I.B.Tauris & Co Ltd

ISBN 1 86064 899 1
EAN 978 1 86064 899 1

A full CIP record for this book is available from the British Library
A full CIP record is available from the Library of Congress

Library of Congress Catalog Card Number: available

Updated in 2003 by Avon DataSet Ltd, Bidford on Avon, Warwickshire B50 4JH
Typeset in Baskerville 10/12pt by The Midlands Book Typesetting Co, Loughborough

Printed and bound in India by Replika Press Pvt. Ltd.

Contents

Preface to the Paperback Edition

Soon after the publication of *Diplomacy in the Middle East* in 2001 an event occurred destined henceforth to be recognizable in numerical shorthand – 9/11. On September 11, 2001 Islamists belonging to a transnational terrorist organization, al-Qa'ida (the Base) commandeered four American commercial airplanes. Two were crashed into and destroyed the twin skyscrapers of New York's World Trade Center, one hit the Pentagon and the fourth, also apparently having Washington as its target, crashed in Pennsylvania after passengers overwhelmed the hijackers.

The terrible deeds accomplished in those few morning hours of September 2001, attacking symbols of America's economic and military global reach and slaughtering almost three thousand individuals, set in motion a response that produced the American-led overthrow of the radical fundamentalist Taliban government ruling in Afghanistan and the scattering, but not destroying, of the terrorist organization al-Qa'ida based there. Set in motion, as well, was the American campaign to force Saddam Husayn from power in Iraq. The claim by the Bush administration that the US had the will and the right to impose regime change in a Middle Eastern country was based on a somewhat shiftingly presented roster of charges, including alleged Iraqi links to al-Qa'ida, but even more the assertion that Iraq, in violation of UN sanctions, was working to produce weapons of mass destruction.

President Bush proclaimed immediately after 9/11 that states supporting or harboring terrorists would be considered enemies of the US. His January 2002 State of the Union address singled out two Middle Eastern states, Iraq and Iran, plus North Korea as constituting an "axis of evil". General statements by him or by administration spokesmen advanced the bold foreign policy agenda of an America prepared to act preemptively against terrorist threats and to impose regime changes when the US deemed it necessary. Action accompanied these words, beginning with the quickly mustered military campaign that overthrew the Taliban in Afghanistan. This has been followed by the build-up of US forces in the Middle East for an attack against the Saddam Husayn regime in Iraq. All such steps were undergirded by a commitment to not just regional but global military predominance. As the official "National Security Strategy of the United States of America", released in September 2002, stated (p. 30), "Our forces will be strong enough to dissuade potential adversaries from pursuing a military build-up in hopes of surpassing, or equaling, the power of the United States."

In the Introduction (p. xii) to *Diplomacy in the Middle East*, written before 9/11, we asked if the post-Cold War world with a single superpower, the U.S., would radically change the multipolar contours of Middle Eastern diplomacy and we prudently admitted that it is too soon to tell. What then of the US actions since 9/11? Certainly, these American actions – the doctrine of preemption and regime change in Afghanistan and Iraq – represent the boldest efforts to manage the Middle East ever advanced by an outside state. This goes well beyond earlier US announcements and actions dating back to the 1947 Truman Doctrine committing the US to defend one part or another of the Middle East against outside aggression or even against internal forces supported by outsiders. In these earlier doctrines (including the 1957 Eisenhower Doctrine and the 1980 Carter Doctrine) the principle of the sovereign state was honored. Now, the Bush posture in its extreme form asserts an American right to decide unilaterally when regime change of a Middle Eastern state is necessary and to take military action if necessary to that end. The Bush administration did back off from its most unilateralist posture by successfully challenging the UN Security Council to get the UN arms inspectors back in to Iraq (withdrawn in 1998) under terms much more stringent for Iraq, but a close reading of President Bush's September 2002 speech to the UN and of later official statements indicates that the US reserved the right to act alone if necessary, which it has now done after failing to get a follow-up explicit green light from the Security Council.

How have the world and the Middle East responded to this assertive American stance? Support for the US action against the Taliban and al-Qa'ida in Afghanistan was widespread with only muted questioning here and there of the necessity or legitimacy of such a response. As for the accompanying American assertion of the right to strike preemptively against threats elsewhere and the explicit campaign for regime change in Iraq, now achieved with, for all practical purposes, only British military support and a very fragile "coalition of the willing", the world reaction, driven by public opinion, has been sharply critical, mitigated here and there only by pragmatic assessment of the likely costs of outright opposition to the world's only superpower. An early case in point was Chancellor Gerhard Schroeder's promise during the September 2002 electoral campaign that if returned to office his government would never commit German troops to action against Iraq. This breaking of ranks with the US administration, daring in the overall context of German-American relations since the late 1940s, probably secured the return to office of Schroeder and his party.

Russia, content to see how the post 9/11 war against terrorism eased diplomatic pressure against Russian repression in Chechnya, but nervous about increased American standing in Central Asia, and eager to get Iraqi debts to Russia paid and a once major Russian standing in Iraq restored, had a mixed bag of considerations.

Finally, Russia lined up with France and Germany in arguing against the justification or the need for the US to act against Saddam Husayn's regime. France even more assertively worked to garner Security Council votes against a second vote that would explicitly authorize immediate American action against Iraq. Only Britain, among the great powers, remained strongly supportive of the American policy toward Iraq (but

Prime Minister Blair has faced severe opposition from elements within his party and, even more, from British public opinion).

As for the states of the Middle East, including Iraq's immediate neighbors, their stated foreign policies appeared to be somewhat puzzling. After all, Kuwait was invaded by the same Iraqi regime of Saddam Husayn in 1990 and the Iraqi army was ejected only by the American-led military campaign in the early months of 1991. The Iraqi juggernaut that overran Kuwait in a day, Saudi Arabia and the oil-rich states of the Gulf surely realized, would be capable of reaching them soon thereafter but for a countervailing outside force. Iran, invaded by Iraq in 1980 and fighting thereafter a brutal war, which ended only eight years later, had no reason to seek Saddam Husayn's survival. And the Syrian regime to the west of Iraq, although also a Ba`thist-ruled state, has actually been for years a bitter rival of the government in Baghdad, even breaching the Ba`thist and pan-Arab golden rule of Arab unity by allying with Iran against Iraq. Yet, all of these states, plus Turkey and Jordan (two other Iraqi neighbors) and all the Arab states farther removed from Iraq have taken a public position against unilateral American military action against Iraq.

How then to explain that such states as these, which experienced Iraqi aggression or witnessed it at close hand, did not accept the American position that Iraq, seeking weapons of mass destruction, constitutes a clear and present danger to them? There are several reasons which apply with different force in these different countries: For all their variety these countries have publics disposed to see American action as simply another phase in the longstanding Western domination of the Middle East. They sympathize with the Iraqi people and sometimes even with Saddam Husayn as well. They compare the adamant American stand against Iraq with what they see as unqualified American support for Israel's harsh actions against the Palestinians, and usually draw the conclusion that this is, indeed, a clash of civilizations – the West led by the US against the Muslim world. For Middle Eastern governments to openly support American policies is not an attractive domestic option.

Moreover, there has been no need to do so. Since the US has staked out a unilateralist position these states can seek to ride out the crisis as "free riders" reaping whatever benefits accrue from American actions against Iraq while avoiding or at least muting the potential confrontation with their own disaffected public. Put differently, the regional states – especially the many weaker neighbors such as Jordan and the states of the Gulf – would have been dangerously exposed if the American campaign against Iraq had ended with the Saddam Husayn regime still in place. Nor did the Middle Eastern political leadership see Iraq, hampered by over a decade of sanctions and seemingly boxed in by no-fly zones and continual US and UK pressure, as an imminent military threat to them.

Iran and Turkey bring somewhat different considerations to this issue. There is no need to rehearse the baleful state of American-Iranian relations ever since 1979 when Ayatullah Khomeini led the revolution overthrowing the pro-Western Pahlavi regime and creating the Islamic Republic. It is sufficient to note that the prospect for liberalization at home and an opening to the US that began with the surprising election of President Muhammad Khatami in 1997 has produced few tangible gains either domestically or in foreign policy. The Islamist hardliners remain in control, and this leadership sees the US as a threat.

There were, it is true, impressive pro-American demonstrations in Iran on the morrow of the 9/11 terrorist attacks in New York and Washington. Also, recent Iranian opinion polls show large majorities favoring relations with the US, but these signs of a deepseated desire for change seem in the short run to have only stiffened the backs of the hardliners against a foreign policy opening.

Interestingly, a certain amount of cooperation existed between the US and Iran in the successful campaign to overthrow the Taliban in Afghanistan, but things fell apart quickly thereafter. It is worth noting that, even though Iran had good reason to cheer the downfall of the Taliban (against whom Iran almost went to war in 1998), the resulting strong position of the US in Afghanistan as well as Central Asia and the American plans for Iraq present a view from Tehran of complete encirclement. And since President Bush as early as January 2002 explicitly included Iran in his "axis of evil" there seems never to have been a sustained will on either side to pursue the prospects of better relations.

The Turkish case can be more simply stated. Turkey does not want an independent or even autonomous Kurdish entity to emerge from the breakup of Iraq, and regime change definitely holds out such a prospect, even though the US has given Turkey assurances on this point. Turkey, uneasy about the de facto autonomy enjoyed in the Kurdish area of Iraq since shortly after the end of the 1991 Gulf War, has been quite forthcoming in indicating that developments that might lead to Kurdish independence in northern Iraq would be unacceptable. The Turkish government, reluctant to break ranks with the US, sensing that Turkish interests would be better protected by being involved, and offered a sizeable financial inducement, actually reached an agreement permitting US to move against Iraq from Turkey, only to have that accord defeated by the Turkish parliament. Thus, all the Middle Eastern states (except Israel) took in one form or another a public position of deploring the prospect of US military action against Iraq, sought a solution short of war and insisted that any action taken must be sanctioned by United Nations. Even so, the public positions of several Middle Eastern states have been matched by actions on the ground accepting the build-up of American military forces to be used when needed against Iraq.

The Middle Eastern states surrounding Iraq have hedged their bets. Whatever their worries, they did not make a sustained effort to create a diplomatic demarche that might seriously challenge these American initiatives. They recognize that the bipolar balancing of the US and the USSR characterizing the Cold War is no longer applicable. Nor does anything resembling the multipolar balancing of several outside great powers such as characterized Middle Eastern diplomacy during that long period of the Eastern Question loom as an immediate prospect. To this extent, the existence of a single superpower since the end of the Cold War and the assertive American policy adopted since 9/11 does appear to have changed the contours of diplomacy in the Middle East, at least for a time.

Official and quasi-official American statements have offered at times breathtaking vistas of not just Iraq but all the Middle East after Saddam Husayn. Under American guidance not only would Iraq become a prosperous pluralist democracy but Iraq's example would pressure other Arab states and Iran to do likewise. The poor, beleagured Palestinian Authority would accept the necessity of its own "regime change", oust Yasir Arafat and bring in sensible people who would strike a fair two-state solution with Israel (it being assumed that Israel led by the likes of Ariel Sharon is disposed to be magnanimous with Palestinians other than Arafat).

And yet the triggering mechanism for all these bold ventures in regime change and state building was 9/11, an atrocity committed not by any state, large or small, but by a nebulous transnational group of religious fanatics who have their own bold vision of regime change and state building. Bipolar thinking might have it that one or the other vision must prevail, but to study that cluster of over 20 states in the Middle East, large and small, rich and poor, is to appeciate the likelihood that neither utopia will be achieved.

Acknowledgements

The group research project resulting in this book has received generous support from the Center of International Studies, the Department of Near Eastern Studies, the Institute for the Transregional Study of the Contemporary Middle East, North Africa and Center Asia and the Program in Near Eastern Studies — all of Princeton University.

Kate Hering, Program in Near Eastern Studies Manager, competently and cheerfully administered this research project from its earliest days. Kathleen O'Neill, Near Eastern Studies Department Manager, kept a benign eye on all developments, and more than once came to the rescue with sound advice and support. Nancy Murphy and Christine Riley, both of the Department of Near Eastern Studies, unfailingly pitched in to help whenever needed.

Introduction

L. Carl Brown

Our story is told in terms of states. The chapters that follow treat the foreign policies of all the states of the Middle East (defined as the entire Arab world, Iran, Israel, and Turkey) plus four outside states, each with a history of intensive involvement in the Middle East—Britain, France, Russia (earlier, the Soviet Union), and the United States.

To interpret Middle Eastern politics by presenting the foreign policy of individual states would seem to be a reasonable approach, as states are the building blocks of international relations. Or is more than that involved? Does organizing this book around the foreign policies of existing states risk offering an incomplete, even a distorted, picture? What about groups that are challenging the state, whether its form of government or its borders? In any case, the size, strength and staying power of each state must be gauged. To evoke that classic maxim of international relations studies, states are not to be seen as so many equal-sized billiard balls.

Alongside this plan of telling the story state by state is another organizing thread that ties together the chapters in this book. Our working assumption is that the study of the foreign policies of these different states will bring out the underlying pattern of international relations in the Middle East, a vast area that has long attracted the attention of the outside great powers. To speak of an underlying pattern implies that Middle Eastern diplomacy differs from that in other parts of the world. In the jargon of international relations specialists, the Middle East is an international relations subsystem. Or, to replace the mechanistic metaphor of system with a richer image, the Middle East has a distinctive diplomatic culture, shaped by history and geography. What are those historical and geographical influences?

The above brief statement dictates the task set for this introductory chapter: to define the Middle East briefly, note several aspects of history and geography pertinent to understanding Middle Eastern diplomacy, and size up the different Middle Eastern states.

Where Is the Middle East?

For purposes of this book, the Middle East includes the Arab countries from Morocco to the Gulf plus Iran, Israel, and Turkey.[1] Other definitions—larger or smaller—exist. For example, the six independent Central Asian Muslim republics carved out of the former Soviet Union (Uzbekistan, Tajikistan, Turkmenistan, Kyrgyzstan, Kazakhstan, and Azerbaijan) might be added, along with Afghanistan, to form a "new Middle East." Some propose including these states and even more to make up a "greater Middle East."[2] On the other hand, many think of a smaller Middle East confined to Egypt, Iran, Turkey, the states of the Fertile Crescent, and Arabia.

Accepting that any definition of the Middle East will be untidy, the justification for our choice is as follows. It includes the Afro-Asian lands that were for centuries held together in the Ottoman Empire plus Morocco and Iran, respectively western and eastern neighbors of the Ottomans, each with its own long-lived political system. Going even farther back in time, the territory thus bounded constitutes the historic core of Islamic civilization. Here are located the lands absorbed into the Islamic ecumene during the early years of the Muslim era. These were the lands of the first two Muslim empires, that of the Umayyads and the `Abbasids (except, interestingly, Anatolia—the Ottoman heartland—where Islamization was the work of later centuries; another exception, in large measure, is Sudan). This definition also covers the lands closest to and most in contact with Europe throughout the centuries, a confrontation that has shaped the history of both. Moreover, this is, in general, the area that Europeans in modern times have identified as a distinguishable entity, even when they have given it a confusing mixture of labels, such as Levant, Near East, and Orient, as well as Middle East. Including the Arabs west and south of Egypt (the Maghrib states and Sudan), instead of the more constricted definition, is defended by the great, if fluctuating and perhaps now ebbing, importance of pan-Arabism in the foreign policies of all Arab states.[3]

The more expanded definitions of the Middle East, on the other hand, do add populations with appreciable Muslim majorities. These states of Central Asia (plus Afghanistan) fit linguistically into the Middle Eastern culture, as they include largely Turkic or Persian speakers (with, admittedly, important dialectical differences). Perhaps, in the future, Central Asia and Afghanistan will increasingly be included in a single "greater Middle East." Such reshuffling would, however, be premature at this time. These Central Asian states are still in the first decade of their independence.

On balance, Middle East as used in this book seems the best solution with the fewest fuzzy edges.

Conceptions of the Past

Our Middle East (along with the Ottoman Balkans) provided the playing field for the jousting of European states from the late eighteenth century to the end of the First World War. European statesmen and scholars dubbed this the era of "the Eastern Question." The question was how the European states could orchestrate a dismembering of the Ottoman Empire (as well as of Iran and Morocco) without upsetting the European balance of power. From the European perspective, the Eastern Question was resolved with fair success until the second decade of the twentieth century, when all Europe sank into the maelstrom of the First World War. Before that catyclysmic event, picking the Ottoman Empire to pieces had occasioned only a single European armed conflict, the Crimean War (1853–1856).

Eastern Question diplomacy always engaged a number of contending European states in a complex multipolar confrontation. In a bipolar confrontation, Britain and Russia concurrently faced off in those parts of the Middle East that a later American secretary of state, John Foster Dulles, would label the *northern tier*. To those nineteenth-century British servants of empire schooled in sports (had not the Duke of Wellington insisted that the Battle of Waterloo was won on the playing fields of Eton?), this was the "Great Game"—a struggle over the land mass from Anatolia to Afghanistan that formed a buffer zone between the British and Russian empires. Britain's goal in the game was to protect India, the jewel in the crown, against incursions of that Eurasian behemoth, Russia. British imperial strategy entailed keeping Russia bottled up in the Black Sea (thus the long-standing British support for the Ottomans—whereas to Russia, Constantinople was, in the words of Czar Alexander I, "the key to the door of my house"), and also well away from India's northern borders by having Iran and Afghanistan as client states at best, buffer states at least.

Historians have customarily seen both the Eastern Question and the Great Game as having ended at different times during the first half of the twentieth century, as one or another of the contenders dropped out. Imperial Russia fell apart in 1917, the Ottoman Empire ceased to exist after 1923, and in 1947 the British Raj dissolved into the states of India and Pakistan. Yet it may be more accurate to see the Eastern Question and the Great Game as having survived in muted form in the years between the two world wars, only to break out afresh thereafter as a new bipolar confrontation in the Middle East between two global blocs led by the United States and the Soviet Union. Certainly, the almost half-century-long Cold War in the Middle East produced great-power proxy battles employing Middle Eastern clients that Palmerston, Czar Nicholas, and Napoleon III would have recognized.

This, however, is only half of the story. The Middle East during these past two centuries has not been simply a playing field for Western diplomatic games, but has also provided its share of the players. To those living in the Middle East the Eastern Question became a "Western Question"—how to deal with intrusive Europe while coping with the ever-present perils and prospects within the region itself.

This Western Question facing the Middle East in modern times can be broken down into a number of separate and contradictory questions: Should we Middle Easterners seek to gain needed strength by adopting Western ways that have produced powerful states in Europe and North America? Or does our salvation lie in resisting alien ways and returning to our own religious and cultural heritage? Is armed resistance feasible? Or can we best protect ourselves by seeking an outside patron who will support us against enemies both at home and abroad? Should we rally around the existing state ruling over us? Or should we seek a new political community with either different borders or different organizational principles (if not both)? If so, should that new state be based on religion, ethnicity, or language?

The salience of these separate questions has fluctuated over the past two centuries, but even a cursory knowledge of modern Middle Eastern history suggests that they have been the defining issues. They remain so. Moreover, in the process new states have been created, old states have been destroyed or modified and a number of would-be states have struggled to emerge.

Blending this Western picture of diplomacy in the modern Middle East (our Eastern Question/Great Game/Cold War continuum) with this same diplomacy seen from within the Middle East (the Western Question, now two centuries old and still thriving) provides the needed balance. The Middle East in modern times has been intensively caught up in great-power politics, and that experience has produced a distinctive pattern of relations among Middle Eastern states and outside states concerned with the Middle East. In the process, Middle Eastern political elites have become conditioned to a diplomacy that balances domestic, regional, and international alignments. The foreign policy of any one Middle Eastern state is a multipolar process that involves many different states within the region and beyond. This has been the diplomatic *modus operandi* spanning the last two centuries. This area "is much like a feather bed: you cannot punch it in one spot without causing it to bulge out in several other places."[4]

Has the world of the 1990s with a single superpower, the United States, changed Middle Eastern diplomacy? It is too soon to tell. Certainly, multipolarity continues within the Middle East itself, and American global predominance may well subside. These first post-Cold War years call into question whether the United States, acting alone, can arrange the Middle East to its satisfaction. Perhaps American diplomacy may even tire of trying to do so. Much more likely is the continuation of a two-centuries-old pattern characterized by many different states and would-be states in constant confrontation.

The burden of the past and, even more important, a people's perception of the past (not at all the same thing) in shaping diplomatic attitudes and actions in the several different states will emerge in the following chapters. For now, a few examples may illustrate the varying approaches to politics that a shared past has produced among the different states.

Egypt's Gamal `Abd al-Nasir, when asked why he did not permit a multiparty system, was said to have replied that if he did one party would be financed and controlled by the British, another by the Americans, and yet another by the Soviets. This is the mindset of a political leader historically conditioned to expect overt and covert interference in his country's affairs by outsiders. Was Ayatollah Khomeini's depiction of the United States as the "great Satan," with the Soviets and British receiving lesser diabolical rankings, unwarranted hyperbole? Not to Iranians who remembered that their country had twice been divided into British and Russian zones of influence. Nor do Iranians view the 1953 Anglo-American coup that overthrew an Iranian prime minister and restored the shah to his throne as ancient history.

President Nixon, recalling the 1970 showdown between the Jordanian government and the Palestinian Liberation Organization (P.L.O.), wrote that King Husayn was in danger of being "overthrown by a Soviet-inspired insurrection," thus depicting this incident in global Cold War terms. In fact, the local crisis was sparked by a small splinter group within the P.L.O., and Syrian intervention was initiated by one faction of the Syrian political leadership. The idea of a Soviet hand behind all important

Syrian activities is belied by the wry comment attributed some years later to the Soviet ambassador in Damascus, "The Syrians take everything from us except advice."

Lord Palmerston, in the early years of Eastern Question diplomacy, defined British imperial interests in the Middle East in a striking image: Britain needed secure passage to India, but it did not seek outright control over that route. Britain's path to India could be compared to Palmerston's traveling from London to Edinburgh. He required accessible inns along the way but had no need to own those inns. This was the British self-image. But the perception of Middle Easterners and others was that the British Empire got into the Middle Eastern innkeeping business in a big way, employing every instrumentality from outright ownership to franchising arrangements. The British self-perception of simply requiring access and the Middle Eastern reading of "access" to mean "control" continued well into the twentieth century.

The United States, which came much later to a position of influence in the Middle East, also had the self-image of seeking no more than access, consistent with the venerable American foreign policy of the "open door." This was seen as long ago as the 1920s, when the American government backed American oil companies in their successful struggle to resist being denied access to major oil exploration prospects in the area. Added to this is the additional American self-image of opposing European colonialism. These perceptions are not lacking in truth. The United States never had colonial holdings in the Middle East, and in the period after 1945 took positions that favored the dismantling of European empires. Even so, the perception in the area, conditioned to expect outside manipulation, was often (not without cause) that the United States wanted free and independent Middle Eastern states—provided that they freely chose to remain within the Western orbit.[5]

Geography and Geopolitics in Brief

Great powers concerned with the Middle East have long formulated foreign policies based on geographical considerations. Even the term "Middle East" was first used in a geostrategic foreign-policy context. In 1902, Captain Alfred Thayer Mahan wrote "The Persian Gulf and International Relations." His Middle East was the area that fanned out from the Persian Gulf; when this usage caught on, a tripartite breakdown of Near, Middle, and Far East prevailed for a time. An American strategist and author of the earlier *The Influence on Sea Power Upon History* (1890), Mahan insisted that Britain would need strong naval bases in the Persian Gulf in order to fend off a likely land-based push from Russia.[6]

Two years later, Sir Halford Mackinder presented a paper on "The Geographical Pivot of History" before the Royal Geographical Society in London, in which he maintained that control of the Eurasian "heartland" could lead to world supremacy. Mahan and Mackinder represent opposite poles in the strategic debate over the relative advantages of sea power and control of coastlands, on the one hand, as opposed to land power and control of the "heartland" on the other. Such thinking—to simplify a complex and at times rather occult reasoning-from-geography—has influenced great-power strategic thinking about the Middle East. Indeed, one can discern such reasoning-from-geography from the early days of the "Great Game" to the 1980 Carter Doctrine and beyond.[7]

Geography, seen from this perspective, has willed that the Middle East, where Europe, Asia, and Africa meet, should become a major hub for world commerce and confrontation. Moreover, the land and sea routes both within and through the Middle East are studded with strategic narrows, control of which decides who has access. For example, the status of the Dardanelles, which controls communication between the Mediterranean and the Black Sea, occupied many a diplomat and scholar throughout the nineteenth and early twentieth centuries. The Turkish straits resurfaced as a diplomatic flash-point when the end of the Second World War brought Soviet pressure on Turkey to offer the U.S.S.R. major concessions there. That incident, in turn, was a major step toward bringing the Cold War to the Middle East.

No less significant in modern history has been the Suez Canal. Britain first opposed the building of the canal, which opened in 1869, then in 1875 became a major shareholder by buying the cash-poor Egyptian khedive's shares in the Suez Canal company. Britain thereafter moved on—largely from concern about canal security—to occupy Egypt in 1882. British troops were to remain in Egypt until early 1956. Only months later, Britain attempted (with France and Israel) a reoccupation of Egypt in an invasion appropriately dubbed the Suez War.

The "lifeline to India" strategic thinking does, in fact, provide a chronological coherence to Britain's growing Middle Eastern imperial holdings: Malta wrested from the French in 1800 (Napoleon's 1798 occupation of Egypt having stirred Britain to action), Aden taken as early as 1839 (important as a coaling station on the route to India), and Cyprus ceded by the Ottomans to Britain in 1878. Thereafter, and with the Suez Canal built and Britain in control of Egypt after 1882, the long-standing British support of the Ottoman Empire could give way to a strategy of drawing a line farther south to protect imperial communications. After the Congress of Berlin, Lord Salisbury mused that perhaps Britain had backed the wrong horse (the Ottoman Empire). What better replacement horse than Egypt and the immediately surrounding areas? From just such geopolitical thinking emerged Britain's Arab policy, including an interest in Palestine (achieved after the First World War) in order to secure in-depth protection of the canal.

Control of the Middle East, or denying control of this area to the enemy, has, in short, figured prominently in the strategic thinking of the great powers for some two centuries, and has made its geographical configurations well known to generations of Western strategic planners.[8]

The military history of the Middle East during the two world wars, in an area peripheral in comparison with the European fronts, also demonstrates this geopolitical thinking. During the First World War, for example, Churchill supported the Dardanelles campaign (1915–1916), a bold and ill-fated Allied effort to knock the Ottoman Empire out of the war and link up with Russia. Then, during the Second World War he championed the strategy of attacking the "soft underbelly" of Axis Europe from the Middle East. To this day some historians single out the 1942 battle of El Alamein (in Egypt, sixty miles west of Alexandria) as being, along with the Soviet victory over Stalingrad at the same time, the turning point of the Second World War. The battle of El Alamein, important as it was, pales in comparison with the Nazi-Soviet struggle at

Stalingrad in terms of deciding the war; but certain military historians argue that Hitler's fatal military mistake was to divert one of his best generals, Rommel, and his Afrika Corps to the Middle East. If Rommel and those German troops tied up in Northern Africa had been on the Russian front, the Nazis might have prevailed. In any case, the perception of the Middle East as a critical strategic area has survived to this day. And the Middle East did provide a critical corridor during the Second World War for Allied supplies to reach the Soviet Union.

In short, the actual geographical configuration of the Middle East as conceptualized in long-standing great-power thinking about that geography provides a meta-narrative in which strategic control of certain critical spaces determines the fate of nations (Dardanelles, Suez, the *northern tier*, to cite only the more prominent). This century has added yet another geographical reality and perception: the Middle East as the world's largest reservoir of petroleum essential to fuel the world's economies. The states that border the Persian Gulf alone (Bahrain, Iran, Iraq, Kuwait, Oman, Qatar, Saudi Arabia, and the United Arab Emirates) possess an estimated two-thirds of the world's proven reserves and account for just under a quarter of world production.

One can thus add to Lord Palmerston's metaphor of a chain of inns securing accommodation through the Middle East a twentieth-century conceit of competing service-station chains. At one time, to pursue the image, the outside powers felt comfortable with leasing arrangements granted by Middle Eastern states to private Western oil companies (often with important state ownership as well). Later, adjusting with more or less good grace to the spate of nationalizations beginning in the 1950s, the Western powers settled for Middle Eastern state ownership provided that those states are neither so strong nor so unfriendly as to become problems. Such hard-eyed thinking figured into such actions as the overthrow of Iran's Prime Minister Musaddiq, the Suez War, and Desert Storm.

Turning now to geography and geopolitics as viewed from within, one of the most striking features is the great diversity in size, population, and wealth of today's Middle Eastern states (see Table 1). The territorial extent of these twenty-one states varies from a state one-third the size of the continental United States (Sudan) to one no larger than a typical American county (Bahrain). Populations range from over 60 million (the big three—Egypt, Iran, and Turkey) to 1/100th of that total or about 600,000 (Bahrain and also Qatar). Differences in wealth range downward from a high of $20,470 per capita G.N.P. in Kuwait, which is well over fifty times that of the lowest (Sudan at $310 and Yemen at $380). Moreover, the unequal distribution of oil wealth produces a situation of several ministates with tiny populations (even smaller when the expatriate work forces are deducted) appearing as so many tempting El Dorados to their larger and poorer neighbors. The population of Bahrain, Kuwait, Oman, Qatar, and the United Arab Emirates, for example, is about 7,630,000, or roughly one-half the population of Cairo. These states plus Saudi Arabia, constituting roughly 10 percent of the Arab world's population, garner about 90 percent of the "Arab" oil revenues. Among the many ironies of Saddam Husayn's invasion of Kuwait is that Iraq, too, is one of the oil-rich states.

Table 1: Basic Statistics on Middle Eastern States

	Population (000s)	Area (000s)	Percent Urban	Per capita G.N.P. U.S.$	Real G.D.P. per capita* 1997 P.P.P.$
Algeria	30,045	920	55	1,520	4,460
Bahrain	633	0.3	90	7,840	16,527
Egypt	63,261	385	43	1,080	3,050
Iraq	21,722	168	68	1,382	3,310
Jordan	4,682	34	79	1,650	3,450
Kuwait	1,866	7	97	20,470	25,314
Lebanon	3,506	4	87	2,970	5,940
Libya	5,691	678	86	6,530	6,697
Mauritania	2,511	398	54	470	1,730
Morocco	28,060	177	49	1,290	3,310
Oman	2,364	120	72	5,950	9,960
Qatar	579	0.4	91	11,606	20,987
Saudi Arabia	20,786	868	80	6,660	10,120
Sudan	33,551	967	25	310	1,560
Syria	15,335	70	52	1,160	3,250
Tunisia	9,380	63	61	1,930	5,300
U.A.E.	2,744	33	84	17,500	19,115
Yemen	16,388	214	24	380	810
Total	260,593	4,709	67	5,340	
Iran	61,531	635	58	2,150	5,817
Israel	5,740	8	91	15,870	18,150
Turkey	64,567	301	69	2,830	6,350
Total	392,431	5,572			
United States	270,000	3,675	76	28,000	

* average

Source: Columns 1–4: *Britannica Book of the Year,* 1999. Last column: United Nations Human Development Report 1999. P.P.P. is Purchasing Power Parity or an index based on the amount of local currency of a country needed to purchase a representative "basket" of basic goods. The conversion to dollars is thus deemed to give a more accurate cost-of-living indicator than would currency exchange rates.

Bahrain, Israel, and Kuwait have in common the fact that, in all three, over 90 percent of the population lives in cities. This might be dismissed as unrepresentative, since Bahrain and Kuwait are virtually city states, and highly modernized Israel has urban percentages in line with those of the developed world (indeed, on the high side). Yet, Saudi Arabia—the desert Araby, par excellence, of Western lore—records an urban ratio of 80 percent. Libya, much of whose territory forms part of the great Sahara desert, is 86 percent urban. At the other end of the scale two states (Sudan and Yemen) have urban populations under 30 percent of the total. With these three exceptions, the states of the Middle East possess, by world standards, a high proportion of the total population living in cities. This is a recent development, however. For example, even when we select four Middle Eastern states that are characterized by a venerable urban legacy, the rural to urban shift over the past fifty years ago is striking (see Table 2). Equally dramatic overall population increases have accompanied this increase in urbanization; for the same four states, the population increase in the last half-century is shown in Table 3. In all four, a scant half century has produced a threefold population increase.

Table 2: Percentage of Urban Population, 1950–1999

	Percentage Urban	
	1950	*1999*
Egypt	31.9	43
Iran	20.0	58
Tunisia	25.9	61
Turkey	21.3	63

Source: The data for 1950 in Tables 2 and 3 are taken from more extensive tables in L. Carl Brown, *Religion and State: The Muslim Approach to Politics* (Columbia University Press, 2000). The 1999 figures are from the *Britannica Book of the Year*, 1999.

Table 3: Population, 1950–1999

	Population (in million rounded)	
	1950	*1999*
Egypt	21	63
Iran	19	62
Tunisia	3	9
Turkey	21	65

This dramatic increase in total population, with a concomitant shift toward urban living, may be set alongside another significant indicator—the great increase in numbers enrolled in state-directed education. Most Middle Eastern countries have moved over the past half century from minimal primary-school enrollments to virtually

100 percent of the primary-school-age cohort actually enrolled. The total enrollments in higher education may seem less impressive, but then even in most of the developed world the numbers enrolled in higher education were quite low until well into this century. Most of all, for these same four Middle Eastern countries the recent increases are striking, ranging in a mere thirty years from fourfold to ninefold (see Table 4). Moreover, graduates in higher education are presumably prepared for, and expect, careers in the modern sector.

Table 4: Percentage of Age Group in Higher Education

	1960	1990
Egypt	5	19
Iran	1	6
Tunisia	1	9
Turkey	3	14

All in all, the growth in population, the rural to urban shift, the increasing centralization of state and society as exemplified by the vastly increased numbers of people who receive state-directed education, and the dramatic disparity of wealth among the several states—all of these factors having been set in motion only during the past two or three generations—provide a recipe for considerable turmoil and instability within the region.

A few other geographical points may be briefly noted. This is an area characterized by a scarcity of water, and the rivers ignore political boundaries. The Tigris-Euphrates system directly involves Turkey, Syria, and Iraq. The Jordan River with its tributaries involves Israel, Jordan, Lebanon, and Syria. Egypt is "the gift of the Nile," but that great river, originating in far-away Ethiopia and East Africa, is equally crucial to Sudan.

Two states, Iraq and Jordan, each have only a single, tightly constricted outlet to the sea. Israel is favorably positioned on the Mediterranean, but its access to the Red Sea and points east is as vulnerable as that of Jordan.

Egypt and Tunisia stand out as states especially accessible to the outside world, with few physical obstacles to centralized control from within. Both have attracted outside interest often leading to domination. Egypt, unlike Tunisia, is large enough to aspire at times to regional predominance.

In terms of certain basic cultural determinants, the states of the Middle East show significant variation. Some fit the well-worn "mosaic" stereotype of a Middle East, with small groups separated from others by religion, language, or ethnicity. Others show considerable cultural uniformity (see Table 5). Although cultural uniformity does not make a nation or deliver legitimacy to existing political institutions, it is usually deemed an asset in state building. A few examples can illustrate the variety found among Middle Eastern states, though it should be kept in mind that the degree of cultural uniformity is only one measure of the strength and viability of states, and not always the most important.

Table 5: Middle Eastern Religious Demography (percentage)

	Sunni	Shi'a	Total Muslim	Christian	Other
Algeria	99.5	a	99.9		
Bahrain	20.5	61.3	81.8	8.5	9.8
Egypt	c.90.0		c.90.0	c.10.0	
Iran	5.6	93.4	99		1.0
Iraq	34.5	62.5	97	3.0	
Israel			14.6	3.2	82.5[b]
Jordan			92.0	8.0	
Kuwait	45.0	30.0	85.0[c]		15.0[d]
Lebanon	21.3	34.0	55.3	37.0	7.1[e]
Libya	97.0		97.0		
Mauritania	99.5			.2	.3
Morocco	mostly Sunni		99.8	1.0	1.0b
Oman	(75.0 Ibadiyya Muslim)		87.7		12.3[f]
Qatar			95.0		5.0
Saudi Arabia	93.3	3.3	96.6	3.0	0.4
Sudan	c.72.0		72.0	c.11.0	17.0[g]
Syria	74.0	12.0[h]	86.0	5.5	8.5[i]
Tunisia	99.5		99.5	3.0	2.0
Turkey	c.80.0	19.8[j]	99.8	.2	
U.A.E.	80.0	16.0	96.0		4.0
Yemen	53.0	46.9	99.9	.1	

Source: Britannica Book of the Year, 1999.

a   0.4% Ibadi Muslim
b   Jewish
c   Includes 10% "other Muslims"
d   Mainly Christian and Hindu
e   Druze
f   Hindu 7.4%, Christian 3.9%, Buddhist & other 1%
g   Traditional religions
h   `Alawite Muslims (not Shi`a)
i   Druze 3%, other 5.5%
j   Of which 14% are Alevi Muslim.

Egypt, Tunisia, Saudi Arabia, Libya, and Jordan demonstrate relatively high cultural uniformity. They are all overwhelmingly Sunni Muslim and Arabic speaking. Only

Egypt has a religious minority of as much as about 10 percent, but the "Egyptianness" of Coptic Christians who have lived there since well before the advent of Islam is beyond dispute. Libya and Tunisia once had significant numbers of European colonial settlers as well as a native Jewish minority, but decolonization plus the push-pull pressures brought by Zionism and the creation of Israel caused the emigration of these communities.

Jordan has an estimated 8 percent Christian minority, but they are Arabic speaking and, as with the Egyptian Copts, trace their roots to pre-Islamic times. Specialists emphasize the important split between Palestinians and Jordanians (those whose geographic roots are west or east of the Jordan River, respectively), but that divide is more a result of modern political history than cultural geography.

Saudi Arabia is overwhelmingly Muslim and, even more important, the majority of its inhabitants are brought together by a distinctive, rigorous school of Sunni Islam dubbed Wahhabism, named after the eighteenth-century religious reformer, Muhammad ibn `Abd al-Wahhab, whose alliance with the house of Saud laid the groundwork for today's state. [9] Specialists stress the differences between the more open western and eastern coastal regions of Saudi Arabia—the Hijaz and al-Hasa, respectively—as opposed to the desert homeland of Wahhabism, al-Najd. In comparison with their neighbors, however, Saudis rate high in uniformity as a people with roots in a desert-cum-oasis ecology marked by distinctions of Arabic dialect and dress. [10] Neighboring Qatar, where Wahhabism is strong, would also rank high in cultural uniformity with a 95 percent Muslim population.

Oman, like Saudi Arabia, is distinguished by the fact that the great majority of its inhabitants belong to a distinctive religious group scarcely found beyond its borders; 75 percent of the population are Ibadi Muslims, a sect found only in Oman plus tiny pockets in the Maghrib.

The tiny states of Kuwait, Bahrain, and the U.A.E. all have both imposing Sunni-Shi`a divisions and large expatriate worker populations, both of which factors militate against cultural uniformity.

The two largest Maghribi states, Morocco and Algeria, possess amazing religious homogeneity, with over 99 percent Muslim populations, all but a few of whom are Sunni Muslims and mainly of the same Maliki school of legal interpretation. Both countries, however, have important ethno-linguistic minorities of Berbers—33 percent in Morocco, 20 percent in Algeria. The Berber-Arab divide, which France sought to play on during the colonial period in a way that largely boomeranged, has not been as imposing an obstacle to national unity as such appreciable percentages would suggest. Still, Berber distinctions are of rising importance in Algeria, especially among the Kabyle Berbers (an estimated 13 percent of the population). The Kabyles are more open to Europe than are others, having been among the first to emigrate to France seeking employment, beginning early in the twentieth century. Though they are often depicted as more secular than the average Arabic-speaking Algerians, it might be more accurate to see them as quite firm in their commitment to Islam but resistant to that variety of fundamentalist Islam that comes with an Arab voice.

The Kabyles are mountaineers, and that serves to emphasize that the Middle East is more than just "the desert and the sown."[11] Throughout the area, the mountains have been just as effective as the desert in helping its peoples elude the control of urban-centered governments that dominate the settled areas. Berber language and culture have held out in the Maghrib because the Berber homelands are in either the desert or the mountains. Similar mountain refuges in the Arab East have sheltered the Christian Maronites and the Druze (an offshoot of Islam) as well as the Kurds. Geography thus helps to explain how the Maronites and the Druze have maintained their religions and the Kurds their distinctive language. Two of these three, the Druze and the Kurds, straddle contemporary political boundaries; the Druze live in Israel, Lebanon, and Syria; the Kurdish spatial geography is even more troublesome, divided among five states (see Table 6). It is perhaps fitting that these three mountain folk are found in the Fertile Crescent, the locus classicus of the mosaic pattern.

Table 6: Distribution of Kurdish Population

	Percentage of population	*Number of Kurds (millions)*
Iran	10.0	5.5
Iraq	23.0	4.1
Turkey	19.0	10.8
Syria	8.0	1.0
Elsewhere		0.7
Estimated total		22.6

Source: David McDowall, "The Kurds: A Historical Background," Special Report, *Britannica Book of the Year*, 1992, p. 375.

Sudan has perhaps the sharpest geographical split of all, with roughly 60 percent of its population in the north, which is overwhelmingly Muslim and largely Arabic speaking; the remaining 40 percent is in the south, where Christianity and various local religions predominate and there is a complex variety of languages and ethnicities.

Iran, Israel, and Turkey might be classified as strong nation-states for reasons more historical and political than cultural and geographical. All have important ethnic, religious, and linguistic minorities.

In short, the Middle East is a complex mix of uniformities and diversities: large states and small, rich states and poor, cultural uniformity and diversity. Yet, for all that, it is a distinctive cultural area, overwhelmingly Muslim, indeed the heartland of Islamic civilization. It is also an area whose diverse countries have all experienced over the past two centuries an intensive confrontation with the West.

The Middle Eastern States

Commentators, past and present, have often depicted Western colonialism as having broken up the Middle East along lines in violation of the more natural historical and geopolitical logic that should guide political boundaries. From a different perspective, a well-regarded Egyptian scholar/diplomat a few years ago dismissively referred to a number of Arab states as no more than "tribes with flags."

Such suggestions that Middle Eastern states are artificial and lacking in the stuff that makes for proper states contain, rather like the mosaic metaphor for Middle Eastern society, some truth but considerable distortion. A number of Middle Eastern states have, in fact, been around for quite a while. Others have had their borders imposed from outside. Some, lacking long historical pedigrees, have nevertheless achieved considerable "stateness" in the pressure-cooker politics of extraordinary challenges. A brief breakdown of these differences is in order.

Leading the list of historic states are Egypt and Iran. True, Egypt was ruled by foreigners for over two millennia until modern times[12]—in a sense until the Free Officers coup in 1952 (since the Muhammad Ali dynasty had Albanian roots). Still, Egypt has been Egypt in terms of politics and the state since the dawn of history.

As for Iran, in October 1971 Shah Muhammad Reza Pahlavi celebrated at Persepolis the 2,500th anniversary of the Persian monarchy. Pedants may point out that he cut a few corners in that calculation. Even so, mention of such august names in imperial annals as Achaeminid, Sassanid, and Safavid suffices to make the point.

Turkey's situation is confused by the long-standing Western tendency to refer to the Ottoman Empire by that name. There was, however, no Turkey until Ataturk pushed through the creation of the Republic of Turkey in 1923. Still, Turks see themselves as the heirs to the Ottoman legacy despite having pulled off a genuine revolution in creating an ethno-linguistic nation-state to replace that sprawling empire.

At the other end of the Middle East, three Maghrib states record several centuries of statehood. Tunisia, the medieval Ifriqiyya (from the Roman "Africa"), had an autonomous existence in the early `Abbasid period with the Aghlabid dynasty. Later, Tunis served as capital of the Hafsids, who ruled over a territory that extended for a time well beyond Tunisia's border. All this is old history, but the beys of the Husaynid dynasty ruled Tunisia (still part of the Ottoman Empire but autonomous) from 1705 until 1957, when Bourguiba's government, newly independent from French rule (1881–1956), abolished the beylicate.

Morocco has had its own rulers through much of the Islamic period, and the present `Alawite dynasty goes back to the mid-seventeenth century. Moroccan nationalists seeking independence from the French (and Spanish) protectorates (1912–1956) hit upon the idea of dubbing the heir to the throne "Prince of the Atlas" in parallel with the British heir, the Prince of Wales. They could argue with some justification that the Moroccan royal dynasty was older than the British.[13]

Emerging from the polemics that accompanied the brutal Algerian war for independence from France (which ruled there for 132 years, until 1962) was the claim that France created an Algeria that had not existed before. Well, not quite. The Algeria that France conquered beginning in 1830 looked back on three full centuries of autonomous rule as the westernmost holding of the Ottoman Empire. Even the existing regional division of the country into three provinces ruled from Oran, Algiers, and Constantine was maintained by the French. Today's Algeria was undoubtedly strongly influenced by the long French presence—the most long-lived, intensive, and harsh example of Western colonialism in the entire Middle East—but Algeria in its existing borders has been around as a political entity for a long time.

Libya became part of the Ottoman Empire in the mid-sixteenth century, and from 1711 to 1835 most of Libya, centered on Tripolitania, was ruled by an autonomous dynasty. Thereafter, the Ottomans restored direct control, and from 1911 Libya came under Italian colonial rule until the Allied victory there during the Second World War. Important political and cultural differences distinguish the westernmost Tripolitania from the eastern Cyrenaica and the Saharan Fezzan; the religo-political Sanusi movement thrives only in the latter two. Even so, Italian colonialism did not redraw boundaries.

The tiny and until recently thinly populated Arab states of the Persian Gulf boast in some cases long dynastic histories. The princely familes in both Kuwait and Bahrain have ruled since the late eighteenth century, and the several separate shaykhly families of the United Arab Emirates have been in power almost as long. Qatar is something of an exception, the ruling family there going back only to roughly the turn of the twentieth century. Admittedly, a case can be made for a sort of "frozen" (if that word may be used for this hot and humid area) state development in the Persian Gulf that began with the long-lived British indirect rule represented in the name Britain gave them, Trucial States, which indicated a tenuous independence in return for truces with Britain that permitted peaceful commerce. Thereafter, following the period of British hegemony, these ministates have been protected by a de facto balance of power precariously achieved by outside powers and Middle Eastern states accepting the implicit principle that no one wants anyone else to control this oil wealth.

Oman, on the other hand, has a long history as a maritime trading state, and, after a century and a half of Portuguese rule, the Al Bu Sa'id, ruling to this day, came to power in 1749. For a time, Oman and Zanzibar were ruled jointly, but they broke up in the 1850s. Soon thereafter Oman began its long decline, victim of disorders within and technological advance abroad, as steamships bypassed both Oman's location and its sailing ships. In any case, Oman in essentially its present border looks back on centuries of history.

As for Saudi Arabia, there have been three Saudi kingdoms. The first was created in the late eighteenth century and then destroyed by the army that Egypt's Muhammad Ali sent in the second decade of the nineteenth century. A second, equally short-lived Saudi dynasty ruled parts of Central Arabia from the mid-nineteenth century until the early 1890s. The kingdom existing to this day was put together by the legendary 'Abd al-Aziz ibn Sa'ud, who began in 1901 to restore Wahhabi rule in Arabia. Control of virtually all of what is now Saudi Arabia was achieved during the 1920s, and in 1932 the kingdom of Saudi Arabia was officially established.

Sudan in its present extensive borders is much more the creation of the Western colonial period, beginning with the Anglo-Egyptian Condominium (1899–1956), but much of the country in its present borders was controlled by Egypt from 1822 until the forces of the Sudanese mahdi expelled them and created the Mahdist state that was overthrown by the Anglo-Egyptian reconquest completed in 1898. Thus there is a core area of Sudan that has been around for a time, but Sudan's southern and western borders do conform to the stereotypical image of lines that imperialists drew on a map, which play havoc with linguistic, religious, and ethnic differences.

This leaves, yet again, the Fertile Crescent as the area most different from the others. It is true that Iraq was the center of the `Abbasid Empire, which had its capital in Baghdad. Syria can look back to a Umayyad dynasty radiating out from Damascus. Israel is seen as a land promised by God (but not a very good fit with Biblical borders). More important, however, is that in all of these states political borders are the work of this century.

In sum, most of the present states of our Middle East have been around for some time in roughly their existing territorial shapes. Colonialism shaped many of them in quite important ways, but—excepting the Fertile Crescent and Sudan—very little spatially. That the majority of these states have long appeared on the map largely in their present bounds says nothing, however, about their forms of government or political development. Moreover, whether continuity of "stateness" fosters continuity of foreign policy remains to be examined. Such matters will be traced in the following chapters.

Each chapter, treating the foreign policy of a specific country, stands alone while also providing yet another case study of the distinctive Middle Eastern diplomatic culture. These chapters can thus be read in any order. They are, however, arranged as follows. The four great powers with significant Middle Eastern interests are presented first. These are followed by Egypt, Israel, Jordan, and Syria. Since the Arab-Israeli confrontation has figured so prominently in Middle Eastern diplomacy since the 1940s, this grouping seems appropriate. Then come the other Arab states that are given individual coverage—Iraq, Morocco, and Saudi Arabia. Thereafter, the two large non-Arab Middle Eastern states—Iran and Turkey—are discussed. In order to achieve a more complete review of Middle Eastern multipolarity, the penultimate chapter provides thumbnail sketches of the foreign policy of the Middle Eastern states not covered in separate chapters.

A concluding chapter returns to the larger question posed—that of making sense of diplomacy as practiced in the Middle East.

Notes

1   "Where Is the Middle East?" is the title of the oft-cited article by Roderic Davison that first appeared in the July 1960 issue of *Foreign Affairs* and has been reprinted in several subsequent anthologies.

2   See, for example, the introduction entitled "Is There a 'New Middle East?'" in David Menashri, ed., *Central Asia Meets the Middle East*, and also Geoffrey Kemp and Robert E. Harkavy, *Strategic Geography and the Changing Middle East*, pp. 13–17.

3   Two Arab states, as defined by membership in the Arab League, are excluded—Djibouti and Somalia. Both are overwhelmingly Somali, not Arab, as measured by language, ethnicity, and culture.

4   E. A. Speiser, *The United States and the Near East*, p. 226.

5   This is like Metternich's witticism that the czar wished his subjects to be free provided that they freely decided to do what he wanted them to do.

6   "The Middle East, if I may adopt a term which I have not seen, will some day need its

Malta, as well as its Gibraltar... . The British Navy should have the facility to concentrate its force, if occasion arises, about Aden, India and the Gulf." Captain Alfred Thayer Mahan, "The Persian Gulf and International Relations."

7   Only minimal changes would be needed to make Mahan's words those of any American military spokesman for the Central Command set up to implement the Carter Doctrine.

8   Illuminating in this context is Michael J. Cohen, *Fighting World War Three from the Middle East: Allied Contingency Plans, 1945–1954*, which sets out the geopolitical role Allied military strategists assigned to the Middle East in their early Cold War contingency planning.

9   Purists would reject the designation "Wahhabi" as derogating from the ineffable unity of God and would prefer the designation Muwahhidun. That, however, best translates as "Unitarian," and to evoke the name of the most latitudinarian of Christians for the most rigorous of Muslims would only be confusing.

10   Even government officials and intellectuals wear the distinctive Saudi dress, unlike their peers elsewhere in the Middle East, who wear Western dress. The same holds true for many of the Gulf Arabs.

11   The often-cited title of Gertrude Bell's classic work published in 1907.

12   That is, from the time of the Persian conquest of Egypt in 343 B.C.E., followed in 332 B.C.E. by Alexander the Great's arrival. Thereafter came Greek, Roman, Byzantine, early Muslim, Mamluk, Ottoman (the Muhammad Ali dynasty remained technically part of the Ottoman Empire), and British rule, with nominal Egyptian independence after 1922. Faruq, the last king, was the first Egyptian ruler to speak Arabic fluently.

13   The Hanoverian succession (following the death of the childless Queen Anne) dates from 1714, whereas `Alawite rule extends back to the 1660s. The "Prince of the Atlas" was the young Hasan, son of Sultan Muhammad V, who later reigned as Hasan II from 1961 until his death in 1999. He was succeeded by his son, now Muhammad VI.

Contributors

Shaul Bakhash, Clarence Robinson Professor of History at George Mason University, is the author of *Reign of the Ayatollahs: Iran and the Islamic Revolution* and *Iran: Monarchy, Bureaucracy and Reform under the Qajars, 1858–1896*. His essays have appeared in scholarly books and journals including *Foreign Policy*, *Journal of Democracy*, and the *Middle East Journal*. He writes frequently for the *New York Review of Books,* and his OpEd pieces have appeared in leading American newspapers. Until 1979 he was a journalist in Iran, reporting at various times for *The Times* of London, the *Financial Times* and the *Economist*.

Laurie A. Brand is professor of international relations at the University of Southern California. She is the author of numerous articles on Jordanian domestic and foreign policy as well as *Jordan's Inter-Arab Relations: The Political Economy of Alliance Making* (1995) and, most recently, *Women, the State and Political Liberalization: Middle Eastern and North African Experiences* (1998).

L. Carl Brown is Garrett Professor in Foreign Affairs Emeritus at Princeton University where he taught from 1966 to 1993 and directed the interdisciplinary Program in Near Eastern Studies. His publications include *International Politics and the Middle East: Old Rules, Dangerous Game* (1984) and *Religion and State: The Muslim Approach to Politics* (2000), and he edited *Centerstage: American Diplomacy since World War II* (1990).

C. Ernest Dawn, a member of the History Department at the University of Illinois from 1949 to 1989, has specialized in the study of Arab nationalism and twentieth-century Fertile Crescent history. He is the author of *From Ottomanism to Arabism: Essays on the Origins of Arab Nationalism* plus numerous book chapters and articles in professional journals. He received his B.A. in History from the University of Chattanooga (1941) and his Ph.D. from Princeton (1948).

Michael Doran received his Ph.D. from Princeton University and is the author of *Pan-Arabism before Nasser* (1999). He taught history at the University of Central Florida for three years, and in September 2000 takes up a position as assistant professor of Near Eastern Studies at Princeton.

Hermann Frederick Eilts was a career U.S. diplomat from 1947 to 1979 with service in the Middle East. He was U.S. ambassador to Saudi Arabia (1965–1970) and to Egypt (1973–1979). From 1979 to 1993 he was Distinguished University Professor and Chairman of Political Science and International Relations Departments at Boston University.

George S. Harris, after almost 40 years of government service, retired in 1995 as director of the Office of Analysis for the Near East and South Asia in the Bureau of Intelligence and Research of the Department of State. He also taught courses on Turkey and the Middle East at the School of Advanced International Studies, Johns Hopkins University, from 1968 to 1981. He is now a consultant on Middle Eastern and Eurasian matters; his publications include *The Origins of Communism in Turkey, Troubled Alliance: Turkish-American Problems in Historical Perspective, 1945–1971*, and *Turkey: Coping with Crisis*.

Rémy Leveau is a professor at the Institut d'Etudes Politiques (Paris) and is scientific advisor for the Arab and Muslim worlds at the Institut Français des Relations Internationales. He spent many years as a teacher and an administrator in the Arab world, including teaching at the Faculty of Law in Rabat and being juridical advisor to the Moroccan Ministry of the Interior from 1955 to 1965, as professor of law at the Université Saint Joseph in Beirut (1975) and as a French official for cultural affairs in Tripoli, Libya, and Cairo, Egypt. His publications include *Le Sabre et le turban* (1993), *Le Fellah marocain: defenseur du Trone* (1985), and a collective work *Islam(s) en Europe* (1998).

Wm. Roger Louis is Kerr Professor of English History and Culture and Distinguished Teaching Professor at the University of Texas at Austin and a Fellow of St. Antony's College, Oxford. His books include *Imperialism at Bay* (1977) and *The British Empire and the Middle East* (1984). He was the Editor-in-Chief of the five-volume *Oxford History of the British Empire* (1998–1999). He is President of the American Historican Association.

Phebe Marr has spent over 40 years as a scholar and an analyst of Southwest Asia, specializing on Iraq and the Arab Gulf. In 1998–1999 she was a fellow at the Woodrow Wilson Center for International Scholars, revising and updating her *The Modern History of Iraq*. Earlier she was a senior fellow at the Institute for National Strategic Studies at the National Defense University, where she prepared long-range studies on US security policy toward the Middle East. She has taught at the University of Tennessee and California State University, Stanislaus, and served as a research analyst in the Government Relations Department of the Arabian American Oil Company. She has written extensively on Iraq, on problems of political and social development in the Middle East, and on US foreign policy.

William B. Quandt is the Edward R. Stettinius professor in the Department of Government and Foreign Affairs where he has taught since 1994. He was previously a Senior Fellow in the Foreign Policy Studies Program at the Brookings Institution where he conducted research on the Middle East, American policy toward the Arab-Israeli conflict, and energy policy. He served as a staff member of the National Security Council from 1972 to 1974 and again from 1977 to 1979, during which time he was actively involved in the Camp David negotiations. He earlier taught at the University of Pennsylvania, MIT, and UCLA. His publications include *Peace Process: American Diplomacy and the Arab-Israeli Conflict since 1967* (1993), *Camp David: Peacemaking and Politics* (1986), and *Between Ballots and Bullets: Algeria's Transition from Authoritarianism* (1998).

Bernard Reich is professor of political science at the George Washington University. He received his Ph.D. in 1964 from the University of Virginia. His specialization is the politics of the Middle East with emphasis on Israel. Among his book are *Quest for Peace: United States-Israeli Relations and the Arab-Israeli Conflict*, *The United States and Israel: Influence in the Special Relationship*, and *Israel: Land of Tradition and Conflict*.

Alvin Z. Rubinstein is professor of political science at the University of Pennsylvania, and a Senior Fellow at the Foreign Policy Research Institute in Philadelphia. His research interests are Soviet and Russian foreign policy, conflict in the Third World, and national security affairs. His publications include *Soviet Foreign Policy since World War II: Imperial and Global* (4th edition 1992), *Red Star on the Nile: The Soviet-Egyptian Influence Relationship since the June War* (1977), *Moscow's Third World Strategy*, and *Imperial Decline: Russia's Changing Role in Asia* (1977), (co-edited) with Stephen J. Blank.

I. William Zartman is the Jacob Blaustein Professor of International Organization and Conflict Resolution and director of the African and Conflict Management Programs at the Paul H. Nitze School of Advanced International Studies of the Johns Hopkins University. He is the author of two books on Morocco, the editor-co-author of a third, and the author and editor of four other books on North Africa. His latest work on the region is *Between Islam and the State*, edited with Charles Butterworth. He has been founding executive secretary, and then president, of the Middle East Studies Association, and founding president of the American Institute of Maghrib Studies, and is president of the Tangier American Legation Museum Society.

PART I

The Four Great Powers

1

France's Arab Policy

Rémy Leveau

In the field of foreign policy, when an image acquires a certain amount of weight, it can become a reality imposed upon the perceptions of all involved.[*] This is the case with France's Arab policy. Whenever rivalries for the control of this region between the superpowers of the time have required, the French regime or government has followed an Arab policy based upon a myth of empire. After the Six-Day War in 1967, when observers looked for signs of a new Arab policy, what they saw was actually a reflection of a more global change in situation, in which the Arab world on one side and Israel on the other were participants in a new political engagement. France's decisions to pull out of NATO's integrated command and to build a nuclear weapon, and de Gaulle's 1963 speech at Phnom Penh condemning American intervention in Vietnam, were, at that time, the fundamental decisions that gave meaning to a new nationalist approach. This approach, ending the decolonization of Algeria and the imperialist adventure, attempted to reconstruct a collective destiny after a crisis that had nearly plunged France into civil war.

It all began with Napoleon Bonaparte's expedition to Egypt in 1798. The expedition, which only lasted three years, was clearly the consequence of the Enlightenment philosophers' perception of Ottoman decadence.[1] This perception had already raised the problem of how to reform and modernize non-European societies, be it through revolution from within or by intervention from without—which would imply the breakup of the Ottoman Empire. The French intervention was, in fact, provoked more by the urgent need the revolutionary leaders felt to find a remote, perilous task for the burdensome victor of the Italian campaigns than by any desire to modernize the Orient. But the element of reform and modernization was nevertheless manifest in the presence of some three hundred scholars and engineers who embarked with Bonaparte. These scholars found the Rosetta stone and studied the flora and fauna of the region as well as the irrigation system and the monuments, both ancient and modern, of Egypt. In three years' work, they imposed upon this country the analytical method put forth by Diderot and d'Alembert, authors of the Encyclopedia. The published results of this research extended over a period going well beyond the fall of Napoleon's Empire, and covered as well most of the modernization projects undertaken in nineteenth-century Egypt, including the project to link the Mediterranean and the Red Sea.

A desire to defeat Bonaparte's war-driven utopia provoked Great Britain's interest in the region, especially in order to protect its interests in India. Thus one can see from the start the three factors that in the long run dominated the development of France's Arab policy: a cultural project to modernize the Arab world; short-term concerns over domestic policy; and international political rivalries. This last aspect is most often evident in the nineteenth century in terms of the Franco-British rivalry, but it had an indirect influence on the European balance of power in general.

Although the first factor was not active at the beginning of the French conquest of Algeria, the other two certainly were. They constituted, from that moment on, an Arab and Islamic policy that was dominated by the rivalry with Great Britain for control over the Mediterranean and the passage to India. In the long run, the building of a colonial empire appeared after 1815 to be a compensation for the impossibility of dominating the continent, which would have drawn Great Britain and Austria into a new conflict. The system that Metternich and Talleyrand put into place neutralized any attempt by France to break with the balance of power, for France was still suspected of harboring revolutionary and expansionist tendencies. These tendencies were channeled into colonial adventures; after the defeat of 1871, the system was reinforced, as Bismarck harbored a plan to facilitate French intervention in Tunisia, thereby creating friction between France and Italy as well as distancing France from any desire to reconquer Alsace-Lorraine.

In the southern reorientation imposed on its expansionist desires, France sought to use its political influence in facing the Ottoman Empire and its dependencies both near and far. France attempted, however, to consolidate its local influence in a lasting way without coming directly into conflict with Great Britain. The abandonment of Egypt's Muhammad Ali (1839–1840) and the backing down at Fashoda (1898) demonstrate the primacy of these choices in terms of the European balance of power. Expansion abroad also served to compensate for France's demographic deficits by bringing in imperial troops that would eventually fight in both world wars. France developed a vision of its regional presence and a long-term project to legitimize its domination over the Muslim populations. The work of the Saint-Simonians in Muhammad Ali's Egypt,[2] the protection of the Christians in Lebanon in 1860, the opening of the Suez Canal in 1869, the intervention of French banks in the management of the Egyptian debt and then of the Ottoman debt all demonstrate the coherence of this regional project. The aid given to Christian religious orders, to *la mission laique* and to the *Alliance française* in the construction of a network of influence that spanned the Ottoman Empire, Iran, and Egypt completed this vision.

Before Bonaparte's invasion of Egypt and then the French conquest of Algeria in 1830, France forged an amicable relationship with the Ottoman Empire, which had, in the time of Francis I and Louis XIV, allowed it to assume the protection of the Eastern Christians who still followed Rome. By virtue of the treaties called "capitulations," French consuls were authorized to withdraw from local jurisdiction a large number of subjects of the empire by registering them as "protégés." These protégés, who came largely from the Christian and Jewish minorities, later constituted a ready-made clientele for French schools established there. Although French influence was maintained on both cultural and political levels thanks to this protection of minorities, however, the affront to the caliph brought about by showing him to be unable to defend the Dar al-Islam against the attacks of miscreants made any deeper political association impossible. The British and the Prussians would profit from this situation to expand political and military cooperation with the Ottoman Empire, progressively setting themselves up as protectors of the empire. The French, who, until the eighteenth century, had benefited from a sympathetic reception, were from this point on considered dangerous predators, although less so than the Russians. The Crimean War would, of course, allow for a new alliance with the Ottomans against Russia, but under British supervision. The occupation of Tunisia in 1882 only deepened the humiliation at a time when the Ottoman Empire was giving in to foreign appetites everywhere.

The Qajar Empire in Persia did not constitute a prize comparable to the Ottoman Empire on the route to India, even though Napoleon himself had dreamed of taking up Alexander's path. French consuls there were more concerned merely to observe Anglo-Russian rivalries, and had enough time on their hands to interest themselves, as Gobineau did, in racial theory or, as others did, in archeology.

In the regions it controlled directly, France established the foundations for what was to be an exemplary empire, a civilizing mission as much as a conquest, in the image of ancient Rome—different from and yet comparable to the British Raj in India. It was the vision of what Prévost-Paradol called a "New France" designing its own empire—less powerful and smaller than that of Great Britain—one that touched the southern shores of the Mediterranean and that would therefore be an integral part of Metropolitan France. "The Mediterranean flows through the center of the empire just as the Seine flows through Paris."[3] Tocqueville had also thought that the installation of a large colonial population of Europeans was the best way to guarantee France's domination in the long run.

In practise, however, it became difficult to reconcile such an objective with the principle of equality, or to consider the interests and needs of the Muslim populations for democratic representation. Under the influence of Ismail Urbain, Napoleon III tried to do just this, by developing while on his travels in the region the concept of an "Arab kingdom" in Algeria.[4] Actually, the realization of a need to consider local populations dates from the creation of the *bureaux arabes* by Bugeaud,[5] as a counterweight to the services more specifically dedicated to helping the *colons*, especially as concerned access to real estate. In the acceptance of French domination by the Muslim populations in Algeria, Napoleon III saw the basis for a peaceful presence following the military conquest. This required that France take responsibility for the interests of these populations, together with instituting a policy of assimilation. But the emperor's personal involvement and his instructions to governors Pélissier and MacMahon were not successful in offsetting the dominant attitude, which sought to impose a European population of Mediterranean origin upon Arab and Berber populations. The confrontation was over the control of the land and the right of suffrage.

Although there were differences in terms of sovereignty, France's extension of its domination to Tunisia in 1882 and to Morocco in 1912 continued the debates about the Algerian model. Despite the efforts of republican statesmen such as Clémenceau,

Herriot, Viollette, and Blum, the *colons* succeeded in their fight against all reformist legislation that was intended to increase the civil rights and resources available to the Muslim populations. These populations suffered under a profoundly unjust domination until the very end, which would cause the revolt of the 1950s. Nonetheless, the contact with French society did exert a cultural influence as well as allow for the dissemination of certain social and behavioral models.

In the Middle East, the First World War transformed the Franco-British rivalry into an uneasy association in order to share the spoils of the Ottoman Empire. The Sykes-Picot accords (1916) still constitute today, along with the Balfour Declaration (1917) and the Crusades, the favorite references that Arabs and Islamists use to illustrate the never-ending plot by the West against Islam. Suspicious of British projects to structure the region by creating an Arab kingdom under British control, the French treated Faisal in Damascus like a rebellious tribal chief and administered the Syrian and Lebanese territories they were entrusted with according to principles that, for more than a century, had proven their effectiveness in the Maghrib; they played upon divisions in language, community, and geography through a direct administration unencumbered by the presence of *colons*. As in the Maghrib, this system produced a confrontation with a French-speaking native elite that soon engaged in nationalist activities. For a long while, this elite counted on the negotiated reformist solutions that were proposed each time the French Left came into power, notably at the time of the Front populaire in 1936. But other priorities of both international and domestic origin always stopped these reforms succeeding. The deputies elected by the *colons* of Algeria, members of Léon Blum's slim majority in Parliament, had no trouble in deferring action.

Even so, the Arab nationalists did not exploit the French defeat of 1940, and resisted the advances of Hitler and Mussolini. The administration and the vast majority of the *colons* remained loyal to the Vichy government both in the Maghrib and in the Middle East. Those who rallied to Free France were marginal types (aristocrats, Freemasons, Jews, socialists). De Gaulle's troops fought in Syria alongside the British against those of Vichy. On the other hand, in 1942, Noguès, then Resident General in Morocco, ordered that the Americans debarking at Kénitra be fired upon. When the civil and military administration of Vichy finally rallied to the cause of the Allies, it attempted to do so by squeezing out de Gaulle and by supporting traditional military leaders such as Giraud and Darlan. Nonetheless, the Maghrib nationalists had an intuitive feeling for de Gaulle, perhaps as a result of the liberal tone of the speech he gave at Brazzaville, and probably also owing to the negative reaction the *colons* had to him. They actively collaborated with the Free French forces in mobilizing troops for the Italian and French campaigns. Oufkir, Ben Bella, Boudiaf, and many others served valiantly as commissioned and noncommissioned officers and were decorated for their war efforts. At the war's end, Muhammad V was made a Compagnon de la Libération by de Gaulle in recognition of the role played by the Moroccan troops in the return to battle of a France that had been defeated in 1940.

The Maghrib nationalists, however, expected, as they did at the end of World War I, a generous and progressive attitude from France with respect to their requests for independence. Once again they were faced with the obtuse and brutal response of a weakened France that was fearful of confronting a decolonization that would destroy its empire and deal the final blow to its world status. The fierce repression of the riots in Setif of May 8, 1945, in which Algerian Muslims participated in celebrating the Allied victory while simultaneously demanding independence, sharply illustrates these contradictions. Thousands died in these riots, which can be considered as the beginning of the war in Algeria inasmuch as they demonstrate a clear break with the attitudes of the colonized people in that country.

Although for a few years France was still able to continue a purely repressive response in the Maghrib owing to the *colon* presence, the proximity of Metropolitan France, and the indifference of the rest of the world, this was not the case in the Middle East. As early as 1943, the Lebanese Maronites, Sunnis, and Shi`ites reached a "national pact" for power sharing and cooperation to achieve independence at the end of the war. Paris could no longer simply bombard Damascus, as in 1925, in order to impose its domination. The regional and worldwide responsibilities of Great Britain obliged it to work against French dreams in the Middle East, whereas, as a result of Algeria's annexation into the French national territory, the Maghrib remained a matter of French domestic politics—a fact that at the time was contested by no one.

It is in this ambiguous context of Franco-British relations that one must situate the attitudes toward Zionism and the birth of the state of Israel. In the beginning, the British support for Herzl's Zionist project seemed like a bizarre way of reinforcing British influence in the region by rendering themselves indispensable as both arbiters and protectors in the conflict between the Jews and Arabs of Palestine, whereas they refused to allow the French to play a similar role (between Christians and Muslims) in Lebanon.

In addition, the French Jewish community had shown no interest in Zionism before World War II. When, after 1945, Jewish terrorist movements began to attack Great Britain they could count on covert support from the French Secret Service, which was thrilled to discomfit a neighbor who had been guilty of bad behavior during the Syro-Lebanese conflict with France in 1945. Léon Blum's rise to power in 1947 facilitated contacts with future Israeli leaders. According to the pattern established in the help given to the Spanish Republicans in 1936, weapons were bought and volunteers recruited. The indirect military support given to the state of Israel was also a function of the not-yet-admitted guilt of the Vichy government in its deportation of French Jews during the German occupation. Moreover, the image of a small state resisting a hostile environment created a wellspring of public support and rendered the sale of weapons a much more acceptable act, and also justified for the elites the assistance given later toward the creation of a strategic nuclear weapon. These two very sensitive programs were jointly developed in order to insure the greatest level of autonomy possible in the West in opposition to both Great Britain and the United States.

The emergence of an Arab nationalist movement after the 1952 revolution in Egypt—a country that was then just as much an adversary of France as of Great Britain, engaged, as it was from 1954, in the Algerian war as well as the opposition to Israel—justified the political and military cooperation that reached its height at the time of the Suez campaign of 1956.

The struggles for independence in the Maghrib were waged in the name of the egalitarian principles put forward by the school of Jules Ferry and disseminated by the French-speaking elites. This rendered the break with the imperial past less brutal and more ambiguous in the Maghrib than in the Middle East. It is in this regard that the years 1956 and 1962 are symbolic. The first date marks the end of a period of Franco-British rivalry in the Mediterranean, the Middle East, and Africa. The nationalization of the Suez Canal and the failure of the Franco-British expedition served as important moments. After these events, the region was caught in the rivalry between the Soviet Union and the United States, polarized by the Israeli-Arab conflict and by the efforts undertaken to assure control of the oil industry. The year 1962, bringing the end of the Algerian conflict, marks also the end of the imperial dream; the economic, political, and cultural consequences continue to be felt today on both sides of the Mediterranean.

From the beginning of the nineteenth century to the middle of the twentieth, through its Arab policy France played skillfully and sometimes powerfully the imperial game that the European powers—Britain, Germany, and to some extent Italy and Spain—all played. This Arab policy was rarely described as such, though with respect to the positioning of the different players involved in the Ottoman Empire, one spoke occasionally of a Muslim policy. In any case, the leaders of the European states felt it important to intervene in the Arab world in order to preserve their ranking in the state system. It was Tocqueville who put forward this idea to justify the occupation of Algeria, although he also analyzed the negative aspects of such intervention. If, at the time of Tocqueville, France's Arab policy made sense, its later expression as well as its final episodes were based on a misconception.

Correcting a Misconception: The Gaullist Policy

The break of 1962 makes sense only if interpreted as the nationalist disengagement from a colonial relationship no longer seen as positive in terms of France's long-term interests. De Gaulle's attitude toward the Algerian conflict was, however, riddled with ambiguity. Having risen to power with the help of the military and the *colons*, who believed that the war could not be won without a total victory over the F.L.N., he had to equivocate. He needed to acquire personal legitimacy by means of a series of national referendums and legislative elections, while at the same time ensuring control over Algeria through military operations undertaken both in the cities and in the country. Thus, with the support of French public opinion, which starting in 1960 wanted to see an end to the conflict, he was able to undertake the withdrawal from Algeria. The separation was painful: there was nearly a civil war, and four attempts were made upon the life of the head of state; there was also a revolt within the army, justified by the Gaullist tradition of disobedience. A double referendum in favor of independence was necessary, one to determine the choice of Algeria, and the other to confirm this choice in metropolitan France. This breaking of ties created a million refugees and caused nearly 100,000 civilian and military casualties for the French side alone. On the Algerian side, losses were estimated at a million dead and disappeared. More than thirty years later, these events still leave an ambiguous mark upon the perceptions of both sides involved in the conflict. In the end, the painful memory of the past is of as much concern to the million French *pieds-noirs* refugees and their descendants as to the veterans of the war and the descendants of the *harkis* (Algerians who served with the French forces during the 1954–1962 war in Algeria), as well as to the descendants of the Algerian immigrants who live in France, whose numbers now greatly surpass those of the European colonists who had lived in the Maghrib.

Even today, each group reacts to current events in the Arab world according to the community to which it belongs. This collective conscience is an integral part of each community and influences the ways in which it integrates into French society. The sad events of the past explain positions taken today, allowing one to better understand a brutal and yet ambiguous separation. As someone who knew Great Britain well, General de Gaulle wished to save France from the decadent and morose atmosphere surrounding the British loss of empire. To accomplish this, he attempted to give France a new role as an autonomous power, without neglecting the alliances necessary to strengthen Europe as a whole. He was careful not to break with his allies, even while being a difficult partner. Another effect of the 1962 rupture was that the Mediterranean became a barrier once again. Despite the efforts made to raise living standards in the region, some saw this barrier as the French refusal to integrate a population of 10 million poor and illiterate Muslims as equals. These perceptions remain powerful even today, and one occasionally has the impression that a sort of collective unconscious continues to influence each side's behavior.

It was in the context of this search for a new worldwide status that France began to develop an Arab policy that appeared to be in direct contradiction of what was expected. The first surprise came from the fact that, despite the emigration to the Metropole of one million refugees, and the assassinations of both *harkis* and European civilians, the decolonization of Algeria was not nearly as catastrophic as had been predicted. The model of Guinea seemed to indicate that a complete and total rupture was inevitable. Nonetheless, an extensive program of cooperation (including military cooperation) between France and Algeria was put into place, inspiring the amazement and at times even the indignation of neighboring countries such as Morocco. This cooperation, however, was the product not of an inexplicably charitable gesture but of a convergence of interests. The Evian accords seemed to preserve the vestiges of the old empire, such as the clauses guaranteeing the status and freedom of circulation, and the choice of citizenship for Europeans living in Algeria and for Algerians in France. Since these clauses were soon to be obsolete, they posed no problem to the two sides engaged in a formal separation.

On the other hand, those clauses which preserved French oil interests, as well as temporary nuclear arms-testing centers in the Sahara and military bases, were scrupulously respected. These were, in fact, essential elements of the worldwide French policy of which the Arab policy was only a part. Observers have, at times, mistaken the part for the whole. General de Gaulle was careful not to reveal his intentions, thereby finding opportunities to reinforce his strengths. Essentially his decisions were focussed elsewhere, depending on the role he wanted France to play in Europe and the world. Seen in this light, the decisions to restart the dialogue with Algeria and to create new contacts with nonaligned countries made sense. These countries were, in fact, following a policy similar to that of France. At the same time, the reconciliation with Adenauer's Germany, the Elysée treaty (1963), and the support for the Common Agricultural Policy were fundamental elements on the new direction France was taking in Europe. At the time, the Arab world took a back seat in terms of priorities and means to French-speaking Africa—and the Arab world could not be considered as a single unit. In the Maghrib, Algeria remained the primary partner. The Bizerte crisis in 1961 with Tunisia, and the Ben Barka conflict in 1965 with Morocco both contributed to the deterioration of the political ties between these countries and France's Fifth Republic.

On the whole, cultural cooperation probably remained the most important element in France's relations with the Maghrib in the long run. It remained a durable if evolving element, with television replacing schools. Beyond whatever choices each state made in this domain, the influence of civil society made its mark and compensated for the decline in public funding. Emigration soon created a transnational domain in which influences and cultural and social models were exchanged. The strongest ties that exist today between France and the Maghrib come from civil society, beyond the destructive effects of governmental policies that attempt to break them by suppressing nearly all north/south contacts. Should one, then, speak of an "Arab policy," or rather of transnational relations that mix domestic and foreign cultural, economic and political influences? In this new domain, states tend to lose their ability to act or even control. With respect to these matters the 1980s marked a turning point, coming on the heels of the independence movements, as a result of the ties created between the north and the south through new immigrants and their images of Europe, images that would soon be reinforced by the television shows picked up on parabolic antennas.

In the Middle East, the situation is profoundly different. The Suez crisis created a deep schism, and the ties that were later established never attained the same human aspect, except perhaps those with Lebanon. After Suez, the rivalry between the Soviet Union and the United States was in place, centered on the Israeli-Arab conflict and the control of oil profits. In this context, the Fourth Republic remained too paralyzed by its inability to administer the decolonization of the Maghrib to do anything other than maintain simple ties of solidarity with the state of Israel and a special cooperation with Lebanon. From his rise to power in 1958 to the end of the Algerian war in 1962, de Gaulle would follow the same path, hindered by difficult diplomatic relations with the principal countries in this region that voted regularly against France in the United Nations. He was far from enthusiastic about the American Middle East policy, but he did not react to the sending of U.S. marines to Beirut in 1958, or to the union of Egypt and Syria.

Having long been pushed off the Middle Eastern scene by his involvement in the Algerian conflict, de Gaulle came back to it at a time when he was going through a general reevaluation of his relations with the United States. Maurice Couve de Murville, his minister of foreign affairs at the time, contributed to this new strategy of distancing within NATO as well as seeking convergence with positions held by the nonaligned countries. Couve, the French ambassador in Cairo in the1950s, did not have a negative view of Nasir's revolution. But Egypt, then heavily dependent on the

Soviet Union for the construction of the Aswan Dam and for reequiping its military, was slow to respond.

It was in this context that the French declared their disapproval of Israel's initiating hostilities in 1967. This disapproval came out of the feeling that the conflict would increase the influence of the two heavyweights, the United States and the Soviet Union, in the region. France's reservations were expressed in the Council of Ministers declaration of June 2, 1967, that "France is not cooperating with any of the states involved in this conflict in any way on any subject. Therefore, whichever state should decide to use military force, wherever this may occur, will not enjoy France's approval nor any kind of support." The Arab world's reaction, at first incredulous, far outstripped the actual extent of France's commitment, and created a symbolic image of de Gaulle as coming to the aid of their mythic leader, Nasir, weakened in defeat.

After 1967, France's Middle East policy sought to emerge from the abyss, and attempted to find a diversified discourse well adapted to the region's situation. But compared to previous positions (before 1940 and even before 1956), the results were meager. Now the rivals were the United States and the Soviet Union, countries that were much more powerful than Great Britain had been. Envious and disdainful of the "commercial diplomacy" of West Germany, France looked for a way to have a greater, more diversified presence than its partners in the European Community without going beyond the "collective declarations" or getting involved in elaborating a truly European political cooperation in the region.[6] Promising security guarantees to Israel became an American problem, and the globalization of the oil market led Washington to consider a region harboring 50 percent of the world's oil reserves as essential to its security. These two factors explain the depth of American commitment as well as the reactions of France which, in 1967, on the heels of the Six-Day War—as in Phnom Penh—would mark a different approach. Israel's increasing tendency to align itself with the American positions doubtless played an important role in General de Gaulle's distancing himself from this country. Additionally, the dangers that Israel was running in Lebanon, through both its violent reactions and its efforts to destabilize Lebanese domestic politics, all contributed to solidifying the French desire to disapprove of its actions.

Although France tried to present a voice distinct from that of the American discourse in the Middle East, notably with respect to a balanced solution to the Palestinian problem, it could not ignore reality. The French found a niche of their own by aligning with states that had taken up the path of a modernization that overcame regional and ethnic divisions. In this respect, Iraq and Egypt were closer and more familiar partners than Saudi Arabia. For a long time, Egypt had expounded, through its jurists and judges, a French concept concerning the role of the state as well as the importance of the legal rules, which today is often in competition with the ideas of those who have attended American universities.

But France scarcely understood that it had contributed to the construction of Arab nation-states that, although often made in France's image, could not but resist direct French influence. De Gaulle, with his own profoundly nationalist point of view, could more easily recognize the Arab nationalism of Nasir and Ben Bella than could the

French Left. Domestic political objectives changed over the years. In the nineteenth century, the Maghrib had been the dumping ground for those who lost revolutions and wars (for example, the rebellious Parisians of 1848 and the inhabitants of Alsace-Lorraine who were exiled in 1871). It was also an expansionist safety valve for ambitious military leaders who would otherwise have threatened the Republic and democracy after 1871. In order to construct its majorities, the Left needed the representatives elected by the *colons* in Algeria, whose support was conditioned by the demand to drop reforms, especially those that would have extended the right to vote to the Muslims without their giving up their personal status. In addition, the traumatic memory of the *pieds-noirs* refugees, the *harkis*, and the veterans of the Algerian war would long influence the images and perceptions of France's relations with the Maghrib.

The transitional period of decolonization seemed therefore to come to an end with the fall of the Iron Curtain and with the Oslo accords. The Gulf War demonstrated the dominant American role in this region as well as the defeat of the strategies of nonaligned countries that had received a warm reception in France. The Oslo accords, however, have been far from successful in bringing peace, and the difficulties of applying their clauses leave room for the intervention of other players should they find it in their interest. Even so, experience has shown that the intervention of a single mid-sized country has neither much meaning nor credibility in the Middle East. In times of crisis, such as during the Gulf War, the validating power of American policy cannot but leave a feeling of helplessness and isolation as soon as one strays from it. Nevertheless, a special French relationship with the Maghrib has been preserved, even though memories of the colonial period and the civil war in Algeria continue to paralyze it. There is still need for an Arab policy that would depend, on the one hand, upon the solidarity of the Muslim community in France and, on the other, upon the strength of the European Community. It is the European Community that should establish well-balanced relations with the surrounding regions, such as the Maghrib and Turkey, which constitute special partners in that they both have large expatriate communities living in Europe.

The fall of the Ottoman Empire was sealed by a primitive peace treaty signed in Sèvres in the spirit of the Versailles treaty. Mustafa Kemal's refusal to recognize it, and his efforts to create a homogenous nation-state that implied a total withdrawal from the Middle East, were recognized by the Herriot government in 1924. At that time, France renounced the idea of expanding its Syrian mandate to part of Anatolia. In 1939, the French even ceded the province (*sandjak*) of Alexandretta (Iskanderun) in order to help maintain Turkey's neutrality in World War II. Later, Turkey became a key element in NATO's arsenal against the Soviet Union, and very quickly became interested in the construction of the European Community. The Europeans did not greet this interest nearly as warmly as they did that of the Greeks, the Spanish and the Portuguese. The 1997 denial of membership was reversed in 1999, but the solution to the Kurdish question remains vital to Europe, especially for Germany, which does not wish to see the conflicts of the Anatolian plateau transferred to German cities. In the end, the integration of the Balkans into the European Union, a possibility since the

Kosovo crisis, would make it both acceptable and necessary to offer the same treatment to Turkey, which would then become a stabilizing factor in the entire region, whereas the Maghrib is neither a logical candidate for, nor in any way desirous of, being a part of the European Union.

Perceptions of Iran have also changed, with Europe taking over the relations with this country. For many years it was considered the privileged domain of Anglo-Russian rivalry; the British dominance became a reality after the Qajar dynasty was overthrown by Reza Shah thanks to the implantation of British Petroleum in the exploitation of oil fields and at the Abadan refinery. France remained outside these rivalries, and was still in this outside position when Musaddiq in the early fifties nationalized the oil industry and temporarily forced the shah into exile. France did participate in the boycott of the Iranian national company and was not unhappy to see the American-orchestrated return of the shah, which put Iran, a country on the border of East-West rivalries, under Washington's lasting influence. On the other hand, years later, after the departure of the shah, France's relations with the regime of Ayatollah Khomeini rapidly deteriorated, to the point where Iran was accused of encouraging the terrorist attacks that occurred in Paris during the summer of 1986. One can find the origin of this confrontation in the French military aid given to Iraq when it engaged in war with Iran (1980–1988) as well as in the French intervention in Lebanon in 1982 following the Israeli invasion. When Iran stopped proselytizing among the Muslim minorities in Europe and contented itself with its role of regional power—having its word in the Middle East conflicts—calmer Franco-Iranian relations were established. But it was through the European dimension of the "critical dialogue" with Iran, in which Germany took the lead, that France reformulated its ties with Iran, while being associated with the uproar around the Mykonos restaurant case.[7]

Enlarging the Field and Increasing the Players

What was perceived from outside, and at times claimed, as France's Arab policy was based upon the East-West blocs, nonalignment, and the construction of nation-states in the Arab world. The Gulf War, the march toward economic globalization, and the reduced role of separate states marked the end of these parameters. The emergence of Islamic movements that reject both the authority of states and certain constraints of globalization only complicates the situation further. In many ways, these changes render a coherent Arab policy even more necessary, but the most important players are no longer the same. Indeed, neither the emergence of regional subsystems capable of protecting each player, nor the balance of economic relations, nor the expansion of new fields of economic relations concerning culture and society are yet perceptible on either the Arab or the European side. In this intermediate phase, however, the influence of the United States remains dominant without guaranteeing an efficient regulation. The control exerted by each state that participates in the separate subsystems is thus downgraded and, more often than not, reduced to an ability to create a nuisance or to block initiatives. A "call to empire" is developing among members of the middle class in the countries of the south, who have been deprived of the politics of nonalignment, cultural opportunities, and grand state projects. Their ability to convert to a global economy is not guaranteed, at least in this generation. The risk of a proletarianization without an opening to the outside world brings about a nostalgic and critical evocation of the good old days of the Arab policies not only of France but also of the Soviet Union. Then, states had real roles to play, which indirectly afforded intermediary elites social mobility.

A new definition of Franco-Arab relations is needed. The goal of playing a role in the Middle East peace process and in the reconfiguring of a region, while respecting the security concerns of the Israelis and the desire for prosperity shared by the Palestinians and the other players in the region, requires greater capacities than those of any single country, even the United States. The United States will remain, however, a privileged partner in dialogue for both sides. The current barriers to the peace process, the risks of collapse, and the increase in rejections coming from identity movements do nonetheless leave room for more balanced support and mediation than those of the current American interventions.

In the Maghrib, where France enjoys political, economic, and cultural influence, the effectiveness of its interventions is weakened by a colonial past that prevents it from doing anything other than supporting the governments currently in power. France also fears that the civil war in Algeria could be waged on its own territory. The Maghrib is not a priority for the United States, which does, however, reserve the right to exert great influence in certain domains. The other European countries have shown some concern without demonstrating the desire to get involved in a way that France would not like.

France, which for many years believed that it could play a role in the Maghrib comparable to that of the United States in the rest of the world, must now be disappointed. During Hassan II's funeral, President Clinton found it the most natural thing in the world to be the first to present his condolences to Muhammad VI in the company of James Baker, who continues to play a role in the arbitration over the Western Sahara conflict. Many of the measures that had been in the domain of bilateral politics, such as agriculture, fishing, and visas, have entered the domain of collective administration. Others are subject to close consultation. In the Europe-Mediterranean partnership one can see a common foreign policy coming into being. France, while desiring this, occasionally gives the impression of being incapable of playing its part correctly in the collective symphony, demonstrating that it sees itself more as a soloist being backed up by the rest of the European orchestra. To continue with this comparison, one might hypothesize that, concerning the important issues (major conflicts, human rights, defense, energy), the United States is already playing the part of soloist, while France is, at best, first violin in a European orchestra playing before a North African audience rarely satisfied with its performance.

Additionally, the confrontations between the Israelis and the Palestinians, and the social and political changes in the Maghrib, are integral parts of the group of issues that greatly concern those populations of Maghrib origin and Muslim culture now living in France. Their loyalty, constantly questioned on the occasion of external tensions such as the Gulf War and generally confirmed by the facts, presupposes the French state's taking into consideration their external ties—be it with regard to the Palestinians or the Maghrib.

If France is to preserve its interests and demonstrate concern for the Arab world on both a governmental and a societal level, it must find a way to reconcile this approach with its first and foremost responsibilities, which today tie it to the European Union. It must take into account the role played in foreign policy and in collective defense by a NATO that is largely dominated by the United States but embraced as well by its European partners.

Moreover, the fifteen states of the European Union lack a coherent foreign policy. The declaration of Venice in 1980, which was largely the product of a Franco-German consensus to recognize the fact of the Palestinian nation, constitutes an important precedent despite its exceptional nature. The choice of a European envoy to the Middle East is another example of an advance in this sense. One can, however, hardly imagine the European Union quickly adopting a policy and naming an executive with the means to act credibly. Once the single-currency stage has been successfully dealt with, one might see groups of states within the European system that will act in concert with respect to certain issues and will agree to abandon certain privileges of sovereignty, as was done with the Schengen accords. Such a strategy would make it easier to develop a common European foreign policy with respect to both the Maghrib and the Middle East.

New Perspectives

A Europe based upon contractual solidarity between states that vary in size and shape casts the central problem in new terms. The first thing to be done is to recognize the importance of the Muslim culture within Europe as the foundation of a collective identity of the populations originating in the Maghrib, Turkey, and the Indian subcontinent. This recognition would validate for these individuals their right to remain citizens of European countries without having to abandon too much of their culture. Beyond assimilating religious difference within a new pluralistic context, this also presupposes accepting, at least in the transitional stage, the principle of double nationality, and the establishment of ties of solidarity with the countries of origin. In these elements one can see sketched out the new bases of what would eventually become a new policy, no longer simply an Arab policy, but also an Arab-Muslim policy, for Europe. This policy would be based on the cultural reconfiguration of the European space through collective regulation, as well as norms and values that would guarantee the legitimate rights of the populations living there.

In this respect, the European courts of justice are the only supranational mechanisms able to fix the customary and progressive bases of the necessary adaptation of the practices of each country. In this area, one thinks first of the problems concerning collective status and behavior (such as the issue of the veil) that create disparities between European countries. One can also imagine that citizenship which influences the free circulation of persons and their right to live where they choose would be the object in the future of harmonizing legislation. It is clearly difficult to manage a population living in a country by cutting it off from any human, cultural, or family contact with its country of origin, as is the intent of the current policy that restricts visas. The right to naturalization must also be adjusted so as to limit conflicts with the countries of origin.

In general, this means a policy of solidarity between Europe and the regions where these populations originate, including economic aid and free circulation of people, capital, and merchandise, as well as mutual security guarantees. The territories affected by these possible commitments would greatly extend the borders of the area currently considered essential for European defense. According to this approach, issues such as the Kurdish question in its regional and Middle Eastern dimensions would have to be solved, if one wants to avoid suffering the consequences in Europe, as the Mykonos case demonstrates.[7] The relations between the Turkish army and the Islamists could also create tensions in German cities. The same is true today of the consequences for French suburbs of the civil war in Algeria. This leads Europe, or at least those states which are determined to contract a strong commitment to domestic and foreign solidarity (probably with the Franco-German dyad at the center), to make possible a common foreign policy that will concern both the Eastern European countries and the Arab-Muslim world.

If the immigration currently flowing into Europe constitutes an important element in a mutual relationship of influence and transnationality with the southern and eastern Mediterranean, this is not the sole determining factor today. Energy needs in Europe are based on a complex balancing of nuclear power (less and less popular with its citizens), oil (susceptible to a world market dominated by the United States), and gas resources. This last resource is provided through a network of pipelines from Siberia, the North Sea, and the Maghrib. Since Spain and Italy have refused to use nuclear power, the fixed supply lines with Algeria that pass through Tunisia on the one hand and Morocco on the other are essential for these two countries. These factors, coupled with Europe's interest in having a partnership with a North African market of about 70 million inhabitants, should push Europe to work toward the unity and stability of these three North African countries. Beyond that, the Maghrib might also be deemed a part of the common European foreign policy (rather than simply a region that France alone is responsible for). This presupposes a European policy on the Algerian civil war, on the Western Sahara and on human rights violations in Tunisia. If Europe is unable to develop a truly autonomous policy concerning these issues, it will find NATO making use of resources which, by expanding its missions beyond its traditional borders, will be a way for the Americans to resolve crises on the model of those in the Balkans.

Although, aside from times of crisis, Europe does not need the United States to solve its problems with the Maghrib, the questions concerning Turkey and the Israeli-Palestinian conflict are more complex. Without the burden of a colonial past, Turkey has developed relations with Germany that are comparable to those between France and the Maghrib. But it has participated in NATO's missions right from the start, and its zones of strategic and defensive importance cover the Balkans, the Straits, the Caucasus, and the Muslim republics of the ex-Soviet Union and the Middle East. Its conflict with Greece over the islands of the Aegean Sea required the personal intervention of President Clinton to prevent the use of force. In addition, the occupation of the northern part of Cyprus by the Turkish army has created a conflict within NATO and is one of the main reasons why Turkey cannot enter the European Union despite favorable attitudes by France and the United States. Germany is now considering (with some reservations) Turkey's entry into the European Community, since, in becoming citizens, the two million Turkish inhabitants in Germany would acquire rights equal to those of Turkish citizens in Turkey. This bundle of criss-crossed interests demonstrates the urgency for a European policy with regard to a country that has for many years been a candidate for entry into the European Union and that is capable of blocking the eastward expansion of NATO.

For all these reasons, a common European policy with regard to Turkey is a priority. This policy should coexist with an American commitment, which one would hope—because of its own needs, including those in dealing with Europe—would have a reasonable amount of weight in the long-term decision-making process. In the domain of the nearby Israeli-Palestinian conflict, which will only be partially resolved by the accords signed in Oslo and Washington for as long as Syria and Lebanon remain outside these agreements, Europe's essential problem is to make itself heard in the concert that the Americans wish to direct. Isolated actions undertaken by individual European states have few chances to succeed, despite the acute interest that France has in Lebanon or that Great Britain has in Jordan. Egypt maintains strong, well-balanced ties with the principal European nations, but the diplomatic, military, and financial commitments made by the United States since the Camp David accords of 1979 to guarantee Israel's defense through negotiated settlements remain dominant. These commitments were renewed after the Gulf War in the accords signed in Madrid, and then by those signed in Washington in 1993.

American aid to Egypt, which since 1979 has been proportional to that given to Israel, contributes to the region's stability. Today, Europe collectively supports the Palestinian Authority by covering 60 percent of its costs, although it has no political power to influence the decisions being made in the current peace process. It was only after the American intervention of December 1996 that an agreement concerning Hebron was reached. No European state alone can claim comparable political power. The Germans remain handicapped in this region by their history, which makes it impossible for them to take a position hostile to Israel. Germany needs a European framework, as was the case with the declaration of Venice in 1980, in order to take a more balanced position. Only consensus mechanisms among the leading European nations can compensate for the lack of a common foreign policy and render valuable the investment of financial support given to the Palestinian Authority. If the Mykonos restaurant case and, before that, the establishment of a critical dialogue led to a coordinated European policy concerning Iran, this is not the case for positions regarding Iraq. Commercial diplomacy and/or humanitarian intervention, and the desire either to support or to combat American positions, have all been characteristic of European attitudes at different times; European states' participation in the Gulf War was never a determining factor in their reactions years later. With respect to Tehran, the Salman Rushdie case and the accusations of state-sponsored terrorism have slowed down what could have been an effort at normalization of relations. With respect to Iraq, its refusal to dismantle its nuclear, chemical, biological, and ballistic weapons arsenal constitutes the primary point of contention for all sides. In both cases it is the United States that necessarily runs the show, along with Great Britain, either directly or through the United Nations.

Conclusion

The reality of France's Arab and Muslim policy was not perceived as such until it became an important part of a vaster imperial project. Paradoxically, it was de Gaulle's break with the empire and the search for an autonomous path for France, one which would bypass the superpowers, that allowed France to come together at times with certain nonaligned Arab countries. This "Arab policy," isolated from its context since the fall of the Soviet bloc, no longer makes any sense, and Europe is not yet a credible collective partner in the context of a U.S.-dominated globalization. Germany's emergence as a major political force in East Europe has allowed it to play a role similar to that of France with the countries of the southern and eastern Mediterranean. This activity has perhaps been motivated by fear of the "Islamic menace" or of waves of immigrants on the Albanian model. Although these fears are largely unfounded, the stability of these Mediterranean countries is necessary to European security as a result of the transnational influences that have been developing for the past twenty years in the fields of economics, culture, and social changes, especially due to south-to-north migrations. The dialogue between the European Union and the Mediterranean region, which is based upon an economic approach, is meant to design a strategy that would compensate for the ruptures that came about during the 1960s. Associating the countries of the south with those of the European Union in a free-trade pact should create the same complementary space as is being created by the ties between the United States, Canada, and Mexico.

Financial aid given primarily to entrepreneurs should incite others to invest and open up the region to international commerce. Although it would be far from the amount of public and private funds invested in Eastern Europe, an annual influx of 3 billion dollars should help create a secure zone by stimulating economic growth. Europe's commitment to this path today is no longer limited to that of France and of the Mediterranean countries of Europe. Rather, in order for this choice to be meaningful, Europe must begin to recognize the place that Islam and Muslims occupy in its culture and society. This is the price of becoming a confident partner with the Arab-Muslim world, transcending what would otherwise seem like a simple aid package meant to buy tranquility for the north. As with the construction of the European Union itself, the heart of the European-Mediterranean relationship is culture, and on this level, thanks to parabolic antennas, communities can better relate to each other than states. Will these communities be able to create a confident relationship with each other in a reasonable amount of time, thus allowing the defects of the human and economic exchanges taking place to be overcome?

Notes

*   An earlier version of this chapter appeared in the French journal *Politique Etrangère* 3 (1997).

1   Henry Laurens, *Les Origines intellectuelles de l'expédition d'Egypte.*

2   Several followers of the utopian socialist Claude-Henri Saint-Simon (1760–1825) made their way to Muhammad Ali's Egypt (and Algeria as well), where they supported the Pasha's bold modernization projects. See Henry Laurens, *Le Royaume impossible*, and Anouar Abdel-Malek, *Idéologie et renaissance nationale*, pp. 189–98.

3   Lucien Anatol Prévost-Paradol was a journalist who, while in the opposition under the Second Empire, ended up rallying to support the government not long before the defeat of 1870; he had decided, among other things, that the policy being undertaken in Algeria was largely a promising one.

4   Ismail Urbain (1812–1884), another of these fascinating Frenchmen linked to the Saint-Simonians, was the principal ideologue to shape Napoleon III's short-lived and ill-fated "Arab kingdom" policy intended to integrate Algerians better into the French Empire. See Edmund Burke III, "Two Critics of French Rule in Algeria: Ismail Urbain and Frantz Fanon."

5   Marshal Thomas Robert Bugeaud (1784–1849), the leading general in the French conquest of Algeria and governor-general there from 1841 to 1847, presided over the system that provided for military administration of the native population—the *bureaux arabes*.

6   Rémy Leveau, "Le Moyen Orient."

7   On September 17, 1992, four members of the Democratic Party of Iranian Kurdistan (P.D.K.) were assassinated in the Mykonos restaurant in Berlin. Very quickly the investigations focussed upon the Iranian secret service, and on April 10, 1997, the German courts sentenced the principal guilty parties to heavy prison terms (life with a minimum of fifteen years to be served) and implicated the Iranian government in having arranged the assassination. As a result of this sentence, the ambassadors of the European Union left Tehran, and an end was put to the "critical dialogue" with Iran.

2

Britain and the Middle East after 1945

Wm. Roger Louis

After World War II, the Middle East formed part of a great British imperial system, with an array of territories that ranged from the crown colony of Cyprus to the mandate of Palestine, to protectorates such as Somaliland, to the protected states in the Gulf such as Kuwait. Just as significant, there were further gradations of domination, an "informal empire" that included states bound to Britain by treaties of alliance such as Iraq and Egypt. In territorial extent the British formal and informal empire in the Middle East extended from Libya in the west to the enclave of the Anglo-Iranian Oil Company at Abadan in Iran in the east. Iraq represented the northernmost country, while in the south the Sudan stretched into tropical Africa and was at once an Arab and an African country. The informal empire—territories where the British held sway but had no direct administration—must be included in any analysis of British imperialism because the British themselves regarded units such as Jordan as an integral part of the British world system. Developments in one part of the Middle East would have repercussions elsewhere. The nationalization of the Anglo-Iranian Oil Company by Muhammad Musaddiq in 1951, for example, influenced Egyptian calculations on the Suez Canal Company and the British base at Suez.

Despite major efforts to meet nationalist challenges, the end of the British era came much more rapidly than most contemporaries had anticipated. In a little over two decades, the British empire virtually disintegrated. In 1967, the British decided to withdraw forces east of Suez. After the British departure from the Gulf in 1971, the history of the British in the Middle East became, in one view, mainly an epilogue, with Britain independently yet rather consistently upholding the American position. "The Americans count on us to be reliable and 'sympathetic, but not sycophantic, allies," commented the British ambassador in Washington in 1967, in a remark that sums up one version of the story from then onward to the end of the century.[1] The other view holds that British imperialism, though diminished and less visible, remains to the present day a vibrant force in the Middle East, above all in the Gulf.

There were four stages in the dissolution of the British Middle Eastern empire, stages that the British themselves did not anticipate. The years 1945–1955 mark the first phase leading to dissolution, though the British tried vigorously to reverse the trend. It was the British view after 1945 that the empire would be recreated and reshaped, not liquidated. As a replacement for India, the Middle East along with

21

Africa and Southeast Asia would be developed economically for the benefit of the indigenous inhabitants as well as the British. The empire after 1945, so went the argument, was in a state of revival and not in the process of decline and collapse. The British would form new alliances with a younger generation of nationalists who demanded reform of the old social order. In the Middle East, the British would, in the phrase of Ernest Bevin, cast their lot with the peasants rather than the pashas. Bevin was foreign secretary in the Labour government from 1945 to 1951, and his influence remains, even today, a source of inspiration. Bevin himself believed, at least initially, that a harmony of interests might be achieved if the British renounced old imperialist ambitions and regarded the Arabs and Iranians as truly equal partners in the effort to develop and defend the Middle East.

Anthony Eden, foreign secretary in the Conservative government from 1951 to 1955 and then prime minister from 1955 to 1957, embraced Bevin's optimistic view that Britain and the peoples of the Middle East might work together in unity. Eden was, however, more skeptical than Bevin about the possibility of aligning Britain's aims with those of the United States and especially the United Nations. In the end, Eden shifted to the view that Britain's position in the Middle East could only be maintained by force. Eden is identified with the catastrophe of the Suez crisis in 1956, when the British and French (and Israeli) invasion of Egypt collapsed under the weight of American protest and economic pressure. The single year 1956 forms the second of the four periods. In the third phase, when American power began to eclipse that of the British, Harold Macmillan, prime minister from 1957 to 1963, attempted to salvage Britain's position in the wake of Suez and the Iraqi revolution of 1958. Macmillan restored Anglo-American relations, which had reached a nadir during the Suez crisis, and he tested the concept that Britain's new and enduring position might rest on an arc of strategic bases stretching from the Mediterranean to the Pacific. The key point would be the base at Aden. The disintegration of the British position in Aden in 1967—the critical year in the fourth and final stage—ended Britain's aspiration to remain a regional power in the Middle East, even though the withdrawal from the Gulf did not occur until four years later.

The roots of Britain's postwar dilemmas extended as far back, at least, as the late nineteenth century, to the problems caused by the Egyptian response to the British occupation of Egypt in 1882; the discovery of oil in Persia at the turn of the century and the eventual issue of royalties to the Iranian government; and the creation of the modern Zionist movement—though in the Zionist case the British involvement did not begin directly until 1917, when the Balfour Declaration promised the Jewish people a national home in Palestine and subsequently provoked Arab protest. How were these three interlocking issues of Egypt and the canal, the oil concession at Abadan, and the question of Palestine regarded in 1945?[2] Could they be solved or were they essentially problems that could merely be contained? We must not let today's vantage point distort the view in 1945. The British in the postwar era examined all options, and retreated only after having exhausted all other possibilities. Their failure to sustain Britain's position in the Middle East makes the story all the more fascinating.

The view that the British should withdraw or at least retrench was, in fact, expressed at the time by Prime Minister Attlee, who believed that Britain's economic and military resources did not permit a sustained presence in the Middle East.[3] Attlee anticipated the solution espoused in the late 1950s and 1960s: that the British might be able to maintain a series of strategic bases stretching from Gibraltar to Cyprus to Aden to Singapore, but withdraw from commitments in most of the Middle East, and specifically from "deficit areas" such as Somaliland. Had Attlee's view prevailed, it might have made the postwar sterling crises less severe and might even have made it possible for Britain to have joined the European Community at an earlier stage. Attlee, however, acquiesced in the postwar consensus forged by Ernest Bevin and the chiefs of staff, who believed that Britain's status as a "world power" had to be sustained and that the problems of the Middle East could be resolved with skill and tenacity. The leaders of the Conservative Party were of the same opinion. There was a consensus in postwar Britain, in Parliament, and generally among the public that Britain's historical position in the Middle East must be maintained. The dilemmas posed by Arab, Iranian, and Jewish nationalism might be acute, but they had to be resolved. If driven out of the Middle East by insurgent nationalism, Britain would decline to the status of a third-rate power and would become, in the phrase of the day, another Belgium.

Old outlooks die hard, and in 1945 there were remnants of authoritarian and indeed arrogant assumptions of a previous age. The Victorians had believed that Britain led the civilized world not only in trade and commerce but also in the art of government. Lesser breeds (Kipling's phrase) might, with British and other Western assistance, modernize their economies and progress toward representative government, but they would require a long period of tutelage before they could stand on their own. The most legendary of British proconsuls in Egypt, Sir Evelyn Baring (Lord Cromer), whose tenure stretched from 1883 to 1907, personified many of the British assumptions of the age when he spoke of the "utter incapacity" of the Egyptian "ruling class."[4] As late as the early 1950s, British officials in Egypt continued to draw inspiration from Cromer's reform of the Egyptian administration, finances, and agriculture. They still believed that the Egyptians were incapable of operating the Suez Canal.

Another such proconsul was Sir Miles Lampson (Lord Killearn), who in 1936 had negotiated the Anglo-Egyptian Treaty, the basis of Britain's position in Egypt, that secured the Canal Zone as a military fortress—of its kind, the largest in the world in 1945. Killearn, like Cromer, was an authoritarian figure.[5] In 1942 he had with a blatant show of military force presented an ultimatum to the Egyptian king, Faruq, to install a Wafd nationalist regime under Nahas Pasha (who collaborated with the British during the rest of the war) or abdicate. This arrogant demonstration of British power rankled with not only Faruq but also the younger military officers and nationalists, not least Gamal `Abd al-Nasir. Killearn, still ambassador in Egypt in 1945, believed that the Egyptians understood only force, which must remain the basis of the British position in Egypt. It was this attitude that the Labour government after World War II attempted to repudiate.

The Labour government pursued a policy of nonintervention as a matter of principle. During the postwar years of Labour rule there was nothing comparable to forcing King Faruq to impose a Wafd government in 1942 or the adventure at Suez in 1956. But the aim was not entirely altruistic; there was an underlying calculation of self-interest. Attlee, Bevin, and their colleagues believed that intervention would undermine rather than sustain British influence in the Middle East. They were reluctant to impose political or economic arrangements that would require British bayonets. That theme runs through Bevin's minutes. Always having to bear in mind the weakness of the British economy and the scarcity of resources, he knew that the British public would not tolerate prolonged colonial warfare or suppression of nationalist movements. The old attitude of British domination as both necessary and beneficent—an attitude still prevalent in official as well as diehard circles—would have to change. If the British system were to endure, it would have to be dismantled and then reconstructed. The history of the British Empire in the Middle East during the first decade after 1945 can be interpreted as an unsuccessful attempt to convert formal rule and alliances to an informal basis of equal partnership and influence. Here is a paradox: the purpose of this transformation was the perpetuation of Britain as a great "world power." Nonintervention thus becomes intervention or hegemony by other means.[6]

Two qualifications need to be made to the Labour government's commitment to the principle of nonintervention. First, Bevin made a virtue of necessity. Britain was now economically dependent on the United States. The American loan of $3.5 billion to Britain in 1946 had significance for the Middle East and the empire at large, as well as for the British Isles. As with the house that Jack built, the United States propped up the British economy, which in turn enabled the British to prop up a fragile system of imperial control and to maintain the garrison at Suez, which in turn propped up a military, air, and naval network that extended throughout the Middle East. British policy, at least implicitly, had to be generally aligned with American policy if the economic relationship were to remain stable. Thus the British would have to prove willing to come to terms with Middle Eastern nationalism and to abolish the remnants of direct control. The relationship came under severe strain in the case of Palestine, and it snapped, temporarily, in the case of Suez. Otherwise the British skillfully played their hand. They managed to maintain for two decades the sterling area in the Middle East and elsewhere, despite American insistence that the closed economic system be opened up. When the British imperial system came to an end in the mid-1960s, decolonization had marched hand in hand with the dismantling of the sterling area.

The second qualification to Labour's principle of nonintervention, at least in the Middle East, lies in the character of Ernest Bevin. Bevin, the strongest man in the Labour government, had worked his way up in the Transport and General Workers' Union, and had served in the wartime coalition government as a member of the War Cabinet.[7] He was the moving force behind British policy in the Middle East, and was respected not merely for his determined views but also for his grasp of essential issues. Harry S. Truman, who disliked him, once spoke of him as "the embodiment of rugged honesty." But he had his shortcomings, not least of which was a volcanic temper and an immense reluctance to remain conciliatory once anyone had, in his view, betrayed him. The Zionists as well as the Egyptians, as will be seen, fell into this category, and by 1949 Bevin's policy of reconciliation was in a shambles. From an Egyptian point of view, there was little difference between him and Winston Churchill, and it is legitimate to ask whether there was ultimately any real distinction between Labour and Tory policies in the Middle East.[8] Since Churchill's tenure as prime minister extended from 1951 to 1955 as well as from 1940 to 1945, the question can be answered in comparative detail.

Would a Conservative government under Churchill's leadership have pursued a different course in attempting to resolve the problems of the postwar period? Bevin and Churchill saw eye to eye on many issues, though Churchill would have evacuated Palestine earlier, and he would assuredly have done it with better grace than Bevin. Nevertheless, there were substantial and divisive differences between the Tory and the Labour outlooks, in particular on the questions of the Canal Zone and the refinery at Abadan. Churchill believed that Suez should continue to provide Britain with a commanding bastion in the Middle East regardless of the loss of India, regardless of Egyptian nationalist protest, and regardless of American criticism of "colonialism." Suez, in his view, remained the keystone of the Middle East and indeed one of the supreme geopolitical positions in the world. He never forgave the Labour government for offering to withdraw British troops from Egypt in the spring of 1946. He also used the word "scuttle" in reference to the evacuation from Abadan in 1951. The differences in Tory and Labour modes of thought were real.

The themes of "development" and "collaboration" after 1945 help to explain the general continuity in British thought. Even the late Victorians would have felt at home in a Cabinet meeting in 1950, when Bevin set out the prospects for development in the Middle East and Africa. There were 25 million people in the Egypt and the Sudan, he said, and the water resources of the upper Nile in Uganda might be harnessed "to develop industries in the Nile Valley which would raise the standard of living in peace and provide a valuable industrial potential for war."[9] In the years after 1945, the British would provide technical assistance in projects of agricultural development, irrigation, education, and many other measures of economic and social welfare. Economically the Middle East, together with Africa, offered as alluring a prospect as India had in the past. Militarily the countries of the Middle East could be brought into a system of defense that would help to offset the manpower and military potential of the Soviet Union. Such were the combined political, economic, and military strands of thought that formed a general policy attempting to preserve Britain as a great power; the Middle East was the principal pillar of Britain's position in the world.

The British would secure their economic and military position only if they could find Arab and other leaders willing to cooperate. During World War II, the British for their own purposes had encouraged the creation of the Arab League, which, it had been hoped, would help to unite the Arabs behind the British wartime cause. In the postwar years, British officials sometimes used the phrase "Frankenstein's monster" to describe this organization partly of their own creation that was at once, in their view, reactionary and fanatically nationalistic. In any event, the British found themselves dependent on what was known as the "old gang" in each of the Arab countries and in the Arab League. The British now pinned their hope on persuading their collaborators to change their ways, while seeking other more moderate and younger nationalists to assist in economic and social development before the initiative passed to the extremists.

There were three major crises in the Middle East that the Labour government faced: the problem of Palestine; nationalization of the oil industry in Iran; and the question of British troops in Egypt, which was inseparable from that of the future of the Sudan.[10]

In Palestine, partition symbolized generally to the British a bankruptcy of policy, the end of the road, and an admission of failure. The British aimed to avert partition and to achieve, in one way or another, a binational state in which there would be religious and political guarantees for both Arabs and Jews. Bevin wanted to create a state in which Arabs and Jews would live and work together as equals.

The model of the binational state could be found in Britain's experience in both Canada and South Africa, though the separate Arab and Jewish units that the British had in mind resembled Swiss cantons. Such a binational state came closer to realization than is commonly remembered. In 1946, a British and American Committee of Inquiry made such a recommendation, but it foundered on President Harry Truman's unwillingness to give it full support. In April 1946 Truman accepted merely one part of the committee's report that recommended the admission to Palestine of 100,000 Jewish refugees. He did so unilaterally, without consulting the British prime minister or foreign secretary. The British and Americans were now acrimoniously at loggerheads at a critical time in the development of the Cold War as well as the Palestine conflict. To the British, a false step in Palestine could lead to disaster in the larger areas not only of Anglo-Arab relations but also of American support of the British Empire, the transfer of power in India, and the confrontation with the Soviet Union.

The critical period in Palestine was from the summer of 1946 to early 1947. In July 1946, the Jewish terrorist or freedom-fighting group Irgun Zvai Leumi blew up the British military headquarters at the King David Hotel in Jerusalem. The explosion at the King David irrevocably changed the public mood in Britain. It caused a powerful impulse to suppress terrorism, but at the same time it strengthened the view that the British should withdraw because of Jewish ingratitude. The British chiefs of staff held that, if Britain was compelled to choose between Arabs and Zionists, the overriding priority would be the need to preserve Arab goodwill. The decisions made at this time took place against the background of the great emotional debate on India, a sense of impending economic disaster, and one of the worst winters and fuel shortages in British history. It was not an easy time for the Labour government, or for the British people.

The two men making the critical decisions on cutting losses were Bevin and Attlee. When the two of them agreed in December 1946 that British troops should be withdrawn from Greece, Attlee aimed at economic and military retrenchment. Bevin also regarded the crisis in the eastern Mediterranean as an economic and military emergency, but beyond that he saw it as an opportunity to win American commitment to a northern tier stretching across Turkey, Iraq, and Iran that would provide a shield against Soviet penetration of the Middle East and Africa. In late 1946, Attlee and Bevin agreed not only on the question of withdrawal of British troops from Greece but also on the issue of submitting the Palestine problem to the United Nations. The key to their thought on the latter problem was that they did not want the British to be held responsible in Arab eyes for a policy of partition. Having presided over deadlock between the Zionists and Arabs, the British now moved to the United Nations in the hope that there would be a better chance that the Arab side would prevail. The British would thus continue to pursue the goal of a binational state, but in the international arena. In the last resort they hoped to avoid the stigma of presiding over partition.

The United Nations strategy was a miscalculation. In the summer of 1947, the United Nations Special Committee on Palestine (Unscop) visited Palestine.[11] British troops and other personnel were bivouacked behind barbed wire in "Bevingrads," in the center of Jerusalem and elsewhere. One-tenth of the armed forces of the entire British Empire now occupied Palestine, a territory the size of Wales. The majority of the members of Unscop voted in favor of partition, which triggered the British decision in September 1947 to evacuate. Against a background of economic anxiety, the decision was made during the crisis over the convertibility of sterling. To the British, Palestine was a small place but a major source of despair. After September 1947, British influence on the Palestine issue diminished. In November, the U.N. General Assembly endorsed partition. According to a British official reporting from New York, American newspapers had built up the fever of excitement to the extent that opponents of partition were regarded as enemies of the American people. The British stayed on until the expiration of the mandate on May 14–15, 1948, but they conducted a rearguard action. They had lost the initiative. The paramount aim remained to keep on good terms with the Americans as well as the Arabs, but the British could not do so as long as the issue of partition continued to poison the atmosphere. Arab nationalism, frustrated in Palestine, could not be appeased. It was the American failure, in British eyes, to curb militant Zionism that went to the heart of the trouble. In the course of the 1948 war, Bevin remarked that the Middle East was "sinking into chaos." The British at this time believed that Israel might become a communist state, if not a Soviet satellite, and that the Middle East was on the verge of revolution. "Another China," was the phrase Bevin used on several occasions to sum up his dire premonition about the Middle East. This was clearly an exaggeration, but it was in line with the general British view of the Middle East in the late 1940s. It is ironic that the British perceived a communist threat in Israel while in most of the Middle East they believed that the Americans exaggerated the dangers of Soviet penetration or communist takeovers.

On Iran, the American and British governments held divergent views, but, on the whole, they agreed that the regime of Muhammad Musaddiq might deteriorate into a revolutionary situation resulting in a communist regime or possibly a Soviet satellite.[12] Musaddiq had an inveterate mistrust of the British. No one who listened to his animated conversation could doubt that he actually believed the British to be responsible for the poverty and general malaise of Iran. Musaddiq himself was a scion of a wealthy Iranian landowning family. Born in 1882, he had first been elected to the Majlis, or Iranian parliament, in 1924. He consistently denounced British attempts to subjugate Iran, in his view, through the Anglo-Iranian Oil Company (A.I.O.C.) in Abadan and the British embassy in Tehran. After becoming prime minister in 1951,

Musaddiq achieved his major aim, the nationalization of A.I.O.C. in the same year.[13] Musaddiq acknowledged that the company was entitled to compensation, but he disagreed with the British on a fundamental point. He held that the foundation of the British position in Iran, the concession agreement of 1933, was both illegal and immoral. In this respect Musaddiq was the forerunner of a later generation of Asian and African nationalists who believed that the Western powers had no right to impose a system of capitalist exploitation. There lingered in Britain, on the other hand, the view that the Iranians had no real right to their own oil because its discovery and development were entirely due to British enterprise. The controversy raised a basic issue for the British, one they could not afford to concede: If Musaddiq's view prevailed, especially on the invalidity of the 1933 concession, then nationalists throughout the world could abrogate British concessions with impunity. The problem was clearly stated by the minister for defense in the Labour government, Emmanuel Shinwell, in May 1951: "Egypt and other Middle Eastern countries would be encouraged to think they could try things on: the next thing might be an attempt to nationalise the Suez Canal."[14]

The decision to intervene in Iran by covert operations was taken by the Conservative government after the election in late 1951 that brought the return of Winston Churchill as prime minister and Anthony Eden as foreign secretary. The Labour government, despite jingoistic sentiment on the part of Herbert Morrison, Bevin's successor as foreign secretary in early 1951, had held firm against military intervention. Attlee decided to keep British policy in line with that of the United States and the United Nations. The prime minister thus upheld a principle championed by Ernest Bevin, who had believed that Britain should use great restraint in interfering in the internal affairs of other countries, not least in Iran. This was a consistent attitude, as can be demonstrated in other places in the Middle East since 1945, above all in Egypt. Attlee and Bevin, however, never indicated that they would refuse categorically to support a policy of intervention. What can be established with certainty is that they persistently checked permanent officials from pursuing a more active or interventionist policy. One cannot say that without exception the Labour government stood in principle against covert operations. It was the Labour foreign secretary, Herbert Morrison, who gave instructions to plan for the overthrow of Musaddiq. In general, however, Attlee and Bevin believed that intervention would lead to unanticipated and undesirable consequences. The Labour government, in short, demonstrated restraint in not taking action against Musaddiq, as did the Truman administration in which Dean Acheson as secretary of state held views that independently coincided with Bevin's. The new Conservative government quickly indicated a much greater willingness to follow an interventionist course. Churchill and Eden worked in concert with the new Eisenhower administration, which included the two Dulles brothers, John Foster as secretary of state and Allen as director of the C.I.A. The early 1950s saw a sea change in the range and nature of covert operations in the Middle East and elsewhere.[15]

The critical month was August 1953. The intelligence agencies of Britain and the United States cooperated in an intervention that led to the fall of the Musaddiq government. The Central Intelligence Agency played a vital part in this venture and, in so doing, eventually established a reputation in Iran as the instrument of Western intervention responsible for the continued rule of the shah. This was a complex operation, its origins and planning mainly British but with vital American financial assistance and with the contribution of a flamboyant and effective intelligence officer, Kermit Roosevelt, who played a key role in its success. On the British side there are two figures useful to identify. The first is C. M. Woodhouse, who had fought with the Greek resistance during the war, became a colonel at the age of twenty-seven, and was later Conservative M.P. for Oxford and still later director of the Institute for International Affairs at Chatham House. In 1951–1952 he headed MI6 in Iran. He deemed joint action by Britain and the United States necessary to prevent the Red Army from marching southward and forging a satellite state in Iran on the model of eastern Europe. Against the background of the Greek civil war, the danger, as he saw it, was that of an internal communist takeover that would provide the opportunity for the Soviets.[16] This was also the American view, held both by the American embassy in Tehran and by the C.I.A. Woodhouse was responsible for the planning and for the initial liaison with the C.I.A. At the highest level, the other person was Churchill, who himself, during a time when Eden was ill, took the initiative in approving the plan to topple Musaddiq.

The British as well as the Americans bear some responsibility for the post-August 1953 course of Iranian history, but it was at this time that, in Iranian demonology, the United States began to eclipse Britain as "the Great Satan." The C.I.A. has lingered on in the public consciousness in Iran as the symbol of foreign intervention. For the British the legacy is more difficult to assess, but perhaps nations, like individuals, cannot be manipulated without a sense on the part of the aggrieved that old scores must eventually be settled. That was certainly Bevin's view. By 1953, however, the British had become convinced that Musaddiq had to be removed. The outcome seemed to demonstrate that the countries of the Middle East could still be coerced or indirectly controlled. The success of the 1953 operation encouraged Anthony Eden to believe that military action against Egypt in 1956 might also be a success.

This leads to the Suez crisis. The problem of the canal and Egypt must be seen from the perspective of Britain's position in Egypt after 1945, the legacy of the Labour government, and Eden's general line of conciliation until close to the time of the Suez crisis itself. The course of action pursued by Eden during the crisis was, as will be seen, very much an aberration for both himself and the course the British had consistently charted since 1945.

The Conservative government under Churchill and Eden had inherited from the Labour government the problems of the Egyptian unilateral abrogation of the Anglo-Egyptian Treaty in October 1951 and guerrilla warfare in the Canal Zone. On "Black Saturday" in late January 1952, mobs swept through Cairo killing, looting, and destroying the symbol of the British occupation, Shepheard's Hotel. Churchill wrote: "The horrible behaviour of the mob puts them lower than the most degraded savages now known.... I doubt whether any relationship is possible with them. They cannot be classed as a civilized power until they have purged themselves."[17] The overthrow of Faruq and the ascendancy of the Egyptian army officers in July 1952 seemed to mark the development of such a purge. The young military officers might not be experienced, and they might harbor anti-British sentiment, but, from the British viewpoint, almost anything was better than the old corrupt regime under Faruq.

The British came quickly to believe that Gamal `Abd al-Nasir was the moving force of the revolution. They judged that Nasir wanted to come to an agreement on the Canal Zone in order to move ahead with economic reconstruction and social reform, and that the dispute over troops in the Canal Zone prevented him from devoting his full concentration to domestic priorities. The British calculated that Nasir would be the best chance, perhaps the last, to reach a lasting reconciliation. According to a key British minute, the opportunity should be seized "to consolidate his [Nasir's] position... . it looks as though he is our best bet."[18]

Both the British and the Egyptians made genuine concessions to reach agreement on the evacuation of British troops from the Canal Zone in 1954.[19] Anthony Eden played a prominent role in the conciliatory tactics that led to temporary reconciliation with Egypt. Though Eden himself was ill for part of this period, and the approach to the Egyptians was very much a collective or team effort, this was an achievement by Eden that must be borne in mind in view of what happened in 1956. Eden was assisted by the 5th Marquess of Salisbury, an experienced statesman who had served as dominions secretary in the wartime coalition, and General Sir Brian Robertson, the commander of British Land Forces in the Middle East, who helped to persuade his fellow military officers that it would be wise to redeploy troops in the Middle East rather than concentrate them at Suez. Robertson's underlying rationale was that nuclear weapons had rendered the Suez base obsolete. In exchange for troop withdrawal, the British would have the right to return in the event of a general war. The withdrawal would be gradual and would take place over a two-year period. Robertson, along with Eden, wooed Churchill away from a diehard position. The British hoped that this would be a permanent settlement that would enable them, in turn, to resolve the Arab-Israeli problem and to create a line of defense in the Middle East along the northern tier.

Eden is often held responsible for the Suez venture, but it was in fact a collective operation with collective responsibility. Eden put his own reputation at risk. Once regarded as the champion of anti-appeasement of Hitler, he now appeared to the hard right of the Tory party as the arch-appeaser of Nasir. By evacuating troops from the Canal Zone, Eden seemed to be sounding an imperial retreat. He himself believed such criticism to be a caricature of his position, but in comparison with Churchill he did have progressive views. During the Suez crisis Eden responded with anger to the American accusation that old-fashioned colonialism motivated him. "It was I who ended the 'so-called colonialism' in Egypt," he exclaimed.[20]

The Suez crisis had its immediate origins in late 1955, when Nasir accepted military assistance from the Soviet Union via Czechoslovakia.[21] By introducing the Soviet Union as a major contender for regional hegemony, Nasir altered the existing balance of power in the Middle East. The Czech arms deal liberated Nasir from the Anglo-American embrace. In consequence John Foster Dulles first orchestrated an Anglo-American–World Bank offer to help build the Aswan High Dam and later abruptly withdrew it. This directly sparked Nasir's decision to nationalize the Suez

Canal Company on July 26, 1956. Eden now attempted to prove that he could rise to the occasion in the tradition of Churchill, but he had a higher aim as well: Britain would demonstrate that it remained the preeminent regional power in the Middle East and, moreover, a world power that could act, if necessary, independently from the United States.

The British prepared for the invasion of Egypt as if they were about to engage German Panzer units in World War II. With more effective and more daring planning, and without the fatal misjudgment about the United States, the military operations in November 1956 might have been a success. Nasir might have been toppled, a more friendly regime in Cairo might have been installed, and the life of the British Empire might have been extended. But it is just as possible that the British might have turned the clock back to 1882 and poisoned sentiment throughout the colonial world, not merely against Britain and France but against the United States as well. In any event, Eden and Harold Macmillan, the chancellor of the exchequer, did indeed make a monumental miscalculation. Eisenhower and John Foster Dulles believed that a British and French invasion would provoke a far-reaching anti-Western reaction. Most irritating to the Americans was the lack of consultation. Eden and Macmillan, as well as other members of the Cabinet, generally thought that the Americans did not want to know about the plans and would acquiesce in a successful operation. There is some evidence that this was true for Dulles but certainly not for Eisenhower, who was outraged. The Eisenhower administration waged virtual economic warfare against the British, forcing them and also the French and the Israelis to withdraw. It was Eden, not Nasir, who was toppled. The Suez venture demonstrated the dependence of Britain on the United States. Suez made it plain for all to see that Britain was doomed both as a colonial power and as a world power unless it acted in concert with the United States.

There was a psychological dimension to the trauma of Suez that has a bearing on subsequent events in the Middle East. Sir Charles Johnston, the governor of Aden, wrote: "One of the worst things that has happened to us ... particularly since Suez, is that in the Middle East we have lost confidence in our ability to deal with situations. The loss of confidence is a very odd thing—it is something which has happened inside ourselves, and bears no particular relation to the facts as observed in the field. Our Suez fiasco seems, in effect, to have left a far deeper mark on ourselves than on the Arabs."[22] Britain had not lost the will or the capacity to deal with colonial insurgency, as would later be proved in places such as Kenya and Malaysia. It had lost the pretense of being a superpower.

Over four decades later, it is still worth reflecting why Suez was so seminal an event and why it so bitterly divided the British people. Part of the explanation is that it split the nation because many believed that Britain should continue to champion the cause of the United Nations and should work in harmony with the United States, while others believed that the issue of security and the prestige of the British Empire overrode other commitments and, moreover, that the United States was aiming to dislodge Britain from the Middle East. These conflicting ideas were apparent in the mind of Lord Salisbury, who had helped to create the United Nations at San Francisco in 1945 and who was Anthony Eden's principal source of strength within the British Cabinet. When Salisbury decided in November 1956 that he could not in good conscience support the government in opposition to the United Nations, Eden himself began to waver and then collapsed. There was a failure of British nerve at the highest level. There was also deception, and this perhaps is the most significant legacy. Even at the time of the crisis there was a general sense that the government, and Eden in particular, had deceived Parliament and the public.

Eden became the scapegoat for a failed policy, but his ideas were representative of, and his policies accepted by, members of the Cabinet.[23] Eden was not a great man, and, for temperamental reasons alone, he probably should never have become prime minister. But he was representative of his age. He believed, as did many of his countrymen, that the British Empire would continue to survive as a Commonwealth, and that Britain would remain a world power. Suez was very much a collective enterprise. Many in the British government and in the country believed that the United States was attempting to dislodge Britain from the Middle East. This was a misapprehension, but sometimes the psychological dimension of such a problem is as important as the reality. The 1956 crisis was one of those rare moments in history when everything suddenly appeared different. Britain was no longer a great world power, certainly not in the Middle East, and within a decade the empire had been liquidated. The British Empire itself was a casualty of the Second World War, shifts in the international economy, and the rising tide of Asian and African nationalism. These great changes had already occurred, but in 1956 they suddenly appeared as a revelation.

In February 1957, in the wake of Suez, Harold Macmillan became prime minister. Macmillan was a political adventurer, able to change course 180 degrees if it served his purpose, as indeed he did during the Suez crisis, when he had been the most aggressive of all ministers at the beginning but then at the height of the emergency had urged an abrupt withdrawal. In 1957, he aimed above all to recapture the benevolence of the United States and, equally, to avert a collision with Arab and African nationalism. He knew that he could not get back on good terms with the Americans unless he demonstrated that the British no longer possessed "a Suez mentality." He responded sympathetically, if ambiguously, to the logic of the chiefs of staff and to certain officials in the Colonial Office and Foreign Office that the British Empire might contract yet prove to be a durable force with a hard core of strategic bases through the Mediterranean to Aden and on to Singapore. The essential elements of the old empire would be retained, not abandoned. Macmillan himself noted, "We only need our 'Gibraltars.'"[24] Aden would be the keystone in the new imperial system, the fortress protecting Britain's position in the Gulf regardless of Adeni or Arab nationalism. This was the grand design in the last decade before the British collapse in 1967.

Macmillan was not inhibited by conventional concepts. He was the single member of the Cabinet in 1956 who attempted to look beyond the crisis to see what might be the result of Nasir's fall. He preferred to regard the possible solution as regional rather than merely Egyptian. He looked forward to a permanent arrangement with the oil-producing states of the Middle East. In the early stages of the Suez crisis, he proposed no less than a post-Nasir era in which a general conference, presumably with

Egyptian participation, would agree to a broad plan for the coordination of oil production, the economic development of the Middle East, and the equitable settlement of boundary disputes, including those with Israel. In one way or another, the United States would be brought in to guarantee the arrangements and probably to pay for them. Macmillan also emphatically believed that there was no alternative to defeating Nasir. "If not, we would rot away."[25] These were apocalyptic thoughts. From the beginning of the Suez crisis he had given the impression, far more than any other member of the Cabinet, of "bellicosity ... beyond all description" and of "wanting to tear Nasser's scalp off with his own fingernails."[26] Macmillan, however, had immediately changed his line when he learned of the run on the pound and the hostility of the United States. The lesson he drew from the episode of Suez was that Britain must always align itself with the United States in the Middle East. Therein lies the explanation of British policy from 1956 onward. If "Nasirism" was to be defeated or at least contained, it would have to be through the revival of the historic Anglo-American alliance of World War II.

The survival of British influence as well as the very existence of some of the ruling elites in the Arab monarchies in the post-1956 period now depended on American support, which was symbolized by the Eisenhower Doctrine. The resolution authorized the president to provide economic and military assistance to Middle Eastern countries that requested "assistance against armed aggression from any country controlled by international communism." The difficulty, which the British fully perceived, was that Nasir was not a communist; nor could it be proved that the Soviet Union "controlled" Egypt. When Lebanon, Jordan, Saudi Arabia, and Iraq became open allies of the United States by adhering to the Eisenhower Doctrine, and thus qualifying for military and economic assistance, Nasir believed that a pro-Western alliance had encircled him. The polarization provided the regional background for the insurrection in Lebanon in May 1958 and for the military coup that liquidated the Iraqi monarchy in July.

The Suez crisis had catapulted Nasir from the status of an Egyptian leader into that of an Arab hero who seemed destined to bring about the unity of the Arab world. The next ten years proved to be critical both for Arab unity and for the continuing presence of the British in the Middle East. From 1958 to 1961, Egypt and Syria achieved unity in the form of the United Arab Republic. Britain responded by following the lead of Iraq and Jordan in a short-lived union between the two countries. From 1962 to 1967, Egypt fought in Yemen against the royalist regime, but other Arab states regarded Nasir's intervention as a bid by Egypt to dominate the Arabian peninsula. In Yemen the British attempted to shore up the imamate against the republican insurgents supported by Egypt. Nasir's Yemen campaign ended in disaster, drawing in one-third of the Egyptian army at an unbearable cost to the Egyptian economy of £E4 billion. The long-term consequences of Egyptian support of the Palestine Liberation Organization were even more cataclysmic. In the 1967 war with Israel, the Egyptian army suffered sweeping and humiliating defeat. Israeli troops captured Sinai and advanced to the Suez Canal, depriving Egypt of the oil fields of the Sinai peninsula and causing the Egyptians to blockade the canal. The year 1967 thus had a double significance for the British. Nasir, the arch-enemy, had been humbled; but in the same year the British were expelled from Aden.

Nasir once described Egypt as moving within the three circles of the Arab world, the broader domain of Islam, and Africa. Britain's three circles, as defined above all by Churchill but articulated just as eloquently by Macmillan, were those of Europe, America, and the Commonwealth. The word "Commonwealth" in the context of the Middle East, at least to British critics, meant British imperialism in a new guise. The British responded to Nasir's Egypt not merely by attempting to enlist the support of the United States but specifically by assisting the monarchies of Iraq, Jordan, and, to a more limited extent, Saudi Arabia; the dispute between Britain and Saudi Arabia over the Buraimi oasis kept the two countries at a distance despite the common enemy of Egypt.[27] From the British perspective, the key to survival in the Middle East lay with Iraq and with the Iraqi leader closely identified with the British, Nuri al-Sa'id, known universally in the West as Nuri Pasha.

Nuri had vigorously pursued the goal of Arab unity, essentially in harmony with British aims in the Middle East. He was the key figure in the calculation of whether the resources of Iraq could be developed and revolution averted. The British believed that Nuri would be the best hope of achieving economic and social reform, specifically through the Development Board established in 1950 to allocate oil revenues for projects such as large-scale dams and irrigation projects.[28] The British as well as Nuri played a critical part in shaping the goals of the Development Board, but it was Nuri's dominating personality that drove its proceedings. If only people would be patient, Nuri stated repeatedly, they would see how prosperous they would become from the investing of the oil money in long-range development projects. Nuri thought that a firm hand controlling and distributing the benefits of the oil riches would eventually lead to general prosperity and political stability. He did not intend, however, to restructure Iraqi society to alleviate the disparity between rich and poor. According to one astute British observer, "There is no sign that Nuri believes in reform. He believes rather in paternal government, the strong hand distributing gifts of welfare, which can be paid for not by taxing the rich but rather by extracting further revenues from the oil companies."[29] There was a case to be made in favor of Nuri's optimism. Oil revenues in Iraq had more than doubled, from £40.0 million in 1952 to £86.4 in 1958.[30] Nuri's gamble was that this huge wealth would create prosperity and bring about a lasting political stability without unduly disturbing the basis of the land system. According to the British ambassador, Sir Michael Wright, in 1957, "The benefits of the oil revenues were beginning to be felt in the lives of the ordinary people and whether in housing, education, health, flood control or irrigation, there was a sense of progress and expanding horizons, and of considerable pride in the manner in which the formidable tasks were being tackled."[31]

To do Nuri justice, at least from a British perspective, Michael Wright probably best summed up Nuri's qualities when he described him as "a sincere patriot working according to his own lights for the betterment of all Iraqis."[32] But the British were right in their assessment that Nuri's plans did not include reform of the landed system of estates and class, and therein lay one of the causes of the impending revolution. The

British found themselves allied not only with a royal family and ruling groups that did not represent the social components of the country but also with a fragile structure of civil and military control. Government in Iraq was still underpinned by the British military presence in the air bases, by British advisors in government departments, and by British influence in controlling the country's most important economic asset, its oil. British sway was nevertheless limited. Ever since the creation of the Iraqi state in the aftermath of the First World War, political power had rested ultimately on shifting Iraqi combinations of the monarchy, the government, the parliament, the civil service, and the army. By the 1950s, however, a political culture had developed that could not find expression in the institutions of the state. An educated class drew inspiration from pan-Arabism or Marxism, or a mixture of the two. The growing mass of urban poor in Baghdad expressed its needs in terms of these new ideologies or in those of a just Islamic society. The intellectual and political climate in Baghdad became increasingly hostile to the British.

The Iraqi revolution of July 1958 was a landmark in the history of the Middle East. It swept away the Hashimite monarchy. The king and other members of the royal family together with Nuri were murdered. What did the British believe that they had achieved in Iraq before "the catastrophe," and what did they hope to salvage? It is a useful question because what was true for Iraq was also true, from the British perspective, for many other countries in the Middle East before and after 1958. Modernization in cooperation with British proved to be a failure, but Iraq did emerge as a modern state during the British era. Iraq acquired not only boundaries but also a system of administration and justice, a constitution, and a bicameral legislature. The British developed an infrastructure of roads, railways, and telegraphs and, not least for British purposes, the strategic airfields at Habbaniyah and Shaiba. They created a central bureaucracy with all the trappings of Western government, including offices with files, typewriters, and telephones. Internal security was provided by the Iraqi Police Force with its own Criminal Investigation Department. The Iraqi Petroleum Company became one of the principal oil producers in the Middle East.[33] All of these things in one way or another served British interests. Yet at the same time British administrators could emphatically claim that they served the Iraqi government in the best tradition of the British civil service.

The British hoped that they had provided a framework of national unity, but the four decades since the birth of the Iraqi state proved to be too short a time to foster a truly national society out of three Ottoman provinces with populations of mixed ethnic origins and religious allegiances. The revolution caught the British off guard; in any event they were not fully appreciative of the intensity of anti-Western sentiment. One official provided a uniquely British description of the volcanic force of the emotions that burst to the surface during the revolution of July 1958 by writing that "if the Russian revolution had been put into execution by the Mau-Mau the effect would not have been very much different."[34] In fact the revolution, though it commanded wide support, was the work of a group of disaffected military officers who had only vague ideological allegiances but were committed to destroying the old social order and ending the common impression that Iraq was a "puppet state" controlled by the British.

Brigadier Abd al-Karim Qasim was the leader of the revolution. Though a passionate Iraqi nationalist, he was wary of conspiracies by his fellow officers, and he was extremely secretive. The British speculated that the Iraqi revolution might follow the pattern of the Egyptian, with sincere if misguided army officers attempting reform. One of the first major British assessments of the new regime described his aims: "Like Nuri, Qasim also wants an independent Iraq, in which Kurds and Arabs, Shias, Sunnis and other minorities will be united and which will be developed in accordance with a long-term economic plan, financed from the oil royalties paid by the Iraq Petroleum Company."[35] Qasim well understood that he needed the oil revenues to finance development projects. The British came to believe that they might be able to live more or less comfortably with the new revolutionary regime. Qasim was an Iraqi nationalist leading an uncertain revolution restricted mainly to Iraq. He did not prove to be an ally or puppet of Nasir, though he turned to the Soviet Union for arms and trade. Most importantly, he was willing to keep the oil flowing; the nationalization of the oil industry did not culminate until 1972, after the British withdrawal from the Gulf and after Libya's nationalization of British Petroleum in the previous year. But a major crisis between the British and Qasim did develop when he threatened to take over Kuwait in 1961. As will be seen, he was deterred by the deployment of British troops. Qasim himself was overthrown and executed during an internal coup d'état in 1963. During the Qasim era there had emerged two bedrock British assumptions about postrevolutionary Iraq. The first was that Kuwait, as the main supplier of oil to western Europe, must be held at any cost against possible Iraqi aggression; the British took comfort from the assurance given by the United States during the period of the Iraqi revolution that American troops would reinforce British forces if Iraq attempted to invade Kuwait. The other accepted truth held that Qasim's successor might be even more bloodthirsty and unsatisfactory. Both assumptions continued to hold true to the end of the century.

The year of crisis for Iraq in 1958 was also one for Lebanon and Jordan. In May, street riots broke out in Beirut, protesting against the pro-Western regime of President Camille Chamoun and threatening civil war. The American and British governments made contingency plans; the Security Council of the United Nations voted in June to send U.N. observers to Lebanon to monitor the movement of troops and arms. By July, Jordan as well as Lebanon appeared to be on the verge of dissolution. Pro-Nasir sentiment was now conspicuous in the two countries and a revolutionary atmosphere seemed to be spreading from Iraq. American marines from the Sixth Fleet landed near Beirut on July 15, and British paratroops were dropped at Amman two days later. Although the show of force proved to be effective and satisfactory, Harold Macmillan was extremely nervous about "Suez in reverse," with the United States playing the part of the principal interventionist power. The crisis ended with the return to stability in Lebanon indicated by the assumption of the office of president by General Fuad Chehab in September, and by the withdrawal of American and British troops from Lebanon and Jordan by the end of October.[36]

During his tenure of office (1958–1964), Chehab proved to be an outstanding Lebanese patriot and statesman. The British persistently underrated him, but he revived the sense of Lebanese national identity, improved the educational system as well as the infrastructure of roads and communications, and promoted social reform. He rose above sectarian loyalties. He kept the army out of politics. But the Chehab system of government did not narrow the gap between rich and poor; nor did it prove strong enough to prevent the descent of Lebanon into civil war and the collapse of the Lebanese economy from the boom of financial services in the 1960s to the shambles of the 1970s. The British remained passive observers when the P.L.O., driven out of Jordan, established its headquarters in Beirut in 1970, and when militias virtually partitioned Lebanon in 1976. Nor did Britain exert any particular influence during the crises in 1978 and 1982, when Israel invaded Lebanon. In a manner reminiscent of previous British interventions, U.S. military forces attempted to reestablish a central Lebanese authority but were compelled to withdraw in 1983 in the face of Syrian-backed Lebanese resistance.

The revolution in Iraq touched even Cyprus, where the year 1958 also marked a turning point.[37] Macmillan thought that the Turks, alarmed at the developments in Iraq and elsewhere, might now work together with the British to avert the danger of civil war on the island. There was a complex interplay of events and personalities. Macmillan brought Archbishop Makarios back from exile in the Seychelles, where he had languished since 1956. Makarios himself set Cyprus on the path toward independence rather than Enosis, or union with Greece, but he also put himself on a collision course with George Grivas, the leader of the underground terrorist or freedom-fighting movement in Cyprus. Whereas Makarios was the charismatic high priest and politician, Grivas was the guerrilla warrior who had a romantic conception of Cyprus as part of the Greek homeland, and who never wavered in his determination to realize his goal. Makarios could never quite make resolute decisions or ultimately distance himself from the "Holy Sacred Oath" binding him and Grivas on Enosis. Macmillan attempted to win over Makarios by offering qualified independence in association with Greece, Turkey, and Britain. The three powers would guarantee the territorial integrity of the island and the constitution (which granted virtual autonomy to the two communities: one 80 percent Greek, the other 20 percent Turkish, but not distributed along ethnic lines). The British calculated that the Greek government—and Makarios—might regard the island's independence as an alternative to civil war and partition, and that Turkey might now be more willing to endorse independence not only for the same reasons but also because of the impending collapse of the Baghdad Pact. Macmillan's initiative represented a break with the policy of previous British governments, and Macmillan himself presided over a critical stage of the island's history by bringing Turkey actively into the equation for a settlement. Did the Macmillan government thereby place Cyprus on the road to partition?

Cyprus held a singular place in British conceptions about security in the Middle East, not least as a point of supreme strategic significance. After the withdrawal from the Suez base in 1954, the island had become the headquarters of British forces in the Middle East. Although Anthony Eden sometimes simplified the problem to the point of caricature, in 1956 he expressed a tenet of British thought when he said that without Cyprus, Britain would not be able defend Britain's general position in the Middle East and might thus lose access to supplies of oil: "No Cyprus, no certain facilities to protect our supply of oil. No oil, unemployment and hunger in Britain. It is as simple as that."[38] Eden believed that Cyprus, like Gibraltar, must remain a permanent part of the empire and could never become independent. Whenever a possible change in the island's status was mentioned, Eden thought of repercussions in Spain as well as Turkey. Cyprus, however, was no adequate substitute for the base at Suez. Nor was it entirely axiomatic that the loss of the island might lead to the loss of oil supplies. Could not oil can be bought and sold without the threat of military action? Could not the British military presence be maintained by strategic bases rather than the occupation of all of the island? The solution devised by the Macmillan government was to offer independence with guarantees to both ethnic communities by Greece, Turkey, and Britain, and with the retention under British sovereignty of military bases at Dhakelia and Akrotiri ("We only need our 'Gibraltars'"). Under those terms Cyprus gained independence in 1960.[39] In the postindependence crises of ethnic violence, Britain refused to intervene in 1964 and refused again in 1974, when Makarios was overthrown by the diehard Greek Cypriots who aimed for union with Greece. The 1974 crisis triggered a Turkish invasion and the partition of the island. The settlement of 1960 might have worked if subsequent British governments had acted as guarantors of the territorial integrity of the island. In the changing political climate of the 1960s and 1970s, however, the British declined to become involved in the Cyprus tangle again. In a comment that accurately sums up the British position after Cypriot independence, George Ball, the American under-secretary of state, remarked that "the British wanted above all to divest themselves of responsibility for Cyprus."[40]

In a pattern that became clear from the late 1960s onward, what held true for disengagement in Cyprus also held true for the rest of the Middle East in the fourth and last phase of Britain's presence in the region. The British withdrew in two stages, from Aden in 1967 and from the Gulf in 1971. The intention, however, was not to liquidate but to stabilize Britain's position and to cling to the essentials of the old empire. As British power shifted from the Mediterranean eastward, Aden and Singapore came into focus as the points of military and naval concentration. The ultimate British Empire would be projected on a wide maritime arc stretching across the Indian Ocean. At a time when British statecraft was becoming increasingly preoccupied with the prospect of a swing toward Europe, the commitment to defense east of Suez actually increased even as British manpower contracted. Part of the reason lay in the fear that turbulence in the Gulf might interfere with Britain's supply of oil. In the year 1967, Britain's annus horribilis, this last great vision of British imperial supremacy shattered on the reality of economic crisis in Britain and the expulsion of British forces from Aden.[41]

In Aden two concepts of grand strategy collided. One was that of the permanent or sovereign base; the other was that of a larger, federated state resting on the popular consent of the inhabitants. The former view held that the British would continue to occupy the base at Aden as a city-port and military garrison despite an anarchic or hostile hinterland. The "Gibraltar" of Aden would become the keystone in the new imperial system with a fortress protecting Britain's position in the Gulf regardless of Adeni or Arab nationalism. "One of the greater heresies of contemporary thought is that a base is useless if situated amidst a hostile population," wrote Julian Amery at the Colonial Office.[42] Amery believed that Aden could be effectively defended, and devil take the hindmost. This notion of a harder, tougher empire unified by strategic bases in the Indian Ocean still appealed to Macmillan as well as permanent officials as they made plans for Britain's continued use of the garrison and base after Aden's independence. In the extensive controversy within official circles about the future of Aden, however, Amery found himself on the losing side. The second and opposing concept held that Britain could not remain in Aden against the will of the peoples of southern Arabia, and that every effort must be made to grant independence to a larger, federated Aden that embraced the protectorate in the hinterland. This was the idea that eventually prevailed. The British pinned their hopes on Aden not as a sovereign base but, in the words of the governor, as "an independent and prosperous Arab State on terms of friendly partnership and association with us."[43]

Aden was linked to a larger struggle in the Arabian peninsula. In September 1962, a revolutionary republican coup d'état overthrew the imam of Yemen, thus beginning the Yemeni civil war. Nasir threw his support behind the republicans while Saudi Arabia and Britain, though secretly, backed the royalists. Just as the British Raj in the previous century had made alliances with the tribes on the frontiers of India to prevent the takeover of Afghanistan by Russia, so the British colonial regime in Aden attempted to unify the tribal sheikhs of the hinterland to prevent the absorption of the Yemen by Egypt. Egypt committed some 70,000 troops in the civil war. But the implications for the British were far greater than the threat posed by the number of Egyptian soldiers. The majority of the 138,000 population in "Aden Town," as the city-port continued to be called, sympathized with Nasir and became increasingly anti-British. The city-port contained some 48,000 immigrant workers from Yemen, and the civil war in Yemen spilled over into Aden. The nationalist or terrorist organizations had conflicting goals, but all aimed to expel the British from southern Arabia. The radical nationalists in Aden drew support from trade unions and immigrant workers, but the leaders had little control over their young followers in the urban jungle of Aden city. The terrorist or freedom-fighting campaign acquired a momentum of its own. In this violent insurrection, no nationalist could afford to be less anti-British than any other.

Since 1839, Aden had occupied a vital place in the British Empire as a coaling station and trading port, and since 1960 (after the withdrawal from Cyprus) as headquarters for the British Middle East Command. In the 1950s, Aden emerged as a major maritime bunkering port that serviced more traffic than any other port except New York. Most ships on the way from Europe to India and all points east put in for fuel and supplies. The refinery at "Little Aden," constructed in 1952 after Musaddiq had evicted the Anglo-Iranian Oil Company from Iran, stood as the most important oil installation in the region. Khormakhsar airfield was the Royal Air Force's busiest station. It was from this military base that the British had deployed forces in Kuwait in 1961 to deter Iraq. The base itself was near Little Aden and about twenty miles from the city-port. The development of the base represented a military commitment as large as any postwar British government had undertaken. It came increasingly to resemble, if smaller, the old base at Suez, with a £5 million cantonment for 2,500 soldiers and

1,000 women and children, air-conditioned barracks, houses, messes, workshops, stores, training grounds, shops, two schools, a hospital, squash courts, a swimming pool, a cinema, and a church.[44] By 1964 there were 8,000 men (and some women) of the Army, Navy, and R.A.F. stationed there. The military complex with its troops, workshops, and communications network represented the last bastion of British power in the Middle East.

In the early 1960s, the city-port would have been immediately recognizable to any visitor as a British colonial city. The immigrant workers created the impression of a volatile urban society, but the British community of soldiers, civil servants, refinery technicians, agricultural advisers, irrigation engineers, doctors, and teachers gave an equally strong impression of a dependency that conformed to the classic traditions of the British colonial presence. The underlying British assumption since the 1950s held that everyone would benefit from the prosperity of the city-port, rather like Nuri Pasha's hope for social gain from oil revenues in Iraq: the greater the economic boom, the greater the chance for an enduring connection between Britain and the city-port and hinterland. But no one doubted the magnitude of the gamble of harnessing the colony and protectorate to a single political purpose.

The area of the colony or city-port extended only over some 75 square miles, but that of the protectorate in the hinterland over 61,000 square miles, roughly the equivalent of England and Wales or half the size of Texas. The protectorate, divided into western and eastern parts, had come formally into shape in 1886, almost half a century after the creation of the colony. In the protectorate, "indirect rule," as in Fiji, Malaya, and Nigeria, found its origins in treaties with individual tribal rulers or shaikhs. By the 1950s, the British hoped that a federation of the shaikhs might stabilize the hinterland against the challenge of radical Arab nationalism. Created in 1959, the federation in the protectorate never achieved a political identity. Sir Kennedy Trevaskis, the federation's principal architect, hoped to forge a viable structure that would be autonomous in its individual tribal units but united under British patronage and protection. Trevaskis was the political agent in the protectorate, and later high commissioner (1963–1965) after the merger of the city-port and the hinterland. During his tenure, the British made improvements in agriculture and communications, and provided significant economic, educational, and medical services in the hinterland. The protectorate's federation, however, remained a conglomeration of individuals and groups united only by the fear of common enemies. Critics often applied the word "feudal" to the attempt by Trevaskis and others to shore up traditional authority and existing social structures, thereby leaving the rulers almost as absolute as before. There was truth in the criticism. The anachronistic social structure of the tribes was increasingly threatened by advancing technology. In the 1950s, transistor radios poured into southern Arabia and undermined the position of the chiefs as well as the basis of British rule, in Macmillan's phrase, with "a wave of poisonous propaganda." The broadcasts of the "Voice of the Arabs" from Cairo exerted a powerful appeal to the inhabitants of the hinterland and city-port alike.

To the prime minister, the tribal rulers had a compelling attraction.[45] He compared the tribesmen to the Scottish highlanders of earlier centuries. By securing the cooperation of the shaikhs, Nasir might be foiled, the position at the base secured in perpetuity, a possible bid for Soviet supremacy in the Indian Ocean thwarted, and the United States assured of Britain's determination to fulfill defense commitments. "They are on our side," Macmillan wrote of the sheikhs. It must not be thought that his ideas were simplistic. Beneath the historical analogies and bold geopolitical views lay a shrewd assessment of the Yemeni nationalists as motivated not by communism but by irredentism, of the crescendo of anticolonial sentiment in the United Nations, and of the necessity to keep British policy in alignment with that of the United States.

Macmillan's conversations about Yemen with President John F. Kennedy took place against the background of the Cuban missile crisis in 1961.[46] Though certain American officials regarded the civil war in southern Arabia as no less than an international emergency, Kennedy himself had no knowledge of the Yemen. "I don't even know where it is," he commented to Macmillan.[47] Kennedy followed the advice of the regional experts in the State Department who favored recognition of the revolutionary regime to conciliate radical Arab nationalism and to persuade Nasir to withdraw the Egyptian troops. Macmillan believed that the new government in Yemen represented Egyptian expansionism, but his assessment of the danger took into account the divergent views of the Foreign Office and the Colonial Office. Summing up the dilemma, he wrote, "If we *recognise* the new revolutionary Government, we shall lose all our friends in the Aden *Protectorate* and the *Colony* may get quite out of hand. If we do *not*, we lose our [Yemen] Embassy (in due course) and all chance of having some influence on the Government."[48] In what he described as a "violent division of opinion" between the Foreign Office (which favored recognition of the new regime in Yemen) and the Colonial Office (which reflected the view of the Aden colonial government in opposing recognition), the prime minister backed the Colonial Office in resisting revolutionary Arab nationalism. With a final throw of the dice in the Great Game, Macmillan moved forward with plans for the merger of the protectorate and the colony. Nasir responded with rhetoric that again soared to the level of his anti-British denunciations in 1956.

The creation of the federation of the colony and protectorate in 1963 symbolized one of the last acts of Britain's imperial will. It took place at a time when comparable federations in the West Indies and Central Africa had either collapsed or were on the brink of dissolution. The aim was admirable. It made geographic, economic, and administrative sense for the resources of the hinterland to be exploited on the basis of the vibrant economy of the city-port and for the city-port itself to have a hinterland in which to develop rather than to achieve eventual independence on the model of Singapore as a city-state. The pooling of resources would allow the financing of large-scale development. The federation, however, had a troubled birth. Apathy rather than protest marked the actual merger, but common people in the back streets of Aden Town sensed that the federation would work to the advantage of the shaikhs and the rich merchants. Even the latter suspected that the wealth of the port would be siphoned off to the desert. There was a hostile reaction from Yemen, Egypt, and the Arab world generally. Nasir proclaimed an all-out war of liberation. When High Commissioner Trevaskis visited New York in late 1963 in an attempt to prevent an adverse judgment at the bar of world opinion, he encountered the full blast of anticolonial sentiment in the U.N. Special Committee on Colonialism and the view that Aden's jails were worse than Hitler's camps. In December, the General Assembly called for the removal of the British base and the independence of Aden.[49] On the eve of the vote, Trevaskis narrowly escaped an assassination attempt at Khormakhsar airport. The public mood now changed. The British felt beleaguered, with Aden regarded as a pariah colony at the United Nations and Aden itself in terrorist insurrection. The initiative had passed to the leaders of the revolution.

In one of its first major acts, the Labour government (1964–1970) sacked Trevaskis, the federation's champion, and reversed course. Aiming to modernize the British economy and radically to reduce defense expenditures, the Labour politicians of the Harold Wilson era found themselves out of harmony with the projected cost of the base and the undemocratic "feudal" shaikhs. The Colonial Office consequently proposed a unitary state based on representative government. The change in direction came as no surprise. The Labour Party had already taken a stand against the federation. In 1962 Denis Healey, who became defense minister in 1964, had attacked "the tying of Aden Colony ... to the reactionary shaykhdoms." The British would now work, in the words of Anthony Greenwood, the colonial secretary, toward "a unitary state on a sound democratic basis."[50] The new stance did not mean giving up the base. When the conflict in Vietnam began to intensify, and with it left-wing anti-American sentiment in the Labour Party, the prime minister pledged not to send British troops to Vietnam. But Wilson desperately needed American support in the economic blizzard that swept over Britain in the mid-1960s. Unemployment stood at a higher level than at any time since 1945, and inflation rose to unprecedented heights. Healey compared defense expenditure to a runaway train. To secure American support for sterling, the British needed, among other things, to hold firm in Aden, and thus to demonstrate that they would fulfill their defense commitments.

The schizophrenic nature of the Labour government helps to explain the indecisive and vacillating policy in Aden, reminiscent of the policy in Palestine three decades earlier. Wilson and Healey accepted responsibilities for the empire in the tradition of Attlee and Bevin. Others sympathized with the liberation movements. Anthony Greenwood, for example, was a member of the Society for Colonial Freedom. Still others, above all Roy Jenkins—who as chancellor of the exchequer in 1967 made a critical difference in the outcome—believed that remnants of the empire such as the base at Aden should be liquidated and that Britain should move into the European Community. As in the case of the plan for the federation, the blueprint for constitutional democracy in Aden was admirable. But critics then and later questioned whether the aim to broaden the representative base of government made sense in the struggle for absolute power that characterized the civil war in southern Arabia. Aden was becoming ungovernable. In 1965–1966, five officers of the Police Special Branch were assassinated within six months. Disaffection spread in the army as well as the police, and in 1967 a mutiny erupted in the federal armed forces. When the revolution moved into the climactic stage, it coincided not only with the Six-Day War between Israel and the Arab countries, in June 1967, but also with the crisis over devaluation. Just as the sterling crisis in 1947 sparked the decision to end the Palestine mandate, so the devaluation controversy two decades later helped to determine the abrupt evacuation of troops from Aden. Palestine may have been a scuttle, but at least the military band played Auld Lang Syne when the last troops departed. British forces withdrew from Aden in a retreat under fire.

In the transition to independence in other colonies, the British usually found collaborators to ensure a stable successor state. In Aden there emerged no equivalent of a Nehru or a Kenyatta, though in the figure of Abdullah al-Asnag, the leader of the trade union movement, the British thought they detected "a kind of fledgling Ernest Bevin" or, in another curious comparison, "the lineaments of another Archbishop Makarios."[51] The dynamic of the revolution, however, drove Asnag and others into extreme opposition to the British. In 1965 he helped to form the Front for the Liberation of Occupied South Yemen (F.L.O.S.Y.), one of two major contenders for power in the revolution. The other was the National Liberation Front (N.L.F.), which had been founded in Yemen two years earlier. Nasir attempted to unite and control the two movements. Indeed it was the failure of the Egyptians to make the N.L.F. their client that led to Nasir's sponsorship of F.L.O.S.Y.[52] Nasir's efforts proved to be futile, as did the British attempt to find a commanding figure in the revolution with whom they could agree on a transfer of power. Asnag himself summed up both the dilemmas, Egyptian and British: "At heart I am a Yemeni."[53]

In early 1966, the political climate began to change with such velocity that it seemed to the British to be a whirlwind of nationalist frenzy. In intensity, anticolonial sentiment resembled that of the Algerian revolution. N.L.F. and F.L.O.S.Y. gunmen battled for control of the streets in Aden. Both organizations turned against the British in terrorist acts to demonstrate that neither was less nationalist than the other. The sponsorship by Egypt of F.L.O.S.Y. and the anticolonial stance of the United Nations now became increasingly irrelevant as the internal balance tilted decisively to the N.L.F. By mid-1967, the British had withdrawn from the hinterland into the city of Aden and were fighting a rearguard action.

Two external events in June 1967 further undermined the British position and simultaneously facilitated the ascendancy of the N.L.F. First, in the Six-Day War that began on June 5, Egypt met with catastrophic defeat. Nasir began immediately to withdraw Egyptian troops from the Yemen. Second, the mutiny of the federal troops on June 20 struck a mortal blow at the military effectiveness of the British, though they reestablished a precarious control over the city of Aden. There were broad consequences. The Six-Day War closed the Suez Canal and strained the British economy as well as the military lines of communication to Aden. It was commonly believed in Aden and throughout the Middle East that the British had supported the Israelis. In Britain there was a shortage of fuel supplies caused by the blocking of the canal. The issue of Aden became part of a debate within a larger debate on the withdrawal of British forces east of Suez and whether or not Britain could afford to remain a world power. When the pound sterling was devalued from $2.80 to $2.40 in November, the new chancellor of the exchequer, Roy Jenkins, argued powerfully that the British could no longer live beyond their means and that the future lay in membership of the

European Community. Events in Aden continued to deteriorate. The Aden government unconditionally ceded authority to the N.L.F. On November 29, the last British troops were lifted by helicopter to a naval task force in the harbor. The military collapse brought to a close 129 years of British rule in Aden. For the British, it marked the end of the Great Game in western Asia.

Historians will long debate whether or not a different course taken by the British in the 1950s and 1960s might have led to the creation of a state more friendly to the west and less inclined to turn to the Soviet Union after 1967. The People's Democratic Republic of Yemen (South Yemen), as the new state was called, relied heavily on economic and military support from the Soviet bloc and Communist China. The civil war in southern Arabia continued to play itself out both within the north and south and within the region as a whole. In North Yemen the army tipped the balance in favor of those attempting to modernize the country as against tribal groups who resisted a strong central government. The discovery of oil and its export, which began in 1987, played a substantial part in the outcome of the regional civil war. In the south, the internal conflict centered on party and Marxist ideology and on persistent hostility to tribal affiliation. Armed conflict broke out between the north and the south in 1971, and hostilities lasted sporadically for the better part of two decades. The civil war has still not entirely ended, but the collapse of support by the Soviet Union in 1989 undermined the position in the south. In any event, the north had the advantages of a larger population and an agricultural base. Not least it possessed the quality of leadership in Ali Abdullah Salih, the president of North Yemen, that the British failed to find in the run up to independence. Salih brought about a union of the two states in 1990.[54] Britain played virtually no part in the internal struggle.

The British reaction to post-independent Aden, or the People's Republic, persistently reflected disillusion. Harold Macmillan commented in retrospect that "our friends were ... abandoned and our enemies comforted."[55] By contrast, the disillusionment of Richard Crossman, a minister in the Labour government, found expression in his relief from the Aden withdrawal: "There'll be one major commitment cut—thank God."[56] The Foreign and Commonwealth Relations Office pondered the lessons. One official observed after the evacuation that "the general British reaction to the Southern Yemen after our withdrawal has been profound indifference."[57] The first British ambassador to the new state reported in 1968 that the Americans now had to deal with many of the problems of the Middle East that had earlier preoccupied the British, but that American squeamishness prevented them from taking a bold and decisive stand: "The Americans ... are far more sensitive to invective and abuse than we are." The British themselves, he observed in a way that linked the issues of Palestine, Cyprus, and Aden, "should stop licking our wounds and try to establish ... the same sort of unsentimental working relationship with the thugs of Aden which we ultimately arrived at with the thugs of Israel and the thugs of Cyprus."[58]

Within four years of the evacuation from Aden, the British withdrew from the Gulf. By 1971, the British presence in the Middle East had dwindled to a mere shadow of its previous self. British statesmen in the decade after 1945 feared that Britain's position would be reduced to that of a second-rate European power or worse—"another

Belgium." There turned out to be some truth in that anxiety, because Britain's influence in the Middle East in the last three decades of the twentieth century did resemble that of a medium-size European state rather than that of a great world power attempting to stand on the same footing as the United States and the Soviet Union. British sway, of course, did not totally come to an end in 1971. The British continued to play an important role, for example, in the peacekeeping operations in Cyprus, in the affairs of Libya, in dealing with the problems of terrorism, in the crises of the oil industry, and in the trauma of the Iranian revolution. But British involvement in these issues was on a different order of magnitude from that of the pre-1971 engagement as a major regional power.

The Middle East itself continued to have a large significance for Britain, even though the influence of Britain as a regional power plummetted.[59] In British trade and commerce, the region counted third in volume after North America and Europe. Middle Eastern wealth in the last quarter of the century accounted for one-third of overseas holdings in British banks, especially deposits from Kuwait and Saudi Arabia. Investments in property in London as well as shares in the stock markets helped to buoy up the British economy. The Middle East provided the greatest overseas market for British building contractors and civil engineers. In the sale of arms, the Middle East in recent decades accounted for 50 percent of British arms exports. The import of oil, however, figured more largely in the 1970s than later. In 1973, the British imported 75 percent of their oil from the Middle East. After the discovery of North Sea oil, Middle Eastern oil reaching Britain dwindled to 14 percent in 1983. Since oil and gas resources in the North Sea will dwindle, dependence on Middle Eastern oil is probably only in abeyance until the end of the first decade or so of the twenty-first century. On the European continent, 75 percent of the oil continues to flow from the Gulf.

In regard to Britain's position in the Gulf, it is important to see the Gulf in relation to both the Middle East as a whole and Anglo-American relations. In broad dimensions, Libya serves as a good example of the way a geographically distant part of the region affected the affairs of the Gulf. The case of Libya illuminates the international problem of oil as well as the mutual reliance of the United States and Britain. The post-1945 government of Libya, indeed the state itself, was in fact a British and American creation behind the façade of the United Nations.[60] As throughout the postwar period, the British reverted to indirect means to achieve traditional aims. In Libya, the British worked under the auspices of the United Nations, and with the indispensable economic support of the United States, to secure Cyrenaica, the eastern province of Libya, as a strategic area that would reinforce Britain's position generally in the Middle East. The American air base at Wheelus Field contributed in a similar way to local as well as regional security. But it was the British who indirectly held sway. By bolstering the authority of the first king of Libya, Sayyid Muhammad Idris, the spiritual and secular leader of the Senussi, the British devised a formula for the stability of the Libyan state. Libya achieved independence in 1951 and Idris's reign lasted until the revolution of 1969.

A decade earlier, oil had been discovered. At the same time that the Iraqi revolution of 1958 sent shock waves through the Middle East, there emerged the possibility of discovering oil reserves of the magnitude of the richest of the Iranian and Saudi fields. Until then the purpose of the presence of British troops had been "to support the Libyan Government against the danger of subversion."[61] The discovery of oil in 1959 transformed the situation. The head of the African Department in the Foreign Office noted that there were prospects of ten to twenty million tons of oil a year—one-half of the Venezuelan production.[62] At a single stroke, Britain might be at least partly freed from dependence on oil produced in the Gulf. By 1970, Libya was the fifth-largest oil producer in the world. But the leader of the 1969 revolution, Mu`ammar Qadhafi, proved to be no friend of either Britain or the United States. He first insisted on the evacuation of foreign troops. British forces withdrew from the principal base at Tobruk in March 1970, and the Americans from Wheelus Field shortly thereafter. In December 1971, in a move connected with developments in the Gulf, Qadhafi ordered the seizure of the assets of British Petroleum on the grounds that there had been British complicity in the Iranian takeover of the disputed islands of Abu Musa and the two Tunbs claimed by two states in the United Arab Emirates. In such a way did the affairs of the Gulf extend as far west as Libya. Libya led the assault on the existing system of oil company contracts, which led to the massive oil price increases of 1973. In 1984, a series of bomb attacks against dissident Libyans in Britain led in turn to anti-Qadhafi demonstrations outside the Libyan Embassy in St. James's Square in London. Shots were fired on the crowd from the embassy. One of them hit a British policewoman, whose death inflamed British opinion. The British and American governments believed that the murder was but one incident in the sponsoring of international terrorism. In 1986, the prime minister, Margaret Thatcher, supported the United States in a bombing raid on Tripoli and Benghazi from bases in Britain.[63] Mrs. Thatcher's action was controversial, but the reaffirmation of the Anglo-American alliance in military as well as economic affairs contributed to the overall isolation and decline of the Libyan economy. Libyan oil revenues fell from $22 billion in 1980 to $6 billion in 1993. Fluctuations in the price of oil and depressed market conditions, of course, accounted for a large part of the drop, but the Anglo-American backing of U.N. sanctions was certainly significant.

Critics of Mrs. Thatcher denounced her support of the U.S. strike on Libya as "slavish", and as evidence of the further decline of British influence.[64] In fact, there were substantial differences in regional outlook and vigorous British dissent. On the issue of Palestine, above all, the British were far more critical of Israel than the Americans, and far more sympathetic to the Palestinian right of self-determination. A good example of the wide Anglo-American ramifications of the Arab-Israeli dispute can be found in the reactions of Kuwait and Bahrain, both of which had a historical interest in the Palestine question. In 1936–1939, events in Palestine helped to focus protests against the ruler in Kuwait—and against the British. In the postwar era, the issue of partition galvanized protest movements in Bahrain. Palestinian teachers and lawyers, as well as laborers in Kuwait and Bahrain, embraced the pan-Arab aspirations of Nasir and supported his crusade against British imperialism. The British thus had good reason to be more sensitive to disaffected Palestinians and to local anti-Zionist sentiment in the Gulf and elsewhere than did the Americans. After Britain joined the

European Community in 1973, British pressure on the United States to respect the Palestinian position acquired ever-greater weight.[65] The younger European genera-tion, and eventually the Americans, possessed a less hostile attitude to the P.L.O. The change in generation helped to encourage a more balanced perspective on the Arab-Israeli dispute than the older and more rigid pro-Israeli line of the United States. In preparing the way for the peace negotiations between Israel and the Arab states at the end of the twentieth century, the British were significant in keeping open lines of communication with the P.L.O. and in persistently arguing that excessive support of Israel might undermine stability in the Gulf.

The system of Gulf politics during the British era lasted some 150 years, and was fundamentally altered only in 1990–1991 by the crisis in Kuwait. Until the middle of the twentieth century, the British "protected states" in the Gulf were remnants of the British Raj in India. The principalities in the Gulf, like others on the outer reaches of India, had been brought under British control during the nineteenth century (the exceptions were Kuwait and Qatar, which remained outside the British sphere until 1899 and 1916, respectively). The senior British official in the Gulf was the Political Resident in Bahrain, who supervised Political Agents in Kuwait, Qatar, the Trucial States (later the United Arab Emirates), and Oman (which in international law was an independent and sovereign state but in effect was a British protected state). The Gulf system survived the Raj. At the time of Indian independence in 1947, protection of oil in the Gulf replaced the defense of India. The Foreign Office took over the supervision of the Gulf territories from the India Office, though the British Resident and Agents functioned like colonial governors. A salient principle evolved from the nineteenth century: the British would control defense and foreign affairs but would intervene only minimally in internal affairs. The British system thus preserved the original pattern of local politics and political rule. The British military and naval presence was essentially regulatory; the Gulf became virtually a British lake. The identification of the names of oil concessions with the names of different rulers helped to perpetuate the political system.[66] The Gulf States were thus "fossilized" until the British departure in 1971. Despite severe challenges, including those of the Iranian revolution and the war between Iran and Iraq of the 1980s, the British legacy endured until 1990–1991.

The British aim from 1971 to the present has been the preservation of the dynastic states on the Arabian peninsula. The abrupt withdrawal in 1971 was the direct conse-quence of the collapse of the British position in Aden, the simultaneous crisis in sterling, and the decision to withdraw all forces east of Suez.[67] In the Gulf itself, the news of the British withdrawal came as an unprecedented shock. The urgency of the situation in 1969 led to intense, indeed frantic, discussions on how best to create a security struc-ture after the British departure, which was confirmed by the new Conservative govern-ment of Edward Heath to take place as scheduled in late 1971. In the run-up to independence, the former Trucial States merged into the new United Arab Emirates (with Ra's al Khaymah joining in 1972). Unification of the seven states offered a defense against possible predators. These included Saudi Arabia, Iran, and Iraq, each of which in different ways could claim to be a successor to the British Empire in all or part of the Gulf. Against them, the British had traditionally pursued a policy of triple containment, a precursor of the policy of dual containment of Iran and Iraq espoused by the United States. There was thus an element of continuity in the transition from the British to the American era in the Gulf, but British sway by no means ceased to exist. By dismantling the system of protected states, the formal British presence disappeared, but invisible or informal influence remained, as will be clear from a brief examination of each case: Oman, the United Arab Emirates, Qatar, Bahrain, and Kuwait.

The key point in the history of Oman for the theme of British post-imperial or post-1971 involvement is the Dhofar rebellion of 1965, but this critical development must be seen in the context of Oman (which was known until 1970 as Muscat and Oman) as a British client state since the nineteenth century. Though much of Oman consists of uninhabitable barren mountains or waterless plateau, it is a vast territory twice the size of the United Kingdom and differs from the other Gulf states in possessing agricultural as well petroleum resources. Oman also has a history as a great maritime state. At its peak in the nineteenth century, Omani rule embraced coastal regions of present-day Pakistan and Iran as well as Zanzibar and the adjacent coast of East Africa. Omani commercial sailing vessels reached as far as New York. The advent of the steamship and modern technology led to the decline of the Oman empire, but the country was also split between the influences of the imam of Oman in the interior and those of the sultan on the coast. By shoring up the authority of the sultan, the British also reduced him into economic and political dependence, even though Oman remained a sovereign state. The story in broad outline thus conforms to the themes of British economic imperialism, but what is remarkable is the degree of direct British intervention in relation to that in other parts of the Gulf. In the 1950s, the British fought against Saudi troops to protect the oasis of Buraimi—believed, erroneously, to contain vast oil deposits—at the strategic point in the interior claimed by Oman and Abu Dhabi; and the British again assisted the sultan of Oman against tribal forces in the interior in 1959 by deploying the Trucial Oman Scouts, troops from Aden, and the R.A.F. From 1965 until a decade later the British intervened decisively in the Dhofar rebellion. This was a critical campaign, the outcome of which set the pattern of Oman's position to the present day.

The Dhofar region was adjacent at the time to what was the British protectorate of Aden. The Dhofar Arabs saw themselves as distinct in language, culture, and history from the Arabs of the capital of Oman, Muscat, some 600 miles away. The Yemen civil war in the mid-1960s now engulfed Dhofar. After the collapse of the British position in Aden in 1967, the new Marxist radical state assisted the Dhofar rebels with arms and ammunition. The People's Democratic Republic of Yemen, as the new Aden state was called, was in turn supported by the Soviet Union and Communist China.[68] Here was a chapter in the Cold War being written on the desert of the Arabian peninsula. The rebellion was anti-British as well as anti-sultan. The British took seriously the rebellion's aim to destroy all of the dynastic regimes in the Gulf. By the late 1970s, Dhofari forces had gained sufficient strength to threaten the overthrow of the sultan of Oman and to seize the straits of Hormuz, which implied Soviet control over the entrance to the Gulf itself. The British responded by committing a British Army Training Team (a designation that allowed the British government to deny a combat role), and eventually elements of the 22nd Special Air Service Regiment. Before full deployment of British military and intelligence units, however, the British assisted in 1970 in the overthrow of Oman's ruler, Sultan bin Taimur—who in the British view was a dangerous anachronism—and his replacement by his son, the present ruler of Oman, Qaboos bin Said, who had been educated at Sandhurst and had served in the British Army.[69] By 1976, Qaboos had not merely pacified Dhofar but also taken immense strides in modernizing the Omani state. In 1980, Oman entered into a military agreement with the United States for air and naval facilities. Both U.S. and British forces made use of bases in Oman before and during the Gulf War in 1990–1991. Oman remains important for U.S. and British operations. At the close of the twentieth century there were well over 500 British military, air, and naval personnel seconded or contracted to Omani forces. Training operations have involved over 5,000 British troops.[70] The British presence in the Gulf may be less visible in Oman and throughout the Gulf than in the pre-1971 era, but it is nonetheless real and significant.

In the United Arab Emirates, the principle of organization at the time of the British departure was a federation of the former Trucial States; the word "trucial" derived from the treaty signed in 1854 by the British and ruling sheikhs who agreed to a "perpetual maritime truce." The British hoped that Bahrain and Qatar would also join the federation, but each chose separate independence. In 1971, the U.A.E. consisted of Abu Dhabi, Dubai, Ajman, Sharjah, Um al-Qaiwain, and Fujairah. Ra's al-Khaymah, on the northern tip of the peninsula, joined the following year. In wealth and prosperity, Abu Dhabi and Dubai even in British times were in a class of their own. The discovery of oil in Abu Dhabi in 1958 led to a growth rate in the 1960s four times that of Kuwait and to a position of unquestioned prominence in the federation. Dubai developed essentially as a city-state that possessed the largest dry dock in the world, and it became one of the leading centers of commerce in the Gulf. The remaining kingdoms were sometimes known as the "dissident five," not merely because of their comparative lack of wealth but also because in 1965 the rulers of Sharjah, Ra's al-Khaymah, Ajman, Um al-Qaiwain, and Fujairah came close to accepting development aid offered by the Arab League and with it unremitting hostility to the British. They were dissuaded only because British authority in the Gulf still had enough strength to depose them.[71]

When the British departed in 1971, they unilaterally abrogated their own treaties guaranteeing British protection. British expatriates in the U.A.E. continued to occupy vital positions in the armed forces and police as well as in such industries as oil and banking, but the withdrawal brought about a major confrontation between Iran and the amirs of Sharjah and, especially, Ra's al-Khaymah. The two rulers claimed, respectively, the islands of Abu Musa and the two Tunbs, about equidistant between Iran and the U.A.E. Both Iran and the two Gulf kingdoms had historic claims, but Britain acquiesced in the Iranian occupation of the islands. The radical Arab world reacted violently; Iraq and Libya broke off relations with Britain. But there were reasons why the British failed to respond as robustly as they might previously have done to support the claims of the former "protected states," which continued in some respects to be British client states. In 1971, Britain faced insurrection in Northern Ireland as well as a prolonged economic crisis and the early oil shocks of the decade. The British had also concluded a contract with Iran for the sale of state-of-the-art Chieftain tanks and communications equipment valued at over £100 million.[72] These were sufficiently persuasive reasons to do nothing, all the more because in the early 1970s the shah, with overwhelming American support, began to take the place of the British as the policeman of the Gulf.

From the vantage point in Bahrain, Iran had been a threat in the past and became ever more so at the time of the British withdrawal.[73] The principal island of Bahrain is about the size of Washington, D.C. There are some thirty other islands in the archipelago, and the cultural and ethnic makeup of Bahraini society, divided roughly between Sunni and Shi`a Arabs, is far from homogenous. The population in 1969 was 200,000—as great as that of the combined Trucial States but small in comparison with that of Iran at over 28 million. Iran had historical claims on the island of Bahrain dating back at least to the eighteenth century. During the British era, Bahrain had developed as the first oil-producing state in the Gulf. Oil began to flow in 1931, but the reserves proved to be minor compared to those in Kuwait and elsewhere. Under British tutelage, Bahrain took the lead in modernization in the Gulf, and could claim the first radio station as well as the first newspaper. Tensions within Bahraini society became severe during the depression of the 1930s, when educated young men as well as merchants failed to find work and resented those who prospered in the oil industry. The ruling family, the Al Khalifah, faced radical or militant demands for reform, but protests were met with a stern combination of resistance and conciliation by the British Resident. When Foreign Secretary Selwyn Lloyd visited Bahrain in 1956, shortly before the Suez crisis, he encountered violent denunciation, the event itself reflecting the turbulence in a society that included Iranians, Indians, Palestinians and others who mainly worked in the oil fields but some of whom filled managerial positions. During the British era, Bahrain had the largest working class in the Gulf. The currents of Arab nationalism ran deep. They were especially strong at such times as the revolt in Palestine in the 1930s and the campaign against British imperialism by Nasir in the 1950s.

The British connection with Bahrain—and the steel frame of British administration—was as sturdy as in any other territory in the Middle East.[74] Bahrain was a British bastion, a strategic point for the Royal Navy, the Army, and the R.A.F. From Bahrain, the Resident administered the foreign and defense affairs of Kuwait, Qatar, the Trucial States, and Oman as well as those of Bahrain itself. British rule in Bahrain was more far-reaching than in any other Gulf state, in part because of the jurisdiction over the large foreign population of workers in the oil fields and in virtually all other sectors of the economy. British expatriates lingered on in significant numbers after the formal withdrawal in 1971. One example illustrates the enduring British influence. After strikes and violence in the oilfields in 1965, the Resident recruited a former colonial officer from Kenya, Ian Henderson, who had served during the Mau-Mau rebellion, to set up and administer the state intelligence service. Under his regime the Bahrain police became an efficient and repressive instrument of the Al Khalifah. Henderson remained at his post until 1998.[75]

The announcement of the British withdrawal of forces east of Suez in 1968 caused consternation, not least as a result of the simultaneous revival of Iran's historic claim to

Bahrain. In 1970, the shah agreed to a referendum that resulted in a resounding demand for independence. Though his motives were not entirely clear, the shah at least managed to ensure that Bahrain would not join the U.A.E., which with Bahrain's membership might have served as more of a counterweight to Iran in the Gulf. Once the British departed, Bahrain had to deal with the shah's ambition to make Iran the dominant regional power. Bahrain consequently aligned itself with Saudi Arabia and the United States. A causeway between the island and Saudi Arabia was completed in 1986. Since 1991, the U.S. Fifth Fleet has anchored at Bahrain.[76] Bahrain has thus stabilized its position in the transition from the British to the American era in the Gulf, but the tensions within Bahraini society remain as turbulent as ever. After the Iranian revolution of 1979, substantial numbers of discontented Bahrainis looked for inspiration to the Iranian Islamic Republic, just as in earlier times they had looked to Nasir's Egypt.

Qatar is perhaps best mentioned in contrast to Bahrain and in comparison with the nature of the British presence. Though Britain's intervention in the nineteenth century frustrated Bahrain's claims to the peninsula of Qatar, it fell under Ottoman sway and did not become part of the British system until 1916, when the British Resident in Bahrain concluded a treaty of protection recognizing the Al Thani dynasty. Oil was not produced until after World War II. The principal town of Doha then had a population of only 12,000. In the 1920s the economy had depended primarily on exploiting the oyster-rich waters of the Gulf, but the pearl industry, which involved nearly half the population, collapsed in 1929 at the onset of the Great Depression. In the 1930s there was a certain lawlessness on the Qatar peninsula, in part because the British Resident regulated the affairs of the kingdom from Bahrain. Though oil had been discovered in 1939, production did not begin until a decade later, and it was only at that time that a British Agent was posted to Doha. He eventually received the support of a Financial Advisor to the ruler, and of two British military officers, one commanding the armed forces and the other heading the police. Qatar thus represented the British Empire in one of its most minuscule proportions, but the stakes were large. By the 1960s, Qatar produced half the amount of oil of neighboring Abu Dhabi and could rank as among the wealthiest states per capita in the world. This was the era of gold-plated cars. The British attempted to regulate abuses, but in fact they could do little to curtail the extravagance of the Al Thani family. After 1971, British expatriates continued to work in the oil industry, banks, and government service, as in the other Gulf states. In 1992 Qatar, like the other Gulf states, concluded a security agreement with the United States. Qatar has consistently held about 0.4 percent of the world's proven oil reserves (though about 5 percent of all the world's gas reserves). Kuwait, by contrast, held 8 to 9 percent of proven oil reserves in the world. During the British era, the significance of Qatar was summed up in the words of a Foreign Office official: "Qatar is an embryo Kuwait in miniature."[77]

Kuwait achieved independence in 1961, a full decade before the British departure from the states of the lower Gulf. British sway had lasted from 1899, when a treaty of protection had excluded other powers and had blocked part of the plan for Germany to create a Berlin-to-Baghdad railway with a terminus in Kuwait. By recognizing the family of the Al Sabah, and by supporting the ruler, the British institutionalized the authority of an extended family, as in other parts of the Gulf. The critical figure in the British era was `Abdallah al-Salim, under whose rule (1950–1965) Kuwait became one of the leading oil producers in the world. The ruler's power, however, was not absolute. Since World War I, a group of notables, who included wealthy merchants as well as members of the Al Sabah family, had been able to check his powers. The British later compared the ruling family to a sort of corporation, even though the ruler himself was the sole beneficiary of the oil revenues.

The British were only one element among several involved in decisions on the investment and distribution of the oil wealth. Oil had been discovered in 1938, and began to flow in 1946. The treaty obligations to Britain obliged the ruler to accept four British advisors. Two became key figures in the customs administration, one in civil aviation, and one in finance. A further British official, a retired general in the Indian Army, took charge of development. His purpose, apart from a misguided though understandable effort to base Kuwaiti development on an Indian model, was to ensure that Kuwait remained in the sterling area and that British firms secured as much of Kuwait's trade as possible. By 1954, there were seven hundred British expatriates working in the oil industry. From the early 1950s, the economy had boomed. Kuwait's revenues increased from $57 to $169 million in the years 1952–1953 alone. If this was the era of gold-plated automobiles in Qatar, in Kuwait it was the time of a clock tower resembling Big Ben in a village that had no electricity.[78] As in the other oil-producing states, the British could not check such questionable innovation, but in the 1950s they did help to shape the thrust of economic development and the creation of the Kuwaiti welfare system.

By the end of the decade, Kuwait was facing ever-increasing pressures from the radical Arab world, above all from Nasir's Egypt, to share its wealth for development in the Middle East rather than investment purposes in London, and to sever the political tie with Britain. After the Iraqi revolution of 1958, Sheikh `Abdallah moved to liquidate Kuwait's semicolonial status. On June 19, 1961, Kuwait became independent, though with a treaty of friendship that included a clause that Britain would defend Kuwait if necessary. Next, `Abd al-Karim Qasim proclaimed that Kuwait formed an integral part of Iraq. This was not a new claim. Iraq had periodically advanced such claims since the 1930s. Before the revolution, Nuri al-Sa`id had proposed including Kuwait as part of a Hashimite federation. In one way or another, Iraqis had viewed Kuwait as a lost province. The British now intervened to establish once and for all that Kuwait must be respected as a sovereign state with no connection to Iraq, whatever the historical connection might have been. "Remembering Suez," Harold Macmillan wrote in his diary, the Cabinet decided on swift and immediate action, "we thought Kassem [Qasim] would seize Kuwait city and territory virtually unopposed."[79]

British intervention in 1961 has subsequently been interpreted as the harbinger of Western determination to save Kuwait in 1990–1991, but at the time the British response was divided and controversial. The British Agent in Kuwait, John Richmond, a man of balanced judgment, did not believe that Qasim possessed the tenacity of purpose or sufficient force to invade Kuwait. Sir William Luce, the Resident in the

Gulf, overruled this conclusion and urged London to prepare for war with Iraq. Luce's view coincided with that of the British military attaché in Baghdad and to some extent with that of the British ambassador, Sir Humphrey Trevelyan, who believed Qasim to be capable of rash action. The key element in the British decision, however, was the military appreciation in London. The chiefs of staff were still smarting from the fiasco of the Suez expedition in 1956. They wanted to demonstrate that Britain had a post-imperial role to play in the Gulf, and they believed that an expeditionary force could be effective if deployed immediately. Richmond received urgent instructions to obtain Sheikh 'Abdallah's request for British assistance. In early July 1961 British forces began to arrive in Kuwait and eventually numbered some 3,500 troops reinforced by HMS *Bulwark* offshore.[80] Rather like the 1958 American invasion in Lebanon, nothing happened. The Kuwaitis went about their daily business, but anti-British sentiment quickly began to develop. "Your troops are occupying our hospitals and our schools. Is this independence?" asked one prominent Kuwaiti.[81] In Kuwait, as elsewhere in the Middle East, radical Arab nationalism held a strong appeal, especially to the younger generation of foreign Arabs who now formed an important part of Kuwait's population.

In 1961, as in 1990, the population of Kuwait demonstrated collective loyalty, but there were rising tensions in Kuwaiti society. The critical point, for the region as well as for Kuwait, was the Iranian revolution of 1979, which at one stroke removed the shah as the principal ally of Britain and the United States in policing the Gulf after the British departure. In Kuwait the revolution drove a wedge between the Sunni and Shi'a, some of whom were of Iranian origin, who formed about 30 percent of the population. There was a link, not least for the British, between the Iranian revolution and the civil war in Lebanon. In 1983, Shi'a groups in Lebanon claimed responsibility for bomb attacks in Kuwait. Of the seventeen arrested for terrorism in Kuwait, two were Lebanese. In retaliation, Terry Waite, the emissary of the archbishop of Canterbury, was kidnapped in Lebanon. In 1987, further major bombing and sabotage occurred in the Kuwait oil fields. During this time, British expatriate officers continued to serve in Kuwait's internal security forces, and others advised on defense. These officers were usually retired, and, as in the other Gulf states, they were not under British command, though usually they had held high rank in the British fighting services.[82] They could perhaps be described as gentlemen mercenaries. They perpetuated British influence as if they were directly employed by the British government. In 1982, for example, several former high-ranking R.A.F. officers advised the amir of Kuwait that the air defense of his country would be difficult if not impossible unless integrated into that of the United Arab Emirates and Saudi Arabia. Their advice was rejected.[83]

The vulnerability of Kuwait became increasingly apparent during the war between Iran and Iraq in the 1980s. Kuwait began to gravitate toward Saudi Arabia, which now emerged as the principal Western ally and, it seemed at the time, the successor to the British Empire in the Gulf. In Britain as in the United States there developed the attitude toward Iran and Iraq that it was "a pity only one side can lose."[84] Especially in the British defense industry, this was an understandable if deplorable view. The Scott Commission in Britain later concluded that British arms merchants had supplied both sides despite a statutory British embargo. The profits, including those in the legitimate market, and especially those based on sales to Saudi Arabia, were unprecedented. In the case of Saudi Arabia alone, British Aerospace in the 1980s concluded agreements in which defense electronics and aircraft contracts would be guaranteed to Britain in a sum estimated at one stage as $7.6 billion—an amount described by two knowledge-able writers as constituting at the time "the largest defence contract in history."[85] British military commitment in the Gulf also remained substantial and is best meas-ured in comparison to the American. At the outbreak of the war between Iran and Iraq in 1980, the British government quickly despatched three ships of the Royal Navy to protect oil tankers and the flow of oil from Kuwait. By 1988, there were seven British vessels and thirty-two U.S. Navy ships. The U.S. naval presence thus dwarfed that of the British, but the latter was significant and had been continuous over the decade. When Iraqi troops invaded Kuwait in August 1990, the British prime minister, Margaret Thatcher, immediately moved to reinforce the British naval contingent.[86]

The Gulf War of 1991 signified a critical break—even if a momentary one—in the continuity of the British geopolitical system in the Gulf that had endured for more than 150 years. One of the component states, Kuwait, temporarily ceased to exist. The fate of the region seemed jeopardized not merely by the takeover of Kuwait but also by the possibility, which seemed plausible at the time, that Saddam Husayn might proceed from Kuwait to invade Saudi Arabia and thus control 65 percent of the world's oil reserves. The extent of the British contribution to the defeat of Iraq and the restoration of Kuwait in 1991 is again best measured against that of the American. In the coalition of forces, American military personnel numbered well over 400,000. British forces amounted to 35,000. Though small in comparison, the British contribution ranked fourth, behind the American, Saudi Arabian, and Egyptian, but well above the level of the French contingent, which was the only other significant European force. In the aftermath of the war, the British bombing of Iraq proved that the British presence continued as a significant military force in the region. The Gulf War did not bring about the fall of Saddam Husayn. But it did ensure the survival of the gulf dynasties at least into the beginning of the next century, and thus contributed to the realization of one of Britain's longstanding aims.

In a more national perspective, British economic and military power since the time of withdrawal from the Gulf in 1971 has been fundamentally different from that of the imperial system that had existed in the Middle East since World War I. In 1945, the British still hoped to remain dominant in the region by dismantling the old empire and by developing the Middle East in partnership with Arab and Iranian nationalists. The Suez crisis of 1956 shattered that vision. The disintegration of the British position in Aden in 1967 marked the end of the British presence in the Middle East. The last shades of red on the map virtually vanished. It was a clear ending, symbolized not only by the fall of Aden but also by the evacuation of all British forces east of Suez. The exit from the Gulf four years later was merely an epilogue, though an important one owing to the arrival of new embassies and the end of the sterling area. In the 1970s and 1980s, it seemed that Iran and then Saudi Arabia might emerge as the successor to Britain as the preeminent power in the Gulf. The role of the United States was not entirely clear. Times of crisis sometimes reveal a new configuration of power, as in 1956 with the British collapse at Suez. The Gulf War of 1991 proved conclusively, for better or worse, that the true successor to the British Empire in the Middle East is the United States.

Notes

1   Sir Patrick Dean to George Brown, Confidential and Guard ("Guard" = not for American eyes), January 1, 1967, F[oreign] and C[ommonwealth] O[ffice] 7/738. All FO, FCO, CAB[inet] O[ffice] DEFE[nce] and PREM[ier] file numbers refer to documents at the Public Record Office, London.

2   For useful works that challenge conventional thought, see Timothy Mitchell, *Colonising Egypt*; and Avi Shlaim, *The Iron Wall, Israel and the Arab World*; for the problem of oil, see especially Jill Crystal, *Oil and Politics in the Gulf*.

3   For Attlee, see especially Kenneth Harris, *Attlee*.

4   See Afaf Lutfi al-Sayyid-Marsot, *Egypt and Cromer: A Study in Anglo-Egyptian Relations*.

5   See Malcolm Yapp, ed., *Politics and Diplomacy in Egypt: The Diaries of Sir Miles Lampson, 1935–1937*.

6   This is the argument in Wm. Roger Louis, *The British Empire in the Middle East, 1945–1951: Arab Nationalism, the United States and Postwar Imperialism*.

7   See Alan Bullock, *Ernest Bevin: Foreign Secretary, 1945–1951*.

8   Churchill referred to Bevin as "a working class John Bull." For Churchill and the Middle East, see Wm. Roger Louis, "Churchill and Egypt," in Robert Blake and Wm. Roger Louis, eds., *Churchill*; see also especially Raymond A. Callahan, *Churchill: Retreat from Empire*.

9   Cabinet Minutes (50) 86, December 14, 1950, CAB 128/18.

10   For the Sudan, which is not dealt with here, see especially M. W. Daly, *Empire on the Nile: The Anglo-Egyptian Sudan, 1898–1934*.

11   For the intervention by the United Nations, see Nathan A. Pelcovits, *The Long Armistice: UN Peacekeeping and the Arab-Israeli Conflict, 1948–1960*.

12   See James A. Bill and Wm. Roger Louis, eds., *Musaddiq, Iranian Nationalism, and Oil*.

13   See especially J. H. Bamberg, *The History of the British Petroleum Company*, Vol. 2, *The Anglo-Iranian Years, 1928–1954*, part 3.

14   Confidential Annex to Chiefs of Staff meeting (51) 86, May 23, 1951, DEFE 4/43.

15   See especially Peter Grose, *Gentleman Spy: The Life of Allen Dulles*.

16   See C. M. Woodhouse, *Something Ventured*, chapters 8 and 9.

17   Churchill to Eden, Private and Personal, January 30, 1952, PREM 11/91.

18   Minute by Roger Allen, April 3, 1954, FO 371/108476.

19   For the background, see John Kent, ed., *Egypt and the Defence of the Middle East*, 3 vols. For regional defense, see Michael J. Cohen, *Fighting World War Three from the Middle East: Allied Contingency Plans, 1945–1954*.

20   Quoted in Iverach McDonald, *The History of The Times*, Vol. 5, *Struggles in War and Peace, 1939–66*, p. 268.

21   For Suez, see Wm. Roger Louis and Roger Owen, eds., *Suez 1956: The Crisis and Its Consequences*; for more recent accounts, see especially W. Scott Lucas, *Divided We Stand: Britain, the US and the Suez Crisis*; Peter L. Hahn, *The United States, Great Britain, and Egypt, 1945–1956*; Steven Z. Freiberger, *Dawn over Suez: The Rise of American Power in the Middle East, 1955–1981*; and Zach Levey, *Israel and the Western Powers, 1952–1960*.

22   Johnston to Sir Roger Stevens, Personal and Confidential, March 16, 1961, CO 1015/2185.

23 The most recent full treatment of Eden is David Dutton, *Anthony Eden: A Life and Reputation*, which strikes a fair balance on Suez.

24 Harold Macmillan, *Riding the Storm, 1956–1959*, p. 692; and Macmillan Diary, February 10, 1959. References to the Macmillan Diaries are copies in the possession of Alistair Horne. I am indebted to Mr. Horne for allowing me to read them. The Diaries have now been deposited in the Bodleian Library, Oxford.

25 Alistair Horne, *Macmillan*, Vol. 1, p. 410.

26 Brendan Bracken to Lord Beaverbrook, November 22, 1956, Beaverbrook Papers (House of Lords Record Office, London).

27 For the Buraimi dispute, see J. B. Kelly, *Arabia, the Gulf, and the West*, chapter 2.

28 See especially Michael Ionides, *Divide and Lose: The Arab Revolt of 1955–1958*.

29 Sir John Troutbeck (Ambassador in Baghdad) to F.O., Confidential, December 9, 1954, FO 371/110991.

30 Edith Penrose and E. F. Penrose, *Iraq: International Relations and National Development*, p. 167. On the British era in Iraq, see especially Marion Farouk-Sluglett and Peter Sluglett, *Iraq since 1958: From Revolution to Dictatorship*; and Phebe Marr, *The Modern History of Iraq*.

31 Wright to F.O., Confidential, February 8, 1957, FO 371/128038.

32 Wright to F.O., Confidential, July 4, 1957, FO 371/128041.

33 The oil production of Iraq, however, was not as vital to the British as was that of Kuwait or Iran. In metric tons the relative production of crude oil by the three states in 1957: Kuwait 57 million, Iran 35 million, Iraq 20 million.

34 C. H. Johnston to E. M. Rose, Secret, July 28, 1958, FO 371/13401.

35 1958 Annual Report, Confidential, January 29, 1959, FO 371/140896.

36 See Irene L. Gendzier, *Notes from the Minefield: United States Intervention in Lebanon and the Middle East, 1945–1958*. For Jordan, see especially Kamal S. Salibi, *The Modern History of Jordan*.

37 The key work is Robert Holland, *Britain and the Revolt in Cyprus, 1954–1959*; see also George Horton Kelling, *Countdown to Rebellion: British Policy in Cyprus, 1939–1955*.

38 Quoted in John Reddaway, *Burdened with Cyprus: The British Connection*, p. 11.

39 For Macmillan's part in the settlement see Horne, *Macmillan*, Vol. 2, pp. 99–104.

40 Quoted in Reddaway, *Burdened with Cyprus*, p.161. See George W. Ball, *The Past Has Another Pattern: Memoirs*, chapter 23.

41 For these themes, see especially John Darwin, *Britain and Decolonisation: The Retreat from Empire in the Post-War World*, pp. 282–88.

42 Minute by Amery, March 10, 1959, CO 1015/1910. Amery was undersecretary of state for the colonies and in the next year conducted the negotiations with Makarios on the sovereign bases in Cyprus.

43 Sir Charles Johnston to Colonial Office, Secret, July 16, 1963, FO 371/168630.

44 See Phillip Darby, *British Defence Policy East of Suez, 1947–1968*, p. 210. "Aden and Its Hinterland," *The Times* (London), December 18, 1959. See also Ritchie Ovendale, *British Defence Policy since 1945*.

45 Harold Macmillan, *At the End of the Day, 1961–1963*, chapter 9.

46 The Cuban crisis cast a long shadow. Ralph Bunche of the United Nations wrote in 1963, "I do not exclude the possibility that Yemen could become a Cuba in the Near East." Brian Urquhart, *Ralph Bunche: An American Life*, p. 365.

47 Macmillan, *At the End of the Day*, p. 271.

48 Macmillan Diary, October 26, 1962. But before a decision was made, the Yemenis broke off relations. It is arguable that the course of the civil war might have been altered had the British taken the initiative and recognized the new regime. See Christopher Gandy, "A Mission to Yemen: August 1962–January 1963."

49 King-yuh Chang, "The United Nations and Decolonization: The Case of Southern Yemen."

50 Quoted in Robin Bidwell, *The Two Yemens*, pp. 146 and 158. See also Fred Halliday, *Revolution and Foreign Policy: The Case of South Yemen, 1967–1987.*

51 Kelly, *Arabia, the Gulf, and the West*, pp. 14 and 22. The Foreign Office held Kelly's historical scholarship in high but not uncritical esteem. See FCO 3/17.

52 See especially Robert W. Stookey, *South Yemen: A Marxist Republic in Arabia*, pp. 55–56 and 62–63. Stookey had served as the U.S. representative in the Yemen during the revolution.

53 Bidwell, *Two Yemens*, p.145.

54 See Robert D. Burrowes, "The Republic of Yemen," especially pp. 197–98.

55 Macmillan, *At the End of the Day*, p. 278.

56 Richard Crossman, *The Diaries of a Cabinet Minister*, Vol. 2, p. 541.

57 Minute by A. J. D. Stirling, FCO 8/284.

58 Sir Robin Hooper to F.O., Confidential, August 22, 1968, FCO 8/284.

59 See especially Rosemary Hollis, "Great Britain."

60 See Wm. Roger Louis, "Libyan Independence, 1951: The Creation of a Client State."

61 W. G. Graham to F.O., Secret, March 31, 1959, FO 371/138738.

62 Minute by Adam Watson, October 15, 1959, FO 371/138785.

63 See Margaret Thatcher, *The Downing Street Years*, pp. 441–49.

64 See, for example, Guy Arnold, *The Maverick State: Gaddafi and the New World Order*, pp. 104–5.

65 On Britain's complex position before and after joining the European Community, see especially Stephen George, *An Awkward Partner: Britain in the European Community.*

66 On all these points, the best historical survey is Rosemarie Said Zahlan, *The Making of the Modern Gulf States: Kuwait, Bahrain, Qatar, the United Arab Emirates, and Oman.*

67 Two articles by D. C. Watt bring these themes together and give an indication of the controversial nature of the debate in Britain at the time: "The Decision to Withdraw from the Gulf," and "Britain and the Indian Ocean."

68 To which, it should be added, some years later, Cuba. This development caused alarm in the United States. For example: "A Cuban intervention force is being trained in armored warfare. The appropriate equipment is being stocked in South Yemen—the entry point... . the Cubans could inject the *coup de grâce* of an armored threat which the small Omani army could not possibly resist... . All the oil of Arabia would come under the direct threat of a radical Cuban-supported (and thus Soviet-sponsored) regime." Edward N. Luttwak, "Cubans in Arabia?" p. 65.

69 See especially Clive Jones and John Stone, "Britain and the Arabian Gulf: New Perspectives on Strategic Influence."

70 Anthony H. Cordesman, *Bahrain, Oman, Qatar, and the UAE: Challenges of Security*, pp. 124–25 and 204–5; and Kelly, *Arabia, the Gulf, and the West*, chapter 3. For historical background see also Ian Skeet, *Muscat and Oman: The End of an Era.*

71 Zahlan, *The Making of the Modern Gulf States*, p. 117. More generally see especially John Duke Anthony, *Arab States of the Lower Gulf: People, Politics, Petroleum*, chapters 4–9; and Cordesman, *Bahrain, Oman, Qatar, and the UAE*, chapter 5.

72 Kelly, *Arabia, The Gulf, and the West*, p. 93.

73 A contemporary account remains especially useful: Denis Wright, "The Changed Balance of Power in the Persian Gulf."

74 See Bernard Burrows, *Footnotes in the Sand: The Gulf in Transition, 1953–1958*, chapter 4.

75 Zahlan, *The Making of the Modern Gulf States*, p. 71.

76 See Cordesman, *Bahrain, Oman, Qatar, and the UAE*, pp. 37–39.

77 Burrows, *Footnotes in the Sand*, p. 145.

78 Zahlan, *The Making of the Modern Gulf States*, p. 42.

79 Macmillan Diary, July 8, 1961.

80 John Bulloch, *The Gulf: A Portrait of Kuwait, Qatar, Bahrain and the UAE*, pp. 62–63. See also Mustafa M. Alani, *Operation Vantage: British Military Intervention in Kuwait 1961*; and Miriam Joyce, "Preserving the Sheikhdom: London, Washington, Iraq and Kuwait, 1958–61."

81 The quotation is from an unpublished paper, "Kuwait 1961," by Sir Marrack Goulding, at that time a young British official in Kuwait. I am grateful to him for allowing me to read his recollections.

82 There were also service personnel still in British ranks but seconded to the Kuwait armed forces. Rosemary Hollis records that there were around a hundred British service personnel on loan to Kuwait in the mid-1980s. Hollis, "Great Britain," pp. 214–215.

83 Jones and Stone, "Britain and the Arabian Gulf: New Perspectives on Strategic Influence," p. 9 n. 32.

84 Zahlan, *The Making of the Modern Gulf States*, p. 174.

85 Jones and Stone, "Britain and the Arabian Gulf: New Perspectives on Strategic Influence," p. 9 n. 32. See also two articles by Clive Jones, "Saudi Arabia after the Gulf War: The Internal-External Security Dilemma," and "The Security of Arab Gulf States and the End of the Cold War."

86 See Thatcher, *The Downing Street Years*, chapter 27.

3

America and the Middle East:
A Fifty-Year Overview

William B. Quandt

There is a paradox at the heart of America's history of involvement with the Middle East. At first glance, it seems as if policy has frequently been based on shaky foundations; policy has often seemed to reflect domestic political forces more than calculations of national interest; and at times the execution of policy has seemed clumsy, if not worse. Regimes closely aligned with America, such as that of the shah of Iran, have been swept away by bitterly anti-American forces. American power has often seemed unable to protect American interests, as during the long ordeal when Americans were held hostage in Lebanon and Iran; and secretaries of state have been known to cringe at the thought of devoting more time and energy to the seemingly hopeless task of peacemaking between Israelis and Arabs.

And yet American interests, as conventionally defined, have been surprisingly well protected in the Middle East over this period, despite mishaps and frequent blunders. When the Middle East is compared to its experience in Southeast Asia, for example, the United States has managed to avoid costly (to America) military engagements. At century's end, the scorecard does not look so bad.

In the immediate post-World War II period, the United States set out to prevent the spread of Soviet influence into the Middle East region, protect access to Middle East oil, and help to create and then nurture a state in Palestine for the Jewish people. Although the Soviet Union competed for influence aggressively in the region, in the end the United States emerged as the stronger power; and Middle East oil, despite disruptions and embargoes, was no more expensive in real terms in 1999 than it had been forty years earlier.[1] Finally, Israel was more secure and economically successful as the new millennium approached than anyone could have imagined when the state was founded in 1948. Although full peace with its Arab neighbors was still elusive, Israel had managed to sign treaties with Egypt and Jordan, and there was some expectation of further agreements with Syria, Lebanon, and perhaps even the Palestinians.

So how can one explain this apparent paradox—clumsy, often flawed policies, yet results that stand up well by comparison with other regions? Part of the answer may be luck, or even more misguided policies by America's global and regional rivals. And part of the answer may be that American policy never remained wedded to a counterproductive track for very long. What many find frustrating about American policy—its shifts and turns—reflects a capacity to adapt, a learning process, and self-correcting mechanisms that have helped to adjust policy after various fiascoes. This has not made for elegant policy formulation, nor are ideologues of left or right happy with the zigs and zags. Middle Easterners complain about America's double standards, the naïveté and lack of sophistication of American policymaking, the frustration of dealing with new presidents and new secretaries of state at frequent intervals. And yet no other country has gained more influence and succeeded better in protecting its interests in the region—certainly not the old colonial powers of Britain and France, and not the Soviet Union (and now Russia).

Historical Legacy

To understand better the evolution of American policy in the region, we need some context and some history. First, the United States did not have a legacy of deep involvement in the Middle East prior to World War II. It had no colonies and it had no regular military presence. Even its commercial and cultural interests were limited, though real. Oil had been discovered by American companies in Saudi Arabia in the 1930s, and soon came to be a major interest, but it was only one of the interests that drew the United States deeply into the region after 1945.

More important than oil was the coming of age of America as a global power during World War II and the onset of the Cold War. Had the United States retreated to isolationism as it did after World War I, oil would have remained a commercial matter rather than a strategic necessity. But the generation of leaders who set America's course after the war were determined not to repeat the errors of the interwar period, and they soon came to see in Stalin's Soviet empire an opponent to be challenged at every turn. The doctrine of containment was devised to address the problem of Soviet power without risking direct military conflict, and still meet challenges in peripheral areas in order to maintain some sort of global balance of power. Thus Americans fought wars in Korea and Vietnam, and a fierce competition was waged between Washington and Moscow in the Middle East, first in Iran and Turkey, and then in the Arab world.

Until 1990, this rivalry with the Soviet Union, this global sense of noblesse—or at least pouvoir—oblige, led the United States to stake out positions on a host of issues in the Middle East, from Israel's right to exist, to the sanctity of borders, to the need for decolonization, to opposition to British-French-Israeli intervention at Suez, to support for Algeria's independence, to protection of the oil of the Persian Gulf, to confessional balances within Lebanon, and dozens of others issues as well. It was inconceivable during this period that the United States would refrain from taking a stand on any significant Middle East issue. For if Washington said nothing, then Moscow might—and that could result in a setback in the propaganda campaign that swept across the region for some forty years. And with words often came commitments, sometimes in the form of economic aid and sometimes in the form of arms. After all, words alone would count for little; credibility was on the line. So involvement flowed from the global rivalry, each side wary of being outmaneuvered.[2]

The Special Relationship with Israel

In the center of this complex mix of issues and interests was Israel. Throughout its existence as a state, Israel has been able to count on support from the United States. Indeed, no country provided Israel with as much aid—economic and military—during its first fifty-plus years of independence. And no country received as much aid from America on a per capita basis as did Israel. By the 1980s it often seemed as if the United States and Israel were formal allies, although no written alliance existed.

But Washington did not always appear to be on such close terms with the Jewish state. At the outset of the Cold War, American officials were often eager to keep their distance from Israel, and there was even serious dissent when President Harry S. Truman rushed to recognize Israel in 1948. Secretary of State George Marshall, among others, thought it was a great blunder to become identified with a state that was so widely disliked by its neighbors. Some thought that American support for Israel would inevitably drive the Arabs into the arms of Moscow.

To a large extent, American support for Israel was rooted in domestic politics. The American Jewish community was relatively small, but it was well organized and focussed in its support for Israel. Many non-Jews also saw Israel as a progressive democracy surrounded by reactionary Arab monarchies. Sentiment, values, politics, and guilt all propelled Americans to help the new Jewish state. At the same time, a hard-headed calculus of interest placed limits on that support. Up until the mid-1960s, almost no American military aid went to Israel, and even economic aid was modest. In addition, Israel was not immune from criticism in official Washington. The Suez crisis in 1956 was just one of the moments when the two countries did not see eye to eye. It was not until after the 1967 war that Israel was generally seen in a positive light in official Washington, and even then American administrations were always concerned with maintaining contacts with some Arab countries.[3]

The net effect on American policy of the special relationship with Israel was to lead successive American presidents to try to find some way to broker an end to the Arab-Israeli conflict. For as long as the conflict endured, there would be tension between the American interests in nurturing Israel and in protecting its oil and other security concerns in surrounding Arab countries. And the existence of the conflict might provide openings for the Soviet Union to advance its influence by selling arms and by providing diplomatic support for the Arabs. With varying degrees of imagination and commitment, each American administration tried to find a solution to the Arab-Israeli conflict.

The special considerations that made the Arab-Israeli arena so compelling and complex for Americans to deal with were largely absent in the so-called *northern tier* area of Turkey and Iran. There the United States perceived a direct Soviet challenge almost immediately after the end of World War II. Soviet troops refused to leave Iran on schedule in 1946, and the U.S.S.R. made threats against the Turkish government, raising alarms in Washington. The response from the Truman administration was immediate. It opposed Soviet expansion in both Iran and Turkey, and promised to send aid and arms to bolster the threatened regimes—the Truman Doctrine. In 1952, Turkey was invited to join NATO as a full member, and from that time onward the

United States treated Turkey as a fully-fledged ally. Only occasionally did Turkey play much of a role in the rest of the Middle East, but when it did it was usually on the same side as the United States.

Iran did not become a NATO member, but its ties to Washington were in many ways as deep. Iran, of course, had oil, and was the dominant regional power in the oil-rich Gulf region. Initially, American companies were not involved in the exploitation and marketing of Iran's oil, but that changed after the 1953 coup to oust the nationalist leader Muhammad Musaddiq and to secure the shah on his throne. For the next twenty-five years, the United States was deeply involved in all aspects of Iranian development. Iran was considered a major asset in the Cold War, and significant American intelligence facilities were located on its territory.

Patterns of Policy

Given the nature of American interests in the Middle East and the peculiarities of American politics, in which domestic forces play a significant part in the formulation of foreign policy, it would have been surprising if American policy had shown consistency and far-sightedness over a long period. Policy often had an experimental quality as various approaches were attempted and then discarded when they were found wanting. Crises tended to force reassessments, and each new president had a tendency to change his foreign policy team and sometimes the policies as well. So we need to look at distinct periods of American foreign policy to get the general picture of how the region was seen by officials in Washington.

Without too much violence to complex realities, we can see one long period from about 1947 to 1967 that was characterized by American activism and containment, both of the Soviet Union and of regional conflicts. From 1967 to 1979, we can see another phase of diplomacy that focused on incremental efforts to resolve the Arab-Israeli conflict while bolstering the role of Iran in the Gulf. The year 1979 marked a return to a preoccupation with Soviet designs on the region, as the shah's regime fell and the Soviets invaded Afghanistan. For much of the next decade, Arab-Israeli diplomacy was placed on the back burner, or at least was allowed to drift, while considerable emphasis was placed on building military capabilities to intervene in the Gulf. The next turning point came at the end of the Cold War and the outbreak of conflict in the Gulf, with Iraq's invasion of Kuwait in August 1990 and the U.S.-led military response. The ensuing decade was one in which attention was paid both to the Gulf region and to Arab-Israeli issues, but with an increasing realization in Washington that the American role was not to impose its own design on the region but rather to deal with the political forces that existed, while trying to encourage those trends that seemed most compatible with American interests. Again a paradox—at the peak of its power as the victor in the Cold War and the Gulf War, the United States reverted to polices of containment in the Gulf and "facilitating" in the Arab-Israeli arena. Those who had worried about Pax Americana in 1990 had as much to fear from the internet as from aggressive American political designs on the Middle East as the decade came to a close.

The Initial Engagement: 1947–1967

The first phase of American diplomacy, from 1947 to 1967, was characterized by a remarkable number of initiatives in the Arab-Israeli arena. Presidents Truman, Eisenhower, Kennedy, and Johnson each brought distinctive views to the conduct of foreign policy in the region, but they were united in seeking to prevent the spread of Soviet influence, in managing—if not resolving—the Arab-Israeli conflict, and in bolstering ties with Turkey and Iran. From the mid-1950s onward, the rise of pan-Arabism and the growing influence of Egypt's Gamal ʿAbd al-Nasir posed particular dilemmas for American policy makers, but on the whole an effort was made to deal with both Arabism and Nasir up through 1964. President Johnson, increasingly preoccupied with Vietnam, had less and less time for the prickly and highly suspicious Nasir, and by the time of the 1967 war little remained of U.S.-Egyptian ties.

The highlights of the early years of this period were the initial support for partition of Palestine into two states, one Jewish and one Arab, in 1947; recognition of Israel in 1948; support for armistice agreements and for a solution to the refugee problem in 1949; and the Tripartite Declaration in 1950, which was aimed at bolstering the armistice regime and regulating arms transfers to the region. Eisenhower and his secretary of state, John Foster Dulles, launched a series of secret political initiatives from 1953 to 1956, some of which involved water-sharing arrangements (the Johnston Plan), whereas others attempted to broker secret contacts between Egyptian and Israeli leaders (the Alpha and Omega projects). Arms and aid were promised to Egypt on certain conditions; the British were urged to leave their base at Suez; and Israel was warned against expanding its territory by force.

Although it supported the British in the creation of the Baghdad Pact in 1954–1955, the United States did not formally join, hoping thereby to retain some credibility with Egypt. All of these efforts to promote an Egyptian-Israeli understanding came to naught, however, and by mid-1956 the United States was pulling back from its courtship of Nasir—the withdrawal of the offer to help finance the Aswan dam was indicative of this new mood—as he edged closer to the Soviet Union.[4] The Suez crisis briefly seemed to reverse this course—Eisenhower backed Egypt against his own allies—but soon Washington was again signaling its intent to contain both Soviet influence and Nasirism (as in the Eisenhower Doctrine of January 1957).[5] Syria was widely perceived by American officials as a target of both Soviet and Nasirist subversion, and there is substantial evidence of a covert effort to topple the government in Damascus, with assistance from Turkey and Iraq. But the net effect of the policy was instead to drive the Syrians into the arms of the Egyptians; the United Arab Republic linked the two countries from 1958 to 1961. Shortly after the unification of Egypt and Syria, Lebanon's simmering crisis seemed to take a turn for the worse. Then, when Iraq exploded in revolution in July 1958, the United States and Britain decided to send troops to Lebanon and Jordan, respectively.[6] This might have seemed like a moment when the two Western powers would try to reverse the tide of Arabism and revolution—indeed, the British pleaded with Washington to join them in such an effort—but cooler heads prevailed, and a diplomatic effort was made to promote a Lebanese settlement that Nasir and Eisenhower were both prepared to live with. From 1958 to 1964, the Middle East seemed to calm down, American relations with Nasir improved, and some observers began to hope that the passage of time would help ease the tensions between Israel and its Arab neighbors. In any event, Nasirism no longer seemed like such a dangerous force once the United Arab Republic was dissolved in 1961 and Nasir's troops became bogged down in North Yemen after 1962.

Elsewhere in the region, this period was one of activism and containment of Soviet power. Iran was one arena for dramatic action. In 1951, Muhammad Musaddiq had come to power as a popular prime minister and immediately set about nationalizing Iran's oil, a precedent that was threatening to American companies in nearby Arab countries. In 1953, the Eisenhower administration, which seemed fascinated with covert actions, joined the British in seeking the ousting of Musaddiq.[7] The operation, named Ajax, succeeded, but thereafter the shah was perceived by many of his countrymen as a Western puppet. After Musaddiq's ousting, American oil companies were given access to a percentage of Iran's oil for the first time.

The Kennedy administration, as if to try to remove this stain of illegitimacy from the shah, encouraged a "white revolution" in Iran. This was the high tide of optimism about America's ability to meet the Soviet challenge by promoting development in third-world countries. The shah might be reluctant to modernize, but the United States would forcefully persuade him to do what was best for his country—or so the development economists in Washington thought. And Iranian society did begin to change as literacy and education spread. But so too did resentment against the growing American presence in the country. Still, by the mid-1960s, the American consensus on Ajax would have been that it had been well worth the effort and that Iran was becoming a model for other developing countries. Among other things, Americans had helped to encourage a discreet relationship between Iran and Israel (and between Turkey and Israel).

A final example of the activism that marked this era was the Kennedy administration's attempt to ward off Israel's nuclear weapons program.[8] One of Kennedy's global policy priorities was to limit the spread of nuclear weapons. In the Middle East, the only country that had a nuclear reactor capable of producing enough plutonium to build bombs was Israel. Kennedy made a strong plea to Prime Minister David Ben-Gurion to sign the Non-Proliferation Treaty and to place the reactor under international safeguards. Ben-Gurion, who was intent upon acquiring a nuclear deterrent, had no intention of acceding to Kennedy's request. Eventually, his successor Levi Eshkol agreed to allow limited inspections of the facility at Dimona (excluding, as we now know, the underground reprocessing and weapons production areas). Based on Israeli assurances that Israel "would not be the first to introduce nuclear weapons" into the area, Kennedy and later Johnson urged the Egyptians to refrain from developing long-range missiles. Kennedy also carried out a long and sophisticated correspondence with Nasir in an attempt to build a better relationship between the two countries.

A brief review of what the United States sought to do during this period reveals a wealth of initiatives, a self-confident (perhaps even arrogant) view of its purposes and prospects in the region, and some successes to offset the numerous errors. The emphasis on containing the Arab-Israeli conflict; the attempt to control the arms race;

the prodding of Nasir and Ben-Gurion to make peace; and the focus on water sharing, refugee rehabilitation, development, and nonproliferation seem sound. More controversial were the covert efforts in Iran and Syria, the abrupt withdrawal of aid for the Aswan dam, and the rhetoric accompanying the Eisenhower Doctrine (which seemed to imply that nationalism and communism were linked). Eisenhower's Suez decision is still debated by historians, but looks both realistic and principled to most observers. Similarly, the intervention in Lebanon in 1958 is still a subject of controversy, but on the whole it seemed to be helpful in cooling the fevered political atmosphere of mid-1958. As of early 1964, one might have had reason, from Washington's standpoint, to feel reasonably confident that American interests were doing well in the Middle East.

The period of apparently successful activism came to a strange and unhappy conclusion between 1964 and 1967. President Lyndon Johnson was not exclusively to blame by any means. This was a period in which the "Arab Cold War" was in full swing, and this had more to do with ambitious leaders in Cairo, Riyadh, and Damascus than anything Washington was doing.[9] Still, Johnson had little patience for the Middle East. He was sympathetic to Israel, but knew little about the region. And, before long, the Vietnam War began to distract him from his domestic agenda and other foreign-policy priorities. In this atmosphere, minor incidents in U.S.-Egyptian relations were allowed to grow in importance. At the same time, American military aid to Israel began to take on significance, although it remained limited in this period.

By the eve of the May 1967 crisis, Nasir was extremely suspicious of Johnson's motives.[10] And as the crisis began to gain momentum, Johnson abandoned the pattern of American interventionism and adopted instead a surprisingly passive stance.[11] By the time he tried to advance a proposal for defusing the crisis, the stage for war was already set. The outbreak of war on June 5, 1967, ushered in a fundamentally new era in U.S. policy toward the region.

From War to Revolution: Coping With Crises, 1967–1979

From 1967 to 1979, three countries occupied pride of place in American dealings with the Middle East: Israel, Iran, and, to a lesser degree, Saudi Arabia. Now diplomatic efforts to resolve the Arab-Israeli conflict moved to center stage, as did efforts to deal with threats to oil interests in the Gulf. This was a crisis-plagued period, with wars in 1967, 1970 (in Jordan), 1973, 1978 (in Lebanon); revolution in Iran in 1978–1979; and oil shocks in 1973 and 1979. Two basic judgments were made in Washington that set this era apart from the preceding one. First, Israel would be actively embraced as a partner. Aid would be provided, along with diplomatic support. The territories that Israel had won in the 1967 war—Sinai, the West Bank and Gaza, and the Golan Heights—could be held as bargaining chips to exchange for real peace, recognition, and security from the Arab neighbors. Israel would be given enough military aid to convince Arab leaders that another round of war was pointless.

The second judgment that emerged a bit later in this period was that the shah of Iran should be treated as a major ally in the region. Rather than press him to reform, as Kennedy had sought to do, the United States should build him up as a regional military power. With his oil wealth, especially after 1973, he could both modernize his country and buy American arms. His tacit alliance with Israel would help promote the cause of keeping Israel strong. And his distaste for Arab radicalism might help contain radical Arabism in the Arabian peninsula.

These policy judgments, it should be noted, were made primarily at the White House. The State Department, because of either inertia or greater knowledge, worried about putting too many eggs in the Israeli and Iranian baskets. State officials tended to see the openings that such a strategy might provide for the Soviets in the Arab world, and they were less sanguine than the White House strategists that keeping Israel strong was enough to persuade the Arabs to make peace. More than in the first period, bureaucratic politics affected the course of policy making. Famous battles were fought between secretaries of state and national security advisers (William Rogers vs. Henry Kissinger over Arab-Israeli policy in the 1969–1971 period; Cyrus Vance vs. Zbigniew Brzezinski over Iran in 1978–1979).

In retrospect, it is striking how quickly after Israel's victory in the Six-Day War American policy shifted emphasis. It was as if policy makers suddenly realized that Israel was no longer a weak state, but rather that it could easily defend itself—and more. In the Vietnam era, that was already a prized quality among friendly states. Iran soon benefitted from the same assessment, as the Nixon administration explicitly began looking for "regional influentials" to act as surrogates for American power—the Nixon Doctrine. Vietnam had shown the pitfalls of trying to play world policeman, but few in Washington were ready for isolationism. Hence the interest in regional surrogates with usable military power.

Whatever one might think of the wisdom of these new American policies, both seemed to enjoy broad support through the 1970s. The tilt toward Israel, coupled with sustained diplomacy on the Arab-Israeli conflict, yielded one huge success, namely, the Egyptian-Israeli peace treaty in spring 1979. Ironically, just a bit earlier that year the shah's regime, on which the United States had counted so strongly, was toppled by an intensely anti-American Islamic revolution. These two developments heightened concern for the stability of Saudi Arabia—the key, more than ever, to the price of oil. And Saudi security would be the central preoccupation of the next phase of American policy.

In this second period, there was again a multiplicity of plans and proposals for dealing with the Arab-Israeli conflict. Most significant in the early years were U.N. Resolution 242 and the Rogers Plan. Resolution 242 set the framework for the basic tradeoff between Israel and its Arab neighbors. In return for peace, recognition, and security, Israel would return captured land to Egypt, Syria, and Jordan. The Palestinians were not mentioned by name, nor were sensitive issues such as Jerusalem addressed. But the "land for peace" formula gave structure to all subsequent diplomacy.

Nixon's secretary of state, William Rogers, is best known in Middle East chronicles for spelling out the implications of 242 on the Israeli-Egyptian front. His proposal, originally intended to be a joint position put forward with the Soviet Union, was initially rejected by both Israel and Egypt when it was introduced in 1969. Ten years later, the two parties signed a peace treaty based almost precisely on the terms of the proposal. But much happened in between.

Kissinger was not a fan of Rogers or the Rogers Plan. He viewed the Middle East through a Cold War lens. This led him to the conclusion that nothing should be done to help Egypt until it had taken its distance from Moscow.[12] Nasir's death in September 1970 did little to change his view, and even when the new Egyptian president, Anwar Sadat, expelled some 15,000 Soviet advisers in mid-1972, Kissinger was slow to respond. The facts that 1972 was a presidential election year, and that the Vietnam negotiations were a major preoccupation for Nixon and Kissinger, help to explain the reaction to Sadat's poorly timed move.

Kissinger's myopia and complacency concerning the Arabs meant that he, like the Israelis from whom he took his cues, was caught by surprise when Egypt and Syria went to war with Israel on October 6, 1973. The war had an adverse impact on U.S.-Soviet relations, but surprisingly it opened the way for a creative period of American-led diplomacy and made possible a dramatic reversal of Egypt's long-standing alliance with Moscow. As U.S.-Egyptian relations gained substance, so also did the prospects for Israeli-Egyptian peace. Kissinger spent long hours working for a series of interim agreements between Israel and both Egypt and Syria.[13] He may have had a blind spot concerning the Palestinians, but he deserves much of the credit for the first breakthroughs toward Arab-Israeli peace.

Kissinger and Nixon also invested heavily in the relationship with the shah of Iran. But this did not turn out as well as the new ties with Cairo. The shah spent lavishly in the American arms market. He did play a certain regional role on behalf of Western interests (as in Oman), but he also turned out to be an unrestrained hawk on oil pricing, which had adverse effects on all oil-importing countries after the 1973 oil shock. And, in the end, the shah fell victim to some of the forces he had unleashed but not understood.

Just as Jimmy Carter was concluding the Kissinger legacy with the Camp David negotiations in September 1978, it became clear to official Washington that the shah was in deep trouble.[14] But what could be done? As it turned out, very little; and in February 1979 Ayatollah Khomeini returned to Iran to install an Islamic republic. Iran went from being the most pro-American country in the region to being the most hostile. One of the few sources of comfort at the time was that Israel and Egypt were ready to conclude their peace negotiations, which they did in March 1979.[15] These two dramatic developments signaled the end of one era and the opening of another. The new one would see much less emphasis on Arab-Israeli peacemaking and much more concern with Gulf security and Saudi stability. For now, more than ever, Saudi Arabia was the key to stable oil prices.

Cold War Revisited: Defending the Gulf, 1979–1990

Carter's last two years as president foreshadowed, in a sense, the themes that came to dominate American policy in the Middle East throughout the 1980s. The first was the preoccupation with Iran and Islamic militancy. In Carter's case, the specific concern was the fate of more than fifty American diplomats held hostage in Tehran. His inability to obtain their release played no small part in his failure to win reelection in November 1980. The second theme that came into sharp focus at the end of 1979 was the perceived Soviet threat to the Persian Gulf region. The immediate trigger for this heightened sensitivity to Soviet ambitions was the Soviet invasion of Afghanistan. Some saw the invasion as a springboard for further Soviet advances toward the Gulf. Instead, Afghanistan turned out to be for Soviet troops what Vietnam had been for Americans in the 1960s. Nonetheless, Carter's initial reaction was to bolster American defenses in the Gulf region and to proclaim the Carter Doctrine, the gist of which was that the United States would be prepared to use force if necessary to prevent any hostile power from dominating the oil resources of the Persian Gulf. During 1979, preparations began for a "Rapid Deployment Force," an initiative that eventually resulted in the creation of a new military force called the Central Command with responsibility for defense of the Gulf region.

Ronald Reagan and his team of foreign policy advisors were more than ready to revert to a Cold War frame of reference for dealing with the Middle East when they came to power in 1981. Israel, already a sentimental favorite with Reagan, was now regularly termed a "strategic asset," a term that had rarely been used in earlier times. Saudi Arabia also became the beneficiary of American support, in part owing to the concern for Gulf security, and in part because the Saudis were awash with petrodollars after the second "oil shock" of 1979 and were one of the few nations that could afford to pay for expensive American military equipment.

Further progress toward Arab-Israeli peace in the 1980s was forestalled not only by the intransigence of the parties to the conflict but also by the Reaganites' aversion to Syria and the P.L.O. Both were seen as radical clients of the Soviet Union. Only Jordan and Lebanon were viewed as potential peace partners with Israel, and the former seemed reluctant to move as long as the P.L.O. was strong, and the latter was inhibited by Syria.

Early in 1982, Israel's ambitious minister of defense Ariel Sharon discussed with American officials a plan that might weaken both Syria and the P.L.O. and thereby revive the chances for Arab-Israeli peace. The plan involved military intervention in Lebanon and support for the Phalangist party, and specifically Bashir Gemayel. The Israelis had supported Bashir for years, and now they saw a chance to bring him to power in Lebanon—on the back of Israeli tanks. Remarkably, the Americans seemed intrigued, despite a few cautionary words expressed about the need for an "internationally recognized provocation." It was not long before such a "provocation" came along, and in mid-1982 Israeli troops drove into Lebanon and proceeded to the outskirts of Beirut. Reagan was alarmed at the possibility of a broader Israeli-Syrian war and firmly told Prime Minister Begin to avoid attacking Syrian troops if possible. Reagan's secretary of state, Alexander Haig, who was persuaded that the Israeli offensive held great strategic potential, threatened to resign, and was soon thereafter dismissed by Reagan and replaced by the more cautious George Shultz.

Sharon's grand design for Lebanon never quite succeeded. The P.L.O. was indeed driven from Lebanon, and Bashir was elected president. But soon thereafter, things began to unravel. Bashir was assassinated and, immediately afterward, Phalangist troops, aided by Israel, carried out massacres against Palestinian civilians in refugee camps on the outskirts of Beirut. A multinational force, including Americans, was rushed back to Lebanon to provide security for Palestinians.

During the early part of 1983, Israel tried to salvage something from its ill-conceived Lebanon adventure. A peace agreement was forced upon the Lebanese government, but was ultimately repudiated under pressure from Syria. The regime in Damascus saw the whole American-Israeli plan for Lebanon with deep suspicion, and mobilized its assets, with help from Iran, to drive American and Israeli forces out of Lebanon. As part of this campaign, the American embassy was bombed, as was the marines' compound near Beirut airport, both with devastating results. In fact, more Americans died in 1983, as a result of hostilities, in Lebanon than in any other year in the Middle East, including the Gulf War of 1991. By early 1984, with his reelection campaign to tend to, Reagan blithely "redeployed offshore" the remaining American forces in Lebanon, ending a sorry episode in American policy in the region.[16]

Reagan's inability to grapple with the complexities of Lebanon and his lack of interest in Arab-Israeli peacemaking stand in contrast to his administration's more purposeful strategy in the Gulf. There the concern with the Soviet Union was less acute than the danger of an Iranian victory in the war with Iraq that had been raging since September 1980. Reagan had pursued the line set by Carter in building American military capabilities to intervene in the Gulf. This required a great deal of skillful diplomacy with countries as diverse as Morocco, Egypt, Kenya, Somalia, and Oman. All of these provided access to facilities for American aircraft and ships to move supplies and personnel from the east coast of the United States to the Gulf. Without much fanfare, this web of relationships was knit together, air and sealift capabilities were developed, and political alliances were adjusted. For example, in 1984 the United States resumed relations with Iraq in a conscious decision to back the embattled Baghdad regime against Khomeini's determined onslaught. Few Americans had illusions that Saddam Husayn's regime was other than brutal and repressive, but the general consensus was that an Iranian victory had to be prevented at all costs, if only to ensure that the Saudi regime and the smaller Gulf regimes would not be swept away by revolution. Despite the embarrassing episode in 1985–1986, when the Reagan administration sent arms to Iran to try to win the release of American hostages in Lebanon, the tilt toward Iraq seemed to represent a fundamental judgment of which of the two regimes was the lesser evil.

In response to a request from Kuwait in 1987, American naval ships began to escort Kuwaiti tankers. The so-called "reflagging" operation also demonstrated that the United States was not prepared to let Iran overrun the vulnerable oil-rich states of the Arabian Peninsula, whatever might happen to Iraq. At the same time, the United States and the Soviet Union, in an intriguing sign that the Cold War was winding down, adopted a joint position in calling for a cease-fire in the Iran-Iraq war. By the middle of 1988, the war had finally come to an end. Neither Iran nor Iraq had registered any gains on the ground; both had suffered enormous losses. But both regimes survived, which is presumably what mattered most to Khomeini and Saddam Husayn. Saudi Arabia and the smaller Gulf states all came through the crisis unscathed, which is what the United States had most sought. For the oil-importing countries, there was the added bonus of an oil glut that sent the price of oil to remarkably low levels after

1986. Thus, despite the debacle of Lebanon and the lack of significant progress in the Arab-Israeli arena during the 1980s, the relative success in terms of protecting American interests in the Gulf more than offset the setback to American interests elsewhere in the region. Or so it seemed as the next phase of American policy unfolded in early 1990.

After the Cold War: Dual Containment and the Peace Process in the 1990s

The end of the Cold War, Saddam's invasion of Kuwait, and the revival of Arab-Israeli peacemaking are the keynotes of this last phase of American involvement in the Middle East. Each of these markers was influenced by the others. As the Soviet Union ceased to play a role in the region, and then ceased to exist altogether, Iraq saw an opportunity to strike at a weak neighbor, especially at a time when many Arabs were frustrated by the lack of progress in the Arab-Israeli arena. Saddam was wrong in his judgment that the United States would acquiesce in the fait accompli rather than risk casualties in a "war for oil."

President George Bush was remarkably successful in mobilizing a broad coalition to oppose Saddam's aggression against Kuwait in August 1990.[17] Not only did the Western allies join American forces in sending troops, but so also did Egypt and Syria. The United Nations played a role in spelling out the conditions that Saddam should meet to avoid a counterattack. In the end, the massive use of force—both air and ground—that began in January 1991 ensured that Iraqi troops would be driven from Kuwait and that Iraqi power would be substantially reduced. The costs of the war were huge—several hundreds of billions by some estimates—most of which were paid by the Gulf states themselves. Indeed, the economic costs to the United States of the war were nil, and the loss of troops was also remarkably low, less than two hundred. The military preparations of the 1980s seemed to have paid off, in what may be a rare example of successful long-range planning.

But the defeat of Iraq left problems in its wake. Saddam survived in power, which meant that his country remained under severe sanctions throughout the 1990s, at huge cost to the well-being of his people. Still, Iraq ceased to be a military threat to the surrounding region, at least as long as some residual American power remained in the vicinity, which it did.

Iraq's defeat was something of a boon for Iran. Khomeini's death in 1989 had opened the way for a gradual move toward greater pragmatism, at least on domestic issues. Iran's foreign policy, however, remained sharply at odds with that of the United States throughout the 1990s. Still, the election of Muhammad Khatami in 1997 seemed to portend a gradual easing of tension between Tehran and Washington.

Perhaps the greatest surprise from the Gulf War was the extent to which it reopened the door for Arab-Israeli peacemaking. Several of the Arab partners of the United States in the campaign against Saddam were eager to see movement on that front. President Bush and his energetic secretary of state, James Baker, devoted much time and energy in 1991 to the organization of a multilateral conference in Madrid to relaunch the various tracks of the Arab-Israeli peace process.[18] Not surprisingly, progress was not easy, especially during the tenure of Likud leader Yitzhak Shamir as

Israel's prime minister. But in mid-1992, Yitzhak Rabin won the Israeli election, and soon demonstrated that Israel was prepared to negotiate seriously.

The United States helped to set the stage for the breakthrough that occurred in 1993. Five years earlier, the outgoing Reagan administration had persuaded the P.L.O. to accept U.N. Resolution 242 and to renounce terrorism in return for the opening of an official dialogue. The dialogue led nowhere and was eventually suspended, but the taboo on dealing with the P.L.O. was lifted. In 1993, Israel followed Washington's lead and began to talk secretly with the P.L.O. through the good offices of Norway. For the first time, a major agreement was worked out by the parties in direct negotiations, without the mediation of the United States. The Oslo accords, although signed with great fanfare on the south lawn of the White House, were only indirectly a result of American diplomacy.

The other track of negotiations between Israel and Syria found the United States more deeply involved, but was not immediately crowned with success. Nonetheless, in 1993 and again in 1995–1996, the two sides came surprisingly close to reaching agreement on general principles. And here Clinton played the role of essential intermediary, somewhat as Carter had between Israel and Egypt.

In mid-1996, the peace process came to an abrupt halt as a result of a series of terrorist attacks carried out by radical Islamist Palestinian groups. An enraged Israeli electorate turned to Benjamin Netanyahu, "Mr. Security," to be the next prime minister, and for the next three years there was little movement on the peace front. With Netanyahu's overwhelming defeat in the election of 1999 and the coming to power of Ehud Barak in mid-1999, many thought that peace talks would resume.

Looking Ahead

This latest phase of American diplomacy can be seen as a partial success—some headway has been made in resolving the Arab-Israeli conflict, and Gulf security has been maintained at manageable costs. But there is much unfinished business. The Palestinian-Israeli relationship remains very fragile; Saddam Husayn clings to power, at great cost to his people, and with no alternative in sight; and change in Iran is painfully slow. Meanwhile, concerns with the development of weapons of mass destruction—especially nuclear weapons—in the region are growing and a series of succession crises can be imagined as aging leaders pass from the scene in Syria, Saudi Arabia, Egypt, and at the head of the P.L.O.

No one can predict with precision what new challenges to American interests will arise in the new millennium, but it is safe to assume that the United States will continue to focus on maintaining Arab-Israeli peace and Gulf security. An abrupt loss of interest in the region is unlikely; hegemonic ambitions will remain in check. Americans know that they have interests in the region, but they have also learned that they cannot easily impose their grand designs.

As our brief overview has shown, for each initiative that might be considered a success there has usually been an unanticipated new challenge to American interests. Musaddiq's ousting in 1953 bought twenty-five years of pro-Western policy in Iran, to be followed by twenty years of hostility to the West. How to judge that one act of policy still remains a challenge for analysts and historians. So also with the other monuments to American policy such as Suez, Lebanon 1958, the management of the May-June crisis of 1967 and the October 1973 war, Kissinger's shuttles, Carter's summitry at Camp David, and Lebanon 1982.

Still, with all the unfinished business, and with all the questionable judgments that American policy makers have made in grappling with Middle East issues over the past fifty years, I return to my initial point. The result of American diplomacy in the Middle East in terms of U.S. interests has not been so bad. Having set out after World War II to support the creation of the new state of Israel without alienating the Arab world, to protect access to oil, and to keep the Soviets at bay, the Americans did just that, not always elegantly, and sometimes at extraordinary cost to peoples of the Middle East, but at little cost to their own interests. And along the way, policy toward the Middle East did not become excessively partisan. Democrats and Republicans generally followed similar approaches; the bureaucratic spats that occurred were more often over tactics than over fundamentals; and only during presidential election years did one really despair of sensible policy making on the Middle East.

In the course of pursuing rather narrowly defined interests in the Middle East, the United States ignored, to a large degree, issues of democracy and governance. To win American support, it was enough that a leader be pro-Western and supportive of the Arab-Israeli peace process. Respect for human rights, transparency, accountability, social justice, development—all of these desirable qualities of democratic government—were less important than fundamental foreign-policy orientations. Saddam Husayn was eligible for support as long as he was in confrontation with the even-more-disliked Ayatollah Khomeini. The fact that he used poison gas against his own people was known but was hardly seen as a reason to reassess the support given him.

As one looks ahead to a Middle East in which the Arab-Israeli conflict may well cease to be such a burning issue and where some type of regional equilibrium returns to the Gulf region, it may be the case that the United States will have the luxury of choosing its friends in the region less for classical strategic reasons than for the quality of their commitment to development and democracy. Some interesting experiments with pluralism and democracy are beginning, often in the small, less strategically located states. Encouragement of these efforts—whether in Qatar, Jordan, Lebanon, or Morocco—could be an important addition to the cultivation of good ties with long-standing friends such as Israel, Turkey, and Egypt. Such a shift of emphasis toward supporting states that do well on democracy and development would mark a significant change from the patterns of the past fifty years. Oil and the money it generates will obviously continue to trump concern with human rights and good governance in some areas, but one can already see that American nongovernmental organizations will keep the spotlight on human rights issues, even when governments choose to ignore them. And American corporations, eager to find profitable places to invest, will also be pressing for suitable economic climates, with respect for the rule of law, upholding of contracts, and the presence of a well-trained work force—not exactly a democratic agenda, but one that encourages a certain kind of open economy and development, both of which may contribute to pluralism and, eventually, democracy. In this new game of nations, in brief, states will only be one set of actors with influence. Americans will continue to be major players in the Middle East game, but not always as diplomats and soldiers, as in the past. The new actors on the scene are likely to be businessmen, computer technicians, representatives of nongovernmental groups, and even rock musicians. America's "soft power" of finance, information, and culture may come to rival its "hard power" of economic and military assistance. The result could be a more balanced set of relations between the world's leading power and countries that remain extremely sensitive about external interference in their affairs.

Notes

1   For the story of oil in the Middle East up to the early 1990s, see Daniel Yergin, *The Prize: The Epic Quest for Oil, Money, and Power*.

2   Avi Shlaim, *War and Peace in the Middle East: A Concise History*, attributes many of the errors of American diplomacy to an extensive preoccupation with global concerns at the expense of understanding the realities of the Middle East region.

3   See Mitchell Bard, *The Water's Edge and Beyond: Defining the Limits to Domestic Influence on United States Middle East Policy*. This empirical analysis shows that when the pro-Israeli lobby clashed directly with the president, it got its way about one-third of the time, generally on issues not involving national security.

4   William Burns, *Economic Aid and American Policy toward Egypt, 1955–1981*.

5   Steven Z. Freiberger, *Dawn over Suez: The Rise of American Power in the Middle East, 1955–1981*.

6   Irene Gendzier, *Notes from the Minefield: United States Intervention in Lebanon and the Middle East, 1945–1958*, makes a strong revisionist case that Lebanon *per se* was a major strategic concern for American policy makers. The conventional attitude, which I share, is that Lebanon was more of a sideshow, and that military intervention would not have occurred in 1958 without the Iraqi revolution.

7   Kermit Roosevelt, *Countercoup: The Struggle for Control of Iran*, provides a relatively frank account of the coup from the perspective of its main instigator.

8   Avner Cohen, *Israel and the Bomb*.

9   Malcolm Kerr, *The Arab Cold War: Gamal `Abd al-Nasir and His Rivals, 1958–1970*.

10   Richard B. Parker, ed., *The Six-Day War: A Retrospective*, provides a novel review of the events leading to the war through the testimony of many of the participants twenty-five years later.

11   William B. Quandt, *Peace Process: American Diplomacy and the Arab-Israeli Conflict since 1967*, chapter 2, analyzes the development of Johnson's "yellow light" policy.

12   Henry Kissinger, *Years of Upheaval*, chapter 6.

13   Edward R. F. Sheehan, *The Arabs, Israelis, and Kissinger: A Secret History of American Diplomacy in the Middle East*.

14   Gary Sick, *All Fall Down: America's Tragic Encounter with Iran*.

15   William B. Quandt, *Camp David: Peacemaking and Politics*.

16   Helena Cobban, *The Superpowers and the Syrian-Israeli Conflict: Beyond Crisis Management?*

17   Bruce Jentleson, *With Friends Like These: Reagan, Bush, and Saddam, 1982–1990*, is a very critical account of the tilt toward Iraq that preceded the 1990–1991 crisis. For the war itself, see Michael R. Gordon and Bernard E. Trainor, *The Generals' War: The Inside Story of the Conflict in the Gulf*.

18   James A. Baker III, with Thomas M. DeFrank, *The Politics of Diplomacy: Revolution, War and Peace, 1989–1992*, chapter 23.

4

The Middle East in Russia's Strategic Prism

Alvin Z. Rubinstein

Few regions of the world have experienced more profound political upheavals in this century than Russia and the Middle East. The term "Middle East" has been in general usage only since 1902, when the American naval historian A. T. Mahan described the region around the Persian Gulf as, viewed from Europe, neither "Near East" nor Far East; Mahan was discussing the geopolitical implications of growing Russian influence in Iran and of German plans to build a railway to Baghdad, then part of the Ottoman Empire. Today, however, it would be shortsighted to limit our notions of "the Middle East" to Mahan's definition. Since the Transcaucasian republics of Georgia, Armenia, and Azerbaijan, and the Central Asian republics of Kazakhstan, Uzbekistan, Turkmenistan, Kyrgyzstan, and Tajikistan became independent nation-states as a consequence of the implosion of the former Soviet Union in December 1991, they have been very much a part—conceptually, culturally, and politically—of the "Greater Middle East," and especially of its Turkic and Iranian dimensions.

Of Russia it can be truly said that it lost the twentieth century, and that in comparison with other major powers it is in far worse condition now than when the century began. The Russia led by Boris Yeltsin into the post-Soviet era was shorn of about 24 percent of its imperial domain and almost 40 percent of its population. The relinquishment of territory in Transcaucasia and Central Asia ended three hundred years of imperial expansion, and left Russia removed from the Middle East arena. The combination of Russia's past history, a persisting imperially-minded outlook, territorial and demographic uncertainties, security concerns, and economic considerations should provide what may be relevant to any assessment of Russia's diplomatic aims in the Greater Middle East. Despite what the evangelists of globalization would have us believe, cyberspace and rampant technological change cannot wither Russia's ambitions nor weakness restrain its political-diplomatic outreach—at least not for another generation or two.

In thinking about any country's foreign policy, context is crucial: thus, although similarities are discernible in many of the determinants and policies that characterized Russian policy during the Czarist, Soviet, and post-Soviet eras, there are differences, and these are all-important in differentiating the style and substance of one Russian regime from another. Any assessment needs to ask: What were the defining strategic characteristics of a particular period? Who were the primary adversaries? What issues loomed large in their rivalry? What was the configuration of power in the region and in the international system? What domestic influences shaped policy perceptions and behavior? What was the ruling elite's outlook?

It is also important to keep in mind that at no time in the nineteenth or twentieth century was the Middle East a vital region of concern for the Russian leadership. Russia's primary security and diplomatic concerns focussed on its western borders in Europe, and, starting with the late nineteenth century and the rise of Japan, its secondary concerns were with East Asia—Japan, the Korean peninsula, and China. Throughout that extended period, Middle East developments were tertiary threats to Russia's rulers.

Nevertheless, the intensity and seriousness of the Soviet-American rivalry in the Middle East during the Khrushchev and Brezhnev periods (mid-1950s to early 1980s) should not be underestimated. The crises were relatively short-lived and infrequent, but the underlying stakes were significant.

The "Great Game"

For the greater part of the nineteenth century, and after it,
up and down the length and breadth of Central Asia, from the Caspian to
the Karakoram and from the Khyber Pass to the confines of Siberia,
through-out the whole of the vast, but rapidly narrowing Tom Tiddler's
ground that separated their respective Empires, Englishmen and Russians,
and men of other races and nationalities too, played what they and their
contemporaries called The Great Game. Played it from various motives
and with varying degrees of success. Played it, on the whole, with
courage and resourcefulness, with dash and initiative, and with no great
attention to any particular set of rules.[1]

The imperial rivalry waged between the expansionist Russian and British empires from the early 1800s to the eve of the First World War encompassed not only Transcaucasia and Central Asia but also an infirm Ottoman Empire, whose coveted jewels were Constantinople and the straits linking the Black Sea and the eastern Mediterranean. Temporarily muted during the period of alliance against Germany in the years 1914 to 1917, the suspicions and fears that underlay the Great Game persisted in modified form until the late 1940s, when the United States supplanted Britain as the dominant Western power in the vast region to the south of the Soviet Union. One legacy of empire is a long historical memory.

Russia's more direct involvement in the Middle East was foreshadowed by two developments: the capture of Kazan from the Muslim Tatars in 1552, which opened up the entire lower Volga River region for settlement and penetration; and, in 1654, the incorporation of Ukraine into the Russian Empire, which ushered in centuries of conflict between the advancing Russian Empire and the retreating Ottoman Empire. Over the course of 250 years, the two fought each other thirteen times: the first was in the period from 1676 to 1681, the last between 1914 and 1918. Under relentless Russian pressure, the Ottoman Turks ceded the northern littoral of the Black Sea and the Crimea, and accorded privileged treatment to Russian subjects of the Ottoman Empire.

By the beginning of the nineteenth century, Britain was the only bar to Russia's unfettered access to the Mediterranean. In order to protect its empire on the Indian subcontinent, Britain was determined to forestall Russia's control of the straits or domination of the land routes between the Mediterranean and the Persian Gulf, and it assumed the role of ultimate guarantor of the Ottoman Empire's survival. However, Constantinople (renamed Istanbul after World War I) and the Bosporus and Dardenelles remained a central objective of Czarist foreign policy.[2] The First World War placed this maximalist Russian ambition within reach, this time with reluctant British acquiescence. In March 1915, as the price for Russia's participation in the war, Britain and France accepted Russia's terms in the secret agreement that came to be known as the Constantinople Agreement, the first of a series among the European members of the Entente for partitioning the Ottoman Empire.[3] But victory in November 1918 found a communist, not a czar, ruling in Moscow, and Britain and France felt relieved of any obligation to respect the accord.

Russian probes into the Caucasus, intermittent in the seventeenth century, were pressed by Peter the Great in the early 1700s, but not until the early decades of the nineteenth century did Russia achieve a decisive breakthrough against the Iranian Empire. By then, Iran, like Ottoman Turkey, was in sharp decline. Dynastic debilitation, economic backwardness, and military weakness left Iran vulnerable to Russian power. As a result, in 1801 Russia annexed Georgia, and a decade later forced Iran to give up "its right to maintain a navy on the Caspian, which thereby became a Russian lake," and to accept Russian interference in Iranian domestic affairs.[4] Fifteen years later, another war and another Russian-imposed treaty: in 1828, Iran surrendered Azerbaijan and part of Armenia, and accepted a commanding Russian political presence in northern Iran. The stage was set for the protracted Great Game between Russia and Britain that was to continue until after the Second World War.

Whereas the Treaty of Torkmanachay of 1828 basically delineated the Russian-Iranian frontier west of the Caspian Sea, to the east of the Caspian there were nomadic tribes and indeterminate khanates in a region of endemic political instability and economic stagnation. This "vast power vacuum, stretching all the way from the Caspian Sea to the borders of China, from Afghanistan to the edge of the Siberian plain, could not fail but exercise an irresistible attraction over the Russians."[5]

The emerging Great Game was stimulated, paradoxically, by Russia's military defeat at the hands of Britain, France, and the Ottoman Empire in the Crimean War (1854–1856). Precipitated by Russia's threatening advances in the Balkans and toward the Straits, the crisis had arisen because Czar Nicholas I thought France was acquiring special privileges in the Ottoman Empire that would give it exclusive rights over Christian churches in Jerusalem. Defeat in the war not only highlighted Russia's military inferiority vis-à-vis Britain and France, but also led to exaggerated Russian fears of the British threat in Central Asia.

In the decade that followed, even as Russian military planners were concentrating on upgrading the army's equipment and logistical infrastructure in Europe against the growing threat from Austria-Hungary and Germany, they were not indifferent to British naval power and its ability to strike at will against Russia's numerous vulnerable coasts. The rumored proposal to expand in Central Asia and heighten British insecurity over India was rejected on the ground that this "might arouse British suspicions, leading to the very rupture with London that had to be avoided at all costs."[6] But developments in the field, coupled with divided counsels and weak institutional controls at the center, set in motion events that acquired a life of their own and ended up reshaping a strategic situation. With small forces and at minimal cost, the Russians conquered the long-anachronistic and weak principalities of Turkestan and Chimkent in 1864, Tashkent in 1865, Samarkand in 1868, Khiva and Bokhara in 1873, Kokand in 1876, and Geok-Tepe in 1881. Although economic considerations such as captive markets and areas for raising cotton were present, the principal driving forces for imperial expansion were "the quest for defensible frontiers on the one hand, conjoined with the excessive ambitions of unruly local commanders willing to gamble that euphoria over easy victories would expunge the consequences of insubordination."[7]

These events merit attention owing to the parallels between the history of late imperial Russia and the Soviet Union in the post-Stalin period, as well as the ways they affected Russian policy in the Middle East. At both times there was the frustrating sense of technological inferiority; the reluctance to retrench from forward positions for fear of displaying any signs of weakness; the intellectual/ideological influence of key individuals in providing a rationale for strategic expansiveness; and the preoccupation with restructuring the economy and society in order to enhance the military's capability. A quest for security was used to justify a policy of expansion; and an expansionist policy mandated an excessively large military.

Russia's dash to the Afghan border led to a "gentleman's agreement" between St. Petersburg and London in January 1873, when they accepted the Oxus (Amu Darya) as Afghanistan's northern border. Minicrises continued, however, and in 1876–1878, the two powers came close to war. Flushed from victories over the faltering Ottoman Turks, Russia made a drive for the Straits and sent a strong military mission to Kabul, setting off alarm bells in British India. Fear that Russia would establish a controlling presence prompted the British to invade Afghanistan (1878–1881). Though an ostensible military success, the attack was costly and induced Britain and Russia to recognize Afghanistan's independence and accept its status as a buffer between them. After a decade of cartological cobbling, Russia and Britain established the 1,200-mile Russian-Afghan border in such a way that British India was insulated from direct contact with Russian territory.

The Great Game between Russia and Britain that had extended Russia's southern rimland from the Balkans to the Pamirs was formally ended in 1907. Facing a worsening strategic environment in Europe and the Far East, the two imperial rivals reached an accommodation in Iran and Afghanistan that lasted until the end of the First World War.

Soviet Diplomacy in the Eras of Lenin and Stalin

After the Bolshevik seizure of power in November 1917, and the civil war and allied intervention that followed, Moscow (the capital was shifted from St. Petersburg in early 1918 because of the threat from advancing German troops) placed a premium on normalizing relations and encouraging the independence of its longtime, long-aggrieved, weak Middle East neighbors: Turkey (now a republic, stripped of its non-Turkic imperial conquests), Iran, and Afghanistan. In so doing, the Soviet Union sought to deprive Britain, its principal threat in the Middle East, of opportunities to intrigue or intervene in Central Asia or the Caucasus. Security transcended ideology.

The Soviet-Turkish accommodation that started in the early 1920s and endured until March 1945 was triggered by a number of convergent considerations: fear of foreign intervention; a commitment to anti-imperialism; a desire to discard the peace settlement imposed by victorious Britain and France; a preference that the straits remain under Turkish control; and a suspicion of the League of Nations, which neither country was initially invited to join. The Russian and Turkish revolutions also shared an ideological commitment to secularism, modernization, and radical social transformation. They differed, though, in important respects: whereas the Russian revolution was international and class-focussed in its outreach, the Turkish was nationalistic, ethnically exclusivist, and inward-looking; whereas the Soviet Union's quest for modernization was doctrinally driven, Turkey's model was eclectic and borrowed from Western European sources; and whereas the U.S.S.R. was activist in foreign policy, Turkey cultivated a balanced form of isolationism.

The treaty of friendship signed by the Soviet Union and Turkey on March 16, 1921, was the first major international treaty for each. It delineated their frontiers in the Caucasus, renounced all former treaties between Czarist and Ottoman rulers, and returned the districts (sanjaks) of Kars and Ardahan, annexed by Russia in 1878, to Turkey, whereas Batum remained part of the Soviet Union. Each had reservations about the other's political aims and attitude, but a cooperative if at times cool relationship served their essential security interests through the dangerous 1930s and the years of the Second World War.

In the period immediately after World War I, Moscow's concern in Iran was to preserve its tenuous hold on the Caucasus and Transcaspia regions by preventing Britain from giving aid to the anti-Bolshevik forces bent on a counterrevolution. When the British failed in their attempt to establish a puppet regime in Tehran, Lenin quickly normalized relations with Iran and encouraged it to resist foreign encroachments. As in Turkey, nationalism—not communism—presented the fledgling Soviet regime with its best prospect to stymie British intervention and enhance its security.

In 1925, Reza Khan, who had taken power four years earlier, abolished the Qajar dynasty and had the Majlis proclaim him Reza Shah Pahlavi. His relations with the U.S.S.R. were correct, but fear of communism and Russian intrigue led him to rely on Germany for assistance and advisers, especially after Hitler came to power in 1933. Knowing of his pro-Nazi sympathies, the Soviet Union and Great Britain, who had forged an alliance shortly after Hitler's invasion of the U.S.S.R. on June 22, 1941, jointly occupied Iran on August 25, 1941, to protect the Persian Gulf oil fields and assure a safe transit route for shipments of war materiel to the beleaguered Soviet Union. Reza Shah was forced to abdicate in favor of his son, Muhammad Reza Shah, and was sent into exile; he died in South Africa in 1944. Iran was divided into two zones of occupation (reminiscent of the 1907 arrangement): the Soviets occupied the northern provinces, the British the southern part of the country, with Tehran treated as a neutral enclave. By a tripartite treaty, the U.S.S.R. and Britain agreed to withdraw from Iranian territory "not later than six months after all hostilities between the Allied powers and Germany and her associates have been suspended by the conclusion of an armistice or armistices, or on the conclusion of peace between them, whichever date is earlier."

Throughout this period, the Soviet-Afghan border was quiet.

The origins of the Soviet-American Cold War in the Middle East

Although the Middle East was not a high priority for Soviet foreign policy at the end of the Second World War, it was there that the Cold War between the Soviet Union and the United States may well have had its first and most concrete manifestations. On March 19, 1945, as the war in Europe was coming to an end, the Soviet government informed the Turkish government that it would not renew the 1925 friendship treaty, due to expire in November. Stalin made what Ankara deemed exorbitant demands: return of Kars and Ardahan, and the granting of military bases in the straits area. At the Potsdam Conference in July, Stalin pressed Truman and Churchill for Turkish territorial concessions and invoked the 1805 and 1833 treaties as the basis for an agreement. His position epitomized classic Russian imperialism. There was no threat; security was not an issue; Stalin merely sought to exploit his strong hand to acquire strategic advantage.

The Western powers supported Turkey, agreeing only to reconsider a revision of the 1936 Montreux Convention, which provided for the passage of warships through the straits, provided that Turkey was not a belligerent. Stalin overplayed a strong hand. Instead of requesting reasonable concessions that might have given him long-term leverage over Turkey and strengthened the domestic position of the sizable sympathetic leftist opposition that was developing, he acted very much the Russian imperialist. By the end of 1946, the onset of the Cold War had become unmistakable in Germany and Eastern Europe, and the United States increasingly assumed the former British role of protector of Turkish independence against Russian threats. On March 12, 1947, President Harry S. Truman asked Congress for the wherewithal to safeguard states threatened by "international communism."

In Iran, too, Stalin was intent on consolidating Moscow's control. Once the war was over, far from withdrawing Soviet forces in accordance with the provisions of the August 1941 agreement, he increased the Soviet military hold on the occupied northern provinces, frustrated Tehran's efforts to reassert central government authority, and encouraged Azeri and Kurdish separatist movements. Iran brought a complaint to the U.N. Security Council in January 1946. Moscow's veto paralyzed the council. Prime Minister Qavam as-Saltaneh, a wily old diplomat, convinced that the West would not resort to force to uphold Iran's independence, decided to negotiate with Stalin. On April 4, 1946, Moscow announced that Soviet troops would be withdrawn within two months; for his part, Qavam agreed to establish a joint Soviet-Iranian oil company before the end of the year, subject to the approval of the Majlis, and to satisfy peacefully, in some unspecified manner, in a way that was consistent with Iranian laws and sovereignty, the demands of the Azeri and Kurdish separatists .

When Soviet troops withdrew on May 9, most Western observers publicly asserted that Stalin's retreat was a result of pressure from the United States and the U.N.

Security Council. But the suspicion was widely held that Qavam had become ensnared in the Kremlin's clever diplomacy. By the end of 1946, however, it was clear that Qavam had outfoxed Stalin: Communist (Tudeh) ministers were removed, and the separatist governments were deposed, as Iranian troops retook control of the northern provinces. And in late 1947, after considerable delay, the Majlis rejected the oil agreement with the Soviet Union and the award of privileged treatment to any foreign country.

Moscow was furious, but in the year and a half since its prospects in Iran had seemed so bright, much had changed in the international environment: the polarizing Cold War in Europe, and America's growing support for countries threatened by the Soviet Union lying beyond the direct control of the Red Army, had raised the costs of armed intervention. Stalin accepted the rebuffs and turned to more serious security challenges in Eastern Europe and the Far East. Kuniholm has observed that it is ultimately unrewarding to quibble over the motives of either the Russians or the Americans in the Near East; rather, "it is preferable to characterize the conflict along the northern tier as another episode in the historical struggle for power in the region, a clash between competing national entities whose interests were intimately related to the world views or philosophies they espoused... . The Russians, in attempting to redefine the balance of power along the northern tier, were doing what they had done for centuries along their southern flank."[8]

Checked by the United States in his efforts to make inroads in Turkey and Iran, Stalin strove to undermine the influence of Britain, whom he considered still a major power in the region. This goal, he realized, could best be achieved through support of the Zionist efforts to establish an independent Jewish state in Palestine. The establishment of the state of Israel on May 15, 1948, and its survival through the first two years of fighting four Arab countries, could not have been accomplished without the extensive military, economic, and diplomatic support of the U.S.S.R. and its East European satellites. As a result, when Stalin died on March 5, 1953, the Soviet Union's prestige and presence in the Arab world was virtually nonexistent; relations with the countries along its southern border were poor; and the U.S.-Soviet Cold War that had already polarized alignments and the environment in Europe and East Asia was spreading to the Middle East.

Khrushchev Globalizes Soviet Strategy

In the struggle for power in the Kremlin after Stalin's death, two processes, interrelated and constantly changing, affected the outcome: one related to domestic policy, the other to foreign policy. Little is known of the ways in which specific individuals or coalitions manipulated these processes. We do know, however, that the triumph of Nikita Khrushchev over Vyacheslav Molotov in the period between late 1954 and early 1955 had enormous implications for Soviet foreign policy toward the third world, in general, and toward the entire Middle East, in particular.[9]

Khrushchev changed the scope of Soviet foreign policy and, by so doing, intensified the emerging rivalry with the United States, which endured almost until the end of Mikhail Gorbachev's tenure as the last ruler of the Soviet Union. He shifted the traditional Russian imperial preoccupation with the Eurasian land mass and security along the borders with contiguous neighbors to a strategy that was global in outreach and ambition. By embarking on a diplomacy of penetration, influence building, and strategic maneuver in the vast noncontiguous regions of the Arab world, southern Asia, Africa, and eventually even Cuba, he upped the strategic ante; and by pushing not only the development of an intercontinental ballistic missile (I.C.B.M.) capability but also a "blue water fleet" that could challenge America's control of the seas, he intensified the military aspects of the Cold War. Khrushchev's chosen approach was by no means the only one possible at the time; indeed, in retrospect, it is incontrovertible that a low-key diplomacy, less belligerently militant, would have brought comparable benefits, perhaps even greater ones, at far less cost and with far fewer tensions with the United States. But Khrushchev, who is often called "the last true believer," was inspired by Leninist formulations on the colonial and dependent areas of the "capitalist" (that is, noncommunist) world. He was a restless ideological and political tinkerer, with a deeply felt innate optimism about the Soviet Union's future and ability to help transform the third world, then in the throes of decolonization, so that it would become an area congenial to Soviet interests. He moved with uncommon verve to project Soviet influence.

A number of important changes in the international and regional environment favored Khrushchev's initiatives and courtship of leading Arab and southern Asian countries. Decolonization brought an end to the European empires and a concomitant increase in the number of newly independent nations operating in the world arena. Soviet leaders awoke to the fact that there were serious regional disputes in the Arab East (as well as in southern Asia and Africa) that could facilitate the U.S.S.R.'s entry into these hitherto exclusively West European colonial preserves.

In addition, intraregional tensions were aggravated and magnified by U.S. policy. In its absorption with the Soviet threat, Washington attempted to globalize containment by persuading Middle East regimes to join U.S.-sponsored alliances directed against the Soviet Union. One illustration may suffice. In the spring of 1953, Secretary of State John Foster Dulles visited Cairo to enlist the new regime headed by Gamal `Abd al-Nasir to sign an agreement that led to the Baghdad Pact. Dulles impressed upon Nasir (in the only personal contact they were destined to have) the urgency of forming a military alliance to safeguard the Middle East against the enemy. Whether it is apocryphal or authentic, Nasir is supposed to have asked, "Who is the enemy?" To Dulles it was international communism; to Nasir it was the continued occupation of Egypt by Britain.

Washington's penchant for "pactitis" enabled the Soviets to present themselves as a counterforce offsetting Western domination, and to offer their wares, military as well as economic. Having experienced Western "capitalism" for longer than they cared to remember, many regional elites in Arab countries looked to "socialism"—and for a time the Soviet Union—for assistance and an alternative model of development.

Finally, there was a greater readiness in post-Stalin Moscow to embrace accommodation with conservative and bourgeois-nationalist leaderships and work with them in areas of mutual interest, notwithstanding their close military ties to the United States. Nowhere was this quintessenial pragmatism and "peaceful coexistence" more evident than in the greatly improved relationships that Moscow enjoyed with Turkey and Iran from the mid-1960s to the late 1970s.

During the Khrushchev years, Moscow learned, belatedly, of the complexities and nationalistic variations shaping intra-Arab world politics. The Arabs had scarcely figured in Czarist imperial policy; they had been Ottoman subjects. Only after the First World War did the contours of the contemporary Arab system of nation-states emerge under the quasi-colonial overlordship of the British and the French. And not until the end of the Second World War did the Arab states become fully independent actors as well as sovereign states. Moscow learned the hard way how difficult it was to deal with inter-Arab rivalries, pursue a policy of balance between two regional rivals, or affix doctrinal labels such as "progressive" or "bourgeois-nationalist" to Arab leaderships. Not even "anti-imperialist" Arabs were easy to pigeonhole, as Khrushchev discovered in trying to balance between Egypt and Iraq in the late 1950s and early 1960s. Truly, as one Egyptian told this writer, "Moscow quickly learned that dealing with Arabs was like swimming in glue."

Policy Objectives and Operational Characteristics 1955–1991

From the perspective of the Soviet Union's Ministry of Foreign Affairs, the Middle East in the latter part of the Soviet period was composed of the following subregions: first, Turkey, Iran, and Afghanistan, in the Department of the of the Countries of the Middle East (Otdel' Stran Srednego Vostoka); second, all the Arab countries—and Israel—except for those in North Africa, in the Department of the Near East (Otdel' Stran Blizhnego Vostoka); and third, the First African Department (Pervyi Afrikanskiy Otdel'), which covered Libya, Tunisia, Algeria, Morocco, Mali, and Mauritania. Moscow's policy toward each subregion and country developed in response to a combination of opportunity and strategic salience. The extensive and often multiple aims may be noted briefly: security, strategic denial, strategic advantage, fostering anti-Americanism, prestige, ideological fulfillment, economic considerations, expansion to acquire territory, and promotion of communist and vanguard parties.

Security. Since the end of the eighteenth century, with the exception of one brief period from the late 1950s to the early 1960s, the Middle East had posed no credible threats to the territorial integrity or internal stability of the Czarist or Soviet state. The implantation of nuclear-tipped medium-range missiles in Turkey and the quest by the United States for air bases to refuel long-range bombers from Arab countries were legitimate Soviet security concerns during the Khrushchev years, but hardly major threats. With the advent of I.C.B.M.s and Polaris submarines in the mid-1960s, the main military threats to Moscow's southern tier or "soft underbelly" stemmed from bases and platforms thousands of miles away.

Strategic denial. Denying advantage to one's adversary is a way of enhancing security. It seeks to undermine and weaken the military position and political situation of an opponent. For the Soviet Union, this meant thwarting U.S. policies, limiting the scope and effectiveness of its alliances and alignments, complicating its diplomacy, diverting its resources to areas and issues that Moscow deemed peripheral to its own concerns (Vietnam was a good example), and preventing the United States from maximizing its regional advantages. In obvious situations, the time-proven proposition, "the enemy of my enemy is my friend," determined Moscow's choice of client. The Soviet government courted regional regimes hostile to those who looked to the West; in the 1950s this led to ties with Egypt and Syria against Western-oriented Iraq (until July 1958); in the 1960s and 1970s, support for Egypt and Syria against Israel, Iraq against Iran, and the People's Democratic Republic of Yemen (P.D.R.Y.) against Oman and Saudi Arabia, and so on. In more subtle fashion, Moscow's diplomacy persuaded an Iran aligned militarily with the United States to refuse the latter permission to base missiles or bombers on Iranian soil, in return for economic and military assistance, a quiescent Tudeh Party, minimal force deployments along their extensive border, and the prompt return of defectors.

Strategic advantage figured prominently in the Kremlin's ties with North Yemen, where it sought port facilities, and with the P.D.R.Y., from which it sought naval and air reconnaissance facilities. Moscow's interest in a foothold on the southwestern part of the Arabian Peninsula (an oft-neglected aspect of Western accounts of the Soviet Union's Middle East policy) explains its willingness to underwrite Egyptian President Nasir's five-year intervention in the North Yemeni civil war from 1962 to 1967. In May 1961, Albania's eviction of the Soviets from the naval base they had enjoyed at Vlone since 1945 prompted an intensified courtship of Egypt, but not until after Egypt's defeat in the 1967 June war did Nasir grant the naval access coveted by Moscow. Over the years, Moscow received far less from Egypt than its generous assistance warranted.

Fostering anti-Americanism encompassed a wide range of techniques that included disinformation, media manipulation, forgeries, planted rumors, misleading radio broadcasts, and outright lies designed to arouse popular hostility toward the United States. These incessant efforts to influence governments and elites were embodied in the Russian phrase *aktivnye meropriyatiya* (active measures).

Prestige is a hoary political status desired by all leaders for self-legitimation. In the Middle East context, it signified to Moscow co-management with the United States in any process seeking to settle the Arab-Israeli conflict, as well as consultation on other regional issues. Soviet leaders were sticklers for form in the matter of being accorded the respect they felt was their due, but basically they were tough bargainers and unwilling to relinquish much to achieve that elusive goal. Not until 1990 and Gorbachev's cooperation with the United States in the crisis occasioned by Iraq's invasion of Kuwait did a Soviet leader make concessions and sacrifice tangible interests (in Iraq) for the sake of improved relations with the United States.

Ideological fulfillment quickly became a minor policy determinant, once initially optimistic expectations were not borne out and Soviet leaders came to appreciate that the Middle East arena was more complex than they had originally expected, and that the "contradictions" yielded confusion, not new syntheses. Ironically, ideological considerations may have played an important role in one of the Soviet Union's unmitigated disasters in the Middle East, namely, the decision to intervene militarily in Afghanistan in December 1979 in order to kill off one set of Afghan communists and replace them with a more manageable cohort.

Economic considerations were rarely taken seriously in decisions to develop a comprehensive relationship with a courted client. To those who could not pay, Moscow was generous; to those who could afford to pay but were prized targets of influence (Iraq, for example), Moscow was patient and forbearing; on the other hand, when it held the upper hand, as it did when Iran and Afghanistan had to sell their natural gas to the Soviet Union for want of any alternative, Moscow drove a hard bargain.

Moscow's main export item to the Middle East was advanced weaponry; financial arrangements and delivery schedules were dictated by political-military aims and urgency, not economics. The oil-rich countries like Iraq and Libya quickly learned that they could buy almost anything they wanted without having to keep up regular payments. Moscow never looked too far ahead with balance-of-payments projections, a mismanagement of a strong position that was to cost it dearly.

Expansion to acquire territory is in the Russian foreign policy tradition, but only as a part of a continental-based empire; Russia had never ventured overseas or beyond contiguous countries in its expansionist phases. After Stalin's abortive efforts to blackmail Turkey and Iran into making far-reaching concessions, Moscow's expansionist impulse did not manifest itself in the Middle East until the takeover of Afghanistan in 1979, and even then there was no indication during the decade-long Soviet occupation of any intent to incorporate Afghanistan, or any part thereof, into the Soviet Union.

Promotion of communist and vanguard parties, always a declared aim of Soviet leaders, was mostly a marginal afterthought in Moscow's diplomacy. On rare occasions, such as the verbal duel between Khrushchev and Nasir in late 1958 and 1959, a fuss was made over Nasir's attacks on Arab communists for their alleged hostility to "Arab nationalism," that is, Egypt's leadership in the Arab world. But far more frequently, Moscow resigned itself to anticommunist manifestations and kept its focus on strengthening bilateral government-to-government relations. In Iran, the Tudeh Party was banned, but this did not prevent the Soviet Union from developing good relations with the shah. Comparable accommodations were made at various times with Turkey, Iraq, Algeria, the Sudan, and Egypt, notwithstanding the persecution of indigenous communists. In Syria, where President Hafiz al-Asad tolerated a small, utterly supportive communist party, the Soviet leadership carefully avoided any untoward interference that might anger him or lead him to reconsider his anti-American course.

With a few notable exceptions, Soviet diplomacy was very much in the Russian tradition. What were familiar were the pragmatism, prudence, and reluctance to become involved in a war with another great power; what was new and distinctive about Soviet behavior in the post-Khrushchev period was the readiness to commit Soviet armed forces to protect prime clients from the consequences of their behavior, and to do so in areas (Egypt, Syria, Sudan, Iraq) remote from any direct threat to vital security interests.

From the record of Soviet diplomacy of the period, it is possible to discern a number of operational principles. First, the Soviet Union pursued a differentiated policy that reflected a keen appreciation of local and regional power realities, and a sharp eye for strategic opportunity. It courted countries that were opposed to U.S. policy as well as countries that were allied to the United States, but sought to maintain correct relations with others. In this way, Moscow's diplomacy worked to fashion a regional environment conducive to the advancement of its geopolitical and military aims in the context of the rivalry with the United States. If tangible military benefits resulted from a particular courtship or commitment, so much the better, but at no time were they prerequisites for the largesse that Moscow dispensed. The main objective was always to enable a client to pursue policies that Moscow deemed generally advantageous to improving the strategic context within which Soviet diplomacy proceeded, rather than to acquire specific influence over the client. Put another way, the aim was to weaken the Soviet Union's principal adversary, the United States. It was this underlying rationale that accounted for the U.S.S.R.'s adapting to the shah's anticommunist conservatism, Sadat's deNasirization, Asad's ambitions and low-intensity war against Israel in Lebanon, Saddam Husayn's crackdown on pro-Soviet Iraqi communists and Kurds, and Khomeini's Islamist outlook. Moscow's disappointments were due primarily to the inconstancy of its clients.

Second, with the exception of Moscow's intervention in Afghanistan, the level and character of Soviet involvement was determined by the Middle East client. Soviet assistance, advisors, and direct military involvement came as a result of invitation, not imposition. Considerations of cost were not a serious constraint on Moscow's commitment.

Third, the Soviet Union proved a reliable patron-protector, openly supportive of clients who requested assistance against external attack, against internal opposition, and against pressure from a U.S.-backed regional rival. Once involved, Moscow stayed the course, irrespective of the military and economic costs or the adverse effect on its relationship with the United States in other spheres of their rivalry in the global arena. Gorbachev's withdrawal from Afghanistan in early 1989 was dramatic evidence of Moscow's retreat from this maximalist imperial policy.

Fourth, to Washington's continual surprise, not until the Gorbachev period did Moscow modify its policies in the Middle East in order to improve relations with the United States.

Moscow's activist diplomacy played an important role—though how much remains a subject of continuing disagreement—in triggering most of the wars waged in the Middle East between 1962 and 1990, from Nasir's 1962 intervention (Egypt's "Vietnam") in the North Yemeni civil war, to the three Arab-Israeli wars of 1967, 1970, and 1973, and the P.D.R.Y.-North Yemen and Afghan wars. Still, it needs to be acknowledged that Moscow's projection of military power on behalf of key clients was accompanied by countervailing diplomatic circumspection and avoidance of behavior that might have been interpreted by Washington as a threat to the survival of its regional clients.

Soon after Gorbachev came to power in March 1985, Soviet foreign policy began to change in the Middle East, among other places. Eager to improve Soviet-American relations and institute a meaningful detente, he accepted major arms control agreements that were complemented by withdrawal from Afghanistan in 1989, restoration of diplomatic relations with Israel in 1990 for the first time since June 1967, a decrease in naval deployments, and regional accommodations in Angola, Nicaragua, and the Horn of Africa. The pièce de résistance was Gorbachev's eventual support in the U.N. Security Council in November 1990 for the use of force against Iraq—long a prime Soviet client—to reverse Baghdad's aggression against Kuwait. But turbulent domestic tides, unexpected and powerful, swept the Soviet Union into the graveyard of past empires before any meaningful accommodation between Moscow and Washington could be consolidated.

Russia and the New Eurasia

When the implosion of the Soviet Union ended 450 years of Russian imperial expansion, Russia could no longer claim to be part of the Middle East. It is now far from Turkey, Iran, and Afghanistan; its new southern borders are contiguous to Georgia and Azerbaijan in Transcaucasia and Kazakhstan in Central Asia, and farther away lie the former republic of Armenia in the Caucasus, and beyond Kazakhstan, Uzbekistan, Turkmenistan, Tajikistan, and Kyrgyzstan in Central Asia. In sharp contrast to the lost empires of its European counterparts, Russia lost considerable defensive contiguous territory along its southern and western periphery, 12 to 15 percent of its ethnic population, and substantial parts of its military-industrial infrastructure. Moscow's primary security concerns along its southern rimland understandably center on the situations developing in the new nation-states of the former Soviet Union.

Given the uninterrupted deterioration and parlous condition of Russia's institutions, the pervasive corruption, and the appalling record of flawed leadership, Russia cannot hope to recreate in the foreseeable future the circumstances that once enabled it to dominate Transcaucasia and Central Asia. Reconquest is out. The Russian army is demoralized, underfinanced, poorly led and trained, and is likely to be preoccupied for decades (perhaps generations) with regime maintenance rather than expansion. The ultranationalists who talk of forcibly reintegrating parts of the former empire are distinguished by their rhetoric, not their grasp of reality. Chechnya is a constant reminder of Russia's military weakness.

Growing increasingly accustomed to ruling in their own nation-state, the new republics find ethnic nationalism a strong agent of cohesion and a difficult barrier for Russia to overcome in today's international system. In addition, Russian emigration from the "Near Abroad" (as Russia calls the non-Russian republics of the former Soviet Union with Russian minorities) is well under way, diminishing Russia's ability to use its nationals as a potential fifth-column force. The exodus, slowed somewhat in recent years because of the horrendous social and economic problems in Russia, is the first Russian demographic retreat since the medieval period.

Another drawback to any imposed Russian return to the region is the diffusion of modern weapons that make military adventurism extremely costly. Occupation of hostile populations for imperialistic purposes is a no-win situation in this day of easily obtained advanced weaponry suitable for harassing foreign invaders.

Finally, the absence of imperial-minded powers with the capability of waging major wars for control of the borderlands south of Russia proper eliminates a prime motive for war, that is, the quest for real estate. There is simply too little—apart from oil, which in any event is cheaper to buy than to fight over—to attract an outside power to seek conquests in this area where ecological damage is incredibly severe.

Why Russia Still Matters

A deeply wounded civilization, Russia lacks leadership, efficient institutions for proper governance, and a viable judicial system appropriate for a modernizing market-oriented society; its elites are rapacious, factious, and unable thus far to shape a consensus on societal transformation. This Russia lacks a coherent approach to the

Middle East. Calling it "the sick man of Europe"—and of Inner Eurasia as well—is no exaggeration. Moreover, compared with the late Soviet period, Russia today lacks a power-projection capability, that is, the ability to intervene quickly and effectively on behalf of a hard-pressed prime client. No longer can Moscow act the patron-protector in Arab or African regional conflicts. Nor can it provide low-interest, long-term loans for would-be clients. Shorn of empire, its focus has shifted, geopolitically, from the Middle East to Transcaucasia and Central Asia.

Notwithstanding all of this, Russia remains an important actor on the Greater Middle East stage, for a number of reasons. First, as a permanent member of the U.N. Security Council, Russia can use its veto power to block resolutions opposed by countries it is trying to shield. This political lever is increasingly important, since the United States and many West Europeans find it domestically prudent and often essential to obtain a U.N. seal of approval for peacekeeping operations that involve their troops under a NATO umbrella. However, when NATO launched air strikes against Serbia on March 24, 1999, to help protect the Albanians living in Serbia's province of Kosovo, it did so without first bringing the matter to the U.N. Security Council; this marked a major departure from its previous interventions and peacekeeping operations in the post-Cold War period. Moscow's veto power is nevertheless one of the few restraints it has on Washington's ambition to manage developments in the Balkans and the Middle East, areas of residual interest to Russian leaders.

Second, however straitened its domestic circumstances and diminished its conventional military capability, Russia remains a nuclear superpower. Washington's policy of promoting denuclearization and nuclear nonproliferation requires Moscow's cooperation, but progress has been slow, and achievements are few in number. Russian suspicions of American intentions have been exacerbated by Washington's championing of NATO expansion, by its hinting at plans to scrap the 1972 anti-ballistic missile treaty in order to embark on a national missile defense program, and by its muddled (and often self-serving) advice on how to develop a market-oriented economy. Progress in the nuclear field, which is essential for global stability, will be increasingly difficult with a Russia in which important political groups blame the United States for worsening their "time of troubles."

Third, Russia is a major exporter of arms (behind the United States, Germany, and Britain), military technology, and skilled engineers and technicians. Because its wares are outperformed and less efficiently supplied with spare parts and servicing in most lucrative markets, it sells wherever possible, notably to China, India, Iran, and Iraq. The main restraints inhere in Moscow's need for payment in hard currency. Rosvooruzhenie, Russia's state arms export agency, has shown few second thoughts about the wisdom of helping these states upgrade their military capabilities. Like that of the United States, Russia's policy is impelled by commercialism and not strategic calculation—with far more persuasive logic, it should be noted. As U.S.-Russian relations deteriorate, Moscow's arms sales to "rogue" regimes are apt to increase, further heightening tensions.

Finally, Russia possesses enormous and as yet underdeveloped energy resources, most of which are to be found in its northern, semiarctic provinces. A massive commitment of foreign investment and technology would be required to produce and export Russian natural gas and petroleum. For the moment, such an enterprise is neither economically nor politically viable. In the future, however, when the price of oil may rise substantially as global demand grows, Russia's reserves could be very important in helping to stabilize Western over-reliance on Persian Gulf oil.

Russia's Geostrategic Situation at the New Millennium

Russia's present strategic environment in the Middle East and Central Eurasia differs profoundly from that of the nineteenth century and most of the twentieth century. First, the dissolution of the U.S.S.R. and the consequent end of Russian rule in Transcaucasia and Central Asia means that Russia is no longer a Middle Eastern power. Russia's primary interests are focused on Kazakhstan and Transcaucasia, and with somewhat lesser urgency on the other four nation-states of Central Asia. However, Russia does not constitute a serious threat to the independence of its former republics.

Second, the high-stakes imperial Great Game waged by Russia and Britain for 150 years, and then by the Soviet Union and the United States for forty-five years, is over. In a throwback to the seventeenth century, Russia finds itself one of several modest regional powers, along with Turkey, Iran, and China, vying for influence and advantage. The United States, the only powerful contestant, remains an uncertain participant, more interested in market share than strategic dominance. At present, America's ostentatiously ambitious involvement has had the effect of coalescing regional actors informally against aspects of U.S. policy—Russia and Iran, Russia and Syria, Russia and Iraq, Turkey and Iran, even Turkey and Iraq, are but a few of the alignments that are cropping up.

Third, Russia's military decline shows few signs of bottoming out, much less being reversed. The once omnipresent and omnivorous military establishment, which absorbed upward of 25 percent of the gross national product in the late Soviet period, has fallen on hard times, characterized by fiscal stringency and pervasive corruption; a lack of discipline, professionalism, and combat readiness; substandard living conditions for and treatment of conscripts; high desertion rates; and bitter bureaucratic and intra-Kremlin intrigues over turf. These make a mockery of the repeated calls for widespread reforms. Russia continues to fall behind other major powers in efforts to keep pace with the technological changes driving the revolution in military affairs. Proposals, of which there are many, to reconfigure Russia's conventional forces into relatively small, mobile units capable of deployment in local conflicts and participation in regional peacekeeping activities, have yet to bear fruit.[10] The dismal performance of the Russian military in Chechnya in 1998 revealed the need for military reforms, but these are as distant and improbable as at any time in the 1990s. Russia's prospects in the realm of naval power are even bleaker.

Fourth, oil and natural gas came of age in the twentieth century. When Russia lost 24 percent of its territory in December 1991, it lost some of the major oil-producing areas of the empire. Although estimated to be sitting on about 10 percent of the world's proven oil reserves, Russia is not likely to be a major oil exporter. Aside from its own domestic needs, it is burdened with an aging infrastructure, shoddy maintenance of its 40,000 miles of pipelines and 85,000 miles of natural gas pipelines, lack of capital to invest in new technology and equipment, and an inefficient work force.[11] Two-thirds of the world's oil reserves are situated in the Persian Gulf and Caspian Sea Basin regions, but Russia may not be in a position to exploit its pipelines, geographic location, or political influence to any significant extent. Unable to nurture the openness and stability that are essential to attract investment and initiative, it seems wedded to intrigues reminiscent of the nineteenth-century Great Game and resistant to the transparency essential for moving its economic interests ahead in the twenty-first century.

Fifth, like much of the Middle East, Russia has been disturbingly affected by the transformation into a nation-state. Elites reared in an imperially dominated environment have found themselves ill prepared to refashion inherited institutions, mediate explosive ethnopolitical animosities and aspirations, and cope with security concerns quite different from any experienced by their predecessors. In an effort to encourage cooperative and integrative processes, in the 1992 to 1994 period, Russia pushed a series of interstate and interministerial treaties with most of the independent republics of the former Soviet Union. The Charter of the Commonwealth of Independent States (C.I.S.) stressed collective security, and was intended to give Moscow an important voice in the managing of peace and security on the vast territory of the former Soviet space. Several years on, the gloss has worn off, and Moscow finds itself viewed with suspicion; its efforts at economic integration have little to show, in part as a result of the continued parlous condition of Russia's economic, industrial, and political institutions. In April 1999, Uzbekistan withdrew from the C.I.S. collective security treaty; should others follow suit, Russia's hopes for the C.I.S. would be seriously hurt. None of this has enhanced Russian prestige in the Middle East.

Sixth, unlike the Czarist and Soviet periods when foreign policy making was, with few and infrequent exceptions, centralized and coherent—with a linkage and logic between policy toward Europe and, for example, policy along the country's southern borders—Russia under Yeltsin has been characterized by a multiplicity of quasi-autonomous institutional centers of domestic influence in conducting aspects of foreign policy with Middle East countries, as well as with China. In contrast to the centralization of policy making authority in the hands of the key organs of the Communist Party of the Soviet Union, post-Soviet Russia has seen the emergence of a number of institutional centers that affect foreign policy. Government ministries (foreign affairs, defense, foreign trade, intelligence, heavy industry, and so on) often act independently of one another.

Russia's relations with Iran, for example, illustrate how complex, potentially dangerous, and out of control the conduct of foreign policy may be. Desperately short of hard currency, individual Russian ministries and firms enter into their own arrangements with Iranian authorities, often without the knowledge of their superiors. The Ministry of Atomic Energy has sold nuclear technology and is helping Iran build a nuclear power plant in Bushehr, on the Persian Gulf. Rosvooruzhenie, the government arms exporting agency, has acknowledged on various occasions that it has sold advanced weaponry, including MiG-29 and Sukhoi-25 aircraft, S-200 air defense systems, and T-72 tanks.[12] More recently, U.S. sources have alleged that Russia has supplied Iran with components for the development of intermediate-range missiles, the Shihab-3 and Shihab-4, with ranges of 800 and 1,300 miles respectively, notwithstanding Russian legislation that forbids such transactions; and the Federal Security Service, the successor to the K.G.B., has been identified as an active recruiter of Russian scientists to help Iran develop its missile technology.[13]

What Does Russia Seek?

For the time being, Moscow's aims in the Middle East stem more from a shared historical memory than geographic determinants. The small group of narrowly based decision makers in Russia today were administrators and advisors during the heyday of the Soviet Union's "imperial moment" in the post-Stalin period. They remember and aspire to preserve as much as possible of the Soviet/Czarist legacy. Though disorganized and often at odds with one another, Moscow-centered elites aim to parlay Russia's seat on the U.N. Security Council and its veto power, past adeptness at diplomatic maneuvering and deal-making with any kind of regime, readiness to satisfy requests for military wares, and remembrances of once-extensive relationships into a foreign policy that perpetuates Russia's great-power status and that advances its interests—which could be national, bureaucratic, or personal in character.

Virtually all of Russia's foreign policy elite, broadly conceived, would consider themselves *derzhavniki*, believers in Russia's great-power status, as well as *gosudarstvenniki*, believers in strong central government. They believe that Russia's status as a nuclear superpower, its extensive interests in Europe, East Asia, and inner Eurasia, and its vast resources merit recognition as a great power. Representatives of all foreign policy persuasions, whether Westernizers or Eurasianists, can agree on this, whether they see Russia as an integral part of the West, or as the center of a unique cultural heritage and civilization, one that—threatened and rejected by the West—should seek allies in the non-West, in China, India, Japan, and the Muslim countries.[14]

The perceived marginalization of Russia by the United States has spawned a politics of resentment among Westernizers and Eurasianists alike. The marginalization is felt in the absence of respect and prestige. Neither is a tangible element of power; yet, inextricably associated as they are with the status due a great power, their absence is quickly felt in the way other actors in the international system respond and in the negative consequences for the leadership in domestic politics. The growing extremism on the left and right strongly reflects the bitterness felt in Russian political life toward the United States, which is blamed for Russia's diminished status.

Ever since the United States pushed NATO enlargement, Western-oriented advocates in Moscow have lost their influence; witness Yevgeny Primakov's replacement of Andrei Kozyrev as foreign minister in January 1996. More than any other event, NATO enlargement is seen by many members of Russia's establishment as an attempt to squeeze Russia out of Europe. Even less critical assessments acknowledge that Russia is being excluded from Europe, "Asianized," with implications of inferiority that are far from complimentary. Then-Foreign Minister Primakov called NATO's expansion to the east "possibly the biggest mistake made since the end of the Cold War."

The first casualty has been trust, most obviously in the arms control field, where multifaceted security-building processes have come virtually to a halt. New nuclear accords are on hold, and with U.S. defense expenditures scheduled to increase in the years ahead—while Russia's of necessity continue to decline—the once-bright prospects for far-reaching cooperative security agreements have dimmed considerably.

All of this has resulted in Russia's intensification of relations with countries that also have reason to mistrust or be dissatisfied with the United States. The greater its sense of isolation and alienation in Europe, the more Russia looks for ways to strengthen relations with non-Western nations. On March 15, 1999, in his annual message to the Duma, President Yeltsin called for intensified efforts to strengthen ties with C.I.S. states and, in particular, to forge stronger connections with China, India, and Japan. But with the balance of power shifting against it and the domestic "time of troubles" showing no sign of abating, Russia has a weak hand to play.

Conclusion

In June 1998, Yevgeny Primakov, then foreign minister, drew on his long career as intelligence officer, diplomat, politician and academic specialist on the Middle East to speculate on Russia's prospects.

Born in 1919, Primakov was trained in international political economy and Middle East studies and speaks Arabic and English. In the 1960s, he was the Middle East correspondent of *Pravda*, the Communist Party's newspaper. In the 1970s, he was director of the Oriental Studies Institute of the U.S.S.R. Academy of Sciences, and then became deputy director of the Institute of World Economy and International Relations—two of the most prestigious foreign policy institutes of the post-Stalin period. In 1988, Gorbachev appointed him to chair the U.S.S.R. Supreme Soviet, and Primakov remained a loyal supporter. After the emergence of the Russian Federation, Yeltsin showed his confidence in Primakov by appointing him, first, to head the Russian Foreign Intelligence Service, then in January 1996 to the post of foreign minister, and in the summer of 1998, to the position of prime minister, until his removal in May 1999.

A year earlier, in May 1998, Primakov spoke at a ceremony commemorating the 200th anniversary of the birth of Prince Alexander M. Gorchakov, Russia's foreign minister during the regin of Alexander II. Drawing on the Gorchakov legacy, Primakov used the occasion to compare the two epochs, the challenges Russia faced, and the lessons to be learned.[15]

Gorchakov became foreign minister in 1856, the year after Russia's defeat in the Crimean War, when "many thought they were present at a funeral for the Russian Empire or at any rate witnessing its transformation into a second-rate power." Russia had been defeated and humiliated. Gorchakov faced two basic options: one, that Russia "resign its great-power status," including even the liquidation of the Ministry of Foreign Affairs, which his predecessor proposed; two, that it push internal changes—without which Russia did not have a bright future—while, at the same time, pursuing an active foreign policy to ensure an environment conducive to internal rejuvenation. On August 21, 1856, Gorchakov answered his critics: "Russia is accused of isolating itself and being silent in the face of facts which harmonize neither with the truth nor with fairness. They say Russia is angry—Russia is not angry. Russia is just concentrating."[16]

Clearly having Russia's situation at the time in mind, Primakov spoke with respect of Gorchakov's skillful maneuvering and adept use of a variety of often contradictory tactics to safeguard and advance Russian foreign policy interests. Some of Gorchakov's ideas, he contended, were still as applicable as they were in his own time. Primakov singled out five relevant lessons from Gorchakov's "arsenal of foreign policy tactics."

First, a weak Russia must not withdraw from the international arena but, on the contrary, must pursue an active foreign policy. Even as Russia strove to implement economic and military reforms (thus far, unsuccessfully), it must vigorously defend its position as a great power and as one of the principal players in the international arena.

Second, Russia should follow a multifaceted policy and avoid a unidimensional approach. In relations with the United States, Western Europe, Japan, China, and India congenial adroitness was important, but at the same time relations with "second-rate" countries must also be assiduously cultivated, because without diversification of foreign connections Russia would not be able to overcome its difficulties or preserve its great-power status.

Third, in what may have been his most important expression of personal sentiment, Primakov left no doubt that he believed Russia was still in a position to play the role of one of the leading powers. In Russia's present circumstances, he declared, it could rely on "its accumulation of political influence, special geopolitical position, early membership in the world's nuclear club, status as a permanent member of the U.N. Security Council, growing economic possibilities, and military production, which establishes the condition for military-technological cooperation with numerous foreign partners." Utilized cleverly, this assortment of diplomatic instruments could be used to frustrate American policies and advance or safeguard Russia's interests.

Fourth, Primakov observed that many countries feared a unipolar arrangement in world politics (that is, a U.S.-dominated world), and their resentments could be mobilized to Russia's advantage.

Fifth, unlike the Gorchakov era, which depended on constantly changing coalitions among the European powers, Russia should now look much farther afield for "constructive partnerships," which, by implication, would be of long-term duration. It may have been with this concept in mind that Prime Minister Primakov suggested, during a visit to India in December 1998, the establishment of a Russian-Chinese-Indian "strategic triangle." Although, in early March 1999, the spokesman for the Ministry of Foreign Affairs said that Russia had no plans to promote such a strategic alliance, Yeltsin himself, in his annual message to the Federal Assembly twelve days later, raised the matter of the importance of drawing closer to India, China, and Japan.

Like Gorchakov, Primakov believed that "there are no constant enemies, but there are constant national interests." Ruefully, he acknowledged, "In the Soviet period, we often deviated from this vitally important truth, and as a result in the circumstances of the time the national interests of our government were sacrificed in the struggle with 'permanent adversaries' and on behalf of 'permanent allies.' Today we have returned to rational pragmatism."

Russia's challenges today are far greater; its domestic condition is far worse than it was in the late nineteenth century; its elites lack the essential cohesiveness of that period, and the newer groups—the financial elites, media moguls, stockholding and insurance companies, and political elites at the local, regional, and national levels—are still in the process of asserting themselves, with as yet unknown consequences, and all are characterized more by confrontation than consensus. Finally, in foreign policy, and particularly in regard to the Middle East, Russia is weaker and more vulnerable than it has been in several centuries. Relative to the United States, it commands limited resources. But since power is no guarantee of influence, nor is economic largesse any assurance of unquestioning fealty, the United States may not be the irresistible arbiter of developments imagined by the unipolarists and proponents of American global leadership. How and when—indeed if—Russia's leaders can turn Gorchakov's tenets into practise is one of the important questions whose answer lies in the next millennium.

Notes

1 Fitzroy Maclean, *A Person from England, and Other Travellers*, Prologue. "Tom Tiddler's ground" was an English phrase for a no-man's land, or a neutral or barren stretch of country between two kingdoms.

2 For example, see S. Goriainov, *Bosfor I Dardenelly*.

3 Cited in J. C. Hurewitz, ed., *The Middle East and North Africa in World Politics: A Documentary Record*, Vol. 2, *British-French Supremacy, 1914–1945*, p. 17.

4 Firuz Kazemzadeh, "Russia and the Middle East," p. 491.

5 Ibid., p. 495.

6 William C. Fuller, Jr., *Strategy and Power in Russia 1600–1914*, p. 289.

7 Ibid.

8 Bruce R. Kuniholm, *The Origins of the Cold War in the Near East: Great Power Conflict and Diplomacy in Iran, Turkey, and Greece*, pp. 429–30.

9 For example, see Alvin Z. Rubinstein, *Moscow's Third World Strategy*, pp. 19–31; and Oles M. Smolansky, *The Soviet Union and the Arab East under Khrushchev*, pp. 23–33.

10 General M. A. Gareyev, "Some Questions of Military Organizational Development."

11 For a far-ranging analysis of the nexus between geography, economics, and politics, see Geoffrey Kemp and Robert E. Harkavy, *Strategic Geography and the Changing Middle East*.

12 For example, Foreign Broadcast Information Service—Soviet Union 96–035 (February 21, 1996), p. 14.

13 *Washington Post*, March 23, 1998.

14 For example, Charles Clover, "Dreams of the Eurasian Heartland: The Reemergence of Geopolitics"; and Oles M. Smolansky, "Russia and the Asia-Pacific Region: Policies and Polemics." A foreshadowing of the Europe First-Eurasianist debate in the opposing camps of Russian elite opinion on foreign policy can be discerned in the 1860s and 1870s, in the competing views of Foreign Minister A. M. Gorchakov and Prince I. Bariatinskii, who was appointed viceroy of the Caucasus and succeeded in bringing Russia's decades-long fighting there to a successful conclusion in 1864. Both men were influential advisers to Czar Alexander II. See Alfred J. Rieber, *The Politics of Autocracy: Letters of Alexander II to Prince A. I. Bariatinskii 1857–1864*, pp. 60–90.

15 E. M. Primakov, "200 Years of A.M. Gorchakov: Russia in World Politics."

16 Ibid., p. 4.

PART II

Israel and the Arabs

5

Egypt:

Pan-Arabism in Historical Context

Michael Doran

More than any other Arab country, Egypt conforms closely to the classic model of the nation-state. The Nile River, a green gash slicing through brown wasteland, has fashioned over the centuries a society that is both homogenous and insulated from the lives of its neighbors, even those who share with it the Arabic language and Islamic religion. The river has also fostered a centralized state. Because it flows north, whereas the prevailing winds blow south, from the earliest of times navigation never presented a serious challenge. With the entire population within a stone's throw of the water, the neck of the peasantry remained within the grasp of the tax collector, who himself stood in easy reach of his superiors. Once the germ of the bureaucratic state found its way to the Nile Valley, therefore, it spread with startling rapidity. Throughout history, larger states often swallowed Egypt; even as an imperial province, however, it retained an independent administrative identity.

This combination of a homogenous population and a long history of statehood invites a power-political analysis of Egyptian foreign relations, because social uniformity and institutional stability give rise to a definition of national interest that transcends changes in government and ideology. Such an analysis properly proceeds from the identification of Egypt as a middle power, or a regional great power. Egypt is the most populous Arab state; among the other regional powers, only Turkey and Iran are its equal in size. By virtue of its geostrategic importance, Cairo has an interest in every major issue in Middle Eastern international politics, and on many occasions it has forced the other Arab capitals to pay deference to its agenda. In short, in the pursuit of its national interest Egypt enjoys greater latitude than its sister Arab states.

Given the susceptibility of Egyptian foreign affairs to a power-political analysis, it is striking that the foreign policy of the `Abd al-Nasir period is almost synonymous with an ideology, pan-Arabism. Of course, ideology and power are not mutually exclusive categories. Beliefs and ideas generate their own power in history, and it would be foolish to deny the pull of pan-Arabism on the imagination of Gamal `Abd al-Nasir and his contemporaries. But institutional and ideological power do not operate according to the same logic: when institutions marry ideas, tensions emerge that force practical choices. A power-political analysis tracks the course of those choices. Without doubt, pan-Arabism had an inherent attraction. It is precisely because of this attraction that it also served as an effective instrument for exploiting Egypt's potential as an intermediary between the global states system and the Arab states subsystem.

The Problem of Britain

In the immediate aftermath of World War II, domestic politics imposed severe limitations on foreign policy.[1] Leaders in Cairo faced a nationalist public that was better organized than ever before, and that demanded an end to British domination. Although "complete independence" had been a central slogan in Egyptian politics for decades, the realities of power had hitherto prevented the major political parties from displaying a steadfast determination to oust the British. As a consequence, in the interwar period Britain had succeeded in holding the balance in Egyptian domestic politics between the Wafd, on the one hand, and the palace and the lesser political parties, on the other. By 1945, however, this pattern was clearly unraveling, in part because the conservative elite in Cairo came under pressure to display a credible and sustained opposition to the presence of British forces on Egyptian soil.

Several factors account for the weakness of the political elite in the face of popular opinion. First, British policies during the war alienated Egyptians of all social classes and discredited the very idea of an alliance with Britain. In theory, the 1936 Anglo-Egyptian Treaty had placed relations between the two countries on a new footing, one that provided Cairo with some measure of control over British behavior. In fact, World War II, just like its predecessor, landed on Egyptian shores tens of thousands of British soldiers who displayed little respect for the local culture. Egyptians felt as powerless as ever to control the foreigners in their midst. This feeling only increased after the events of February 1942, when the British compelled King Faruq by force of arms to appoint a Wafdist government. The humiliation of the king taught two simple lessons: it was in fact the foreigners who held sway over supposedly sovereign Egyptian institutions; and the basic premise of the 1936 treaty—that Britain and Egypt were allies of equal standing—was a sham. Many Egyptians concluded, therefore, that only the complete and unconditional evacuation of British troops would secure independence for their country.

The fractiousness of the political parties further undermined the status of the conservative elite and contributed to the rising nationalist tide. The behavior of the Wafd government that Britain had foisted on the country exacerbated divisions among the old guard. In late 1944, with the war drawing to a close, the enemies of the Wafd toppled the party from power and then leveled against it serious accusations of corruption. In the fight of its life, the Wafd responded to the attacks by playing the nationalist card, calling for a complete, immediate, and unconditional withdrawal of British troops. While the traditional parties were at each other's throats, a number of radical groups—including the Muslim Brotherhood, the Communist Party, and the Young Egypt movement—began to flex their muscles. Their power was considerable: the Muslim Brothers alone boasted a mass following that numbered in the hundreds of thousands. These radical organizations all added their voices to the anti-British chant. With the Wafd, the Muslim Brothers, and a host of other organizations all playing to a public that had grown exasperated with Britain, the non-Wafdist governments who ruled Egypt between 1945 and 1950 had no choice but to demonstrate their commitment to the nationalist cause.

But evicting the foreigners was no easy matter. The British regarded the Suez Canal and the military bases that flanked it as vital imperial turf, and they were not prepared to evacuate their forces without receiving guarantees that, in time of war, they would be allowed to return. In 1947, the Egyptian prime minister, Isma`il Sidqi, attempted to strike a compromise between competing claims by conceding limited base rights to the British, but the Egyptian public rejected the notion. This public opposition to a military alliance in *any* form must be seen as a primary cause of the failure of the Bevin-Sidqi Agreement, even though historians traditionally attribute the breakdown in negotiations to conflict over Sudan, which was indeed a second point of contention between the two sides.

By early 1947 the middle ground between Egypt and Britain had been eliminated: no government in Cairo could sign an agreement with Britain and still hope to remain legitimate at home, and yet the Egyptians did not have the power to oust the British, who occupied the Canal Zone with thousands of troops. This deadlock set the stage for the disruptions that culminated in the burning of Cairo in January 1952, an event that itself helped to trigger the revolution. Egypt's new rulers regarded the British problem as the first priority. In the words of one, "In fact, the justification for our having come into existence as the Free Officers organization and for our having carried out the revolution was to free Egypt from the hand of the British occupation. The problem of the evacuation [of the British troops] became the prime concern of all of us. In fact, it was our first thought, because if the evacuation were not fully carried out, then the revolution would be far from realizing its goal and would lose the justification for its existence."[2]

The Global and Regional Systems, 1945–1952

The Anglo-Egyptian conflict was so central to political life in Cairo that it informed all aspects of Egyptian foreign policy in the postwar era. Consequently, Egyptian leaders surveyed the international horizon in search of anti-British allies.

In this regard, the rise of the United States and the Soviet Union gave Cairo some reason for optimism, because these powers might have been persuaded to weigh in on the side of Egypt against the British Empire. `Abd al-Nasir would fully realize this potential, of course, in 1956. However, in the first decade after World War II the continued presence of thousands of British troops in the Canal Zone limited Cairo's options. For one thing, this military threat made it impossible to appeal directly to the Soviet Union for aid.[3] An agreement similar, say, to the Czech arms deal of September 1955 would have met with an immediate crackdown by the British forces, which had the means on hand to unseat the government. Cairo did, however, possess an American option. Since the United States was the senior partner in the Anglo-American alliance, a request to Washington for aid against Britain entailed none of the dangers inherent in a request to Moscow. The Egyptians did, in fact, turn to the Americans, among whom a number of important voices recommended support for Egyptian nationalism; in the end, however, Washington decided in favor of qualified support for Britain in the Anglo-Egyptian dispute. Thus the Truman administration made sympathetic noises but refused to help Cairo oust the British.

Although the Egyptians courted frustration in the great-power arena, they did find some satisfaction in the sphere of inter-Arab politics. Between 1943 and 1945, Cairo led the movement to establish the Arab League, which extended its regional influence in a manner that weakened Britain. As the League rose up, two blocs of Arab states crystalized: the Hashimite powers of Iraq and Jordan stood poised against Egypt, Syria, and Saudi Arabia, a grouping that I have dubbed elsewhere the Triangle Alliance. The Hashimite bloc stood for a continuation of the British regional order, which the Triangle Alliance sought to destroy. In theory, the Arab League functioned as the representative of collective Arab aspirations, but it actually served as the instrument, in general, of the Triangle Alliance and, in particular, of Egypt.

In fact, Egypt founded the League primarily in order to prevent British attempts to establish a new Middle Eastern order coordinated solely with its Hashimite allies.[4] In February 1943, British Foreign Secretary Anthony Eden repeated an earlier statement in support of any scheme for greater Arab unity—political, cultural, and economic—that "commands general approval." Eden's statement came on the heels of an Iraqi proposal for Fertile Crescent unity that envisioned two stages: first, Syria, Lebanon, Palestine, and Transjordan would unify in a Greater Syrian state; second, Iraq and the enlarged Syria would form a federation open to the accession of other Arab countries. The Iraqi and British initiatives immediately sparked the interest of Amman. The Amir 'Abdallah, who had for twenty years called for the unity of the Syrian lands, responded immediately to the Iraqi and British initiatives. In April he issued a proclamation inviting representatives from Syria, Lebanon, and Palestine to Amman, where a conference would convene in order to plan the unification of Greater Syria. In short, if the Egyptians had remained aloof, then the British and their Hashimite allies would have enjoyed a free hand in reorganizing the postwar Middle East.

Thus the League projected Egyptian power into the Arab arena, organizing the anti-British forces into the nucleus of a new regional order. The Saudi and Syrian allies of Egypt, of course, had their own reasons for opposing the British and Hashimite plans. Ever since 1925, the year they expelled the Hashimites from Arabia, the Saudis had regarded Amman and Baghdad as their most formidable rivals—so much so that they based their regional policies on the goal of containing Hashimite expansion. For their part, the Syrians looked upon the Hashimite plans for reorganizing the region with a fear that bordered on paranoia. Unlike the Saudis, who enjoyed the benefits of a well-organized polity, growing oil revenues, and staunch American protection, the Syrians were internally divided, poor in resources, and had no close relations with any great power.

The position that Egypt and its friends took on pan-Arabism suffered from one serious weakness: it stood opposed to the popular notion of integral Arab unity, the idea of wiping out the illegitimate borders drawn by the European powers. The Triangle Alliance therefore lobbied against the Hashimite plans by appealing to the equally popular principles of anti-imperialism and anti-Zionism. Its propaganda claimed that any form of Arab unity that excluded Egypt, the most powerful Arab state, would simply allow the British to assert control by proxy over Greater Syria. The Triangle Alliance made similar claims with regard to Zionist influence, which, it argued, the British-dominated governments in Amman and Baghdad would be powerless to block on their own. Fortunately for Cairo, the principles of anti-imperialism and anti-Zionism were indeed powerful; consequently, the spotlight never fell on its own selfish opposition to erasing borders in the name of Arab unity.

That Cairo regarded its role in the Arab world as an asset in its negotiations with Britain became explicit in 1947. In that year, King Faruq explained to the British that any attempt to establish a new relationship with the Arab world must first pass muster with Egypt, which he described as the "keystone in the arch," the most important Arab country.[5] London, ever hopeful that the Arab League might one day support its aspirations for a broad Anglo-Arab alliance, was surprisingly slow to recognize the anti-British role that the League played. Owing in no small measure to the activities of the Triangle Alliance, now coordinated within the framework of the League, Egypt helped to frustrate almost all major attempts by Britain and the Hashimites to revitalize the existing Anglo-Arab alliances. Prior to the Anglo-Egyptian Agreement of October 1954 (which, as we shall see, was itself problematic), the sole British success was the Anglo-Jordanian Agreement of 1946.

The First Arab-Israeli War

The fundamental goal of Cairo's policy in the 1948 Arab-Israeli war was to maintain the dominant position of Egypt within the Arab arena. Failure to do so would have gravely weakened Egypt's international position, itself the basis of any hope that Cairo had of ousting the British.

In 1948, the primary threat to Egyptian regional status came not from Iraq, as sometimes presumed, but from Jordan. When the United Nations partition resolution sparked a war between the Arabs and Jews of Palestine, the Jordanian army was the only regular Arab force that stood prepared to intervene on behalf of the Palestinians. For their part, the leaders in Cairo hesitated to commit their army because they considered it unprepared, and because they feared that the war would expose weaknesses that Britain would exploit to its own advantage. At the eleventh hour, however, Egypt decided in favor of intervention. Public opinion certainly played a role in this decision, but subsequent Egyptian moves in both diplomatic and military arenas demonstrate that much more was also at stake. In the final analysis, Cairo decided in favor of war on the basis of a familiar calculation: failure to take action would have given the Hashimites a free hand in reorganizing the region.

The worst nightmare of the Triangle Alliance fixated on the possibility of a British-endorsed agreement to partition Palestine between Jordan and Israel.[6] The Triangle Alliance reasoned, on the basis of sound political judgment, that in return for King `Abdallah's acceptance of Israel's existence, Tel Aviv might support the Greater Syria scheme of its Hashimite neighbor. Shukri al-Quwatli, the president of Syria, expressed this fear clearly when he first heard, in April 1948, that King `Abdallah would in fact intervene in Palestine with British approval. Upon receiving the news, the Syrian President confided to associates as follows: "King `Abdallah wants to deceive [us], and the British are exploiting the opportunity to impose a treaty on our country, because our independence is a thorn in their eyes. They want our army to move first [against the Israelis], so that it will be destroyed. Then they will pretend to come to our aid, but in exchange they will demand the price of our enslavement. They want to pave the way for `Abdallah to spread his influence in Palestine and Syria. This is a trick that I will not allow them to play on me."[7] This passage reflects the fears not just of the Syrian president but of the entire Triangle Alliance. The somewhat paranoid belief in a detailed British plot should not blind us to the fact that President al-Quwatli's fears accurately depicted the deepest political motives of his Hashimite neighbors.

Although the Syrian leader did misjudge British policy, his apprehension was not unfounded in this regard either. British claims of neutrality in the matter of Greater Syria meant little to the Triangle Alliance—because London might change its policy, or the Hashimite powers might present the British with a fait accompli. It is worth remembering that many of the leaders of the Triangle Alliance had watched in the aftermath of World War I as Britain established the modern state system; it hardly took a flight of fancy to believe that in the aftermath of World War II it might reorganize the region. Moreover, during the 1948 war the United Nations mediator, Count Folke Bernadotte, reinforced the anti-British fears of the Triangle Alliance by advancing peace plans that aggrandized Jordan. Bernadotte's proposals proved that the Triangle Alliance did indeed confront in Palestine international forces that favored either the Hashimites or the Israelis. None of the great powers, for instance, supported the Triangle Alliance's vision of a new order in Palestine, which included the suppression of Zionism and the establishment of a Palestinian state independent of Jordan.

The power of Jordan and the policies of the great powers forced hard choices on Cairo. Had Egypt failed to enter the war, Jordan would have inevitably expanded into Arab Palestine, either with tacit Israeli acceptance or with only a limited Jordanian-Israeli conflict, one that would have left Jordan still capable of threatening the independence of Syria. Such an outcome would have led, in the worst-case scenario, to the absorption of Syria into a larger Hashimite state; in the best case, it would simply have turned Syria into a British satellite. In either case, the Triangle Alliance would have ceased to function as a platform for projecting Egyptian power into the global arena. Alliance maintenance, therefore, dictated not just entering the war but fighting it so as to weaken Jordan and, thereby, to frustrate plans for strengthening the British Empire.

Popular concern for the plight of the Palestinians could not generate enough political will to close the chasm that separated Egyptian and Jordanian state interests. Consequently, the Israelis managed to fight each of the Arab powers separately, and on Israeli terms. The 1948 war, therefore, was both politically and militarily a debacle for the elite in Cairo. Nonetheless, the abject nature of the failure against the Jewish enemy has blinded us somewhat to the limited successes of Cairo's policies toward its Arab enemies: the Triangle Alliance did frustrate any Jordanian-Israeli cooperation, and the war left Jordan so weakened as no to longer pose a threat to Syria.

A Grand Strategy

The failure of the Egyptian army in the war called into question the pan-Arab orientation; in 1949 voices advocating the abandonment of the Arab League again made themselves heard in Cairo. The forces that had in the first place impelled Egypt to establish the League and to fight in Palestine were not transient, however. They had the deepest roots in Egyptian politics; therefore, shortly after the defeat, Cairo again reaffirmed its commitment to pan-Arabism. Two factors account for this continuity in policy: the Syrian question and the question of regional defense.

The war destabilized Syria, forcing hard choices on Egypt. In 1949, Syria suffered three coups d'état in rapid succession, and this instability gave rise to a sense of insecurity which, in turn, strengthened a current of opinion in favor of unity with Iraq. Proponents argued that Syria was so weak that it would fall under Israeli domination; federation with Iraq would, they argued, both protect the country and satisfy the yearning of nationalists for Arab unity. Consequently, Egypt yet again faced the reality that inaction on its part would give the Hashimites a free hand to reshape the Fertile Crescent. Cairo rediscovered why it had founded the Arab League in the first place: to counter Hashimite expansionism.

In an effort to deny the Iraqis and their supporters in Syria the use of the Israeli threat as a pretext for a Syrian-Iraqi union, the Egyptians resuscitated well-rehearsed pan-Arab themes. They claimed that the most effective plan of defense against Israel was the one that included all of the Arab states—and Egypt in particular, since it was the largest and most powerful. They further claimed that any union with Iraq would be rotten at its core, because Baghdad stood in thrall to the British. As a counterweight to plans for an Iraqi-Syrian federation, Cairo proposed the creation of an Arab League Collective Security Pact (A.L.C.S.P.), an organization that would create a centralized command in charge of all Arab armies.[8] The Hashimite states hesitated before ratifying the A.L.C.S.P., but, in the prevailing pan-Arab political climate, both eventually dropped their opposition. The pact finally came into force in February 1952, after Amman ratified it.

While the A.L.C.S.P. supplied Cairo with ideological weaponry for fighting Iraqi propaganda in Syria, it also served an important role in relations with the great powers. In the early 1950s, Britain and the United States placed before the Arab states a series of proposals—the Middle Eastern Command, the Middle Eastern Defense Organization, and the Baghdad Pact—for creating a system of regional defense. For the Egyptians, all of these schemes spelled the continuation of the British occupation, because they sought to modify rather than dismantle the existing British security system, at the center of which stood the web of military facilities that flanked the Suez Canal. Cairo designed the A.L.C.S.P., therefore, to function as an indigenous alternative to the web of Anglo-Arab military alliances.

The A.L.C.S.P. envisioned an independent bloc of Arab states, led by Egypt, that would cooperate in matters of defense and present a common face to the outside world. It presupposed dismantling the British network of military bases, of course, and creating a new regional order. In that case, the status of the Triangle Alliance would have increased in direct proportion to the decrease in Hashimite power, which rested on the British connection. In terms of popular ideology, the A.L.C.S.P. appealed to anti-imperialist sentiment and to the popular attitude that Arabs should rely on Arabs in matters of defense. It therefore fostered a political environment throughout the Arab world that made it very difficult, for instance, for Baghdad to ignore Egypt and negotiate a new Anglo-Iraqi military alliance. In the event of such an Iraqi attempt, which actually did materialize in 1955, Cairo could charge Baghdad not with offending Egyptian national interest but with stabbing the entire Arab nation in the back.

The A.L.C.S.P., then, was the expression of a grand strategy, a comprehensive political vision that tied together policies in all the major spheres of public life—the domestic, inter-Arab, Arab-Israeli, and great-power arenas. The very notion of the Arab League had always contained a latent blueprint for international revolution but, especially in the period before 1947, other strands of Egyptian policy had muted the revolutionary components of the organization. The advent of the A.L.C.S.P. demonstrated that, even before the 1952 revolution, the Egyptian elite was harnessing the power of Fertile Crescent Arab nationalism so as to compel the Arab states to cooperate on Egypt's terms in matters of defense and, thereby, to create an independent Arab bloc. At the top of the Arab pyramid, of course, would sit Egypt, which would act as the intermediary between the Arab world and the West. Only one thing stood in the way of realizing this bold vision: the British security system.

The Sources of `Abd al-Nasir's Foreign Policy

Much of the scholarship on the early `Abd al-Nasir period takes it as axiomatic that the Free Officers, in foreign policy as in domestic, radically departed from the traditions of the late Faruq era. In fact, however, the Free Officers inherited the grand strategy of the old regime: `Abd al-Nasir and his associates continued to work for an independent Arab bloc based on a system of regional defense defined by the A.L.C.S.P. To this end, they maintained the alliance with Syria and Saudi Arabia, while seeking complete independence from Britain by using American power as a counterbalance to British influence.

Why have these continuities largely escaped notice? Lack of scholarly interest in the foreign policy of the Faruq era provides a partial explanation. More importantly, on three occasions in the aftermath of the revolution the Free Officers departed dramatically from the course charted by their predecessors; so radical were these policy changes that they created the lasting impression of discontinuity in foreign affairs. In the first two years, the Revolutionary Command Council made two significant concessions to long-standing British demands: first, it recognized the Sudanese right to self-determination; and second, it ratified the 1954 Anglo-Egyptian Agreement, which allowed the British the right to return to the Canal Zone bases in the event of an attack on the Arab states, Turkey, or Iran. These signs of apparent deference to British and Western interests gave way by late 1955 to growing cooperation with the Soviet bloc, and to the leading role that Egypt played in the Non-Aligned Movement. Thus, the early `Abd al-Nasir period began with concessions to the West that contradicted fundamental nationalist principles, and it ended with an unprecedented level of cooperation with the communist bloc.

On the face of it, such dramatic deviations in policy prove that the rise of the Free Officers signaled a break with foreign-policy traditions. Indeed, perceptive Egyptian observers themselves arrived at this very conclusion. For instance, the famous Egyptian author Tawfiq al-Hakim writes that "a person who carefully studies the political, military and social events that took place in Egypt throughout the rule of `Abd al-Nasir will find that their true unseen motor force was 'excitation and reaction,' and not calm, composed and serious thought built up on the basis of a long-term view of things."[9]

In fact, however, `Abd al-Nasir's policy deviations were tactical rather than strategic. Take, for instance, the concessions to Britain in the realm of defense. Khalid Muhi`l-Din explains them as follows:

The truth is that I often spoke to `Abd al-Nasir ... about the evacuation problem, and about the agreement on Britain's right to return. My point of view was that concluding an agreement with Britain that included her right to return would strengthen the imperialist camp and give it strategic advantages that would increase the chances of a world war and, thereby, increase the chances of Britain returning to occupy Egypt. But `Abd al-Nasir understood that the evacuation was the dream of every Egyptian, and that it was very important for us to realize for the Egyptians their dream. He always emphasized that carrying out the evacuation would be an historic victory. If, after that, the British would want to return, we would prevent them, because, hopefully, we would have acquired the requisite amount of strength.[10]

Pretending to accept the future right of the British forces to return was the price of immediately ousting the foreigners from Egypt. `Abd al-Nasir understood that the mere removal of British troops from Egyptian soil would create new opportunities for destroying the British regional security system. A similar rationale informed the decision to accept the principle of self-determination for the Sudan: Cairo calculated that the Sudanese forces favoring union with Egypt would prevail, and the "Unity of the Nile Valley" would finally be realized.[11]

`Abd al-Nasir's hostility to the British security system certainly ran as deep as that of the pashas, but his method of undermining British influence had been unthinkable in their day. The Free Officers provided themselves with unprecedented room for maneuver in Anglo-Egyptian affairs by banning party politics. Politicians in the Faruq era could never have contemplated making concessions that, privately, they had no intention of honoring, because the competition between political parties forced the pre-Revolutionary leadership to demonstrate public fidelity to nationalist principles.

Secretly, then, `Abd al-Nasir and his associates worked to replace the British regional security system with an Arab bloc. But in order to win British and American acceptance of a total British withdrawal, they partially hid their uncompromising position on Western security interests. Of course, at home `Abd al-Nasir's concessions to Britain were unpopular; they forced supporters of the Anglo-Egyptian Agreement to defend it as the lesser of two evils. Tawfiq al-Hakim's testimony is again apposite. A defender of the concessions to Britain, he answered `Abd al-Nasir's critics as follows: "I used to respond that as long as we had got rid of the occupation, in whatever way, it was better than perpetual stalemate and constituted a decisive point leading to movement and a start in building the renaissance of Egypt. The revolution had eliminated this abscess from the face of Egypt so that it could devote itself to something more important. Now, at last, the country was moving toward the desired economic growth."[12] This point of view did not rouse emotional support in Cairo, but it did play well in Washington and London, where `Abd al-Nasir's apparent deference to Western interests won him considerable goodwill. He earned the reputation of being a pragmatic military man who sought to overcome the long-standing conflict with Britain in order to build the economy of Egypt.

The perception that `Abd al-Nasir's foreign-policy goals stemmed directly from domestic economic concerns is central to the "excitation-and-reaction" interpretation of his foreign policy. According to this view, it was the Arab-Israeli border war of 1955–1956, not opposition to the British security system itself, that forced Cairo into close relations with the Soviet Union. `Abd al-Nasir himself promoted this view, which persists in scholarly work down to the present, finding expression in most of the literature on the international politics of the period.[13] This perspective, however, suffers from a serious analytical weakness: it explains only the triangle of relations that linked Egypt, the great powers, and Israel; it excludes, that is, inter-Arab affairs. Consequently, if we factor Egypt's policies toward the Arab states into the equation, then we arrive at a very different understanding of events.

The one issue that dominated inter-Arab relations for three years preceding the Suez Crisis was the struggle over the Baghdad Pact.[14] Even before the Free Officers began the negotiations that culminated in the Anglo-Egyptian Agreement, both Washington and London were pursuing the goal of creating an alliance that would link together the United States, Britain, the Arab countries, Turkey, Iran, and Pakistan. Cairo abhorred such an alliance, both because it would revitalize the British security system and because it would allow Iraq to serve as the pivot of the Western powers in the Arab world. To examine the unbroken Egyptian record of condemnation of Anglo-Arab alliances is to recognize the truth of Khalid Muhi'l-Din's observation that `Abd al-Nasir never had any intention of actually allowing the British to return to the Canal Zone bases. `Abd al-Nasir, that is, never made his peace with the status quo in the international arena in order to focus on domestic affairs. The notion of international revolution, of overturning the existing order in the region, was implicit in his foreign policy from the moment he took power. Thus, Ahmad Hamrush, the Free Officers' historian, writes that "the signing of the Evacuation Agreement was not the end of the struggle with British imperialism; rather, it was the beginning of the next stage," the struggle over the Baghdad Pact.[15]

The "excitation-and-reaction" interpretation of Egyptian policy ignores the link between the rise of the Baghdad Pact and the decision of the Free Officers to concede limited base rights in Egypt to the British. In 1954, `Abd al-Nasir perceived that the coordination of British and American policy in the region gave the Western powers enough clout to ignore the protests of Cairo and the Arab League and to establish with Iraq a new alliance, one that would probably seek other Arab adherents. Therefore, if the Free Officers had remained publicly faithful to hallowed nationalist principles, then Cairo would have remained mired in the Anglo-Egyptian conflict while Britain and America placed a hammerlock on the Arab world. The Baghdad Pact would have come into being while thousands of British troops remained ensconced on Egyptian territory. The regional role of Iraq and Jordan would have expanded considerably, while the authority of Egypt in international affairs would have contracted in direct proportion.

The Border War with Israel

On February 28, 1955, Israel launched the Gaza Raid, which initiated a lengthy border war that culminated in the Israeli invasion of the Sinai in 1956. As we noted before, according to the dominant interpretation of `Abd al-Nasir's foreign relations, Israel's aggressive border policies diverted Cairo's attention away from its domestic economic priorities.[16] In typical reactive fashion, so the argument goes, `Abd al-Nasir turned to the Soviet Union for military aid in order to shore up his legitimacy among his officer corps.

Undoubtedly the Gaza Raid did make a deep impression on the Egyptian elite, but the threat that it represented to Cairo was not exclusively or even primarily military in nature. The key to understanding the Egyptian view of the aggressive Israeli border policy is the fact that it coincided, almost to the day, with the signing of the Baghdad Pact. Egyptian propaganda immediately linked the two issues, depicting the pact and the Israeli strike as two prongs of a conspiracy designed to force the Arabs to submit to both Israel and Britain. The Egyptians may well have believed their own propaganda, which, though it sounded absurd to British and American ears, did in fact reflect power-political realities as viewed from Cairo. This was so because the containment of Israel required Egypt to request the diplomatic aid of the Western powers, who of course expected something in return for their efforts. In 1955, both London and Washington were seeking an Egyptian-Israeli peace agreement as part of their general strategy to dampen down local conflicts that stood in the way of Western-Arab cooperation in the Cold War.[17] As a consequence, if `Abd al-Nasir had actively sought the support of the Western powers against Israel, he would have been forced to acquiesce in their plans for regional defense. Thus, although the Israeli government was not, as Egyptian propaganda alleged, directly coordinating its border policies with the West, the project of bringing the Israeli military to heel did in fact entail the subservience of Cairo to Washington and London.

The Gaza Raid, then, was not a turning point; rather, it intensified Egypt's priorities, which remained those of destroying the British order and replacing it with an Arab bloc dominated by the Triangle Alliance. But the Israeli military confrontation did provide Cairo with new tactics for pursuing its traditional grand strategy.

The 1955–1956 border war with Israel gave Cairo an explanation, tailored to sensibilities in Washington, for concluding the famous Czech arms deal in September 1955. Cairo explained its growing involvement with Moscow not as a rejection of the West per se but rather as a necessity of self-defense and regime stability. Since Israeli border policies aroused the ire of the great powers, Egyptian claims in this regard indeed found sympathetic ears, particularly in Washington. At the time, Cairo had a vital need for American sympathy. In accordance with the Anglo-Egyptian Agreement, the last British soldier did not leave the Canal Zone until June of 1956. That is to say that `Abd al-Nasir was conducting his struggle against the Baghdad Pact in 1955 while Egypt was still under British occupation, and he had good reason to fear that his attacks on the British security system might jeopardize the withdrawal of British forces. As would become readily apparent during the Suez crisis, the sympathy of Washington functioned as a valuable insurance policy against British reprisals.

Whereas in conversations with Washington, Cairo stressed the Israeli threat to 'Abd al-Nasir's regime, in its broadcasts to the Arab world it emphasized the Egyptian threat to Zionism. By openly organizing guerrilla operations against Israel, 'Abd al-Nasir projected an image of uncompromising nationalist resistance. This image served Cairo's anti-British goals well. The signing of the Baghdad Pact had prompted 'Abd al-Nasir to initiate a hostile propaganda campaign against the Iraqi regime, which stood accused of breaking Arab ranks in order to please its British masters. In this context, the violence on the Egyptian-Israeli border testified dramatically to the veracity of Cairo's claim to be the defender of Arab nationalist principles at a moment when the Hashimite states were stabbing the Arab nation in the back. (Saddam Husayn's use of anti-Zionism in 1990–1991 in an attempt to break up the pro-Western Arab coalition bears a striking resemblance to 'Abd al-Nasir's tactics.)

The Czech arms deal, as has gone largely unnoticed, played a particularly important role in this propaganda campaign, because it allowed Cairo to argue before the Arab world that there existed an independent Arab alternative to the British security system. In broadcasts that reached every corner of the region, Cairo Radio took the line that, whereas in the past the Arab states had no choice but to maintain good relations with the West, they now could look to Egypt and the Soviet bloc for assistance. According to Egyptian broadcasts, supplies from the communist world, in contrast to those from the West, came with no strings attached: no demands for base rights, and no onerous political entanglements such as an imposed peace with Israel. The Baghdad Pact, so the propaganda went, spelled perpetual subservience to Zionism and imperialism, whereas an independent Arab bloc led by Cairo would be faithful to the priorities and values of the Arab world.

The power of the Egyptian propaganda expressed itself clearly in late 1955 and early 1956 when a series of riots erupted in Jordan in response to attempts by the Turkish and British governments to bring Amman into the Baghdad Pact. These events brought home to all observers that the Baghdad Pact would never gain legitimacy in the Arab world. Within two months, Amman compounded the blow to British prestige by dismissing the British officers in the Jordanian army.

Historians now recognize that the drift of Jordan out of the British orbit set the immediate stage for the Suez Crisis, the events of which are so well known that they require no retelling here.[18] This well-told tale, however, does deserve revision with regard to two points. First, the incompatibility between British and Egyptian regional strategies suggests that the nationalization of the Suez Canal was not a hasty decision taken in response to the American refusal to fund the Aswan High Dam. On the contrary, it represented the logical culmination of the Free Officers' drive for independence. With regard to the timing of the nationalization decree, more important than Dulles's famous rebuff of 'Abd al-Nasir was the fact that the last British soldier left the Canal Zone in June 1956.[19] With the British military threat a thing of the past, the Suez Canal Company, the worst symbol of British economic exploitation, hung before Egyptian nationalists like a plum ripe for the picking.

Second, the nationalization, like the Arab-Israeli border war, also played a role in the Egyptian campaign to destroy the Baghdad Pact. It functioned as an exhilarating display of freedom from Britain at the very moment when Egyptian propaganda worked to persuade the entire Arab world that the period of subservience to the imperial powers had indeed ended.

Pan-Arabism and State Interest, 1955–1961

As we have seen, throughout the postwar period Egyptian policy was bound up with Fertile Crescent pan-Arab nationalism. Supporters of this doctrine argued that the European powers had divided the Arab nation while supporting the establishment of Israel, a state that thrived on the Arab divisions that the Europeans had created. The goal of nationalist action, therefore, was to end European political and economic domination of the region, erase the illegitimate borders, and confront Zionism. From 1945 to 1973, Egypt presented its major policies in terms that affirmed the three core values of pan-Arab nationalists: anti-imperialism, anti-Zionism, and Arab unity. But the interests of Cairo and the pan-Arab agenda, though tied to each other, were never identical; rather, they existed in a dynamic tension.

For a brief moment, from 1955 to 1958, events unfolded so as to create the impression that pan-Arabism was the exclusive motor of Egyptian policy. After all, first Egypt fought simultaneously the European imperial powers and Israel; then, second, it united with Syria. Nothing spells a greater commitment to the three core pan-Arab values than does this sequence of events; obviously, the pan-Arab ideal was a determinant of `Abd al-Nasir's policies. But it was not the only determinant. If one examines events closely, one discovers more ambiguity in the relationship between Egyptian state interest and pan-Arabism than appears at first glance.

Take, for instance, the establishment of the United Arab Republic (U.A.R.). Traditionally, the idea of erasing borders had actually threatened Cairo, because it had the effect of legitimising Hashimite schemes for absorbing the territories of neighboring states. Thus, `Abd al-Nasir's decision in favor of unity reversed a long-standing Egyptian policy against altering the territorial status quo in the Fertile Crescent. On the face of it, then, the rise of the U.A.R. was a striking example of pan-Arabism reshaping Egyptian foreign policy. It is important to remember, however, that Cairo decided in favor of union with Syria at a moment when political authority in Damascus was disintegrating. If Egypt had failed to take action, another power—the United States, the Soviet Union, or Iraq—would inevitably have filled the vacuum in Damascus. Syria would have spun out of the Egyptian orbit. In other words, `Abd al-Nasir broke with tradition with respect to erasing borders in order to follow tradition with respect to denying Syria to rival powers.

One discerns a similar ambiguity in the relationship between Egyptian state interest and the principle of anti-Zionism. As we have seen, Egypt confronted Israel in 1948 and 1956 in a manner designed to weaken Britain and her allies. It should come as no surprise, therefore, that the Egyptian-Israeli border grew quiet after the British security system had crumbled. From 1958 to 1961, Cairo devoted its energies to maintaining its authority in Syria. With this primary goal in mind, conflict with Israel would have exposed tensions between Cairo and Damascus, and would have called into question `Abd al-Nasir's ability to defend Syria effectively. As a consequence, in order to champion the principle of Arab unity in the form of the U.A.R., Egyptian policy played down the principle of anti-Zionism.

To point to the conflicts between ideology and state interest is not to deny the intrinsic power of the pan-Arab ideal. Indeed, it is impossible to understand Egyptian policy in the postwar period if one fails to realize that Cairo, even while conducting normal relations with existing states, cultivated a relationship, both direct and indirect, with a pan-Arab constituency in the Fertile Crescent. The very need to maintain a tacit alliance with this constituency, whose power augmented the power of the Egyptian state, meant that displaying fidelity to pan-Arabism was itself a vital state interest. Nonetheless, policy often contradicted principle.

Ironically, it was in the period prior to the foundation of the U.A.R. that `Abd al-Nasir cultivated his Fertile Crescent pan-Arab audience most effectively. As long as Cairo's main concern was to uproot British bases, its policies enjoyed the support of a wide spectrum of groups, from communists to religious nationalists—groups that had nothing in common except a desire to destroy the British order. Once the British security system had fallen, however, these groups had no positive principle around which to rally, and the differences between them moved to center stage in the classic fashion of protest alliances that crumble after success.

This process clearly helped to erode the legitimacy of the U.A.R., which rose up with a bang in 1958 only to collapse with a whimper in 1961.[20] By all accounts, the Syrian public greeted the idea of union with unprecedented enthusiasm, which was, of course, stoked by the image of `Abd al-Nasir as the champion of all Arabs. After the establishment of the union, however, he stopped being a mere symbol, and became directly responsible for the maintenance of order, the allocation of scarce resources, and the mundane day-to-day responsibilities of government. In Syria, `Abd al-Nasir now stood for a particular social order; he represented the haves to the have-nots; he symbolized bureaucratic hierarchy rather than equality for all. Enthusiasm quickly gave way to disappointment, because the union raised expectations that no political order in this world could ever satisfy.

To a certain extent, a transient set of international alignments had helped to build `Abd al-Nasir's reputation. Prior to the establishment of the U.A.R., an elegant symmetry between global and regional orders appeared to be emerging: a bloc of Arab nationalist states, led by Egypt and supported by the Soviet Union, was squaring off against a bloc of conservative Arab clients of Britain and the United States. The announcement in 1957 of the Eisenhower Doctrine (which was clearly designed to contain `Abd al-Nasir) and the rise of the U.A.R. (the dream of pan-Arabists) further reinforced this impression. When viewed through the prism of the pan-Arab value system, these alignments produced no strange bedfellows.

But the symmetry did not last long. The Iraqi Revolution brought to power `Abd al-Karim Qasim, who boasted unimpeachable anti-imperialist credentials, but who nonetheless did not enjoy good relations with `Abd al-Nasir.[21] The Egyptian-Iraqi conflict reappeared, but in a form that was in some ways more threatening to Cairo. In the past, Egyptian anti-British propaganda had hit Baghdad hard, because Iraqi nationalists had in fact viewed their own rulers as puppets of the British. But Qasim was a character altogether different from the Hashimites. With close ties to the Communist Party and an open channel to the Soviet Union, he hardly looked the part of a British stooge. Cairo's propaganda machine, therefore, had a harder time diminishing him in the eyes of his own public, but not for want of trying. `Abd al-Nasir impugned Qasim's commitment to Arab independence, branding him a puppet—now of Britain, now of the Soviet Union. The claim that Qasim was the puppet of masters who stood on opposite sides in the Cold War did not resonate with Iraqi nationalists as powerfully as had Cairo's anti-Hashimite propaganda. The problem appeared even more starkly in 1961, when Qasim played the Iraqi nationalist card by laying claim to Kuwait. In that case, `Abd al-Nasir found himself in the altogether uncomfortable position of being on the same side as the British with regard to the question of erasing the Kuwait-Iraq border. The symmetry between global and regional systems that had made `Abd al-Nasir's struggle appear, in the eyes of Arab nationalists, as a clear-cut case of good versus evil had disappeared; international politics were again producing strange bedfellows.

These developments had a significant impact on grand strategy. Originally, Cairo had sought to lead a comprehensive regional bloc that would provide Egypt with a platform from which to play the role of intermediary between the West and the Arabs. By 1958, however, the possibility of creating such a bloc was more remote than ever. When the entire Arab world had been under the Western power penumbra, Cairo had hoped to convince Washington to ease out the British and replace the imperial network of defense with an Arab League system. Once the Soviet Union had entered the balance, however, the development of a comprehensive regional organization would have required either the support of both superpowers, or the defeat of one of them. Neither of these conditions could have been met.[22]

In addition, in the period after Suez, local opposition to Egypt stiffened in direct proportion to the rise in `Abd al-Nasir's reputation. Under pressure from Washington and out of fear of pan-Arabism, Riyadh distanced itself from Cairo, thus ending the powerful alliance with Egypt that had been a fixture of the local scene since 1945. Jordan and Lebanon increased internal security measures, and both demonstrated a willingness to turn to the Western powers to prevent a pan-Arab coup. As already noted, the Iraqi revolution brought to power a new rival, one that enjoyed an independent relationship with Moscow. To many observers in 1958, Egypt appeared on the verge of unifying the entire Arab world. `Abd al-Nasir's reputation indeed soared, but the Egyptian sphere of influence actually contracted, being now limited to Syria. Egypt captured the moral high ground in the Arab world, but it was nonetheless losing turf.[23]

In order to preserve its sphere of interest, Cairo had no choice but to position itself between the superpowers. Thus, `Abd al-Nasir maintained cordial relations with Washington, to which he presented the Egyptian presence in Damascus as a means of preventing Syria from becoming a Soviet satellite. This development, although it did not destroy Cairo's relations with Moscow, certainly weakened them, as did the Egyptian propaganda campaign depicting Qasim as a communist stooge. Although Egypt indeed remained the most powerful single force in Arab politics, in fact its interests no longer dovetailed with those of either superpower, nor could it command the loyalty of all Arab nationalists. Despite the appearance of unrivaled power, `Abd al-Nasir could not plausibly hope to place Egypt in the role of intermediary between a comprehensive regional bloc and the outside world. Instead, he used his limited sphere of interest and his extraordinary ideological clout to extract favors from both superpowers—for instance, the Aswan High Dam from the Soviet Union and economic aid from the United States.

Collapse of the U.A.R. and the Six-Day War

The fall of the U.A.R. in 1961 further eroded the Egyptian position. For the first time in the postwar period, Damascus and Cairo were at odds, and the very idea of Arab unity suffered a severe blow. With Syria and Iraq now both led by Arab nationalist regimes, and with Saudi Arabia and Jordan aligned with the United States, Egypt was almost completely isolated in the regional system, at the very moment when it embarked on an ambitious experiment in socialist economics.

`Abd al-Nasir responded to these developments in two ways: by adopting a posture of ideological purity, and by projecting Egyptian forces abroad.[24] First, in the realm of ideology, he turned isolation into a virtue, presenting Egypt's solitary position as proof that it alone remained committed to Arab nationalism while others, such as the Syrian secessionists, pursued their selfish interests. Cairo openly proclaimed the right of Egypt, as the guardian of the pan-Arab flame, to intervene on behalf of the Arab nation in the domestic affairs of sister states. Second, Egypt opened up a new sphere of influence by involving itself, in 1962, in the civil war in Yemen, supporting the republican revolutionaries against the monarchists, who enjoyed the backing of Riyadh. This involvement transformed Cairo into a major factor in the balance of power in the Arabian peninsula; more particularly, it directly threatened Saudi Arabia, the most important client of the United States.

The trade-off in benefits between spheres of influence in Arabia and in the Fertile Crescent was not equal. The Yemen intervention quickly turned into a fiasco. It was a textbook case of military overreach, analogous to the American and Soviet adventures in, respectively, Vietnam and Afghanistan. Being mired in such a war had severe diplomatic repercussions for Cairo. By involving himself in a proxy war against Saudi Arabia, `Abd al-Nasir harmed his relations with Washington and forced himself ultimately into an uncomfortable dependence on the Soviet Union. Although the alliance with Moscow did reinforce `Abd al-Nasir's claim—as part of the new ideological purity—to be the foremost opponent of imperialism, it pushed Egypt out of the middle ground between the great powers, the space that it had habitually occupied since 1955. Egypt now laid claim to a territory exclusively within the Soviet sphere. The dangers inherent in this position became all too apparent in 1967, when Washington, in stark contrast to its behavior in 1956, displayed no interest in restraining the Israelis.

The commitment to ideological purity continued to project Cairo's influence into the Fertile Crescent, but this apparent benefit came at a high cost. The images of both the U.A.R. and `Abd al-Nasir continued to haunt the politics of Syria. As rival nationalist factions battled for control of the state, the vitality of the pan-Arab ideal combined with Syrian political fragmentation to form a volatile mix. In terms of domestic legiti-macy, a succession of leaders in Damascus claimed the right to rule on the basis of pan-Arab principles; to do so, however, was almost by definition to submit to the authority of `Abd al-Nasir, who still held the moral high ground in Arab politics. In order to justify operating independently of Cairo, therefore, leaders in Damascus found it expedient to discredit `Abd al-Nasir in terms of the prevailing value system. They found a convenient instrument for this project in the Arab-Israeli conflict.[25]

In terms of commitment to core pan-Arab principles, Egypt was clearly vulnerable with regard to anti-Zionism, which had never been the first priority of Cairo. Especially now that the British security system was a thing of the past, there was no specifically Egyptian motive for confronting Israel. By `Abd al-Nasir's own public admissions, war in the near future was to be avoided—because Israel's military was too strong, its rela-tions to Washington too close, and the Arabs too divided; in addition, of course, the flower of the Egyptian army was fighting in Yemen. Sensing a chink in `Abd al-Nasir's armor of ideological purity, Damascus championed its unwavering commitment to armed anti-Zionism. By promoting the interests of Palestinian commandos and organ-izing raids into Israel, Syria embarrassed Cairo. In addition, it also threatened Jordan, which defended its own unwillingness to fight by pointing to the weak Egyptian resist-ance to Israel. In summary, by adopting its new ideological purity, Cairo invited taunts from all sides of the Arab political spectrum; as a result of its commitment in Yemen, it did not have the resources to make good its claims to Arab leadership.

The radicalism of Damascus placed `Abd al-Nasir on the horns of a dilemma. On the one hand, he could have renounced war with Israel, thereby abandoning his posi-tion as the preeminent Arab nationalist and losing considerable authority in the Fertile Crescent. Naturally, his clout in Moscow would have diminished in direct proportion. On the other hand, he could have joined in the border conflict, thereby suffering the unpredictable consequences of an Arab-Israeli war. He sought a middle ground, attempting to remain the dominant player in the Fertile Crescent by supporting pro-Palestinian political initiatives—such as the formation of the Palestinian Liberation Organization—that, while demonstrating a commitment to the principle of anti-Zionism, would not actually drag Egypt into a war.

This middle ground, however, was difficult to hold. The dynamic of pan-Arab one-upmanship led to disastrous consequences in the form of the Six-Day War. In May 1967, Egyptian-Israeli relations deteriorated precipitously against the background of an escalating border conflict between Syria and Israel. The Soviet Union encour-aged the Egyptians to intervene by passing on to Cairo false reports of Israeli troop concentrations on the Syrian border. After having learned that the reports were false, `Abd al-Nasir ordered the removal from the Sinai of the United Nations buffer forces, which had been moved into place as part of a tacit Egyptian-Israeli agreement in 1957, and which had become, in the propaganda of `Abd al-Nasir's rivals, a symbol of Egyp-tian unwillingness to confront Israel. He then proceeded to remilitarize the peninsula and to announce the closure of the Straits of Tiran to Israeli shipping.[26]

The blockade and the remilitarization overturned the post-Suez status quo in the Sinai, and created circumstances that made an Israeli attack inevitable. There is no doubt that `Abd al-Nasir realized the danger; it appears that even the Soviet Union, which had set the ball rolling, attempted to slow down the pace of events when they began spiraling out of control. Why, then, did the seasoned Egyptian leader act so recklessly?

Egypt remilitarized the Sinai with an eye to gaining political advantage in the Arab arena, not to attacking Israel.[27] Undoubtedly `Abd al-Nasir was operating on instincts honed during the Suez crisis. He envisioned a war in which the Egyptian forces would hold out long enough for the superpowers to intervene, and that would reaffirm his nationalist reputation in the Arab world. The benefits of such a scenario would have been considerable. Another political success against Israel would certainly have allowed `Abd al-Nasir to silence his conservative Arab critics, but the Saudis and the Jordanians were not the main target of his actions. More important were the Syrians. Success would have given him the political clout to bring the Ba`thi government, which was suffering a legitimacy crisis, firmly under his authority. Cairo's behavior in 1967 should be read not as an attempt to come to the aid of Damascus but, rather, as an attempt to dominate it. If Syria had been returned firmly to the Egyptian orbit, Cairo would have enjoyed considerably more clout in Moscow. With the war in Yemen going badly, `Abd al-Nasir was in danger of losing altogether the Egyptian sphere of interest, the prime source of Cairo's international clout.

Obviously, the Egyptians did not foresee a lightning Israeli victory. In this regard, they made two miscalculations. The first was military: they failed to gauge correctly the power of their enemy. Unorthodox Israeli tactics—compounded, perhaps, by poor communication between `Abd al-Nasir and his chief of staff—account for this mistake.[28] The second miscalculation was political: Cairo probably misread American intentions. A view has developed in Egypt that `Abd al-Nasir was the victim of a premeditated American plan to cut him down.[29] This line of reasoning is certainly overblown. By downplaying his role in precipitating the war, it begs the question, "If a trap existed, then why did `Abd al-Nasir make himself such easy prey?" Nonetheless, this theory does highlight an important aspect of the strategic setting: the United States adopted the stance of passive observer as Egypt stood exposed, for the first time in its history, to the full brunt of Israeli power. In 1948, it was the British that had stopped the Israelis before they occupied Egyptian territory; and in 1956, it was the United States that had halted the Suez War and rolled back the Israelis from the Sinai. Consequently, political instincts honed in the 1940s and 1950s, when Egypt had occupied the middle ground between the great powers, were of no use to `Abd al-Nasir in the polarized world of the Cold War.

A War for Peace

The Israeli victory in 1967 sounded the death knell for `Abd al-Nasir's strident pan-Arabism and, therefore, marks a significant turning point in Egyptian foreign policy.[30] To be sure, `Abd al-Nasir himself did not proclaim the end of pan-Arabism, and it is unlikely that he, whose political personality was synonymous with it, could have made peace with Israel in the manner of his successor. Nonetheless, the signs of significant change were obvious: a hasty retreat from Yemen, a rapprochement with Saudi Arabia, and a new approach to Israel. This last factor was the least obvious at the time but, in retrospect, the most far-reaching.

From 1948 until 1967, the problem of Israeli power had never been a central concern of Cairo, which tailored its policies toward Israel, in war and in peace, with an eye to their impact on the wider Arab arena. The goal of Cairo's Israel policy was, from 1948 to 1956, to destroy the British security system; from 1957 to 1967, to hold the balance in Arab affairs, thereby commanding the respect of the great powers. It is impossible, as we have seen, to understand inter-Arab politics in the 1960s (including the slide to war in 1967) without first recognizing the derivative nature of Cairo's Israel policy. After 1967, however, the question of how to handle Israeli power no longer appeared in the eyes of the Egyptian elite as a component of Egypt's Arab policy. It was now a problem in its own right. Thereafter—in the War of Attrition and the 1973 war—Egypt confronted Israel in order to change the strategic balance between the two countries themselves rather than to alter inter-Arab alignments.

The unprecedented level of inter-Arab cooperation in 1973 testifies to the change. All preceding Arab-Israeli wars had erupted amid extreme inter-Arab discord; public competition between the Arab regimes regarding the Palestine question had in fact played a role both in precipitating those wars and in determining their outcome. By contrast, secret planning between Arab regimes rather than public recrimination preceded the 1973 war. The military coordination that Egypt achieved with Syria and the diplomatic cooperation with Saudi Arabia were made possible precisely because Egypt did not seek to best its sister Arab states.

Since pan-Arab symbolism played only a small role in the 1973 war, Cairo succeeded in calibrating precisely its political and military goals.[31] President Anwar al-Sadat designed the attack not to destroy the Israelis but to bloody them enough to force them to make concessions. He also sought to generate superpower intervention in order to subject Israel to significant international pressure. In addition, he planned for a limited victory that would generate for him enough legitimacy at home to sell an honorable peace to his public.

To say that Israeli power became a problem in its own right is not, however, to suggest that it became the central issue in Cairo's diplomacy. As would befit a middle power, Egypt attempted to reach a settlement with Israel as part of a grand strategy: Sadat sought nothing less than to effect a tectonic shift in foreign policy—namely, to move Egypt into the American camp.

Politically, economically, and militarily, the price of pan-Arabism had become prohibitive. Failure in the Yemen adventure and the Six-Day War brought home to the leadership in Cairo the unbearable political and military cost of Arab leadership. This awareness coincided with the realization that the socialist experiment had failed. The stagnation of the state-run economy was causing Cairo enough hardship without the additional costs of the 1967 war, which closed the Suez Canal and denied Egypt access to the oil fields in the Sinai desert. Domestic economic factors, therefore, militated in favor not just of peace with Israel but also of alignment with the United States, which alone could provide the foreign aid and the access to international investment funds necessary to revive the flagging economy. In short, Sadat's peace diplomacy was part and parcel of his economic liberalization at home and his turn toward the West.

The Peace Imperative

The decision to make peace with Israel precipitated a bitter divorce between Egypt and the Arab world. That Sadat had no more use for Nasirist pan-Arabism became readily apparent in 1977, when he traveled to Jerusalem and made his famous appeal to the Israelis for peace. By opening up a direct channel to Israel, Sadat was also sending a message to Washington: Egypt would negotiate alone, not as part of an Arab coalition. At the time, Jimmy Carter and his advisors were wedded to the notion of a comprehensive peace agreement, one that would include not only all of the Arab belligerents, but the Soviet Union as well. Sadat, however, saw little benefit in allowing foreign governments to negotiate the fate of Egyptian interests. Thus Cairo decided to go it alone; in response, Baghdad quickly seized the mantle of Arab leadership. Following the signing of the 1978 Camp David accords, the Iraqis took the lead in organizing an Arab boycott of Egypt: most Arab regimes broke off relations with Cairo, and the headquarters of the Arab League moved to Tunis.

The Arab states' decision to ostracize Egypt did not shake the foundations of the new policies. The Egyptian-Israeli peace agreement and the American alliance have certainly withstood the test of time. The assassination of Sadat in 1981 did not result in a return to the policies of `Abd al-Nasir. In 1982, tensions did develop between Cairo and Jerusalem when the Israelis, having used the peace agreement to secure their southern border, felt free to move northward, invading Lebanon with an impunity that deeply embarrassed Egypt. But these tensions did not in any way threaten to destroy the peace agreement or the alliance with the United States. In 1990–91, Cairo even went so far as to side with Washington in a war against a sister Arab country.

Nonetheless, signs have never been wanting of Egyptian discontent with both the peace agreement and the subordinate regional role to which Egypt has been consigned.[32] Islamic radicals and ex-Nasirists are not the only critics of the new American order. Many Egyptians from all walks of life find aspects of the Sadat orientation humiliating. They perceive an invidious connection between, on the one hand, Cairo's subservience to America and Israel in the international arena and, on the other, the slavish devotion to American culture demonstrated by the *nouveaux riches* beneficiaries of Sadat's economic liberalization. This discontent, which finds constant expression in both the news media and popular culture, has kept the Egyptian-Israeli relationship from developing into a warm friendship. On occasion, it has also created friction with the United States.

However, the economic realities underpinning the Sadat orientation have tended to overwhelm the Islamist and Nasirist cultural challenges. An examination of Egypt's foreign exchange accounts demonstrates the importance of peace to Cairo. Foreign currency enters the Egyptian economy thanks primarily to oil, tourism, Suez Canal tolls, and worker remittances—sources that had been severely reduced, if not eliminated altogether, by the Six-Day War. These are not the only economic benefits of peace. In addition, the alliance with the United States brings in more than $2 billion a year in direct aid. It also helps grease economic relations with other Western countries, and results in occasional windfalls, such as the decision by Washington to reward Egyptian support in the Gulf War by canceling Cairo's $7 billion military debt. A return to a policy of confrontation with Israel and the United States would jeopardize all of these sources of income, and would require defense expenditure beyond the means of Egypt. In 1994, the Egyptian GNP stood at $43 billion, whereas Israel, with less than one tenth the population, had a GNP of $78 billion.

The Ghost of ʿAbd al-Nasir

Yet the ghost of ʿAbd al-Nasir refuses to recede quietly into the night. The 1980s saw the gradual erosion of the Arab boycott of Egypt, and in the course of the last decade Cairo has once again laid claim to Arab leadership.[33] While the Mubarak regime has not asserted its authority with anything like the stridency of ʿAbd al-Nasir in the 1950s, the parallels are nonetheless striking. For example, the election of Benjamin Netanyahu in 1996 prompted Egypt to convene a pan-Arab summit conference designed to place the new Israeli government before an Arab consensus on the peace process. As the following analysis, which appeared in al-Wafd, indicates, the Egyptian press draped the conference in Nasirist robes:

You thought that Arab unity had collapsed, or that the glow of Arab struggle had died away. But it turned out that it was glowing under the ashes, and when the wind of challenge blew from Israel, the Goliath woke up. You will find that the Egyptian people ... are supportive of President Mubarak's Arab approach, because he put Egypt in its rightful place at the head of the Arab convoy.[34]

This resuscitation of Nasirist themes certainly has domestic roots. Without doubt, the Mubarak regime relishes the opportunity to fashion policies that give expression to the popular criticism of Israel. Arguably, however, developments in the international system have played an equally important role in raising the ghost of ʿAbd al-Nasir.

During the last decade, regional alignments have mimicked those of the 1950s. The collapse of the Soviet Union and the advent of the Gulf War led to the resurrection of the Triangle Alliance—the alignment, that is, between Egypt, Syria, and Saudi Arabia that helped to catapult ʿAbd al-Nasir to fame. As in the 1940s and 1950s, the specter of Iraqi power prompted both Riyadh and Damascus to turn toward Cairo for diplomatic support. The Syrians, in particular, felt a powerful need for friends, because the fall of the Soviet Union and the defeat of Iran in the Iran-Iraq war had left them exposed. But this time, when the Triangle Alliance faced off against Iraq and Jordan, the nationalist polarities were reversed. In the 1950s, it was Cairo that had played the anti-Zionist and anti-imperialist cards against the Hashimite supporters of the Baghdad Pact. By contrast, in the Gulf War it was Baghdad that adopted the role of defender of Palestine, thus painting its Arab rivals as traitors to the political values of the Arab nation. The attempt, of course, failed. With Iraq crippled for the last ten years by a regime of United Nations sanctions, the role of defender of Arab unity has again migrated back to Cairo.

Although the Triangle Alliance had first reemerged in response to the Iraqi threat, it continued to function throughout the 1990s. The lonely position of Syria in the new regional order is the key to understanding this longevity. The entire Middle East, of course, now lies under the shadow of American power. In addition, in recent years a strategic bond has developed between Turkey and Israel—a friendship based in part on a mutual distrust of Syria. Since both the Turks and the Israelis enjoy very strong ties with Washington, the Syrians have found it expedient to balance the power of their foes by turning to Egypt and Saudi Arabia, the two Arab states with the greatest clout in the American capital. For their part, the Egyptians find in the Triangle Alliance a sphere of interest the very existence of which forces the Americans to respect Cairo as their primary interlocutor in Arab affairs. Cairo has augmented the power of the alliance by periodically pleading the causes of Libya, Iraq, and the Palestinians.

The Egyptian rediscovery of pan-Arab themes in the mid-1990s is, therefore, best understood as a weapon in the competition for influence over the policies of the United States. It is in this context that we should understand, for instance, Cairo's dispute with Washington in 1994–95 over the Nuclear Nonproliferation Treaty. The Egyptians refused to adhere to the treaty so long as the Israelis themselves refrained from signing it. Although leaders in Cairo undoubtedly believed that they stood on the side of the angels in this dispute, they found the nuclear issue attractive for at least two practical reasons: it struck a popular chord in the Arab world as a whole, and it held out the hope of raising the price for Washington of strategic cooperation with Israel. In the event, however, the Egyptians buckled under American pressure and signed the treaty. It remains to be seen whether they receive any tangible benefits for their decision to compromise.

The Mubarak regime's appeal to pan-Arab sentiment and its participation in the Triangle Alliance are both strikingly reminiscent of Nasirism, but the decision to please Washington on the nuclear non proliferation issue demonstrates that the current Egyptian bid for Arab leadership is conducted within narrow limits, of whose nature Cairo is painfully conscious. By contrast, when `Abd al-Nasir aggressively took up the cause of pan-Arabism in the 1950s, his policies benefited from a state of discord among the great powers, whose rivalries opened up a field on which Egypt could roam freely. Today, however, American power permits no such latitude. Given the economic dependence of Egypt on the United States, the Mubarak regime is deeply aware that it cannot win in a sustained battle with Washington. Moreover, the Triangle Alliance in the 1950s was a wholeheartedly revisionist alignment: Cairo, Damascus, and Riyadh all shared a desire to break the spine of the British security system. Today, neither Cairo nor Riyadh wants the United States to quit the Middle East.

The pan-Arabism of the 1990s simply has no potential for shaking the region with anything approximating the force that it mustered in the 1950s and 1960s. At that time, Cairo derived its power in part from the vitality of the pan-Arab ideal in the Fertile Crescent, and from the weakness of the surrounding states. Today, pan-Arabism has waned, and the other Arab states have sunk deep roots in their societies. Therefore, the theme of Arab solidarity that currently issues from Cairo is not designed to create a new order: it is part of a process of bargaining with Washington.

But it is too early to consign Egypt to the status of a minor power. The American ascendancy, like the British before it, will pass. An unexpected decline in the fortunes of the United States, or the arrival of a great-power competitor (in the form of a revitalized Russia or a united Europe) will again allow Egypt to contemplate playing one great power off against the other by organizing the Arab forces opposed to the current American order. Though poor and weakened, Egypt remains a middle power. It will, therefore, continue to search for a means of forcing the great powers to respect its interests. Nasirist pan-Arabism itself has died, but, as its ghost in the Mubarak era demonstrates, the function that it served in Egyptian foreign policy lies dormant, not dead.

Notes

1 For a more detailed presentation of some issues discussed in this section, see Michael Doran, *Pan-Arabism before Nasser: Egyptian Power Politics and the Palestine Question*, chapter 1.
2 Khalid Muhi'l-Din, *Wa'l-an atakallim*, pp. 192–93.
3 For a revision of our understanding of the attitude of the old regime toward the Soviet Union, see Rami Ginat, "British Concoction or Bilateral Decision?" and *The Soviet Union and Egypt, 1945–1955*.
4 On the foundation of the Arab League, see Yehoshua Porath, *In Search of Arab Unity*. My analysis does not follow Porath's account directly, but it does rely on it.
5 On this proposal, see Doran, *Pan-Arabism*, chapter 3.
6 For a detailed development of this argument, see Doran, *Pan-Arabism*.
7 Taha al-Hashimi, *Mudhakkirat Taha al-Hashimi*, Vol. 2, p. 166.
8 On the genesis of the Arab League Collective Security Pact, see Avraham Sela, *The Decline of the Arab-Israeli Conflict: Middle East Politics and the Quest for Regional Order*, pp. 41–43.
9 Tawfiq al-Hakim, *The Return of Consciousness*, p. 21.
10 Khalid Muhi'l-Din, *Wa'l-an atakallim*, p. 194. See the related statements in Ahmad Hamrush, *Mujtama` Jamal `Abd al-Nasir*, p. 34.
11 Gabriel R. Warburg, "The Sudan's Path to Independence: *Continuity and Change in Egypt's Policy toward the Sudan*."
12 Al-Hakim, *The Return of Consciousness*, p. 30.
13 For two recent versions, see Keith Kyle, *Suez*; and W. Scott Lucas, *Divided We Stand: Britain, the US and the Suez Crisis*.
14 For the most exhaustive treatment, see Elie Podeh, *The Quest for Hegemony in the Arab World: The Struggle over the Baghdad Pact*; for the classic discussion, see Patrick Seale, *The Struggle for Syria*.
15 Hamrush, *Mujtama`*, p. 39.
16 For a detailed account of the border war, see Benny Morris, *Israel's Border Wars 1949–1956*. Morris's view of Egyptian motivation is consistent with the standard accounts.
17 See the analysis of Shimon Shamir, "The Collapse of Project Alpha."
18 On the place of Jordan in the Suez Crisis, see particularly Lucas, *Divided We Stand*.
19 This according to `Abd al-Latif al-Baghdadi, *Mudhakkirat `Abd al-Latif al-Baghdadi*, Vol. 1, p. 318. For confirmation that this time line weighed on `Abd al-Nasir's mind, note his request to Amman for a delay in ousting the British officers from the Jordanian army until after June; quoted in Kyle, *Suez*, p. 91.
20 For a perceptive account of this process, see Malcolm Kerr, *The Arab Cold War: Gamal `Abd el-Nasir and His Rivals, 1958–1970*, chapter 1.
21 On the Egyptian-Iraqi split, see Fawaz Gerges, *The Superpowers and the Middle East: Regional and International Politics, 1955–1967*, chapter 5; and Malik Mufti, *Sovereign Creations*, chapter 8.
22 See the analysis of the homeostatic nature of the Arab states subsystem in L. Carl Brown, *International Politics and the Middle East: Old Rules, Dangerous Game*, pp. 169–72.
23 Stephen M. Walt, *The Origins of Alliances*, pp. 68–80.
24 Kerr, *The Arab Cold War*, chapter 2.
25 This is a major theme of Sela, *Decline of the Arab-Israeli Conflict*.

26 For the latest discussion of all aspects of the Six-Day War, see Richard B. Parker, ed., *The Six-Day War: A Retrospective*.

27 Various dimensions of this position are developed in L. Carl Brown, "Nasser and the June 1967 War: Plan or Improvisation?"; C. Ernest Dawn, "The Egyptian Remilitarization of the Sinai, May 1967"; Kerr, *The Arab Cold War*; and Sela, *Decline of the Arab-Israeli Conflict.*

28 The military-miscalculation theory is developed cogently in Nadav Safran, *Israel: the Embattled Ally*, chapter 15.

29 Muhammad Hasanayn Haykal, *1967-al-Infijar.*

30 This position was first brought to wide attention in the influential article by Fouad Ajami, "The End of Pan-Arabism."

31 For a comprehensive analysis of Egyptian foreign policy, 1967–1977, see Yoram Meital, *Egypt's Struggle for Peace.*

32 Shimon Shamir, "Basic Dilemmas of the Mubarak Regime."

33 For two perceptive analyses, see Gregory Aftandilian, *Egypt's Bid for Arab Leadership* (New York: Council on Foreign Relations, 1993); and Fouad Ajami, "The Sorrows of Egypt," *Foreign Affairs* 74, no. 5 (September/October 1995): 72–88.

34 *Al-Wafd*, 26 June, as reported in Foreign Broadcasts Information Service, 5 July 1996; quoted in Ami Ayalon, "Egypt," *Middle East Contemporary Survey*, Vol. XX (1996), p. 281.

6

Israeli Foreign Policy

Bernard Reich

Israel is in and of the Middle East in its ultimate foreign-policy goals—it fits into the underlying pattern of Middle Eastern (and indeed most other) states in seeking security and well-being for its people. In Israel's case that means ensuring its survival in a hostile region, with security and well-being for Israelis, but also for Jews worldwide.

Since its inception, Israeli policy has been characterized by a general consistency of policy objectives, a constancy in approach, and continuity in substance—this despite changes in government and styles of governance over the first five decades of independence. The objectives, or core goals, have been to achieve peace, universal recognition and acceptance, security, and economic as well as social well-being.

The policy to achieve these objectives has been marked by pragmatism in approach displayed by a small group of decision makers, constituting the political elite of the country and headed by the prime minister. Given the small size of the polity and of the political decision-making elite, personalities have been important in the formulation and execution of foreign policy, and there has been a significant centralization of foreign policy at the highest levels of the government. Major decisions are made at the senior levels of the government and often by the most senior ministers, especially the prime minister, on a continuing basis. In instances seen as central to the survival and security of the state, especially in recent decades, it has been the prime minister who has concentrated the ultimate decisions in his or her office.

Israeli foreign policy, and its formulation, is a complex phenomenon composed of intersecting elements of security, defense, and foreign policies that are inextricably intertwined. Although all countries think in terms of security and survival, and these must be the ultimate objectives of foreign policy, in the case of Israel these elements have been connected since the inception of the state as a result of an existential threat that was identified even before independence. Indeed, Arab opposition to the Palestine partition plan adopted by the United Nations in November 1947, and the Arab League declaration of war against the new state upon its declaration of independence, were seen as additional evidence of this Arab design to prevent the creation of Israel and, later, to ensure its demise. The concept of an existential threat has informed Israeli foreign policy since the independence of the state, and still influences the views of a large portion of the population. It was this perception that the Arabs had a goal of destroying Israel that was summed up in the term "politicide" coined by Yehoshafat Harkabi in the 1960s to refer to the destruction of a state.[1]

The decades of Israeli independence have been marked by dramatic changes in regional conditions, and also by a significant alteration in the international environment. The inception, evolution, and eventual end of the Cold War, and its manifestation in the bipolarity of the international system and later in the establishment of an American hegemony, have led to changes in Israeli approaches and policies even as the ultimate objectives of Israeli foreign policy have been marked by continuity of major themes.

It is useful to recall that, despite a broad Israeli consensus and general agreement on the objectives of peace, security, and well-being, Israelis generally have strongly-held and often divergent views on most political issues, including foreign policy. There is the old saw, which refers to the multiplicity and intensity of political views, that if there are two Israelis there are three political parties to reflect their viewpoints. That continues to describe the political landscape in Israel and is manifest in the fact that all Israeli governments since the inception of the state have been coalitions, as no single party has ever achieved an absolute majority in the Knesset (parliament). Indeed, the fractionalization of the parliament reached its zenith with the 1999 election, which brought more parties to parliament than in any previous election. Thus, when Ehud Barak formed his government in the summer of 1999 he was faced with the daunting task of compromising more party perspectives and policies than his predecessors as he continued the efforts to achieve peace with the Arabs. In this case, the intersection of local and foreign politics became even more obvious than usual.

Foreign Policy Perceptions and Lenses

Policies on issues of political (and security) import result from Israeli perspectives of the threat and the challenge as seen through a series of lenses. In this respect, Israel is no different from other states. Its singularity lies in the fact that it has an atypical set, and a larger number, of lenses through which it views the world and which affect its approaches to foreign policy.

The central lens is that Israel is a Jewish state. This brings both Jewish history and contemporary Jewish concerns to the forefront of politics and policy. Unique to Israel are the impact of Jewish history on its current perspectives and the special role Israel adopts with regard to the diaspora.[2]

Israel's policy is conditioned by its view of Jewish history as a history of negatives. The great watersheds in Jewish history are negative events—the destructions of the Temple, the exiles of the Jews from the Holy Land, the creation of the concept of the diaspora, anti-Semitism (the Jewish Question), persecution and discrimination, and the Holocaust. Among the symbolic locations of modern Israel are Masada, Yad Vashem, and the Western (or Wailing) Wall—each a symbol of and memorial to a great negative event in Jewish history. The creation of the state was something of an aberration (in the sense that it was a positive event), but even that was short-lived, as the Arab states soon launched the wars that were designed to restore Palestine to the Palestinians and eliminate the newly reestablished Jewish state.

Israel's history since independence is often recounted in terms of the wars it has fought with its Arab neighbors who have challenged its right to exist. During its first fifty years of independence, it fought six major wars and engaged in countless skirmishes with its Arab neighbors in an effort to achieve the peace and stability essential for domestic development. Israeli thinking is reflected in such phrases as "never again," in which it is suggested that the horrors of the past cannot be allowed to be repeated in the modern world.

Israelis have a strong sense of history, and this has been reflected in their education and in their mind-set. Israeli leaders have often spoken of the "ghetto mentality" that reflects a sense of history, isolation, and victimization. Israeli history, based on Jewish history, provides the basis for attitudes that condition thinking about foreign and security policy. Jewish history, which derives from the Biblical period and sees the Bible as a recording of history (in addition to its other dimensions), thus provides a basis for foreign policy. It contributes to an Israeli sense of isolation and insecurity. This springs from the Biblical concept reflected in Numbers 23:9: "Lo, it is a people that shall dwell alone, and shall not be reckoned among the nations." But isolation and separation from the mainstream of the international community are not simply of Biblical dimensions but are still a factor in modern history, as is reflected in Israel's position in the United Nations and other international organizations and its exclusion from Arab-dominated regional organizations.

The Zionist lens is an extension of the Jewish one. Israel is the creation of political Zionism as described and defined by Theodor Herzl. It is a movement that, at least in part, achieved its ultimate objective—the solution to the Jewish Question (anti-Semitism), especially in nineteenth- and twentieth-century Europe—with the independence of Israel in 1948. Zionism sought to create a sovereign Jewish state that would serve as a haven for imperiled and persecuted Jews, and that would also serve as a "Jewish" focus, thereby helping to ensure the long-term survival of the Jewish people. The Jewish state would, therefore, engage in "ingathering the exiles" as a mechanism for dealing with anti-Semitism. Thus, the goal was not simply a state, but a secure Jewish state for its people, in Israel and outside. Zionism was and remains today the ideology of the state with which an overwhelming majority of Israelis (Jews) identify.

In his pamphlet *Der Judenstaat (The Jewish State)*, published in Vienna in February 1896, Herzl wrote: "The idea which I have developed in this pamphlet is a very old one; it is the restoration of the Jewish State.... The Jewish question still exists. It would be foolish to deny it.... The nations in whose midst Jews live are all either covertly or openly Anti-Semitic."[3] His solution to the problem was to be found in the restoration of the Jewish state. "The whole plan is in its essence perfectly simple.... Let the sovereignty be granted us over a portion of the globe large enough to satisfy the rightful requirements of a nation; the rest we shall manage for ourselves."[4] Herzl's preference was Palestine because it was "our ever-memorable historic home." When the World Zionist Organization came into being as a result of the meeting in Basle, Switzerland, in August 1897, it established the Basle Program, which proclaimed: "The aim of Zionism is to create for the Jewish people a home in Palestine secured by public law."[5]

Israel's declaration of independence formally declared "the establishment of a Jewish state in Eretz-Israel, to be known as the State of Israel." The Law of Return, passed by the Knesset on July 5, 1950, established this principle as a legal requirement of the state. By granting virtually any Jew the right to immigrate to and become a citizen of the Jewish state it formalized a connection between the state and the people, and created a foreign-policy requirement for the state. Israel's history is marked by the immigration to Palestine (*aliyah*) patterns of the late nineteenth and early twentieth centuries prior to Israel's independence and by the postindependence waves of immigration (*aliyot*) of European Holocaust survivors, Jews of the Arab world, and, later, the Jews of Ethiopia, and the former Soviet Union. Each affected the nature of the state and its politics and foreign policy in its own way.

Israel is the modern world's only Jewish state, and as such is concerned not simply with remaining a Jewish state (whose exact nature remains the subject of continuing and substantial controversy), but also with being a Jewish state that generates myriad special requirements and obligations for foreign-policy makers and implementors. Thus, for example, Israeli diplomats and representatives abroad have responsibilities that flow from their accreditation to a foreign government, but also assume responsibilities in relation to the Jewish community in the countries to which they are posted. Walter Eytan, the first director-general of Israel's Ministry of Foreign Affairs, described the phenomenon in these terms: "It is a commonplace of our Foreign Service that every Envoy Extraordinary and Minister Plenipotentiary of Israel has a dual function. He is Minister Plenipotentiary to the country to which he is accredited—and Envoy Extraordinary to its Jews. This has come to be accepted generally—by other governments in the 'free' world, by the Jews of the diaspora, and by everyone in Israel."[6] The links to local Jewish communities serve numerous purposes, from ensuring their well-being to gaining support from them for the objectives of the Jewish state; from charity and other forms of economic support to the political imperative of ensuring safe local conditions. It is a two-directional connection in which the local Jewish leadership and populace work with the Israeli representative to ensure their mutual benefit and their well-being. And it follows the Judaic requirement to be responsible for one another. These links are informational, cultural, economic, and social. And, at times, they are mutually beneficial in the political and diplomatic realms. There is the ultimate factor of protecting endangered or distressed Jewish communities wherever they may be. Promoting and facilitating the emigration of distressed Jews (and Jewish communities) and other Jews who wish to become immigrants to the Jewish state and citizens thereof has been a major element of Israeli politics and policy, foreign policy and diplomacy, from the beginning.

The Zionist lens is increasingly subject to reinterpretation and modification, but its central premises remain unshakable—the creation and continued existence of a Jewish state. Although it is now fashionable to talk in terms of post-Zionism, that is more of an academic concept than an operational element of foreign policy. Associated with post-Zionism is the growing development of "revisionist" history, which reexamines and revisits older events and policies and suggest that, perhaps, interpretations an decisions based on them were incorrect and erroneous. The school of "new historians" often referred to as revisionists, that has developed in Israel over the last decade and has emerged to prominence after the Oslo accords (1973) has sought to correct the historical record and portray Israel "accurately," not in the idealistic tones of Zionist historians.[7] Their goal is to demythologize Israel and its history, but although they have engendered substantial academic and general interest, and have revealed dark moments in Israel's history as well as that of the Zionist movement, they remain controversial and, in some ways, create newer myths. But the more significant question is: Do they reveal "opportunities lost" in the quest for peace or suggest that the course of events might have been substantially different in the Arab-Israeli relationship (or indeed in Israel's other relationships) had the record been exposed then? The dominant response must be: It wasn't, and rewriting the scenarios now cannot alter the foreign policies pursued then. "What might have been if only we knew then what we know now" is an area for speculation but does not provide a basis for a study of policy making that focusses on the then-perceived reality.

The concept of politicide clearly identifies the security lens and the military, diplomatic, political, and economic threat posed by a hostile Arab world, thus generating the need for arms and aid; diplomatic and political support, whether in general in the international community, or in specific votes in the United Nations; and economic linkages for aid and trade. Recognizing its geographic vulnerability and political isolation, and faced from the first days of independence with a political-military threat and the armed hostility of the Arab world, Israel soon identified the need for the support of at least one major ally or power. After it became apparent that the initial flirtation with nonalignment (a posture attempted until July 1950) was diplomatically and politically impossible, Israel assumed its natural posture of a Western orientation; coincident with the Korean War, it began a serious quest for a major Western power as an ally. The initial success was with France, and that led to a tacit alliance;[8] but from the outset Israel also pursued good relations (to include arms and political support) with each of the major powers. This need for support was highlighted in the negotiations between Israel and Syria in 1999 and 2000, when the security factor emerged as a dominant concern of Israel, and much of the discussion focussed on the roles that external powers (especially the United States) might play in ensuring security through various mechanisms such as peacekeeping forces and/or financial assistance.

The primary goal—the central concern—of Israeli policy throughout more than five decades lies at the obvious nexus of foreign and security policy; it is and has been to enhance the security of the state. This objective has various components, and the policies to achieve them are even more numerous. A closely connected second objective is to establish, sustain, and expand peaceful relations with the Arab states of the Middle East and North Africa—not just the bordering neighbors but also those beyond, in the broader Arab world. This would enhance the overall security of the state, but is also a goal in and of itself: clearly it would alleviate the geographic isolation of Israel within its region and facilitate trade and other exchanges with its neighbors.

A third objective is to protect Jewish minorities everywhere, and to establish and sustain links between them and Israel as the world's only Jewish state. Israel seeks to oppose anti-Semitism wherever it may exist or arise, and to secure and assure Jewish immigration to Israel from endangered as well as more secure locations. This helps those Jewish communities and also contributes to Israel's well-being.

The Circle Concept of Foreign Policy

One can envisage Israeli foreign policy, to achieve its objectives, using a conceptual model composed of a series of concentric circles with itself at the center. From this center it perceives not only the threats and concerns of, but also the possibilities and opportunities provided by, a series of bounded sectors, each different from the other and separated from it, but nevertheless affected by it. The "circles" provide a useful way of thinking conceptually about the issues and content of Israeli foreign policy.

At the center is Israel, a small state located in an Arab world much larger than it in both size and population. In the armistice lines that existed from 1949 to 1967, Israel covered some 8,000 square miles, with a population, at independence, of some 900,000 people. In 2000 its population exceed 6 million, but even with the occupied territories it is only about 10,800 square miles in size. It is poorly endowed with natural resources despite its location in a region renowned for its oil resources.

Small Israel is immediately surrounded (in concept as well as in reality) by what was (and to some extent still is) a hostile Arab world. There has been some progress in reducing the threat and hostility posed by its neighbors, but the process is far from complete. This has led to a sense of insecurity and a consequent effort to alter that situation and to be accepted in the region and beyond. But in the year 2000 Israel still did not enjoy full diplomatic recognition in the international community, even beyond the wall of Arab hostility and opposition. The six major Arab-Israeli wars conditioned Israel's perceptions of its place in the international system and were important turning points in its domestic development and foreign policy.

The first Arab-Israeli war, known in Israel as the War of Independence, was long and costly: Israel lost some 4,000 soldiers and 2,000 civilians, about 1 percent of the Jewish population. But at the same time, when the war ended in 1949, Israel was in control of about one-third more territory (some 2,500 square miles) than it had been allocated by the United Nations partition plan. The area was acquired at the expense of the projected Arab state of Palestine. Jerusalem was divided between Israel and Jordan rather than becoming the international city envisioned by the United Nations. The war did not end in a formal peace between Israel and its neighbors but in armistice agreements that were intended to be the first steps toward peace. Peace did not follow, and the early 1950s were characterized by a heightening of tension in the area that was manifested in acts of sabotage, shootings, and cross-border attacks. Were chances for peace missed by Israel? The record suggests that no significant opportunities were ignored. The give-and-take necessary for a successful outcome was never launched, and the concessions required were not likely. In the period from 1951 to 1956, there were numerous armed clashes with Arab forces inside Israeli territory, and other hostile acts were committed by infiltrators who came primarily from Egyptian and Jordanian territory. Israel and its Arab neighbors, especially newly revolutionary Egypt, sought arms for defense and security. The situation continued to deteriorate until Israel, in collusion with Britain and France, invaded Egypt in October 1956.

For a decade after the 1956 war, there was no large-scale outbreak of hostilities between Israel and the Arab states, although tensions remained high, and there was no movement toward peace. By the spring of 1967, conditions had reached the point of probable conflict that could not be averted by international efforts. The *casus belli* of the announced closure of the Strait of Tiran led to an Israeli preemptive strike against Egypt.

The June 1967 Six-Day War arguably had the greatest impact on Israel of all the wars it has fought. Israel's significant victory and subsequent control of substantial amounts of Arab territory altered the regional and domestic situation and generated considerable discussion in Israel on appropriate (and new?) policies to secure peace. Between 1949 and 1967, Israel was prepared for peace with the Arab states on the basis of the 1949 armistice lines, with minor modifications, but after the events of May and June 1967, the stark reality of "politicide" began to enter into these considerations, and many in Israel argued for a need to change the security situation. The newly occupied territories gave Israel an enhanced strategic position with more defensible borders and early-warning time as a result of greater strategic depth. Religious and ideological-historical claims to territory reinforced this view. The status of these territories has been the focus of the peace process ever since.

The 1969–1970 War of Attrition did not alter the situation meaningfully, although it placed the Arab-Israeli conflict squarely in the international strategic arena, with American and Soviet interest heightened by clashes between Israeli and Soviet pilots in the Suez Canal Zone. A growing Soviet presence in Egypt, coupled with the supply to Egypt of new and more sophisticated military equipment, evoked growing United States interest and concern that was evidenced by the increased involvement of Richard Nixon and Henry Kissinger.

The 1973 Arab-Israeli war (Yom Kippur/Ramadan War) took Israel by surprise. After the invading Egyptian and Syrian armies scored initial successes, Israel ultimately was able to reverse the tide, although not fully. For Israel the war was accompanied by significant political and diplomatic disappointments, and by domestic economic, psychological, and political stress. The war eroded the optimism and self-assurance of a population that had believed that the Arabs would not attack, given the relative strength of the two sides. The prewar euphoria was replaced by a more sober and realistic outlook that helped to foster political and social maturity. There was a greater turning inward by Israelis, who also became more cautious, questioned attitudes and policy more, and were more critical of both the system and the people who ran it. The outcome of the war made initial military disengagements between Israel and Egypt (1974) and Israel and Syria (1974) necessary and possible.

The immediate environment had been in flux since the first post-Yom Kippur War agreements, and continued to undergo change as efforts to achieve a negotiated peace continued. But the breakthrough was not a direct result of Israeli foreign policy, despite a three-decade quest for peace. Anwar Sadat's initiative of 1977 made peace negotiations possible; the bilateral Egypt-Israel issues were subject to compromise, and an agreement was struck with the assistance of the United States. By the spring of 1979, an Egypt-Israel peace treaty was signed and, in the years that followed, was fully implemented. Nevertheless, relations have rarely been warm or friendly. But although many have focussed on the cold or frozen nature of the peace between the two former adversaries, the central element is that peace has been established and sustained, despite numerous challenges. The agreement removed from the battlefield what was then the most serious Arab military threat to Israel and the country with which it had fought five wars (in 1948–1949, 1956, 1967, 1969–1970, and 1973). Although Israeli security was enhanced, the broader concept of Arab hostility and threat was not notably eased when it became apparent that the remainder of the Arab world was more interested in distancing itself from Egypt, and condemning and ostracizing it, than in following its example. The next peace treaty was not signed for a decade and a half.

The war in Lebanon (Operation Peace for Galilee) that began with the Israeli invasion of June 1982 was designed to eliminate the Palestinian presence in Lebanon, which threatened Israel's northern sector. Defense Minister Ariel Sharon appeared determined to project Israeli military power, where opportunities presented themselves, in pursuit of Israel's national interests. The dispatch of Israeli forces into Lebanon, primarily and ostensibly to destroy the P.L.O. military infrastructure, was accompanied, at least in Sharon's conception, by broader goals—to weaken the P.L.O. politically, particularly on the West Bank; to expel the Syrian army from Lebanon; and to create a new political situation that might lead Lebanon to become the second Arab state to make peace with Israel. The war was the first to generate internal protests and significant opposition in Israel. It was followed by an American-brokered agreement signed on May 17, 1983, that would have improved the regional situation and brought greater security to both Israel and Lebanon. The abrogation of this agreement by Lebanon, under significant outside pressure, has led Israel to sustain a military presence in southern Lebanon (Israel's "security zone"), a festering problem debated extensively within Israel and an agenda item in Israeli-Syrian negotiations until its termination in 2000.

The signing of the Declaration of Principles (D.O.P.), the so-called Oslo accords, between Israel and the Palestine Liberation Organization on the White House lawn in Washington in September 1993 suggested a changing environment and the potential for enhanced regional security and cooperation. Among other elements, the P.L.O. recognized Israel's right to exist in peace and security, a crucial breakthrough in Arab thinking and a major positive element for Israel's position in the region, especially once appropriate agreements were reached to implement this acceptance. Since 1993, Israel has made significant progress in its quest for peace and security and improved relations with its Arab neighbors, though not without some setbacks.

The D.O.P. also facilitated the possibility for other negotiations, most prominently between Israel and Jordan. The two neighbors, who had held substantial secret negotiations over many decades, shifted these discussions to the official and public domain after the signing of the D.O.P. By the fall of 1994, Israel and Jordan were prepared to sign a peace agreement that resolved the main issues between them—primarily peace, borders, and water distribution. The peace between the two states has been marked by a relatively warm relationship, unlike that between Israel and Egypt, that has been sustained despite the death of King Husayn and the succession of his son, King 'Abdallah II.

Progress in making peace with the P.L.O. and with Syria (and, consequently, Lebanon) has gone through positive and negative phases since the Madrid Peace

Conference of 1991, but the overall result has been a general improvement in Israel's situation with its immediate neighbors and a decrease in the prospects for conflict along its borders. The Oslo accords also facilitated Israel's broader international acceptance, as numerous states thereafter regarded relations with the Jewish state as an acceptable option.

The threat from the broader Arab world has also changed, with a number of states in both North Africa and the Persian Gulf sectors establishing links, official and unofficial, formal and informal, with Israel in various sectors. At the same time, the threat has not ended, and some Arab states, especially Iraq and Libya, and some Arab organizations continue to suggest that the resolution of the Arab-Israeli conflict can occur only with the elimination of Israel.

The overriding, monolithic threat posed by the Arab world to Israel has been altered. Israel's most potent memory of wars and incidents, of terrorism and security threats, from the Arab world has been replaced by a more multifaceted perception of the Arab world. A focus on war has been partially supplanted by negotiations for further treaties of peace and for the establishment of normalized relations. Some Israelis think beyond that point and focus on "regional cooperation"—indeed, Prime Minister Ehud Barak appointed Shimon Peres as minister in charge of regional cooperation in his 1999 government—in which a more peaceful and prosperous Middle East will be marked by closer cooperation between Israel and the Arab states, not just Israel's immediate neighbors. Shimon Peres has referred to the process by which Israel's relations with its Arab neighbors (especially the Palestinians and Jordan) improved and changed dramatically since the Madrid Conference as the "art of the impossible." By whatever rubric we refer to it, the process continues.

Crucially, after more than five decades of independence Israel has neither succumbed to, nor been fully successful in utilizing, the six major Arab-Israeli wars to assure its security and well-being. Despite victories in combat (some major and clear, others less so), Israel has not succeeded in converting military accomplishment into full peace with the Arabs (to include the Palestinians). At the same time, a reassessment of war and peace suggests that full-scale war between Israel and its recalcitrant neighbors is unlikely in the near term, either because of a balance of terror or because it is now clear that neither side in this Arab-Israeli conflict has been able to achieve its objectives through combat.

The negotiation and signing of the Israel-P.L.O. Declaration of Principles ushered in a new era in the politics of the Middle East, and changed forever and irreversibly the Arab-Israeli conflict and other factors linked to it. Nevertheless, it did not bring peace even as it moved Israel closer to its acceptance by its Arab neighbors. Despite the euphoria generated by the events of that day and some of the implementation that followed, delays in putting the agreement and subsequent ones into effect were inevitable, as was vocal and violent opposition to the process or some of its parts that soon emerged in Israel as well as among the Palestinians and in the Arab states that supported them.

The circle of Arab hostility around Israel, acting to fence it in and to prevent its incorporation in the broader international community, is itself encircled by a group of states located "beyond the fence" with a special role that is potentially helpful in alleviating the Arab threat. Surrounded by a wall of Arab hostility—isolated in its immediate neighborhood—Israel soon after independence launched efforts to "jump the fence" of Arab military encirclement and establish relations with regional states of consequence beyond the fence.[9] It sought links with local non-Arab states; much of the focus was on Turkey and Iran to the north and to a lesser extent on Ethiopia, Kenya, and Uganda in the south.

Both Iran and Turkey gained attention because of their geographical and religious positions and their historical relations with the Arab states. Tensions over borders, colonial pasts, and religious-ideological differences between these two Muslim but non-Arab states and the Arab world suggested opportunities for Israel to develop ties that would enhance its regional position and, perhaps, contribute to its security and assist in resolving the Arab-Israeli conflict. Although both states voted against the U.N. partition plan that created Israel, they soon established diplomatic relations, albeit limited in scope. Over time these improved and became increasingly complex.

Israel's relationship with Iran during the shah's reign was multifaceted and important in a number of areas, although, to a great extent, secret. It involved several Israeli concerns—the well-being of Iran's ancient Jewish population, the security of Israel's essential oil supply, and a shared wariness of Arab radicals. But with the ousting of the shah and the coming to power of the Islamic revolutionary regime, all ties were severed, and Iran became passionate and intense in its opposition to the Jewish state, in its support of the Palestinians, and in its opposition to peace efforts to resolve outstanding elements of the Arab-Israeli conflict. Opposition to Israeli control of Jerusalem became a constant Iranian theme. Iran's state sponsorship of terrorism (and support of anti-Israel terrorist organizations) and its pursuit of programs to develop weapons of mass destruction concerned Israel (and others), which perceived negative goals and objectives, including potential targetting of Israel.

The relationship with Turkey evolved differently and in a more positive direction. Long-standing animosities between Arabs and Turks contributed to an improved Israel-Turkish relationship. Despite tensions generated by Turkey's opposition to the partition plan of 1947 and the creation of Israel, ties have evolved to the point where Israel and Turkey today have a strongly positive political/economic relationship and an extensive strategic connection that some have likened to an alliance. The current links are seen by both as beneficial, particularly in their respective dealings with Syria, a bordering neighbor and adversary for both.

To Israel's south, just beyond the Arab states of Egypt and the Sudan, and across the Red Sea from Yemen and South Yemen, were three states of consequence—Ethiopia, Kenya, and Uganda. Each was regionally important and proved to be a valuable asset to the Jewish state (albeit only for a relatively short period in the case of Uganda), although not to the same extent as Iran and Turkey. All these states provided Israel with a means to "jump" the Arab fence and gain support for its position in the international system from important local actors.

Ethiopia was a regional power of some significance, had a long period of independence, was located strategically, and had a "Jewish" community of ancient origins.

Israel's approach to Christian Ethiopia was built on Christian Coptic foundations and on the legend and folk history of the emperor's descent from the Biblical-era connections of the Queen of Sheba to King Solomon of Israel. The Ethiopian and Egyptian Coptic churches often competed with each other, and consequently tensions often existed between the two states. The fact that Ethiopia had a relatively sizable Jewish community also suggested a linkage that ultimately led to the transfer of that community to Israel. Ethiopia's leadership in the Organization of African Unity (O.A.U.) also proved a useful factor in helping to assure Israel's position.

Kenya was strategically located, important in African politics, and desirous of technical assistance for development. Israel early established close links that were demonstrated during the 1976 raid to rescue Israeli hostages at Entebbe, when Israeli forces were able to facilitate their operation by utilizing Kenyan facilities. The Uganda connection, established on grounds similar to those in the case of Kenya, was broken in early 1972, but only after a multifaceted link had been established.

The third circle was different—less significant (except in numbers) but involved in a more straightforward relationship based on Israeli technical aid and other assistance. Located in Africa, Asia, and Latin America, the third world (nonaligned, developing) states had strength in numbers (well in excess of a hundred states today), but were not significant political or strategic players in the international community. They had and have votes in the major international organizations and could be a force in those bodies as a consequence of their numbers and usual cohesion. Overwhelmingly this is the bloc composed of states that are often seen as politically unstable, and that have not achieved significant economic and social development. They are in need of technical and economic assistance, a need Israel can address. This circle, then, relates directly to a Biblical-Zionist concept—an essentially idealist approach of Israel as a "light to the nations" as described in the Old Testament (Isaiah 49:6). Accordingly, Israel becomes an international factor—a state that provides technical and other assistance to "the nations" as an element of foreign and security policy.

The emergence of the new states of Africa and Asia in the 1950s and 1960s led Israel to pursue a policy in keeping with Afro-Asian aspirations for economic development and modernization. In an effort to befriend these states and to secure their support, Israel's multifaceted program focussed on technical assistance, exchange and training programs, loans, joint economic enterprises, and trade. The program grew dramatically over time and remains an element of Israeli policy. It had successes in economic and social terms, and also proved politically beneficial in various international venues. Third-world support helped to prevent the United Nations from adopting anti-Israel measures after the 1967 war, and in the early 1970s a committee of African presidents worked to achieve Arab-Israeli negotiations (albeit without success). The nadir of the program was reached at the time of the 1973 war, when virtually all of the African states with which Israel had established relations broke those ties in support of the Arab effort to regain the territories lost in the 1967 war. For some Israelis this reflected a policy failure, although some of the states have reestablished close links, and some sustained informal but significant ties despite their official actions (for example Kenya, as demonstrated during Israel's Entebbe operation in 1976).

Smaller in size, the fourth circle comprises the developed and economically advanced, industrialized states of Europe, plus Japan, Korea, and Canada. The European states are primarily those of substantial economic development and long history as independent states, and some as colonial powers. Most are also O.E.C.D. and European Union members. Japan and Korea, although clearly important economic powers and, in the case of Japan, a significant political actor, differ from the other members of this group in history and background.

Europe posed an interesting challenge and presented a significant opportunity. As Israel sought links to a significant power for military and economic assistance, Europe seemed a logic choice. A tacit alliance with France was supplemented by links with Great Britain and Germany and a formalized relationship with the European Economic Community (E.E.C.) and, now, the European Union (E.U.). The establishment of the E.E.C. in 1957 and its evolution into the E.U. opened a new and major area of concern for Israeli foreign policy. Over time it has been successful in establishing economic links not only with the E.E.C. and E.U. as a group, albeit within limitations, but also with various European states (especially France and Germany) on a bilateral basis. France proved a useful supplier of military aid, whereas Germany was an indispensable factor in Israel's economic development.

In its approach to the European states, Israel sought to focus on its Judeo-Christian heritage (its Biblical links to Christianity), its historical connection, and on a "guilt complex" relating to the Holocaust and Europe's responsibilities derived therefrom. Israel's political and moral arguments have stressed its fundamental ties to Europe—a natural affinity to Western Europe in general outlook as well as in geographic, cultural, and social orientation. The Holocaust has led to complex relationships with the European states, especially Germany, which ultimately have been indispensable for Israel's security and well-being.

The superpowers (the United States and the Soviet Union) from World War II to the 1990s comprised the fifth circle, that is, the encompassing major players of the international system. Clearly, in the case of the Soviet Union, the relationship was not simply with the superpower itself but also with its bloc partners. From its independence to the 1990s, Israel, like all other states, had to operate within the confines of the Cold War. But there were multiple factors whose cumulative impact was greater for Israel than for most others. Both of the superpowers were also significant as the residences of large segments of the world's Jewish population. Thus these states had dual significance.

Israel initially pursued a policy of nonidentification, neutralism, or nonalignment, and was initially somewhat successful in that posture. Whereas other states often tried to play off the United States and the Soviet Union to secure from them the benefits of alliance, Israel was unable to do so in its earliest days of independence. The United States and the Soviet Union both sought Israel's allegiance when it became independent, and it joined the United Nations with the support of both superpowers. Soon, however, it became clear that nonidentification would give way to a pro-Western orientation and later to a United States-Israel connection or alignment. The special relationship (or "alliance," as seen by some) between the United States and Israel developed only later and remains unformalized by treaty even today.

The lens of Zionism and the associated "ingathering of the exiles" required concern for Jewish communities elsewhere and a potential of emigration from their imperiled locations to the haven of the Jewish state. Thus in focussing on the superpowers, Israel had an additional concern for the world's largest Jewish communities; the United States still has the world's largest, and the Soviet Union once had the world's second, and today has the third, largest.

During the Cold War, the focus of Israeli attention through the Jewish-Zionist lens was to assure the security and well-being of Jewish communities elsewhere and close links between them and Israel. The American-Jewish community's relationship with Israel has been indispensable. From the earliest years to the present, with occasional low points, Israel has benefitted from the economic and philanthropic aid and political support provided by American Jewry. Indeed, from Chaim Weizmann's arranged meeting with Truman before Israeli statehood to lobbying by Israel's friends and supporters today, the pattern has been persistent and consistent in securing the covenant between Israel and the United States. The end of the Cold War has not altered the relationship.

Applying the Zionist-Jewish lens to the Soviet Union provides a different perspective. Anti-Semitism was (and arguably is) an endemic feature of Russian society and history. Not only were Soviet Jews unable to assist the Jewish state in its birth and consolidation, but also during the Cold War Israel was unable to protect them, nor could it secure large-scale emigration of those at risk. This began to change in the last years of the Gorbachev era, but emigration to Israel became a continuous flow only with the end of the Soviet Union and of the Cold War.

Over time, the United States has changed from a power providing limited direct support for Israel to the world's only superpower linked to Israel in a free-trade area, and a crucial provider of political, diplomatic, and strategic support as well as economic aid.

There is a widespread misperception that United States support for Israel has been a major element of United States Middle East policy since the creation of the state. In fact, United States economic and military assistance was far more substantial to other regional states (such as Turkey, Iran, and Greece—in part reflected by the Truman Doctrine of 1947) than to Israel until the Kennedy-Johnson and, later, Nixon years. Israeli efforts to secure a formal relationship with the United States in the mid-1950s were rebuffed by the Eisenhower-Dulles administration, and it was Britain and France that collaborated with Israel in the Suez War (without American knowledge). It was also then that the Eisenhower administration forced Israel to withdraw from the territories it occupied in the conflict under pain of sanctions. Since then, United States diplomatic-political backing for Israel in the United Nations and elsewhere has been marked by the post-1967 war efforts reflected in Johnson's Five Principles of Peace speech of June 19, 1967, and United Nations Security Council Resolution 242, which is substantially similar in its approach to peace.

United States military aid and military sales to Israel were negligible in amount and unimpressive in content until the Kennedy administration sold Israel Hawk missiles and the Johnson administration sold it modern jet aircraft. It is useful to recall that the well-regarded Israel Air Force of the 1967 war was primarily equipped with modern French jet aircraft, not those of the United States. The first Phantom (F-4) jet aircraft arrived in Israel only in 1969. Total United States military aid to Israel was less than $1 million until the Kennedy tenure, and increased dramatically to substantial levels first with the Nixon administration and then in the wake of the Camp David Accords (1978)—the so-called "Camp David dividend." A well-developed strategic link derives from the Reagan administration, from the president's perception of Israel as a "strategic asset" and the subsequent Memorandum of Understanding (1981), although the Nixon administration certainly valued the support of King Husayn of Jordan during Black September (1970).

Israel's special relationship with the United States—revolving around a broadly conceived ideological factor based on positive perception and sentiment evident in public opinion and official statements, and manifest in political and diplomatic support and military and economic assistance—has not been enshrined in a legally binding commitment joining the two in a formal alliance. Despite the extensive links that have developed, the widespread belief in the existence of the commitment, and the assurances contained in various specific agreements, the exact nature and extent of the U.S. commitment to Israel remains imprecise. Israel has no mutual security treaty with the United States, nor is it a member of any alliance system requiring the United States to take up arms automatically on its behalf. The American commitment to Israel has taken the generalized form of presidential statements (rather than formal documents), which have reaffirmed interest in supporting the political independence and territorial integrity of all Middle East states, including Israel. Although it has largely been assumed by both parties that the United States would come to Israel's assistance should it be gravely threatened, the United States is not committed to specific actions in particular circumstances. These unspecific arrangements have been codified in the Sinai II accords of 1975 and in memoranda of understanding since 1981. Israeli leaders continue to be interested in military and economic assistance as the primary tangible expression of the U.S. commitment, and have been particularly cautious about potential U.S. participation in a conflict, fearing that combat losses might lead to a situation analogous to that in Vietnam.

The United States is today an indispensable if not a fully dependable ally. It provides Israel, through one form or another, with economic (governmental and private), technical, military, political, diplomatic, and moral support. It is seen as the ultimate resource against potential enemies; it is the source of Israel's sophisticated military hardware; and its interest in lasting peace is central to the Arab-Israel peace process. Although there is this positive relationship, there is also an Israeli reluctance, bred of history, to abdicate security to another party's judgment and action. Israel will continue to consider its perceptions of threat and security as decisive. In Israel's elite and collective popular judgment, the special relationship must be sustained. It has been a vital foundation of Israel's security and foreign policy for years.

The two states maintain a remarkable degree of parallelism and congruence on broad policy goals. The policy consensus includes the need to prevent war, at both regional and international levels, as well as the need to maintain Israel's existence and security and to help provide for its economic well-being. At the same time, however, there was, is, and will be a divergence of interests that derives from a difference of perspective and overall policy environment. The United States has broader concerns that result from its global obligations, whereas Israel's perspective is conditioned by its more restricted environment and lesser responsibilities. Israel's horizon is more narrowly defined, and is essentially limited to the survival of the state and a concern for Jewish communities and individuals that goes beyond the frontiers of the Jewish state. Thus there has been and will continue to be discord on issues relating to the Arab-Israeli conflict, and particularly the future of the Palestinians. There has also been a divergence on methods and techniques to be employed, as well as discord on specific issues.

Nevertheless, the objective of securing the special relationship that exists between Israel and the United States has developed over the years and is now a central focus of foreign policy objectives.[10] This was not always so to the same extent. At Israel's birth, the United States seemed to be a dispassionate, almost an uninterested, midwife—its role was essential and unconventional, but also unpredictable and hotly debated in U.S. policy circles. Today, more than fifty years later, some of the policy debate continues, and there are periods of discord in the relationship. Some of these reflect personality and related differences between U.S. and Israeli leaders. But there is little doubt about the overall nature of U.S. support for its small and still embattled ally.

In all relationships there are limits to the ability of one party to influence the other, and limits beyond which a state will not go (and concessions it will not make) given its perception of its national interest. As with other states, Israel has imposed limits ("red lines") for its behavior and policies, and there is an ultimate "independence" of action that Israel ascribes to itself. Many have assumed that, as a result of the overwhelming importance of the United States to Israel (and especially owing to the vast amounts of aid and political-diplomatic support), the United States retains the ability to "influence" Israel to move in certain directions and adopt certain policies. There is, in fact, a wide range of actions that Israel is likely to take at the suggestion of the United States. At the same time, Israel is able to forestall such suggestions for a variety of reasons, some relating to the nature of the American political system (including checks and balances, the role of public opinion, the importance of lobbying groups, and so on) and others that are a direct consequence of its own self-perception. For Israel, as for other states, core values and vital national interests are not subject to compromise or policy modification, even under substantial external influence from an important and close friend. Reflecting the perspective of numerous Israeli leaders before and since, Yitzhak Shamir noted in the Knesset in September 1982, "On the fundamental life-and-death issues ... we have no choice but to stand by our position firmly, strongly and clearly, even against our great friend the United States." For the Jewish state, the ultimate decisions on peace, security, and well-being remain in the hands of its senior decision makers.

Barak and After

The accession of Ehud Barak to the post of prime minister in 1999, as in previous changes in government and prime minister, once again raised questions about

135

continuity and discontinuity in Israeli foreign policy. Each prime minister and each government in Israel has pursued similar foreign and security objectives—the quest for peace with its neighbors and security accompanied by economic well-being—but often with modified policies. Each maker of high policy brought a different background to office and pursued policy in an altered environment from that of his or her predecessor. Each has had a different constellation of advisors, despite substantial continuity in senior cabinet posts by a rather small and cohesive decision-making elite. Over time, several elements of divergence on method and policy to secure the goals have emerged.

Differences that developed within the Jewish leadership in the preindependence period in Palestine and elsewhere were soon reflected in the new state after independence. The division between the Zionist mainstream led by David Ben-Gurion and the Revisionist movement of Vladimir Zeev Jabotinsky that developed over the question of the British Mandate, the partition of Palestine, the creation of Transjordan, and related themes, was reflected in the tension between Ben-Gurion and Menachem Begin, as well as in the continuing rivalry and visions of Labor (One Israel), on the one hand, and Herut and Likud, on the other. The pragmatism of the Labor/Ben-Gurion response to British policy versus the hard line of the Revisionists (Herut-Likud) of Jabotinsky (and later Begin), who focussed on less compromising outlooks, continues to be reflected in Israeli politics in the new century. Within this broad division of the Zionist mainstream versus Revisionist concepts there were further tensions and divisions. The differences between Ben-Gurion and his Labor successor as prime minister, Moshe Sharett, on approaches to the Arabs has long been recorded as an important subtext of Israeli policy in the 1950s, but there were also differences that emerged in the triumvirate of Prime Minister Yitzhak Rabin, Defense Minister Shimon Peres, and Foreign Minister Yigal Allon in the post-October War Labor government (1974–1977), when each promoted an approach at variance with the others. Similarly, differences on the right were especially noteworthy between Menachem Begin and his defense minister, Ariel (Arik) Sharon, particularly over the war in Lebanon and dealings with the Palestinians. Thus, whether between political right and political left, or within each camp, Israel has been characterized by consistency in objective but often by divergence in policy to achieve those ends.

The United States was an early stop on Barak's first policy tour. The reasons for this could be found in the concerns the United States has shown for Israeli wellbeing over the decades, and in its role as a source of diplomatic, political, strategic, and economic support. Especially in the security sector, which Barak focusses on, the United States is indispensable. It is a source of weapons systems, and assists in the development of new military technology. There is a need to coordinate on matters relating to terrorism, and the United States is essential to formulating responses to the development in the region of weapons of mass destruction, especially by Iran and Iraq. Closely connected to this was the need for peace with the Arabs and acceptance in the region and beyond. Thus, their agenda focussed on the peace process. Clinton remained concerned with the diplomacy of Oslo and Wye, whereas Barak seemed to prefer moving to a final agreement before relinquishing a series of tangible assets (including land).

Peace and security, security and peace, in either order, remain the central themes and goals of Israeli national life more than five decades after independence. This combination of concerns has preoccupied Israel's governments and its leaders since independence. Peace and security have eluded Israel from the outset despite massive efforts and singular concentration on these themes. The lack of peace contributes to a lack of security, and peace has thus far been achieved only with Egypt and Jordan. The treaty with the former was signed in 1979, that with the latter in 1994, both very long after the independence of Israel and almost as long after the armistice agreements of 1949 that were to be stepping-stones to full peace accords between Israel and the Arab world. Insecurity across unrecognized and unaccepted borders has been a constant reminder of the initial Arab opposition to Israel's creation and of the failure to convert armistice lines to final borders. Barak saw the threat from Syria as more substantial than that of the Palestinians, hence his willingness to focus on a deal with President Assad of Syria as a means of resolving the major military concern and also of dealing with the Lebanon matter and Israeli troops there. Continuation of negotiations with the Palestinians remained important, and it was on parallel tracks that Barak sought to move to achieve Israel's ultimate foreign policy objective: peace and acceptance in the Middle East as a sine qua non for Israel's overall security and wellbeing in the broader international community.

Notes

1   See Yehoshafat Harkabi, *Fedayeen Action and Arab Strategy.*
2   The term "diaspora" is employed in this discussion in its original meaning. Derived from the Greek word for dispersion, it is used here to refer to the scattering of the Jewish communities outside of Palestine (or modern Israel) after the Babylonian exile and continuing to this day.
3   Theodor Herzl, *The Jewish State*, in Bernard Reich, ed., *Arab-Israeli Conflict and Conciliation: A Documentary History*, pp. 17–18.
4   Ibid., p. 18.
5   "Basle Program" in Bernard Reich, ed., *Arab-Israeli Conflict and Conciliation: A Documentary History*, pp 18–19.
6   Walter Eytan, *The First Ten Years: A Diplomatic History of Israel*, pp. 192–93.
7   Among the newer and more comprehensive of these are Avi Shlaim, *The Iron Wall: Israel and the Arab World since 1948*, and Benny Morris, *Righteous Victims: A History of the Zionist-Arab Conflict, 1881–1999.*
8   The concept of a tacit alliance between Israel and France is derived from Sylvia K. Crosbie, *A Tacit Alliance: France and Israel from Suez to the Six-Day War.*
9   Some early Israeli official thinking about this concept can be found in Yaacov Shimoni, "Israel in the Pattern of Middle East Politics."
10 For a detailed evaluation of the relationship, see Bernard Reich, *Quest for Peace: United States-Israel Relations and the Arab-Israeli Conflict*; Reich, *The United States and Israel: Influence in the Special Relationship*; and Reich, *Securing the Covenant: United States-Israel Relations after the Cold War.*

7

In Search of Budget Security:

A Reexamination of Jordanian Foreign Policy

Laurie A. Brand

The end of the Cold War has triggered reconsiderations of the meaning and ways of studying "security."* The traditional notions of security as measured by numbers of tanks and warheads have given way to a more comprehensive and nuanced understanding of the potential sources of threat, and one important addition to the literature has been the increasing attention devoted to the role of domestic politics and economics in security-related issues.[1] The concept of "economic security" has also commanded growing interest. Applied at first to considerations of the apparent trade-offs between military and broader economic investment, the term is now used to cover such diverse issues as debt, trade, and population growth.[2]

The Hashimite Kingdom of Jordan and its foreign policy present interesting challenges to traditional notions of security. As the state with the longest border with Israel, the kingdom has been a party to the Arab-Israeli conflict since 1948. It is a small state, traditionally described as vulnerable. To the extent that the kingdom has received scholarly attention at all—and in the field of international relations such attention was long minimal—most analysts have been preoccupied with state-level factors such as geostrategic location and relative military might, and have focused almost exclusively on Jordan's role in this conflict and its attendant concerns. They have then derived from this analysis more general explanations of the kingdom's foreign policy.

The problem with relying on such a monocausal explanation is that Jordan's regional position cannot always or—as this paper will argue—even in most cases account for critical foreign-policy moves; indeed, in some instances it can account for both the move taken and its opposite. As the brief case discussions below illustrate, Jordan's place in the regional system cannot, for example, explain the Jordanian-Syrian alliance of 1975–1977, the Jordanian-Iraqi alignment beginning in 1979, the kingdom's attempted rapprochement with Syria in 1983, or its reestablishment of ties with Egypt in 1984. Yet all of these were key, and in some cases controversial, foreign-policy moves.

The explanatory framework developed in the larger work of which this is a part does not deny the role of external factors (regional or systemic) in conditioning or constraining Jordan's foreign-policy options; indeed, it lays them out clearly in the beginning.[3] Nonetheless, it argues for examining another set of factors that have been more specifically determinant in many key foreign-policy decisions. International relations have traditionally been explained in terms of balancing or bandwagoning based on relative power or threat.[4] The evidence suggests, however, that economic variables, particularly the structure of the kingdom's budget and revenue sources and the financial imperatives they imply, can often better explain a foreign policy or an alliance shift.

Such an approach rarely appears in analyses of Middle East politics. To the extent that domestic factors have been used to explain the kingdom's (or the king's) behavior, most attention has focussed on the purported impact of the presence of large numbers of Jordanians of Palestinian origin in constraining what—it is implied—would have otherwise been a more forthcoming policy on a potential peace settlement with Israel. The effects of foreign aid, trade, and domestic economic structure have been neglected by most authors examining regional interstate relations.[5] For example, Paul Noble has argued that whereas other state systems relied heavily on military and economic capabilities, in the case of the Arab states, only modest military and economic means were available, at least in the 1950s and 1960s.[6] Neither Noble's study nor any other has attempted to discuss the role that economic factors might have played. But even if economic factors are shown to have played only a minor role in foreign policy considerations prior to 1970, one should not assume that the nature and bases of Arab politics have remained unchanged since the 1950s. In Dessouki and Korany's *The Foreign Policies of Arab States*, the first serious attempt to theorize about this subject, economic factors are viewed as policy inputs or national attributes, but national economic structure is not discussed as an independent variable capable of explaining foreign policy, except in the case of Egypt. To the degree that economic factors are considered more broadly, the question is posed in terms of dependence on foreign aid and degree of economic development.[7]

The contention here is not that such issues are unimportant but that the picture is incomplete and thus severely undermines the explanation. Rather than examining only the way in which economic factors may constrain foreign policy, one may also legitimately ask: Given a state's economic structure, what sort of foreign-policy behavior may be expected? That is, to what degree are a leadership's or a regime's estimates of its own economic needs and weaknesses a *source* of foreign policy—the independent variable—rather than mere measures of capability to carry out foreign policy constructed on the basis of other factors?

This approach leads to another difference in the way that thinking about the foreign policies of countries of the developing world (and, indeed, beyond) should be conceptualized. Foreign policy has been a major component of the national security policies of states. Security, as it has traditionally been defined, involved protection of sovereign territory, of a country's boundaries, from violation or aggression from outside. The implication was that a state/country had a single, knowable, and (based on relative power position) generally unchanging national interest that was pursued or upheld by the leadership as part of its trust to defend the nation. In fact, of course, whereas military threats from abroad are most easily countered in the name of a unitary national interest, when one moves to another level or another type of threat, the "national" interest may be much less apparent or compelling. In many issue areas, indeed, particularly economic ones, it is difficult to make a case for a single national interest that would dictate a particular policy response from which all citizens would benefit (even if not equally). Hence, it is useful to think of the concept of national security and its accompanying discourse as constructed by a unitary leadership or coalition of elites in order to secure *its* best interests. In other words, what one is in fact examining is "leadership" security, a set of policies by which a political and/or an economic elite tries to legitimate or reinforce its own position, perhaps at times even at the expense of a broader national interest.[8] It is this focus that leads to the concept of budget security used here: the notion that a leadership will make state solvency a basic element of its efforts to maintain power, and will construct foreign policy in such a way as to achieve that goal.

Although myriad factors may influence the foreign-policy decisions of a country as economically and politically vulnerable as Jordan, this chapter argues that the domestic political economy is the key to an understanding of the kingdom's foreign policy and, specifically, its alliance behavior. Numerous sources or types of data are needed to substantiate such an argument. The first and most obvious are statistics on trade and aid relationships as well as domestic revenue sources and spending patterns. Such information makes clear which sectors are most important or most vulnerable, and which external relationships underpin or contribute to budget security. Yet, although statistical data may serve as part of the evidence, they do not by themselves indicate the degree to which such patterns are the result of conscious, targeted policy. Nor do they tell whether or to what extent decisionmakers may be constrained by societal or institutional forces that might push policy choices in a particular direction. Before proceeding with discussions of Jordan's relations with three key Arab states—Syria, Iraq, and Egypt—to explore the "budget security" argument, therefore, the process of economic decision-making must be briefly explored.

The Economic Decision-Making Process in Jordan

To make a case regarding budget security, it must first be shown that state decisionmakers are aware of and responsive to the central role that the various sources of state income play in maintaining state solvency. Second, there must be substantial overlap between economic and political decision-making groups, or at least very close coordination between them. Third, either societal forces that might lobby for their own interests must be in relative accord with the decision-making group or the decisionmakers must enjoy relative autonomy from such societal forces so that they are able to proceed without significant concern for the preferences of these actors.

Three models have traditionally been used to explain decisionmaking at the national level. The first gives primacy to a state's place and relative power position in the international system. The second, society-centered, approach looks for explanations of state policy choices in the jockeying for power and influence by domestic, civil society groups. Finally, the state-centered approach argues for examining the role of the state as structure and actor in determining or affecting policy choices, and assumes that the preferences of such actors are at least partially separable from societal or interest group pressures.[9]

In the case of Jordan, the system-level approach would first focus on the country's geographic location, which not only places it at an important transit point to and from the Arabian Peninsula and the Gulf, but also situates it at the eastern end of the Mediterranean, with all that has meant for British and American strategic interests as well as for Israeli security concerns. Hence an important element in the system-level approach would be the larger context of the Arab-Israeli conflict in which Jordan has found itself since the late 1940s. Second, as part of the evaluation of Jordan's strength (or vulnerability), such an approach would note that the kingdom is resource poor, and that, until the economic crisis of the late 1980s, the kingdom was able to live well largely due to external largess or rents.[10] The problem with this approach is that it is static and has difficulty explaining variation in policy orientations that do not coincide with major shifts in military, economic, or political power positions.

The second, society-centered, model would seek to determine which societal groups have been in a position to play a role in influencing economic policy making. One salient distinction is that between the public and private sectors, all the more important in the Jordanian case because of the long-standing, if eroding, communal divide that underlies it. For historical reasons, Jordanians of Palestinian origin have overwhelmingly constituted the private sector in Jordan, whereas Transjordanians have been disproportionately represented in the state bureaucracy, including the various security and armed forces. This distinction can be exaggerated, for there are significant examples of crosscutting networks. Even so, the degree of coincidence of these two fracture lines—public sector/private sector and Transjordanian/Palestinian—as well as popular perceptions of them cannot be overlooked as markers of domestic constituencies. Nor can the size of the sectors: each of the communities probably accounts for about 50 percent of the population.[11] In 1986, it was estimated that the public sector employed 45 percent of the country's work force, contributed 50 percent of capital formation, and was responsible for 30 percent of exports.[12] Although much more could be said on this point, the statistics support a picture of a relatively large state sector and a relatively undersized private sector.

The question to be answered in assessing a society-centered approach, however, is whether these or any other interest groups have played consistent, effective roles in influencing economic decisionmaking. In Jordan, from 1957 until 1989, civil society was largely circumscribed by the martial law regime.[13] That said, two institutions with potential clout in economic policy, the chambers of commerce and industry, have been in existence throughout much of the kingdom's history. Yet, by members' own admission, the government consulted the Chamber of Industry only infrequently in the 1970s.[14] The annual reports of the Chamber of Commerce reinforce this picture. Although the record is incomplete, the annual reports for 1975–1990 list fewer than twenty formal meetings, four with the prime minister and one with the crown prince. In a number of cases, it was decided that joint committees of various sorts should be established to address key issues; that such committees are not mentioned subsequently indicates their short unproductive lives.[15]

The record since the beginning of the political liberalization in 1989 is somewhat different, as will be discussed later. Nonetheless, although the members of these chambers were some of the wealthiest men in the kingdom, their official lobbying organizations seem not to have served them particularly well in the pre-1989 period, even under the putative pro-private-sector governments of Zayd al-Rifa`i (1973–1976, 1985–1989).[16] Numerous factors help to explain the lack of power of the business community, including conflicting interests between sectors, a strong suspicion of the private sector among bureaucrats who could facilitate their work, and the martial law regime, which certainly did not encourage overt protest. Moreover, the small size of the private sector's contribution to the economy, as well as its dependence upon the state for many of its contracts and other activities, has not given it the bargaining power vis-à-vis the state that a larger, more independent private sector might have. That said, it would be wrong to leave the impression that businessmen in Jordan have been under siege. Red tape and bureaucratic inertia are certainly facts of life, but Jordan has a substantial stratum of successful businessmen who are aware that part of the reason for their success lies not only in the availability of contracts from the state but also in the relatively stable domestic climate that the state provided during the years of authoritarian rule and martial law. Moreover, when the health of the private sector was at stake in the early 1980s, the state initiated a policy of export credits to Iraq, in addition to making overtures to expand trade ties with both Syria and Egypt. The impetus for such policies may be deduced as having come from the private sector, even if its concerns were not articulated formally through one of the chambers. In sum, it appears that during the period prior to 1989, nongovernmental societal actors, although not devoid of influence, nonetheless did not play a clear and consistent role in articulating or advocating their interests as part of the economic policy-making process.

It remains to be determined whether a state-centered approach provides a better framework for analyzing policy making in the kingdom. Interviewees made clear that, even for what would appear to be relatively minor matters, economic decisionmaking is highly centralized in the kingdom.[17] Most decisions are made at cabinet level or above, not even at the level of individual ministries. Moreover, from 1967 until 1990, economic decisionmaking was increasingly monopolized by what came to be called the Economic Security Committee. Composed of the ministers of finance, trade and industry, and transport, and the governor of the Central Bank, it was initially assembled to solve problems that resulted from the severing of the West Bank from Jordan as a result of the Israeli occupation. Since parliamentary life was largely inoperative after 1967 and suspended from 1974 to 1984, however, the committee's mandate gradually broadened. It increasingly came to be used to overturn and bypass existing laws when they proved inconvenient or an obstacle to powerful interests. Its decisions were not published, and many of its acts were discovered only after the full extent of the economic crisis of late 1988 unfolded.[18]

At the top of the pyramid of decision-making power—economic or political—is the king, followed by the crown prince. During Husayn's reign, he, the crown prince, the prime minister, and the chief of the royal court were the decision-making circle on issues of foreign policy. (They were, in effect, the diplomatic corps.) Testimony of a number of interviewees close to or formerly part of the upper echelons of economic and political decisionmaking indicated, however, that the king himself was not particularly interested in economic matters, and certainly not in details. He rarely had an economic briefing; when he did, he reportedly focussed primarily on issues that related to the military budget. In addition, according to such testimony, always present in the king's calculations were the sociopolitical underpinnings of the regime—the Palestinian/Transjordanian divide. In the case of the budget, the king's uppermost concern during the period under study was to pay the salaries of the members of the army and the security apparatus, who have traditionally been recruited from Transjordanian tribes.[19]

Beyond the king, crown prince, and prime minister, the economic decisionmaking group differed little from the foreign-policy group. The king had certain advisors and confidants both within and outside the government whose friendship and proximity gave them access to him, and hence the opportunity to lobby for certain policies. For domestic economic matters to have an influence on upper-level decision making, however, they had to be of real consequence—large loans, the devaluation of the dinar, and the like—so as to sweep consideration of them up to the highest levels.[20]

Finally, Jordan's strategic significance to a range of international actors led not only to its initial establishment as a modern state but also to its continuing ability to draw on those actors for substantial support in the form of grants-in-aid for the military, the bureaucracy, and development as well as a host of concessional loans and other forms of budgetary assistance. Whether as a result of inertia, lack of experience, or conscious policy choice based on evaluation of domestic political and economic trade-offs, the state leadership, in its early decades, appears to have been content to develop a heavy reliance on external sources of support rather than choosing to push more actively for expansion of the domestic productive base.

The state, therefore, gradually evolved as primarily a distributor of rents collected from outside, rather than as an extractor of resources from within.[21] The longer this relationship between state and citizen continued, the more people's expectations of the state's distributive role became set, and the more difficult it became to break such a pattern or attempt to encourage new patterns. What also appears to have developed through the emergence of the allocator-recipient relationship is a degree of state autonomy from the citizenry in the realm of both economic and political decision-making. Although martial law and its many constraints were clearly key factors in discouraging popular input into the decisionmaking processes, as long as the state was "providing for its own" through the distribution of rents from abroad, dissatisfaction was less likely to be expressed.

Given such a pattern of development, the state also made the collection of funds that enabled it to continue to play its allocative role a primary focus of its foreign policy, since this role was essential to leadership/regime survival. Therefore, economic policymaking during most of the period under study—certainly when it concerned external issues, but also to a large extent when domestic issues were at stake—was the preserve of a handful of decisionmakers whose primary focus was securing state revenue sources and finessing or overcoming economic constraints so that the distributive policies, particularly those that affected the critical military and security bureaucracies, could continue. The argument made here thus builds on the state-centered approach to the extent that it stresses the importance of state political structures and institutions, as opposed to so-called civil-society ones, as preeminent in shaping economic decision making. It argues, however, that those making the decisions were guided by their understanding of the nature of the Jordanian economy, especially the structure or composition of state revenues. And these considerations frequently played decisive roles in influencing the course of Jordan's foreign policy.

The final step necessary to substantiate the argument involves the presentation of empirical material. Here we must show that as a consequence of an awareness of the critical role that external sources of finance played in maintaining state security, foreign policy—particularly in the form of alliance and realignment decisions—was used by decision makers precisely to reinforce or bolster the budget. We now turn, therefore, to several case studies of Jordan's external relations in its Arab environment during the post-1973 period to demonstrate that an explanation in terms of domestic economic structure best captures the variables accounting for Jordanian alliance behavior.

Syrian-Jordanian Relations

The period 1974–1977 witnessed an unprecedented rapprochement between Jordan and Syria. Relations not only warmed, but approached formal unity.[22] Regional conditions—the situation in the area following the 1973 war, Egyptian President Anwar Sadat's growing ties with the United States, the outbreak of civil war in Lebanon—all certainly influenced the course of relations. However, economic concerns, which have not previously been factored into the analysis of this bilateral relationship, clearly played a key role. First, on a regional level, Jordan and Syria, given the structures of their economies and the nature of their reliance on Arab Gulf state financial aid, found common cause during this period in approaching the oil states with a united front (begging together rather than separately). Indeed, both faced potentially severe budget crises at home without such aid. By working together and ostensibly moving toward political unity and greater economic integration (through a variety of joint committees in 1975–1976), they appear to have succeeded in convincing these states to provide them with the support they had already figured into their annual budget calculations and which, by all accounts, they desperately needed.[23] Moreover, it seems not to have been coincidental that these moves toward unity gradually lost steam shortly after the January 1977 meetings in Riyadh in which the financial aid the two states were demanding was approved. The evidence therefore strongly suggests that the potential political threat that a federal unity between these two represented to the Gulf states (especially Saudi Arabia, with which Jordan share a border) served a purpose akin to extortion, although the funds had in fact already been promised.

In terms of the immediate bilateral relationship rather than the Gulf state target, it appears that Jordanian policymakers were far less keen on movement toward real political integration than their Syrian counterparts seemed to be.[24] Economic cooperation with Syria, on the other hand, was a basic Jordanian concern and a primary tool of statecraft that was aimed at achieving greater budget and economic security. Here, Jordan was largely seeking to alter the conditions that had enabled Syria to close its border with the kingdom in 1970, during the September conflict. Through pushing for greater economic integration, Amman sought to lay the groundwork for stronger and deeper economic ties with Damascus so that Syrian decisionmakers would be forced to think twice before again closing the joint border. Economic cooperation developed during this period to include attempts to lower barriers to trade, to increase industrial integration through participation in shared projects, and jointly to exploit the Yarmuk River waters.[25]

Jordan's gradual move toward Iraq, beginning in late 1978 (to be explained below), eventually made a political break with Syria inevitable, given the poor state of Syrian-Iraqi relations. During the early period of the cooling of Jordanian-Syrian relations, in 1978–1979, economic meetings and interaction continued, if without the intensity of the previous three years. Although some of the joint ventures (a Syrian-Jordanian commercial bank and a free zone on the border) were unable to survive the deterioration in relations, others, remarkably, continued to function normally. Bilateral trade did drop, although it is unclear how much of the drop was due to the political situation and how much to Syrian austerity measures unrelated to relations with Jordan. Through it all, however, the border remained open, a critical fact for a country dependent upon transit trade. The bases of economic integration or cooperation that the Jordanians had viewed as critical to preventing a repetition of 1970 had succeeded at least in part in playing their economic security role. Thanks to the initiatives of the 1975–1977 period, even in the most difficult of days Jordan managed to avoid the economic damage that the 1970 border closure had caused.

The Jordanians tried to reconcile with Syria in 1983. At this stage, their goal appears to have been the reopening of the oil pipeline through Syria from Iraq in order to secure relief for both the Jordanian and the Iraqi economy in the context of the war-induced regional recession.[26] This rapprochement attempt failed, and the Syrians launched a period of "coercive diplomacy," consisting of a series of sabotage and assassination attempts against Jordanian targets.[27] The Syrians did not respond positively until their economic relations with Iran had deteriorated and Jordan appeared to offer the prospect of economic (perhaps as well as political) relief. If political considerations had in fact outweighed economic ones, the Syrians might well have sought reconciliation with Jordan somewhat earlier, since, following its humiliation in its 1982 confrontation with Israel, Damascus was left militarily weakened and strategically vulnerable. It is true that in 1984, after a renewed reconciliation had been set in motion, even economic problems with Iran would not allow Syria to excuse Jordan's rapprochement with Egypt and its warming relations with the P.L.O. Given Syrian regional concerns at the time (Egypt's peace with Israel, Israel's position in Lebanon, and Syria's feud with the P.L.O.), this was simply too great a threat to Syrian political and military security. After sufficient fury had been demonstrated, however, the return of the pro-Syrian Zayd al-Rifa`i to the Jordanian prime ministership seemed to open the way for the improvement in ties that Amman sought in order to end inter-Arab feuding and to reenergize trade. As a result, the two sides held serious discussions that were aimed at reviving bilateral trade and revitalizing the joint companies, although the unity discussions of the mid-1970s were not resurrected.

Jordan's reconciliation with Syria certainly helped to ease Damascus' isolation (which stemmed from its support for Iran). It also lay the groundwork for moving toward a unified Arab stance on the Iran-Iraq war, with an eye to ending that conflict. Even so, while Jordan was striving for good relations with the Syrians and engaging in mediation to repair strained inter-Arab ties, the primary state in its calculations during this period was Iraq. The 1986–1990 period witnessed a number of fluctuations in Jordanian-Syrian ties, but nothing that dramatically changed the course of the relationship. The two continued to differ over policy in Lebanon—as Jordan allowed Syria's archenemy, Iraq, to ship arms to its erstwhile ally in Lebanon, General Michel Aoun—but economic relations seemed to recover, particularly in the realm of trade, although by the end of the period Jordan's own austerity measures made clear the need to cut imports, regardless of provenance.

Jordanian-Iraqi Relations

The record of political relations between Jordan and Iraq during the mid-1970s is mixed, as Iraq, preoccupied with a domestic Kurdish insurgency, involved itself in regional affairs in largely disruptive or subversive ways. The economic record, on the other hand, is different. Beginning in 1975, as its feuding with Syria intensified, Iraq began to manifest interest in expanding its access to the port of Aqaba. To that end, it started to provide support for various forms of infrastructural development that both increased the port's capabilities and facilitated moving goods through it. By the time bilateral political relations began to improve in 1978, trade and infrastructural links had already been established between Jordan and Iraq. The most significant development for Jordan's budget security concerns, however, was the Iraqi push for greater Arab economic support of the "confrontation states" at the November 1978 Arab summit held in response to Egypt's signing of the Camp David accords. At a critical time of decline in expected Arab aid, Iraq stepped in to offer and promote support. Iraqi actual and potential largess served as the foundation for Jordan's gradual shift away from alignment with Syria in the next two years.[28]

The Baghdad summits of November 1978 and March 1979, and Saddam Husayn's role there in mobilizing Arab financial support for the confrontation states, must have seemed a budgetary dream come true for the Jordanians. Political relations continued to warm, and King Husayn was an early and strong supporter of the Iraqi war effort launched in the fall of 1980 against Iran. Trade increased, and a series of joint economic projects was initiated to reinforce ties further. Equally important, unrequited aid from a variety of official and nonofficial Iraqi sources poured into Jordan, with Iraqi state development aid largely targeting the further expansion of the Aqaba port and access to it. With the outbreak of war and Iraq's effective loss of the Gulf as an import and export lane, the Aqaba link had only increased in importance. Jordan was only too willing to oblige Iraq and take further economic advantage of Baghdad's interest.[29]

On the economic front, 1981 began as a good year with aid, loans, and joint projects high on the bilateral agenda. As the war continued, however, and Iraq grew harder pressed economically, particularly after Arab aid to Baghdad began to drop as early as 1983, Iraqi aid to Jordan also dwindled, and Jordanian private-sector activity, which had boomed after the initial outbreak of war, faced the impact of serious Iraqi austerity measures by mid-1982. To support its exporters, Jordan introduced an export credit program for 1983; and by 1984 it had reached an oil barter agreement with the Iraqis to facilitate payment for Jordanian products. Had the war ended shortly thereafter, these stopgap measures might have worked. But Jordanian decisionmakers had, unwittingly perhaps, allowed the kingdom to be drawn into a deeper economic relationship that ultimately threatened the very national economic security the relationship had initially been developed to serve.

As the battles dragged on, and the political ramifications and negative economic impact of the war became clearer, the king undertook what mediation he could to encourage the Iraqis to end the fighting. Political relations remained close and indeed expanded, as a Jordanian-Iraqi-Egyptian axis crystalized. Very early in the war effort, Egypt had begun supplying Iraq with weaponry and personnel, and Jordan served as the transit country. The establishment of the Arab Bridge Company for Maritime Navigation among the three, as well as its connection to the existing Iraqi-Jordanian Land Transport Company, was further evidence of the importance and raison d'être of the relationship.

A ceasefire in the Iran-Iraq war was not reached until August 1988, and, in the meantime, the ceiling set on the export credits program had been violated by both the Iraqis and the Jordanian private sector, to the tune of several hundred million dollars. Before the war's end, Iraq was not interested in addressing this problem; after the war, its own financial distress put it in no position to help reverse the damage done as a result of drawing down Jordan's foreign exchange reserves. By the late summer of 1988, Jordan was again in need of an external bailout.

To a certain extent, one could argue that once again Jordan sought an alliance shift in order to address budgetary difficulties. The establishment in February 1989 of the Arab Cooperation Council, joining Jordan, Egypt, Iraq, and Yemen, was intended to ease Jordan's growing economic problems by creating a larger market for both labor and goods, and encouraging greater cooperation and integration—although by this time the dinar had already crashed and Jordan had begun negotiations with the I.M.F. to reschedule its external debt. If the founding of the A.C.C. was not as dramatic a shift or solution as, for example, Jordan's move away from Syria and toward Iraq in 1978–1979, part of the explanation lay in the options Jordan had. Unlike the situation in 1978, in 1988, Amman was not being actively courted by another Arab state with wealth and power. In 1988 there was no alternative alliance partner who was willing to offer a bailout or a better deal. Jordan could only hope to build on the economic basis it had laid in the early and mid-1980s, no doubt assuming that the end of the Iran-Iraq war would enable Baghdad to return to its prewar position of prominence and economic power in the region. Unfortunately for the Jordanian regime, the problems were too serious and time was running out.

Jordanian-Egyptian Relations

By the mid-1970s, Jordanian-Egyptian relations had begun to warm after years of feuding that stemmed from regional rivalries and opposing orientations in external relations (with Jordan usually in the Western camp and Egypt allied with the Soviet Union). After Egypt's move away from the Soviet Union and expression of interest in pushing forward a regional peace process, a major obstacle to improved bilateral relations was removed, although Jordan's close ties with Syria at the time prevented a full flowering of the relationship. However, the Egyptian-Syrian rapprochement of 1976 and the subsequent discussions of a 1977 Geneva peace conference finally made a further warming of Jordanian-Egyptian ties both possible and necessary, if they were to attend with a united front.

However, Sadat's November 1977 trip to Jerusalem and his subsequent opening of negotiations with Israel ultimately preempted a Geneva conference. King Husayn initially reacted cautiously to the Egyptian president's dramatic initiative. It was only after the similarly cautious Gulf oil states clearly joined the opposition that Jordan took a firmer stand. The financial incentives from these states (and Iraq) served as a reward of sorts for breaking ties with Egypt. In addition, Jordan's heavy reliance on inter-Arab trade meant that the king could ill afford to oppose the Arab League position. As a result, Jordan remained a "confrontation state," and joint economic projects (similar to those initiated earlier with Syria) that had been proposed with Egypt were tabled. Jordan adhered to the Arab League-imposed economic sanctions against Cairo.

Nevertheless, breaking diplomatic relations with Egypt did not mean that Amman completely closed the door. Indeed, Jordan adhered to the letter, but often not the spirit, of the anti-Egypt boycott. It quickly restored flights between the two capitals, and Egyptian labor continued to be recruited to the kingdom. By mid-April 1983, Jordan had taken what appeared to be a bold step in restoring private-sector trade relations with Egypt—arguing that only the public sector was covered by the Arab League boycott—at the same time that it attempted to revive trade ties with Syria.[30] Whereas the Syrians balked, the success of the new policy toward Egypt went almost unnoticed, a lucky development for the Jordanian private sector, which was in desperate need of alternatives to the war-plagued Iraqi market. The security and prosperity of the Jordanian private sector appears to have been a major concern in both of these rapprochement initiatives.[31]

A revival of relations with Egypt, even before the official reestablishment of ties, was possible in part as a result of the role Egypt played in supporting the Iraqi war effort and in part through the shrinking of the Iraqi market for Jordanian exports and the impact of this on the Jordanian private sector. Also crucial was the October 1981 assassination of Sadat. The king believed that the Arab world needed Egypt, particularly as it was facing a threat from the east (Iran), but it had been difficult to contemplate restoring ties with the author of Egypt's separate peace with Israel. Once Sadat was gone, it was easier politically to work with his successor. The restoration of political ties came in September 1984. Although Jordan was strongly criticized by Syria and at least rhetorically by the Gulf states, aside from a number of acts of domestic subversion against Jordan carried out at Syria's behest, no state moved to reprimand or punish the kingdom.

Subsequently, political relations between Egypt and the kingdom expanded to include coordination on the Iran-Iraq war, P.L.O.-Jordanian relations, and the peace process. Egypt's involvement in the war effort eventually created a trilateral Jorda-nian-Egyptian-Iraqi axis, despite Baghdad's failure to restore official ties with Cairo at the time. As noted above, the axis was formalized in the founding of the Arab Cooper-ation Council in February 1989. Bilateral economic ties also developed during this period. Indeed, they had preceded the official reestablishment of formal diplomatic relations. Developments in bilateral trade were of particular importance: targets for trade levels were raised dramatically, and a new, if still minor, role was given to the two countries' respective private sectors.

Summary

Each of these three case studies reveals examples of alliance shifts as well as attempts at reparation of relations. In all cases, although the importance of the broader regional and political context is taken into account, it nonetheless appears that economic factors triggered the foreign policy decision. There is no other way to explain convincingly the Syrian-Jordanian unity moves in the mid-1970s, the Jordanian move away from Syria and into an Iraqi embrace 1978–1979, and Jordan's risking of Arab League wrath in reestablishing relations with Egypt in 1984. In all of these cases, the move was made not simply for economic advantage but because of pressing economic needs that a shift in relations could directly and immediately affect. The argument is not that leaderships will act in a state's economic best interest—a banal conclusion. Rather, it is that economic imperatives associated with shoring up or maintaining state solvency can drive foreign policy decision making.

The Gulf War

Any reader familiar with the 1990–1991 Gulf crisis and war will probably have wondered by now how budget security can be applied to Jordan's alliance behavior during this period. Indeed, the reader may be tempted to conclude that Jordanian decision making during this crisis completely undermines the preceding argument. Although I do not insist that domestic economic structure alone tells the whole tale, this section attempts to explain why the Gulf crisis does not invalidate the argument developed above.[32]

In the first place, there were clearly strong economic considerations at work that militated against Jordan's cutting ties with Iraq through adhering to the U.N.-imposed sanctions. The discussion above briefly surveyed the increasing interdependence of Jordanian-Iraqi political and economic relations. During the first three quarters of 1989, Jordan relied on Iraq for 82.5 percent of its petroleum.[33] Iraq was Jordan's number one trading partner. Thus, implementing sanctions threatened not just future Iraqi good will but also a very real and important market for Jordan's exports.

The equation, however, is not quite so simple, because Jordan also relied heavily upon Kuwait and Saudi Arabia for aid and markets.[34] The issue of Kuwait, after the invasion, was somewhat moot, since the occupation of the country meant that, at least temporarily, it was lost as a market to Jordan no matter what position the king took. Jordan also faced a disruption in the flow of remittances from its large expatriate community in Kuwait, a factor that might have argued for a more circumspect, long-term-oriented policy in order to ensure the economic and employment future of this community. Although Gulf state largess had clearly been on the wane during the 1980s, Saudi Arabia and Kuwait remained the most likely potential Arab sources of aid and concessionary loans.[35] In the wake of the invasion, both states indicated their willingness to reward support for the anti-Iraq coalition. Saudi Arabia agreed to provide half of Jordan's crude oil needs in order to encourage Jordan to line up with the coalition. Conversely, when that policy of "encouragement" did not work, on September 20, 1990, Saudi Arabia announced that it was ending its oil shipments to Jordan; it closed its border to Jordanian traffic and expelled Jordanian diplomats.

As the crisis unfolded, Jordan had several options, all unappealing. To join the coalition would have meant the loss of Iraqi markets and oil, although after the sanctions were imposed, Iraqi markets were largely closed (despite the leakage) no matter what position the kingdom took. The sanctions also meant that Kuwait was temporarily lost as a market; the future of its relations with Jordan would be determined by the outcome of the crisis. Here, there were two possible positive and two possible negative outcomes. If Jordan joined the coalition and it was victorious, or if Jordan sided with Iraq and it was able to hold out, Jordan stood to win. If, on the other hand, Jordan chose to side with the future loser (whether Iraq or the coalition), at the least access to Kuwait would have been lost—which is, of course, what happened.

Joining the coalition would have offered Jordan the possibility of increased Arab and Western aid to offset losses incurred during the crisis, whereas failure to join the coalition both ruled out any such assistance and offered no other options. Acquiescing in coalition policy would also probably have meant swift and more substantial financial assistance for Jordan to address the (largely South Asian) refugee problem it faced as those fleeing Kuwait poured across its borders. In the event, as the crisis unfolded, and Amman remained outside the coalition, the international community was slow to assist Jordan in its efforts to provide relief to the incoming refugees.

Any attempt at financial accounting of the positive and negative impact of each of these options would be at best imprecise. Nonetheless, from the standpoint of short-term budget security, the pro-coalition option would appear to have been, at least on the surface, the wiser strategy. Why, then, did the king act otherwise?

It may be argued that the king's sense of Arabism, which by all accounts was quite strong, motivated him to seek an inter-Arab solution and ultimately to refuse to abandon Iraq. Then, however, one would have to be able to argue why such a sense of Arabism led him to stand more firmly behind Arab Iraq than Arab Kuwait. One could also argue that the king simply miscalculated, although his survival for over four decades as monarch of a small and vulnerable country certainly suggests that it would have been the uncommon exception. More plausible is that the traditional bases or factors used to assess options had changed, and the king was reacting to the new environment.

One of the key components of the new environment was popular opinion, the "Jordanian street." The argument has long been made that Husayn had to take into account his domestic constituency. The reference has generally meant the Palestinian component of the population, the implication being that the king could not take certain steps if they were likely to upset the kingdom's Palestinians. Yet this community's size and importance had not stopped Husayn taking a number of unpopular steps over the years, most notably the military assaults against the Palestinian resistance in 1970–1971. Hence, if one wants to argue that the king was always sensitive to "the street" one must also be able to explain the occasions on which he was apparently able to ignore it. It would seem prudent to reexamine those past crises in which popular opinion has been deemed to have played an influential role to determine if in fact its role was as central as it has been described. In any case, the case still has to be made for why the pressures from below had special significance in the Gulf crisis and how they related to the concept of budget security.

The basis of the argument here is that developments in the 1980s, in particular the evolution of a serious economic crisis, gradually undermined the traditional bases of budget and regime support. When the crisis finally exploded in economic riots in April 1989, following the announcement of I.M.F.-mandated austerity measures, the regime reacted by launching a process of political liberalization, a survival strategy aimed at defusing discontent while setting the stage for significant changes in the political and economic systems. As a result of the relaxation of political repression that accompanied the liberalization, by the time of the Gulf crisis, Jordanians were better positioned to express publicly and vocally their position on any issue. In fact, spring 1990 had witnessed unprecedented demonstrations in the kingdom related to events in Palestine.

In sum, the economic crisis of the late 1980s meant that the government's distributional capabilities had severely declined. With no new external financial savior available, the state budget could no longer sustain the regime's part of the "political acquiescence in exchange for allocation and domestic security" bargain. Therefore, as the kingdom continued along the path of debt rescheduling and belt tightening, when severe rioting ensued in April 1989, the king initiated a process of political liberalization that led to Jordan's first free elections in thirty-three years.

In addition, given the state's waning distributional capabilities in the context of a popular political liberalization process, the state would have been hard pressed financially, even with a massive infusion from Kuwait or Saudi Arabia, to call up and sustain the repression needed to silence its pro-Iraqi population into acceptance of a pro-coalition stance. Moreover, given that the traditional institutions of coercion—the army and the intelligence apparatus—were overwhelmingly staffed with Transjordanians, who were as enamored of Saddam as were the Palestinians, the cost to the regime, in both material and legitimacy terms, would have been tremendous. It seems unlikely that it would ever have crossed the king's mind to fight his population—across the communal divide—in the way he probably would have had to do, had he chosen a clear pro-coalition position.

Hence by 1990, budget security for Jordan had a much more important domestic component than at any other time during the period under consideration in this paper. The degree of state autonomy suggested by the state-centered model had begun to give way to greater societal importance. That was clear from the role the private sector or some of its members appear to have played in influencing the course of relations with Egypt and Iraq during the Iran-Iraq war. With the revenue and aid from the oil states dwindling and unlikely to be restored on a long-term basis, the economic crisis of 1988–1989 further increased the importance of domestic extraction for supporting the budget. Add to this the unparalleled and unified Jordanian popular mobilization that accompanied the invasion of Kuwait, and the resources (both material and moral) that would have been needed to check or repress this outpouring of emotion, and one has the most important components in explaining Jordanian policy toward the coalition and Iraq.

The argument here is not just that pressures from below had a greater impact on Jordanian foreign policy in the period following the liberalization than they did before. There is a budget-security aspect to the economic crisis as well. A state can deal with an economic crisis in two major ways: it can seek a short-term fix, which involves securing additional revenues rather quickly and avoiding painful domestic economic restructuring; or it can attempt to address the crisis through a series of policies that amount to restructuring. The second strategy, which is perhaps sounder for the national economy in the long run is, nonetheless, potentially subversive in the short run, because diversifying may require upsetting standing sociopolitical coalitions.

The brief case studies show that, in the past, the Jordanian government, like many others, had chosen to avoid the restructuring option on numerous occasions. It preferred to maintain budget security through the quick-fix, aid-infusion model. It jointly sought Gulf aid with Syria in the mid-1970s. Later that same decade, it shifted its alliance from Syria to Iraq when Iraq offered greater financial incentives. At some point, however, one may run out of such options. At that point, the leadership must bite the bullet and face socioeconomic and political choices that may threaten its power or the coalition of the forces that underpin it. Such was the situation that confronted the Jordanian leadership in spring 1989 when, in the context of economic restructuring, it launched a process of political liberalization.

Jordanian-Israeli Peace

Before concluding, it is useful to examine the most recent foreign-policy challenges, those associated with the move toward Arab-Israeli peace following the Gulf war, and explore their economic aspects. With the destruction of Iraq and the curtailment of its regional power, there was little question that Jordan would make its way to the U.S.-Russian-sponsored Middle East peace talks that began in Madrid in October 1991. Little progress was made, however, until the so-called Oslo agreement of August 1993 was announced, thereby reenergizing the Arab-Israeli negotiations. An examination of the Jordanian response to the unfolding of events since the signing of the Palestinian-Israeli accord further reinforces the salience of the budget security argument.

In the first place, it is clear that old habits die hard. The promises made by various members of the international community to provide development aid and other assistance to help support and institutionalize the peace struck a resonant chord with Jordanian decision makers. A number of years of austerity had not erased the sweet memory of the kingdom's former aid addiction. New infusions of money in the quick-fix tradition could well help ease the country's continuing struggle with belt tightening, which was leaving increasing numbers of Jordanians below the poverty line.

Selling the peace process in Jordan raised numerous sensitive issues that potentially threatened stability, many of which could be calmed or soothed (or so decisionmakers appeared to believe) if new aid commitments were secured. A population that feels itself to be less under siege economically and understands that the peace process is responsible for bringing relief is less likely to take an openly oppositional stance. Moreover, the political atmosphere in Jordan in 1993–1994 was somewhat changed from the excitement, ferment, and uncertainty that followed the beginning of the liberalization. In 1990, at the time of the outbreak of the Gulf crisis, the outlines of the liberalization were not yet clear, and the king and his advisors were still learning how to manage a liberalization along lines acceptable to them. This was a time of great uncertainty for the regime. By the time of the elections of 1993, however, and certainly in their wake, the ruling circle could be sure of a number of key variables. The secular opposition had been shown to be without substantial mass following or appeal. The Islamists had had their power in the Parliament cut, largely thanks to a late summer 1993 amendment to the electoral law. A substantial degree of freedom of the press and expression had not only served as a safety valve to release pent-up frustration but had also allowed the regime better to chart the political spectrum and gauge its power. In addition, the swift and crushing defeat of Iraq had sapped many Jordanians of the mobilizing energy they had manifested during the Gulf crisis. It left them more pliable, if not convinced, when it came to Jordan's own signing of peace accords—much less likely to constitute a domestic oppositional front that could pose a threat if the regime moved in a direction that it found displeasing.

But there was another element as well: intercommunal relations. First, the fact that P.L.O. chief Yasir `Arafat and his people had negotiated in secret, outside the realm of coordination with any other Arab leader, led not only to expressions of anger by the king but also to Jordanian perceptions of Palestinian ingratitude and to strong voices of concern that Jordan needed to secure its own interests, since the Palestinians had moved unilaterally to secure theirs. Closely related to this issue, in the discussions of aid or foreign investment that might be attracted or courted as a result of the peace, Jordanian policy makers and editorialists expressed great concern that the kingdom not be shortchanged; hence the Jordanian demand that the kingdom be compensated for the years that it had hosted its large Palestinian refugee population. To be sure, the demand reflected in part a desire for recognition of Amman's contributions, but it also reaffirmed a fact of central concern, for varying reasons, to the country's Palestinian and Transjordanian populations alike: that the refugees should be eligible to return to a Palestinian state. Even if there should be substantial Palestinian repatriation, a larger issue concerns many Transjordanians: since a majority of the kingdom's wealth is held by Palestinians (which is certainly the perception), either Jordan, without external assistance, will become an economic colony of the Palestinian state (or possibly Israel), or a wealthy and ascendant Palestinian bourgeoisie—whether it returns to Palestine or continues to reside in Jordan—will eventually control the country.

Thus, in addition to the regime's more secure position in 1993–1994 than in 1990, the differences in intercommunal perceptions of the threats versus the potential benefits of the peace process meant that a broad cross-communal coalition (such as emerged during the Gulf crisis) was unlikely to challenge the regime. Therefore, the king could take the controversial move of quickly signing first a peace accord and then a full agreement (in July and October 1994 respectively) despite clearly identifiable opposition to the move. The financial rewards were potentially substantial (if oversold), and the threat of a domestic backlash was under control.

Conclusions

Consideration of how to ensure or reinforce state budget security (solvency) can play a key role in directing a leadership's foreign-policy decisionmaking. However, as the last two cases have shown, the bases upon which budget security rests may shift, just as its centrality in decision making may vary. From a fair degree of autonomy from society, thanks to Jordan's ability to rely for years on external grants-in-aid to keep it solvent, the Jordanian state gradually descended into insolvency by the late 1980s. Arab aid had declined, state calculations were not substantially revised, and the various attempts at quick fixes (not involving domestic economic structural reform) had not succeeded.

Hence, after the riots of 1989, a shaken regime found itself forced to make concessions to Jordanian society in the form of political liberalization. This happened, of course, against the backdrop of increasing state belt-tightening and the implementation of a range of policies called for by the I.M.F. that weighed more and more heavily on Jordan's middle and lower classes. It was in the early stages of these shifts in regime policy that Saddam Husayn invaded Kuwait, and the economic and political shifts already under way help to explain the king's subsequent policy course.

Jordan's participation in the Middle East peace process—or perhaps, more accurately, the nature of its participation in the process—can also be clarified by using the concept of budget security. Iraq's defeat and the combined U.S. and Soviet pressure to attend the conference left little room for any Middle Eastern actor to stay away from Madrid. Likewise, although most admit that Jordan and Israel had largely worked out the details of their agreement, the king's decision not to move ahead with a unilateral announcement of an accord was certainly due to a combination of political and economic factors. Once the Palestinians had their Oslo, Jordan could move swiftly ahead. A *Jordan Times* report of summer 1994 noted that when the king was made aware of the difference in economic benefits that would attend an end to the state of war between Jordan and Israel, rather than simply a declaration of an end to the state of belligerency, he quickly moved toward the former.

Developments since the signing of the Jordanian-Israeli peace treaty are in some ways reminiscent of the pre-1989 period, as the king did his best to court Israeli and American good will in the hope of securing more aid and more foreign investment, even though Jordan's adoption of an openly anti-Iraqi policy and its flirtation with joining a United States-sponsored Turkish-Israeli axis were unpopular at home. Yet two developments demonstrate that despite a clear retrenchment in the political liberalization Jordan has not returned to pre-1989 business as usual. Both relate to the growing voice of the private sector. The first is the open displeasure that certain segments of the business community displayed regarding the regime's anti-Iraq tilt in 1995, and the continuing visits to Iraq by Jordanian trade and industry delegations, despite the regime's official position. The other development has been the support in some sectors of the business community for the peace treaty, given the tourism and other private-sector investment opportunities they are working to take advantage of.

Both of these developments indicate a shift in the relative weight of factors that influence regime thinking on revenue sources and, by extension, extra-regime influence on foreign policy (economic or otherwise). None of this is to say that the king is no longer the final arbiter, although the passing of King Husayn in February 1999 and the assumption of the throne by his eldest son, `Abdallah, leaves open the possibility for change. The evidence does suggest, however, that the regime will face a more complex set of considerations when making foreign policy. The budget security concept can help explain regime policy formation, even as the environment in which it is constructed—one in which the state as a primary recipient of external rents is in retreat—continues to shift toward one in which certain societal actors play a more prominent role.

Notes

*   For research support that made this project possible, I would like to thank the School of International Relations, University of Southern California. Much of this article is based on my book *Jordan's Inter-Arab Relations: The Political Economy of Alliance Making*.

1   Examples have included Jack Snyder, *Myths of Empire: Domestic Politics and International Ambition*, and Helen Milner, "International Theories of Cooperation among Nations: Strengths and Weaknesses." The work of such scholars as Peter Katzenstein and Peter Gourevitch has long been in this tradition, but was not generally viewed as within the realm of security studies.

2   For early uses, see, for example, such works as Nicole Ball's *Security and Economy in the Third World*.

3   Brand, *Jordan's Inter-Arab Relations*.

4   Balance-of-power theory has long been central to the realist paradigm of international relations. Balancing behavior involves a state's allying or aligning itself with other states to counter a perceived threat. In bandwagoning behavior, a state aligns itself with the threatening power so as to avoid as far as possible the impact of opposing such a state and losing to it. Stephen Walt's *The Origins of Alliances* explores the concepts in great detail.

5   This is clear in a number of classic works on the "Arab system": Malcolm Kerr, *The Arab Cold War: Gamal `Abd al-Nasir and His Rivals, 1958–1970*; Patrick Seale, *The Struggle for Syria: A Study in Postwar Arab Politics, 1945–1959*; and Alan Taylor, *The Arab Balance of Power*.

6   Paul Noble, "The Arab System: Pressures, Constraints, and Opportunities," pp. 60–61.

7   Ali E. Hillal Dessouki, "The Primacy of Economics: The Foreign Policy of Egypt."

8   See Stephen R. David, "Explaining Third World Alliances."

9   For a useful summary and discussion of the utility of these three approaches, see John G. Ikenberry, David A. Lake, and Michael Mastanduno, "Introduction: Approaches to Explaining American Foreign Economic Policy," p. 4.

10   For a discussion of the concept of rent as used here and of the "rentier state," which gained great currency in Middle Eastern studies beginning in the late 1980s, see especially Giacomo Luciani, "Allocation vs. Production States."

11   Not surprisingly, this percentage is a point of major disagreement between the two communities, and the Jordanian state, which conducted the most recent census in late 1995, has refused to release the information. Palestinians have long said that they constitute between 60 and 70

percent of the kingdom's population. This was certainly close to the truth when the kingdom included the West Bank. Following the disengagement of July 1988, however, the 60–70 percent figures are unrealistic estimates. On the other hand, the rise in Transjordanian nationalism has led to a contention on that side of the communal divide that Palestinians constitute only between 35 and 40 percent of the population (depending upon whom one asks).

12   These figures actually understate the state's role, since the private sector has depended for much of its contribution to the economy on contracts generated by the state. Moreover, statistics on the state sector in Jordan have generally not included some establishments that look private but have a large state component.

13   For a discussion of civil society in Jordan, see Laurie A. Brand, "In the Beginning Was the State: The Quest for Civil Society in Jordan."

14   I interviewed a number of members of these chambers during fall 1991 and summer 1992.

15   Federation of Jordanian Chambers of Commerce, annual reports, selected years.

16   Private sector influence does, however, appear to have been exercised on an individual and ad hoc basis. The rather small group of decisionmakers is bound by a network of family, school, regional, or business ties. These ties opened the doors for informal lobbying on a variety of issues. This form of interest articulation was likely to take place on an individual or a small-group, not a broad sectoral, basis. In this way, it was not at all difficult for certain select businessmen to gain the ear of the relevant decisionmaker. The beginning of political liberalization in 1989 opened the way for more open and effective lobbying by more formal organizations, but much business in the kingdom continues to be conducted on the basis of individual contacts and ties.

17   For the larger study from which this is taken, I interviewed numerous former ministers, economic policy advisors, economists, and mid-to-upper-level employees in a number of key economy-related ministries.

18   For a full discussion, see Brand, *Jordan's Inter-Arab Relations*, pp. 66–69.

19   Author's interview with Jawad al-`Anani, former minister of supply, minister of labor, and minister of industry and trade, July 20, 1992.

20   Author's interview with Tahir Kan`an, former minister of planning and minister of occupied territories affairs, June 22, 1992.

21   See Luciani, *The Arab State*.

22   The most detailed discussion of the unity and integration talks of this period is Syrian Arab News Agency and Jordanian News Agency, *Masirat al-Takamul bayna Suriya w-al-Urdunn: 'Ala Darb al-Wahdah*.

23   Author's interview with Zayd al-Rifa`i, former prime minister of Jordan, July 11, 1992. See also Brand, *Jordan's Inter-Arab Relations*, pp. 154–55. The 1974 aid promised by Rabat had not been forthcoming to either Syria or Jordan, and in January 1976, Saudi Arabia had suspended development aid to Syria.

24   Author's interview with Rifa`i; author's interview with Mudar Badran, former prime minister of Jordan, July 19, 1993.

25   For details of trade agreements with Syria as well as discussions of joint companies, see Hashimite Kingdom of Jordan, Ministry of Trade, *Majmu`at al-Ittifaqiyyat al-Iqtisadiyyah w-al-Tujariyyah bayna al-Mamlakah al-Urdunniyyah al-Hashimiyyah w-al-Duwal al-`Arabiyyah* (hereafter, *Majmu`at*).

26   Economist Intelligence Unit, *Quarterly Economic Report: Syria and Jordan*, no. 3 (1983): 17.

27   Patrick Seale uses the phrase "coercive diplomacy" in *Asad of Syria: The Struggle for the Middle East*, p. 465.

28   For details of trade agreements with Iraq as well as discussions of joint companies, see *Majmu`at*, vol. 2.

29 See Brand, *Jordan's Inter-Arab Relations*, pp. 206–9.

30 *Middle East Economic Digest*, March 11, 1983.

31 For details of trade agreements with Egypt as well as discussions of joint companies, see *Majmu`at*, vol. 1.

32 For a lengthier discussion of this argument and the attendant evidence, see Laurie A. Brand, "Liberalization and Changing Political Coalitions: The Bases of Jordan's 1990–91 Gulf Crisis Policy."

33 See *Middle East Economic Survey* no. 33 (1989), p. 47; *Washington Post*, January 9, 1990. For trade statistics see Hashimite Kingdom of Jordan, *Statistical Abstract*, selected years.

34 See Hashimite Kingdom of Jordan, *Statistical Abstract*, selected years.

35 Only Saudi Arabia had continued to pay in full the commitment it had made at the March 1979 Baghdad summit (Baghdad II). By 1984, Jordan was receiving only about half of the nearly $670 million per annum it had been promised at that meeting.

8

The Foreign Policy of Syria

C. Ernest Dawn

Middle Eastern international relations have been aptly characterized as involving two concomitant factors, both of which have long endured, indeed since the "Eastern Question" emerged two centuries ago. First, a vulnerable regional political system (the Ottoman Middle East) was exposed to a threatening, expanding neighboring system (Europe). Both sides reacted to the resulting opportunities and threats. Second, both political systems were characterized by a multiplicity of autonomous political entities, a number of distinct states on the European side matched in the Middle East by what might be dubbed states, de facto states, and would-be states. They differed in size and strength from great powers to non-state ethnic or religious groupings such as the Armenians, Druze, or Maronites (and, I would add, political factions and individuals), but all interacted in a kaleidoscopic, multilateral fashion.

Most participants in the interaction between the two systems depicted, if they did not view, the interaction as a conflict of homogeneous entities. In fact, alliances across the divide have been the rule. Not only have polities within one system allied with polities in the other system against intrasystem rivals, but groups within polities have also allied with groups within rival polities within both their own system and the rival system. Perhaps the most notable result of this process in the twentieth century was the creation of the Syrian Arab Republic, the self-styled "Beating Heart of Arabism," in territory where at the beginning of the preceding century both Syria and Arab nationalism were totally unknown concepts.

Europe since 1914 (including the United States) has been by far more powerful than the Middle East. Even today, when regional armies in the Middle East have sometimes reached massive size, the materiel is largely of foreign, mostly Western, origin and, even more important, whenever combat endures beyond a short period, all regional actors, including Israel, must depend on the outside for re-supply. The disparity in material power between the two regions has been accompanied by a cleavage in culture that antedated the disparity in power. The Ottoman territories were Islamic, Europe was Christian. Through the many centuries of contact, in each region the prevailing religion was considered to be inseparable from the distinctive culture. When the great gap in material wealth and power became obvious, the self-view of the Islamic East was severely injured. As is the common, probably universal, reaction in such cases, intellectuals and politicians concentrated on defense of the injured self-view.

The leadership in the Ottoman lands searched for the secret of Western might and prosperity. They found it not only in Western science and technology but also, notably, in the patriotism and nationalism of the European peoples, seen as the ultimate source of European greatness. Since patriotism and nationalism were believed to be the source of European power and glory, those who possessed or aspired to office and benefits in the Ottoman state began to regard the empire as a nation-state. The Ottoman nation had not always been lowly and abased, they learned from history. Instead, the Islamic people in the past had created a great civilization, in fact modernity itself, which the West had borrowed, while the Islamic people deviated from true Islam. So the Ottoman elites set about reviving the moribund Ottoman patriotism that in the past, they believed, had created the essentials of modern civilization. In constructing an Ottoman nation in an Ottoman fatherland, the Ottoman elites were following the common pattern in the construction of nationalism. Those who would create the nation are contenders for power, and the arena of their contention is almost always an existing state that they seek to capture, secede from, or perhaps merge with some larger polity. As possessors of or contenders for office and benefits in the Ottoman state, most of the Arab elites readily adopted Ottomanism, and most of them remained loyal to the empire until its collapse in 1918.

Contenders for office and benefits within a state, even at the highest level, are based in a specific locality. Consequently, politics begins as competition for office and benefits in the family and the neighborhood, and extends outward and upward through a variety of territorial divisions, commonly administrative but also at least partly demographic, or geographic, to culminate in the supreme state organ. It is a rare polity whose elites do not present themselves to their constituencies as representatives and agents of their immediate friends and neighbors. Thus, when the Arab elites in the region that the West called Syria, vaguely defined as extending from the Mediterranean to the desert and from the Taurus to Sinai, examined their history as depicted by Europeans, they discovered that the Syrians had been a great civilized people in the past. Like the Turcophone Ottomanists, those newly conscious of their Syrianness appealed to a past civilization that had used the Arabic language. As a result, the new Syrianists also took pride in their Arabness, though Syrianism predominated, and most retained Ottomanism as the highest loyalty. Ottoman Syrianism was most popular among the Greek Orthodox, especially those located in Beirut, but many Maronites espoused the doctrine. Most notably, Maronite notables who dominated the administration of the autonomous province of Mount Lebanon could speak with pride of their Arab Syrianism while insisting on the complete autonomy of the Mountain.

Ottomanism and Ottomanist Syrianism were ideologies created or adopted by notables who succeeded in holding, or at least in having their turn in, office. In every locality and within every religious community, however, there were unsuccessful or discontented notables who dissented. Some Greek Orthodox and most Greek Catholic notables favored an independent Syria under French protection. A very important opposition faction of Maronite notables differed from the dominant faction by seeking an independent Lebanon under French protection, in which the Maronites would hold a favored position, even though the lands that they claimed as the Lebanese homeland did not have a Maronite majority. Political factionalism has thus been at least as important as confessionalism. By the beginning of the twentieth century, major opposition Sunni notables who were mostly inhabitants of the provinces of Beirut, Damascus, and Hama, had become Arab nationalists; they initially argued that as the true Islam of the ancestors was Arab, the religious and cultural leadership of the Ottoman Empire should be Arab, and then, when their demands were rejected by the Young Turks, they promoted complete Arab independence. Syrianism had a place in their self-view, but it was decidedly subordinate to Arabism.

The Ottoman collapse in 1918 eliminated Ottomanism. Arabism was left as the predominant ideology. By the 1930s, among Arabs, especially in geographical Syria and Iraq, a vision of history that offered solace and hope became widespread. In this vision, modernity, as exemplified by the West, was Islamic in origin, bestowed by the Deity on the Arabs through the Prophet Muhammad. Although the Europeans had borrowed the elements of modernity from Islam, the true believers corrupted true Islam. In fact, the Arabs were the chosen people even before Islam. The various Semitic peoples of the Ancient Near East were Arabs who migrated from Arabia into the Fertile Crescent, where they created the ancient civilizations. The Islamic expansion was the final and complete divine mission bestowed on the Arabs who, inspired by God's perfect revelation, created the first civilization based on reason. Unfortunately, the Arabs, despite their many virtues, were easily corrupted by foreigners who took advantage of Arab dissensions that were engendered by Arab individualism. In this historical vision, the Arabs were victims of their imperialist neighbors, especially the Aryans such as the Persians and Greeks, who plunged the ancient Arabs into the Jahaliya, from which the Prophet rescued them by the preaching of Islam, and most notably the Europeans, who imprisoned the Arabs in a second Jahaliya. To escape their present abasement, the Arabs must return to the true Islam of the ancestors, eliminate the traitorous collaborators with Western imperialism, restore Arab unity, and then lead in the revival of all Islam. The internal enemies were the tyrannical rulers and the obscurantist 'ulama', who for their selfish purposes had impoverished the masses by imprisoning them in superstition. It was even suggested that the true Islam of the ancestors was socialist in character.

Such is the historical vision expounded in Darwish al-Miqdadi's textbooks, which were widely used during the 1930s, in the works of Michel `Aflaq and the Nasirists, and in the school textbooks of Ba`thist Syria and Iraq and Nasirist Egypt. It must be emphasized that this version of Arabism is based squarely on Islamic modernism. It is not a doctrine of secular nationalism. Gamal `Abd al-Nasir was an Islamic modernist. "Religion is a fundamental pillar of the revolution," Nasir said to the president of Iraq in 1967. Later in the same year, Nasir said to Simone de Beauvoir, "We do not want you to accept the saying that Islam may be an obstacle to development. In my opinion, the distinctive feature of Islam is that it is a religion open to all ages and all stages of development. I always quote the Prophet Muhammad calling the people to practice ijtihad in the face of the innovations of the ages, 'you are the best informed concerning the things of your world.'" Among the Arabs a long succession of Christian intellectuals have held Islam in high esteem as the source, or at least the mark, of

Arab greatness, as the true expression of the Arab genius that all Arabs must take pride in and love.

The Ottoman collapse left the people of geographical Syria face-to-face with European imperialism. Britain and France utilized the confessional and factional rivalries among the inhabitants, but the latter were able to use similar rivalries between Britain and France and even within each of the two imperialist countries. The collapse of Russia and Germany, along with American isolationism, left Britain and France the only powers capable of intervention, but these two powers were bitter rivals. Attempting to restrict if not exclude French influence, the British utilized the doctrine of national self-determination, newly dominant in 1918, in place of the older doctrine of the white man's burden, which was transformed into the League of Nations mandate. The British, immediately after the end of the First World War, were in the advantageous position of being the occupying power in all the lands except the future Lebanon, and they supported a group that proclaimed the independence of a Syrian Arab state in its natural frontiers from the Taurus to Sinai and from the Mediterranean to the desert, and the economic federation of that Syrian Arab state with the brother Arab Iraq. When challenged by France, which moved militarily against the Syrian Arab state, the British acted as great powers usually have done in the Middle East: they decided that maintaining acceptable ties with other great powers had precedence over relations with regional clients or would-be clients. Thus, the British had to content themselves with Palestine (east and west of the Jordan) and leave the rest of the Syrian lands to France.

The population of the French mandated territories was sharply divided regarding the future. At one extreme, among the Maronites the clergy and an important group of notables favored independence for Lebanon under French tutelage and protection, in complete separation from the Arabs. Similarly, the leaders of two compact confessional minorities, the `Alawites and the Druze of the interior, tended to favor independence or autonomy under the French. At the other extreme, most Sunnis outside the Ottoman province of Beirut insisted on an independent Syria that included Lebanon completely free of the French presence. This position was supported by some opposition Sunni and Shi^ca notables in greater Lebanon. The Greek Orthodox, most of the leading Maronites, and the dominant Sunni notables of Beirut province would accept a united Syria under French mandate, but were opposed to a completely independent united Syrian state. French efforts to bridge the gap were fruitless. Through the 1920s and into the 1930s, the advocates of an independent united Syria would not accept Lebanese independence or a French presence. Consequently, although some French officials favored a united Syrian state, the influential French friends of the Maronite separatists, and consequently the Syrian minorities (`Alawites and Druze), ensured that Syrian unity died as soon as it was embodied in an administrative change. In addition to the Maronite separatists, the French were supported by other Maronites, Orthodox, Druze, Sunnis, and Shi^ca in Lebanon, who were favorable to Syrian unity under French mandate but insisted on Lebanese independence if the French presence were terminated. In the 1930s, a group of notables throughout the French mandated territories, including leading Maronite notables and the patriarch, formed an alliance on the principle of guaranteeing the independence and territorial integrity of Lebanon, provided it had "an Arab face." France, weakened by defeat in Europe, was no match for this coalition, which in 1943, with the support of Britain, the United States, and the Soviet Union, gained control of Lebanon and Syria and won independence for the two countries.

With the creation of the Syrian Arab Republic, Syrianist Arabism became the overwhelmingly dominant ideology. Explicit sectarian independence was given up by the `Alawites and Druze. Non-Arab Syrianism, however, was adopted by some Greek Orthodox and a few `Alawites and Sunnis who joined the secret Lebanon-based Syrian National (later Social National) Party in advocating the creation of a Greater Syria (later Fertile Crescent plus, incongruously, Cyprus) that was to be totally separate from Arab lands and peoples. The dominance of Syrian Arab nationalism did not put an end to factionalism. Pre-Ba`thist Syrian politics might be considered to be, and was sometimes declared by participants to be, a contest between Damascus and Aleppo, with occasional appeals to the claims of Homs and Hama. In fact, Syrian politics was dominated by two great rival coalitions: one, later to be called the National Party, was composed of the dominant factions of Damascus and Hama and the opposition factions of Aleppo and Homs; the other, later to be called the People's Party, joined together the dominant factions of Aleppo and Homs with the opposition factions of Damascus and Hama.

The creation of a sovereign Syria with fixed boundaries did not eliminate the practise of alliances by Syrian factions with non-Syrian political elements against their Syrian rivals. Among the independent Arab states, Syria has been ostensibly the most faction-ridden state. Quite possibly, the sense of identity and state formation have shallower roots in Syria than elsewhere. Egypt possessed a state formed through generations, even centuries, or some might say millennia, of independence or autonomy. Iraq and Jordan had monarchies created by Arab nationalist monarchs, protected and assisted by a British presence devoted to an Arab nationalist policy. Lebanon's major component, Mount Lebanon, had a long history of autonomy, and there the French applied a consistent policy. Syria had no such history, and the French frequently shifted abruptly in futile attempts to find a policy satisfactory to both particularists and nationalists. This helps to explain why Syrian oppositions have so frequently engaged in joint action with non-Syrians.

Syrian opposition factions (most of them later united as the People's Party) from the very foundation of independent Syria pointed to the deficiencies of the 1943 state as measured by the norms of Arabism. The government was strongly attacked for not gaining Syria's natural frontiers, especially for renouncing the claim to Lebanon, and for rejecting offers of Arab union from Iraq or Jordan. The internal opposition's position was dangerous to the government as a result of the appeal that Arab union had to many Syrians and the advantages possessed by the neighboring suitors. Jordan had some advocates in Syria, but its small size and relative lack of resources greatly limited its appeal. Iraq, however, a major oil-producer that possessed other resources superior to Syria's, had a much greater following in Syria. Undoubtedly, the Syrian opposition's turn to Iraq or Jordan was strongly motivated in part by the desire for support against their Syrian enemies, but they also genuinely believed union to be necessary, as did many Syrians. Concern for Arab unity was fed by strong fears for Syria's security. France had withdrawn from Syria with the greatest reluctance, and showed every sign of seeking to return. The Zionists were a greatly feared enemy believed to be bent on dominion from the Euphrates to Sinai. Even for an Arab country, Syria was woefully weak militarily, and lacked the financial resources to increase its military strength. Moreover, in the early post-war period, the only source of arms and financial assistance was the West, in fact the United States. The two Hashimite kingdoms were tied by treaties to Britain and both monarchs and government urged alliance with Turkey and the West in the emerging cold war.

Hashimite foreign policy had many opponents in the Arab countries. In the established Arabist self-view, the West (with the United States now added to Europe) was the millennial enemy, ever seeking to subjugate and exploit the Arabs. That great threat must be defeated if the Arab nation was to survive. Many believed that the British sought to gain control of Syria through the annexation of Syria by Iraq or Jordan, or the formation of an anti-Soviet Middle East alliance including Turkey and the Arabs. The Hashimite monarchs and governments were considered by many to be creations and puppets of the British. Nevertheless, in 1943–44, the Hashimite states were the only Arab states offering some form of unity or cooperation to Syria. The two obvious alternatives to Iraq or Jordan were Saudi Arabia, a nascent giant oil-producer, projected to be super-wealthy, and Egypt, by far the most important Arab state. Egypt's cultural and educational leadership of the Arabs was without rival. It was the most populous and the richest Arab country; it possessed the greatest military force in the Arab countries, and was among the few (unlike Iraq) located so that it possessed the capability of immediate military intervention in Palestine. War against the Zionists without Egypt was unthinkable. From the standpoint of the rulers of Syria, Egyptian military power, unlike Iraqi and Jordanian, was located a very safe distance from Syria. But neither of the two alternatives to the Hashimites in 1943–44 had any enthusiasm for Arab unity. Both were keenly aware of Arab military shortcomings in the face of impending threats.

In response to Syria's problems, the government of 1943–1949 utilized Arab nationalism in the formulation of a policy that has been embraced by all governments ever since. Lebanese independence and territorial integrity was justified by Lebanon's acknowledgment of and fidelity to its Arab character by freeing itself in perpetuity from any non-Arab presence instead of remaining a base for imperialism in the Arab homeland. Syria, the doctrine asserts, favors Greater Syrian union, but only in a democratic republican form and free of foreign domination. Syrian unity, however, was subordinate to full comprehensive Arab unity, which must be led by the big brother, Egypt. Egyptian and Saudi fears of the unbearable collective security obligations inherent in Arab union were overcome by the threat to them posed by the Hashimites. The Saudi-Hashimite rivalry, which antedated 1914, was not closed with the Saudi expulsion of the Hashimites from Arabia. Moreover, Iraq demonstrated tendencies that were independent of Hashimite dynastic ambitions by laying claim to Kuwait in 1939. Egypt had no traditional interests east of Sinai, though opposition elements had been advocating Arabism since the late 1920s, and from 1936 on the Palestinian uprising resulted in popular and elite demonstrations of support for the Palestinians. The great Egyptian interest was the total expulsion of the British from the Nile Valley. Iraqi and Jordanian achievement of Fertile Crescent and Greater Syrian union would have created a large pro-British Arab state, an intolerable threat to the total independence and unity of the Nile Valley. So the Egyptians and the Saudis, after much hesitation, answered the Syrian call. The government of 1943–1949 joined with Egypt, Saudi Arabia, and Lebanon in forming the Arab League on the basis of the sovereignty and territorial integrity of the Arab countries (in the case of the Palestinians, the right to self-determination). In response to the expressed desire for closer association than the League provided, Syria supported an unsuccessful Iraqi proposal that the League have a collective security character. Syria agreed with Iraq and Jordan that member states could enter into closer association, but also agreed with Egypt and Saudi Arabia that the League had the right to monitor the external relations of the members. The League pact included a provision regarding closer associations. Although it did not provide for League authority over the affairs of its members, its existence provided a rationalization for accusing governments of violating the Arab consensus, and the League meetings very frequently acted as if such authority was provided for in the pact.

The notion of comprehensive Arab unity provided an ideological tool for the founding fathers of independent Syria, to counter both their internal enemies and the expansionist Iraqis and Jordanians who were pushing for Fertile Crescent unity. At the same time, comprehensive Arab unity put limitations on the Syrian government. The fidelity to Arabism of every act was subject to debate not only within Syria but also in other Arab countries. In the interstate Arab debate, Syria generally sided with Egypt as a result of their having common adversaries, Iraq and Jordan. It was a partnership of unequals. Egypt was unparalleled in its cultural and political influence among the Arabs. Moreover, Egypt was the largest and richest Arab country, with the greatest military force, and geography made it the Arab country with the greatest potential for military intervention in Palestine. Alignment with Egypt very soon led Syria into an act that the Syrian government was loath to take. When war between Zionists and Arabs broke out in Palestine in 1947, Syria followed Egypt in opposing intervention by the Arab states. When the war turned against the Palestinian Arabs, however, Jordan and Iraq called for and promised military intervention. Egypt, fearing expansion by the British-allied Hashimites, then decided to intervene. Syria reluctantly followed the Egyptian lead.

Failure in Palestine resulted in increased attacks by the opposition and in deep cleavages within the government coalition. In less than six years, the Syrian government that achieved independence was torn apart by violent popular demonstrations, first fights in parliament, only to be overthrown by a military coup in 1949. From then on, cabinets were made and unmade by coups carried out by factions within the officer corps in alliance with civilian factions. In the course of the protracted conflict, the old nationalist leaders who composed the two great alliances continued to fight each other rather than join together against an increasingly dangerous adversary, the Ba'th, a coalition of provincial notables, including Sunnis, Druze, and 'Alawites, together with dissident members of some of the old elite families. The Ba`th was especially successful in gaining followers in the army. Not even the subordination of Syria to Egypt in the United Arab Republic, or the resultant Syrian united front that overthrew the U.A.R., could suppress factionalism. Even after the victory of the Ba`th in 1963, factionalism, with frequent cabinet changes and purges and reassignment of officers and officials, remained dominant until Hafiz al-Asad came to power in 1970.

The defeat in Palestine heightened Syrian security concerns, but did not eliminate factionalism. In the contest for office, some Syrians turned to Iraq for assistance against their Syrian competitors as well as to strengthen defense against non-Arab enemies. During the rapid succession of military coup-installed governments in 1949 (there were three military coups in that one year), apparent imminent agreement between Syria and Iraq was aborted twice by Egyptian and Saudi financial assistance to Syria. Instead, the Egyptian-sponsored Arab League Collective Security Pact of 1950 was intended to provide a security framework that would render unnecessary any Fertile Crescent unity scheme, which was strongly opposed by both Egypt and Saudi Arabia. Still, security remained a central concern of the Syrian elite. The pact's deficiencies were demonstrated in 1951 during border clashes between Syrian and Israeli forces, when only Iraq made even a show of coming to Syria's assistance. Some of those who opposed and finally brought down the anti-Iraqi regime of Adib al-Shishakli were receiving financial assistance from Iraq. Soon after Shishakli's overthrow by a military uprising in February 1954, two unsuccessful efforts to create a Syro-Iraqi union of some sort were made, one by members of the cabinets, the other by an army cabal.

The West offered one solution to Syria's security problem. Led by the United States, it offered arms and money and the guarantee of existing frontiers both in the Tripartite Declaration of 1950 and in the projected Middle East Defense Organization proposed by the United States in late 1951. Similar benefits were contained in the Baghdad Pact, which the British, with silent American consent, promoted in 1954–1955. Some elements in the governments of Syria at the time were attracted to the proposals, but none could accept any of them publicly. All the Western proposals were denounced by some and ultimately by all as being designed to protect Israel. The Arabs demanded that the West provide arms and financial assistance "without strings," that is, without limitation to defense and internal security, meaning that they could be used against Israel.

Once again, the Syrian government's espousal of comprehensive Arab unity contributed to limiting its action. The Egyptian government and news media had long since been carrying out vicious campaigns against any Arab governments or individuals who favored Arab defense ties to the West, most notably in an attempt to expel Jordan from the League in 1950. After the July 1952 coup, the new military government in Egypt remained silent while it negotiated with the British, but after the conclusion of a new treaty in July 1954 and the beginning of British troop withdrawal, as well as Nasir's suppression of his rivals, Egypt redoubled its efforts against Arabs who favored alliance with the West, even though the new Anglo-Egyptian treaty bound Egypt to Britain in the defense of the Arab states and Turkey. As a result of the Egyptian campaign, Syria had to denounce the Baghdad Pact and enter into a defensive alliance with Egypt.

After Egypt's dramatic demarche of purchasing arms from the Soviet bloc (the so-called Czech arms deal announced in September 1955) and the nationalization of the Suez Canal in July 1956, Egyptian influence throughout the Arab world reached new heights, and nowhere more so than in Syria. Not even Israel's victory in the Suez War could diminish Nasir's standing in Syria. Israel's victory could be explained away as the result of imperialist intervention, and the canal remained in Egyptian hands. Those elements in Syria which favored solving Syria's security problem by defense ties with the West were silenced. No one spoke out in favor of the Eisenhower Doctrine. The security problem, however, remained.

To much of the Arab populace, Arab nationalism was the answer to the security problem: a united Arab nation, it was asserted, could defeat all the Arabs' enemies. Not many of those who ruled Syria believed this. Some of the most zealous ideologues admitted Syria's need for non-Arab assistance. Arabist ideology depicted Russia as a part of the eternal enemy, the West, but respected Arab nationalists had argued since 1918 that the anti-imperialist Soviet Union was a potential ally of the Arabs against the common enemy, Western imperialism. Thus, when the Western proposals were debated, some Syrians argued that Syria (and the Arabs) must seek support from the Soviet Union. At the time, however, the Soviet Union was not providing arms and money to noncommunist (or to many communist) states. This all changed soon after the death of Stalin in 1953, and the Soviet transformation into a supplier of arms and money was quickly exploited by one Syrian contender for power. Khalid al-`Azm, foreign and defense minister and active candidate for president, who counted the Syrian Communists among his allies, was successful in engineering trade, cultural, economic, and arms agreements with the Soviet Union.

`Azm's enhanced political position as a result of his success in gaining Soviet assistance frightened the other contenders. As a result, the remnants of the old leadership and the Ba`th intensified their calls for federation with Egypt. The proposed federation, however, would preserve Syria's internal independence. Nasir was not interested. `Azm initiated even closer ties with the Soviet Union. Finally, he and his allies sought to circumvent their rivals by offering Nasir complete union, an action that forced the other competitors to join in making the offer. To the Syrians' surprise, Nasir accepted the offer.

The formation of the United Arab Republic (U.A.R.) merely added competition between the Syrian and Egyptian leaderships to competition among the Syrians. Nasir reduced the most important Ba`thists to ciphers. In September 1961, a coup carried out by conservative officers in Syria put an end to the union. The government was restored to traditional civilian leaders, but neither they nor the dominant officers had moved beyond the traditional factionalism. Pro-union sentiment remained strong, and Nasir unleashed a relentless propaganda attack against the secessionists. The result was a return to the continual civilian and military intrigues and maneuvers of the pre-U.A.R. days. In February 1963, a Ba`th-dominated group of officers in the Iraqi army carried out a successful coup. In March, a similar coup took place in Syria. The Ba`thist victories in early 1963 had to satisfy the widespread desire to restore the Arab union. The Iraqis and Syrians met with Nasir. An agreement to reestablish union was reached, but the Syrians and Egyptians had used the meeting in attempts to outmaneuver each other. Soon after the meeting, Egypt and Syria were engaged in a fiery propaganda war.

The rule of the Ba'th in Syria did not put an end to the internal competition, which pitted civilians against military and kept both sectors in constant anarchy. The military branch of the Syrian Ba'th quickly became dominant. From the beginning, the new regime was based on elements, especially, but by no means entirely, in the military, that were hostile to 'Aflaq and Bitar, who retained the nominal supreme political offices even as they were being stripped of influence and power. In February 1966, these elements, now led by the 'Alawite officers Salah al-Jadid and Hafiz al-Asad, carried out a successful coup. Jadid had already given up the military in favor of leadership of the Ba'th Party. Publicly, he was regarded as the first of two equals, and he dominated the civilian government. Asad, however, already commander of the air force, became minister of defense. After a coup in February 1966, 'Aflaq and Bitar fled Syria and were expelled from the party.

Almost from the start, the Ba'thists in Syria concentrated their fire on Nasir. Their Arabist enthusiasm was undoubtedly designed for internal consumption, but almost surely the Syrians believed that they were the leading edge of the Arab revolution that would sweep away the corrupt old regimes, including Nasir, and cleanse the Arab homeland of imperialism. Syrian propaganda accusing Nasir of betraying Arabism contributed to the failure of a compromise settlement between Egypt and Saudi Arabia over Yemen. Most importantly, the Syrian Ba'thists revived the Palestine question. Syria, in comparison with Egypt and Jordan, possessed an advantage vis-à-vis Israel. The Egyptian and Jordanian frontiers were much more open to Israeli military retaliation than Syria's short frontier along the brink of the heavily fortified Golan Heights. As a result, most Israeli retaliation against Syrian action was limited to air strikes, unlike the incursion of ground forces in Jordan and Egypt. These two, since 1956, had restrained Palestinian irregular action against Israel. But Ba'thist Syria sounded the alarm about Israel's drainage and water diversion projects, and called for united Arab military action. In response, Nasir took the lead in establishing the P.L.O. and the Arab Summit in order to prevent rash action against Israel. The Syrian Ba'thists, however, supported Fatah and the other new Palestinian organizations in carrying out irregular warfare against Israel. Syria also taunted Egypt with charges of cowardice, of hiding behind United Nations forces. Israel retaliated harshly, first against Jordan but finally, in early 1967, by air action deep within Syria, together with threats of stronger intervention. At this point, massive antigovernment demonstrations in Syria threatened the regime. To force Nasir to action, the Syrians and their Soviet friends passed to the Egyptians false intelligence of a massive Israeli troop concentration on the Syrian frontier. The result was the Six-Day War of June 1967.

The Israeli victory did not destroy the enthusiasm of the ruling clique in Damascus, whose members shared some common interpretations of Vietnam and Algeria as proof of the inevitable victory of this people's war. In their view, the Palestinian organizations were the shock troops of the people's war. The Israeli victory had discredited both the Egyptian policy of postponing war until the regular armies were ready and the

Egyptian-controlled leadership of the P.L.O. As a result, `Arafat took over the P.L.O. and carried on armed activities from bases in Lebanon and Jordan.

Syrian enthusiasm for action was undoubtedly encouraged by continued support from the Soviet Union, whose embrace had for the first time become support for the regime. Earlier Soviet ties to Syria were essentially ties to individuals: `Azm and important senior officers. As the Ba`th under `Aflaq and Bitar had always been strongly anti-communist, the Soviet Union at first was suspicious of the new regime. The suspicion dissipated as the two founders of the party were reduced to figureheads and Syrian Communists were admitted to the political structure. The Soviets provided diplomatic support and massive economic and military assistance, which continued after the Israeli victory. Thus fortified, the Ba`th regime, under the leadership of Jadid, in rhetoric and action claimed a virtually unique position as the vanguard in the struggle against imperialism and its Zionist lackeys. In addition to encouraging and assisting the Palestinians, the designated main force against Zionism, the Syrian army fired on Israeli positions in the Golan. In September 1970, Jadid sent Syrian troops into Jordan to assist the Palestinians during King Husayn's "Black September" campaign to drive them from his kingdom.

The Jadid regime presented itself as the one true hero and savior of Arabism. It joined Jordan and Egypt as "confrontation states," the first line of defense against Israel, in claiming and receiving financial assistance from the oil-producing states, and in September 1968 it joined Jordan and Iraq in the Eastern Command. At the same time, however, it pointedly set itself apart and demonstrated both its fidelity to Arabism and the tepidness, even treason, of other Arab states by rejecting U.N. Security Council Resolution 242, the Khartoum Conference decisions, and the Rogers Plan—unlike Jordan and Egypt, which had accepted these commitments to the use of diplomacy and political means rather than force. The regime's most powerful neighbor and most dangerous competitor, Iraq, received special attention. The ruling Iraqi Ba`thists who came to power in July 1968, soon to be dominated by General Ahmad Hasan al-Bakr and his kinsman and aide, Saddam Husayn, had been since 1963, and remained, allies of `Aflaq and Bitar. Syrian Ba`thist dissidents in exile in Lebanon welcomed the new Iraqi regime at the outset; in November 1970, `Aflaq himself moved to Baghdad. The Jadid faction in Syria soon began attacking the Iraqi regime as a traitor to Ba`thism. The Iraqis replied in kind. The resulting long-lasting cold war between the two Ba`ths thus, like earlier episodes in Syria's history, originated in the rivalries of competitors for office in the two polities who formed alliances across state frontiers. At the same time, however, like those earlier episodes, the intra-Ba`th conflict represented a conflict between polities whose geographical location and political culture made them competitors.

Ideology blinded the Jadidites to realities. Egypt under Faruq and Nasir had used Arabism very effectively to discipline Iraq and Jordan when their policies were perceived as threatening Egyptian interest. Nasir, in his campaign, had utilized the widespread populist revolutionary brand of Arabism. Chastened by the Suez War, Nasir attempted to dampen Arab nationalist fervor with respect to Israel, but the Ba`thists attacked him with the same brand of Arabism that he had used against his enemies and forced him into the course that led to disaster. The 1967 catastrophe finally convinced the Egyptians that their course had been unwise. Egypt changed course, but, as Barnett explains, it followed the customary behavior of political actors—individuals or states—and modified the definition of Arab nationalist norms by following the Hashimite and Saudi interpretations that made respect for state sovereignty a principle of Arabism. Clearly, Egypt intended to be the sole author of its policy. Following the war, there was considerable discussion in Egyptian books and news media of the suggestion that the liberation of Palestine should be left to the Palestinians. Egypt's War of Attrition was aimed at the recovery of Egyptian assets, not the liberation of Palestine. Despite the pan-Arab outcry against King Husayn, Nasir did nothing at the end of his life. His successor, Sadat, did even less. Husayn was allowed to eliminate the P.L.O. in Jordan.

The Jadidites attempted to fill Nasir's shoes by sending troops into Jordan. Before the June war, such action had produced major effects in all Arab countries. Syrian activism and propaganda, after all, had provoked Nasir to take steps that led to war. Nasirist attacks on Jordan and Iraq had shaken governments. Now those who ruled Egypt could successfully withstand such attacks and give them up as an instrument of policy. Syria, or any other Arab country, could not replace Egypt. Egyptian books, periodicals, newspapers, radio, movies, and television were very popular throughout the Arab world, and in every Arab country important people had been educated in Egyptian schools. Even more important was Egypt's military position. Egypt was by far the strongest of the Arab states, but its influence was not the result of threatening other Arab states. To the geographical difficulties of action abroad, demonstrated by the Palestine and Yemen wars, was added the existence of Israel, which prevented intervention in the Fertile Crescent. On the other hand, war against Israel without Egypt was unthinkable. As Syria possessed none of Egypt's advantages, Jadid's attempt to assume Nasir's mantle failed. Asad, minister of defense and commander of the air force, refused to commit the latter to Jadid's intervention, which failed. In November 1970, Asad ousted Jadid and began the creation of a new regime.

Asad shared Nasir's later understanding of Arabism, not Jadid's. The goal remained the defeat of imperialism and in particular securing the rights of the Palestinians, and Arab union remained the ultimate fulfillment of Arab aspirations. The existence of sovereign Arab states, however, was inescapable in Asad's view. He argued that given the realities, the sovereign Arab states must cooperate against the common enemies. From the start, Asad expressed his opposition to Jadid's populist revolutionism and urged the need to work with the other Arab states, especially Egypt, even advocating closer relations with Ba`thist Iraq. Proper Arab cooperation would, of course, result in Syria's achieving its legitimate aspirations. Asad held the common view that Jordan, Palestine, and Lebanon were parts of natural Syria, which had been disjointed by imperialism. At the same time, like Shukri al-Quwatli and others, he accepted the sovereignty and independence of the several parts as long as they cooperated with Syria against their common enemies. The superpowers constituted the great, but distant, enemy of the Arabs. Asad aimed at an Arab bloc strong enough to withstand pressure from either the United States or the Soviet Union. Like Nasir, he understood how to utilize the superpowers' rivalry to Syria's advantage. The immediate mortal threat was Israel, which occupied the land of the Palestinians and part of the Syrian Arab Republic and, in the Syrian view, claimed all the land from the Euphrates to the Nile.

Asad was pragmatic in applying his principles. He prepared for better relations with the United States by terminating some restriction on the TransArabian Pipeline (Tapline) that went through Syria. Moreover, in accordance with his own political views, and appealing to the Syrian mercantile and industrial class, he eliminated Marxist and pro-Soviet rhetoric from official statements. The United States, enthralled by the notion that Iran and Israel secured its interests in the Middle East, paid little attention to Asad and continued the massive supply of military goods to its two chosen allies. Asad held cordial conversations in Moscow in early 1971, and one year later signed an agreement on economic cooperation. There was a lessening of anti-Iraqi propaganda, but the threat of Iraqi Ba`th-supported Syrian dissidents kept such propaganda alive until early 1972. Asad centered his hopes on Egypt. One of his first acts was to announce that Syria would join the Federation of Arab Republics recently projected by Egypt, Libya, and Sudan, and Syria joined with the first two in establishing it in April 1971. Most important, Syria joined Egypt in planning and preparing for the war they launched against Israel in October 1973.

The October War was not as fruitful for Syria as it was for Egypt. Syria failed to regain the Golan, but Egypt regained the Suez Canal, thanks at least in part to American restraints on Israel. Moreover, the Americans obviously were neglecting Syria in favor of brokering an Egypt-Israeli peace, while the Egyptians manifestly had little interest in anything beyond the recovery of Sinai. Israel, which was receiving massive American economic, military, and diplomatic aid, put its hopes in agreement with Egypt. The Asad government, in the face of considerable criticism, nevertheless adhered to its American-brokered disengagement agreement with Israel and had some slight success in improving its reputation with the U.S. government. Syria was successful in using inter-Arab diplomacy to establish the principle that no Arab state should make a separate peace with Israel, but this did not prevent Egypt from negotiating separately with Israel and the United States. Syria even entered into a special arrangement with Jordan in July 1975, and in September 1976 established the Unified Political Command with Egypt. Neither agreement produced any lasting benefits, and Syria's most important Arab neighbors, Iraq and the P.L.O., offered problems, not solutions.

Tension between Iraq and Syria arose in part over material benefits, notably transit rights and royalties for Iraqi oil pipelines across Syria, which were the subject of a dispute in 1972–1973, and the division of Euphrates waters, which occasioned a more serious conflict beginning in early 1975. But the more important source of the conflict was rivalry between aspirants to the leadership of the Arab nation, a rivalry that had taken the form of Iraqi expansionism in the 1930s, 1940s, and 1950s. Thus, the October War produced a flaming war of words over Iraq's role in it and Syria's acceptance of a cease-fire and of U.N. Security Council Resolutions 242 and 338. At the time, Iraq was heavily burdened with a military campaign against Iranian-supported Kurds, which was attended by occasional encounters with Iranian forces. Syria, in May 1975, received a substantial financial credit from Iran. In March 1975, a settlement with Iran allowed Iraq to suppress the Kurdish resistance. At the same time, Iraq broadcast strenuous complaints about Syria's use of Euphrates waters. The propaganda war was intense. Syria now attacked the Irano-Iraqi accord as a betrayal of the Arab nation.

The Asad government sought to use the P.L.O. Syria provided major assistance to the Palestinians when they established themselves in Lebanon after their expulsion from Jordan, but the Palestinians resisted Syria's efforts to control them. Within a few years, the Palestinians became a major military force in Lebanon, where the national army was by intention weak in relation to the forces of local magnates. The Palestinians were soon carrying out frequent operations against and into Israel. Israeli responses, with ground and air forces, increased in numbers and severity, and Israel established ties with some Christian Lebanese groups and created a Christian army in southern Lebanon. The threat of massive Israeli intervention grew. The P.L.O.-Israeli war in the south exacerbated some old Lebanese divisions. In April 1975, civil war broke out between defenders of the old regime, mostly Maronites, and its opponents, mostly Muslims, who were joined by the Palestinians. In December, Saddam Husayn demonstrated Iraqi support for the rebels when he led a delegation to Lebanon. In January 1976, Syria sent units of its Palestinian force into Lebanon to support the rebels, but when the Palestinians and antigovernment forces were nearing a major victory, Syrian support was shifted to the Christians. Syrian regulars then entered in force. Syria represented its intervention as being at the request of the Lebanese government. The Asad government clearly aimed to prevent either a Palestinian- or an Israeli-dominated government in Lebanon. Iraq opposed the Syrian intervention from the start, but to no avail. Syria was now, with the virtual withdrawal of Egypt, the only significant "confrontation state" with Israel. As such, Syria received legal approval from the Arab League, and major financial assistance from Saudi Arabia and the other oil-producing states. The Syrian troops were dubbed first the Arab Peace Force and then the Arab Deterrent Force. Iraq, whose government had claimed Kuwait in 1939, and in addition in 1961 threatened occupation, was not likely to have the support of the Gulf states and the Saudis, especially after its agreement with Iran. The Asad government's careful treatment of the United States was also productive. The Americans brokered a sub rosa agreement with Israel that established spheres of influence. By October 1976, Syria's opponents, the P.L.O. and the Lebanese antigovernment forces, were defeated.

All Syria's foreign difficulties ran through Lebanon. In keeping with the agreement with Israel, southern Lebanon was free of Syrian troops. The area was thus open to the P.L.O., which rapidly expanded its activities from bases there. Israel continued to assist the supply and training of Maronite forces throughout Lebanon. The new Begin government, from spring 1977 on, increased support for the southern Christian force, and in September sent the Israel Defense Force (I.D.F.) into Lebanon. P.L.O. action from south Lebanon against Israel greatly increased. In response, Israel carried out a large-scale offensive to the Litani River in March 1978. By this time, a very important Maronite faction had initiated armed resistance to the Syrians. The Maronites approached the Begin government, which announced that it would oppose Syrian "genocide" of the Lebanese Christians.

As Syrian confrontation with Israel was intensifying, the Syrian effort to maintain as a principle of Arabism the doctrine of no separate negotiation with Israel was meeting with failure. Sadat visited Jerusalem in November 1977, and signed the Camp David accords in September 1978 and a peace treaty with Israel in March 1979. Both Syria and Iraq called for common Arab action but, in 1977–1978, Iraq utilized the crisis in an unsuccessful attempt to defame and isolate the Asad regime. Iraq's campaign against Syria failed to win support when Libya, the P.L.O., South Yemen, Algeria, and Syria formed the Iraqi-boycotted Front of Steadfastness and Confrontation in December 1977. Camp David was followed by a rapprochement between Syria and Iraq. As a result, the Baghdad summit in December 1978 resolved on the expulsion of Egypt from the Arab League. Syria was again given additional Arab financial assistance. Syria and Iraq began the implementation of agreements to work for complete unity between the two regimes. Each side seems to have been using the union project for its own purposes; the Iraqis appear to have been providing ideological cover for Saddam Husayn's elimination of his rivals. The rapprochement disintegrated almost immediately after Husayn secured his position in summer 1979. The rivalry continued, as before, by means of propaganda, of terrorist activities and subversion carried on by each regime in the other's territory, and of troop concentrations on the border. In this conflict, Iraq was joined by Jordan and some Maronites in Lebanon, who were supported and aided by Israel. They provided bases, matériel, and training to Islamic forces that became increasingly active in Syria, especially in Hama, where they had become important in the 1940s. In 1981–1982, Hama was the scene of a major rebellion that was ruthlessly suppressed, with great destruction and loss of life.

The Asad government, confronted by Israel and Iraq, sought to compensate for the loss of Egypt. First, Syria would itself build up to "military parity" with Israel. The rapid expansion of the armed forces began. In October 1980, a new treaty with the Soviets was signed, and the latter provided massive quantities of materiel and large numbers of advisors. Second, Syria turned to Iran. After unsuccessful approaches to the shah, Syria went to the Iranian Shi`a opposition, and after the revolution immediately lauded the Khomeini regime. At the same time, the Syrians courted the Shi`a of Lebanon. When Iraq attacked Iran in September 1980, Syria charged Iraq with fighting the friend of the Arabs instead of the common enemy, Israel. Syria, moreover, sold important military supplies to Iran. In return, Syria received Iranian oil on very favorable terms.

Syria's insistence on the expulsion of Egypt from the Arab League and alliance with Iran against Iraq created a deep rift within the League. Iraq sought and received the cooperation and support of Egypt and Jordan. The Arabian oil-producing states silently opposed Egypt's banishment and, despite their distrust of Iraq, were fearful of the prospect of Iranian success. But they continued to provide financial assistance to Syria. Libya, however, was firmly in the Syrian camp. Qadhafi took the initiative in working for union with Syria, and this union was announced in September 1980. Although the union was never realized, lip service was paid to the principle as late at May 1985. Libya reportedly provided major financial assistance to Syria. The Gulf states and Libya were surely motivated by Syria's position as the only Arab state in actual combat with Israel.

The Israel Defense Force during June–August 1982 advanced to Beirut, inflicted heavy losses on Syrian forces, and compelled them to withdraw from a few strategic locations. The P.L.O., defeated by the I.D.F., evacuated Beirut under an American-mediated agreement. A Lebanese government headed by an anti-Syrian Maronite was installed, and in May 1983 a Lebanese-Israeli political agreement was signed. The Israeli victory was deceptive. The main Syrian military position that controlled the Beirut-Damascus highway and access to the upper Bi`qa was so strong that the I.D.F. could not break it at an acceptable price. As long as Syrian forces held this position, Israeli invasion of Syria by way of Lebanon or Hawran would be extremely difficult and costly to the I.D.F. If Syria had not occupied these positions in Lebanon before the Israeli invasion, the I.D.F. would have been able to occupy them and establish control by friendly Maronites. In this case, the Israeli position would have been invulnerable to Syrian attack, and Israel would have gained great retaliatory capabilities against Syria. The strength of the Syrian position allowed Syria to remain in Lebanon and organize and assist Druze and Shi`a forces in carrying out irregular warfare against the I.D.F. Moreover, the twists and turns of the Reagan administration's policy permitted Syria to appear as the Arab champion against Israel's imperialist patron, the United States. Even before the Israeli invasion, the U.S.-Israel strategic agreement and other actions were used to reinforce the customary identification of America as the enemy. Thinking that Syria had been defeated, the Americans proposed in the Reagan Plan to isolate Syria by having Jordan negotiate with Israel for Palestinian self-government in the West Bank and Gaza. Although American and French troops were introduced as a peacekeeping force, the United States sponsored the pro-Israeli Maronite government and its army and mediated its treaty with Israel. Finally, American naval and air power was employed against Syrian-backed Lebanese forces. So, Lebanese forces, allied with and assisted by Syria, attacked not only the Maronite government forces but also Israeli, American, and French targets. Especially spectacular were bombing attacks on the U.S. Embassy and U.S., French, and Israeli military installations. American naval and air action against Syrian-supported militias and Syrian positions culminated in the loss of two aircraft and the Syrian capture of one pilot. The final result was the evacuation of the Americans and French in early 1984, and, finally, the withdrawal of the I.D.F. In early 1984, the Lebanese government abrogated the 1983 agreement with Israel. Attacks on the Israeli-controlled security zone in the south, and occasionally action from it against Israel, continued until the Israeli withdrawal from South Lebanon in June 2000. Israel charged Syria with responsibility for the attacks, but Syria was not the object of Israeli retaliation.

Syria's status as the sole Arab state at war with Israel did not prevent active opposition to its policies by other Arab states. Egypt and Jordan continued to support Iraq. Relations with `Arafat, who believed Syria had betrayed the P.L.O. during the Israeli invasion, greatly worsened. Syria turned to anti-`Arafat Palestinians, who, with Syrian assistance, drove `Arafat from Lebanon in autumn 1983. `Arafat then made peace with Egypt and responded favorably to King Husayn's overtures regarding the Reagan plan for Jordanian-P.L.O. negotiations with Israel about the West Bank. Jordan resumed diplomatic relations with Egypt in September 1984. In response, in May 1985, Syria's Lebanese Shi`a friends began attacks on the remaining Palestinian camps in Lebanon. Moreover, anti-`Arafat Palestinians based in Syria and Libya carried out a terrorist campaign against Jordanian, U.S., and Israeli targets. `Arafat's purely personal concord with Husayn was rejected by the P.L.O. Executive Committee. Beginning in the latter part of 1985, relations between Jordan and Syria became friendly, and Asad visited Amman in May 1986. Jordan then joined in the effort at mediating the Iraqi-Syrian conflict that the Arabian oil producers had been engaged in since September 1982. Seeming successes in these efforts aided Syria. Iran had been attempting to collect Syria's unpaid debts for Iranian oil, but fearing Iraqi-Syrian agreement, instead made new deals in 1986 and 1987 that were very favorable to Syria. Nevertheless, the search for Arab consensus continued. The Amman summit in November 1987 passed resolutions proclaiming solidarity with Iraq against Iran, and authorized League states to establish diplomatic relations with Egypt, but granted substantial financial assistance to Syria.

The Amman summit was a turning point. The authorization of diplomatic relations with Egypt legitimized Egypt's agreements with Israel and thus annulled the keystone of Syrian policy, the principle of Arab unanimity with reference to Israel. Syria still successfully opposed Egypt's readmission to the League, but this ran against the current. In June 1988, the P.L.O. announced its recognition of Israel and renunciation of terrorism, and its willingness to negotiate with Israel. Syria, meanwhile, was facing the loss of vital external support. The Soviet Union, under Gorbachev since 1985, had reduced its financial and logistical support. Then, in August 1988, Iraq, having cleared its territory of the enemy, signed a cease-fire with Iran and soon began to assist General Aoun, a claimant to the premiership of Lebanon, in his armed conflict with the rival Syrian-backed government.

Ever adaptable, Syria ended its hostility to Egypt, which was readmitted to the League in May 1989, and resumed diplomatic relations late that year. Relations with the Soviet Union and its successors continued as before in word and deed. Syria still bought its arms from the Eastern Bloc. The United States was depicted as Israel's essential backer, and Secretary of State George Schultz's 1988 peace initiative met with failure and bitter criticism, but public statements and interviews with American political figures were aimed at mollifying the Americans. There was a dramatic improvement during the first two years of the Bush administration, even though that administration initially followed Israel in preferring negotiations between Israel, the Palestinians, and Jordan.

Syria's cultivation of Egypt and the United States was rewarded in Lebanon. General Aoun's campaign against his Lebanese rivals and the Syrians produced an Arab League mediation effort that resulted in the Ta`if Agreement in October 1989; this recognized a special relationship between Lebanon and Syria. The United States approved the agreement, and its promise of amity was fulfilled when Syria joined the United States, Egypt, and the Arabian oil producers in opposing Iraq in Kuwait in 1990–1991. General Aoun was defeated in October 1990. In the following May, Syria's special position in Lebanon was embodied in a Treaty of Fraternity, Cooperation, and Coordination between the two countries. Syria also was awarded substantial financial assistance by the Arabian oil-producing states.

Since the October War, Syria had insisted that Arab negotiations with Israel be carried out by the Arabs collectively for the purpose of reaching a comprehensive settlement on the basis of U.N. resolutions under the auspices of the Security Council. But Egypt, Jordan, and the P.L.O. went their separate ways. After Desert Storm, Syria seemed finally to have succeeded. In June 1991, the P.L.O. announced acceptance of collective negotiations. In July, Syria accepted an American invitation to the Madrid peace conference. That conference honored Arab collectivity in word only. The serious negotiations were to be separate bilateral talks. Even the appearance of Syrian victory faded away. The P.L.O. and Israel signed the Oslo accords in August 1993, and Jordan and Israel reached a nonbelligerency agreement in July 1994. Nevertheless, Syria has maintained that peace with Israel must be approved by all the Arabs, that no Arab entity by itself can cede any land or right. Syria expounded this position in public and implemented it in many negotiations with Israel between August 1992 and March 1996, and again in late 1999–early 2000. Syria thus retains the option of denouncing any agreement between the P.L.O. and Israel as a betrayal of Arabism. Whatever Syria's goal, the Asad regime has shown no sign that it regards peace with Israel as an urgent matter. It may be that Syria is waiting for a final settlement between Israel and the P.L.O. so that it can claim that it remained true to Arab nationalism even if the P.L.O. did not. Syria can then either settle with Israel or shift to rejectionism.

Syria considers American pressure on Israel to be the most effective instrument of restraint at the present time. At the same time, Syria continues to make a show of its friendship with Russia, and continues to buy arms from both it and former Eastern Bloc countries. Syria's military position in Lebanon is firm and established by treaty. Syria also demonstrates its friendship with Islamic Iran. In Lebanon, Shi`a guerrillas have fought against Israel in the south with Israel retaliating against Lebanon, not Syria. Moreover, Syria provides recognition and approval to the new Palestinian militants, Hamas and Islamic Jihad, in addition to the older rejectionist factions of the P.L.O. Syria's chief Arab enemy, Iraq, is now restricted by American-led U.N. action. But Iraq's long-range potential and ambition to expand in the Peninsula means that the Gulf states will continue their support for Syria, the only Arab state in a position to counter Iraqi expansionism. Finally, Syria can proclaim to all the Arabs that it stood alone to the end in opposing Zionist-imperialist aggression.

Syria continues to enjoy geographically bestowed advantages with respect to Israel in comparison with Jordan and Egypt. The Golan Heights are under Israeli occupation, but the territory is not especially valuable economically, as Sinai and the Suez Canal were to Egypt and the West Bank was to Jordan. Moreover, although Syria is no longer able to shell Israeli territory from heavily fortified positions, it is still relatively secure from Israeli invasion. The Syrian military positions in Lebanon protect Syria from invasion via Lebanon, and these positions are so strongly held that in 1982 Israel could not break them at an acceptable price. Syria's size, configuration, and terrain render invasion by the only remaining route, via Hawran, extremely difficult. Syria therefore has no need to rush to peace with Israel.

Syrian Arab nationalism combined with geography to condition Syrian external relations decisively. Enemies or threats to Arabism necessarily were enemies or threats to Syria. Thus Syria was obligated to oppose imperialism, vaguely the West, and, most specifically, its instrument in the Arab homeland, Zionism (later Israel), but Syria as one of the four Arab neighbors of Palestine was especially vulnerable to Zionist power, which was greatly feared even before 1948. On the other hand, Arabism provided Syria with allies against Zionism, but at the same time also posed a threat to the regime by legitimizing the expansionist ambitions of other Arab states and the collaboration with them of Syrian opposition groups. The threat of Arabism was especially great in the case of two of Syria's neighbors, Jordan and Iraq, both expansionist. Jordan was too small and poor to pose a great threat, but Iraq was a formidable threat because of its superior size and resources. Arabism provided allies against Iraq ambition. Egypt and Saudi Arabia could be counted on to oppose Iraq. The first government of independent Syria set the course by forming the Arab League in alliance with Egypt, Saudi Arabia, and Lebanon. The League pact guaranteed the sovereignty and territorial integrity of the member states, principles acceptable to all the governments. Many in Syria, however, fervently believed the Syrian Arab Republic should be a part of Greater Syria or of a Fertile Crescent union. In response, the Syrian government had already reached an agreement with the Lebanese government whereby Syrian recognition of Lebanon was on the condition that Lebanon follow an Arab policy and not become a base for imperialism. Although the independence of Jordan and Lebanon and the Palestinians' right to self-determination were recognized, Syria's claim to Greater Syria was never renounced. Instead, a Republic of Greater Syria, free of foreign domination, with Damascus as its capital was put forward as the ideal. In the formation of the Arab League, Syria supported a successful Iraqi provision of the pact that permitted special arrangements between League members. Syria also supported an unsuccessful Iraqi proposal to include a collective security obligation in the pact. Finally, Syria supported an unsuccessful Egyptian proposal to make the external relations of the members subject to monitoring by the League. Both proposals remained fundamental principles of Syrian foreign policy.

Syria's policy worked well at the beginning, but failure in Palestine ushered in a decade of extreme political instability marked by frequent coups carried out by cabals composed of civilian politicians and army officers. Some competitors looked to Iraq for assistance against their Syrian rivals as well as security from Israeli attack. The Iraqis were interested, but the anti-Iraqis won out with assistance from Egypt and Saudi Arabia, including the Arab League Collective Security Pact. Although many in the Syrian leadership favored alignment or alliance with NATO, Egypt under both the monarchy and Nasir was able, through propaganda and subversion, to mobilize over-whelming opposition. After Nasir's deals with the Soviet Union, pro-Soviet sentiment grew in Syria, but the Syrian government was so much an unstable collection of warring factions that Soviet assistance was provided to the minister of defense, whose allies included the largely Kurdish Syrian Communist Party, instead of the Syrian government. The threat of dominance by the minister of defense was met by the formation in 1958, of the United Arab Republic which began a period of Egyptian dominance followed by civil war and instability. The first, pre-Asad, Ba'th regime (1963–70) abandoned independent Syria's original foreign policy in favor of attempting to become the center and leader of Arabism, displacing not only Iraq but Nasrist Egypt as well, which was attacked as preferring diplomacy to armed struggle. The result was the 1967 defeat and the failed intervention in Jordan in 1970.

The Asad government returned to the policy of independent Syria's founding government. Iraq and Israel, which now occupied Syria's Golan as well as Palestine, continued to be great problems. In the contest with Iraq, Asad's Syria replaced Egypt with Iran and justified its action by charging Iraq with betraying Arabism by attacking an ally against imperialism and Zionism. Syria received financial support from the Gulf states (and probably will continue to do so) because it was the only Arab check to Iraqi ambitions in the Gulf. Asad's Syria has insisted that Arab problems with Israel must be settled by the Arabs collectively. Initially, Syria relied on Egypt and followed its lead in using diplomacy as well as military means. Egypt's defection was not a fatal blow. Syria possesses geographical military advantages vis-à-vis Israel that Egypt and Jordan lack, so Israeli action against Syria has been much more subdued than against Egypt and Jordan. Syria, as the only Arab state actually engaging Israel in combat, now could and did claim and receive financial support from the oil-producing Arab states. As the Arab champion confronting Israel, Syria secured its position in Lebanon. Expanding ties with the Soviet Union established by the first Ba`thist regime, Asad's Syria built up a significant armed force and continued to procure matériel from the former Eastern Bloc. At the same time, relations with the United States improved greatly. Iraqi ambitions in the Gulf created a wartime alliance with the United States. Syria has failed to achieve control of the policies of Jordan and the P.L.O., but Syria still insists that no one, not even the P.L.O., can cede Arab territory or rights, and maintains close relations with maximalist Palestinian groups and Lebanese Shi`a which continue to practice irregular warfare.

On June 10, 2000, Hafiz al-Asad died, and Syrian laws were hastily changed to make it possible for his son, Bashar, to replace him as president. It is too soon to tell whether the son will follow the policies of his father, too soon even to know if the Asad regime will long survive the death of the man who brought Syria a distinctive authoritarian stability. The many different changes of government from the 1940s to 1970 gave way to thirty years of rule by a single individual, Hafiz al-Asad. He put in place a Syrian foreign policy based on Syrian state interests and recognizing the reality of other states with their interests, even while adroitly preaching Arab unity. Moreover, that posture held up, paradoxically, while Syria maintained close ties with non-Arab Iran.

Asad's long years of authoritarian rule simplified Syrian politics by holding in check the many internal divisions and alliances of past years that transcended state boundaries. The old perceptions of Syrian domestic politics as divided along lines of, for example, Damascus versus Aleppo or pro- and anti-Hashimites no longer exist. Whether, in the process, the Asad regime strengthened state institutions or contributed to the making of a Syrian nation-state by fostering a sense of Syrianness on the part of its people is quite another issue, not explored here.

In any case, the foreign policy of Syria after Hafiz al-Asad will surely remain one of multipolar complexity.

PART III

The Larger Arab World

9

Iraq: Balancing Foreign and Domestic Realities

Phebe Marr

At the close of World War II, Iraq was a relatively new state firmly planted in the Western alliance, with oil resources and a reasonable potential to become a viable nation-state. Fifty years later, at the millennium, Iraq is considered a state in crisis. Two decades of war and international sanctions have devastated its economy and population, eroded its sovereignty, and left it isolated regionally and internationally. Yet the government responsible for this situation and the institutional structures supporting it have survived.

The anomalies inherent in this situation raise fundamental questions, not just about the regime but about the structure of the state, the institutions and ideology that sustain it, and the interrelationship between these structures and international and regional environment. Is the state, as it has come to be structured, a viable entity? Can it continue to exist within its present borders and structure without unacceptable levels of force? If it needs a new structure and orientation, in what direction? How will this be related to the region? Can Iraq, with its strong anticolonial legacy, fit into an increasingly interdependent world led by the former colonial powers?

Historians and political analysts of modern Iraq have focussed on two major realities structuring Iraq's foreign policy—the creation of the state by foreign powers and its continued subjection to foreign control and manipulation, and the fractiousness of its domestic power structure and the foreign policy constraints this has imposed on the state.

The weakness of Iraq in the international environment has frequently been emphasized by Arab writers, particularly those who espouse dependency theory.[1] In this view, Iraq, like many other third-world states, suffers from a global asymmetry of power, low levels of institutionalization, artificial boundaries, and a fractionalization of its domestic population—all of which weaken its ability to develop an autonomous foreign policy.[2] Iraq's reliance on foreign companies for oil development (until 1972) and its continued dependence on foreign (mainly Western) markets fit the same model.[3] However, although there is undeniable truth in dependency analysis, it has its limitations. As some have noted,[4] it must be modified to take account of national leadership, the ability to use and mobilize existing resources, and skill in negotiating with outside forces, all of which can mitigate dependency. This caveat seems particularly relevant to Iraq.

At the other end of the spectrum are writers who focus on Iraq's domestic conditions and the need for regime control as the dominant factor in its foreign policy.[5] In this view, Iraq's vulnerability is due less to its creation by and dependency on the great powers than to its multilayered society, which creates numerous possibilities for disorder as various domestic constituencies vie for control of the state. Iraq must continually balance its requirements for outside protection or support against its need for domestic stability.

Whatever the emphasis, all of these schools reflect the complexity of Iraq as a state structure and the difficulty of balancing its multiple requirements—domestic, regional, and international. Different regimes have balanced these factors in different ways. None has yet found the balance that would provide sustained stability.

Constant Themes

The "Nation-State Project"

Three major themes have been continuous in the foreign policy of Iraq since 1945. The first has been the major project of the state since its formation in 1921: How to make a nation—or at least a cohesive state—out of the territory and population bequeathed it by the mandate, and, at the same time, how to situate this state in a neighborhood of equally diverse countries. At the domestic level, this project has involved integration at several levels.

The most important has been the transformation of a multiethnic, multisectarian society into a national community with a broad common identity, sufficient to hold the state together by consensual means rather than by force. This issue has been complicated by the fact that many of Iraq's leaders, including some of its founders, have never accepted the state as the final statement of Iraq's political destiny. Rather, they have envisioned Iraq as part of a larger Arab "nation," bound by ties of language, culture, and sometimes religion. These aspirations have most often focused on neighboring Fertile Crescent countries—Jordan, Syria, and Egypt. (Kuwait is an exception and is more often envisioned as a legitimate extension of the Iraqi state.) For much of Iraq's history, especially its early, formative years, the national and cultural vision presented to its population was more pan-Arab than Iraqi, although politicians, when confronted with actual opportunities for unification, have always pulled back from the brink or been compelled to do so by others.[6]

This vision, from Sati-l-Husri to Michel `Aflaq, has been almost wholly secular and language-based. Hence, it has had the broadest support among the majority Arab-speaking constituency in Iraq (75–80 percent of the population), whether Sunni, Shi`a, or Christian. Although strong pan-Arab policies have sometime originated with Arab Shi`a (as in the Ba`th Party Command of February 1963 and various Shi`a ministers under the monarchy),[7] the vision has received its strongest support among Sunni Arabs and Christians, both a minority (the former 15–20 percent of the population; the latter less than 3 percent). Pan-Arab sentiments have been strongest among Arabs living in geographic proximity to neighboring states, whose populations they have frequently engaged in economic and social interactions, with whom they have cultural affinities, and to whom they sometimes look for political support.[8]

But Iraq has also had to adjust to another reality: two strong non-Arab neighbors, Turkey to the north and Iran to the east, both larger and more powerful than any—or all—of the Arab states bordering Iraq. Here, too, there are ties with domestic constituencies. Although Turkish and Persian speakers in Iraq have always been few (less than 5 percent of the population), the ties of the Kurdish population in the north to Kurds in Turkey and Iran, and religious and cultural links between its majority Shi`a population in the south with Iran, have been problematic. Kurds constitute 15 to 20 percent of the population; Arab Shi`a, at least 60 percent.

The issue of Kurdish identity has been the most serious challenge to the "nation-state" project, posing a linguistic and ethnic challenge, rather than a religious or even a cultural one. Kurds, though mainly Sunni, have been largely secular in political outlook, like their Arab compatriots, but a constantly growing sense of Kurdish identity and a desire for self-government have checked not only pan-Arab visions of Iraq's future but also prevailing concepts of Iraqi state structure. The issue of Kurdish separatism, which has reached acute proportions since the Second Gulf War, has also made border maintenance with Turkey and Iran problematic. The fact that Kurdish populations, with similar identities, straddle the borders of Iraq, Turkey, and Iran[9] has provided a means and a justification for foreign intervention and even threats to Iraq's resources, such as oil and water.[10] On the other hand, central governments in all these states share a common desire to keep the Kurdish challenge contained and have, on occasion, cooperated to do so.[11]

Ties of culture, religion, and propinquity between the Shi`a Arab population and Iran have always been more ambiguous and difficult to measure. All indications are that Iraqi Shi`a identification with language (Arabic) and homeland (Iraq) is far stronger than their religious and cultural links with Iran, but the emergence in 1979 of an Islamic Republic in Shi`a Iran, together with the development of a vigorous Shi`a Islamic movement in Iraq (especially since the 1970s), has changed that equation, although it is not clear by how much.[12] Those Iraqi Shi`a for whom a religious identification is paramount have always been inclined to look for leadership to the clerical establishment in Najaf and Karbala, whose ties to Shi`a Iran have been stronger than those of more secular Iraqi Shi`a. It is now more difficult to separate a Shi`a religious identity from Iran, its embodiment. In addition, there are family ties with large numbers (probably over half a million) of Iraqi Shi`a exiles who reside in Iran.[13]

Creating a national identity has also involved integration of another kind—socioeconomic. Iraq, like other third-world states, has had to accommodate the tensions arising from urbanization, the emergence of new social classes, and other phenomena associated with ongoing modernization. Iraq's changing social structure (the development of an educated middle class, the emergence of an unskilled or semiskilled working class, the appearance of urban slums adjacent to affluent residential areas) has created new socioeconomic fault lines that have complicated the process of national integration. Although new classes frequently cut across ethnic and sectarian lines (there have always been rich landlords and merchants as well as poor and middle-class elements among Shi`a and Sunnis, Kurds and Arabs), it is also true that many of Iraq's have-nots, particularly among its peasantry and its urban migrants, were Shi`a and

Kurds, which has fed a sense of alienation already established on other grounds in these communities.

Modernization has also hastened the importation and development of new ideologies (communism, socialism, Arab nationalism), creating new political and intellectual constituencies that competed for power with more traditional groups. In the post-World War II period, these new ideological groups formed a growing opposition to the power structure. They looked abroad for political models and support from the Soviet Union, from the nonaligned movement, and from regional opponents of the regime. The growth of Iraq's oil wealth has also played a role, both positive and negative, in the nation-building process and in its foreign policy. Oil resources certainly provided Iraq with potential for development and a social lubricant for easing tensions. But as oil wealth grew and became an increasingly dominant portion of its domestic G.D.P. (28 percent in 1958; 63 percent in 1979),[14] control over its production and distribution of its benefits became a contentious issue that caused not only domestic instability but also foreign problems. Slowness of development and maldistribution of oil benefits, especially in the 1950s, sharpened social (and ideological) divisions, and hastened the overthrow of the monarchy. In the late 1950s and the 1960s, the issue of foreign control over Iraq's oil production also caused serious domestic and foreign problems.

Growing oil wealth in the Arab Gulf states also caused a shift in Iraq's perception of its regional position. Iraqis increasingly came to resent the growing affluence of the Arab Gulf monarchies, with their much smaller populations and much higher standards of living, as well as their increasing dependence on Western military protection. Meanwhile, the uses to which Iraq's own oil resources were put, particularly after 1980, created fears and anxieties on the part of its neighbors. Iraq's growing military and its not-so-secret development of weapons of mass destruction (W.M.D.), together with an increasingly expressed desire for regional leadership, created unease that resulted in constant attempts by neighbors to check and balance its power and to thwart its goals.

The Struggle for Independence

A second major theme influencing Iraq's foreign policy has been the strong desire for independence from great-power intrusion. A creation of Great Britain, existing under its imperialist rule as a mandate for the first formative decade of its history, and more indirectly under its advisors and a system of treaties and bases until 1958, Iraq in its early decades was dominated by an intense and prolonged struggle for independence. In 1941, during World War II, Great Britain reoccupied Iraq and replaced an independent, anti-British government with one more satisfactory to the Allies. This colonial legacy of intrusion and manipulation has left an indelible impact on Iraq's foreign policy.

Although direct interference by foreign powers in Iraq's decision-making process diminished considerably in the post-World War II period, dislike—and suspicion—of foreign interference, especially by Great Britain or the United States, its successor as the leading Western power in the Middle East, has dominated most regimes as well as the mind of the public. Anti-imperialism has been nourished not only by this history but also by ideologies prevalent in the postwar period, whether Leftist or nationalist. The rhetoric generated by this attitude, and support for it among intellectuals and other constituencies, have made cooperative policies with the West extremely difficult,[15] especially in the post-1958 period, after the pro-Western monarchy was replaced by a military regime that was driven in large measure by popular opposition to Western policies in the region. Thereafter, Iraq turned to the Soviet Union and the communist bloc both for political and military support and as a substitute for the Western alliance.

Economic disentanglement from the West proved more difficult, however. With rising oil prices in the mid-1970s, Iraq gained a greater degree of international autonomy and economic independence. It also achieved a better balance between the two Cold War blocs. This balance was fairly well managed, even during the Iran-Iraq war, when Iraq required support from both sides. But this period did not last long. The Iran-Iraq war reduced Iraq's economic strength, although the country emerged from the war with a greatly enlarged and more potent military arm, a factor that may have caused it to misassess its regional and global position. Reduced oil revenues and growing debt ultimately increased Iraq's economic dependence on the West and its regional Gulf allies, a dependence it was not able to break in the war's aftermath. These new constraints led, in part, to Iraq's invasion of Kuwait, which, in turn, resulted in a reimposition of foreign control over much of its foreign and domestic policy. As its behavior since 1990 illustrates, however, the strength of this desire for independence and freedom from foreign interference has not ended. Rather it has reached new intensity, as exhibited in defiance of foreign control which, despite the costs, appears to have at least the acquiescence of critical numbers of the regime's support groups.

The Role of Geography

A third major continuity in Iraq's foreign policy has been the role of geography. Here, too, Iraq has faced constraints and limitations (border problems and limited access to the Gulf) as well as opportunities (a rich endowment in resources). Iraq's geographic location in the region has imposed special burdens on its foreign policy: it is bordered not only by two large non-Arab states, Turkey and Iran, but by four Arab neighbors as well, two of them (Syria and Saudi Arabia) major players in the region. The other two, Kuwait and Jordan, are much weaker. Moreover, Iraq's Arab hinterland is differentiated: on the west, it faces the Fertile Crescent; on the south, the Gulf, both with different interests and cultural orientations. This geostrategic environment requires multiple roles and a high degree of sophistication and flexibility to manage.

Iraq's borders, drawn up by foreign powers and for the most part imposed on Iraq, are still not completely settled or accepted by the population. Border issues have been a constant irritant with most of Iraq's neighbors, especially at the head of the Gulf, where Iraq's boundaries leave it with only about twenty-six miles directly on the Gulf. Its main port, Basra, lies seventy miles up the Shatt al-'Arab (the confluence of the Tigris and Euphrates), a river it must share with Iran. This riverine boundary has been contested for decades. A second port, Umm Qasr, is situated on the Khor 'Abd Allah channel, a second Gulf estuary, which Iraq shares with Kuwait. Two Kuwaiti islands, Warba and Bubayan, control the entrance to this channel. A strong desire to modify these borders, which limit Iraq's access to the Gulf, has been a powerful motive in Iraq's two Gulf wars.

Although Iraq is bordered to the west and south by weaker Arab neighbors, its sense of vulnerability has been enhanced by its dependence on these neighbors for much of the export of its major resource (oil). Pipelines running through their territory (Syria, Saudi Arabia, and also Turkey to the north) have often been cut off in times of trouble, which has emphasized Iraq's geographic vulnerability as an almost landlocked power.[16]

A similar situation exists with respect to Iraq's water resources. The headwaters of both the Tigris and Euphrates, as well as the tributaries of the former, lie in Turkey and Iran, whereas the middle reaches of the Euphrates flow though Syria on the way to Iraq. Some 48 percent of Iraq's arable land is dependent on Tigris and Euphrates irrigation. The Tigris irrigates about 2.2 million hectares; the Euphrates, one million.[17] Iraq is vulnerable to water interdiction from all three neighbors, and water problems have been an increasingly contentious issue with both Syria and Turkey. Since the early 1970s, Turkey has moved to dam the headwaters of the Euphrates and Tigris in a massive irrigation project (the Southeast Anatolia Project or GAP) that has interfered with downstream flow in Syria and Iraq. When the GAP project is finally completed, it will reduce Euphrates flows to Iraq by 50 to 60 percent.[18] Syria, too, has installed irrigation projects on its portion of the Euphrates, causing serious hardship in Iraq. In 1975, Iraq and Syria nearly came to blows over greatly reduced Euphrates flow, which caused drought and endangered millions of Iraqi farmers.[19]

Finally, as indicated, human geography has played a profound role in Iraq's foreign policy. Arbitrary borders have divided Iraq's multiethnic, multisectarian population from communities of similar background in neighboring states, providing ample opportunity for cross-border interactions and frictions that can cause problems for the central government in Baghdad. These dynamics have given neighbors frequent justification for intervention and have made defense of clear-cut borders difficult. Today, much of Iraq's northern border with Turkey and Iran, in Kurdish-controlled areas, has virtually disappeared. Turkish troops frequently cross this border to control Kurdish guerrillas from Turkey. Iran supports cross-border military activities by dissident Iraqis (both Kurdish and Shi`a) in the north and the south. Iraq, too, has played this game with Turkey's Kurdish dissidents, with the Arabs in Iran's Khuzistan province, and, on occasion, with Iran's Baluch population in the east of the country.

This rather negative picture, however, should not be left as the dominant one. If geography has imposed constraints on Iraq, it has also provided the country with rich resources and, through their development, with the potential for enhanced power and foreign influence. Iraq, although a middle-sized country on the world scale, has a very favorable resource balance. A country of about 22 million (in the year 2000), it has sufficient manpower to build and maintain a modern industrial/service economy and to provide a reasonable domestic market for its goods and services. In the course of recent decades, Iraq has produced an impressive educated middle class, which by the late 1970s constituted about 35 percent of the urban population, 22 percent of the total.[20] (This middle class has since declined under the impact of wars and sanctions.) Iraq is also fortunate in possessing water resources for agriculture (both rainfed and irrigated) and abundant oil, a precious source of hard currency for investment and development. Iraq's proven oil reserves have been estimated at over 100 billion barrels, second only to those of Saudi Arabia, with large as yet unexplored and exploited areas in the Western Desert. But as recent history has proved, it is management of these resources rather than their mere possession that is critical in the development of a country's power and success in its foreign policy.

Changes in Iraq's Foreign Policy

In the post-World War II period, these themes have been constant factors in Iraq's foreign policy, providing the underlying structure of its relations with the outside world. But as all observers know, there have also been sharp and turbulent shifts in Iraq's foreign policy and in the international and regional environment with which it has had to deal. Of these changes, three have been most significant. First have been the major domestic upheavals in Iraq's political life, which have brought to power new political leaderships with different perceptions and different foreign policy orientations. The two sharpest changes have occurred with the military revolt that overthrew the British-established monarchy in 1958 and ushered in a decade of unstable military rule, and the coup of 1968 that ended that period and brought the current Ba'th regime to power.

The second source of shifts in policy has been wars and economic sanctions. Iraq has been in a state of war for almost half of the period since 1980 and under economic siege for the other half. Wars—and their outcome—have eroded Iraq's sovereignty over its territory (especially in the Kurdish area of the north), weakened its economy and society, and isolated it regionally and internationally. Its overall power in the region has been reduced along with its ability to play any regional role.

The third source of change has been the major alteration in its regional and international environment. A revolution in neighboring Iran brought to power a proselytizing Islamic regime that changed the balance of ideological forces in the region, created problems on Iraq's eastern border, and challenged Iraq's domestic stability. Also important is the fact that with the end of the Cold War and the collapse of the Soviet Union, Iraq has lost an important international supporter and a buffer against Western intrusion in the region. Iraq has had serious problems in coping with both of these latter changes.

These transformations in Iraq's domestic, regional, and international environment have brought a shift in the balance of forces, inside and outside Iraq, that shape its foreign policy. Although the most important of these has been the leadership and its skill in managing Iraq's environment, there is little doubt that the environment itself has been turbulent, problematic, and difficult to deal with. The nature of the dynamics—and the ways in which different leaders have dealt with both continuities and changes—can best be understood by examining three different regimes and their very different foreign policies. The first is that of the monarchy, especially at the peak of its development in the mid 1950s, before its demise; the second is that of the unstable military leadership that took its place, especially in the mid-1960s when the military regime of `Abd al-Salam `Arif appeared to have stabilized the situation; and the third is the current Ba`th regime, which has gone through several phases. An examination of these three regimes at a few critical points will allow us to see how the balance of forces, internally and externally, changed, and how these changes shaped Iraq's foreign policy direction.

The Monarchy

It is fair to say that by the 1950s, Iraq's major project—its development as a nation-state—had been well launched. The infrastructure of the state had grown—in roads, bridges, and communications facilities—thereby extending the rule of the central government into most regions of the state. By the postwar period, a national government, including a sizable bureaucracy, a growing military and police force—both nationally recruited—and a parliamentary system that, though flawed, included all ethnic and sectarian communities had been established and were executing laws throughout the state.[21] A national education system, small by current standards, was educating a small but growing elite. After a revision of the oil agreement with the Iraq Petroleum Company in 1952, oil began to flow in more substantial quantities and helped supply the revenues for a national development program initiated in 1950.

In this postwar period, some progress was also made on ethnic and sectarian integration. Persistent, though episodic, Kurdish revolts of the 1920s, 1930s, and early 1940s had petered out by the end of World War II, a trend that was helped by the exile of the legendary Kurdish leader Mulla Mustafa Barzani in 1945. Although the core of the military and bureaucratic leadership in Baghdad remained predominantly Arab Sunni, more efforts were made to integrate Shi`a, Kurds, and others into the leadership structure, some in visible positions. The postwar period, for example, saw four Shi`a (Salih Jabr, Muhammad al-Sadr, Fadhil al-Jamali, and `Abd al-Wahhab Mirjan) and two Kurds (Nur ad-Din Mahmud and Ahmad Mukhtar Baban) as prime ministers.[22] In education, a succession of foreign missions began to bring back a new generation of educated Shi`a and Kurds. These factors helped produce a postwar period of relative domestic tranquility on the ethnic and sectarian front. Although some of this was undoubtedly due to social and political mobility for Iraqi Shi`a and Kurds, particularly among the upper and middle classes, it was also helped by an unspoken "Iraqi First" policy in foreign affairs, one that focussed on Iraqi rather than on pan-Arab interests, and on good relations with Turkey and Iran.

Domestically, the monarchy did less well in balancing the social asymmetries produced by modernization and economic development. The process of development was slow and lopsided. Accelerated urbanization, maldistribution of landed and urban wealth, and underdevelopment of the countryside were not addressed sufficiently or in time. Meanwhile, modern education and urban employment created new constituencies that the regime was unwilling or unable to accommodate. Among these, Leftists, communists, and those desirous of an economic redistribution of wealth and social change looked abroad to the Soviet Union as a model and possible supporter. Others were more moved by the nationalist vision espoused by Gamal `Abd al-Nasir and the newly emerging ideology of Arab socialism, which focussed less on social reform (although that was included) than on Arab unity and independence from Western control. The leadership of the monarchy in its last years proved unable to deal adequately with either the new constituencies or the visions they elaborated.

In foreign affairs, Iraq had gradually reduced the control of global powers, mainly Great Britain, over its domestic affairs, although the old regime's step-by-step approach did not produce complete independence nor did it satisfy those anxious for it. The later 1950s also saw a shift away from previous attempts at Arab integration schemes (in 1949 and 1953–1954), most of which had foundered on the bedrock of national interests.[23] The apex of the old regime's foreign policy was the Baghdad Pact concluded in 1955, a security instrument that included three of Iraq's non-Arab neighbors—Turkey, Iran and Pakistan—as well as its foreign protector, Great Britain, but no other Arab countries.[24] After a domestic struggle over the issue, Jordan refused to join, while Egypt became an implacable adversary of the pact and of Iraq's participation in it. The pact revealed how far Iraq's leaders had moved from the old Arab nationalist agenda that had been their desideratum in the early decades toward one centered on the Iraqi state. It was also an attempt to resolve Iraq's old contradiction between its need for foreign protection and the strong domestic desire for independence. The pact was designed to downplay the old colonial tie by regionalizing Iraq's alliance with Britain, although the pact's failure to include any Arab partners proved to be fateful.

As the pact made clear, monarchical Iraq was still part of the Western system—and dependent on the West for defense, for management of much of its oil resources (still under the control of a Western consortium), and for much of its economic development. Increasingly, the Soviet Union was excluded from the spectrum. Just as the Communist Party and the Left were seen as the chief domestic threat and forcefully repressed, the Soviet Union assumed the role of the chief foreign threat. The Baghdad Pact openly brought Iraq into a Western regional alliance designed to be a territorial buffer against Soviet expansion into the Middle East. Preparatory to the pact, in 1955, Iraq took the ultimate step of breaking diplomatic relations with the Soviet Union, and threw in its lot completely with the West.

In the end, the leadership of the old regime was defeated not by the Cold War or by Soviet machinations but by new regional and domestic forces. Although the regime may have been successful in getting Western protection and resources, and in gradually reducing Western interference in its domestic affairs, it failed on two grounds. It did not shift its domestic base of support from the upper and landed classes to new constituencies, especially the middle and working classes, which were captured by the opposition (both Leftist and Arab nationalist) which also gained a foothold in the military. In foreign affairs, the Baghdad Pact, an alliance with Iraq's non-Arab neighbors and an extension of its alliance with the West, alienated the pro-Arab and pro-independence constituencies among its domestic population, as well as the strongest Arab power at the time, Egypt. The combination was to prove fatal, and in July 1958 the regime was overthrown by a military coup.

The Period of Military Regimes

The period between the overthrow of the monarchy in 1958 and the establishment of the current Ba`th regime in 1968 can be seen as a transitional period: one of domestic upheaval and turbulence, but also of substantive change in the two main drivers of foreign policy—the balance of domestic forces and relationships with the major global powers. The military revolt ended the monarchy and the semifunctional parliamentary institutions that had sustained it, as well as the social and political position of the landed and urban upper classes. Power gravitated to the new middle class, represented by army officers, bureaucrats, and the intelligentsia, who had constituted the backbone of the opposition. But this did not mean a new homogeneity of outlook. Rather, the divisions on critical issues already imbedded in the opposition—over the domestic structure of the state (the Iraqi project), Iraq's regional role, and its relations with outside powers—now came to the fore. A continuous ten-year struggle for control of the state apparatus ensued.

The question of Iraq's integration into a larger pan-Arab union led by Nasir was the first issue to emerge. It was settled rapidly, though not finally, in the early days of the new regime in favor of an Iraqi First policy that would concentrate on Iraq and reform of its social and economic structure. The leader of this faction, `Abd al-Karim Qasim, was supported by Leftist elements among the former opposition, including the Communists, as well as by dispossessed elements in the social structure such as rural peasants and the urban lower classes (often Shi`a). This policy also appealed to many Kurds and minorities, such as the Christians.

Qasim's regime (1958–1963) sponsored the most far-reaching attempt to restructure the Iraqi state up to that point, by introducing land reform; a redistribution of wealth, privilege, and political power; and economic benefits extended to the poor.[25] In a new dispensation for the Kurds, Mulla Mustafa and his Kurdish Democratic Party supporters were invited back to Iraq to share power.[26] The presidency of the new republic was, symbolically, made a triumvirate of Iraq's three main ethnic and sectarian communities—a Kurd, an Arab Sunni, and an Arab Shi`a.

On the international front, as well, the Qasim regime made a sharp shift. Iraq ceased its participation in the Baghdad Pact, and the structure of its alliance with Great Britain and the United States was dismantled. As a substitute, Iraq turned to the Soviet Union. Formal ties were restored, an extensive economic agreement was signed, and Russian technicians replaced the departing Americans and British. By late 1958, Iraq had begun importing Russian arms and equipment, tying Iraq's military establishment to the Soviet Union from then on.[27] Neither Qasim nor his successors, however, afforded the new partner access to bases or other privileges previously given to the West. Iraq achieved a greater measure of independence but less international support.

Qasim also began the long process of dismantling Iraq's dependence on the foreign-owned Iraq Petroleum Company's control of its oil resources. In 1959, his regime began a long and acrimonious dispute with the company that resulted in 1961 in Public Law 80, which deprived the company of 99.5 percent of its concessionary territory and limited it to its producing fields, mainly in Kirkuk.[28]

The results of both steps were significant. They brought Iraq closer to one of its long-cherished goals—political and economic independence of great-power control.

No longer was Iraq enmeshed in the Western alliance system, although economic and cultural ties were not completely severed. Diplomatic relations continued, as did Iraq's strong trade ties with the West. Iraq's best students, including those on government missions, continued to go to the West. But these links were now supplemented by those with the communist bloc.

These beginnings proved unsustainable, however. The political and economic restructuring, although it dismantled the underpinnings of the old regime, did not lay a new foundation. The attempt at Kurdish integration also failed, and the start of a new Kurdish revolt in 1960 did much to weaken and undermine the regime. But it was alienation from the Arab world and the dramatic shift to the Left (especially the Communists) that did most to bring about the fall of the Qasim regime. The two were related. Qasim's early refusal to follow his partner, `Arif, into a union with Egypt turned Nasir and his local supporters against him; in need of domestic political support, Qasim found it in the Iraqi Communist Party. Although the honeymoon with the Communist Party did not last long, it was enough to turn the nationalist element against him. The last straw was Qasim's ineptitude in making a claim to Kuwait in 1961, an act that brought British forces back to the region (temporarily) and turned the rest of the Arab world against Iraq.[29] Among domestic forces, the regime faced severe opposition from those who supported pan-Arab aspirations and opposed the Left. The Ba`th Party was the group best organized and most motivated to take advantage of this situation, and in February 1963 it overthrew the Qasim regime.

The Ba`th coup put a decisive end to Communist influence on the government, already seriously on the wane, but it failed to solve the key issue of pan-Arabism and Iraq's national identity. For nine months (February to November 1963), the Ba`th regime plunged the country into a frenzy of pan-Arab politics, aimed at eventual integration with Syria (which also came under a Ba`th regime in March 1963) or Egypt or both. Although the attempt failed, Iraq probably came closer then to a pan-Arab restructuring, with all that would imply for a loss of national sovereignty, than at any other time since its founding.[30]

Such a restructuring was, of course, problematic for the Kurds. Although the Ba`th made an attempt to come to terms with the Kurds, they failed to do so. The issue of Shi`a identity did not yet present a similar problem. The elected Ba`th Party Regional Command at the time of the 1963 coup had a majority of Shi`a and a strong, nonsectarian orientation. (Once the Ba`th Party came to power, however, the officers in the military wing of the party were added to the command structure, thus shifting the composition of the leadership in favor of Arab Sunnis.)[31]

The Ba`th Party's downfall in November 1963 came largely from the willingness—indeed, the eagerness—of many of its civilian members to sacrifice Iraq's sovereignty and the vested interests of the new ruling elite on the altar of pan-Arabism. A fratricidal struggle within the party enabled others to oust it from power.[32] Ba`th problems were compounded by their leaders' youth and inexperience, their narrow domestic power base (they reputedly came to power with no more than 800 full party members),[33] and their lack of broad support from Iraq's major constituencies (Kurds, conservative Sunnis and Shi`a, and the majority of the lower classes).

In the end, the party was eased out of power by pragmatists within their own pan-Arab ranks. A military contingent under `Abd al-Salam `Arif outmaneuvered its Ba`thist colleagues and instituted a more Iraq-centered regime of military officers and civilian technocrats. The new leadership was moderately pan-Arab and had some strong Nasirite elements, but `Arif and his cohorts proved to be wary of any real integrationist schemes. Within the regime, a succession of purges and new military appointments produced a leadership more conservative in composition, and indeed in outlook. `Arif, an Arab Sunni whose family was from al-Ramadi, increasingly drew on military men from Dulaim and other cities and towns in the Arab Sunni triangle north and east of Baghdad. As a result, the regime became more Arab Sunni in orientation, and less appealing to Shi`a.

Although the situation stabilized somewhat under `Arif, two issues—that of social reform and pan-Arabism, that is, the nature of the state and its regional role—remained alive and contributed to a continuous social and political struggle. The nationalization of Iraq's industry in the mid-1960s and other attempts by Arab nationalists to align Iraq's social and political structure more closely with that of Egypt in preparation for more integration were contentious. The unresolved Kurdish issue also came to the fore, and a low-level war with the Kurds became a running sore that undermined an already weak regime.

The issue of Iraq's relations with the West also remained a serious bone of contention within the regime. The main arena, this time, was the development of Iraq's oil resources, particularly the rich oil reserves in the south, which had been taken out of the Iraq Petroleum Company's control under the Qasim regime. Some favored Iraq's independent development of these resources under a newly established national company (with some help from abroad); others favored some cooperation with I.P.C. This issue was still unresolved when the regime was overthrown in 1968. The Arab defeat by Israel in 1967, a debacle in which the Iraqi army participated, further undermined the legitimacy of the regime, which had originally come to power on a pan-Arab program.[34] Finally, in July 1968, the regime was overthrown by a combination of army officers and the Ba`th Party, and by the end of July 1968 the current regime had complete control. The decade of military rule (1958–1968) finally broke both Iraq's military dependency on the West and direct Western interference in its domestic affairs. But it left two very negative legacies for foreign and domestic politics. One was a progressive increase in authoritarianism and repression at home, as well as the use of state violence to enforce stability and regime survival. Qasim's experiment with civilian political parties collapsed in 1961, and military men ruled from then on. Sham trials and executions, begun under Qasim, intensified under the Ba`th, as did the use of torture. Ubiquitous intelligence and security services grew apace, as did the suppression of dissent. These now became institutionalized as the *"mukhabarat* [intelligence] state" took shape.

The second legacy was a concomitant loss of the political and diplomatic skills needed for peaceful conflict resolution. Regime changes, attempted coups, trials, and executions rapidly eroded Iraq's pool of political talent and diplomatic knowledge, that had slowly accumulated under the old regime. This pool, never very large, was now depleted as youthful rebels and professional military, with entirely different skills and experience (in mass mobilization and coercive control) took over.[35] These tendencies were to grow under the succeeding regime.

The Current Ba`th Regime, 1968–2000

The current Ba`th regime began its three decades of rule with a thin political base of 5,000 members and a ruthless determination to maintain power.[36] In a series of trials and executions based on accusations of foreign and domestic threats—some real, some imagined—the regime eliminated its opponents with a brutality unmatched even by the standards of its authoritarian predecessors. The most serious attempt to wrest control of the regime from within (the attempted coup by Security Director Nadhim Qazar in 1973) was successfully put down, and thereafter the regime settled down to a stability enforced by draconian measures. However, it had difficulty in stabilizing the situation in the north. A 1970 agreement with the Kurds did not last, and by 1974 military engagement was again in full swing. This time the Kurds were supported by Iran, Israel, and the United States. It was not until after the Algiers Accord in 1975 that Ba`th control was firmly extended over the entire country.

Meanwhile, the regime consolidated its position on a new basis at home. Military officers who had helped make the coup were gradually eliminated from top positions (sometimes physically), except for the president, Ahmad Hasan al-Bakr, the figure with the most public stature and legitimacy and the one who could keep the military in line. The civilian party apparatus was put in control of both the bureaucracy and the military, but was gradually reduced to an administrative and ideological arm of the government. The intelligence and security apparatus was strengthened and given paramount importance. Most importantly, this security system, as well as the party apparatus, was increasingly brought under the control of Bakr's younger kinsman, Saddam Husayn, while key security positions were gradually filled by their kin or by colleagues drawn from their hometown of Tikrit.[37] This kinship relationship was neither so prevalent nor so visible in the 1970s as it later became, but it was sufficiently noticeable to generate party and public criticism, which prompted the regime, in 1976, to outlaw the public use of family names that indicated tribal or town connections.

Once power was consolidated domestically, the regime showed that it had learned the lessons of 1963. It gradually developed a better balance in its foreign relations and a new ideological paradigm to complement it. On the issue of independence, in 1972 the regime took the final though risky step of nationalizing Iraq's oil resources, thus ending the control by foreign oil companies over Iraq's major resource. This step was enormously popular and helped legitimize the regime, especially among Leftists, who had always favored this move. The immediate costs—in delayed oil revenue—were minimal (the dispute was settled in February 1973), and it put Iraq in a good position to reap the full benefits of the oil price rises of the late 1970s. It also gave the country greater measure of economic and political independence of the West, although it could be argued that Iraq's increased oil revenues made its economy more, not less, dependent on oil and its Western markets than before.

With respect to the great powers, by the mid-1970s Iraq had begun to shift its policy away from heavy dependence on the Soviet Union and to position itself to deal more judiciously with both Cold War blocs.[38] With cash to buy the best in technology and equipment, Iraq now purchased more from the West, including the United States.[39] Although Iraq had broken diplomatic relations with the United States in 1967, as a response to U.S. support for Israel in the Six-Day War, its business ties with great United power grew, as did de facto diplomatic relations with the U.S. Interest Section in Baghdad. Security relations, including training of security and intelligence personnel, were still confined to the communist bloc, especially East Germany and Romania. Independence was also maintained by increasing foreign reserves and avoiding foreign debt, thus eliminating any necessity for transparency or any need for intrusion from the Club of Paris or the International Monetary Fund.[40]

On the regional side, there was also a noticeable shift. Iraq's intense involvement in pan-Arab affairs and Fertile Crescent politics was greatly diminished. Indeed, the retreat was striking. Relations with Syria, where an opposing wing of the party remained in power, were hostile.[41] By contrast, relations with Jordan improved (particularly as a balance to Syria), and economic ties increased.[42] Although Iraq fought in the 1973 war, it withdrew its troops as soon as the cease-fire (which it did not accept) was signed. Thereafter, support for Egypt deteriorated as it engaged in peace talks with Israel. Instead, Iraq shrewdly profited from Egypt's isolation during and after its negotiations with Israel by organizing an Arab summit in November 1978 that was designed to punish Egypt and to counteract the Camp David agreement. In the bargain, Iraq succeeded in boosting its regional leadership role. In 1980, it promulgated an Arab Charter, endorsed by most Arab states, and put forth a bid to host the nonaligned summit in 1982.

In fact, Iraq's main focus, especially in the 1970s, turned toward the Gulf and its non-Arab neighbor to the east, Iran. The British withdrawal from the Gulf in 1971, Iraq's increased dependence on oil exports (especially from its southern fields), and the shah's emergence as the Gulf's "policeman"[43] all riveted Iraq's attention on this region. The shah's aggressive stance, sparked in part by Iraq's radical rhetoric, encouraged this focus. His hostility to the new Ba`th regime, his enforcement of Iran's boundary claims on the Shatt, and his support (with Israel and the United States) of the Iraqi Kurdish rebellion in northern Iraq nearly caused an open war between the two countries.[44] Outgunned, however, Iraq took a pragmatic course, and in 1975 concluded the Algiers Agreement with the shah. This agreement gave Iran half of the Shatt in return for the shah's abandonment of support for the Kurds.

Accompanying this foreign policy evolution was a new ideological orientation that was centered on Iraq's interests and its prosperity, rather than on radical pan-Arabism. This new framework marked a trend toward pragmatism, already under way, which attempted a new balance between the old contradiction of Iraq's identity as a state and its Arab role in the region. Integrative pan-Arab policies were clearly forsaken.[45] Iraq, as a state, was the new desideratum, and loyalty to it was paramount. But Iraq itself was now defined as "Arab" in a cultural sense, a definition designed to include the Kurds. More important was Iraq's regional role, which was now one of defender of the Arab world from non-Arab threats (Iran) and a model of political and economic development.[46] This formulation was designed to appeal to a broad constituency in Iraq, including all those desirous of seeing a strong Iraqi state capable of taking a leading role in the region. Indeed, by the late 1970s, with the Kurdish issue seemingly settled and Egypt temporarily out of the picture, this formulation came close to reality.

The new ideological formulation also had an economic side—socialism—borrowed from the communists and the Left. Increased state control of the economy, and a massive development program that distributed benefits such as health, education, and employment more widely than before,[47] appealed to Leftist elements and, of course, to the lower and lower middle classes, who saw increased social mobility.[48] It also helped reduce discontent in Shi`a and Kurdish regions, although it did not entirely eliminate it. Middle-class complicity in the regime's authoritarianism was likewise obtained by greater wealth, access to travel, and other economic privileges.

This new foreign-policy orientation and the domestic forces supporting it reached their peak in 1979, when Saddam Husayn took over as president.[49] Shortly thereafter it began to unravel, mainly under the impetus of two major changes outside Iraq's control: the revolution in Iran and the end of the Cold War. It was the former that was of immediate concern to Iraq. Although the Iranian revolution itself was a dramatic event that had a direct impact on the region, it was the response of Iraq (and mainly Saddam Husayn) that put the gains made by Iraq thus far—economic, political, and international—at risk.

Historians and analysts may long debate the motives for Iraq's attack on Iran in September 1980. Some cite Iran's provocations—inciting Iraq's Shi`a to overthrow the regime and abetting the revival of the Kurdish movement—as the major cause, and see Iraq's military action as mainly defensive, designed to protect the regime and the structure of power.[50] Others have claimed that the Iranian revolution and the apparent collapse of Iran's military and government institutions were viewed as an opportunity by Saddam and his planners to recoup their losses on the Shatt (never really accepted), destroy the new regime's power, and possibly even make permanent gains in Khuzistan, previously thought beyond Iraq's capability.[51]

Although no definitive answer can be given on motives, there is now wide agreement that initiating a land war with Iran (which Iraq expected to win quickly) was a gross strategic miscalculation. The war dragged on for eight years—the better part of a decade.[52] The human toll (over half a million killed and wounded), the costs in loss of oil income ($100 to $200 billion),[53] and the debt eventually owed to Gulf ($50 billion) and international powers, mainly European ($30 to $35 billion) began a reversal of Iraq's previous economic position. The same was true of its regional and international role. The shift in venue of the nonaligned summit to be held in Baghdad in 1982, the formation of the Gulf Cooperation Council (G.C.C.) in 1981, specifically excluding Baghdad, and Syrian support for Iran in the war were all testaments to Iraq's reversal of fortune and its overreach. Meanwhile, previous gains on the home front were also lost. Although the Shi`a of the south fought for eight years against Iran, their loyalty to the regime, though probably not to the state, was deeply frayed. Many Iraqi Shi`a ended up in Iran through expulsion, capture, or desertion; there they would form a nucleus of opposition to the regime.[54] In the north, the Kurdish insurgency, under new leadership, regained life, and gave the regime one of its most serious challenges during the war with Iran.

Despite these costs, however, the war's ultimate outcome—capitulation of Iran to a cease-fire it had been rejecting for six years—seemed to demonstrate the strength of the regime's domestic reorganization and the hold of its security structure. Although its population was only a third of Iran's in size, Iraq was able to mobilize an army almost twice the size of Iran's, and it won the diplomatic battle in getting help from the West in arms sales, credits, and loans, and in a U.S. military presence in the Gulf to protect its allies, the Arab Gulf states. These factors helped tip the balance in its favor.[55] And it was able to sustain the loss of its offshore oil export facilities by expanding its pipeline through Turkey and building a new one to connect with a Saudi pipeline to the Red Sea, and by financial help from the wealthy Gulf states. The price of this support—financially and politically—would only come due in the war's aftermath. Indeed, Iraq's reconquest of Fao in 1988, its last-minute push into Iranian territory, and Iran's acceptance of a cease-fire in July 1988 allowed Iraq to claim a "victory," and even to achieve new stature in the eyes of the Arab world for having stood off revolutionary Iran for almost a decade.

But the victory was to prove increasingly hollow. Iraq emerged from the war economically dependent on the West and its regional allies. By 1990, debt to Europe had reached over $40 billion, $10 billion more than in 1988; the annual interest on the debt was $6 to $7 billion.[56] Both had to be repaid to restore Iraq's creditworthiness. The inability of Iraq to restore oil exports immediately and the multiple demands on its resources (including an expensive W.M.D. program) made its post-war oil income inadequate.[57] When oil prices dropped in 1990, Iraq was vulnerable.

On another plane, Iraq also suffered from the end of the Cold War, and the loss of the Soviet Union as a supporter and a balance against the West, at a time when it had become increasingly dependent on the West economically. Ideologically, the blow was also severe. As former Eastern European satellites scrambled to join the European Union and NATO, the collapse of the communist vision and its model of state-controlled socialism was clear to all, especially those in Baghdad who had depended on Eastern Europe for security training and the Soviet Union for material and moral backing.[58]

Iraq may have been slow to appreciate the changed nature of its financial and economic situation in the wake of the Iran-Iraq war and the degree of its dependence on outside financing.[59] It may also have overestimated its domestic security, which had held up so well during the eight-year war with Iran. In August 1990, after a decision apparently made within the narrowest political circles, Iraq invaded Kuwait in an effort to force a solution to the problems of its own financial difficulties, its borders with Kuwait, and other unresolved issues.[60] It also appeared to feel it could assert its new leadership role in the region and absorb the costs.

The outcome of this decision is too well known to repeat in detail. Iraq miscalculated the degree of opposition it would face in the Arab world, especially from Saudi Arabia and Egypt, key regional players, and from the United States, which took a much firmer position than had been anticipated. The costs to the regime of miscalculation this time were far higher than those of the Iran-Iraq war. They included not only defeat in the war and much destruction of its military (and ultimately its W.M.D.

program), but also a spontaneous uprising in the south and the north of the country that temporarily put fourteen out of Iraq's eighteen provinces in rebel hands. The regime had never been closer to being overthrown.

Under an international sanctions regime, Iraq lost all control over its oil exports and saw drastic erosion of its domestic economy. Two no-fly zones, north of the 36th parallel and south of the 33rd parallel,[61] still patrolled in 2000 by Western forces (essentially the United States and Great Britain)[62] ended Iraq's sovereignty over much of its air space. Meanwhile, withdrawal of Iraqi troops from a large swath of territory in the north, running roughly south and east from Zakho to Kalar and Kifri, left much, though not all, of the Kurdish region under real Kurdish control for the first time in Iraq's modern history.[63] In the Gulf, the coalition (mainly the United States) drew down their forces after the war but left a robust naval and air armada to enforce these restrictions. An intrusive international weapons inspection regime began dismantling Iraq's nuclear program, and had reduced much of the remainder of its W.M.D. program by the time it was expelled in December 1998.

In the course of the Gulf War, virtually all Western countries and most regional powers broke diplomatic relations with Iraq. By the end of the decade, Iraq's regional isolation had been eased, but the country was still considered a pariah state by the most important global powers. An increasingly deplorable economic and political situation was, by 2000, causing massive inflation, disinvestment by the population, deaths from malnutrition (estimated at 4,500 a month in the mid-1990s)[64], and a serious depletion of the educated middle class as Iraqis left the country by the thousands. Fixing the responsibility for the harmful effects of the postwar settlement (whether on the Iraqi regime or the West, essentially the United States) remained a contentious issue, but there is little disagreement on the outcome. The two Gulf wars, but particularly the second, can only be considered foreign-policy disasters of the first order.

Domestically, another kind of imbalance became apparent in the wake of the Gulf War, although its origins occurred earlier. In an effort to shore up a badly shaken regime, the hold of Saddam's family over the sinews of power intensified and was gradually extended to the younger generation, especially his sons—Udayy, who plays a key role in the informal economy, and Qusayy, who dominates the security mechanism. By the end of the decade, members of the Albu Nasr clan and Saddam's nuclear and extended family dominated the key security functions.[65] At a broader level, important military and security posts came to be occupied by recruits from Arab Sunni tribes from the triangle north and east of Baghdad, such as the Dulaim, the Ubaid, and others. A few Shi`a tribes were included, but the composition of this leadership was overwhelmingly Arab Sunni. Even among second- and third-tier technocrats, party members, and bureaucrats, the mix favored the Arab Sunnis, although there were more Shi`a among this group. Among these Sunnis, however, the older, more established classes had completely lost power, a phenomenon characterized by many as the "ruralization" of society. Many if not most of this new political class came from small towns and rural areas, and brought with them increasing attachments to their localities rather than to the country as a whole. Isolation within Iraq, as well as outside it, grew.[66]

Buttressing this political class was a new commercial and economic stratum.[67] Although also heavily Arab Sunni, this group included more Kurds and Shi`a, especially from tribal families well positioned to take advantage of the new situation. In the 1990s, this class burgeoned, positioning itself to make money in the gray and black areas of the economy not controlled by the international sanctions. Illicit as well as legal oil trade, smuggling of prohibited goods, currency speculation, and such private-sector agricultural and manufacturing activities as could be conducted under sanctions were their stock in trade. None of this could be undertaken without close ties to Saddam's family, and especially to his son Udayy.

This new informal (and highly personal) structure, together with the ability to rely on the larger institutional structures of the party and the various units of the military, gave the regime a seemingly unshakable base—small but solid, from which it seemingly could not be dislodged despite repeated, and drastic, foreign-policy failures. Indeed, it may be said that control has been consolidated not by a broad based, multiethnic, multisectarian power base but by concentration on a narrow group from one geographic region of the country, and on one ethnic and sectarian community. Even among this group it is drawn not from its well-educated and more sophisticated elements but from its more rural and parochial members.

Impact on Foreign Policy

This structure at the top has had its impact on Iraq's diplomatic apparatus as well as its methods and style. To the erosion of diplomatic talent and experience under way since 1958 was now added a new problem, which began in the 1980s but intensified in the 1990s—the growing distance between the top leadership actually making decisions and the specialized bureaucratic cadres, particularly those in foreign affairs, with expertise on the subject at hand. Within the Ministry of Foreign Affairs there remained a repository of diplomatic skill and experience, but the extent to which its members were able to give advice, or the extent to which it was taken, is questionable. All the evidence points to a top political elite with less and less contact with the outside world and more and more suspicion and distrust of it, and a domestic atmosphere of fear that has prohibited discussion, let alone debate, in inner circles.[68]

The leadership has come to rely instead on the intelligence and security apparatus for decisions in foreign policy, and often for its conduct as well. This group, as indicated, not only has little foreign experience but is also intensely distrustful of it. Information is a commodity to be closely guarded, not shared or discussed, and too much of the wrong kind may prove fatal.[69] As a result, the expertise that does exist in foreign affairs has been crippled. At times, it may be drawn on; at others, disregarded. Meanwhile, the regime has extended to foreign affairs the modus operandi by which it governs domestically: manipulation and sometimes offers of reward, interlaced with recourse to force, threats and intimidation.[70] Even when there may be a justified position or a real grievance, this style has left an indelible impression as an aggressive, episodic, and unpredictable government, extremely difficult to deal with. Meanwhile, some of the Iraqis outside the country, now possibly numbering upward of three million, have developed an increasingly active lobby against the government. Although they cannot effect change inside Iraq, they have influenced outside perceptions of the Iraqi government through published works, and have enough clout with London and Washington, to forestall policies favored by the Iraqi regime.[71]

The Iraqi regime also uses ideology and symbolism to appeal to its main base of support.[72] Although the regime still emphasizes Iraq as a (potential) Arab leader, rich in oil resources and an educated population, the country's independence and its steadfastness in maintaining it are fiercely stressed. At the same time, the regime stresses the negative results that would ensue from its disappearance—chaos, collapse, and long-term instability. Unspoken, though clearly understood, is the idea that the groups which have benefitted, even if precariously, from Ba'th rule—the party, the military, the new economic groups, and the upwardly mobile provincial Arab Sunnis from northeast Iraq—would lose their positions. These themes, negative and positive, are designed to appeal to the Arab—and mainly Sunni Arab—elite now in power. A number of secular Shi'a can also identify with these aims and fears as they seek to integrate. The themes are not likely to appeal to the bulk of the Kurdish population or to religious Shi'a or Sunnis (the latter growing in number), but are sufficient to generate complicity, if not support, from the main power base.

Conclusion

Iraq has come full cycle since the days of the monarchy, when it was largely integrated into the Western alliance system and allied with its two non-Western neighbors in the Baghdad Pact. This foreign policy coincided with a period when ethnic and sectarian tensions were reduced, and Shi'a and Kurds were increasingly assimilated into the leadership structure. Repression, although present, was moderate by today's standards. Economic development and oil revenues were just starting to increase and make an impact. But the regime failed to meet the domestic challenge of modernization and the regional challenge of growing pan-Arabism, and it neglected its Arab constituency at home. Nor did the Western alliance system protect it from domestic and regional challenges to stability.

A half century later, Iraq is ruled by a narrowly based group that tends to exclude Kurds and limit Shi'a, but that caters to an Arab constituency by using pan-Arab rhetoric on which it takes little or no action. Its political isolation—regionally and internationally—although gradually improving, is extreme; its domestic economy is a shambles, and its sovereignty greatly eroded. But after thirty-two years, the regime's hold on power shows few overt signs of cracking. Unlike its predecessors (including the Ba'th regime of 1963), it has given overwhelming priority to domestic political security and its hold on power. By establishing kinship links and developing institutional structures (the party, the security system, and multiple military forces) as well as control of the media, it has managed to maintain support among a critical core. The results for society and the economy have been extremely negative; so, too, has been the effect on its regional and international position. Whether this formula will continue to be successful is open to question. But the lesson of history that this regime appears to have learned is an old one: all politics is local.

Notes

1   See Tareq Y. Ismael, *International Relations of the Contemporary Middle East: A Study in World Politics*, in particular, chapter 2, "Domestic Sources of Middle East Foreign Policy" by Jacqueline Ismael.

2   Bahgat Korany and Ali E. Hillal Dessouki, *The Foreign Policies of Arab States: The Challenge of Change*, chapter 1.

3   See, for example, J. Ismael, "Domestic Sources"; and Peter Sluglett, "Progress Postponed: Iraqi Oil Policy, Past, Present and Future," in Kate Gillespie and Clement Moore Henry, eds., *Oil in the New World Order*.

4   Korany and Dessouki, *Foreign Policies*, chapter 2.

5   Amatzia Baram, *Building toward Crisis: Saddam Husayn's Strategy for Survival*; Shahram Chubin and Charles Tripp, *Iran and Iraq at War*; Charles Tripp, "Symbol and Strategy: Iraq and the War for Kuwait"; Tripp, "Iraq"; and Ahmad Yousef Ahmad, "The Dialectics of Domestic Environment and Role Performance in the Foreign Policy of Iraq."

6   This was the case in the attempts at union with Syria in 1949 (thwarted by Syria); of the Hashimite schemes in the mid-1950s (opposed behind the scenes by Nuri al-Sa'id); of 'Abd al-Salam 'Arif's overtures to Egypt in 1958 (opposed by 'Abd al-Karim Qasim); of the failed Ba'th attempts with Egypt and Syria in 1963 (a major contributing factor in their overthrow); of the more modest attempts by Nasirites in the mid-1960s (opposed, ironically, by 'Arif, then president of Iraq), and of the discussions with Syria in 1978–1979 (which preceded Saddam Husayn's takeover as president in Iraq). The only exception was the short-lived union with Jordan in 1958, which helped precipitate the fall of the old regime. In all these attempts, Iraq was unwilling to relinquish sovereignty and resources to others unless it could control the resulting political entity, a formulation resisted by others.

7   Of the eight members of the Ba'th Regional Command at the time of the February 1963 coup, five were Shi'a, including Ali Salih Sa'di, the secretary general. In the mid-1950s, Fadhil al-Jamali (prime minister, 1953–1954, and foreign minister, 1954) and 'Abd al-Karim al-Uzri (minister of finance, 1953–1954, and development, 1954) were strong advocates of Arab unity and worked for it.

8   The reasons for this affinity have been questioned by a number of scholars. Natural bonds of trade and travel between the Arabs of Mosul and the small towns of the Euphrates bordering Syria and Jordan are one reason cited. Tribal ties that cross frontiers are another. But pan-Arabism is also an ideology that goes beyond the Sunni community, and appeals to numerous Shi'a, as well; hence it should not be equated merely with religious or even communal identity. For a good exposition of this, see Nikolaos van Dam, "Middle Eastern Political Cliches: Takriti and Sunni rule in Iraq: Alawi rule in Syria."

9   Kurdish population estimates vary, depending on the source. There are probably a little over 4 million Kurds in Iraq. There are about 13 million in Turkey, where they constitute over 23 percent of the population; in Iran they are about 5–6 million or 10 to 12 percent of the population. There are fewer than a million in Syria, and there are smaller numbers in Armenia, Azerbaijan, and Europe. See David McDowall, *A Modern History of the Kurds*, pp. 3–4; and Mehrdad R. Izady, *The Kurds*, p. 116.

10 In the mid-1970s, Iran's military support for the Kurdish dissidents (along with that of Israel and the United States) was strong enough to compel Iraqi concessions to Iran on the Shatt al-'Arab. During the Iran-Iraq war, Iranian troops, supported by Iraqi Kurdish opposition, threatened Iraq's Derbendikhan Dam near Halabja. Part of Iraq's pipeline through Turkey runs through Kurdish territory, and hence is subject to interdiction. Turkey has repeatedly intervened militarily in the north since the Second Gulf War in an attempt to control cross-border actions by its own dissident Kurds, now situated in northern Iraq.

11 Several times in the aftermath of the Second Gulf War, Turkey, Syria, and Iran have met to discuss common strategy on "containing" the Kurdish-controlled zone in northern Iraq.

12 The growth of an organized (underground) Shi`a opposition in Iraq has now been described in a rich and growing literature too voluminous to detail here. Its most important indigenous movement, the Da`wah, began in the late 1950s under the impetus of a young cleric in Najaf, Muhammad Baqr al-Sadr. His writings in the 1960s and 1970s popularized a Shi`a identity. Open confrontation with the Ba`th government grew in the 1970s, with open clashes in 1974 and 1977, and concomitant repression by the regime. With the coming of the Iranian revolution in 1979, Sadr and some other Iraqi clerics supported Khomeini and the Islamic Republic, and gathered a sufficient following among the Shi`a to constitute an open threat to the regime and the entire structure of the Iraqi state. Sadr was executed by the regime in 1980. A new movement, organized under the umbrella of the Supreme Assembly for the Islamic Revolution in Iraq (S.A.I.R.I.), was established in 1982 in Iran, among a growing group of Iraqi Shi`a exiles there. It is headed by Muhammad Baqr al-Hakim from another leading family of Iraqi Shi`a clerics. This group includes a number of Iraqi Shi`a organizations. It played a role in supporting the Shi`a uprising in the south of Iraq in 1991 and continues guerilla activities across the border from Iran. The degree of support commanded by these organizations is not known, but there has clearly been an increase in Shi`a consciousness since the 1960s.

13 The numbers of Iraqis in Iran can only be estimated. These include Iraqi Shi`a of Iranian origin expelled from Iraq, starting in 1972, but largely in 1980 and thereafter, as well as war defectors and those who have fled the persecution of the Iraqi government. Figures range as high as a million, but a more likely number is around 600,000.

14 Phebe Marr, *The Modern History of Iraq*, p.164.

15 J. Ismael, "Domestic Sources," p. 32.

16 The pipeline through Syria to the Mediterranean was closed by Syria in 1956 and in 1966–1967, and was finally shut down during the Iran-Iraq war. These problems prompted Iraq's construction of a "strategic" pipeline running from the northern fields south to Iraq's offshore Gulf terminals at Mina-l-Bakr and Khor al-Amaya south of Fao, in 1975. The pipelines through Turkey and Saudi Arabia were closed down in the wake of the Second Gulf War.

17 Phebe Marr, "Turkey and Iraq," p. 47.

18 Thomas Naff and Ruth C. Matson, *Water in the Middle East: Conflict or Cooperation?*, p. 97.

19 Marr, "Turkey and Iraq," p. 47. The completion of the Tabqa Dam in Syria and its subsequent activation, along with the Keban Dam in Turkey, caused serious water displacement when both dams were being filled in 1975. Syria did not release compensatory flows, as it had done the previous year, indicating that the dispute may have been more political than technical, but the episode does illustrate Iraq's vulnerability.

20 Marr, *Modern History*, p. 279.

21 One exception to the formal extension of national law throughout the country was the Tribal Disputes Code, initiated by the British during the mandate and still in effect in 1958. In tribal areas, it allowed shaikhs and aghas to settle civil conflicts outside the jurisdiction of the central government. These tribal leaders were also landlords who dominated parliament. See Marr, *Modern History*, p. 135.

22 Hassan al-`Alawi, *Al-Shi`a wal-Dawlah-l-Qawmiyyah fi-l-Iraq*, pp. 198–99. At lower levels, Arab Sunnis maintained a disproportionate dominance. One study has found that among top decision makers between 1945 and 1958, 60 percent were Arab Sunni; 21 percent Arab Shi`a, and 15 percent Kurds. See Marr, *Modern History*, p. 144.

23 In 1949, a year of three coups in Syria, Iraqi politicians worked for some kind of union, which fizzled out by the end of the year. In the mid-1950s, schemes centering on unity with

Syria were largely initiated by Crown Prince `Abd al-Ilah in a vain attempt to find a Hashimite role for himself in the region after young Prince Faisal II would come of age in 1953. By this time, veteran statesman Nuri al-Sa`id was firmly opposed to these efforts.

24 The United States was an "observer" in the pact, but did not officially join.

25 These included rent ceilings, a cut in working hours, and income tax and housing relief.

26 The temporary constitution promulgated by the new regime publicly recognized Kurds and Arabs as partners for the first time.

27 In 1959, Iraq formally seceded from the Baghdad Pact, thereby annulling its military agreement with Great Britain, and the R.A.F. was withdrawn from its base in Habaniyyah.

28 The law put the rich Rumailah field in the south in government hands. Iraqi regimes were not able to develop these fields, however, because they were legally threatened by the expropriated companies, a situation that did not end until nationalization of oil in 1972. From 1961 to the mid-1970s, Iraq's production and market share were frozen. Some consider this a high price to have been paid. See Centre for Global Energy Studies, *Oil Production Capacity in the Gulf*, Vol. 4, section 3, p. 76.

29 In 1961, the rest of the Arab world supported Kuwait, which had just announced its independence from Britain. Iraq proclaimed that it would reconsider diplomatic relations with those who recognized Kuwait, and gradually withdrew its ambassadors (but not all its diplomatic staff) from a long list of Arab (and other) countries, thus isolating itself.

30 In February 1963, the new Ba`th regime turned to Egypt for unity. When a second Ba`th coup occurred in Syria in March, Syria was added to the discussions. Although unity was agreed on in principle it proved difficult in practise, and Egypt and Iraq had second thoughts. The two Ba`th regimes continued discussions, but when, in November 1963, a Syrian delegation arrived in Baghdad to help mediate a local dispute, it was viewed as interfering in Iraq's domestic affairs. Unity talks ended when a moderate faction, under `Arif, took over the government in Iraq, ending purely Ba`th rule. See "Les relations syro-irakiennes: Quarante ans de rivalité," *Cahiers de l'Orient* 6 (2nd trimester, 1987): 208–10.

31 Hani al-Fukaiki, *Awkar al-Hazimah*, p. 268. Batatu notes that in the period before the party came to power (1952–1963) the top command was over 50 percent Shi`a, almost 40 percent Arab Sunni. From 1963 to 1970, the figures were 85 percent Arab Sunni, a mere 5 percent Arab Shi`a; Hanna Batatu, *The Old Social Classes and Revolutionary Movements of Iraq*, p. 1,078.

32 These struggles are graphically illustrated in al-Fukaiki, *Awkar*, and in Ali Karim Sa`id, *'Iraq 8 Shabat 1963*, based on Talib Shabib's recollections.

33 Batatu, *Old Social Classes*, p. 1,010.

34 The regime was also weakened by the death of `Abd al-Salam `Arif in April 1996, in a helicopter crash. He was succeeded as president by his brother, a much weaker figure.

35 In the cabinets of the old regime between 1948 and 1958, only 6 percent of the ministers were former military officers; 12 percent were lawyers, 31 percent civil servants, and 11 percent businessmen. Between 1958 and 1968, the number of former military men rose to 29 percent; lawyers remained the same; civil servants dropped to 17 percent, and only 1 percent were businessmen. See Marr, "Iraq's Leadership Dilemma," p. 196. Another good example is the Ba`th National Council of the Revolutionary Command in 1963: of the eighteen members, eight were Ba`th Party activists and organizers; the rest army officers. See Batatu, *Old Social Classes*, pp. 1,004–6.

36 Marr, *Modern History*, p. 213.

37 Bakr and Saddam Husayn come from the same tribe, the Albu Nasr, but from different clans or extended families. For a description of the Albu Nasr tribe and its clan relationships, see Baram, *Building toward Crisis*, chapter 2.

38 The early 1970s represented a high point in Soviet influence. The Ba`th's need for Soviet support to help stabilize its domestic situation diminished with the end of the oil crisis in 1972/1973 and the Algiers Agreement of 1975, which ended the threat from both the Kurds and Iran.

39 From 1974 to 1985, with the exception of one year, U.S. exports to Iraq greatly exceeded those of the Soviet Union. By 1985, Soviet exports had dropped to sixteenth place. Iraq, General Statistical Organization, General Statistical Office, *Annual Abstract of Statistics*, various years.

40 By 1980, Iraq had reserves of $35 billion and an oil income of over $26 billion annually. See Sluglett, "Progress Postponed," p. 236.

41 This was partly a family feud within the Ba`th Party. With the access of the `Aflaq wing of the party to power in Baghdad in 1968, relations deteriorated markedly, except for a few years, a situation that was not changed by Hafiz al-Asad's accession to power in Syria in 1970. The two countries squabbled over pipeline fees in 1972, the terms of the Arab-Israeli cease-fire in 1973, water in 1975, and Syria's entry into Lebanon in 1976. By 1978 there were acts of sabotage in each other's capital. See "Relations syro-irakiennes," pp. 212–20.

42 In 1979, Saddam Husayn visited Jordan, the first Iraqi head of state to do so since 1958. Economic, military, and political agreements followed, including an expansion of Aqaba port to help relieve Iraq's port problem.

43 The shah's role was encouraged by the emergence of the so-called U.S. "two-pillar" policy in the Gulf, a strategy initiated in the early 1970s by President Nixon. It was designed to encourage regional leaders to take responsibility for regional stability. In 1972, a major arms sale was concluded with Iran, and the shah stepped forward to assume the position of guardian of Gulf security. This sale was balanced by more modest support to Saudi Arabia, the second "pillar."

44 This phase of the conflict on the Shatt began in 1969 and continued until 1975. The shah's occupation in 1971 of three islands at the foot of the Gulf, claimed by Arab Gulf states, also caused Iraq to focus on the exit from the Gulf at the Strait of Hormuz.

45 For a good exposition of this evolution, see Amatzia Baram, *Culture, History and Ideology in the Formation of Ba`thist Iraq, 1968–1989*, chapter 11. Baram cites Saddam Husayn in a press interview, saying: "The question of linking unity to the removal of boundaries is no longer acceptable to present Arab mentality... . The Arab reality is that Arabs are now twenty-two states, and we have to behave accordingly." See interview with Kuwaiti editors, Fez, September 8, 1982, in Baram, *Culture*, p. 121.

46 For an exposition of this thinking, see an extensive interview with Saddam Husayn, 1979, in Fuad Matar, *Saddam Husain, the Man, the Cause, the Future*, chapter 8.

47 Education up to the university level and health services, including hospitalization, were free, and from 1968 to 1983, school enrollment doubled. The Ba`th also pushed land distribution, agricultural coops, and, for a time, collective farms. Meanwhile, the share of the public sector in domestic production rose from 31 percent in 1968 to 80 percent in 1977, although the percentage varied from sector to sector. See Marr, *Modern History*, pp. 240–42.

48 By 1978/1979, the regime had split with the Iraq Communist Party and many Communists had fled to Europe or gone underground. See Tripp, "Iraq," p. 192.

49 In July 1979, Bakr was "retired" as president, and within days, Saddam undertook a brutal purge of the party, executing five Revolutionary Command Council members and dozens of other key party officials, while accusations of plotting with Syria flew about. The episode came amid the rising "Shi`a" challenge, domestically and from Iran, and in retrospect may have been a prelude to the Iran-Iraq war.

50 For this view, see Majid Khadduri, *The Gulf War: The Origins and Implications of the Iraq-Iran Conflict*.

51 For this view, see Chubin and Tripp, *Iran and Iraq at War*. Although Ba`thists had sometimes talked of "liberating" the Arab population in Khuzistan (formerly Muhammarah), this was not a goal consciously pursued until the war.

52 Iraq made rapid gains in occupying Iranian territory, mainly in Khuzistan, but by 1982 Iranian forces had regrouped and pushed Iraq back across its frontier. Iraq then asked for a cease-fire and a settlement, but Iran miscalculated by continuing the war for another six years, attempting to capture Iraqi territory and overthrow the regime.

53 In 1980, Iraq was earning $26 billion a year from oil; by 1983, with a drastic cut in exports and a drop in oil prices, it earned $7 to $8 billion. It is dificult to predict what prices and production would have been had the war not occurred, but Iraq's oil income is not likely to have been below $100 billion for these years and could easily have been higher than $200 billion.

54 By the mid-1980s, this opposition, organized under the S.A.I.R.I. umbrella, was fielding a military force that numbered in the thousands, and that participated with Iranians in the war against Iraq on both the northern and southern fronts.

55 The United States reestablished diplomatic relations with Iraq in 1984, and was extending agricultural credits of $1 billion by the end of the war. The United States also provided critical military intelligence and other support during the war.

56 Phebe Marr, "Iraq in the 90s: Oil Revenues, Debt Management, Spending Priorities," *Middle East Executive Reports*, Washington, D.C., June 1990, p. 13.

57 Although Iraq's oil income picked up after the war, the country still had to repair major destruction to oil installations and its offshore export facilities before it could return to prewar levels. Moreover, it was attempting to spend scarce resources on at least four areas: military technology (essentially W.M.D.), reconstruction; consumer imports (especially food); and debt repayment. Reconciling these priorities proved impossible. See Marr, "Iraq's Uncertain Future."

58 Press articles in the United States pointedly compared the Iraqi ruler to Ceausescu in Romania and opined that his fate might (and should) be the same. See, for example, David Korn, "Don't Deal with Dictators."

59 Iraq's ability to roll over its debt during the Iran-Iraq war led it to believe it could continue this practice in the war's aftermath, relying on incoming oil revenues to cover expenses, and discounting future revenues in favor of loans. It refused debt rescheduling because this would have given European creditors some control over its fiscal policy, yet it continued to spend on multiple programs it could not afford, such as weapons of mass destruction.

60 As with the Iran-Iraq war, Iraq's motives cannot be known with certainty, but its decision must be set against a background of long frustration over lack of direct access to the Gulf and the desire to eliminate Kuwaiti control over the Khor `Abd Allah estuary. Kuwait was also seen as being "used" by the United States and the West to prevent Iraq's economic revival, through such methods as overproduction of its OPEC oil quota, refusal to cancel Iraq's debts, and its unwillingness to provide substantial sums of money for postwar reconstruction. These long-festering issues were now coupled with the changing global situation and the emergence of the United States as the leading power, especially in the Gulf. In this context, the Iraqi regime appears to have seen its leadership position threatened domestically and regionally.

61 The southern no-fly zone was originally fixed at the 32nd parallel. It was moved up to the 33rd (virtually the outskirts of Baghdad) in 1996 in retaliation for the regime's attack on Irbil.

62   France also participated in enforcing the southern zone up to the 32nd parallel until late 1998.

63   This region is clearly delineated by a map in Sarah Graham-Brown, *Sanctioning Saddam: The Politics of Intervention in Iraq*, pp. xviii–xix.

64   Figures vary widely and none can be accepted at face value. This assessment was made in a Unicef report, October 1996. The best study of the impact of the stanctions regime on Iraq is Graham-Brown, *Sanctioning Saddam*.

65   Baram, *Building toward Crisis*, chapter 2.

66   This process was accompanied by the reemergence of tribal influence. The government increasingly relied on tribal leaders to keep law and order at the local level in return for benefits such as land grants and economic favors. This trend was related to the shrinking of the state apparatus in the 1990s. See Amatzia Baram, "Neo-Tribalism in Iraq: Saddam Husayn's Tribal Policies, 1991–1995," and Faleh Abd al-Jabbar, "The Reconstruction and Deconstruction of Iraq's Tribes: Tribalism under Patrimonial Totalitarianism."

67   For the development of this phenomenon, see Kiren Aziz Chaudhry, "On the Way to Market: Economic Liberalization and Iraq's Invasion of Kuwait," and Isam al-Khafaji, "War as a Vehicle for the Rise and Demise of a State Controlled Society."

68   A telling critique of Iraq's diplomatic service and its performance in the Gulf War is offered by Sa`d al-Bazzaz, who faults it, among other things, for emphasizing "the principle of loyalty at the expense of performance." See Sa`d al-Bazzaz, *Harb Talidu Ukhra*, p. 472.

69   For an account of this phenomenon by a former chief of military intelligence who escaped, see Wafiq al-Samarra'i, *Hatam al-Bawabah-l-Sharqiyyah*.

70   For example, Iraq has held out postsanctions oil concessions to potential supporters, such as France and Russia, while raising the military and political costs of containment to its adversaries (the United States and Great Britain) through repeated challenges such as expelling the weapons-inspection regime.

71   A good example of works that have greatly influenced Western perceptions of the Iraqi regime is those of Kanan Makiya (Samir al-Khalil), *The Republic of Fear* and *Cruelty and Silence*.

72   See Charles Tripp, "Symbol and Strategy: Iraq and the War for Kuwait."

10

Morocco

I. William Zartman

Geography, history, and people making choices have made Morocco, and have in turn made Moroccan foreign policy. Geography has placed the country at the crossroads of many worlds, giving it several overlapping identities. History has left it on the fringes of all those worlds of which it is a part. Its decision-making structures have been a product of that geohistory, which they in turn have made. To this is added present-day domestic needs, to which all foreign policy responds and which it defends. In all this, Morocco is like every other country, but as a result of all this, there is no other Morocco.

The foreign policy of independent Morocco is essentially that crafted for nearly three decades by King Hassan II. In 1999, that leadership disappeared, to be succeeded by the new hand of Muhammad VI. The historic ship of state has a new governor, to test the freedom of action that his inheritance allows.

Geopolitics

When the Mediterranean waters broke through the chain of mountains that begins in the Atlantic with the Canaries and marches north in three columns from North Africa into Spain, Corsica-Sardinia, and Italy, they left the northwest corner of Africa cut off from its natural prolongation, which formed its own Iberian peninsula, walled off from the rest of Europe by a pile of mountains pushed up by tectonic forces. That sluice between the Mediterranean and the Atlantic has been tantalizing to population movements over millennia. The waters that flow westward through it have carried sailors from the cradle of civilization in the Fertile Crescent to the western end of the Mediterranean, to colonize the south Spanish and north Moroccan shores; the land that forms the hinterlands of those shores has also borne soldiers westward and—on momentous occasions—to burst across the water for the conquest of the opposite shores. The latitudinal movement bore Carthaginians and Romans westward to Morocco and Iberia; the longitudinal movement carried Carthaginians north to Spain and France, than Vandals south into North Africa, then Arabs north again into Spain and France, then French and Spanish south into North Africa, and now North Africans (though not yet as conquerors) into Europe.

Loves and hates followed as a consequence. It is too early to know whether Europe (mainly France) marked Morocco as deeply as Morocco had earlier marked Spain; France stayed in control of Morocco for only about a tenth of the time Morocco had been in control of Spain. But the dual experience confirmed the geographic fact that Morocco is closer to Europe than is any other part of the Afro-Arab world (with Tunisia second). "Africa stops at the Pyrenees," claims a popular saying, but it could just as well say, "Europe stops at the Atlas." In the seventeenth century, the great Sultan Moulay Ismail quite naturally asked King Louis XIV for the hand of his cousin, the Grande Demoiselle, and was slightly peeved that he was refused. In 1987, Hassan II quite naturally applied for outright membership in the European Community, and was slightly peeved that he was refused.

The same king was the only known Arab ruler to say, "As a Westerner, as a Muslim... . "[1] Morocco is the only Arab country that is both Mediterranean and Atlantic—and the latter shore is socially and economically the more important. Although this enabled the Arab conqueror Uqba ben Nafi' to ride his horse into the ocean in 682 crying, "If there was more land, I would keep on going," it also means that Morocco was the first Axis territory on which the Allies landed in 1942, and that it was the only Arab country to have U.S. Strategic Air Command bases both before and after independence (even if against its will). The fact that the Land of the Far West (al-Maghrib al-Aqsa) is the westernmost prolongation of Arabia brings it into close contact with the American as well as the European component of the West.

But Morocco is also the northern prolongation of Africa. Historic times have seen Moroccan forces extending the Sharifian Empire as far south as the Niger River inland delta, when Sultan Ahmad al-Mansur took Timbuktu in 1591. The gold and salt trade that long tied Morocco to West Africa has more recently been replaced by trade in modern commodities, and Morocco's population includes an admixture of Black Africans.[2] The great cities of Morocco on either side of the Atlas Mountains grew rich as entrepots for the trans-Saharan trade—Sijilmassa and the other cities of the Tafilelt (home of the current `Alawi dynasty), Marrakesh, even Fez and Meknes. Its historic ties deep into the land of the Blacks (bilad al-sudan) resonate today in the Morocco irredenta issue.

All of these elements have combined to form the basis of Moroccan identity, and so of its foreign policy. Morocco is an Arab Muslim country, part of the Arab world and its councils. It is a member of the League of Arab States, and of the ad hoc body that has essentially replaced the League since the late 1970s, the Arab Summit Conference. Morocco is also member of the Organization of the Islamic Conference, and King Hassan and now King Muhammad chaired and chair its al-Quds Committee. It has been actively involved in Arab causes, and played an important role as a moderate leader in the Middle East peace process.

Before the creation of the Organization of African Unity (O.A.U.), the Casablanca Group in 1961 grouped Morocco with three more radical African states plus the Algerian exile government in a bid to define African unity. Morocco was then a founding member of O.A.U. in 1963, belonging until its resignation upon the admission of the Sahrawi Arab Democratic Republic in 1981.[3] Since these founding days, Morocco has been involved in African politics.

Finally, it has been in a constant relationship with Europe, and more broadly with the Atlantic West, since independence. Its institutional tie with the European

Community (E.C.) and, since 1995, the European Union, has been its association agreement, initially signed just after independence in 1957, and renewed and revised regularly thereafter. One interpretation of the request for E.C. membership was that it was a ploy to claim better terms in the upcoming negotiations for the 1995 association agreement.[4]

There are no institutional ties with the broader Atlantic or NATO world. In the Cold War, Morocco played a clever game of balancing ties to both the Soviet Union, on a commercial basis, and the United States, on a political basis. [5] There was never any doubt that it was a nonaligned part of the Western world, but its careful relations with the Soviet Union supported its Saharan claims and neutralized the eastward ties of its rival neighbor, Algeria (both elements to be discussed below).

All of these worlds combined to triangulate Morocco's position in North Africa, the center of its circles of interest. The Maghrib is an island in physical and human geography, circumscribed by seas of water and sand to the north and south. As a regional system it is structured on a rivalry between neighbors equal in population but unequal in wealth—Morocco and Algeria. Owing to its oil and gas deposits, Algeria since independence has had a per-capita G.N.P. of at least twice that of Morocco. Despite their great social similarities, the two states have invented a rivalry that turns history into mythology and mythology into a reading of history. Facing the historic monarchy of Morocco (its `Alawi dynasty dating from 1666) is the new revolutionary state of Algeria. Moroccan society and polity were preserved by the French protectorate of only forty years, whereas Algerian society was more revolutionized by 130 years of direct French rule than it was by the seven years of revolutionary war. Those parallel facts allow for hostile readings of past acts and present intentions on either side of the only recently recognized boundary. Tunisia has played a mediating role in the system, Libya a spoiler role after 1969 and, more recently, Mauritania a dummy role.

The brotherly rivalry that forms the basis of the Maghribi system has passed through stages of conflict and cooperation. It has been Tunisia's role to raise an appeal to cooperation whenever conflict comes too close to tearing the region apart. Cooperation has been institutionalized at four periods since Moroccan independence—1958, when the parties of the three neighbors met in Tangier to plan collaboration; 1964–1967, when the Moroccan-Algerian border dispute was managed and the Maghribi Permanent Consultative Committee was established; 1972–1974, when Morocco and Algeria completed their border and cooperated on the Western Sahara; and 1987–1994, when the Arab Maghrib Union (U.M.A., established in Marrakesh in 1989) was in preparation and then in initial operation.[6] In between these high points were valleys of conflict, including the Moroccan-Algerian border war of 1963, the Saharan dispute after 1974, and the bipolar system created by the Algerian-Tunisian-Mauritanian Friendship Treaty of 1983, which sparked the Moroccan-Libyan Arab-African Union of 1984–1986. The nature of the regional system is to restrain intensity in either direction, keeping these moments of conflict from destroying the system and the moments of cooperation from eliminating the states.

Concentric Circles

These geopolitical components have produced policies that benefitted from Morocco's Maghribi, Arab, African, Mediterranean, and Atlantic location and history to play on all four arenas. As may be expected, they act as concentric circles, with loyalty and membership most intense in the center rings and freedom of action greatest toward the periphery. Yet even in the innermost circles, Morocco has retained an autonomy that balances its roles as a team player, and this will be examined in the next section.

Within the Maghrib, a number of models of relations have been pursued by member countries—integration, pluralism, hegemony. Morocco's model is pluralism, which grows out of its position in the region—neither center nor periphery, unique in its attributes, locked in a rivalry with its neighbor, able to ally but not to unite or suffer hegemony. It is the underlying pattern of the classical balance of power, as practiced in Europe and other areas where there have been a number of roughly equal states. Its dynamics allow for short-lived alliances to check hegemony. Such a model of relations has a basic configuration, referred to as Kautilyan after the ancient Indian statesman who spelled out its underlying principle: "My neighbor is my enemy; my neighbor's neighbor is my friend."[7] The result is a loose checkerboard of relations, with boundary matters playing an important part.

When Morocco and Algeria became independent, in 1956 and 1962, respectively, there was not even a disputed boundary all the way between them; after the first 500 kilometers from the Mediterranean, there was no boundary at all until the western end of Algeria. After the 1963 war, which ended in a draw, a committee of the O.A.U. studied the problem to let it cool down, and in 1972 the two neighbors signed an agreement delimiting and providing for the demarcation of a boundary. Scarcely had the bilateral boundary been settled, however, when the Spanish or Western Saharan question arose between the two countries. Morocco understood that it had an agreement from Algeria for its claims in 1974, and therefore felt betrayed as well as contested when Algeria took up the cause of the Popular Liberation Front for Saqiet el-Hamra and Rio de Oro (Polisario). Thereafter, through numerous changes in government (except during the brief presidency of Muhammad Boudiaf, assassinated in 1991), the Algerian military insisted on a hard line in the Saharan issue, and King Hassan came to consider Algeria the major enemy of Morocco throughout his life.

During the fourth period of Maghribi cooperation, 1987–1994, Morocco hoped that the agreement on the U.M.A. would set aside contention on the Saharan issue, but a terrorist attack in Marrakesh in the summer of 1994 convinced Morocco of Algerian intentions to destabilize the monarchy, and it "froze" its membership in the U.M.A. and called for suspension, which effectively occurred. Morocco's relations with the other three members of the union have been positive but scarcely engaging, and economic exchanges among the five countries constitute no more than 5 percent of their total trade.

Morocco's policy among Arab states has been one of moderate leadership. The Royal Armed Forces (F.A.R.) took part in crucial Arab encounters. They were in position on the Golan Heights when the October 1973 Arab-Israeli war broke out, and they were sent to Saudi Arabia to protect the Holy Places (but not to join the coalition against Iraq) in January 1991, when the Second Gulf War broke out. But Morocco has above all worked to support Egypt in the peace process and was host to the initial Egyptian-Israeli meetings that led to President Anwar Sadat's visit to Jerusalem in 1977. Thereafter, Fez, Casablanca, and Rabat were the sites of Arab summits in 1981, 1989, and 1996, respectively, and King Hassan sought to play the conciliatory role of a good host. Within a wider circle, King Hassan's chairmanship of the al-Quds (Jerusalem) Committee of the Islamic Conference Organization was used to buttress and deploy his prestige in the cause of the recovery of Jerusalem. The Arab League has long been behind Morocco on the Saharan issue, and so Morocco has a freer hand in Arab politics.[8] Hassan II was a constant participant in the Arab Summit Conference, the successor institution to the less active Arab League. He enjoyed close relations with other monarchial families of the Arab world but above all with the Saudis, many of whom have vacation palaces on the Moroccan coast and sponsor economic ventures in Morocco, including financing the Saharan war for many years in the 1970s and 1980s.

On the African front, Morocco's position has been different. As with the Arabs, Morocco's policy among African states has been one of moderate leadership. But during the radical era of the O.A.U. in the 1970s, the moderates were outflanked by the activism of Algeria, Libya, and the Afro-Marxists south of the Sahara. When the Polisario's government in exile was admitted to the O.A.U., Morocco left, making good a threat it had brandished for a long time. Morocco has continued to have good relations with many O.A.U. members and has long been a leader of a moderate group particularly concerned with communist activities on the continent. The F.A.R. was sent to Congo (Zaire) as part of the U.N. operations in the early 1960s, and again against dissident invasions from Angola in 1977 and 1978. Moroccan troops provided presidential bodyguards in Gabon, Cameroun, Equatorial Guinea, and Togo; Zairean president Mobutu Sese Seko went in exile to die in Morocco in 1998 (as did the shah of Iran nearly two decades earlier).

As a Mediterranean country, a former French and Spanish protectorate, the source of a large expatriate minority in France and its neighbors, and a major trader with Europe, Morocco sees its history, economy, and hence politics tied up with its trans-Mediterranean relations. France and Spain are its most important partners, and Morocco has been careful to keep those relations on a good working level. In addition to official relations, it has had to deal with both countries' important socialist parties and their penchant for criticizing the monarchy, sometimes by applying counter-pressure, sometimes by making a virtue out of concessions. For example, Danielle Mitterrand, the former French president's wife, was a vigorous critic of human rights and political prisoners' conditions in Morocco in the 1980s; in answer, the king released almost all political prisoners and hosted a world congress of Amnesty International in the early 1990s. The Spanish socialists have also been critical of Moroccan policy in former Spanish (Western) Sahara; even as it sets up royal relations with King Juan Carlos, Morocco continues to remind Spain that the three Spanish enclaves on the north Moroccan coast could be claimed and captured any time, just as the Sidi Ifni enclave in the south was in 1969.

Europe, in the form of the European Union (E.U.), has risen in importance for Morocco to the same level as its most important members. Morocco continues to aspire to the closest of associations with the E.U., an aspiration sharpened by perpetual rivalry for European attention among the three Maghribi states and also by Morocco's position as the least developed economically but arguably most stable politically of the three. Europe too has its left-wing critics of the monarchy; this has kept that relationship from being taken for granted by either side. But Morocco renewed its association agreement in 1995, a bit later than Tunisia; Algeria has still not followed suit. The agreement endorses structural adjustment measures and opens Morocco to duty-free competition in significant sectors.

The outermost circle is the global arena of the superpowers, in the singular since 1991. Morocco never had bad relations with the Soviet Union, and in 1978 it came out the winner in a Soviet $2 billion phosphate and $300 million fishing agreement that implicitly recognized Morocco's claim to the Western Sahara. King Hassan listed himself as an "advisor of American presidents," and made sure he was invited to visit every one of them for golf, horseback riding, and politics. The first country to recognize the United States and to share a friendship treaty still in force since 1787, Morocco has maintained a close relationship with Washington as a partner with integrity in Middle East matters and also south of the Sahara. Although its strategic importance in the Mediterranean and Africa has waned with the passing of the Cold War, and in the Middle East with the return of the peace process to the Levantine principals, its history and geography have not changed, and its relevance to American policy remains.

National Integrity

Although much of Morocco's historical tradition can be read out of its geopolitics, there is an additional aspect of its character that derives directly from its historical experience. Throughout its history, Morocco has been not just a part of North Africa, West Arabia, the western Mediterranean, or the Euro-African crossroads, but a particular part of those regions. Morocco per se has a long tradition of national coherence and national integrity that gives it autonomy within all its worlds, a tradition of separate action and separate ability to act that gave a historical pedestal to the policy initiatives of Hassan II.

Morocco was its own province of the Roman Empire but, more important, it was its own caliphate in the Muslim world, independent of the Arab kingdoms and the successor community of the East. In the short time when the Maghrib was undifferentiatedly united, in the eleventh and twelfth centuries, it was from the base of the Moroccan Almohad and Almoravid kingdoms. When the rest of the Arabo-Muslim world fell to the Ottoman Empire, Morocco was independent, the only separate Arab entity and the only separate Muslim entity east of Persia. Under the French, it was a separate colonial possession, and not a colony but a protectorate, from 1912 to 1956. Its current dynasty is the latest in a more or less unbroken succession of twelve centuries of dynasties. Even within the Maghrib, Morocco's view of cooperation is not a thrust at leadership to rival Algeria's pretentions, but a program of cooperation among units within a pluralistic region.

As a result, national integrity is a central tenet of Moroccan policy, and independent démarches are a policy characteristic. This has affected Morocco in two very different ways. On one hand, it has given its foreign policy a mission of striking out in new and innovative directions within the framework already outlined; on the other hand, it has designated the territorial question as a coin of membership in the national community.

In all the worlds to which it belongs, Morocco is a freewheeling member, unconstrained by any external consensus. This makes it a valuable if an unpredictable participant, capable of initiatives and independent actions. Its démarche to the E.C., its early role in the Middle East peace process, and its unique participation in the Second Gulf War have been mentioned. A striking example with many instances is its position, in both domestic and foreign policy, toward Jews. Successive kings have cultivated the small Jewish community in Morocco, made its members their advisors, and extolled their role in Morocco. For twenty years, delegations from Israel have visited the country.[9] King Hassan made a point of visiting former Moroccan Jewish communities abroad and reminding them that Moroccan citizenship cannot be lost. He entertained close ties with the American Jewish community.

The territorial or irredentist issue is more complicated. With colonization, the Moroccan kingdom was divided up into French and Spanish colonial pieces, in some places without even a boundary, as noted. With independence, those pieces came back together (the Moroccan term is "retrocession"), one by one, unlike almost any other colonial possession. The French, northern Spanish, and international zones received their independence in 1956; the southern Spanish protectorate (Tarfaya) followed in 1958, and Ifni in 1969. By that time, the one area still under colonial rule was the Spanish Sahara, Morocco having recognized the independence of Mauritania in 1969. When the Spanish withdrew in 1974, Morocco negotiated a treaty, along with Mauritania, to receive the territory, and it received agreement from the Yemaa, the territorial assembly under the Spanish.

However, the Polisario was also active, enjoying support and sanctuary from Algeria, also eliciting a vote of support from the Yemaa, and declaring itself a Sahrawi Arab Democratic Republic that eventually received recognition from a majority of O.A.U. members and then the O.A.U. itself. The Saharan issue was then taken up by the United Nations, which in 1988 established a plan for a settlement through a cease-fire and referendum. Although the cease-fire has been respected, with Morocco in control of most of the territory, progress toward the referendum has been slow and contested by both parties all along the way. For Moroccans, the Sahara is a deep and popular issue, the last piece of the country (and of a much reduced irredenta) to be returned. The fact that the F.A.R. expended considerable effort to recover it de facto also makes it an issue on which compromise is difficult and—for the monarchy—dangerous.

Domestic Issues

Domestic concerns and resources are the basis of any sound and durable foreign policy. Morocco's domestic concerns are varied, but knitted together they form the material of its political positions and initiatives. Several are particularly important: national cohesion in regard to subversion, the Sahara, Islam, and economic resources including water and oil.

As the governors of a newly independent state and an old nation with a modernizing political system, Moroccan leaders need to guide the evolution of their country through dangerous rapids. Government, which derives from the Greek word for "steering" and is related to the French word for "rudder," reflects its original meaning intensely in countries such as Morocco where tradition and modernity converge and diverge to make up the flow of politics. Foreign policy is an important aspect of these activities. In Morocco, three aspects are of particular importance: the protection of the political system against external subversion, the Western Sahara as the issue that raises the question of national integrity within the political system, and the danger of fundamentalist Islamic opposition to the established political system.

Morocco has been the target of externally based infiltration that has linked up with internal dissident elements. In the 1960s and 1970s, this took the form of left-wing antimonarchist opposition from a wing of the Socialist Party, the National Union of Popular Forces (U.N.F.P.), with alleged subversion coming from Algeria. Trials of suspects were held, and relations with the neighbor suffered, but the problem was finally brought under control by King Hassan's negotiations with the political parties, the replacement of the U.N.F.P. by the Socialist Union, and the restructuring of the political system. When relations with Algeria soured again in the mid-1990s, subversion was once more part of the conflict. Whether subversion and charges of subversion are part of state policy or merely incite state reactions is not always clear.

The Saharan issue, already discussed, has been the touchstone of the new political system restructured by King Hassan in the mid-1970s, and therefore the central issue of Moroccan foreign policy. So much effort has been expended on recovering the last piece of Moroccan territory that softness on the part of any political actor—a political party or the king himself—would weaken its political position greatly, not just as a result of the role of the army but owing to widespread public sentiment.

The issue of Muslim fundamentalism is still more complicated. Morocco has escaped the problems that have plagued its Maghribi neighbors and other Arab Muslim states, for a number of reasons: the position of the monarch as caliph of the west and descendent of the Prophet (*sharif*); the attention that the king has paid to his position of religious leadership and his cultivation of the religious authorities (*'ulama'*); and the fact that the kingdom is accustomed to rural prophets who are summarily suppressed when they rise to challenge urban religion. But the Islamic issue is important for national cohesion, precisely because religion is so important to the position of the monarchy, the historic center of the political system. So Morocco, although a deeply religious society, has little patience with religious deviants such as Libya's Qadhafi or religious fanatics such as the Iranian revolutionaries. This domestic concern is also felt in its foreign relations.[10]

A basic law of foreign policy is that its ends and means always bring each other into balance.[11] When the means outrun the ends, the goals are expanded to meet them, and when the means fall short, the ends will be trimmed. When the goals expand, the means must be found for them or they will be pulled in again; when the goals contract, the means will be allowed to fall off, or will drive the ends up again. Morocco is not richly endowed with the physical resources of an ambitious foreign policy, so it needs to cultivate its means and adjust its goals to them.

Economic resources are limited in Morocco, which has pursued a policy of agricultural development for export rather than import substitution or heavy industrial development. Morocco's small oil reserves are nearly exhausted, and new prospecting in the Sahara has not yet produced oil. Morocco therefore is an energy consumer, not a producer. It taps the new gas line from Algeria to Spain, but its energy sources are mainly thermo- and hydroelectric, as its terrain greatly favors an extended system of dams for irrigation and electricity. However, this focus on agriculture and hydropower also means great vulnerability to the whims of the weather, particularly drought. Morocco is in a water-deficit area, a pressure already felt in the northern (Rif) zone and certain to increase over the coming decades.[12] Its main raw material is phosphate, so important that Morocco was able to quadruple the price in the mid-1970s in imitation of the oil price rise; unfortunately, the phosphate market then took a downturn.

This quick economic picture points to the fact that Morocco does not have the luxury of a wide ranging policy of broad leadership. It cannot aspire to guidance of the third world nor even to hegemony of its region, as does Algeria or Libya. At the same time, it has some very specific interests to protect, including both the Saharan issue and its general need for favorable economic conditions. This means that its policy is concentrated on its domestic needs, and that its ability to take the initiatives that it does depends on its ability to protect its independence with more powerful allies and to capitalize on other nonmaterial assets, such as the prestigious position of the monarchy and the two-seas location of the country.

Policy-making Structures

Morocco is a historic monarchy, not a new creation. The king, who reigns and rules, is the center of the political system. The late King Hassan accomplished the extraordinary task of maintaining and, after the mid-1970s, renewing a multiparty political system that grew out of the vigorous nationalist movement while at the same time preserving the position of the monarchy. This evolution is being accelerated by King Muhammad VI, and requires delicate political engineering.

In foreign affairs even more than in domestic affairs, Morocco's policies and relations are the king's domain. Relations among Arab and African states are already highly personalized through the head of state, and Morocco is no exception. King Hassan's was a very personal diplomacy, capitalizing on ties among Arab kings, Arab and African presidents, and European and American parliamentarians and presidents. In the conduct of foreign affairs, the Sahara dossier is located in the palace, and other issues are under the king's close supervision. His ambassadors are his personal envoys, and he looks for personal representatives of the heads of important states in his capital.

The king is supported by the normal structure of foreign-policy agencies, including a foreign and other ministries, embassies and their chiefs of mission, and delegations to the United Nations and other conferences, periodic or ad hoc. The king follows their activities closely. Some of his envoys are skillful, some are not. The royal dominance probably explains in large measure the fact that Morocco has not contributed international statesmen to world diplomacy as have some other third-world states.[13] As a result of the importance of foreign policy to specific national interests, political parties are also important players, both as pressures and as supporters and envoys, in the dynamics of Moroccan foreign policy.

Conclusions

Owing to the importance of the monarchy to Moroccan politics, foreign as well as domestic, the country is going through a crucial turning point at the turn of the century. Three decades of Hassan II, with his political skill and prestige in the world as well as on the domestic scene, have been succeeded by the rule of his son, a young man (at thirty-six, only a few years older than his father's age at accession) with various kinds of preparation for the job.

For all his preparation, Muhammad VI's instincts are quite different from those of his father and were only starting to appear at the beginning of 2000; the same is true of his skills. The king is popularly known as "the king of the poor" as a result of his concern for the condition of the broader Moroccan population, and this populist focus translates into a greater concern—for example, for the indigenous population of the Sahara. He has rid himself of many of the old Makhzen lieutenants of Hassan II, including Interior Minister Dris Basri, Hassan's main instrument of Saharan policy, but his own foreign policy team was not yet in place by early 2000. A good example of his personal style is found in early relations with Algeria. At the time of his father's funeral and soon thereafter, Muhammad sought and reciprocated a friendly turn of relations with the new Algerian president, Abdulaziz Bouteflika. But when Bouteflika launched into one of his mercurial attacks on his neighbor at the U.N. General Assembly in October 1999, Muhammad did not respond in kind, merely noting to his advisors that Bouteflika had made his mess and it was his business to get out of it. Moroccan newspapers cried casus belli, but the king remained calm. The king is said to have kept a private list of things he learned from his father, with one column of things to imitate and other of things not to repeat. It is not known what the two columns contain.

Muhammad VI's style is certain to be different, and style was much of his father's strength. A new style for new times can be the strength of the son as well, just as his father personified a very different style from that of Muhammad V. The givens, however, remain the same. The historical and geopolitical heritage of the country present the tasks and habits to address, and the domestic needs and resources give him the tools to use. There is little doubt that the same interests of national cohesion and resource protection will guide Moroccan policy, and that the circle within which it operates will continue to surround the country in the same hierarchy. Other new young leaders are on the scene at the same time, notably in Jordan, and the preponderance of aging leaders at the end of their constitutional or actuarial mandates in most of the other countries of the Arab world and some of the African countries means that the new king will have new younger colleagues to work with. Morocco under

Muhammad VI will continue to be an exciting actor with a useful role to play and important challenges to meet, with expectations of both stability and initiative in that role.

Notes

1   Hassan II, *Discours et interviews 3 mars 1978–3 mars 1979*, pp. 295, 306, 308.
2   E . W. Bovill, *The Golden Trade of the Moors*.
3   See I. William Zartman, *Ripe for Resolution: Conflict and Intervention in Africa*, chapter 2; Khadija Mohsen-Finan, *Sahara Occidental: Les enjeux d'un Conflit Régional*.
4   John Damis, "Morocco's 1995 Association Agreement with the European Union."
5   See I. William Zartman, "Superpower Cooperation in North Africa and the Horn of Africa."
6   See I. William Zartman, "The Ups and Downs of Maghrib Unity."
7   Kautilya, *Arthasastra,* translated by R. Shamasastry, p. 289.
8   Jamal Sa'd, *The Problem of Mauritania*.
9   Mark Tessler, "Moroccan-Israeli Relations and the Reasons for Moroccan Receptivity to Contact with Israel."
10 See I. William Zartman, "Explaining the Nearly Inexplicable: The Absence of Islam in Moroccan Foreign Policy."
11 Walter Lippman, *U.S. Foreign Policy: Shield of the Republic*.
12 Will Swearingen and Abdellatif Bencherifa, eds., *The North African Environment at Risk*.
13 The Moroccan foreign minister was, however, a co-mediator, along with his Saudi and Algerian colleagues, at the 1989 Ta'if Agreement that ended the Lebanese civil war.

11

Saudi Arabia's Foreign Policy

Hermann Frederick Eilts

To borrow an aphorism of the late U.S. Secretary of State Dean Acheson, the national purpose of the Kingdom of Saudi Arabia, like that of any other country, is "to survive, perchance to prosper," but with the added proviso "under the Al Saud dynasty." Survival has translated into security from frequently perceived, putative external predation. Prospering has meant internal economic development together with promotion of its national interests in the world at large. In both spheres, the kingdom has enjoyed eminent success, though not without travail. Its diplomatic instruments, apart from its moral authority in the Arab and Islamic worlds, have largely been its vast petroleum resources and the financial leverage that these have vouchsafed the kingdom. Its diplomatic style has been both proactive in its efforts to resolve Arab and Islamic problems and reactive where its special interests have been threatened. Patience and pragmatism have marked its approach to foreign affairs.

The foreign policy of the founder of the third and present Saudi polity, King `Abd al-Aziz ibn `Abd ar-Rahman al-Saud, commonly known as Ibn Saud, has generally been pursued by his successor sons, Kings Saud, Faisal, Khalid, and now Fahd, with only minor aberrations. To be sure, Saudi foreign policy has evolved and has adapted to changing times and circumstances in the world at large and in the Middle East in particular. From the relatively unknown and impoverished Arab chieftaincy that emerged at the end of World War II—which, ironically, still had to import kerosene!—it metamorphosed into a nation state.[1]

The present Saudi state first came into existence through the daring of the exiled Ibn Saud and a small band of followers, who, in 1902, retook Riyadh from a usurping dynasty. In the ensuing three decades, as a result of the military prowess and religious zeal of Ibn Saud's Wahhabi tribal supporters, the adjoining provinces of al-Ahsa in the east, Jabal Shammar in the north, Hijaz in the west, and `Asir in the southwest were added to the ruler's original Najd domains. In 1932, the dual monarchy of Najd and Hijaz was consolidated into a unitary state and renamed the Kingdom of Saudi Arabia.

Two years later, the kingdom fought its first war—a brief and successful seven-week long campaign against the imamate of Yemen, largely over ownership of the Najran sector of `Asir. Contrary to the expectations of some Saudi and British observers, Ibn Saud did not seek to exploit his victory by taking over most of Yemen. Instead, in the

219

resulting Treaty of Ta'if of 1934—which still governs Saudi-Yemeni relations—Saudi-occupied Hodaidah and its environs were returned to imamic rule. The
kingdom's southeastern boundary with Yemen was also tentatively agreed upon and
subsequently demarcated from the Red Sea coast to the eastern escarpment of the
Hijaz mountain range. In the Rub' al-Khali, or Empty Quarter, no border delineation
was attempted. Saudi Arabia and Yemen still dispute ownership over parts of that
desert area.

Elsewhere in the Arabian peninsula, the kingdom's borders with Kuwait, Iraq, and
what was still dubbed Transjordan were unilaterally drawn in, 1922 and 1925 respectively, by the British protectors of those states. In the southeast, Saudi Arabia's limi-
trophes (rather than precise boundaries) with the series of small Trucial shaikhdoms
(six of which later became the United Arab Emirates or U.A.E.) and Oman were likewise determined by the British. Pursuant to a series of earlier treaties with these small
statelets, Britain had extended a protective umbrella over them. Citing traditional
tribal loyalties, as evidenced by Saudi tax collections (*zakat*) among the tribes of the
area, Saudi Arabia regarded the traditional grazing grounds of these tribes as rightfully
belonging to it.

As early as 1934, an Anglo-Saudi frontier dispute arose as each side proposed lines
to define its respective territorial claims. The resulting impasse effectively deferred the
issue until the postwar period. From the late 1940s onward, these arid areas, previously
considered usable solely for pastoralism, were increasingly coveted by all interested
parties. Oil was now believed to lie beneath their desert sands.

Saudi Arabia is today a major international economic force with a respected political influence on the world scene, yet the kingdom emerged from World War II as a
relatively weak state whose future was tenuous. Its quest for modernization and international status would come slowly as its oil resources were exploited and its revenues
correspondingly enhanced. It entered a new postwar international environment, whose
global political dynamics soon embraced the Cold War dichotomy. The Saudi leadership, although only peripherally concerned, had perforce to conduct its overall foreign
policy in that general East-West global framework. It focussed particularly on the
ever-fractious emerging Middle East region, where its primary national interests lay.
As early as 1945, as an Arab and a conservatively Muslim state, the kingdom became a
charter member of the newly organized Arab League.

The Saudi state was first recognized by the Soviet Union in February 1926 and by
Britain, France, and the Netherlands shortly thereafter. Like most other Arabian
peninsular polities, and despite border disputes, it looked largely to Britain for external
help.[2] Internally, in a virtual civil war from 1928 to 1930, Ibn Saud succeeded in
crushing rebellious Ikhwan tribes, thereby buttressing his rule.[3] Treaties of friendship
were concluded with Persia and Germany in 1929, and with Turkey, Iraq, Egypt, and
France in 1931. Not until November 1933 was a provisional executive agreement
concluded between Saudi Arabia and the United States, after three years of leisurely
negotiations.[4]

Such official foreign recognition aside, a more portentous Saudi-American bond
developed in 1933. In that year, Ibn Saud awarded a petroleum concession in al-Ahsa

province to an American oil company, the Standard Oil Company of California (Socal). Both before and during the war, the Saudi monarch's principal source of income, the annual Muslim pilgrimage dues, was sharply curtailed because of the worldwide depression and the exigencies of wartime travel. In consequence, an impecunious Saudi government sought emergency assistance from Britain in the form of foodstuffs and silver riyals, needed to insure tribal fealty. Subsequent U.S. participation in such an economic aid program was a logical corollary of the Socal concession. (By 1945 the concessionaire had become the Arabian American Oil Company—Aramco—after three other major American oil companies joined the consortium.) During the war, too, the U.S. government recognized the likely magnitude and future importance of Saudi Arabian oil reserves when Secretary of Interior Harold Ickes unsuccessfully sought to buy out all or at least part of the Socal concession. Ibn Saud was willing to permit such a transaction, but the American oil company was adamant in its determination to retain unfettered ownership of its promising Saudi properties.

Until World War II, only a British and an Egyptian legation had been maintained in Jidda, where the Saudi government preferred to keep foreign diplomatic missions. In 1941, a resident U.S. legation was established in Jidda. Three years later, not without some initial Saudi hesitation, since an earlier Iraqi request to open a consulate in al-Ahsa had been refused, an American consulate (later elevated to consulate general) was established in Dhahran. The rationale for doing so was the requirement for consular services for the American oil technicians working there. Concurrently, again with reluctant Saudi agreement and even more grudging British acquiescence, U.S. military engineers commenced building an airport at Dhahran. The airport was initially conceived by the United States as a staging base for the Far East theater of operations, but Japan's surrender while construction was still under way made that facility militarily redundant. As a gesture of goodwill—especially after Ibn Saud's successful meeting with President Franklin D. Roosevelt aboard the U.S.S. *Quincy* in the Great Bitter Lakes in 1945—it was completed by the United States and transferred to Saudi Arabia as an international airport. Lacking the indigenous trained personnel to operate that facility, Ibn Saud requested the U.S. Air Force to do so, and later contracted with private American companies to perform that function.

In the immediate postwar period, some tensions existed between the United States and Britain for influence in the kingdom, which the sagacious Saudi ruler initially sought to manage by insisting that the British and Americans resolve their outstanding differences. Where possible, he shrewdly used such differences in order to further his kingdom's still limited international position. Determined to loosen what he saw as British hegemonic ambitions in the Arabian peninsula, he sought a closer tie with the United States. At U.S. and British urging, Ibn Saud had also been persuaded to jettison his previous nominal policy of neutralism in the European conflict and to declare war on Germany, even as the war was ending. The kingdom was thus able to participate in the San Francisco conference, and became a charter member of the newly organized United Nations.

For many years thereafter, Saudi Arabia eschewed foreign involvements as much as possible except in Arab and Islamic contexts. Its primary concern was resolving its still outstanding peninsular problems. In the overall Arab context, it sought to promote

Arab unity, although it retained its misgivings about suspected Egyptian, Iraqi, and even Jordanian aspirations. Inevitably, too, following the establishment of Israel in 1948, the kingdom became emotionally involved in the Arab-Israeli conflict.

Conceptually, the kingdom's foreign policy has been a function of several discrete but interactive factors: its Arab identity and its status as the largest entity of the Arabian peninsula; its unique Islamic legacy as the guardian of the sacred places of Islam; its vast petroleum resources and resultant international financial influence; and its omnipresent security concerns in relation to possible external threats. As its self-confidence grew, it also sought to broaden its associations elsewhere in the world. Paradoxically, its emergent role in international circles has been disproportionate to its relatively sparse population.[5]

The Arab Factor

The foremost factor in Saudi foreign policy is the kingdom's strong adherence to traditional Arabism. As a member of the Arab League, it has staunchly espoused Arab values and causes. This has translated into support for the removal of foreign, non-Arab colonial regimes from Arab entities, including those in the Arabian peninsula. As a corollary, it has been hostile to Israel, and has condemned the latter as a usurper of Palestinian rights and, after the 1967 Arab-Israeli war, of occupied Arab territories. It has been a consistent proponent of Arab unity, not in any federal sense but as an agglomeration of like-minded independent Arab states cooperating to achieve common aims. Regrettably, the pursuit of these objectives has not spared the kingdom from persistent internecine differences among Arab states. Its successive leaders have sought to resolve such differences by peaceful means.

Though they disclaimed any hegemonic aims, Saudi leaders view their country, by virtue of its size, affluence, and Arab and Islamic credentials, as first among equals among its Arabian peninsular confrères. At the end of the Second World War, the Saudi border disputes with virtually all of its British-protected neighbors ranked high among issues that required early resolution. Yet, paradoxically, much as the continued British political and military presence in parts of their frontiers and in adjacent regions was vexatious to the Saudi leadership, it also offered a measure of security.

In 1949, the latent frontier controversy flared anew. It began with the unresolved Saudi-Qatari border, but soon centered on the collection of oases known as Buraimi (seven belonged to Abu Dhabi, one to Oman). Although warned off by the British, the Saudis militarily occupied the Buraimi oasis in 1952, only to be expelled eventually by British-officered Trucial levies. Largely at the urging of the United States, Saudi Arabia agreed to arbitration. Its request for U.S. arbitration was declined and, instead, an international arbitration tribunal was convened. That effort collapsed in a welter of conflicting British and Saudi charges of subornation.[6] The border issue rankled, and had much to do with souring Ibn Saud's views on Britain. To show displeasure with the sultanate of Oman, the Saudis openly and in Arab League circles supported the rebellious Ibadi Imam of Oman and his tribal supporters.

Not until 1974, by which time the British had militarily withdrawn from the Gulf, was a settlement reached with Abu Dhabi, due in large part to the efforts of the minister of the interior, Prince Fahd ibn ʿAbd al-Aziz. In return for the retention of its Buraimi oases, Abu Dhabi ceded two strips of territory to Saudi Arabia. Essential honor was thus retained by both sides. The Saudi-Qatari border was formally fixed in 1965, but revised some thirty years later. An agreement on the Saudi-Omani border was amicably negotiated in 1993.

The military coup of 1962 in Yemen, which overthrew the Zaidi imamate and established a Yemeni republican regime, profoundly shocked the Saudi leadership. Not only had another Arab monarchy fallen, but in addition suspected Egyptian instigation and subsequent visible Egyptian military support for the Yemeni republican regime seemed to threaten the kingdom's peninsular interests. Saudi financial and arms support for the Yemeni royalists followed, bringing the kingdom and Egypt to the cusp of war. Saudi positions in and around Najran and Jizan were attacked by Egyptian aircraft from Yemen. Concurrently, Egyptian support for Saudi dissidents, whose aim was suspected to be the overthrow of the Saudi monarchy, aggravated the controversy. Eventual U.S. mediation and the deployment of U.N. peacekeepers assuaged tensions, but produced little more than a standoff. Not until the Egyptian defeat in the June 1967 Arab-Israeli war were their troops finally withdrawn. Three years later Saudi Arabia, convinced by then that the restoration of the Yemeni imamate was impractical, reluctantly recognized the Yemen Arab Republic (Y.A.R.).[7]

Yet the Y.A.R. remained a source of concern to Saudi Arabia, both owing to its political structure and because its leaders sporadically revived irredentist claims to the Jizan and Najran areas or staked out positions in the undemarcated Rubʿ al-Khali region. In response, the Saudi authorities sometimes resorted to subsidizing the powerful Hashid tribal shaikh of North Yemen to weaken San'a republican governments. Saudi leaders also sought to forestall any unification of North and South Yemen. To their chagrin, however, the two Yemens joined in 1990, a union not finally confirmed until after another North-South Yemeni civil war four years later. The united Yemeni entity confronts Saudi Arabia with a demographically larger—but also poorer, despite recent oil finds—state on its southwestern border.[8]

Because the Y.A.R. supported Saddam Husayn during the Gulf War, Saudi Arabia expelled almost a million Yemenis, citing security reasons. Some had resided in the kingdom for many years, and enjoyed privileges not accorded to any other Arab expatriates. The Saudi action placed an enormous economic burden on the Yemen Republic, and inevitably added to prevailing tensions between the two neighbors.

Saudi Arabia was especially displeased when, in the late 1980s, the Y.A.R. awarded oil concessions to foreign companies in parts of the disputed Rubʿ al-Khali area. Beside protesting the Yemeni action, it warned such foreign concessionaires that they were subject to arrest if they sought to operate in areas that Riyadh claimed. The Saudis have emphasized their firm intention to control such areas as well as several disputed Red Sea islands, and have occasionally deployed military forces to assert their claim. Although Yemen agreed not to press its residual claim to Najran and Jizan for another of the twenty-year periods stipulated in the Treaty of Taʿif, the Rubʿ al-Khali border issue remained unresolved until June 2000 when a definitive land and sea border agreement was signed between the two countries and is now being implemented.

The kingdom's relations with Kuwait, despite sharp differences before the Second World War and sporadic Saudi concern about private smuggling from its neighboring amirate, have in postwar years been neighborly. Riyadh has demonstrably supported Kuwait's independence. Thus, a small Saudi military contingent was sent to Kuwait in August 1961 to join the British forces deployed there in response to the threatened invasion of the newly independent amirate by the Iraqi government of `Abd al-Karim Qasim. Whatever the military limitations of that Saudi unit, its political symbolism was considerable: Saudi Arabia supported Kuwait's independence. If Kuwait fell, an Iraqi threat to the kingdom's al-Ahsa province might also loom. The Saudi unit subsequently became part of an Arab League force sent to Kuwait to take over from the British defenders.

The British-created, nominally undivided Saudi Arabian-Kuwaiti Neutral Zone was in fact divided through amicable bilateral diplomacy in 1975, thereby eliminating a sometimes controversial area of overlapping authority. Further cementing fraternal ties between the two states, Saudi Arabia allowed a Kuwaiti government-in-exile to be established in Ta`if in August 1990, following the Iraqi invasion of Kuwait. Equally importantly, it permitted foreign troops, under a U.S.-organized United Nations coalition, to use Saudi territory as a staging base for the liberation of Kuwait. Saudi armed forces participated in the U.N. coalition's liberation of Kuwait six months later and the reestablishment of Sabah family rule there. But the Saudi leadership retains nagging misgivings about perceived Kuwaiti liberal tendencies, such as the Kuwaiti National Assembly, female suffrage, and most recently allowing women to serve in the Kuwaiti armed forces.

Another instance of the kingdom's preoccupation with Arabian peninsular affairs was the organization in 1981, largely as a result of Riyadh's urging, of the Gulf Cooperation Council (G.C.C.). Consisting of the six Arab polities that line the western shore of the Persian/Arabian Gulf, the G.C.C. was envisioned as a regional collective security, economic, and cultural organization, designed to enhance cooperation among its members in these several spheres. In the almost two decades of the G.C.C.'s existence, commendable progress has been made in economic and cultural cooperation, but less in the contemplated security sphere. The inevitable numerical preponderance of Saudis in the G.C.C. military force has worried some of the smaller member states. They fear that such a force could become an instrument for Saudi Arabian control, and some also prefer to retain their own sources of military supply.[9]

In fact, the Saudis have usually—but not always—shown commendable sensitivity to the concerns of the smaller G.C.C. states. Beside providing leadership, they have participated constructively in the regularly scheduled G.C.C. meetings of chiefs of state and ministers. They have also sought to mediate various issues that exist between G.C.C. states, such as the Bahraini-Qatari boundary dispute and their own border dispute with Qatar. Saudi Arabia attaches considerable importance to the G.C.C., and has refused occasional Iraqi requests to join that organization. The kingdom has regularly endorsed G.C.C. resolutions calling upon Iran to return the Abu Musa and Tunbs islands to their former Sharjah and Ra`s al-Khaima owners. Yet Saudi efforts, beginning in 1998, to effect a Saudi-Iranian rapprochement displeased the neighboring

United Arab Emirates. In the absence of any satisfactory resolution to the island dispute, it feared that the kingdom was striking out on its own and without, in this instance, adequate consideration of other G.C.C. member states' concerns. Qatari mediation was required to ease Saudi-U.A.E. strains. (Iran has rejected arbitration, but has expressed willingness to conduct direct talks with the U.A.E. parties.) The scornful comment of the Saudi minister of defense that opposing a possible Saudi-Iranian reconciliation was "childish" has kept the controversy alive. In fact, a split of sorts has long existed in the G.C.C., with Saudi Arabia and Bahrain on one side and the remaining states on the other. To the Gulf states, Saudi Arabia, whether it likes it or not, is sometimes viewed as the colossus of the Arabian peninsula.

In the broader Arab context, Saudi Arabia, like its fellow Arab states, soon found itself enmeshed in the hardy differences that characterize those regional polities, and also involved with the challenge of Israel. Persistent inter-Arab bickering has perennially run counter to the vision of Arab unity, however much the kingdom has sought to further the latter objective.

In the years immediately after the Second World War, Saudi Arabia retained a deep distrust of the British-created Hashimite monarchies of Jordan and Iraq, and of the potential irredentist aspirations of those states, especially with respect to Hijaz. Ibn Saud suspected that these aspirations might be encouraged by the British mandatory power. In the case of Jordan, Saudi Arabia refused to accede to the British-imposed transfer of Ma'an and Aqaba in 1925, and did not finally do so until 1965. In the case of Iraq, it was sharply critical of that country's role in the organization of the Baghdad Pact in 1955, echoing the Egyptian charge that this represented foreign-encouraged disunity in Arab ranks. Occasional suggestions that Saudi Arabia join the Baghdad Pact were spurned. Distrust of Iraq was aggravated by the overthrow of the Hashimite monarchy by a military coup in 1958 and its replacement by a Ba`th Party republic. The continuing Iraqi threat to newly independent Kuwait was likewise worrisome. Nevertheless, the Saudi-Iraqi border, including the elimination of the Neutral Zone, was amicably negotiated between 1975 and 1979.

Most significantly, in the context of their Arabism, the Saudis gave generous financial aid to Iraq—as much $21 billion, according to Saudi estimates—during the protracted Iraq-Iran war in the 1980s. Free access to Saudi ports for food and materials required by the Iraqi regime was likewise made available. And substantial quantities of Saudi oil were provided to Iraq to sell abroad on Baghdad's account after wartime conditions closed the latter's own production facilities. When an exhausted Iranian regime finally accepted a U.N.-proposed cease-fire in 1988, it was King Fahd who persuaded a reluctant Saddam Husayn to do likewise.

Saudi uneasiness about Iraqi reliability was revived when, in 1989, Saddam Husayn sponsored the Arab Cooperation Council, embracing Iraq, Jordan, Egypt, and Yemen. The new organization raised Saudi fears that Iraq might support vestigial Yemeni irridentist claims to its territories. Accordingly, King Fahd, during a visit to Baghdad later that year, signed a nonaggression pact with Iraq, the first such agreement in the Arab world. The Saudi monarch's action was troubling to Kuwait, which was already experiencing problems with Iraq, especially since it was negotiated outside the G.C.C. context. The agreement left the Sabah amirate exposed, especially after Iraq rebuffed a subsequent Kuwaiti request for a similar nonaggression pact.

In fact, the kingdom's attempt to forge a special bilateral tie with Iraq soon proved ephemeral. In July 1990, Saudi Arabia's attempts to mitigate Iraqi-Kuwaiti tensions, through friendly mediation and a generous offer of a monetary contribution to an Iraqi financial demand of Kuwait, aborted when the Iraqi delegates to a Saudi-convened trilateral conference in Jidda unceremoniously left. Within days thereafter, Iraq invaded Kuwait and appeared threateningly astride the kingdom's northeastern border.

Notwithstanding the ultimate defeat of Iraq in February 1991, the kingdom has ever since remained wary of its northern neighbor. Nevertheless, considerable Saudi official and public sympathy exists for the plight of the Iraqi people that results from the U.N.-imposed economic restrictions. Saudi Arabia would clearly like a less aggressive government in Baghdad, but strongly opposes any breakup of the Iraqi state. It abjures any possible Iranian-dominated Shi`i state on its northeastern border.

Over the years, Saudi Arabia's relations with Egypt have similarly fluctuated. Immediately after the Second World War, subliminal rivalry existed between the two states when both Ibn Saud and King Faruq were mooted as potential candidates for a revived Islamic caliphate. Nothing ever came of this, and there is no evidence that Ibn Saud aspired to any such distinction. The advent of the Egyptian republic after the military coup of 1952 troubled the Saudi regime as the largest Arab monarchy imploded. The kingdom nevertheless sought to forge good relations with the Egyptian regime of Gamal `Abd al-Nasir. The death of Ibn Saud in 1953 signaled, at least for a time, a lessening of Saudi dependence upon the United States, and both King Saud and Prince Faisal dabbled for a time with the Nasirist doctrine of "positive neutralism." In this context, a U.S. Point IV mission was expelled by the Saudis in 1954. For a time, too, King Saud became for a time the principal financier of radical Nasirist activities in the Arab world. Saudi Arabia strongly supported Egypt during the tripartite Anglo-French-Israeli invasion of Egypt in 1956. In that year, the kingdom also associated itself with Egypt and Syria in a loose cooperation pact. Moreover, protesting the British participation in the Suez attack, Saudi Arabia severed diplomatic relations with Britain and did not resume them until 1961.

Before long, however, a fundamental incompatibility between the Saudi system and Nasirist values became increasingly evident. There were reports of an Egyptian-inspired assassination attempt against King Saud, and the Saudi ruler gradually came to suspect Nasir of seeking to subvert his family monarchy. Relations further deteriorated when King Saud, following a visit to Washington in 1957 (where he somewhat equivocally embraced the so-called Eisenhower Doctrine, in which the United States pledged armed support as necessary against overt communist aggression), attempted unsuccessfully to persuade Nasir and King Husayn of Jordan to do the same. Somewhat naïvely, the Eisenhower administration had concluded that King Saud might be built up as a counterpoise to the Egyptian leader in the Arab world.

The final rupture came in 1958, when King Saud was publicly accused by the Egyptians and Syrians of conspiring to assassinate Nasir, and a check allegedly drawn by the Saudi ruler for this purpose was publicly displayed as evidence of the latter's perfidy. Entrusted to the ubiquitous Shaikh Yusuf Yasin, a Syrian advisor of the Saudi monarch, the affair—whatever its true purpose may have been, which remains in dispute—had been bungled. Although King Saud sought to explain that funds he was providing to the Syrians were intended to be used against the growing communist presence in Syria, the Saudi monarch's image at home and abroad was irretrievably tarnished. Henceforth the Saudi regime was cast by Nasirist media as foremost among the "reactionaries" as opposed to the "progressives" of the Arab world. Still residually sensitive to such Nasirist propaganda attacks, Saudi Arabia unexpectedly terminated U.S. Air Force usage of the Dhahran airfield in 1961, hoping thereby to reduce the kingdom's vulnerability to radical Arab criticisms.

The resultant weakening of King Saud and his replacement by Prince Faisal, first temporarily and then permanently in 1964, did not still Egyptian media attacks on the kingdom. To be sure, Faisal remained for a time an advocate of "positive neutralism," but the Egyptian involvement in the 1962 Yemen rebellion once again alarmed the Saudi leadership and dictated a renewed quest for U.S. security support. From the Saudi point of view, Nasir persistently disregarded his obligations to disengage from Yemen, and the Saudis remained convinced that the Y.A.R. could not survive without Egyptian physical support. Faisal's distruct of Nasir became indelible.

Despite these lingering Saudi-Egyptian tensions, Saudi Arabia shared in general Arab pride when Nasir, in May 1967, closed the Straits of Tiran to Israeli-bound shipping, and asserted that the Gulf of Aqaba was an "Arab sea," one that the riparian Arab states (Saudi Arabia, Egypt and Jordan—Israel's port of Eilat was conveniently ignored) had a legal right to close. Saudi leaders officially viewed the Aqaba waterway in this same light, although some privately considered Nasir's action as untimely. Still, widespread Saudi official and public hope existed that Egypt, supported by the other Arab states, would finally prevail. The earlier Arab humiliation would then be cleansed.

In the first days of the June Six-Day War, the Saudi media carried totally unsubstantiated reports of alleged Arab military successes everywhere, which resulted in strong pressure from the Saudi military to enter the war. The officer corps wished to be part of the presumed imminent Arab victory. Fortunately, the clear-sightedness of the Saudi leadership, coupled with the short duration of the conflict, kept Saudi Arabia out of that war. Although the Saudi leaders and public were gratified by the resultant Egyptian withdrawal from Yemen, the sheer magnitude and rapidity of Israel's defeat of Egypt, Syria, and Jordan, and the loss of East Jerusalem to Israel, appalled them. Saudi leaders, beginning with King Faisal, have ever since consistently demanded that Israel leave occupied Arab areas and have interpreted U.N. Resolution 242 of 1967 as requiring such unconditional withdrawal.

The Egyptian defeat also enabled the Saudis once again to assert a leadership role in inter-Arab affairs. At an Arab chiefs-of-state conference, held in Khartoum in September 1967, King Faisal took the initiative to offer a substantial financial subsidy to a badly weakened Egypt and persuaded Kuwait and Libya to join in that effort. Nominally such aid was to continue only until the "consequences of the Israeli aggression" were removed, which the donors expected would be no more than a year or so.

In fact, it continued until the 1973 Arab-Israeli war. With Anwar Sadat's assumption of the Egyptian presidency in 1971, Saudi Arabian-Egyptian ties once again became close. Indeed, during the 1973 Arab-Israeli war, and afterward as well, Saudi Arabia supported Egypt financially and morally. Annoyed, however, at the Egyptian media's repeated brandishing of the "Arab oil weapon" as if it were their own, the Saudis quietly but firmly stressed that they, not the Egyptians or other Arabs, would decide when and where Saudi oil would be used coercively.

Saudi Arabia has consistently sought to effect a peaceful resolution of other inter-Arab disputes, Thus, in North Africa, it worked to bring the Moroccan government and the dissident Polisario together. In the Lebanese civil war from 1975 to 1990, it used its good offices to try to achieve a settlement between the bitterly antagonist confessional groups of that country. And in 1999 it played a significant role in persuading Libyan leader Mu`ammar al-Qadhafi to turn over to a special court in the Hague two Libyans suspected of complicity in the Pan-American aircraft bombing incident of 1989 over Lockerbie, Scotland, thereby enabling U.N. economic sanctions on Libya to be suspended.

Antipathy to and distrust of Israel have suffused Saudi Arabian foreign policy from the inception of the Jewish state in 1948 to the present. This frequently led to strains in the Saudi-U.S. relationship. There were, in fact, early fears in Washington that Ibn Saud might, as a retaliatory measure, cancel the American oil concession. The ruler assured U.S. representatives that he had no intention of doing so. Yet he and his successors were embittered that the Truman administration failed, in their view, to honor a pledge made by President Roosevelt to consult with the kingdom before adopting any new policy with respect to a Jewish state. Saudi leaders have remained resentful of U.S. support for Israel ever since.

Twice, once in the immediate aftermath of the June 1967 war and again during the 1973 conflict, the kingdom imposed a partial embargo on the export of Saudi oil to the United States. Nevertheless, during the 1967 embargo, King Faisal agreed that American naval vessels in the Red Sea, which had shortly before been deployed as a deterrent to Egyptian attacks from Yemen against Saudi installations, might covertly be bunkered from Saudi oil barges at sea and out of sight of land. In the event, such offshore bunkering proved to be unnecessary. The first such Saudi oil embargo lasted only four weeks. It was intended primarily a as a show of solidarity with fellow Arab states and to mollify outraged Saudi public (and military) opinion, which ascribed the stunning Israeli military success to U.S. complicity. The second oil embargo, in 1973, lasted some five months. Even after an Egyptian-Israeli disengagement agreement (Sinai I) was brokered by the United States in January 1974, King Faisal declined to lift the oil embargo until a similar Syrian-Israeli disengagement agreement had been achieved. Not until the latter was accomplished in May 1974 were Saudi oil shipments to the United States resumed.

Token Saudi military units were sent to Jordan in both the 1948 and the 1967 Arab-Israeli conflicts. Although those units were not involved in hostilities, King Faisal could observe after the 1967 conflict that the kingdom, too, had lost territory as a result of Israeli "aggression." The two small, Saudi-owned but unpopulated islands of Tiran and Sanafir at the entrance of the Straits of Tiran had earlier been lent to Egypt in the context of the Arab Collective Security Pact. Fortified by the latter, they were seized by Israeli forces during the brief Sinai campaign. The Saudi monarch declined a U.S.-brokered Israeli offer to return one of the two islands, insisting that any such return must be in the context of the evacuation of all Israeli-occupied Arab territories. The islands were quietly recovered by Saudi Arabia following the signing of the Egyptian-Israeli peace treaty in 1979.

In related spheres, Saudi Arabia has from the inception of the Arab secondary economic boycott against Israel adhered to that proscription. Incidents like the al-Aqsa Mosque burning in Jerusalem in 1969 by a demented Christian zealot were ascribed by King Faisal to Israeli instigation. That otherwise moderate Saudi ruler never tired of subjecting his foreign visitors to lengthy disquisitions on the alleged iniquities of the Israeli Zionists. The latter's treatment of Palestinian refugees was always a prominent theme in such Saudi criticisms. The Saudi Arabian government has regularly pressed for implementation of U.N. General Assembly resolutions critical of Israeli treatment of the Palestinians. By the same token, it has deplored U.S. vetoes of similar Security Council resolutions, scoffing at U.S. explanations that most such resolutions were unbalanced.

Although relatively few Palestinians were admitted into the kingdom for resettlement purposes, Saudi Arabia strongly supported the Palestine Liberation Organization (P.L.O.), and gave it generous financial grants. Its generosity was poorly rewarded when P.L.O. leader Yasir `Arafat appeared to be supporting Saddam Husayn's 1990 invasion of Kuwait. As a result, Saudi aid to the P.L.O. ceased for a number of years. Beginning in 1998, however, Saudi Arabia resumed limited economic aid to the Palestinians. It has also given cautious but qualified support for U.S.- brokered peace negotiations. On the whole, however, it believes that the Europeans are more reliable with respect to Arab quarrels. Although it recognizes the European Union's limited capabilities, the Saudis endorse that organization's pronouncements in favor of a Palestinian state.

Saudi rulers have nonetheless moved appreciably from the 1967 Khartoum conference consensus of "no peace, no recognition, and no negotiations" with Israel. King Faisal subsequently formulated the position that the details of any Arab-Israeli peace should be negotiated by the "confrontation" states, namely, Egypt, Jordan, Syria, and Lebanon. With a single exception, whatever those states decided would be agreed to by Saudi Arabia. The exception was Jerusalem, where the Saudi monarch, by virtue of the kingdom's custodianship of the Islamic holy places, believed it should have a voice. In August 1981, at an Arab summit in Fez, Crown Prince Fahd endorsed the concept of a two-state solution to the Palestinian-Israeli imbroglio. Among the eight points that came to be known as the Fahd plan was a call for Israel to dismantle its settlements in the occupied areas and to withdraw to pre-June 1967 borders. Repatriation of Palestinian refugees was sought. So was an independent Palestinian state, with East Jerusalem as its capital.[10] The United Nations should guarantee respect for the principle that all Middle East states live in peace. Israel summarily rejected the proposal, but the Reagan administration termed it a "positive" step. Implicitly, it acknowledged the existence of Israel. The previous year, Saudi religious leaders had declared a *jihad* against Israel for declaring Jerusalem to be the undivided and eternal capital of the Israeli state.

The year before that, however, in 1979, following the conclusion of the U.S.-brokered Egyptian-Israeli peace treaty in 1979, Saudi Arabia had severed diplomatic relations with Egypt and terminated all economic aid to that country. Only consular relations were maintained. The kingdom had the previous year joined with other Arab League states, following a conference in Baghdad, in an ill-advised, undignified, and abortive offer of money to Sadat not to sign any peace treaty with Israel. Similarly, as a gesture of protest against Egypt's having unilaterally made peace with Israel, Saudi Arabia supported the removal of the Arab League headquarters from Cairo to Tunis.

By 1987, the kingdom, like most other Arab states, had decided that a rapprochement with Egypt was desirable, and diplomatic ties were resumed. When, three years later, Saddam Husayn invaded Kuwait and threatened Saudi Arabia, the kingdom's leaders welcomed Egyptian President Husni Mubarak's success in persuading ten members of the Arab League to condemn the Iraqi aggression. At Saudi request, and pursuant to the Arab Collective Security Pact, Egypt also deployed some 25,000 Egyptian troops to the kingdom to participate in the U.N. coalition that liberated Kuwait and ended the Iraqi menace to Saudi Arabia. The presence of such Egyptian troops (and those of Syria, Morocco, and other Islamic countries) eased King Fahd's domestic problem in countering misgivings among rigidly conservative elements of the Saudi public for having invited large numbers of foreign, non-Muslim troops into the "holy land of Islam."

In the period immediately after the Gulf War, both Saudi Arabia and Kuwait gave consideration to a new defense arrangement that would involve G.C.C., Egyptian, and Syrian troops. Dubbed the G.C.C. plus two, this would have either replaced a continuing U.S. military presence or complemented such a presence. Although soon tabled, the notion has been periodically reviewed by Saudi leaders. Yet the idea of a permanent Egyptian and Syrian troop presence in Saudi Arabia is hardly congenial to the Saudi authorities; nor is the prohibitive cost of maintaining such Egyptian and Syrian troops in the kingdom attractive.

Saudi Arabia has sometimes suggested that it will never recognize Israel, regardless of what other Arab states may eventually do. The Saudi leadership is likewise opposed to the U.S. idea of a Middle East Development Bank, which the kingdom would in the main be expected to fund. Such a bank would presumably finance infrastructural and related development projects throughout the region, including in Israel. But the kingdom's leaders are also aware that various fellow Arab states, notably Morocco, Tunisia, Qatar, and Oman (as well as Egypt and Jordan, which have peace treaties with Israel) have in recent years signaled a desire for economic, consular, and even political ties with Israel. In all likelihood, Saudi Arabia will be among the last of the Arab states to regularize its relations with Israel. Much will depend on the eventual outcome of the Palestinian-Israeli and putative resumed Syrian- (and Lebanese-) Israeli peace talks. As Crown Prince 'Abdallah indicated when visiting Washington in September 1998, Saudi Arabia supports the U.S.-sponsored peace process, but on the clear understanding that it must assure legitimate Palestinian rights. In effect, the Fahd plan remains the basis of pertinent Saudi policy. Saudi Arabia also supports the return of Syrian territory and Israeli withdrawal from south Lebanon.

The Islamic Factor

Closely related to the Arab factor has been the Islamic factor. Makkah, whose centrality in the Islamic world is attested by the annual *haj*, the Qur'anically prescribed Muslim pilgrimage, is in Hijaz. The importance of this factor is indicated by the fact that the present ruler, King Fahd, has discarded any royal title and designated himself instead as "Custodian of the Holy Places." Since its seizure of Hijaz in 1925, the kingdom has viewed itself as having a special responsibility to the entire global Islamic community for caring for the Haram al-Sharif Mosque in Makkah and the Prophet Muhammad's tomb in Madinah—this despite deep-seated Hanbali-Wahhabi aversion to tombs and saint worship. The proper discharge of that global responsibility has been a cardinal element of Saudi Arabian foreign policy. Indeed, from the outset of his rule over Hijaz, Ibn Saud saw to it that Muslim pilgrims were not harassed by Wahhabi zealots. His successors have followed his example.

The task of managing, in a relatively short timespan each year, the arrival and departure of two million or more Muslim pilgrims from all parts of the world, most of them non-Arab, has placed an extraordinary burden on the Saudi authorities, The contingents of pilgrims are often led by senior officials of Muslim countries.[11] Keenly aware that its global image in the broader Islamic world depends upon the successful administration of the *haj*, the Saudi Arabian government has spent vast sums of money in improving inland transportation to Makkah, building pilgrim hostels, and improving medical services for pilgrims.

By the same token, Saudi Arabia is sensitive to occasional criticism from foreign Muslim communities and states of its management of the annual pilgrimage, and occasional inferences that the holy places of Islam should be placed under some kind of international Islamic administration. This lay behind its concern over the 1979 seizure by Saudi Wahhabi millenarians of the Grand Mosque in Makkah. Similarly, past Iranian Islamic Republic charges of alleged Saudi mismanagement of the annual pilgrimage have been deeply resented. Any notion of international Islamic administration of the *haj* is totally unacceptable to the Saudi leadership.

The Saudi authorities have generally insisted that the *haj* be apolitical, although that stricture has not prevented occasional valedictory sermons at Jabal Rahmah, the climax of the annual pilgrimage on the Plain of `Arafat, from deploring Israeli occupation of Jerusalem. Saudis were nevertheless embarrassed when, in the late 1980s, Iranian Shi`i pilgrims publicly castigated the United States (and Israel). In later years the Saudi authorities segregated such Iranian contingents to a separate area where they could vent their spleen.

Owing to the large numbers of foreign Muslim pilgrims, the Saudi Arabian government has in recent years had to establish quotas, based on population, for the various Muslim states sending pilgrim contingents. Some Muslim savants and governments grumble at any such restrictions, but the foreign currency constraints of many Muslim countries have facilitated the kingdom's quota efforts.

Apart from its spiritual significance, the annual *haj* offers opportunities for official discussions with visiting foreign leaders to encourage political and other cooperation among Islamic states on matters of common concern. Indeed, the concept of Islamic cooperation—though not an Islamic pact, as has sometimes been suggested—was initiated by King Faisal in 1970 when he convened the first Islamic foreign ministers' conference in Jidda. In part, his action represented a conscious political counterpoise to the radical Arab states, which misread its purposes and saw it as an attempt to weaken the Arab League. By thus asserting his leadership role in the Muslim world, the king mainly sought to rally pan-Islamic solidarity to recover what was by then Israeli-held Jerusalem. At Saudi urging, a permanent Islamic secretariat was established in Jidda to maintain dialogue with the Muslim states on matters of common concern. A second, even larger Islamic conference was held in Lahore in 1974, which resulted in a unanimous call for Israel to withdraw from occupied Arab lands. At Saudi behest, it also established an Islamic Solidarity Fund, to which King Faisal personally contributed over $10 million, to assist in the economic development of the poorer Muslim states. Such Islamic conferences have become annual affairs.

In implementation of the Islamic aspect of its foreign policy, the kingdom has over the years extended considerable sums of money to poorer Arab and African states in support of local Islamic organizations and for the construction and maintenance of mosques in such countries. Saudi funding has also been given to various Islamic organizations abroad, such as the Muslim Brotherhood in Egypt, and Hamas in Israeli-occupied Palestine and elsewhere. In such instances, to the extent that the Saudi Arabian government acknowledges such contributions, it insists that its purpose is the promotion of legitimate humanitarian and educational causes and not the encouragement of internal instability—though there are some foreign misgivings about whether recipients use such funds for benign purposes. The decline in Saudi revenues in the past five years due to lower world oil prices has perforce constrained such support for foreign Muslim groups, but this may only be a temporary phenomenon.

Saudi Arabia has not been immune to Islamic sectarianism, which has on occasion spilled over into the foreign relations sphere. Of its indigenous population of fifteen million, some 95 percent are Sunni Muslims. Approximately half a million Twelver Shi'i Muslims live in al-Ahsa province. Traditional Wahhabi animosity to Shi's as presumed heretics has sometimes animated domestic politics and provided a fertile field of political exploitation by the Iranian regime of Ayatollah Khomeini and his successors. Shi'i insurgency in al-Ahsa province was incited in 1980, and possibly Iranian-inspired Shi'i dissident groups were evident in the Khobar Towers bombing incident of 1996. Such Iranian propaganda attacks upon the Saudi royal family eased somewhat with the death of Khomeini. Since the election of Muhammad Khatami in 1997, there have been distinct signs of a Saudi Arabian-Iranian rapprochement. There have been visits by senior officials of each country to the other's capitals, during which fraternal Islamic relations and a desire for mutual cooperation were pledged.

Of other Muslim countries, Pakistan has been closest to Saudi Arabia. The kingdom was one of the first states to recognize that country in 1948, and a warm dialogue has ever since existed between the two. Numerous Pakistanis work in Saudi Arabia, and the kingdom has occasionally sought Pakistani help in the form of military specialists. Saudi Arabia has supported Pakistani claims to Kashmir, and, according to some unconfirmed sources, may even have contributed to the funding of Pakistan's nuclear weapons capability. After Pakistan tested its first nuclear weapon in May 1998, Saudi Minister of Defense Prince Sultan publicly lauded Pakistan as the first Muslim country to possess a nuclear capability. Since then he has visited nuclear and missile construction plants in Pakistan, and, much to U.S. distress, Saudi Arabia may be on the verge of purchasing Pakistani medium-range missiles to replace the aging Chinese weaponry bought a decade ago.

During the protracted Eritrean insurgency, Saudi Arabia also supported Eritrean Muslim aspirations for independence from Ethiopia; and it has provided financial and relief support to Albanian Muslims in Kosovo.

The Petroleum-financial Factor

In an energy-driven world in which Saudi Arabia sits atop at least 25 percent of known world petroleum reserves, the kingdom's oil policies are inevitably an integral part of its foreign relations. Similarly, its oil-derived revenues, growing until recently, have been a major factor in enhancing its international image. Its use of these instruments of foreign relations has developed slowly.

In the first two decades after the Second World War, the production, disposal, and pricing of Saudi oil were largely in the hands of its foreign concessionaire, Aramco, and the latter's four parent companies. They determined production levels, and they fixed prices, including occasional reductions, on the basis of international oil-market conditions. Their contractual obligations to the kingdom were met by stipulated royalty and tax payments. Seldom was there any government-to-government involvement. On their part, the Saudi authorities sometimes sought the presumed influence of the Aramco parent companies to lobby U.S. administrations on political issues such as Israel—usually to no avail. From a Saudi point of view, this arrangement became increasingly unsatisfactory.

Spearheaded by Saudi Arabia and Venezuela in 1961, the oil-producing countries joined in the Organization of Oil Producing Countries (OPEC) in a common effort to assert a greater voice in all aspects of their oil assets. A decade later, the sometimes painful collective bargaining finally brought an agreement in which oil-pricing decisions were shared between the producing countries and their foreign concessionaires. Thereafter, the OPEC states, including Saudi Arabia, were gradually able to assume unilateral control of oil prices, thereby drawing in increased revenues. Significantly, that initial shift—the beginning of what would eventually be a total takeover by Middle Eastern states of their oil holdings—made the Saudi Arabian government the determinant of its oil policies. In a seminal change, not only private purchasers but also foreign governments now dealt with it on petroleum matters.[12]

In the heady early days of OPEC successes against the foreign oil companies, a split soon developed among member states on production and pricing issues. Some, such as Iran, Algeria, Iraq, and Libya, sought steep production cuts in order to raise world oil prices. For its part, Saudi Arabia, while no less anxious to maximize oil revenues, which were needed for its internal Five Year Development programs, sought to keep oil price rises within reasonable limits.

Saudi Arabia prevailed in OPEC circles, largely as a result of its expansive and expandable production facilities. In effect, these made it the "swing" producer in global oil economics. In the 1980s and early 1990s it could and did expand or contract its production levels between eight million and ten million bpd, depending upon overall global demand and supply factors. If necessary, it was known to be able to expand production at short notice to as much as twelve million bpd. It thus regulated world oil supply, and despite occasional short-term price spikes that resulted from particular Middle East problems, effectively kept oil prices within reasonable limits.

Economic as well as political considerations figured in the Saudi decision to maintain price moderation. Largely dependent as it is upon oil-derived income, it had two economic alternatives: it could cut production levels in order to raise global oil prices, or it could maintain or even increase its already high production levels, which would also bring greater earnings to its coffers. It consciously opted for the latter, believing that, by thus encouraging oil-price moderation, it would garner greater political respect from the United States and Western Europe. This, some Saudis believed, would benefit the overall Arab cause. From an international monetary point of view, it was a responsible move. And Saudi petroleum officials were beguiled with the clear leadership role that their "swing" production capability gave them in OPEC circles. They were prepared to incur the ire of some fellow OPEC members and of Saudi conservationists.

Unfortunately for Saudi Arabia, the oil-market glut after the Gulf War of 1990–1991 resulted in a precipitous decline in global oil prices and a corresponding drop in Saudi oil income. The high costs of that war also adversely affected its financial position. These factors forced the kingdom to abandon its "swing" producer role. Saudi internal development programs had to be decelerated, and the kingdom's ability to use economic aid as an instrument of foreign policy was also sharply curtailed. At a rump session of OPEC in May 1999, the kingdom agreed to a three percent reduction in its oil production as a means of raising global oil prices. It did so on the explicit understanding that other OPEC (and, it was hoped, non-OPEC) states would do likewise.

Beset by recurrent budgetary deficits, senior Saudi officials intimated in 1998 and 1999 that Saudi Arabia might welcome the reentry of foreign oil companies, including American ones, into the kingdom's energy exploitation sector. Foreign investment is again being sought. This has whetted the appetites of foreign companies, and a new Saudi-United States energy agreement was signed with the U.S. secretary of energy during the latter's visit to the kingdom in February 1999. Such Saudi interest has been limited, however, to natural gas exploitation. Whether foreign companies will be permitted to reengage in upstream oil production remains to be seen.

The petroleum factor had other international ramifications. Starting in 1973, following the Iranian lead of twenty years earlier, various Arab governments, beginning with Libya, took steps to nationalize foreign oil companies. For its part, Saudi

Arabia also pressed Aramco on this issue, but handled the matter with considerable skill and avoided a major controversy. Instead of unilaterally taking over the foreign oil installations, as happened in Iraq, Libya, and elsewhere, the Saudi Arabian government incrementally increased its equity participation in Aramco until it was finally the sole owner of the enterprise. Mutually agreed-upon compensation was paid to the former owners. Saudi Aramco, the successor organization, has generally maintained its predecessor's policies, and many American and other foreign employees remain on its payroll. The generally amicable Saudi takeover of Aramco did not roil Saudi Arabian-U.S. bilateral ties. On the contrary, the kingdom's international image was enhanced by its sensitive handling of a delicate subject.

In the heyday of its high oil income, Saudi Arabia engaged in a series of Five Year Development programs, which emphasized infrastructure, education, building construction, and so on. Much of the manual labor associated with these successive programs was expatriate. Though the workers were privately employed, this situation has occasionally brought the kingdom into conflict with foreign states, both Muslim and non-Muslim, for alleged mistreatment of foreign expatriates. The Saudi authorities are sensitive to their heavy dependence upon expatriate labor for the construction and maintenance of their modern installations. They are pressing for greater "Saudization" of the labor force, but the kingdom's reliance on expatriate workers remains high. On another level, the kingdom's reduced oil income in the past five years has required the Saudi government to request deferred payments to some foreign suppliers and contractors, including those in the defense sector. This has tended to reduce the kingdom's international credit rating. The government clearly hopes that this situation will be redressed before long if world oil prices strengthen.

A major derivative of Saudi Arabia's oil bounty has been its financial earnings from petroleum and the attendant influence that this gives the kingdom in international financial markets. Foreign governments, including the United States as well as European and Asian states, assiduously seek Saudi official and private investments in their bonds or enterprises. The kingdom is a member of the International Monetary Fund and enjoys Special Drawing Rights from that organization because of its monetary participation. Until recently, Saudi Arabian economic aid abroad was as much as three percent of its G.D.P. on a per-capita basis, larger than that of any other donor country.

The Security Factor

Among the several factors influencing Saudi Arabian foreign policy, security from potential external predation has been preeminent. The nagging fear of a threat from some of its neighbors, prompted in part by rival dynastic ambitions as well as the proliferation of republics in the Middle East and their sometime castigation of Saud family rule, along with suspected foreign covetousness of the vast Saudi oil resources, have combined to elevate this factor to top priority in the Saudi leadership's international calculations. Inevitably, the Saudi external threat perception has evolved in the postwar years. In large measure, it has dictated Saudi Arabia's foreign security alignments.

At the end of the Second World War, Ibn Saud cast the security dimension of his kingdom in two directions. First was the Arab dimension, when the kingdom in June

1950 joined four other Arab states in signing a Joint Defense and Economic Treaty—commonly known as the Arab Collective Security Pact—consistent with Article 51 of the U.N. Charter, which legitimized Arab collective defense. At the same time, the Saudi ruler maintained close relations with Britain—this, despite his persistent problems with that country over Arabian peninsular borders. For a time, the kingdom depended upon a small British military mission to train a Saudi army.

Uncertain of British intentions, however, as previously recounted, Ibn Saud had during the war years moved closer to the United States. That trend continued throughout the remainder of his reign. There emerged, not without occasional controversy, an increasingly close Saudi Arabian-U.S. security link, which in the totality of the relationship between the two countries effectively came to outweigh regular Saudi displeasure with United States support for Israel.

Problems with the British over boundaries with the Trucial States, which culminated in the Buraimi oasis imbroglio, contributed to the dismissal of the British military training mission, which was replaced for a short period by an Egyptian one. Increasingly, however, Ibn Saud came to look on the United States as his primary support against external threats. He sought arms and a military alliance, but was initially rebuffed by Washington. By 1949, Ibn Saud had come to suspect a British plot to "encircle" his kingdom with Hashimite rulers, specifically Jordan and Iraq in the north, the imamate of Yemen to the southwest, and the British-supported or protected states of Kuwait, the Trucial States, Bahrain, and the Aden colony and protectorates in the south and southwest.[13]

Far-fetched though this perception may have been, it was held almost paranoically by the Saudi monarch. What might be called a modified "encirclement syndrome" became a feature of Saudi foreign-policy thinking for many years. The nature of the suspected external threats altered with evolving circumstances in the Middle East—Nasir's Egypt, a communist-oriented Sudan, a Ba`th dominated Iraq, the Yemen Arab Republic, or any combination of these—but the fixation persisted. Despite U.S. efforts during the Cold War period to instill into Saudi governmental thinking a putative Soviet threat, the Saudi authorities never saw this a major source of concern. Although they excoriated communism and rejected occasional Soviet offers to resume diplomatic relations, including offers of arms aid, they also found it convenient in dealing with the United States at various times to label Egypt, Sudan, the two Yemeni states, and Iraq as communist "proxies," and were in fact genuinely concerned about those states' ambitions.

As the Saudi regime came increasingly to rely on the United States, especially after President Harry Truman wrote to Ibn Saud on October 30, 1950, declaring U.S. support for the political independence and territorial integrity of the kingdom, security cooperation between the two countries inexorably became a major element of Saudi foreign policy. An agreement for U.S. Air Force use of the Dhahran airfield was concluded in 1950 and was renewed five years later. At Saudi request, a United States Military Training Mission was deployed to the kingdom in 1953 to train the Saudi army, air force, and navy, and substantial quantities of American military equipment were bought by the Saudi Arabian government. A U.S. Corps of Engineers mission was also engaged to plan and supervise construction of various infrastructural projects, such as a TV station and three military cantonments. In 1970, U.S. training and equipment sales were extended to the Saudi national guard, at Prince `Abdallah's specific request. Up to that time, the national guard had been exclusively British trained.

During the critical period of the 1960s, when Saudi-Egyptian tensions were high because of events in Yemen, President Kennedy, at King Faisal's request, deployed a squadron of American aircraft to the kingdom as a tangible demonstration of U.S. support. Saudi Arabia likewise welcomed visits of U.S. naval vessels to its ports, including one to Jizan, for the same purpose.[14] The Saudi Arabian government was at times critical that such military deployments, nominally stationed in defense of the kingdom, were reluctant to engage intruding Egyptian aircraft, and was later incensed to learn that the American planes were in fact unarmed; but it grudgingly recognized that it had no other feasible recourse for needed external security support.

With the British military departure from the Gulf region in 1971, the Saudi regime—like the Nixon administration—feared that a vacuum might develop in that strategically important area. Somewhat paradoxically, considering earlier Saudi concerns about the British presence in the Arabian peninsula, thought was even given in Saudi leadership circles to paying the British to retain some military presence in the Gulf region. The Labour government, determined to withdraw from previous British commitments there, scuttled any such design.

At U.S. urging, Saudi Arabia instead forged a measure of security cooperation with the shah of Iran. To be sure, there were some serious birth pangs over conflictual views on the independence of Bahrain, different, millennium-old, Islamic sectarian rivalries, and residual Saudi resentment over Iran's earlier insistence on revising an already agreed-upon median line in the Gulf, to the latter's advantage. These were overcome, and what came to be known as the "twin pillars" policy evolved. In order to maintain future security in the Gulf, Saudi Arabia and Iran agreed to cooperate in the defense of that region, and received increased quantities of American weaponry. For Saudi Arabia, this soon engendered worries that Iran, as the larger state, would dominate the Gulf region. King Faisal, in particular, was disturbed by Iran's intervention, at Omani request, in the Dhofar rebellion of the early 1970s.[15] The demise of the shah's government in 1979 and its replacement by a highly conservative Shi`i clerically-dominated government brought the incipient security cooperation between the two states to an end. For a time Saudi worried about the new Iranian government's attitude toward the kingdom and the Saud family.

In the protracted Iraq-Iran war from 1980 to 1988, Saudi Arabia gave strong financial, logistic, and moral support to Iraq as a fellow Arab state. It did so not because of great confidence in Saddam Husayn, but largely out of concern that an Iranian victory might bring about the dismemberment of Iraq and produce a rump Shi`i state on its northeastern flank. The organization of the G.C.C. was one Saudi response to that conflict. The kingdom also welcomed the deployment of additional U.S. and other foreign naval vessels to the Gulf to convoy oil tankers and provide umbrella protection against possible Iranian attacks. The shooting down by a Saudi air force plane of an intruding Iranian aircraft in 1984 seemed briefly to threaten direct Iranian hostilities against the kingdom, but happily this failed to materialize. At Saudi request, President Ronald Reagan was also able to obtain reluctant congressional approval for the sale of some AWAC aircraft to the kingdom. As a further precaution during this tense period, the kingdom engaged a number of Pakistani mercenary troops to assist in its defense.

The final stalemate in the Iraqi-Iranian conflict and Khomeini's death a year later offered momentary relief to the Saudi regime. But this was short lived. Saddam Husayn's invasion of Kuwait in August 1990, despite earnest Saudi efforts to mediate Iraqi-Kuwaiti tensions, suddenly posed an imminent threat, despite the Saudi-Iraqi nonaggression pact of the previous year. Since neither Saudi Arabia's indigenous military forces nor those of the G.C.C. had the capability to withstand a possible Iraqi attack on the kingdom, King Fahd, albeit reluctantly, agreed to a U.S. proposal that we should invite American forces into the kingdom in order to deter the Iraqi threat and eventually to liberate Kuwait. Sensitive to the misgivings of his Wahhabi subjects to having non-Muslim military in the holy land of Islam, the king prudently obtained a *fatwa*, or religious advisory opinion, from the late Shaikh `Abd al-Aziz bin Baz, the mufti of Saudi Arabia, legitimizing the presence of such troops in defense of Islamic territories. The American troops, it was stipulated from the outset, would leave the kingdom once the Iraqi threat was removed.

Egyptian, Syrian, and Moroccan troop contingents were also deployed, upon Saudi invitation and in the context of the Arab Collective Security Pact, as were troops from Britain, France, and thirty other states, some of them Muslim. The military operation was internationally legitimized through a U.N. resolution; a U.N. imprimatur was essential to Saudi Arabia. A total of 700,000 foreign troops, 500,000 of whom were American, were ultimately deployed to Saudi Arabia and the Gulf region. Whereas the American and British troops were under U.S. operational command, most others (except the French, who retained their own command) were under a Saudi general, Prince Khalid bin Sultan, the eldest son of the Saudi Arabian minister of defense.[16] Symbolically salient for the kingdom's image abroad and at home, a joint Saudi-Qatari force, under the latter's command, ultimately liberated the Saudi oil town of al-Khafji from Iraqi occupation.

Following Iraq's defeat in February 1991, most of the foreign troops departed. Nevertheless, Saudi concerns about possible external threats remained. It was feared that Iraq, though momentarily defeated, might at some point in the future seek to renew its aggressive actions. And Iran, even after Khomeini's death, was still considered as potentially hostile. Hence, in response to a U.S. proposal, Saudi Arabia reluctantly agreed that some 5,000 American military personnel, mainly U.S. Air Force, remain in the kingdom, ostensibly for purposes of conducting aerial monitoring over the southern U.N. exclusionary no-overflight zone of Iraq. Some British and French air squadrons were also retained.

That the retention of such a body of American military personnel troubled some Saudi conservatives was graphically evident in the bombings of U.S. military installations in Riyadh and Khobar Towers, in 1995 and 1996 respectively. The bulk of the

American contingent still in Saudi Arabia has since been moved to an installation at al-Kharj, which has a lower public profile. There has also been some Saudi resentment at attempted F.B.I. involvement in the Saudi Ministry of Interior investigations of the bombing incidents. The Saudi minister of the interior, Prince Naif ibn `Abd al-Aziz, is clearly not anxious to allow Americans to probe potential internal dissidence. Saudi Arabia has refused to allow U.S. aircraft based on its soil to participate in the bombing of Iraq.

The extraordinary effort of the Bush administration in deploying such a large body of American troops to Saudi Arabia and the Gulf, the largest such deployment since the Vietnam War, has graphically demonstrated the credibility of the American security commitment to the kingdom. At the same time, it has heightened concern among many Saudi leaders that the kingdom might appear to be simply a satrapy of the United States in the Middle East region, all the more so since the United States remains widely viewed in the region as pro-Israeli. The American embrace has often been felt by Saudi leaders to be overwhelming and undesirably intrusive. Moreover, the inclusion of Saudi Arabia in the annual State Department human rights reports as a sometime violator because of arbitrary imprisonments and *shari'a* court procedures and judgments is resented by Saudi officialdom as unwarranted U.S. interference in the kingdom's internal affairs. As such, it has touched a raw Saudi nerve with respect to considerations of sovereignty. The kingdom's leaders, despite their continued reliance upon the United States for security against stronger foreign states, often lean over backward to demonstrate their independence on other matters. The Americans, they charge, have a tendency to try to dictate their foreign affairs, for example their relations with Iran and Pakistan. Close though it is, the Saudi-U.S. tie is at best ambivalent. Saudi leaders wish to keep it that way.

As King Fahd, who has consistently placed great reliance upon the United States, has become increasingly ill, Crown Prince `Abdallah ibn `Abd al-Aziz, his half brother, has assumed greater executive functions in determining the kingdom's foreign policies. Although `Abdallah may be expected to retain a close Saudi-U.S. tie, he has long harbored doubts about U.S. policy in the Middle East, especially with respect to Israel. The crown prince's visit to the United States in September 1998, as well as to various European countries and Japan, was generally viewed in Washington as reinforcing the Saudi-U.S. link, although his parallel overtures to Iran and the resultant Saudi-Iranian rapprochement have worried some senior U.S. officials. With respect to Iran, Prince `Abdallah has made it clear that Saudi Arabia will go its own way and will not be led by the United States. Indeed, he argues—as do many European states and Japan—that constructive engagement with Iran is desirable, will strengthen moderates in that country, and could even assist in an eventual U.S.-Iranian accommodation.

In the view of many Saudis, Iran is a permanent neighbor; in contrast, the United States is an outside, transitory phenomenon. It thus behooves Saudi Arabia to explore prospects of improved ties with a seemingly more moderate Iran. Nor do the Saudis relish their visible dependence upon a U.S. security umbrella. Unlike its immediate Arab neighbors, the kingdom declined to conclude a new agreement with the United States for this purpose, contending that earlier bilateral military accords were still valid and sufficient. Were it practical in present circumstances, one suspects that many would prefer to revert to earlier Saudi-U.S. "over the horizon" defense concepts.

The World at Large

As Saudi Arabia became increasingly important in international affairs, for reasons already cited, its relations with the broader global community grew. As a small state, the kingdom has emphasized the importance of the United Nations. In that forum, Saudi Arabia has regularly caucused with both the Arab and the Islamic conference blocs, and maintains close liaison with the African bloc. It has generally supported resolutions introduced by members of those groups, even when they have been opposed by the United States. It has also regularly supported anti-Israeli resolutions in the General Assembly, despite U.S. representations to do otherwise. Even as it acknowledges the futility of most such General Assembly resolutions, Saudi Arabia considers that they reflect the true sentiment of the international community at large, regardless of Security Council decisions. It sees the General Assembly as a forum to voice smaller states' hopes and grievances. A distinguished Saudi diplomat, Ambassador Samir Shihabi, served as elected president of the General Assembly in the 1980s.

Before qualified indigenous Saudis were available to head Saudi Arabia's mission to the U.N., for a time non-Saudi nationals were utilized for this purpose. In the 1950s, the mission designated Ahmad Shuqairi, a forceful Palestinian nationalist, for that function. By doing so, it in effect gave the still nascent Palestine Liberation Organization a prominent voice in U.N. circles that it could never have had on its own at the time. Shuqairi was followed by the flamboyant Lebanese Jamil Baroodi, whose intemperate vilifications of U.S. support for Israel antagonized many of his hearers. Baroodi was kept on, however, because Prince (later King) Faisal felt a sense of obligation to him for having looked after the prince's sons when the latter were studying in the United States. Neither of these men had any influence in Riyadh, and they were often the bane of the Saudi Foreign Ministry in Jidda, since they constantly ignored their instructions. Their vitriolic denunciations of the United States (and Israel) could, of course, be adduced, as necessary, with other Arabs to demonstrate uncompromising Saudi support for the Arab cause. In contrast, pertinent Saudi diplomatic representations to U.S. and Western diplomats in Jidda were always much more moderate in tone.

Moreover, despite its heavy reliance upon the United States for security assistance, Saudi Arabia has sought to diversify its sources of arms. Britain, whatever past Saudi concerns over British policies in the Gulf and Middle East may have been, has remained a major supplier of armaments, especially aircraft. In 1965, Saudi Arabia reluctantly accepted the so-called Jenkins-MacNamara agreement, according to which Britain would sell Lightning fighter aircraft and military communications equipment to the kingdom, and the United States would sell Patriot ground-to-air missiles. As a result of congressional opposition to U.S. sales of fighter aircraft to Saudi Arabia, due to that country's anti-Israeli stance, the kingdom subsequently also bought Tornado aircraft from Britain. After Britain's grant of political asylum to a Saudi dissident, however, Saudi Arabis warned that British firms might be boycotted, but this did not materialize. French and Swedish military equipment have likewise been purchased.

And, much to U.S. chagrin, medium-range ground-to-air missiles were bought from the People's Republic of China against a supposed Iranian threat.

The kingdom's diplomatic relations with most European and Far Eastern countries have been correct. A Japanese oil company has had a concession agreement from Saudi Arabia (and separately with Kuwait) for the offshore areas of the former Saudi-Kuwaiti Neutral Zone, but, when the original agreement was due to expire, extended negotiations throughout 1999 did not lead to a renewal of the concession. For many years, Saudi Arabia declined to establish formal ties with the Soviet Union, but has done so with the emergent Russian Republic. Apart from Venezuela, a fellow OPEC member, the kingdom has limited contacts with South American states. After recognizing only Taiwan, Saudi Arabia established diplomatic relations with Beijing in the 1980s.

In southwest Asia, following the Soviet invasion of Afghanistan, the kingdom endorsed the position of the nonaligned states, which rejected any interference in the region by the superpowers. Through funds, arms, and volunteers, the Saudis supported *mujahidin* efforts to oust the Soviet invaders. It cooperated with Pakistan in this attempt and, its aforementioned pronouncement notwithstanding, did not object to covert U.S. aid to the *mujahidin*. Since the Soviet withdrawal, it has endorsed the Taliban government there. Relations with the latter have become strained, however, as a result of Kabul's harboring of the Saudi dissident Usama bin Ladin. In protest, the kingdom has suspended relations at the ambassadorial level. Seeking to mollify Saudi concerns, the Taliban authorities have pledged to curb the Saudi exile's activities while he is their "guest." Elsewhere, Saudi Arabia strongly supported the U.N. anti-apartheid sanctions on the former South African government until that situation was corrected in 1994. The previous South African government's relations with Israel were also a factor in the kingdom's attitude.

Saudi Foreign Policy Modalities

The foreign policy of Saudi Arabia is determined in the first instance by the reigning monarch. This has been so from the time of Ibn Saud, though King Fahd's recent incapacitation has given Crown Prince `Abdallah a more prominent role in foreign-policy decisions. It has sometimes been suggested that family consensus is a major determinant, but this should not be overstated. In contrast to major family matters, such as succession, where family consensus is necessary, foreign-policy issues are much more closely held. Only a few senior Saudi princes are involved in foreign-policy determination. They may be consulted, along with the senior technocrats concerned with or knowledgeable about a particular situation, but in the final analysis decisions are taken by the ruling monarch. His ministers and bureaucrats implement them and, in that process, may indeed seek to interpret royal decisions as they deem fit. Routine matters are entrusted to the appropriate ministers or bureaucrats.

Depending upon the issue, and in the absence of qualified Saudi nationals, Saudi rulers have consulted concerned members of Al Saud and trusted nonroyal counselors. In Ibn Saud's time, these included the Lebanese Druze Shaikh Fuad Hamza, the Syrians Shaikh Yusuf Yassin and Khairaddine Zirikli, the Libyan Shaikh Khalid

Gargani, and the Egyptian Shaikh Hafiz Wahba, each of whom was given particular foreign policy-watching briefs. Thus, Fuad Hamza dealt with Yemeni affairs; Yusuf Yassin with Syrian affairs (and was reportedly the ubiquitous emissary for the alleged plot to persuade the Syrian intelligence chief, Colonel Abdul Hamid Sarraj, to assassinate Nasir); Wahba involved himself in everything that he could, including U.S. ties, until he was again shipped off as Saudi ambassador to London; Gargani was also used in the Buraimi dispute, though Yusuf Yassin was the Saudi representative who was caught trying to influence the abortive arbitral tribunal. The system of using such foreign advisors was notoriously inefficient and frequently lent itself to overlapping assignments. Moreover, it created bitter palace rivalries and intrigues.

During his brief flirtation with "positive neutralism," King Saud relied mainly on the advice of his sons and at times on that of his half brothers, Prince Talal and Prince Misha`al. Both were skeptical of any close Saudi-U.S. ties. Talal and two other half brothers subsequently defected to Egypt, returning several years later without any positions. Both believed that Saudi Arabia should work more closely with Egypt rather than the United States. Prince Misha`al, in his capacity as minister of defense, sought greater Egyptian military training and arms aid. In the event, their views failed to carry the day. And the vacillating King Saud himself, after being deposed in 1964, went with his immediate family to Greece, but shortly thereafter was invited by Nasir to reside in Cairo. There, Prince (by now King) Faisal's house, which the Egyptian authorities had confiscated, was made available to the exiled king. Ever erratic, he allowed himself to be used by the Egyptians to denounce his successor's policies toward the Yemen revolution. As the person who had initially begun Saudi support for the Yemeni royalists, the former King Saud hardly enhanced his image by his turnabout. His defection was nevertheless embarrassing for King Faisal and his regime.

King Faisal used a forum in which those of his counselors who chose to appear would "sit" with him, as it was called, in his office as he pondered specific issues and, when asked, proffer advice. Dr. Rashad Pharaoun was the most prominent such counselor, but the former Egyptian secretary-general of the Arab League, `Abd ar-Rahman Azzam Pasha, who was then living in Saudi Arabia, and occasionally the Palestinian Jamal al-Husayni were at times also consulted. They had no specific briefs, however. When King Khalid assumed the throne, it was widely expected that he would have little interest in foreign affairs and would rely largely on his half brother, Prince Fahd, to handle such matters; but Khalid involved himself in foreign-policy decisions more than had been expected. Until his recent illness, King Fahd was active in determining Saudi foreign policy, sometimes relying on members of his family and his in-laws for advice and counsel. Crown Prince `Abdallah's sources of advice are still being developed, though the foreign minister, Prince Saud ibn Faisal, is said to be one trusted advisor.

A Foreign Ministry was established in Jidda in the early 1930s. In Ibn Saud's days, his second son, Amir Faisal, was named foreign minister (as well as viceroy of Hijaz), and initially Shaikh Fuad Hamza and then Shaikh Yusuf Yassin were successively designated deputy foreign minister. In their absences from Jidda, which were frequent, Khairaddine Zirikli was the principal local Foreign Ministry official for foreign diplomats. King Faisal, with his long experience in foreign affairs and his photographic memory, had little need of outside counsel. During Faisal's reign, the Foreign Ministry in Jidda was more effectively organized by Sayyid Umar Saqqaf, who held the post of deputy foreign minister. It was still small, however, and consisted of an undersecretary, an Arab Bureau, a Political Bureau, and European and African sections. By then there was a handful of Saudis who had graduated from the American universities in Beirut or Cairo and were qualified to assume such functions.

The ministers responsible for various functions have also been involved in foreign-policy matters. They provide technical advice and recommendations. Thus, Prince Sultan, who has been minister of defense for twenty-five years or more, has had a major voice in security policy. Petroleum ministers, such as Shaikh Zaki Yamani, Shaikh Hisham Nazir, and the present incumbent, Shaikh Ali Na`imi, have provided counsel to reigning monarchs on oil issues. The successive finance ministers and the director of the Saudi Arabian Monetary Agency have frequently been called upon for advice on financial matters. The director of intelligence, Prince Turki ibn Faisal, is likewise a source of information and maintains contacts with selected foreign intelligence organizations.

Since Prince Saud ibn Faisal became foreign minister in 1980, he has reorganized the Foreign Ministry and made it a much more efficient and responsive organization, better able to meet the kingdom's growing foreign-policy needs. Under the minister, four deputy ministers now supervise separate spheres of activity. One is charged with political affairs and oversees separate sections for the Arab League, the Arab countries, Afro-Asian ties, Palestinian matters, and United Nations and Islamic affairs. Relations with Western states and supervision of the Legal Advisor's office likewise fall under his area of responsibility. Additionally, he supervises separate sections for Arabian peninsular and Arabian Gulf affairs. A second deputy minister handles economic and cultural affairs as well as the ministry's research requirements. Still another is charged with consular and pilgrimage matters. A fourth handles the various aspects of Foreign Ministry administration, including finance, personnel, archives, requisite translation services, warehousing, maintenance, protocol, and communications.[17]

In the mid-1980s, the Saudi Arabian government moved all foreign embassies from Jidda to a newly built diplomatic quarter of Riyadh, thereby placing them closer to the seat of authority. No longer do foreign diplomats have to travel to Riyadh for senior-level discussions, as was previously the case. A number of Islamic countries that send annual pilgrimage contingents have, with Saudi concurrence, retained consulates in Jidda, as has the United States. The U.S. consulate general in Dhahran, still the sole foreign consular office in al-Ahsa, likewise remains open, largely owing to the large number of private Americans in Saudi Aramco's employ.

For its part, the Saudi Arabian government maintains embassies, with consular sections, in some 120 countries, along with a diplomatic mission to the United Nations in New York, and an Arab League office in Cairo. It has also established various educational missions abroad, including one in Houston, Texas, to handle the large number of Saudi students studying in the United States and in other foreign countries. King Fahd often uses the Saudi ambassador in Washington, Prince Bandar bin Sultan, for special missions such as the missile purchase from the People's Republic of China and mediation with Qadhafi on the Lockerbie bombing suspects.

Since `Abd al-'Aziz Ibn Sa'ud began the process of creating the modern Saudi state by capturing Riyadh with a handful of followers in 1902 there have been changes that no one then, nor even for many decades after, could have dreamed of. Much of the vast Arabian peninsula has been united into a single polity for the first time in centuries. Saudi Arabia with its enormous fossil fuel reserves has become a major force in the international politics of oil. And the kingdom has moved the Arabian peninsula from its earlier position of being somewhat peripheral to regional politics to center-stage. At the same time, as this chapter has sought to indicate, alongside these changes occurring throughout the last century can be charted a considerable consistency in the Saudi approach to diplomacy.

Notes

1   For the earlier Saudi polities, see R. Bayly Winder, *Saudi Arabia in the Nineteenth Century*. For the transition from Arab chieftaincy to state, see Joseph Kostiner, *The Making of Saudi Arabia*, and Christine Moss Helms, *The Cohesion of Saudi Arabia*, especially pp. 181–97.

2   For pre-Second World War Anglo-Saudi relations, see Clive Leatherdale, *Britain and Saudi Arabia, 1925–1939*.

3   Helms, *Cohesion*, pp. 225–34.

4   For the negotiations leading up to the exchange of notes between the U.S. ambassador and the Saudi minister in London, see United States Department of State, *The Foreign Relations of the United States, 1933, Diplomatic Papers*, Vol. 2, pp. 986–1,001.

5   William B. Quandt, *Saudi Arabia in the 1980s: Foreign Policy, Security and Oil*.

6   For the Saudi claim, see *Memorial of the Kingdom of Saudi Arabia* (Riyadh, 1955), 4 vols.; the British challenge to the memorial is summarized in J. B. Kelly, *Eastern Arabian Frontiers*.

7   Saeed M. Badeeb, *The Saudi-Egyptian Conflict over North Yemen, 1962–1970*, especially pp. 46–108.

8   F. Gregory Gause III, *Saudi-Yemeni Relations, Domestic Structures and Foreign Influence*.

9   For some of the G.C.C. activities, see Joseph Wright Twinam, *The Gulf, Cooperation and Council*, and J. E. Peterson, *Defending Arabia*, especially pp. 185–242.

10   Mark Tessler, *A History of the Israeli-Palestinian Conflict*, pp. 537–38.

11   For some of the logistical problems facing the Saudis with respect to the annual *haj*, see David E. Long, *The Hajj Today*.

12   Shaikh Ahmed Zaki Yamani, "Saudi Arabia—Consumer-Producer Understanding"; also Quandt, *Saudi Arabia in the 1980s*, pp. 123–38.

13   Nadav Safran, *Saudi Arabia: The Ceaseless Quest for Security*, citing a dispatch from the American consul in Dhahran of May 10, 1949. Also David E. Long, *The United States and Saudi Arabia: Ambivalent Allies*, especially pp. 33–72, and Joseph Kechichian, "Trends in Saudi National Security."

14   Parker T. Hart, *The United States and Saudi Arabia: Birth of a Security Partnership*, especially pp. 202–36.

15   Safran, *Saudi Arabia*, pp. 128–29.

16   For somewhat different Saudi and American views of the conduct of the Gulf War, see General H. Norman Schwarzkopf, with Peter Petre, *The Autobiography: It Doesn't Take a Hero*; and H.R.H. General Khaled bin Sultan, with Patrick Seale, *Desert Warrior*.

17   Fouad al-Farsy, *Modernity and Tradition: The Saudi Equation*, p. 65.

PART IV

The Other Middle East

12

Iran's Foreign Policy under the Islamic Republic, 1979–2000

Shaul Bakhash

The impact of the 1979 Islamic revolution on Iran's foreign policy has been the subject of considerable debate among scholars and analysts. Some have discerned a post-revolution foreign policy dominated by ideological considerations. Others have argued that Iran is no exception to the rule that the geostrategic interests of states determine foreign policy; and that, inevitably, Iran's foreign policy has continued to be character-ized by the same geostrategic considerations and priorities that defined foreign policy under the monarchy. In fact, the Islamic revolution and the ideas and ideology to which it gave birth have significantly reshaped Iranian foreign policy. There are conti-nuities across the watershed of the revolution, but the transformations in foreign policy orientation are also striking.

Under the monarchy, the United States was a close ally, and the shah took pride in his close relations with Western Europe. Iran had excellent relations with Israel. In the Middle East and the Persian Gulf, Iran identified most often with the Arab monarchies and the conservative Arab states, including Saudi Arabia, the Gulf amirates, Jordan, Morocco, and Sadat's Egypt. Relations with the radical Arab states—Syria, Iraq, and Libya—were generally strained. Iran under the shah was, in essence, a status-quo power and served as an element of stability in the Persian Gulf.

By contrast, under the Islamic Republic, the United States has come to be regarded by Iran as the "great Satan" and an enemy of the Islamic Republic. Diplo-matic relations were broken in 1979, and the rupture continued two decades after the revolution. Diplomatic relations with Britain, France, and Germany were frequently disrupted by minor and major incidents that derived primarily from the political and foreign-policy attitudes generated by the revolution. On the Arab-Israeli conflict, Iran took the position that Israel was an illegitimate state that had no right to exist. After 1990, Iran remained intractably hostile to the Oslo peace process. For a decade after the revolution, diplomatic relations with Egypt, Morocco, and Jordan remained broken, while Iran moved closer to the Arab radicals. Syria became its closest Arab ally, Libya was considered a friend, and Iran acted with alacrity to support the radical Islamic regime that seized power in Sudan in the early 1990s. In the first decade after the revolution, Iran was with good reason seen as a disruptive element in the Persian Gulf region rather than a source of stability. At the very least, Iran adopted a rhetoric against Saudi Arabia and the Gulf amirates that these states viewed as an attack on their legitimacy. Iran saw itself, and behaved, as an anti-status-quo power.

Revolution and Foreign Policy

Several elements contributed to these altered directions in Iran's foreign policy. Iran's new rulers saw their revolution as a model and catalyst for Islamic revolutions throughout the region and sought, at various times, to advance such revolutions by example, word, material support, and action. Even after hopes for a wider upheaval in the Persian Gulf and Arab Middle East began to wane, Iran's new leaders continued to treat Islam as the preeminent weapon for the world's exploited peoples to use against the great powers. In the Iranian view, for centuries the great powers had been exploiting Muslims, looting their resources and threatening their culture.

Iran's leaders, moreover, claimed for the dominant figure of the Iranian revolution, Ayatollah Khomeini, a kind of spiritual leadership for Muslims everywhere. Khomeini took his role as spiritual leader and spokesman for the Muslim world with utter serious- ness. His words and actions implied a transnational Islamic responsibility that extended beyond Iran's borders. In January 1989, for example, Khomeini addressed a letter to Mikhael Gorbachev in which he applauded the Soviet leader for abandoning the false god of communism, urged him to avoid the equally false god of capitalism, and advised him to return to God, read the Qur'an, and study the Islamic mystics and philosophers. Again, it was as a defender of the world's Muslim community against the supposed insults and blasphemous content of the novel *The Satanic Verses* that Khomeini condemned the author, Salman Rushdie, to death. Khomeini addressed his last will and testament not only to the people of Iran but also "to all the Muslim nations and the oppressed of the world."

Khomeini and his lieutenants felt little compunction in publicly denouncing other Muslim heads of state, arguing it was an Islamic duty to denounce the tyrant, the corrupt leader who had strayed from the Islamic path. In his last will and testament, a document intended as a guide to policy for his successors, Khomeini described King Husayn of Jordan as a "criminal peddler" and King Hassan of Morocco and President Mubarak of Egypt as American lackeys and associates of "criminal Israel." He called for the public cursing of the rulers of Saudi Arabia for their alleged "treachery" against the house of God.

Khomeini's successor, Ali Khamenei, aspired to a similar role as spokesman for the world Islamic community. He championed the cause of Muslims in Bosnia and the West Bank, Somalia and Lebanon. He argued that the Palestinian question and the ultimate disposition of Jerusalem were "an Islamic matter" on which presumably all Muslims, not just Palestinians, must have a say. He repeatedly urged the Islamic world to unite and gird itself for a struggle with the exploitative, threatening West. In these ways he sought to assert Iran's primacy among Muslim states, to capture for himself the prestige and authority that he believes Khomeini enjoyed among Muslims world- wide, and also to bolster his position at home.

This universalistic streak in Iran's postrevolution ideology was strongest in the first decade following the revolution, but its influence on foreign policy continued well into the 1990s. Iran's leaders supported Islamic movements beyond their own borders out of both conviction and calculation. The support that Iran lent to these movements by word or deed was a token of Iran's own Islamic credentials and helped boost the regime's standing, or so the leadership thought, with constituencies at home. It served as a means of projecting Iranian influence abroad and allowed Iran to create for itself a presence in Lebanon or to become a player, if only briefly, in Bosnia or in the politics of the Arab-Israeli conflict. As such, Islam served the same purpose for Iran as Arab nationalism had for Egypt under Nasir. Supporting Islamic causes abroad was also an attempt to secure leverage against countries like the United States and Israel that were hostile to Iran. Iran used the Shi`ite Hizbullah party to drive American marines out of Lebanon, to harass Israeli troops in that country, and to take American hostages who were then used (not necessarily successfully) to influence American policy toward Iran.

Resistance to Western cultural hegemony, suspicion of Western motives, and unease with even the appearance of friendly traffic with the West was another element in the revolutionary legacy that impacted on foreign policy. The revolution, after all, defined itself in part against what was seen as the shah's excessive deference toward the United States and his excessive zeal for Westernization. The revolution, by contrast, stressed Islamic authenticity and identity. The postrevolution period was characterized by repeated attacks on Western cultural influence and the liberal intelligentsia that were its presumed agents. In 1993, the Supreme Leader, Khamenei, revived a campaign against Western cultural influence. The term he employed, "cultural onslaught," was added to the revolutionary lexicon; it was a code word for the supposedly corrupting influences of the West fostered by liberals and reformers. In the 1996 parliamentary elections and the 1997 presidential elections, Khamenei tried to rouse public opinion for or against various candidates or political factions by asserting that the people would not vote for "an American Islam" or for those who would be "soft" on America. Twenty years after the revolution, conservatives were still trying to taint their opponents with the "American" or "Western" brush. Such rhetoric, used in part for domestic political advantage, nevertheless bred an environment hostile to normal relations with European countries and America.

The propensity for "revolutionary" posturing and action also remained a legacy of the revolution and exacerbated Iran's relations with the Arab states of the Persian Gulf, the United States and the Western European countries. In the months immediately following the revolution, clerical propagandists fanned out in the Gulf amirates to preach the need for Islamic revolution. One senior cleric warned the amir of Bahrain that he would call on the Bahrainis to overthrow him if he did not treat his people with greater consideration. Ayatollah Montazeri, a senior cleric who at one time was expected to succeed Khomeini as Iran's leader, in the early 1980s denounced the Saudi ruling family as "a bunch of pleasure-seekers and mercenaries," and asked, "How long must Satan rule in the house of God?" For years, Iranians on the annual *haj* pilgrimage to Mecca acted on Khomeini's instructions to "disavow the infidel" by organizing demonstrations against Israel, America, and the "world-devouring" great powers. These demonstrations almost invariably led to clashes with the Saudi authorities. Iran changed tack only after inept handling of the demonstrators by the Saudi police in 1987 led to riots in which over 400 pilgrims, 270 of them Iranians, were killed. Diplomatic relations between the two countries were broken as a result and not resumed for three years.

In addition, there existed a plethora of government organizations that acted independently, sometimes with and sometimes without government sanction. The security agencies felt free to pursue policies which, even if officially sanctioned, did not always coincide with government policy. The government often appeared to be pursuing contradictory policies. For example, after 1990, Iran actively sought better relations with the countries of the European Union. Yet in these years, Iranian agents carried out a string of assassinations of Iranian dissidents in European capitals and cities, including Paris, Berlin and Vienna. Well into the second decade after the revolution, it was often difficult to know whether such operations were the result of decisions taken by the government, by its agencies acting independently, or by rogue elements within the regime.

The examples are legion. In 1982, following the Israeli invasion of Lebanon, Muhammad Montazeri, the senior cleric's son, flew armed Iranian volunteers to Lebanon to fight the Israelis. He prevailed in his enterprise although the government was opposed and tried forcibly to stop him. Shapour Bakhtiar, a former prime minister and opposition figure, was assassinated in Paris by Iranian agents on the eve of a long-planned state visit to Tehran by French President François Mitterrand. The Mitterrand trip, the first by a European head of state to the Islamic Republic and therefore of considerable importance to Iran, was canceled. In May 1987, the second-ranking British diplomat in Tehran was pulled out of his car and beaten after an Iranian consular officer was arrested in Manchester on shoplifting charges. In June of that year, the French embassy in Tehran was surrounded by a mob, and French diplomats were prevented from leaving the embassy or the country, after the French police tried to question an Iranian embassy employee in Paris in connection with a series of bombings that had taken place in the French capital the previous year. These incidents led to a rupture of diplomatic relations with both Britain and France. In 1996, the German federal prosecutor issued a warrant for the arrest of Iran's minister of intelligence for involvement in the 1992 assassination in Berlin of the leader of the Kurdish Democratic Party of Iran and three others. The trial of the Iranian agents charged with the assassination was underway when Belgian officials in Antwerp boarded an Iranian ship bound for Germany. They found on board mortar shells, a rocket launcher, and 250 kilos of TNT.

The consequences for foreign policy of a government impelled by conflicting priorities and impulses and competing power centers is well illustrated by the politics of the Rushdie affair. In 1988, Ayatollah Khomeini had endorsed an annual budget for 1989–1990 and a five-year development plan that authorized the government to borrow abroad and to permit foreign investment. Both had been taboos in the revolutionary lexicon. The development plan itself was to mark a new era of economic reconstruction and engagement with Europe. The foreign ministry moved to repair relations with half a dozen countries, including Britain, France and Germany. Yet in February 1989, Khomeini wrecked months of careful Iranian fence mending in Europe by issuing his "death decree" against Rushdie. Countries of the European Community withdrew their ambassadors from Iran, and discussions on industrial projects with West Germany, France, and other countries were suspended.

The Rushdie affair continued to bedevil Iran's relations with the European states for several years. Although Khomeini himself died in 1989, it was considered unthinkable to declare void a decree issued by the revered founder of the Islamic Republic. In the early 1990s, Rafsanjani, as president, tried to find formulas by which he could explain away the decree. But he backed off under attacks from clerics looking for domestic political advantage or convinced that an abandonment of Khomeini's ruling amounted to a betrayal of Khomeini and the revolution. Discussions between Iran and European states in 1992 led to a declaration by Iran that it would respect international law in this matter, implying that Iran would not attempt to assassinate Rushdie. Almost immediately, 180 deputies in the 270-member Majlis signed a letter affirming Khomeini's edict. In 1994, Iran promised the Europeans that it would put in writing an undertaking not to kill Rushdie. But at the last minute, at a meeting with E.U. officials, Iran's representative refused to put his signature to the document. It was not until September 1997, following the election of Muhammad Khatami to the presidency, that Iran's foreign minister handed the Europeans an undertaking that they found acceptable, declaring that Iran would not attempt to carry out Khomeini's decree. Only then did the E.U. ambassadors return to Tehran.

Postrevolution foreign policy was obviously characterized by a strain of pragmatism, as well. Iran, for example, did not allow President Asad's harsh repression of the Muslim Brotherhood to influence the close relations with Syria, its one reliable Arab ally. During the Iran-Iraq war, Iran was careful to maintain correct relations with Abu Dhabi—a principal transit port for imports into Iran—despite the fact that it joined other Gulf states in siding with Iraq in the war.

There were numerous deliberate attempts to reshape foreign policy in a more pragmatic direction. One such attempt was made in 1984, following criticism of a spate of visits abroad by the foreign minister and the speaker of the Majlis, Rafsanjani, who was beginning to play an increasingly important role in shaping foreign policy. The visits were designed to secure Iran arms and greater international support in the war with Iraq; but to the guardians of the revolutionary flame, these visits and the quest for help abroad smacked of pandering. Khomeini had to step in to defend the new policy. In widely publicized remarks, he attributed the criticism of the foreign visits to Iran's enemies. He noted that the Prophet had sent emissaries to all parts of the world, and that for Iran not to do so now meant courting defeat and annihilation. This came to be known as Khomeini's "open window" policy. It was clearly controversial, and Khomeini had to invoke the example of the Prophet to justify it. In the following months, Khomeini's lieutenants tried to use his remarks to diminish Iran's international isolation; but, as already noted, the "open window" policy was undercut by the actions and rhetoric of officials, government agencies, and Khomeini himself.

Postrevolution foreign policy, then, was the product not only of traditional Iranian geostrategic interests but also of a worldview and of Iran's place in it that was born out of the revolution. Its principal themes included a belief in the worldwide relevance, especially to Muslims, of the Iranian revolution; a belief in the revolution's exportability; a commitment, at least in the early years of the revolution, to altering the nature of regimes in the Persian Gulf and the regional balance of power; a conviction that certain aspects of Western culture were threatening to Iran's cultural and national identity; a suspicion of Western, and particularly American, intentions toward Iran; a revolutionary ideology that attached value to a truculent, muscular posture in international relations, and that considered friendship with the West a sellout of revolutionary principles; and a willingness to use unconventional means, including assassination and hostage taking, to achieve foreign-policy ends. Foreign policy was also significantly influenced by domestic politics and rivalries; by the conflicting agendas of different government agencies or quasi-independent groups acting with only partial government sanction; and by the propensity of the government itself to pursue several conflicting foreign-policy goals at the same time. Again and again, the government seemed unable to agree on priorities aimed, for example, at securing the goodwill of both conservative regimes in the Middle East and the Islamic radicals who wished to overthrow them; and at catering both to domestic constituencies committed to export the revolution and to technocrats who argued that Iran must secure foreign investment to rescue its deteriorating oil industry.

Postrevolution foreign policy is thus best understood as the result of a dialectic between what, in shorthand, can be described as pragmatic and ideological considerations, between traditional Iranian foreign-policy orientations and a worldview generated by the revolution. The relative strength of ideology and pragmatism has tended to wax and wane, depending on domestic and international factors, personalities, and the nature of the issues involved. Most often, foreign policy has run on parallel tracks: it has been both ideological and pragmatic in temper, both revisionist and traditional in intent. The pragmatic strain in foreign policy has tended to be more in evidence in the second decade following the revolution, but the worldview generated by the revolution has continued to exert an influence, and the trend toward pragmatism has resembled a bumpy road rather than a smooth progression.

Pragmatism in the Post-Khomeini Era

A more concerted attempt to mute the ideological and reinforce the pragmatic strain in foreign policy came with the election of Rafsanjani as president in 1989. Several factors made a new foreign-policy initiative possible. Perhaps most importantly, Iran's devastating war with Iraq had come to an end in 1988. This removed a major irritant in Iran's relations with the Persian Gulf states and the Western European countries. The eight-year war left the country physically and emotionally exhausted, and considerably drained revolutionary fervor. It was ready to devote its energies to repairing war damage and reviving a much-battered economy. Khomeini's death in 1989 removed a powerful, domineering presence, and allowed his lieutenants more flexibility in domestic and foreign policy. Rafsanjani, the new president, had a reputation as a pragmatist and deal maker. He put together a team of technocrats focussed on economic development, launched what he described as the "era of reconstruction," and set about repairing Iran's foreign relations.

The 1990–1991 American-led war to expel Iraq from Kuwait also proved favorable to Rafsanjani's initiative. Iran acted out of national interest when it refused to acquiesce in the Iraqi annexation of Kuwait, but Rafsanjani enhanced his reputation as a pragmatist by siding, in effect, with the aims of the American-led alliance. He consolidated his position at home and confirmed that more moderate men were at the helm in Tehran by facing down a faction in the Majlis that urged an alliance with Iraq against the United States. Rafsanjani used the cover of the war to reestablish diplomatic relations with Egypt, Saudi Arabia, Jordan, and Morocco—all controversial measures. After the war, he used Iranian influence to help secure the release of American hostages being held by Iranian-supported groups in Lebanon. He launched a major effort to repair relations with the Arab states of the Persian Gulf and with the European countries.

The policy yielded results. Although relations with Egypt remained difficult, relations with the Persian Gulf states, Morocco, and Jordan markedly improved. The E.U. countries, led by Germany, conducted a substantial trade with Iran. When Iran ran into balance-of-payments difficulties in 1993–1994, foreign creditors, primarily Japan, Germany, and other European states, agreed to reschedule about $12 billion in Iranian debt. American pressure limited but failed to stop arms sales and technology transfer to Iran by China and Russia. In 1995, the American oil firm Conoco signed a $1 billion agreement to help develop Iranian offshore oilfields. The deal proved abortive when a presidential order banned American companies from investing in Iran's oil industry and forced Conoco to cancel the agreement. Nevertheless, Iran's to Conoco indicated a new willingness to deal with the American companies. Moreover, the French firm Total promptly signed the deal that Conoco canceled—the first of its kind since the revolution. Iran then went on to sign a number of agreements with French, Russian, and other companies to develop Iran's oil and gas resources.

The success of the Rafsanjani initiative was limited by opposition at home, the government's own actions, and persistent problems with the United States abroad. Hardline clerics and parliamentarians frustrated Rafsanjani's attempts to explain away Khomeini's edict against Rushdie. The assassination of Iranian dissidents in Europe eventually seriously strained relations with at least some European countries. There continued to be reports of Iranian involvement either directly or through surrogates in terrorist acts. Argentina claimed evidence that linked the Iranian-backed Hizbullah of Lebanon with the 1992 bombing of the Israeli embassy in Buenos Aires, in which twenty-nine people were killed, and the 1994 bombing of a Jewish Center in the capital, in which eighty-six people lost their lives. Some reports blamed agents trained in Iran for the 1996 bombing of Khobar Towers outside Dharan, Saudi Arabia, in which nineteen American servicemen were killed. The bombing took place in the seventh year of the Rafsanjani presidency. The anti-American and anti-Israeli rhetoric out of Tehran continued unabated.

Moreover, America continued to express concern over Iran's weapons programs, its opposition to the Arab-Israeli peace process, its support for groups like Hizbullah in Lebanon and Hamas on the West Bank that used violence to undermine the Arab-Israeli peace process, and evidence of Iranian support for terrorist groups. The

United States blocked World Bank loans to Iran. American opposition was decisive in excluding Iran from pipeline projects to carry oil and gas from fields in Central Asia and Azerbaijan to markets abroad. America also pressured its European allies and Japan not to invest in Iran or extend to Iran loans, credits, and significant trading privileges. Such pressure did not stop, but did reduce the extent of, European and Japanese involvement in the Iranian economy.

The Clinton administration tightened America's own sanctions against Iran. President Clinton, as noted, signed an order in March 1995 that barred American firms from investing in Iran's oil industry. In April, he signed an order that banned all American trade with Iran. In April 1996 he signed a bill that required the president to impose a range of sanctions against foreign firms investing more than $40 million in Iran's oil and gas industry. By the end of Rafsanjani's second term, his foreign initiative appeared to have lost steam. Nevertheless, he had begun a process that his successor as president, Muhammad Khatami, was able to continue.

In his 1997 election campaign, Khatami ran on a platform of political liberalization at home and "friction-reduction" or détente abroad. His message resonated with the electorate. Nearly 80 percent of eligible voters cast ballots; 70 percent of them voted for Khatami. He thus came to office with a strong public mandate. Unlike Rafsanjani, who perfected a style that was ambiguous and shifting in both tone and gesture, Khatami articulated clear and consistent domestic and foreign policies, and seemed far better able to win trust both at home and abroad. The rapid improvement in Iran-Saudi relations in the Khatami period was largely attributable to a meeting between Khatami and Saudi Crown Prince `Abdallah during the Islamic summit in Tehran in December 1997. `Abdallah came away from this encounter persuaded that Khatami was sincere and would keep his word regarding foreign-policy moderation.

Khatami moved in the first few months of his presidency to deal with at least three of the issues of greatest concern to the United States. At the Islamic summit in Tehran in December 1997, he privately told Yasser `Arafat that Iran would acquiesce in any agreement with Israel acceptable to the Palestinian people. In January of 1998, in a now famous interview with CNN, he condemned terrorism and attacks on innocent civilians, and he also invited Americans to join in a "thoughtful dialogue" with the Iranian people. The invitation to a "dialogue" led to a program of exchanges between Iran and America that involving scholars, filmmakers, artists, and athletes; there was an expectation that government-to-government exchanges would eventually follow. In an address to the U.N. General Assembly in September 1998, Khatami called for a "dialogue of civilizations." He also declared the Rushdie affair "completely finished," and his foreign minister, as noted, gave the Europeans a written commitment that the Iranian government would not enforce Khomeini's death edict. Hardliners in Tehran tried to generate the usual uproar regarding this supposed retreat from revolutionary principles, but the government remained firm, and the protests against its "neutral" stance on the Khomeini edict had little effect.

The pattern observable in previous years, of pragmatic intentions undercut by the legacy of the revolution, domestic politics, and competing priorities, reasserted itself. For example, the Supreme Leader, Khamenei, who almost certainly had endorsed the idea of a "dialogue" between the Iranian and American people and the assurance Khatami gave to `Arafat, very soon reverted to harsh attacks on the United States, and adamantly ruled out negotiations or diplomatic relations with America. Khamenei also began to suggest that `Arafat did not represent the will of the Palestinian people (thus implicitly absolving Iran of the undertaking to be guided by whatever agreement with the Israelis the Palestinian people endorsed). He strongly attacked both the Wye Plantation accords signed by `Arafat and the Palestinians, and the resumption of negotiations between Syria and Israel in 1999. This was an indication of unresolved tensions in the shaping of foreign policy, although by the end of 1999 the pragmatic strain in Iranian foreign policy appeared stronger, the ideological and "revolutionary" strain weaker, than at any time under the Islamic Republic.

Foreign Policy Fundamentals

By the end of 1999, it was also possible to identify a number of consistent and fundamental principles in Iranian foreign policy.

First, like the shah's government, the Islamic Republic came to attach primary importance to stability along its own borders and good relations with neighboring states. It reserved support for radical Islamic movements for the "far abroad," for places distant from Iran's borders like Lebanon, Sudan, or the West Bank. Along its own borders, it no longer supported militant Islamic groups against their own governments. For example, Iran did not allow sectarian conflict and attacks on the Shi`ite community in Pakistan to mar relations with that country. It expressed sympathy with fellow Muslims in Kashmir, but was careful not to take sides in the India-Pakistan conflict over Kashmir. Iran continued to support one of the warring factions in Afghanistan, but once the Taliban gained substantial control over the country, it resisted the temptation to get deeply mired in Afghanistan's civil war. It did not try to stir up Islamic sentiments in the newly independent republics in Central Asia and the Caucasus. It stood on the sidelines in the civil war in Tajikistan in which 20,000 to 50,000 persons—largely Muslims—lost their lives. Most often, Iran sought to cast itself in the role of peacemaker among Muslims and between Muslims and their neighbors. At one time or another, it tried to mediate disputes between warring factions in Afghanistan and Tajikistan; the rival Kurdish parties in Iraq the governments of Azerbaijan and Armenia; and even the amir of Bahrain and his Shi`ite subjects.

After Iraq was expelled from Kuwait, Iran showed restraint in the limited aid it extended to fellow Shi`ites when Saddam Husayn brutally crushed an uprising in southern Iraq. It stood back even as Iraqi troops bombarded Shi`ism's holiest shrines. In stark contrast to the 1980s, when Iran pursued its war into Iraq with the aim of toppling Saddam Husayn and installing an Islamic government in Baghdad, the regime had grown chary of military or open-ended entanglements along its own borders. Concerned lest the autonomous enclave the United States helped create in Iraqi Kurdistan lead to the breakup of Iraq, Iran joined Syria and Turkey in affirming a commitment to Iraq's territorial integrity. Occasional friction in relations notwithstanding, Iran appeared dedicated to maintaining good relations with Turkey—a policy that has survived growing (and, for Iran, alarming) military cooperation between Turkey and Israel. President Khatami continued a policy of strengthening ties with the Persian Gulf states. For example, while highly critical of the American military presence in the Persian Gulf, Iran refrained from criticizing Kuwait for permitting Americans to be based on Kuwaiti soil. Iran strongly opposed the Oslo peace process, but its criticism of Oman and Qatar for recognizing Israel was muted.

Second, Iran's foreign policy is shaped by overriding security concerns. Iraq's invasion of Iran in 1980, the eight-year war with that country, and the sense that Iran received virtually no support from the international community in the face of naked aggression have left deep scars on the national psyche. Moreover, Iran with good reason feels it lives in a dangerous neighborhood. Instability is endemic along its border with Afghanistan, and constantly possible along the borders with the former Soviet republics in Central Asia and the Caucasus. Iraq remains an unpredictable and menacing presence, and there is no certainty concerning Saddam Husayn's regional ambitions and weapons capability. Given America's hostility to Iran, huge military presence in the Persian Gulf and uncertainty about its intentions another source of concern. Military cooperation between Israel and Turkey, and the possibility that Arab-Israeli peace might lead to an Israeli diplomatic, commercial, and perhaps military presence in the Arabian Peninsula, reinforce Iran's perpetual fear of encirclement.

Third, Iran has deliberately sought to foster relations with other great or regional powers as a counter to the United States. If the 1980s were characterized by tension between Iran and the Soviet Union over Afghanistan, the suppression of the Iranian Tudeh (Communist) Party, and the anti-imperialist rhetoric generated by the revolution, the 1990s were characterized by care on Iran's part to reinforce ties with Russia. Iran, for example, did not seriously try to compete with Russia for influence in the newly independent republics in Central Asia and the Caucasus; its criticism of the war Russia conducted against Muslim militants in Chechnya was strikingly muted. Iran also cultivated China, an important source of weapons and weapons technology; the E.U. states and Japan as important trade partners; and regional powers like India.

Historically, Iran dealt with the great powers either by seeking to secure some room for maneuver by balancing one against another or by invoking one to check the other, more threatening one. In the nineteenth century, a weak Iran attempted to maintain its independence by playing off Britain and Russia against one another. At times, it also sought protection from an expansionist Russian through closer alliance with Britain. In the 1950s, Prime Minister Muhammad Musaddiq coined the term "negative equilibrium," to describe the manner in which Iran would avoid falling under the influence of either Britain or the Soviet Union. The shah in the 1950s sought protection against a perceived threat from the north by tying Iran closely to the United States. In the later 1960s and 1970s, he felt strong and stable enough to seek good relations with the Soviet Union even as he maintained his close, informal alliance with America. The shah also made it a practise in his later years to develop close trade and diplomatic ties with a host of other powers, including the European states and China.

The Islamic Republic's great-power diplomacy in the 1990s was therefore a return to a well-established tradition, with some difference. The United States, considered a friend and potential ally since early in the twentieth century, was uncharacteristically cast in the role of potential enemy (although this view could change); and no single country (like Britain in the nineteenth and early twentieth centuries or the United States in the mid-twentieth century) emerged as Iran's principal great-power partner.

Fourth, beginning with the Rafsanjani presidency in 1989, and in sharp contrast to the first decade following the revolution, Iran has been seeking substantial foreign investment, particularly in the oil sector. Iranian officials are well aware that the huge sums required to repair and expand the neglected oil and gas industry cannot be generated at home and must come from abroad. This goal, however, has encountered formidable obstacles, some historical, many the result of the revolution.

The revolution reinforced a deep historical fear among Iranians of rulers willing to "sell" the country to foreigners, and of control and exploitation of Iran's valuable natural resources by foreign firms or governments. The tobacco monopoly protests of 1890–1891, the constitutional revolution of 1905–1906, and the oil nationalization movement of 1951–1953 were all partly reactions to a sense of foreign domination and exploitation. The Islamic revolution was also, in part, a response to what many Iranians perceived to be the excessive role of foreign firms and multinationals in the Iranian economy. After the revolution, there was a massive exodus of foreign firms and personnel, and the government took steps to take over or nationalize numerous large foreign-related enterprises, including oil operations—either as a matter of policy or because it felt compelled to do so as a result of the disorders following the fall of the monarchy. Revolutionary rhetoric subsequently stressed economic independence and autarchy, and reinforced sentiments against foreign borrowing, foreign investment, or a foreign economic presence in Iran. The question of foreign involvement in the Iranian economy carries with it powerful historical and revolutionary baggage. Provisions in the 1985 budget and the first development plan that allowed for foreign borrowing and investment were, as noted, controversial. In the 1990s, Iran began to permit foreign participation in developing oil resources; but, significantly, foreign participation was confined to offshore fields. Until the end of 1999, the government still felt it could not risk permitting onshore foreign involvement in the energy industry.

In addition, the legal framework was not conducive to large-scale foreign investment. Red tape, overlapping jurisdictions of government departments, labor laws overly protective of the labor force, a court system easily manipulated by politics, the continued insecurity of property, weak guarantees for private investment, and conflicting government policies all discouraged significant private investment, whether domestic or foreign. The hold on the economy exercised by the Foundation for the Disinherited and other para-statal foundations that controlled hundreds of expropriated and nationalized enterprises discouraged competition and a larger role for the private sector. The pursuit of foreign investment and the integration of Iran into the international economy, like some other elements of foreign policy, therefore remained tied to major and controversial issues of domestic politics and policy.

Finally, Iran continued, as under the shah, to view itself as a regional power and to aspire to a large regional and even international role. The shah had cultivated a sense of the greatness of Iran by virtue of its size, population, history, and imperial past. The Islamic Republic cultivated a sense of the greatness of Iran on the same basis, but rather than the imperial past it stressed the centrality of the revolution itself and of Iran's Islamic credentials. But as the second decade of the Islamic Republic was coming to an end, the concept of that role was changing. Iran was no longer in the business of exporting the revolution or, with a few exceptions, appealing over the heads of governments to the Islamic masses. The government, rather, took pride in its role as president of the Islamic Conference Organization, and in speaking for the community of Muslim states. Iran still aspired to a leadership role among the Persian Gulf states. It argued, for example, against the American military presence in the Gulf, and for a Gulf defense system maintained by the regional states themselves. But such a leadership role for Iran was not on the cards, given the Shi`ite-Sunni divide, lingering Arab suspicions of the country, and its diminished military and economic clout. The Islamic Republic, like the monarchy, entertained a sense of Iran's weight, its rightful role, in the region and on the international scene. But unlike the shah's government, or even the Islamic Republic in the early years, Iran at the beginning of the twenty-first century no longer seemed certain what that role should be, or how it could fulfill it.

13

Turkey's Foreign Policy: Independent or Reactive?

George S. Harris

Turkey's basic foreign-policy orientations, like those of all states, reflect its history and geography. Some of its foreign-policy directions grew out of the geopolitical reality of sitting astride the exit to the Black Sea and of serving as a land bridge to the Middle East from Europe and Russia. Others evolved from Ottoman experience and the legacy of the dismemberment of that extensive and long-lasting empire. Still others derived from its ethnic composition and status as a predominantly Islamic state on the border of the Christian world. Mustafa Kemal Ataturk, founder of modern Turkey, gave operational impetus to some directions, which enjoy increased standing from that fact. And finally, some choices came about in response to the onset of the Cold War, its weakening, and its eventual demise. Because the fundamental lines of Turkish foreign policy are so solidly based in Turkey's experience and place in the world, they have remarkable staying power no matter what the nature of the government in Ankara might be.

A constant throughout Turkish history since the fifteenth century has been its position controlling the straits of the Bosporus and the Dardanelles, which connect the Black Sea and the Mediterranean. Possession of this vital waterway brought Turkey into perennial conflict with the Russians, whether the czars, the Bolsheviks, or in more attenuated form the post-Soviet Russian state. Conclusion in 1936 of the Montreux Convention regulating the Black Sea exit met Turkey's primary requirement: to gain recognition for the principle of its sovereignty over this passageway, with authority to apply agreed-upon controls as it saw fit. At the same time, Moscow saw the accord as meeting long-term Russian interests in the principle of free and secure commercial transit to the Mediterranean. But controversy over the application of these principles, which peaked during Stalin's last years, continues to set Moscow and Ankara at odds, now over the passage of large oil tankers that the Turks insist must be restricted to reduce the danger of accidents that could threaten Turkey's largest city.

The influence of geography on Turkey's destiny is also visible in the natural-resource deficit imposed on the modern country by the loss of oil-rich Arab lands in the breakup of the Ottoman Empire. Had the Turks been able to sustain, for example, the claim to Mosul province that they pressed until 1925 (and which President Ozal reputedly considered reviving during Desert Storm),[1] they would long since have had the economic and financial strength to meet the material criteria for inclusion in the European Union. But having lost these areas, Turkey was less able to deal with its recurring economic crises. Nonetheless, since gaining the district (*sanjaq*) of Alexandretta (called the "Hatay" by the Turks) in 1939, Turkey has not advanced claims on the territory of other nations. Rather, it seeks to ensure energy supplies both through commercial transactions with Moscow, a key natural-gas supplier, and through negotiating an amicable triangular relationship between the Caucasus, Russia, and itself.

Although the Turks have remained sincere in their renunciation of imperial desires, the memory of losing these territories still influences foreign policy considerations. This partly explains why the Turks have proven so tenacious in their claims to the Aegean seabed with its possible oil deposits. Domestic political pressures make Turkish leaders unwilling to be perceived as once more giving up natural resources to which the country has a plausible claim. Thus the Turks insist that the eastern portion of the Aegean basin is an extension of the Anatolian continental shelf and not a prolongation of the underpinnings of the Greek islands that dot the Turkish coast. Similar considerations lie in part behind Turkish insistence that a Greek declaration of a twelve-mile limit in the Aegean would be a casus belli.

Despite nationalistic rhetoric that focusses on the Turkish nature of modern Turkey, it remains a multiethnic state. Its Kurds have fit contentiously into the nation-state; segments of this minority have rebelled from time to time, a circumstance that has impelled Ankara to maintain a large standing army for use as a last resort to hold the country together. And concern over Kurdish separatism has conditioned Turkey's relationship with Iraq, whose northern sector has periodically fallen under de facto Kurdish control. Turkish leaders have, as well, often voiced fears that Western powers, especially the United States, were covertly aiding Turkey's Kurds in the southeast in their bid for special status.

Turkey's population is nominally about 98 percent Muslim; a small, though significant, part of this majority feels a strong political commitment to its Islamic identity, an orientation that at times it seeks to have reflected in foreign policy, against the will of the majority. To curry favor with these voters, Ankara governments have generally in recent decades made a conscious effort to give a more Islamic cast to foreign-policy actions, although without abandoning the majority view that secular considerations, particular those of the military, take precedence.

Foreign policy in modern Turkey has been the preserve of prime ministers and presidents. Particularly since the mid-1950s, foreign ministers have often been technicians drawn from the ranks of diplomats. Even when politicians have been chosen, they have operated as advisors rather than as formulators of major foreign policy initiatives. The Turkish diplomatic corps has evolved from a French-educated organization, drawn largely from the elite Galatasaray School, to a much more diverse body today, educated in many different universities, with far more competence in English and German than in the past. But the corps remains conservative and nationalistic in orientation. It is said to prefer to follow the majority in the United Nations and/or NATO, as the case may be, than to urge riskier courses. In Turgut Ozal's words: "In the view of the Foreign Ministry, before setting policy, look around," then do what everyone else is doing, for that will be considered successful.[2]

The battle that the modern Turkish state waged to come into being out of the ruins of the Ottoman Empire had lasting consequences. From the start, the new Turkish Republic was surrounded by old adversaries. Although Ataturk and Vladimir Lenin established an alliance of convenience against the Western world after the Russian revolution, the Turks remained wary of their northern neighbor, especially as communism seemed to threaten to subvert Turkish nationalism, and the liquidation of the independent Caucasian states brought Soviet power to Turkey's borders. No trace of this uneasy cooperation survived the Second World War, as Moscow reverted to its age-old role as the bogeyman whose territorial ambitions threatened Turkey's integrity during the intense phases of the Cold War.

Other neighbors nourished irredentist claims against Turkey, as well. The hostility of the Arabs, who had just broken away from Turkish rule, was muted at first by being under European mandate control. But after Turkey secured French cooperation to acquire Alexandretta from its Syrian mandate, relations with Damascus soured. Once Syria gained freedom, it pressed for return of this province. To this day, Syrian maps regularly show this area as within the borders of the Syrian state. At the same time, Kurdish restiveness in northern Iraq periodically troubled Ankara regimes that feared the spread of Kurdish separatism inside Turkey. Although Ataturk orchestrated a remarkable rapprochement with Greece, starting in the 1920s, efforts by Greeks and Greek Cypriots to join the island with the Hellenic motherland would set Athens and Ankara at odds after the mid-1950s. In that atmosphere, irreconcilable claims on the Aegean seabed between the two would even lead to occasional threats of armed clashes.

Accordingly, therefore, Turkey's leaders have consistently believed that they inhabit a hostile neighborhood and need to be prepared for the worst. As a result, the primary foreign-policy concern of the Turkish Republic has always been to protect and nurture its national existence. All governments have done so by building up their military establishment and by creating defensive alliances, occasionally with regional states when that was possible or, more significantly, with stronger powers outside the region. Detente in the Cold War or even its disappearance thus have not affected the basic perception that defense of the state is a continuing urgent requirement.

Turkish regimes have universally seen modernization and development at home as essential parts of their drive to undergird national independence. Eager to move faster than Turkey's limited natural resources would permit, its leaders have consistently believed that their country must enlist foreign assistance in this endeavor. Hence, political and defense ties were augmented with economic relations, first stressing aid but more recently broadening to an emphasis on trade. In sum, the perception of continuing threat has moved Turkey in the direction of increasing its links with the outside world and integrating itself into a more complex global order.

At the same time, Turkey's paramount concerns have profoundly influenced the underlying direction of the Turkish Republic. For over a century, leaders of both the Ottoman Empire and its successor republic had envied Western power, seeing it as a source of strength and something to be emulated. In line with this understanding, even though the main adversaries of the emergence of modern Turkey were European states, Ataturk set the new republic on the path of adopting European forms at home, and he prepared the way for alliance with the West as the primary foreign-policy goal. And this understanding is behind the strong desire among the elite and most of the populace to see Turkey become a fully-fledged member of the European Union.

A Western orientation has remained a constant in Turkey's approach, yet there has always been some ambivalence in the Turkish attitude. Ottoman experiences with the Europeans in the nineteenth and early twentieth centuries were mixed. Memories of financial control exercised by Europeans in bygone days have made governments since the Young Turks' days sensitive to infringements on their sovereignty as well as to foreign economic entanglements. The first consideration has meant that Ankara regimes are extremely wary of the activities of foreign forces on Turkish territory. And before the 1980s, skittishness about bending to economic influence from abroad inhibited Turkey governments from erecting sufficient incentives to attract foreign capital.

Since the Second World War, relations with the United States have lain at the base of the Turkish foreign-policy construct. The arrival in 1946 of the battleship *Missouri*, bringing back the body of a Turkish ambassador to Washington who had died in the United States, opened this key relationship for Turkey, and demonstrated the reach of American power. The extension of American aid under the Truman Doctrine in 1947, and the inclusion of Turkey in the scope of the Marshall Plan a few years later, suggested that the country enjoyed the protection of the U.S. defense umbrella as well as access to economic and military aid. With Turkey's eventual accession to NATO in 1952, major party leaders felt assured that their country had gained immeasurable security. And relations with the world's greatest superpower have been a part of Turkey's sense of security ever since, whether it be to neutralize Soviet threats or more recently to supply Patriot missiles to guard against Iraqi Scuds in Desert Storm and its aftermath.[3]

The long alliance in NATO and with the United States has in the main met the expectations invested in it by Turks of almost all persuasions. But the course of this relationship has often been troubled. To a considerable extent this reflects Turkey's domestic influences on its foreign policy, for Turkey is a country that has experienced a considerable degree of internal political disruption. That raises a number of questions: Under what circumstances does this impact become clear? And indeed, can Turkey have an independent, activist foreign policy when facing difficulties in domestic policy? Or does the domestic disorder predispose Turkey's foreign policy to be largely reactive and primarily derivative of its superpower relationships? Moreover, to the extent that Turkey can take independent initiatives, is that a function of the strength of individual leaders who may at a given times be directing Turkish affairs, or is there something of a geopolitical or an institutional nature that gives Turkey greater individual initiative and a more successful foreign policy at some times rather than at others? To try to answer these questions, it appears useful to look back on various periods of modern Turkish history to see how the nature of its domestic regime may have helped or hindered its foreign policy.

When the Turkish Republic was established, it became evident from the beginning that the new state had a sense of direction based on consistent leadership. It had a political system flexible enough to meet challenges but bold enough to initiate far-reaching social reforms, and a leadership that was dominant enough to speak for the population. Most scholars have attributed much of the initiative of the young Turkish Republic to the personality of its founder, Mustafa Kemal Ataturk. That included a nonideological, pragmatic, but activist approach that, combined with his charisma, gave him a position unrivaled in modern Turkey.

One way to disaggregate Ataturk's personality from the institutional strengths that Turkey enjoyed is to compare his policies with those of his successor, Ismet Inonu, in terms of boldness and activism. Even on cursory inspection, it is clear that Ataturk acted decisively and took risks, where Inonu was cautious and hesitant. Inonu always wanted to be sure how things would turn out before venturing along a new policy line. Thus at Nyon in 1937, when the question of hunting down unidentified submarines in the Mediterranean came up, Ataturk was determined to join Britain and France in agreeing that these submarines could be sunk if they refused to identify themselves, whereas Inonu believed Turkey should not join in such activities, at least until Ankara had concluded a alignment with Britain to protect it in case the submarine in question turned out to be Italian or Russian.[4]

Indeed, this difference in approach was the final issue over which Ataturk and Inonu broke in 1937. Inonu protested that his orders not to sign the agreement were ignored, whereas the Turkish negotiator in Nyon followed instructions given by Ataturk from the dinner table (where, by implication, alcohol was served). Once the dispute was framed in such a personal manner, Inonu had to resign as prime minister. But one can see a similar difference in boldness and activism in policy toward the *sanjaq* of Alexandretta, which under Ataturk's direction was acquired by Turkey from Syria through a policy that seemed at the time to carry a high risk of war.

Although the personality of the leader thus clearly had a bearing on the conduct and success of foreign policy, the domestic political structure erected by Ataturk favored an ability to act decisively and independently in foreign policy. Despite his innate caution, Inonu in his own way had full control of Turkish foreign policy when he became president. In fact, his independent foreign policy was highly successful during the Second World War in avoiding the fate of neighboring states of similar size, even when challenged by Nazi Germany or Stalin's Soviet Union. And under his direction, as well, Turkey laid the groundwork that would end in alliance with the West.

The structure responsible for this was based above all on the Ataturk constitution, which called for a one-house Assembly, which exercised all legislative and executive power and was not even subject to check by an independent judiciary. With an Assembly elected under a majority-vote system, the political scene tended toward a two-party rather than a multiparty competition. That meant that the majority party, under the firm control of its leader (and there were only two from the beginning of the republic until 1950), could act quickly and decisively in crisis or to take advantage of opportunities. It could even override the constitution, if that seemed necessary, with a simple majority vote, as Menderes's party did, for example, on May 20, 1959. At that time, it passed a law to give the government authority to conclude executive agreements that did not have to be brought to parliament for approval for six months, an arrangement that was contrary to the previous provisions of the Ataturk constitution.[5]

This structure also meant that the government of Adnan Menderes could peremptorily send troops to Korea in its bid to enter NATO, without having to risk a difficult debate to bring the opposition into agreement.[6] On its face, sending troops abroad seemed to violate Ataturk's hallowed formula of "Peace at Home and Peace Abroad." Indeed, the Republican People's Party caucus, meeting the day after the decision to send troops, advanced the claim that the process violated the constitution. But according to the prevailing constitutional interpretation of the day, the majority party could and did brush off this charge without a second thought.

Similarly, constitutional practice of the First Republic allowed Turkey to create the Baghdad Pact without having to go through a lengthy argument to justify a Middle East link to Kemalists who were used to focusing on Western Europe and were skeptical of Middle East connections. It even made it possible for the Menderes government to agree with the United States to station the nuclear-tipped Jupiter missiles in Izmir without informing the Republican People's Party leaders or taking their views into account.[7] These liquid-fueled, medium-range missiles were outmoded when the Turks agreed to receive them in 1959. Yet the Turkish military establishment viewed them as adding luster to their armaments and was reluctant to give them up when Polaris submarines in the Mediterranean were soon able to take on this role of striking at the heartland of the Soviet Union if necessary.[8]

For the most part, those policy decisions may have been reasonable exercises of power, but there are obvious dangers in having so powerful a centralized authority both for domestic politics and for foreign policy making. In the end, it was abuses of domestic power that did in the Menderes regime and led to a colonels' coup in 1960. Having settled in power, as their first act the new rulers junked the Ataturk constitution, to which they attributed the excesses of the Democrat Party regime.

With the replacement of the Ataturk constitution by the liberal 1961 constitution, the decisiveness of the past was seriously undermined. The principle of the unity of power was replaced by a system of checks and balances that relied on judicial controls and the dilution of legislative power. These constitutional changes, which were complemented by an electoral system based on proportional representation to assure a strong opposition presence in parliament, worked only too well. They encouraged political fragmentation that in turn often made coalition government the norm after the return to civilian rule in 1962. It was no accident that Makarios launched his bid to change the Cyprus constitution at the end of November 1963, just at a time when the New Turkey Party and Republican Peasants' Nation Party had withdrawn from their coalition with the Republican People's Party, leaving Turkey with only a caretaker regime. Even in the latter part of the 1960s, when the Justice Party was able for a time to command a majority in the lower house, the presence of a Senate diluted the ruling party's power. Additionally, the introduction of a Supreme Court gave Turks, with their legal bent, another avenue to challenge government decisions. But more important was the establishment of the National Security Council, where the top military brass could convey their views on matters of security, both internal and external, to the civilian leaders.

As a result of these changes that created new players in the foreign affairs arena, the foreign-policy process in Turkey after 1961 involved bargaining among the political parties and between the civilian and military wings of government. In particular, foreign policy became handled as a natural component of the security nexus that formed the central concern of the Turkish military establishment.

This bargaining was visible in the Cuban missile crisis of October 1962. At that time, the desire of the Turkish military leaders to keep the Jupiter medium-range missiles appears to have been behind Prime Minister Inonu's premature public rejection of a trade-off of missiles in Turkey for those in Cuba. Inonu seems also to have been distracted by the military plotting that surrounded Colonel Talat Aydemir's abortive military coup attempts at this period. These were serious challenges to the regime, and marked the only time in Republican history that segments of the military actually arrayed themselves against the chain of command. Thus domestic problems appear to have played a role in a puzzling foreign-policy mistake by Inonu in publicly ruling out a missile trade just at the time that the United States was making such a trade-off behind Turkey's back.[9]

The need to coordinate domestic forces to formulate foreign policy also played a major role in June 1964, when Inonu made sure the American embassy had advance warning of Turkey's intention to land troops on Cyprus.[10] He ordered his foreign minister to tell the Americans of Turkish intentions, it is reasonable to believe, because he wanted to head off domestic pressures for a landing on the island and he knew that the United States would not approve of a military operation against the Greek community on Cyprus. Given Inonu's well-known caution, he must have expected the Americans to provide him with ammunition to argue against those from the senior command of the armed forces who believed that they were ready to carry out this difficult operation. Inonu also wanted to be able to resist those civilian politicians who were pressing for Turkey to intervene militarily on the island. Inonu was clearly aware that the military had never made a sea landing, and if Turkish troops were thrown back it would bring numberless "catastrophes."[11] But Inonu certainly did not expect President Lyndon Johnson to respond as he did with a blunt letter calling into question NATO's defense obligations in the event of a Soviet reaction to a Turkish landing on Cyprus.

Another example of the problem in coordinating foreign policy under the Turkish system after 1961 was again related to Cyprus. This time it involved differences between the armed forces and the civilian command in the 1967 crisis, when the air force refused to carry out a bombing mission against the island that the cabinet had directed. There is evidence that the other services, as well, had reservations about the concomitant decision of the civilians to prepare to carry out a landing without clarifying the political goals.[12] Indeed, the military raised so many objections that the government eventually welcomed U.S. Special Envoy Cyrus Vance's help in defusing the crisis, even though originally Turkish Foreign Minister Ihsan Caglayangil had strongly urged that President Cevdet Sunay not receive Vance.[13] These examples show the extent to which bargaining between elements of government had become necessary under the 1961 constitutional structure even in those years when there was no coalition government.

What happened in 1974 to permit much more decisive action to be taken in respect to Cyprus, even though the Turkish leadership recognized that the United States was opposed? In 1974, the provocative and highly threatening nature of the Cyprus crisis united the civilian and military wings of the government. Athens had sponsored a coup against the president of Cyprus, Archbishop Makarios, which led to clashes all over the island between supporters of the archbishop and those of the puppet Nikos Sampson, who replaced him. The Cyprus constitution had clearly been violated by the ousting of Makarios, raising the possibility that Athens would run the island, effectively carrying out *enosis* (union with Greece) to the detriment of Turkish interests. Moreover, the horrors of past massacres of Turkish Cypriots raised great fears of a repetition. Prime Minister Bulent Ecevit was at the height of his personal popularity; his sympathy for and standing with the armed forces were also strong. By this time, the Turkish military leaders felt sufficiently prepared and equipped to be confident of victory, so whatever bargaining may have gone on was quick and simple. The military would obey the command to intervene this time.

The Turkish military performance would leave a legacy of foreign-policy problems that still beset Turkey. The Turkish forces used an intervention plan that called them to give first priority to protecting the Turkish enclaves rather than seeking to capture Nicosia International Airport in the first hours to allow immediate resupply. As a result of logistical problems in landing tanks that were to follow behind the troops, Turkish forces fell well short of their strategic objectives before a cease-fire was imposed under strong international pressure from all of Ankara's allies and the United Nations. Numerous concentrations of Turkish Cypriots were left outside the area under the control of Ankara's soldiers.[14]

The Turkish intervention had immediate political repercussions. On Cyprus, the puppet regime of Nikos Sampson melted away overnight, to be replaced by the respected Glafkos Clerides; in Athens, the poorly regarded junta also fell, giving way to the elder statesman Karamanlis. These new rulers sent representatives to Geneva to a peace conference with the Turks. But when negotiations rapidly stalemated, Ankara ordered a second wave of military action in August to extend the Turkish zone to include a majority of the Turkish population. Unfortunately for Turkey, whereas the first operation was accepted by the international community as necessary to deal with a junta in Athens generally regarded as odious, the second wave, after democratic forces were in place, has never been accepted by the outside world as legitimate. On the Cyprus issue, Turkey has been politically on the defensive ever since.

When we look at Turkey's foreign-policy performance from the viewpoint of its domestic political weakness, it is clear beyond dispute that Turkey was hurt by a lack of coherence in its political scene following the military stages of the confrontation. The Ecevit government resigned in early September 1974, just after the fighting ended; the fall ushered in a six-month interregnum under a caretaker cabinet that was refused a vote of confidence. It was during the tenure of this cabinet that the U.S. Congress debated and then voted to impose an embargo on military sales to Turkey.

The formation of the caretaker cabinet in Ankara led directly to disarray in the Turkish embassy in Washington. The Turkish ambassador to Washington, Melih Esenbel, had been recalled to Ankara in the fall of 1974 to serve as foreign minister in the new government, and had left the Turkish embassy in Washington under the care of a chargé d'affaires. When the new government failed to gain a vote of confidence and continued for a full six months in a caretaker capacity, Esenbel remained in Ankara as acting foreign minister and did not send a replacement ambassador, or even a mission headed by a senior ambassador, to argue the Turkish case in Washington during this critical period. Thus the Turkish embassy in Washington remained under-staffed and unable to speak with maximum authority for Turkey during debates when the U.S. Congress needed all the explanation it could get of the Turkish position and the rationale for Turkish policy. In that way, the political incoherence in Ankara directly weakened Turkish diplomacy with its major ally and hurt Turkey's ability to influence legislation that turned out to damage Turkish-American relations badly.

At this critical time, the Turkish authorities depended solely on the American diplomats to argue their case in Washington. Ankara had great confidence in Henry Kissinger, and the Turkish leaders clearly did not understand the intensity of congres-sional hostility toward the secretary of state in the aftermath of Nixon's resignation from the presidency. Ambassador William Macomber worked as hard as he could to explain the Turkish cause. He returned to Washington for brief periods several times during the months when the House and Senate were considering the embargo. But he lacked much help from the Turkish side. Many Turkish critics in Ankara complained that the U.S. Congress did not understand the justice of Turkey's position, yet the Turkish government still made no effective lobbying effort in Washington. More-over—perhaps not surprisingly, especially given its domestic weakness—the Turkish government did not see the need to go all out to move fast enough on the diplomatic track to offer a settlement that would appear reasonable to the international commu-nity, even though the outlines of such a deal, involving land for peace, were beginning to become visible when the American embargo was finally imposed in February 1975. The bargaining was over the percentage of the island that would be in the Turkish zone, with Ankara demanding some 32 percent and Washington considering that something around 25 percent could be sold to the Greek side. Once the embargo took effect, however, negotiations stopped in their tracks and no one has been able to make a deal since. In fact, Turkish diplomacy has not been able to achieve its aims of gaining political recognition for the Turkish community.[15]

By the mid-1970s, a new factor that reflected the domestic balance of forces was apparent in Turkey. The National Salvation Party became an indispensable partner in forming coalition governments. This party had an interest in supporting Arab causes and generally in strengthening ties with the Islamic world. And at least in part thanks to the pressure from Erbakan's National Salvation Party, Turkey even began to support anti-Israeli resolutions in the United Nations, and the Turkish government allowed the P.L.O. to open an office in Ankara. (Later Prime Minister Turgut Ozal would take pride in announcing that Turkey was the first NATO country to give offi-cial recognition to the Palestinian state.)[16] Also as a reflection of Erbakan's desires, Turkey increased its participation in the Organization of the Islamic Conference.

This emphasis on the Islamic world would eventually conflict with the interests of the secular forces in Turkey. It was not a coincidence that the disrespect of the

National Salvation Party for the Turkish national symbols and its slighting of the Turkish military command on August 30, coupled with its successful drive to remove the secularist foreign minister, Hayrettin Erkmen, for failing to support Islamist causes, were the final straws in triggering the military intervention in politics in 1980.[17] In the longer run, the effort to promote an Islamic orientation for Turkey's foreign policy would be scaled back while the relationship with Israel would be greatly strengthened under pressure from the Turkish military.

The Soviet invasion of Afghanistan in December 1979 pushed Turkey toward the United States. The Demirel minority government saw a threat to Turkish interests from the Soviets moving into Afghanistan, where Moscow's troops seemed a more immediate threat to Gulf oil. Previously, the Demirel government had been unwilling to allow the United States to use Incirlik airbase in connection with the Iranian hostage crisis because public opinion led by the Republican People's Party and the National Salvation Party warned against sacrificing friendly Iran for the sake of the West. Forti-fied by the signing of a new Defense and Economic Cooperation Agreement (D.E.C.A.) with the United States at the end of March 1980, the Turkish authorities became bolder in actions against Moscow at this time. But although Washington made clear its view that the D.E.C.A. should permit operations in areas outside of NATO, the most the Demirel minority government felt itself able to do was to avoid taking a public position on this matter. Indeed, Foreign Minister Erkmen, just before he was brought down in the no-confidence vote, said about possible American use of Incirlik in connection with Afghanistan, "We'll think about that when the time comes."[18]

The military intervention of September 12, 1980, ended the 1961 liberal constitu-tion period in which foreign-policy making had become a shared responsibility between civilians and military. With the abolition of parliament, and with General Kenan Evren in charge, unilateral foreign-policy decision making was the order of the day. As president, General Evren could speak for the armed forces, whereas other domestic political actors had no say. Thus when Rauf Denktash announced that the Turkish Federated State of Cyprus had become the Turkish Republic of Northern Cyprus in November 1983, the military regime in Ankara, in its last days before handing power over to the newly elected regime of Turgut Ozal, wasted no time in extending recognition to the self-proclaimed republic. It is still unclear how this announcement came about and what the role of Ankara was in the birth of this state. But, in any event, Turkey's overt actions themselves showed a decisiveness in Turkish foreign-policy making which arose because the military rulers were not beholden to other constituencies.

This activism, however, did not translate into a larger success. Turkey's recognition of the Turkish Republic of Northern Cyprus was not followed by other states. The way had not been prepared. So Turkish Cyprus would remain a responsibility of Turkey, while Cyprus would remain a weak point in Turkey's relations with all its NATO part-ners, including the United States.

The military intervention in 1980 formed an important turning point in Turkey's position in the world. It disrupted Turkey's relations with its European partners in lasting fashion. The interruption in democratic procedure, the arrest of Suleyman

Demirel and Bulent Ecevit, and the broad jailing of socialists and communists gave ammunition to enemies of Turkey in Europe. The view that the Turks did not meet European norms of behavior became influential in determining European relations with Ankara. And these negative judgments would only be strengthened by the rise of Islamic politics in Turkey. As a result, the European members of NATO began to move away from seeing Turkey as a candidate for political membership in the European Community. That meant that Turkey was thrown back to heavy dependence on the United States for political backing. The search for a multidimensional foreign policy, originally set off by the need to find allies in Cyprus diplomacy after the Johnson letter of 1964 called into question NATO's commitment, was dealt a severe blow by the growing hostility of Europe toward Turkey.

After the military rulers took over on September 12, 1980, Turkey moved closer to the United States in the military realm as well as the political, signing a memorandum for the joint use and modernization of some air bases and the construction of facilities at Mus and Erzurum. But it would be Turgut Ozal who would take a giant step toward creating a new post-Cold War basis on which the current closeness of relations with the United States would be built. Ozal's ability to dominate and direct Turkey's foreign policy masked to some degree its essential weakness in the 1980s. His policies of opening Turkey to the outside world laid the basis for deepening economic relations with Europe as well as with the United States.

Ozal's experience in the United States during his stint of several years at the World Bank had well prepared him for the role of integrating Turkey into the world economy. It disposed him to recognize that the aid mentality, which decades of reliance on the United States had made the measure of Turkish-American relations, was bad for both Turks and Americans. Thus his slogan of "Trade not Aid" suited the mood of America, where the Cold War was winding down. Yet, at least in part because the military had become a more powerful pressure group after 1980 than before, even an Ozal regime could not apply this new philosophy of independence from aid to Turkey's military relationship with the United States.

The Turkish constitution of 1982 moved part way back from the extreme liberalism of the 1961 constitution toward a less constricted executive. It abandoned the concept of a Senate and accorded the president some ill-defined power to assure the smooth running of the state. But it would be the personality of the president and his prime minister, rather than any clear constitutional prescription, that would determine who made policy in both domestic and foreign policy. In short, the new constitution did not represent a long-term fix for coherent foreign-policy making. And given the frequent requirement for coalition building that the continuing reliance on proportional representation mandated, it would be exceptional for Turkish foreign policy to be able to display the independence and initiative it had at some times in the past.

Ozal, however, was an exceptional figure. Like Ataturk and then Inonu, he was determined to control Turkey's foreign policy even after he became president of the Turkish Republic in 1989 and was no longer formally responsible for the operation of the government. To do so required that he not be challenged by the leader of the majority party, so Ozal arranged for a successor to be head of the Motherland Party, and hence at that time prime minister, one who would not challenge his decisions. That was key to Ozal having his way, and we have the testimony of the chief of the Turkish General Staff, General Necip Torumtay, to the effectiveness of this strategy during the Gulf War.[19]

Ozal was operating at that important time at the end of the Cold War, when there was unusual fluidity and uncertainty in foreign relationships. Without his firm sense of where Turkey should be, it is entirely possible that Ankara would have fallen sufficiently out of step with its allies to have been cast adrift from almost all its Western moorings. It might have been left with only its NATO partnership if it had not acted quickly to cut the Iraqi pipeline, and it could possibly have faced an Allied blockade of the Yumurtalik oil terminal on the Mediterranean. But Ozal immediately saw the need and opportunity to solidify Turkey's relations with the United States, and to make sure that Washington recognized Turkey's continuing strategic importance in a post-Cold-War world. Acting decisively in crisis times, Ozal overcame Turkey's parliamentary disarray to pursue a much stronger foreign policy than the fragmenting domestic scene would normally have allowed. In fact, operating from a post that was not responsible to parliament, he took advantage of parliamentary weakness to act on his own initiative. In large measure, Turkey can thank Ozal, and Ozal alone, for its current closeness with the United States. In contrast, other political leaders at the time expressed suspicion or even hostility toward the United States. Indeed, under this pressure, until the Gulf War opened new horizons, even Ozal had felt forced to cut back the scope of U.S. military action after Senator Robert Dole introduced a pro-Armenian resolution in 1987.

There were reasons why the Turks might not have been expected to cooperate closely with the United States during the Gulf War of 1990-1991. Domestic political coherence was beginning to weaken in Turkey, and the dominance of the Motherland Party was fast waning. Even American support for the Turkish military had been eroding. In 1990, the U.S. Air Force opposed upgrading F-16s for Turkey. Washington also had unilaterally withdrawn from Erhac and Eskisehir air bases. Negotiations to extend the Defense and Economic Cooperation Agreement, which was to expire at the end of 1990, were proving sticky, as the Turkish side was insisting on more assistance than the United States felt it could give. Finally, renewed political pressures in the U.S. Congress over Cyprus were disturbing the relationship between Turkey and the United States.

At the same time, Iraq had been Turkey's traditional good neighbor. Ankara and Baghdad had long shared common policies toward Kurdish dissidence. Turkey had come to terms with the loss of Mosul (though Ozal would later raise suspicions that he was considering reopening that issue after much of northern Iraq fell outside of Baghdad's authority). Moreover, American aims in the Gulf War did not include ousting Saddam Husayn, hence there was no assurance that Iraq would have new leadership at the end of this conflict. Thus Ozal had to confront substantial foreign-policy arguments suggesting that Turkey not actively side with the United States in allowing military action from its soil.

Yet, on the other hand, there were good reasons beyond merely currying favor with its superpower patron for why Turkey should collaborate closely with the United

States. Iraq had run roughshod over Turkish interests at times in the conflict with Iran, for example, opening fire on Turkish tankers during the Iran-Iraq war. Saddam's forces had continued to bomb Tehran during Ozal's trip there in 1988. Even more important, the Iraqis had not renewed the hot-pursuit agreement that expired in 1988, which allowed Turkish troops to conduct operations in northern Iraq near the Turkish border. And Iraq was constantly raising the Euphrates water problem, insisting that relations could not be correct as long as water issues were unresolved.

Although there were thus pros and cons about joining the United States against Iraq, Ozal saw the Kuwait problem as Turkey's opportunity to gain a new strategic position in the world. Indeed, the Gulf War would prove to be another turning point in Turkey's international position. And this time, developments would validate Ozal's vision of a new strategic importance for Turkey in the world, at least to its important American ally.

When the temper of the times is ripe and a personality comes along who can seize opportunities, it is possible to act decisively even when the basic structural underpinnings are weak. That is the lesson of the Ozal era. For Ozal did not ask for the recommendations of the Foreign Ministry. He did not keep the chief of the General Staff, General Necip Torumtay, informed as to his telephone diplomacy with President George Bush, although the Turkish armed forces needed to be prepared to cope with the effects of Turkish Gulf War policy. He acted as a one-man band, and General Torumtay says that Yildirim Akbulut, the prime minister, kept silent in Ozal's presence and went along with whatever the president decided.[20] That only enhanced Ozal's stature and made him seem strong and decisive in the eyes of his American interlocutors.

As a result, scholars who have inspected Turkey's Gulf War diplomacy generally have seen personal diplomacy by Ozal as dominating the course of foreign policy during that conflict.[21] But it is important to remember that, although in form Ozal conducted private, individual diplomacy without consulting the organs formally charged with the conduct of Turkey's foreign relations, his overall decisions lay within the established consensus on what Turkish foreign policy should be.[22] And this consistency with the general course and principles of what mainstream opinion held was in Turkey's interest meant that the stamp Ozal put on policy would outlast his life.

There was wide agreement in Turkey that Ankara should follow the United Nations decisions. Indeed, that is just what Turkey did. It took no part in the actual fighting, but in conformity with U.N. resolutions, it assisted those countries that were enforcing them.

Ozal kept Turkey's relations with the United States on track during a difficult and critical period. He did so through taking decisive decisions consistent with U.N. resolutions, such as shutting off the oil pipeline from Iraq, though he apparently told the United States he would do this even before the Security Council vote, and also by allowing U.S. planes to operate from Incirlik. Such permission was critical in earning Washington's goodwill and assistance in meeting some of the costs of compliance with U.N. directives. That decisive cooperation laid the groundwork for establishing the greater closeness with Washington that would become the hallmark of Turkish foreign policy in the final years of the twentieth century.

Ozal, however, did not in the final analysis take such extreme measures as sending troops to the Gulf, a course he clearly considered and probably would have liked to follow. In this, he apparently heeded the advice of the Turkish General Staff and the Foreign Ministry.[23] Ozal's approach was built on ostentatious posturing, but in fact ran only a limited risk. There was little danger that Iraq could attack Turkey while coping with U.S. troops in the south. The most Turkey risked, in fact, was a few missiles against Incirlik, with a low probability they would hit a significant target. And Washington rushed Patriots to Turkey to minimize even that possibility. On the other hand, in exchange for that limited risk, Turkey positioned itself to be able to demand compensation for its cooperation.

Indeed, Washington came through for Turkey. After the war, the F-16 joint production program was put into high gear. With the United States running interference, Turkey got $3 billion in aid from the Gulf states. Washington itself provided $3.5 billion in excess military equipment, and raised textile quotas at least 100 percent across the board. Even the European Union raised its textile quotas by a third.[24] Although Turkey has argued that this did not make up for the $30 billion loss of revenue from closing the oil pipeline, the cost to Turkey of not closing the pipeline would have been enormous politically, and the international community would have closed the line anyway, with no prospect of any compensation. So Turkey under Ozal made a virtue of necessity and emerged with some gain, or at least reduced loss.

The Gulf War raised the level of Turkey's Kurdish problem as both a domestic and a foreign policy issue. Although the P.K.K. (the Kurdish initials for the Kurdish Labor Party) had begun violence in eastern Turkey in 1984, by 1990 this insurrection was still only sputtering along. The Gulf War events provided a climate in which its intensity and scope increased to become a major war that cost Turkey billions of dollars for the military effort. Beyond its monetary cost, the struggle entailed a high cost with Europe in human rights, and much wear and tear on relations with the United States, despite Washington's constant willingness to recognize that Turkey faced a severe terrorist problem. This recognition set the United States apart from its European NATO allies. Yet there is no doubt that the P.K.K. issue undermined the effectiveness of Turkish diplomacy around the world.

The Gulf War did not solve the Iraqi problem. Saddam Husayn was left in power. The problem for the United States was to keep him under pressure. Turkey after Ozal's death in 1993 has thus found Iraqi policy a challenging problem. The United States created Operation Provide Comfort, at President Ozal's request, to stop the flow of Kurdish refugees into Turkey. But many Turkish leaders, from Bulent Ecevit to Necmettin Erbakan, were suspicious that this operation, whatever its original rationale, was serving to create an independent Kurdish state.[25] And in 1996, when the Islam-oriented Refah Party came to head the government coalition in Turkey, it had the scope of Provide Comfort reduced. The endeavor was renamed Northern Watch and continued basically as an air operation alone.

Turkey was not the only state to develop reservations about the embargo regime applied against Iraq. Moscow and Beijing also seemed interested in resuming economic relations with Baghdad. This obvious weakening of the international coalition encouraged Saddam Husayn to challenge the U.N. Special Commission. And inside Turkey, the suggestion of international sympathy for Saddam encouraged some civilian factions to question whether Ankara's cooperation with Washington toward northern Iraq was in Turkey's best interests.

On the other hand, by 1997 the Turkish military had become concerned about Iraqi missiles that could reach Konya, as well as Iraqi weapons of mass destruction.[26] The Turkish armed forces even appeared to be ready to support a U.S. military strike against Iraq to destroy weapons of mass destruction. This military concern was evidently stronger than fears that U.S. policy would lead to a Kurdish state. And in view of the role that the United States was credited with playing in helping Turkey capture P.K.K. leader Ocalan in 1999, even a previous skeptic like Prime Minister Bulent Ecevit began to recognize the benefits of cooperating closely with the United States. In this environment, particularly after Iraqi Deputy Premier Tarik Aziz overplayed his hand in demanding that Turkey break with the United States early in 1999, U.S. military action against military targets in the no-fly zone of northern Iraq experienced a high degree of acceptance by the Turkish government.

Prospects

Turkey's multidimensional foreign policy is today more heavily centered on relations with the United States than the architects of that policy probably ever intended. The bases of that relationship have changed, however, to reflect the realities of a post-Cold-War world. Ties with the United States are far less involved with an aid relationship which the U.S. Congress can routinely control or heavily influence; nor do they now consist heavily of military facilities directed at monitoring Soviet military developments, which would lead to an American military presence that would raise questions of extraterritoriality. Instead, Washington and Ankara have a mutuality of interest in combating terrorism, in securing energy routes through Turkey for Caspian Basin oil, in containing Saddam Huseyn's weapons of mass destruction, and in keeping the Turkish armed forces modernized at tolerable cost to Turkey. These common interests provide a healthier environment in which to cooperate than there was at many times in the past.

From the Turkish side, the need for support from a superpower in dealing with the E.U., or at least American neutrality in disputes with Greece, argues strongly for continuing an intimate relationship with Washington, even if at times its costs run high. And generally, the United States has proved a useful ally, especially since the Gulf War, showing itself much more understanding of the terrorism that lies behind the Kurdish problem in Turkey than have Turkey's European partners, who did not help Turkey during Ocalan's exodus to Europe in the months before his capture. In fact, Washington's recent willingness to deliver frigates and to proceed down the path of selling helicopters has also strengthened cooperation. Turkish/Israeli relations have had some positive impact on ties to the United States, as well.

Cyprus, of course, remains a locus of potential friction with the United States. Washington's interest in promoting a solution may at times cause irritation in Ankara. But both sides recognize the need to keep the corrosive effects within tolerable bounds.

Hence, flurries of discord do not last long and are not apt to cause the major problems they once did in Turkish-American relations.

Another area where relations could run into problems is in U.S. interest in using Turkish facilities for operations in northern Iraq. American policy toward containing and eventually bringing down Saddam Husayn has involved supporting an autonomous Kurdish area adjacent to Turkey's borders. In the past, that has been a subject of contention, and, if the Turkish leaders are disappointed in other matters, it could again be. Yet the important Turkish military command sees benefit in cooperating with the United States in regard to Iraq. And as long as American action seems plausibly covered by U.N. resolutions, there is a good chance that sporadic bombing of Iraqi military installations above the 36th parallel from the Turkish base at Incirlik by American and British warplanes will not disrupt present relations with Ankara.

Beyond this strong center of relations with the United States, Turkey's foreign-policy construct is in some disarray. Relations with Europe have been strained for most of the past two decades over questions about Turkey's democratic practices, Islamic politics, and human rights performance. Turkish foreign policy has been frustrated by the growing influence of Greece on common European foreign-policy positions, and European failure to act resolutely against ethnic terrorism. The willingness of Europe to discuss the entry of Cyprus into the European Union at a time when Turkey's eventual candidacy was in doubt appeared symptomatic of Europe's increasing unwillingness to take into consideration Turkey's point of view. European pressure not to execute Kurdish leader Ocalan only increases the already serious tensions within the present Turkish coalition. Although in December 1999 the Europeans reinstated Turkish candidacy for the European Union in the aftermath of earthquake diplomacy with Greece (each country having reacted supportively to the damaging earthquake in the other's country), this is far from enough to assure that the larger problems with Europe will be solved in the near future.

Turkey's policies with regard to the Middle East and its fellow Islamic states have also had mixed success. The end of the oil boom reduced the importance of these states to Turkey. The Middle East has proved less of a road to riches than Europe has been, for all the problems with European relations. Although Turkey still hopes to increase exports to the Middle East, especially of agricultural products from the fields irrigated by the Ataturk Dam complex, the money is in the developed world, not in the oil economies, for some time to come. The efforts of Necmettin Erbakan to foster the politics of D-8 (a grouping of eight Islamic developing countries), and his travels when the Refah Party was in power to Islamic states, especially those at odds with the United States, did not pay dividends for Turkey.[27] A new turn to the Islamic world is not likely to be tried again soon, whereas ties with Israel seem destined to grow as a result of their strong support by the Turkish military leadership and because they offer an additional lobbying arm in the United States.

The one success, after many years of failure, has been with Syria which, after Turkish troops mobilized on its border, abandoned the P.K.K. There are now even signs that water issues are less of a problem between the two states. Turkey seems willing to assure more water. A cynic might say that Syria may have extracted valuable concessions from Turkey in exchange for the P.K.K., which was a card that cost Syria nothing and was never part of its primary foreign-policy agenda.

Central Asia's Turkic states have not fully met the rosy expectations at the end of the Cold War, when Turkey hoped to be the bridge to the outside world for these landlocked states. Turkish governmental educational ventures and the efforts of Fetullah Gulen, leader of Turkey's Nurcular sect, who has led a movement to create high-standard schools in Russia and Central Asia, may yet pay off in the distant future in increasing Turkey's influence. But these states are so poor that relations with them can hardly play a major role in the life of a state with an economy the size of Turkey's. And politically, they offer little if anything as their regimes seem to have questionable long-term stability. What the second post-Cold-War generation of leaders in these states will be is, moreover, hard to divine. But there are no signs that they will give Turkey political support in the Cyprus question, which is the one area in which their help could be important for Turkey.

Russia is important to Turkey as a supplier of energy and a trading partner, but its fragile political and economic scene limits the relationship that Moscow can have with Ankara. Russia is more fragmented politically than Turkey and has far less democratic tradition on which to build, so Ankara cannot rely very heavily on Moscow. The Russians eventually did cooperate in denying Ocalan refuge, but what it could do as an encore is not readily apparent. And Moscow's opposition to the NATO military operation to defend the Kosovars raises another point of difference, as does Russian determination to bring the Chechens to heel through military operations.

So the picture for Turkey is not the balanced multidimensional foreign policy it has desired since 1964. Rather its foreign policy remains based on an alignment with the United States that basically meets Turkey's requirements, but still gives the U.S. Congress some hold over weapons sales—hence an ability to disturb ties from time to time for essentially domestic reasons. Otherwise, however, Turkey and the United States seem to have worked out the major problems to meet their mutual requirements tolerably for the moment. But Turkey is likely to have a reactive foreign policy largely set by these parameters, at least until its gets its domestic house in much better shape. That could be quite far off, as political fragmentation seems certain to be the bane of Turkey's existence for a long time to come. Turkey's politicians seem to lack the will and vision to reshape the rules of the political game in a way more suited to Turkey's national interests.

Moreover, the Kurdish problem may be further from solution than many Turkish leaders and the Turkish public seem to have expected in the flush of victory with the capture of Ocalan. Military operations continue, though at a much lower level than in the recent past. There seems little will among the senior politicians to take full advantage of the current lull in insurrection to fashion a more lasting solution. With the current coalition dependent on a strongly anti-Kurdish party, and with factions of the P.K.K. not certain to obey Ocalan's call to cease terrorist operations, human-rights issues may well continue to disturb Turkey's ties with its NATO allies.

In short, domestic political weakness will tend to be reflected in general weakness in Turkish foreign policy. Hence it is far from certain that Turkey will be able to take advantage of its recent acceptance as a full candidate for the E.U. Turkey is likely to be largely reactive in its foreign policy and closely bound to the positions of the United States, whose general diplomatic support lies at the base of Turkey's approach to foreign problems.

One can see the impact of political incoherence, especially at times of crisis and when unusually strong leaders are not on the scene. It is always difficult to pursue an independent, activist foreign policy in a world filled with larger, more powerful states. But when foreign policy is run by fragile coalitions, let alone minority governments, the problem of decisive action becomes greater. Mobilizing on the Syrian border to press for the extradition of P.K.K. leader Abdullah Ocalan was clearly the product of military initiative, as the Turkish generals insisted that cutting off support from outside Turkey for the Kurdish insurgency was necessary to complement the gains they were scoring on the ground at home. The civilians, who had for some time recognized military primacy in security issues, gave the military its head in this activist step. That worked. But in general it is far easier to orchestrate a small-force action, such as capturing Ocalan with the help of a major superpower ally, than it is to deal with a neighboring state like Iraq in an imaginative way to obviate the need for continuing military action in the region by the United States. And bold moves to take advantage of the easing of hostility in the relationship with Greece in the wake of the good feeling engendered by mutual earthquake aid at the end of 1999 are highly unlikely. To devise solutions that could cut through the Cyprus stalemate is likely to defy even the more solidly based coalition that took power in Turkey after the April 18, 1999, elections. Already demands to carry out the death penalty on Ocalan threaten to fracture the coalition and disrupt Ankara's chances of gaining European Union membership expeditiously, as many in Turkey desire.

Turkey frequently seems to be awaiting another Ataturk to escape the coils of a political system that encourages stalemate. But institutional changes to strengthen government would have a greater chance of allowing Turkey a more satisfying and successful foreign policy than does hoping for a personality, which at best may appear only rarely. Yet, at present, there seems little chance of Turkey's reforming its political system to assure majority rule, and hence to achieve the structure for a less reactive and more satisfactory foreign policy.

Notes

1   Mahmut Bali Aykan, *Türkiye'nin Kuveyt Krisi (1990–1991) Politikasi: 1998 Yılından Geriye Yönelik Bir Yeniden Değerlendirme*, p. 52.

2   Ibid., p. 30.

3   After U.S. and British planes from Incirlik airbase struck Iraqi radar and other targets in northern Iraq in January 1999, the Pentagon rushed Patriots to Turkey to deal with possible retaliation by Iraqi Scuds against Turkish territory. See "Patriot Fuzeleri Geliyor" (Patriot Missiles Are Coming), *Cumhuriyet*, January 15, 1999, p. 1.

4   Interview with Sukru Kaya, October 15, 1954. See also Feridun Kandemir, *Siyasi Dargınlıklar: Atatük-İnönü, İnönü-Mareşal Dargınlığı*, pp. 17–26.

5   Mümtaz Soysal, *Dis Politika ve Parlamento*, pp. 205–7.

6   Ibid., pp. 196–97; Fahri Belen, *Demokrasinden Diktatörluge: On Senelik Siyasi Hayatımıza Dair Tenkit ve Tahliller*, p. 24.

7   Nur Bilge Criss, "Strategic Nuclear Missiles in Turkey: The Jupiter Affair, 1959–1963," p. 99.

8   George S. Harris, *Troubled Alliance: Turkish-American Problems in Historical Perspective, 1945–1971*, pp. 92–93.

9   Ibid., p. 117.

10 Metin Toker, *Demokrasimizin Ismet Pasa'li Yillari 1944–1973*, p. 206.

11 Cüneyt Arcayürek, *Cüneyt Arcayürek Açıklıyor—4: Yeni Demokrasi Yeni Arayışlar: 1960–1965*, p. 282.

12 Cüneyt Arcayürek, *Cüneyt Arcayürek Açıklıyor—5: Demirel Dönemi: 12 Mart Darbesi: 1965–1971*, pp. 120–21.

13 Interview with former Cyprus desk officer Ilter Turkmen, April 8, 1980; Parker T. Hart, *Two NATO Allies at the Threshold of War: Cyprus, a Firsthand Account of Crisis Management, 1965–1968*, pp. 69–70.

14 Mehmet Ali Birand, *30 Sicak Gun*, pp. 235–37, 259.

15 The author was acting political counselor in the American embassy during January and February 1975, when these negotiations were taking place.

16 "Filistin'i Taniyan Ilk NATO Ülkesiyiz," *Hurriyet*, November 16, 1988, p. 10.

17 Cüneyt Arcayürek, *Cüneyt Arcayürek Açıklıyor—10: Demokrasi Dur. 12 Eylül 1980*, p. 398.

18 *Cumhuriyet*, September 4, 1980; Mehmet Ali Birand, *The Generals' Coup in Turkey: An Inside Story of 12 September 1980*, p. 162.

19 Necip Torumtay, *Orgeneral Torumtay'in Anilari*, p. 109.

20 Ibid.

21 For example, Sabri Sayari, "Turkey: The Changing European Security Environment and the Gulf Crisis"; Strobe Talbott, "Status Quo Ante: The US and Its Allies."

22 This point is cogently argued in Aykan, *Türkiye'nin Kuveyt Krisi*.

23 Ibid., pp. 50–51.

24 Ibid., pp. 60–61.

25 Ibid., p. 72; "Dogu Meselesi Inanc Beraberligi ile Cozulur," *Tercuman*, September 28, 1992, report of an interview with Erbakan.

26 Aykan, *Türkiye'nin Kuveyt Krisi*, pp. 73–74.

27 Erol Mütercimler, *21. Yüzyil ve Türkiye "Yüksek Strategi,"* pp. 462–63, and "Erbakan'dan Gizli Diplomasiye Devam."

PART V

Rounding Out the Area

14

The Other Middle Eastern States

L. Carl Brown

Summary statements about the foreign policy of each regional state not covered separately are presented in this chapter, starting with Lebanon and proceeding clockwise to Mauritania.

Lebanon

The image of the Middle East as a mosaic of many distinctive religious, ethnic, or linguistic groups belies the reality that most states of the area have populations with clear majorities. The mosaic trope does, however, fit only the Fertile Crescent, and within that region (which includes Iraq, Israel, Jordan, Lebanon, Syria, and a prospective Palestinian state) Lebanon stands out as the extreme example of religious diversity. No religious community in Lebanon accounts for a majority of the population. The Shi`i Muslims are the largest single group, followed by Sunni Muslims and Maronite Christians, rounded out by many other Christian denominations and the Druze.[1] Lebanon's religious diversity lies at the heart not just of domestic politics but of its foreign policy, too.

Lebanon's answer to this plethora of religions has been a highly institutionalized form of communal politics. The president of the republic must be a Maronite, the prime minister a Sunni Muslim, and the speaker of the National Assembly a Shi`i Muslim. Earlier, seats in the National Assembly were allocated in multiples of eleven (six Christian, five Muslim), with roughly equivalent quotas governing positions in other governmental institutions. Later, in 1989, as the devastating civil war that began in 1975 was finally winding down, an agreement was reached that divided governmental positions on a fifty-fifty Muslim-Christian basis. The three top offices remain as before, but the powers of the two posts earmarked for Muslims, prime minister and speaker of the National Assembly, are expanded.

The diplomatic impact of these religious differences has been that the Muslims identified with neighboring Muslim Arabs whereas Christians, especially the Maronites, have sought a Lebanon more attached to France and the West. This meant that the Christians, fearing that they would become an insignificant minority in any larger Arab polity, sought an independent Lebanon controlled by Christians, whereas the Muslims favored absorption into a greater Syria or any other form that pan-Arabism might take. Ironically, the best chance the Maronites would have had for a Lebanon securely dominated by Christian forces and capable of resisting Arabist pressures was jeopardized in 1920. In that year Maronite leaders convinced French officials, just as the French mandate over Lebanon and Syria was being organized, to create a "Greater Lebanon" by adding territories that did not contain nearly as high a proportion of Christians as were to be found in historic Mount Lebanon. This also produced a continuing Syrian irredentist claim against Lebanon. Any possibility that Lebanon as expanded would have a Christian majority (Maronites plus other Christians) was soon lost—differential birth and emigration rates between Christians and Muslims ensured as much.

Destined thus to be a country of multiple minorities, Lebanon during the years of the Second World War was the scene of an inspired political arrangement. This was the so-called National Pact of 1943. In brief, the Christian leadership agreed that Lebanon would be part of the Arab world and would cut its leading strings to France and the West. The Muslims, in turn, would respect the independence and territorial integrity of Lebanon in its existing borders. This paved the way for Lebanese independence.

The history of Lebanon since the mid-1940s can be told in terms of three interacting developments that have buffeted this national pact idea: the Arab-Israeli conflict, the Cold War in the Middle East, and the evolving demographic and relative power situation within Lebanon.

The creation of Israel and the first Arab-Israeli war in 1948 brought thousands of Palestinian refugees to Lebanon, most of them destined to live in refugee camps. Being overwhelmingly Muslim, these Palestinians, if given Lebanese citizenship, would have upset the existing balance of religious communities. Instead, with few exceptions who were granted citizenship (usually Christians), Palestinians remained a politically alien and alienated population in Lebanon.

At the same time, although Lebanon has dutifully joined the other Arab states in the war against Israel, Lebanese attitudes toward Israel were ambivalent and skewed along religious lines. Some asked why Lebanon could not be a state serving as a haven for Christian Arabs, just as Israel was put forward as a haven for Jews. In any case, a neighboring non-Muslim state could perhaps serve as a counterweight to possible pressures from the Arab states with their decisive Muslim majorities.

In the resulting diplomacy over the years, Lebanon's official stance was consistently within the Arab political consensus, but secret discussions with Israel (even well before 1948) reflected the underlying temptation to challenge if not replace the National Pact emphasis on Lebanon's Arabness. Such a diplomatic revolution appeared possible with the 1982 Israeli invasion of Lebanon to oust the P.L.O. forces, and the American-brokered Israeli-Lebanese agreement the following year. Resistance from Syria and from within Lebanon soon brought on the abrogation of this agreement.

The peak of pan-Arabism came in the 1950s when Egypt's Nasir seemed likely to become the Arab world's Bismarck. This fervor for Arab unity was also tied into the Cold War struggle. Ever since the 1955 Czech-Egyptian arms deal, Washington had feared that Nasirism would facilitate Soviet penetration of the Arab world. The 1957 Eisenhower Doctrine (coming after the Suez War, which discredited in Arab eyes the

British and the French, who had colluded with Israel to attack Egypt) was viewed in the region, and with good reason, as an American attempt to woo the Arabs away from Nasir. Most Arab leaders, whatever reservations some of them had about Nasir, steered clear of such an unpopular public position. The Lebanese government, led by President Camille Chamoun, was more inclined to go along with U.S. policy. A battle for control of Lebanon ensued, with claims (only spottily verified) of infiltration of Nasirist partisans from neighboring Syria (which in February 1958 had merged with Egypt to form the United Arab Republic). When July 1958 brought the violent overthrow of the pro-Western Hashimite regime in Iraq, the Lebanese government appealed for help, and President Eisenhower sent troops to Lebanon. The negotiations that followed quickly got U.S. troops out of Lebanon, and a new Lebanese administration replaced Chamoun. In substance this amounted to restoration of the National Pact—a Lebanon assured of its independence but definitely part of the Arab world, not a Western beachhead.

The June 1967 war brought Israeli occupation of the West Bank and Gaza (essentially the area that the United Nations in its 1947 partition plan had earmarked for a Palestinian state) and produced yet another exodus of Palestinians fated to become refugees. The June war also stimulated the transformation of the P.L.O. into a more independent and militant nationalist movement.

The P.L.O., needing an Arab territory from which to launch raids into Israel, was attracted to Lebanon. Egypt and Syria, whatever their pro-Palestinian rhetoric, would permit no independent P.L.O. activities from across their borders with Israel. Jordan tried with some success to police its extensive border with Israel. Only Lebanon lacked a strong enough central government and army to do the job along its border. Moreover, in a series of clumsy and even cynical moves the Arab states imposed a settlement in Lebanon that provided the P.L.O. a status in that country that made them virtually a state within the state of Lebanon. The main symbol of this settlement was the so-called Cairo Agreement brokered by Nasir in 1969.

A year later, in 1970, in a fratricidal war the P.L.O. challenged King Husayn in truncated Jordan (the West Bank that was lost to Israel in 1967 had been absorbed into the Jordanian state following the 1948 Arab-Israeli war). King Husayn prevailed, and the defeated P.L.O., ousted from Jordan, made their way to Lebanon to join fellow P.L.O. forces already there.

Added to the mounting problems throughout these years was the growing numbers of Lebanese Shi`ites (with a markedly higher birthrate than the Christians). By this time clearly the largest single religious community in Lebanon, the Shi`ites were also developing organizational muscle and a populist program. These Shi`ites could, as underdogs, identify with the Palestinians in Lebanon, but did not always do so. It was the Shi`ites in South Lebanon who bore the brunt of Israeli reprisal actions against P.L.O. incursions. The Shi`ite image of the situation was of a larger Arab world passionately supporting the P.L.O. in speech but content to let the Lebanese areas of great Shi`ite concentration pay the price in this grotesque proxy war. They saw a Lebanese government unable to protect them, and P.L.O. cadres often less than politic in dealing with those who happened to live in the lands they had chosen as their last available bases for guerilla war against Israel.

Thus, by the 1970s a weak and divided government presided over a weak and divided population. Both were harassed by outside neighbors, especially Israel and Syria. A changing demographic balance led the have-nots to believe that they had little to lose by taking on the status quo, while the haves sensed that they must act lest things get worse. A banal incident sufficed to set in motion a terrible civil war destined to last for roughly fifteen years, with casualties estimated in the tens of thousands.

The years 1975–1990 brought the ill-fated Israeli effort to bring about a decisive diplomatic realignment by, first, evicting the P.L.O. from Lebanon, the last territory bordering Israel from which Palestinians were able to operate militarily, however weak and totally indecisive such P.L.O. military probes were in fact; and, second, creating a Christian-dominated client state in Lebanon.

The Israelis achieved only the first goal, and even that to no avail. Soon the Lebanese Shi`ites, especially the political and military party, Hizbullah, more than matched the military nuisance posed earlier by the P.L.O. Moreover, the result of events since 1982 has been a Lebanon with a southern strip of its land occupied by Israeli troops (until May 2000, when Israeli Prime Minister Barak ordered their withdrawal), and with Syrian troops dominant in the rest of the country.

Little Lebanon can only employ the diplomacy of the weak. It can only regain some margin of maneuver by making pluralist domestic politics sufficiently attractive to all Lebanese that they can in united fashion balance off the outside powers. Lebanese once did that, in 1943. It did not manage, after 1989–1990, to achieve an updated national pact that just might have moved toward getting both Israeli and Syrian armies out of Lebanon. The immediate prospect is that Lebanon will remain virtually a client state of Syria. Still, if, after Israeli withdrawal from Lebanon, Hizbullah is integrated into a revivified domestic political system, and the other religio-political forces can conceptualize the idea of a truly independent Lebanon as a better deal than any available alternative (and a strong case can be made for this), then Lebanon may be granted a second chance to pursue a foreign policy based on pluralistic politics at home.

Kuwait and the Gulf States

Like Lebanon, Kuwait is a small state surrounded by powerful neighbors. The equivalent of Lebanon's immediate neighbors—Israel, Jordan, and Syria—are the imposing triad of Iran, Iraq, and Saudi Arabia. The parallel to Syria's irredentist claims to parts of Lebanon, moreover, is the Iraqi claim to all of Kuwait. Both states, too weak to confront or opt out of the Arab state system, rely on diplomatic balancing and accommodation.

Kuwait is also to be classified with its fellow Gulf states (Bahrain, Qatar, United Arab Emirates, and Oman) along the Arabian littoral of the Arab/Persian Gulf.[2] They all have scanty populations. Only Mauritania needs to be added to provide a list of the six least populous countries in the Arab world. The combined population of all five Gulf states (somewhat more than eight million) is just slightly more than one-third that of Iraq and about one-seventh that of Iran. Even this modest population looms large when contrasted with that of just a few decades ago, before the age of oil wealth.

With such a thin population base and, until the modern discovery and exploitation of oil, an equally thin resource base, these states have played subordinate roles in regional and international politics. This is not to say that the Gulf inhabitants have been an archaic, unenterprising lot. Graceful dhows whose design represented a masterful adaptation to prevailing monsoon winds engaged in trade from the Gulf to East Africa, India, and the Indies. Indeed, the commercial enterprise of Oman achieved imperial proportions, beginning in the last years of the seventeenth century, with the occupation of coastal areas in the Indian subcontinent as well as the island of Zanzibar, controling from there much of the East African coastal regions with lucrative trade in ivory and slaves. A later sultan actually moved his capital from Muscat (Oman) to Zanzibar in 1841, and it was only upon his death in 1856 that Muscat and Zanzibar were divided into two sultanates. Thus, for a time Oman was an Arab equivalent of Portugal in early modern times. Both expanded from quite meager populations and resource bases to engage in extensive maritime exploits.

By later in the nineteenth century, however, Oman and the other Gulf states were becoming a backwater, having lost out to steamships, redirected trade routes (such as the 1869 opening of the Suez Canal), the abolition of the slave trade, and the overwhelming economic and political power of Europe.

Modern European penetration into the Gulf came from the principal naval power of the day, Great Britain.[3] Operating from India, the British brought imperial order to the region in a series of bilateral treaties with the several small states plus truces imposed among them all. Thus, for example, the area of what is now the United Arab Emirates, which had earlier been dubbed the "Pirate Coast," came to be known as the Trucial Coast. It became the U.A.E. only in 1971.[4] This pattern of informal imperial control remained in place, not seriously challenged by regional or outside powers, until roughly after the Second World War when the worldwide movement toward decolonization and the equally worldwide thirst for oil restored the Gulf states to regional and international attention.

The transition to new power balances can be sketched in the following broad brush strokes: Britain, in its post-World War II scaling down of imperial commitments, maintained a strong presence in the Gulf until the end of the 1960s, having resisted in the previous two decades efforts to challenge the status quo in the Gulf by such diverse regional actors as Saudi Arabia, Iraq, and the Dhofar rebels in the hinterland of Oman.[5] By the 1970s, all states of the Gulf had achieved independence, but they lacked the military might to defend themselves. They even lacked adequate military prowess to hold out against an aggressive neighbor for a few days before help could come from farther away. This was harshly demonstrated by the one-day Iraqi conquest of Kuwait in August 1990.

Yet these oil-rich states offered attractive prizes. A massive oil field was discovered in Kuwait as long ago as 1938, and oil was found even earlier in Bahrain (1932) but in limited amounts. Qatar began its oil exports in the late 1940s. As for the U.A.E., oil was discovered in Abu Dhabi in 1958, and eight years later (1966) in Dubai. In Oman, oil exports became economically significant only in the 1970s. All together, the Gulf states (including Saudi Arabia) account for just slightly less than one-half of world proven oil reserves and roughly one-quarter of world gas reserves. If these reserves were controlled by any one power the changes in power balances would be dramatic, and even more so if a single power also controlled Iran or Iraq, both major oil and gas producers.

The existing arrangement of states and wealth in the Gulf is maintained, it can be suggested, by classic multipolar balance-of-power procedures. Any state attempting a quick coup against one or more of the Gulf states can expect a reaction from the other states involved, which will counter the gain sought. This, too, is the lesson of the August 1990 Iraqi invasion of Kuwait.[6] This was seen in less dramatic fashion in the British support to Oman and what became the U.A.E. against Saudi efforts to claim the Buraimi oasis as part of its territory. Similar balance-of-power realities kept in check the earlier Iranian claim to Bahrain, and have thus far kept Iran from grabbing more than minor offshore islands (Abu Musa and the Tunbs) claimed by the U.A.E.

That, in general, is the situation as viewed from outside. What, then, of the view from within? What are the foreign policies of the Gulf states themselves? The creation of the U.A.E. in 1971 (with Ra's al-Khaymah joining the following year) can be seen as a modest effort toward creating some strength through union, but the extent to which Britain played a role in making this union possible can hardly be exaggerated. The original idea was to include Bahrain and Qatar, but both chose to remain independent.

In response to the threats provoked by the Iran-Iraq war (1980–1988), all the Gulf states plus Saudi Arabia (the clear leader in this venture) joined together in 1981 to create the Gulf Cooperation Council (G.C.C.). This brought together all the Arab states bordering the Gulf (except Iraq) and all the littoral states of the Gulf (except Iraq and Iran), but now almost a generation later its achievements appear modest—especially in matters of defense. Still, it seems only fair to note that even a G.C.C. with a seriously planned and implemented military doctrine might not be secure without support from one or more outside powers, either with bases in the Gulf or forces solidly available "over the horizon." Moreover, the other states have reservations about being in a Saudi-dominated alliance.

In any case, the actual foreign policies of the several Gulf states remain strikingly independent when measured by their strategic vulnerability. Sometimes they balance off outsiders brilliantly, as Kuwait did in the latter years of the Iran-Iraq war by playing off the Soviet Union and the United States in the tanker-flagging issue. But it was the same Kuwait that relied too much on balances in confronting Iraq in 1990. Nor does their collective vulnerability to outside forces restrain them from disputes among themselves, such as the one that pitted Qatar against Bahrain over ownership of offshore islands. At times they even dare to challenge the overall Arab consensus—witness Qatar's tentative moves toward commercial relations with Israel.

Oil wealth has also been a mixed blessing. The skylines of Abu Dhabi, Dubai, Doha, and Kuwait City present impressive modern El Dorados, but this striking infrastructure of economic modernity was built and is largely maintained by foreign workers ineligible for citizenship. Nor is there always the cohesion needed among the native population to produce the kind of loyalty that a nation-state generally inspires. Bahrain, for example, has a Shi`ite majority governed (not very benignly) by a Sunni dynasty. And the seven different "states" making up the U.A.E., in their differing levels of wealth and tribal disputes, often call into question whether these amirates are, in fact, united.

A cynical interpretation might be to recall the label "tribes with flags" given such states by an Egyptian observer, and see them as engaged in carpe diem diplomacy. It is as if to say, "We will take our chances on the checks and balances characteristic of international politics in this region, since we can't change that system or build up enough strength from within to provide adequate insurance." A more charitable interpretation would see these states as wrestling with a unique set of advantages and liabilities for which no master plan for state building offers attractive answers. What then remains is for these states to live with their contradictions—some more effectively than others—like so many Arab Candides cultivating their desert gardens.

Yemen

What is now the sizeable state of Yemen (the fourth largest Arab state in area, the sixth largest in population) has existed in its present political form only since 1990, when the merger of North and South Yemen was achieved.[7] It is a natural union, perhaps, in terms of language, religion, and culture, but a united Yemen also presents many contrasts. When civil war broke out in Yemen in 1962, Western journalists covering the events could not resist repeating the saying that Yemen was rushing headlong into the fourteenth century. Imams Yahya (r. 1904–1948) and Ahmad (r. 1948–1962), ruling from their mountain fastness (the capital San'a', a veritable Shangri-la of high-rise adobe buildings, is 7,250 feet above sea level), willfully kept Yemen frozen in time.

During these same years, the thriving port of Aden was the very model of economic modernity, and those South Yemenis destined to achieve independence from Britain in 1967 lived in a world of trade unionism and Marxist ideology. The name of this new state, People's Democratic Republic of Yemen, accurately reflected their aspirations. Even South Yemen, however, offered radically different life styles that could not easily fit into a single polity. The vast hinterland beyond Aden and the coast was given over to tribes and nomadism.

Occupying the southwestern corner of the Arabian peninsula, Yemen, the Arabia Felix of the ancients, has been only partially integrated into larger Middle Eastern empires throughout the centuries. The Ottomans are considered to have ruled the area from 1517 to 1636 and then from about 1870 to 1918, but even in these two periods Ottoman control usually extended only slightly inland from the coastal regions. In the interior, throughout the entire period, rule by the different dynasties of Zaydi Shi'i imams prevailed. Yemen never experienced Western colonial control— sharing this distinction with only one other Arab land, that which is now Saudi Arabia.

South Yemen, by contrast, was absorbed into the British Empire. Aden was captured as early as 1839 and became a major fueling port along the maritime route to India. As there was, however, no strong strategic or economic need to control the interior, that vast, thinly populated area was essentially left to its traditional tribal patterns of politics with an indirect, even leisurely, British oversight.

The great changes that moved the two Yemens toward their present political structure and foreign-policy orientation took place in the decade of the sixties. The 1962 civil war in Yemen began as a coup against the new imam, Badr, by Nasirist army officers. Badr escaped to the mountainous north and began a struggle to recover power. He found support from Saudi Arabia, which was not eager to see antimonarchical revolutions in the Arabian peninsula. Egypt then backed the Republicans by sending troops to Yemen. This intervention proved sufficient to buttress the Republic but not enough to defeat the imam's forces. The United States, fearing Soviet penetration of Arabia, sought to mediate between Egypt and Saudi Arabia.

On and off, Egyptian-Saudi negotiations periodically resumed and then failed throughout the sixties, and the evacuation of Egyptian troops came only after Egypt's disastrous defeat in the June 1967 war against Israel. Thereafter, surprisingly, instead of a royalist victory a stalemate ensued. Then, with a changed leadership in republican ranks (more acceptable to Saudi Arabia) and divisions within the dynasty, the way was paved for the end of the imamate and for a republican regime that coopted some of the royalist forces.

In the same decade, the British, in the last years of imperial downsizing, were working toward leaving in place a pro-British Federation of South Arabia in which radical Aden would be adequately checked by being mixed in with the several different traditional sultanates. The nationalists in Aden successfully resisted this plan, and even forced a speeded British evacuation by November 1967. As an added complexity, the winning party, the National Liberation Front, had won out over the Egyptian-supported nationalists, the Front for the Liberation of Occupied South Yemen (F.L.O.S.Y.).

Thus, by the end of the sixties, the imamate had become a secular republic, and its southern neighbor was a Marxist People's Republic. These developments, moreover, had taken place with the active intervention of Egypt, Saudi Arabia, the United States, Britain, and the Soviet Union. Somewhat later, China, and even Cuba (with small numbers of Soviet-sponsored troops and military advisors), became involved. Indeed, Yemen's triangular road system built in these years revealed a country able to reap some profit from Cold War rivalries. The road from Ta'izz to San`a' was begun by the United States, and after relations were broken it was completed by West Germany. The road from San`a' to Hodeida was built by China, and from Hodeida to Ta'izz by the Soviet Union.

Neither of the Yemens thereafter was able to settle down to statehood. Both confronted a several economic blow with the closing of the Suez Canal in June 1967, and South Yemen's bold domestic programs (including strikingly advanced women's liberation projects) were not matched by political stabilization. The first president was ousted within two years, the second executed in 1978, the third resigned two years later and went into exile in the Soviet Union, and the fourth was overthrown in 1986.

In Yemen, one president was deposed in 1974 by an army officer who was himself assassinated in 1977. His successor was killed one year later by a bomb believed sent from South Yemen. There was even a brief war between the two Yemens in 1979.

Thereafter somewhat more stability at the top was realized. `Ali `Abdallah Salih, president of Yemen since 1978, continued in that capacity after union in 1990, and the

South Yemeni president since 1986, Haidar Abu Bakr `Atas, became prime minister of the united Yemen.

The very year of Yemeni unity brought the Iraqi invasion of Kuwait and a Yemeni decision that cost the country dearly. Refusing to go along with the American-led coalition assembled to drive Iraq out of Kuwait, Yemen felt the wrath of Saudi Arabia and the United States. Perhaps a million Yemenis working in Saudi Arabia were expelled, and U.S. aid was reduced to a pittance. The following years have brought violence, assassinations, and the taking of foreign hostages (all subsequently released unharmed until 1999, when hostages were killed). Tension between north and south has also been present, but not strong enough to produce a breakdown. On the positive side of the ledger, the 1990s brought border agreements with Oman and Eritrea, and some progress with the Saudis. Modest amounts of oil have been discovered and are now being exported. In 1999, `Ali `Abdallah Salih was reelected overwhelmingly in Yemen's first direct presidential election.

A united Yemen, with reasonably good relations with its neighbors, and neither so strong nor so rich as to attract the fears or cupidity of others, seems capable of holding its own—if it can stay united and work toward a better domestic stability.

Sudan

The largest country in the entire continent of Africa, Sudan edges out Algeria and Saudi Arabia as the largest country in the Arab world. With almost one million square miles, it is one-third the size of the continental United States. Sudan is also the second most populous Arab state, with somewhat more than 50 percent of the population of first-ranked Egypt.

Sudan, however, does not cut a figure in international politics commensurate with its size and population. This can be explained by a combination of two factors—its poverty (only Yemen and Mauritania among the Arab states rank lower in per capita G.N.P.) and its diversity.[8] Sudan has been too much caught up in state building to be tempted to an assertive foreign policy. Moreover, it is not lacking in resources, but the existing level of its economic (and political) infrastructure has limited the country's attractiveness to outside interests, benign or otherwise.

The great divide in Sudan is that between north and south, the former largely Arabic-speaking and Muslim and the latter peopled with a crazy quilt of tribes, languages, and religions. Almost all of the estimated 17 percent of the total population listed as following diverse "traditional beliefs" and the 11 percent who are Christian are located in the south, or are southerners who have migrated northward seeking refuge from the civil war that has for years ravaged the southern half of Sudan. In addition, there are the many non-Arabic-speaking Muslims in the south.

The short answer as to why Sudan has been torn by a seemingly endless civil war is that north and south represent two different cultures, the one essentially Arabo-Islamic and the other not. With the wisdom of hindsight, several observers have suggested that Sudan's borders should have been drawn differently, placing most of the south in other East African states such as Kenya and Uganda. Indeed, following the establishment of the Anglo-Egyptian Condominium soon after the reconquest of the Sudan

(1896–1898), different boundaries were considered. In the end, however, the worst possible decision was reached. A more extensive Sudan that included the south was decided upon, but the British authorities determined that the south would be separately administered; education would be in languages other than Arabic and would be in the hands of Christian missionaries. Restrictions on the entry of northerners into the region were put in place. Thus, Sudan's roughly half century of colonial rule did not—as usually happened elsewhere—foster north-south interactions between different tribes, languages, and religions.

In the northern part of the country, the colonial period brought centralizing moves that fostered nation building, but all these only widened the differences between the two parts of the country.

In addition to this important and continuing factor of the north-south split is the distinctive experience of Sudan—especially the north—in modern times. In the 1820s, Sudan was conquered by the armies of Egypt's Muhammad Ali, and remained under Egyptian control until the 1880s, when the Sudanese Mahdi and his followers freed Sudan from foreign rule. By this time Britain had occupied Egypt (1882), and when Britain decided a decade later that Sudan must be regained (for reasons of European imperial rivalries in dividing up Africa), this could only be justified as restoring Egyptian sovereignty.[9] Not wishing that, the British imposed upon Sudan (and Egypt) a diplomatic innovation—two colonial overlords over one colonized country, the Anglo-Egyptian Condominium. It was never an equal partnership, and by the 1920s the rule over Sudan was a completely British performance; Egypt retained only a marginal presence in such matters as monitoring Nile waters.

Stemming from this, a distinctive bifurcated pattern of colonial nationalism developed, with some seeking independence while others called for union with Egypt. These contending options were championed by the two major religio-political forces in Northern Sudan. The Ansar (organized in the Umma Party) under the leadership of the posthumous son of the Mahdi, Sayyid ʿAbd al-Rahman al-Madhi, sought independence, while the leading Sudanese Sufi brotherhood, the Khatmiyya (organized in the National Unionist Party), led by Sayyid ʿAli Mirghani, opted for union with Egypt.[10] Then, in a bargain reminiscent of the 1943 Lebanese national pact, politicians in the two camps realized that independence beholden neither to Egypt nor Britain should suit all concerned. That was what happened, but after independence was gained on January 1, 1956, the internal struggle continued, overlaid by foreign involvement in the Middle East following the lines of the Cold War. This took the form in the 1950s and 1960s of Britain and, increasingly, the United States seeking to line up Sudan in their disputes with Nasir's Egypt supported by the Soviet bloc.

Sudan's role in regional or Cold War diplomacy was muted in comparison with, for example, that of Jordan, Lebanon, Syria, or Yemen—all of which provided the setting for one or more Middle Eastern diplomatic showdowns. No outside state or bloc scored decisive wins in a Sudan that groped for an elusive domestic stability.

The first military coup was as early as 1958. Then General Ibrahim Abbud's six-year rule was brought to an end in 1964. There followed five frustrating years of inept civilian rule before Jaʿfar Numeiri grabbed power in 1969 and remained in office until he was overthrown in 1985. Numeiri himself changed course so often that the relatively long stretch of time during which he was in charge offered scant stability. Putting down an attempted communist coup in 1971 (with Libyan and Egyptian help), Numeiri moved in the following year to offer the south considerable autonomy, formulated in the February 1972 Addis Ababa Agreement. Later, however, believing that he was losing support (the Islamist leader, Hasan Turabi, back from his foreign studies, was a rapidly rising force), Numeiri shifted to a fundamentalist Islamic policy.

By the early 1980s, Numeiri had imposed the Shari'ah (Islamic law) and completely reversed his earlier liberal policy toward the south. His last years in power brought oppressive abuse even in the north, epitomized by his encouragement of the shocking heresy trial and execution of a venerable Muslim leader, Muhammad Taha.

Another coup in 1985 ousted Numeiri, but the civilian government of Sadiq al-Mahdi (the great-grandson of the Mahdi) proved as feckless as the brief civilian rule in the mid-sixties. Yet another coup in 1989 brought to power yet another general, 'Umar Hasan Ahmad al-Bashir, who rules to this day. With Hasan Turabi, until recently, as his ideological eminence grise, al-Bashir has presided over an Islamist government that tried unsuccessfully to end war in the south with a military victory.

During the years of Islamist rule from Khartoum and a continuing civil war in the south, Sudanese foreign policy has been ideologically driven and contentious. It has included ties with Islamist Iran (Iranian troops reportedly participated in the campaign against the southerners in the early 1990s); support of Saddam Husayn's invasion of Kuwait (in return for which thousands of Sudanese workers were expelled from Saudi Arabia); provision of a haven to sundry guerilla groups; involvement in cross-border skirmishes and diplomatic confrontations with Eritrea, Ethiopia, and Uganda; and see-saw swings in relations with Libya.

Relations with the United States and also with Egypt reached new lows during these years. In 1992, Sudan was added to the United States' list of states supporting terrorism.[11] Six years later, the United States bombed a Sudanese pharmaceutical factory alleged (without positive proof) to be producing weapons of biological warfare. The nadir with Egypt came with the Egyptian charge that the Sudanese government was behind a foiled assassination attempt on President Husni Mubarak in 1995.

At the same time, the Sudanese forces opposing the Islamist regime (both southerners and northerners) have not been able to work together consistently, nor, even at their strongest, do they appear capable of overthrowing the government in Khartoum or even of imposing radical changes. Tentative moves by Khartoum to settle with domestic opponents and even to reach detente with some of its neighbors (such as Egypt and Eritrea) took place in 1999. Whether these augur the kind of basic policy changes that might permit a breakthrough to peace, or are simply short-term tactical shifts, remains to be seen.

Libya

Libyan foreign policy can be divided into two distinct periods separated by the year 1969. Before that time, Libya had experienced somewhat less than a generation of independence. It was the first state of Arab Africa (except Egypt) to achieve that status.

This was not because it was better prepared for independence than the others in terms of existing political or economic institutions: quite the contrary. Libya at the time of independence was a thinly populated and impoverished country. Moreover, battles during the Second World War that pitted the British Army against the Italian forces and Rommel's Afrika Korps had destroyed much of the basic infrastructure that had been created during the years of Italian colonization, beginning in 1911. Libya achieved independence in 1951 simply because the outside powers could agree on no other alternative.

Libya started its independent life as a monarchy. The leader of the Sanusi brotherhood, Idris, became Libya's first and only king. The Sanusis, having fought with distinction alongside British forces against the Axis, were supported by the British. They were not without support in the eastern and southern parts of Libya, but those living in the somewhat more advanced and more urban province of Tripolitania were not so favorably disposed to Sanusi rule. In any case, during the 1950s Libya survived largely on British and American subventions and, in turn, offered military bases to both.

Then, in 1959, oil was discovered in commercial quantities, and Libya began a rapid move from rags to riches. The Sanusi dynasty made few and feeble efforts to adjust to the new situation which included—in addition to wealth—a Middle Eastern environment dominated by Nasirist pan-Arabism. Libya as a client state of the Western powers, hosting foreign military bases, was by this time an anachronism. A military coup one decade later, in 1969, easily brought down the dynasty, which offered no resistance.

Since 1969, Libya has experienced the consistency of having had a single person in charge, Mu`ammar al-Qadhafi, but his has been an erratic and a revolutionary leadership. The very bases of Libyan state and society have been radically changed, and many Libyan actions in the international arena have challenged and often violated prevailing diplomatic norms. Libya thus, after 1969, moved rapidly from being a modest, status-quo state to a system-challenging state, limited only by the fact that even with oil wealth and a rapid population increase in recent years it remains merely a middling regional power.

Appraisals of Qadhafi and the Libya he has produced are seldom restrained. To many observers, both his fellow Arab leaders and outsiders, he is at best dangerously erratic and at worst hopelessly unhinged. Moreover, he and the Libyan regime that he directs have confronted the region and the world with a long list of actions that substantiate such negative appraisals.[12] Still, it is not a bad rule of thumb to assume that a leader who remains in power for over thirty years must be tapping some core of support or at least acquiescence. Qadhafi may perhaps be seen as a latter-day Nasirist and populist who is more consistent (and thus less realistic?) in both his pan-Arabism and his populism than were Nasir and most Arab leaders of the radical Left.

Under Qadhafi, Libya has sought union—and in some cases achieved it briefly—with Algeria, Chad, Egypt, Morocco, Sudan, Syria, and Tunisia. And all these efforts were in a period when Arab leaders and most Arab people had begun to view such mergers from the top as mere theater.

Qadhafi's Libya also reflects the deep-seated regional desire to break free of outside domination. The very first months following the overthrow of the monarchy brought action to get American and British military bases evacuated. Soon thereafter came nationalization of foreign banks, confiscation of Italian property and—by stages—nationalization of the oil industry.

Also, in a step evoking Nasirism Redux, in 1974 Libya concluded a major arms agreement with the Soviet Union. Again, like Nasir, Qadhafi took care to resist Arab communists. Three years earlier, it should be recalled, Libya had helped Numeiri of Sudan put down a communist putsch.

Libya's neighbors and outsiders might look with greater sympathy on Qadhafi's ideology and actions if they were confined to Libya itself. The very nature of the ideology and certainly its implementation, however, have meant active intervention in the domestic politics of other states. Libya's efforts for unity with Egypt (even accepting Egyptian leadership) in the period leading up to the October 1973 Arab-Israeli War were, once clearly rebuffed, replaced by confrontational acts that came close to provoking an Egyptian military response. As for its western neighbor, Tunisia: when the union of the two states, announced in 1974, quickly fell apart, Libya became aggressive. The most dangerous incident was a Libyan-sponsored attempted coup that started in the southern Tunisian city of Gafsa in 1980.[13]

Libya's southern neighbor, Chad, experienced in the early 1980s two different Libyan military interventions plus the usual announcement of an impending union between the two states. Libya's ambitions in Chad, opposed by all its neighbors, were stymied by a combination of Western (especially French) military response,[14] a less than brilliant Libyan military campaign (the best chance of success for Libya being a quick, successful strike that would present the world with a fait accompli), and a very confused domestic situation in Chad itself (with would-be outside patrons being obliged to support a changing cast of Chadian clients).

Libya's stormiest foreign relations have been with the United States. Qadhafi had declared the Gulf of Surt to be territorial waters, and sought to bar entry by any outsider without Libyan permission. The United States took the position that these were international waters, and in 1981 planes from the Sixth Fleet shot down two Libyan jets that challenged them in this area. Then, in 1986, U.S. planes bombed Tripoli and Benghazi in retaliation for terrorist incidents in Europe that the United States claimed that Libya had arranged. The next incident in this cycle of violence was the terrorist bomb that exploded Pan-Am flight 103 over Lockerbie, Scotland, in 1988. This brought U.N. sanctions against Libya, and an extended confrontation with it over the American and British demand that two Libyan intelligence agents suspected of planning the bombing be extradited for trial. Only in April 1999 were the two released into Dutch custody for trial.

Scores of other such incidents could be cited, including assassinations of disaffected Libyans living abroad and the disappearance (and almost certainly arranged assassination) of the popular Lebanese Shi'ite leader Musa Sadr during a visit to Libya in 1978, or an attempt to assassinate the U.S. ambassador to Egypt. Yet an appraisal of these turbulent thirty-plus years of Qadhafi's diplomacy seems to confirm the homeostatic nature of balance-of-power politics in the Middle East. Libya has failed to achieve union with any Arab state. No border changes have been effected. Qadhafi has seemingly backed off from indiscriminate support of expatriated resistance groups (even, for a time, the I.R.A.) and terrorism. And the international community, with sanctions against Libya being lifted, appears ready to get back to business as usual.[15]

Tunisia

After Egypt, Tunisia is perhaps the Arab country with the greatest number of factors facilitating national unity. Its uniformity is reflected in a population that is almost 100 per cent Arabic speaking (with miniscule pockets of Berber speakers in the extreme south) and Muslim. Nor does Tunisia offer any significant split within Islam. The population is overwhelmingly Sunni Muslim, with only small groups of Ibadi Muslims (who trace their roots back to the Kharijites of the early Islamic period) in and around the island of Djerba. Almost all of Tunisia's Jewish population has left for Europe or Israel, as have the once significant numbers of European settlers (7–8 per cent of the total population) who came during the years of the French Protectorate (1881–1956).

Moreover, a government in Tunisia can gain ready access to all parts of the country from the one dominant city, the capital Tunis (of which Carthage is now a suburb). Tunisia can look back on centuries of independent or at least autonomous political existence in essentially its present borders. Although incorporated into the Ottoman Empire in 1574, Tunisia soon gained autonomy. Indeed, a single dynasty of beys, the Husaynids, ruled in Tunisia from the early years of the eighteenth century until 1957, when the beylicate was abolished. Even French colonial rule in Tunisia, although intensive and harsh, brought increased centralization and institution building conducive to national cohesion.

An especially well organized nationalist movement, the Neo-Destour, under the leadership of Habib Bourguiba, gained independence for Tunisia and was situated to implement a distinctive foreign policy.[16] At a time when neighboring Algeria was locked in a brutal struggle for independence from France (gained only in 1962), and Nasir's Egypt emerged from the Anglo-French-Israeli invasion at Suez championing Arab unity, decolonization, positive neutralism and ties to the Soviet bloc, Bourguiba's Tunisia adopted a pro-Western orientation. Bourguiba, in March 1956, even stated publicly that if Tunisia had to choose between the Arab League and NATO it should, he believed, choose NATO.[17]

This pro-Western stance was a good tactic at the time. Independence for Tunisia (and Morocco) had been accelerated in the 1950s as France cut down its commitments in order to concentrate on keeping Algeria French. The position of the Algerians who sought independence was naturally that a unified front of Maghribi resistance to France would be most effective. Tunisia needed to walk a narrow line in maintaining that step-by-step dismantling of the French imperial holdings was the best, if not the only, option. At the same time, Tunisia had to convince France that a Maghrib of independent states closely tied to France was the optimal outcome. Then, after Algerian independence, Tunisia needed support from the West in order to balance possible threats from its larger neighbor or from Nasirist pan-Arab pressures, or even from Qadhafi's Libya after 1969.

Ties with France were not easy in these circumstances, and another aspect of Tunisia's balancing diplomacy was to seek support from the United States and other Western powers. This was demonstrated in 1958 when France, claiming the right of hot pursuit, bombed the Tunisian village of Sadiet Sidi Yusuf, where units of the Algerian National Liberation Army (A.L.N. in the French abbreviation) were located.[18] An Anglo-American mediating mission (the Murphy-Beeley) sought to settle the crisis. The Tunisian policy of bringing France and the West to see that all the Maghrib might be lost without a settlement in Algeria seemed to be working.

The limits of confrontational diplomacy with France were, however, demonstrated in the 1961 Bizerte incident. When all parties sensed that a settlement granting Algerian independence was only a matter of time, Bourguiba feared that certain border and other arrangements would be at Tunisia's expense. His ploy of restricting French rights to an air base in Bizerte was intended simply to send the message, "Please do not overlook Tunisia's interests." Unfortunately, he misjudged the man receiving his message. De Gaulle responded with a short, brutal battle that left hundreds killed and wounded. Tunisia had to accommodate as best it could to this setback, and work toward restoring relations with France. Tunisia was obliged as well to live with a Gaullist policy of giving greater importance to strengthening ties with Algeria, which achieved independence the following year.

Other such bumps along the road occurred, but in the long run none permanently drove Tunisia off course from a diplomacy of sustaining ties to the West while working to maintain good relations with its neighbors in the Maghrib and the Arab world at large. In classic balance-of-power terms, this has called for such tactics as lining up with Morocco to balance pressure from Algeria or vice versa. It has meant, above all, avoiding bad relations with both of its immediate neighbors, Algeria and Libya, lest a quick strike produce a hard-to-reverse fait accompli before help could arrive from farther away.

Bourguiba's diplomacy clearly required a secure foundation of domestic support. The overthrow of regimes in Iraq (1958) and Libya (1969), to cite only two, indicated the perils of moderate and pro-Western politics in a time of Nasirist sentiment for Arab unity and radical third-worldism. In positive terms, Bourguiba's government in Tunisia's early postwar years earned considerable popularity with a dynamic developmental program fueled by a consortium of Western aid donors.

Yet Bourguiba never felt completely secure from those Tunisians, small in number but organized and armed for guerilla activity, who rejected the idea of independence achieved in stages and championed unified resistance of all three Maghribi states against the French. These found their leader in Salah bin Yusuf, earlier a close collaborator of Bourguiba, who broke with him in 1955. Once agreement on independence had been reached between the Bourguibists and the French, the two cooperated militarily in putting down armed resistance in the Tunisian south. Bin Yusuf as well as many of these guerilla were driven out of Tunisia or went underground.

By January 1957, Bin Yusuf was in Cairo supporting Nasirist policy. The following year, disturbances in Tunisia believed to have been organized by Egypt led to a break in diplomatic relations between the two countries (one of several periods of strained relations with Egypt over the years). A plot to assassinate Bourguiba, announced in December 1962, was also attributed to the Yusufist forces. By this time, however, Bin Yusuf himself had been assassinated, in August 1961. The timing of that assassination is significant. Tunisia was reeling from the bloody battle of Bizerte the previous month, and the Algerian freedom movement (F.L.N.) was destined to achieve independence soon. Since the F.L.N., with its diplomacy of armed resistance, had good ties with the Tunisian Yusufists, his death removed the threat that Bin Yusuf might return to Tunisia "on an F.L.N. tank."[19]

Never was Bourguiba's diplomacy, attuned to the needs of a small power making its way prudently in a multipolar environment, more sharply contrasted with the heroic (or flamboyant) rhetorical style of the Arab East than during his ill-fated visit in 1965 to the Mashriq where, at Jericho, he deplored the Arab all-or-nothing policy that had brought Palestinians to exile and refugee camps. Bourguiba recommended, instead, that the Arabs accept the 1947 U.N. Partition Resolution and work, in Bourguibist step-by-step fashion, toward gaining as much as possible of Palestinian rights. Bourguiba was pilloried by the Arab press for recommending a realistic diplomacy that was more than a generation ahead of its time.

With the passing of time, however, and as Bourguiba's long tenure in office wound down (he was replaced in 1987 by Zayn al-'Abdin bin Ali in a quiet coup), Tunisia has been able to gain a greater standing in the Arab East.[20]

When the 1982 Israeli invasion of Lebanon drove the P.L.O. out, Tunisia was chosen as the country most acceptable to all parties where the P.L.O. might go. Even earlier, when the Arab states decided to punish Egypt for signing a peace treaty with Israel (1979), the headquarters of the Arab League was moved from Cairo to Tunis. It remained in Tunis from 1979 to 1990. The Israeli air attack on the outskirts of Tunis in October 1985, which sought to destroy the P.L.O. headquarters, brought Tunisia further in line with other Arab states and provoked a crisis in U.S.-Tunisian relations. It was thus not surprising that Tunisia in 1990–1991, heeding domestic pressure, opposed the American-led coalition to oust Iraq from Kuwait. From another, long-term, perspective, the Tunisian government has over the years lost much of its earlier domestic popularity. Seen increasingly as authoritarian and facing a challenge from Islamists (although not as great as that which has confronted the Algerian government), the Tunisian regime is more inclined now to follow rather than lead its public. This requires a diplomacy of moving more in line with Arabist and Islamist ideologies prevailing throughout the region.

Even so, the essential principles of a balanced Tunisian diplomacy remains intact: maintain good ties with the West, especially France and the United States; play the balance-of-power diplomatic game in the region; and quietly push for looser forms of interstate unity, such as the Arab Maghribi Union established in 1989.

Algeria

Algeria is the extreme case of intense colonialism. The French conquest began in 1830, and French rule ended 132 years later, in 1962. Pacification (that colonial euphemism) of the country took years, and created a tradition of violence and mutual distrust between colonizer and colonized. A significant immigration of European settlers poured into the country, and during the last six decades or so of *Algerie française* these *colons* accounted for about 10 percent of the total population, and controlled not only all the important but even the mid-level political and economic posts too. And the country was, in law as well as fact, *Algerie française*, Algeria having been juridically absorbed into the metropole and constituting three French *départements*. With almost no native Algerians granted full French citizenship, it was the *colons* who voted to send representatives to the French National Assembly, and in the multiparty Third and Fourth Republics those few deputies from Algeria could make or break governments.

Decolonization in Algeria was, accordingly, difficult. The possibility of a charismatic leader or a nationalist party able to negotiate independence after a minimum of violence—as was the case with most decolonizations—was ruled out. Independence came only following an eight-year-long armed struggle (1954–1962) in which thousands of Algerians were killed and an estimated one-third of the population displaced from their home areas (many of which were destroyed).[21] There was also no orderly transfer of power at the time of independence. Leaders of the Algerian Provisional Government found themselves at odds with contingents of the military who had managed to stay in Algeria, with the units of the Algerian army (A.L.N.) that the French forces had forced out of Algeria into Morocco and Tunisia, and with those rallying around Ahmad Ben Bella, a founder and leader of the F.L.N. who, captured by the French in 1956, had spent the rest of the war imprisoned in France. The various forces making up the F.L.N. barely escaped sliding into their own internecine war before Ahmad Ben Bella, supported by—among others—Colonel Houari Boumedienne, gained power.[22]

It was an inauspicious beginning. A party and a people radicalized by their struggle for independence, rightly proud of their achievement, and putting themselves forward as the proven model of revolutionary revolt against first-world domination, were woefully lacking in the trained personnel and working institutions to make a going concern of their state.[23] Within a year Algeria was involved in a brief war with Morocco over border delineation. This event was a harbinger of things to come—an ongoing rivalry between these two giants of the Maghrib.

Ben Bella was overthrown in 1965 by Boumedienne, who remained in power until his death in December 1978. Boumedienne's tenure brought the institutionalization of a tightly controlled state. Abundant gas and oil resources at a time when world prices greatly increased gave Algeria the working capital needed to put in place a command economy along socialist lines. These were also the years of Algeria's most significant and ideologically driven interventions in foreign relations. Supporting decolonization in Africa and elsewhere, championing the Palestinians, and lining up consistently with the hard-line positions in Middle Eastern issues, Algeria also rallied the nations of the "South" against the dominant "North" around the concept of the New International Economic Order proclaimed by Boumedienne himself in his 1974 speech to the U.N. General Assembly. Such a policy perspective viewed the United States as leading the hegemonic Western camp that was to be resisted. Nor did usually strong U.S. support for Morocco sit well with those ruling in Algiers. Even so, Algeria's commercial relations with the United States (as with Europe) moved along fairly smoothly, as if on an entirely different track.

Since the mid-1970s, Algeria has confronted Morocco over the Western Sahara, a vast desert expanse (103,000 square miles) with a tiny population (perhaps 200,000). Morocco's annexation of the area, after the departure of the Spanish, was resisted by a nationalist group of the native Sahrawis (the Polisario), who were fully supported in their resistance by Algeria. The confrontation with both the Polisario and Algeria (and with others such as Libya, which often joined in) has continued in an ebb-and-flow fashion ever since.

The post-Boumedienne years brought a certain liberalization at home, with acceptance of a multiparty system and also a pragmatic foreign policy. Emblematic of the latter was the very effective role Algeria played during 1980–1981 in bringing the United States and Iran together to settle the crisis created when the Iranians stormed the American Embassy in Tehran and held those caught there hostage for 444 days.

Algeria's domestic liberalization was accompanied by, and to a large extent a response to, a sharply declining economic situation set off by falling oil prices plus the cumulative problems of a command economy that had not worked very well. With the somber rollcall of trends so characteristic of many third-world countries—a rapidly increasing population, massive influx from countryside to the cities, painfully high unemployment rates reaching at least 40 percent of the working-age population, and a small governing elite no longer shielded by the aura of having achieved independence—Algeria was ripe for the stern challenge of disorder if not even revolution. The major organized resistance was the Islamic Salvation Front (F.I.S. in the French abbreviation). The year 1988 brought widespread riots in Algiers and other major cities. The army, sent in to restore order, killed at least 159 (this was the official figure—others suggest more than 500). This began the process of alienation between army and people. Ironically, 1988 brought important moves in foreign affairs toward a general detente among the five Maghrib states leading to the creation in February 1989 of the Arab Maghrib Union.

The government of Chadli Bendjedid, having used the stick of the army, then tried to use the carrot of more liberalization. This set in motion a process that led to national elections in which the F.I.S. was on the way to winning overwhelmingly. In January 1992, just before the runoff elections were to be held (a F.I.S. majority already being assured), the army intervened, canceled the elections, and forced Bendjedid to step down.[24] This brought in its wake a civil war that pitted the Islamists against the army, with the hapless Algerian population caught in the middle. Before the worst of this warfare was ended, in 1999, the violence had claimed the lives of some 100,000 Algerians. The Islamists organized in the Army of Islamic Salvation accepted a truce in 1997, and agreed to lay down their arms in 1999. In a narrow sense, the army had won, but there were rumblings among pockets of Islamists about again taking up arms. More important, the army, now the acknowledged *pouvoir* (the French term Algerians use to describe government), emerged with little popularity. The 1999 election of Abdelaziz Bouteflika, seen as the army candidate, as president was unopposed when the other six candidates dropped out protesting that the elections would be rigged. He received a sizeable 75 percent majority of the votes, but only an estimated 23 percent of the electorate bothered to vote.

In sum, from the mid-1980s to the present, Algeria's foreign relations may be seen as marking time until some acceptable measure of domestic stability can be reached. This will be difficult, but at least the major actors in Algeria's international relations, past and present, have an interest in an Algeria restored to domestic health. Certainly France and Europe in general perceive the need for stability on the southern shores of the Mediterranean, given the great numbers of Algerians and Maghribis now living in Europe. They don't want civil strife transferred to their countries, and the fear of massive migrations to Europe in the event of chaos in the Maghrib is ever in their thinking. These considerations, although less pressingly felt, are shared by the United States. The Tunisian government, also facing a loss of popularity and an Islamist challenge (although much milder), needs a stable Algeria. Even Morocco, where the potential for rivalry with Algeria remains, can see that a spillover effect of what Algeria suffered in the late 1980s and early 1990s is destabilizing for all.

Mauritania

Mauritania, like Sudan, is a large area that serves as a border zone between Arab Africa and Black Africa. Unlike Sudan, however, whose ecological features such as the Nile Valley and the tropical south make possible large human settlements, Mauritania offers a thinly populated desert ecology. Another difference is that whereas Sudan is characterized by a major political and cultural division between Muslims and non-Muslims, Mauritania is 99.5 percent Muslim. The social divisions there are essentially along racial lines, made even sharper in that the descendants of Arab and Berber tribesmen (the Moors) dominated and often enslaved the Blacks, who constitute about 30 percent of the total population.

France, which had controlled coastal Senegal since the early nineteenth century, and which had established all of that country as a French colony by the 1880s, was positioned to incorporate the Moors into the French imperial structure in the years from the 1890s to 1909. First a territory in French West Africa, and later a colony, Mauritania was for a time administered from Saint-Louis in Senegal. In a phased process of decolonization, Mauritania established a government under Moktar Ould Daddah, and in 1958 voted to become a member of the French Community. After just two years, in 1960, Mauritania became independent and was accepted into the United Nations a year later.

Two other dates serve to underscore Mauritania's principal problems and prospects in foreign relations. It was a founding member of the Organization of African Unity, established in 1963, but joined the Arab League only a decade later, in 1973. Mauritania was, in short, torn between a northward orientation toward the Maghrib and the Arab world or southward toward Senegal and Black Africa. The majority of the population and most of the dominant Moorish elite was culturally drawn toward the Maghrib and the Arab world, but that orientation posed a major problem. Morocco claimed all of Mauritania, and managed to block its first effort to join the United Nations (the Soviet Union, courting favor with Morocco, used its veto). Mauritania was accepted the following year, when the Soviets reversed themselves in a bargain that brought membership to Mongolia as well. Only in 1969 did Morocco change course and recognize Mauritanian independence. This paved the way for the country's later admission into the Arab League.

Mauritania was later caught up in the problem of the Western Sahara, contiguous to both Mauritania and Morocco. When the Spanish departed in 1976, the former Spanish Sahara was divided between Mauritania and Morocco, with the latter taking the larger share and the north, rich in phosphate resources. Mauritania also shared with Morocco the problem of coping with Sahrawi resistance under the aegis of the Polisario, which was supported by Algeria. Mauritania, unlike Morocco, lacked the resources and the motivation to continue the fight against the Polisario. In 1979, Mauritania renounced its claim to the Western Sahara and signed a peace agreement with the Polisario. This, in turn, angered Morocco, which immediately occupied that part of the Western Sahara held by Mauritania. Diplomatic relations with Morocco were restored only in 1985.

The ill-fated involvement in the Western Sahara had earlier contributed to the mounting difficulties that brought about the overthrow of Ould Daddah in 1978. From that date until 1992, Mauritania was ruled by military officers. That year brought the establishment of a multiparty democracy, with presidential elections bringing to power Maaouya Taya, himself an army colonel and formerly head of the military government. His party gained control of the local councils in 1999 elections, which were boycotted by opposition parties. The announcement that the runner-up in the 1992 presidential election would be brought to trial suggests that an adequately institutionalized Mauritanian polity remains elusive.

With a small and impoverished population, Mauritania is fated to play a minor role in foreign affairs. This role, properly used, can be a blessing. It can avoid unwanted pressures from outsiders by continuing to rely on France, still its major trading partner, and keeping manageable ties with its powerful Arab neighbors, Morocco and Algeria, while not completely ignoring its other neighbors, Senegal and Mali. An interesting recent development, that could be interpreted in two quite contradictory ways concerning the Mauritanian approach to diplomacy, is that, in October 1999, Mauritania established ambassador-level ties with Israel, which was irritating especially to Libya as well as to several other Arab states.

Notes

1 Without a proper census since the 1930s, all Lebanese population estimates can only be approximations that will not go uncontested.

2 Arabs have insisted that this body of water, long known as the Persian Gulf, be called the Arab Gulf. The situation is such that to designate the Gulf as either Arab or Persian becomes a political statement. Seeking to avoid that problem, many simply refer to "the Gulf," and that available dodge will be adopted here.

3 Not to forget the fascinating but short-lived Portuguese conquests in the sixteenth century.

4 As the name implies, the U.A.E. is actually a federation of Abu Dhabi, Dubai, and five smaller amirates–Sharja, Ra's al-Khaymah, Fujayra, Umm al-Quwayn, and `Ajman.

5 See the chapter by Wm. Roger Louis, especially pp. 47–55, for details.

6 It can be rightly countered that it was not multipolar balance-of-power politics but decisive American leadership that got Iraq out of Kuwait. That inter-Arab diplomacy alone would

have saved Kuwait does seem doubtful, but some rearrangement of balances that would have deprived Iraq of all the gain and produced new power relations not completely different from the old was possible. This would have been almost certainly at Kuwait's expense, but that often happens in balance-of-power politics—witness the crass carving up of Poland in eighteenth-century Europe.

7   These two territories, now a single state, will be dubbed Yemen and South Yemen when the period before 1990 is being referred to.

8   The U.N. real G.D.P. per capita (perhaps a better gauge, as it is based on what can be bought of basic needs in the local market) ranks Sudan slightly lower than Mauritania: Mauritania $1,730, Sudan $1,560.

9   After Kitchener's army had defeated the "dervishes" (as they were called) of the Khalifah who succeeded Muhammad Ahmad al-Mahdi at the Battle of Omdurman (1898), he and a small party hurried upstream to the remove village of Fashoda in southern Sudan. There he confronted the French Captain Marchand coming with a small party from West Africa to claim these territories for France. The resulting "Fashoda incident", in which the British forced the outmanned French to stand down, almost brought the two countries to war.

10   As the names of the two leaders were quite a mouthful for the English speaker, the acronyms SAR (Sayyid `Abd al-Rahman) and SAM (Sayyid `Ali Mirghani) were often used. This bipolor image of pro- and anti-union politics skips over important details. For example, Sayyid `Ali's Khatmiyya later split with the National Unionist Party led by Ismail al-Azhari and formed their own party, and other political groupings existed even in the north. This bipolar image will suffice, however, as a simplified presentation of the major factor in Sudanese politics during these years.

11   It should be noted, however, that Usama bin Ladin, now viewed by the United States as the principal paymaster and perhaps mastermind of Islamist international terrorism, was expelled from Sudan in 1996 in response to U.S. pressure.

12   Early on, Qadhafi resigned from various official positions. In the same spirit, he has from time to time pushed through utopian anarchist schemes that would do away with or at least downgrade the state (thus, the neologism *jamahuriyya*, literally "publics" or "peoples," or replaced embassies with People's Bureaux). Even so, there is no doubt that he has been and remains the de facto ruler of Libya.

13   There was also Algerian involvement, but Tunisia, which needed the support of its large neighbor to the west, kept quiet about that and accepted the pledge (probably true) of new Algerian President Chadli Bendjedid (replacing Boumedienne, who had recently died) that he knew nothing about the matter.

14   President Reagan, in pushing for French action against Libya in Chad, stated that this country was in the French "sphere of influence." This was probably the first time that an American official used the phrase "sphere of influence" in other than a negative sense. The idealist and Wilsonian tradition in American diplomacy deemed "spheres-of-influence" politics unacceptable.

15   Libya has transferred over $30 million to France to compensate families of the victims of a French commercial flight brought down by a terrorist bomb over Niger in 1989. This followed a French court's judgment of in-absentia life sentences against six Libyans, including Qadhafi's brother-in-law. France seems prepared to turn over a new leaf, but one French judge has demanded that Qadhafi himself be investigated for his possible role in the bombing. See *Britannica Book of the Year* 2000, pp. 457–58.

16   The nationalists also implemented impressive domestic reforms, including the boldest legal changes granting rights to women in the entire Muslim world since those of Ataturk some three decades earlier.

17 "Habib Bourguiba's Policy for Independent Tunisia," *The Times* (London), March 22, 1956, as cited in Nicole Grimaud, *La Tunisie à la recherche de sa securité*, p. 25.

18 In a narrowly military sense, the French army "won" its war in Algeria, for by the late 1950s it had pushed most of the A.L.N. across the borders into either Tunisia or Morocco. In such a war, however, those resisting colonial rule win by not losing. Eventually, the F.L.N. convinced France (notably de Gaulle, to his great credit) that Algeria under these circumstances was a liablity.

19 This is the way an informed Tunisian stated the issue in 1960. See Clement Henry Moore, *Tunisia since Independence: The Dynamics of One-Party Government*, p. 70.

20 All this was done with a deft touch of legality. Medical experts declared Bourguiba unable to continue in office. In his eighties at the time (the precise date of his birth is unclear), he lived cloistered in his native town of Monastir until his death on April 6, 2000.

21 Figures for the losses during those eight years of war vary wildly. French estimates, for example, give the figure of 250,000 for the number of Algerians killed, whereas Algerian estimates are 1,500,000. Whatever the exact figures, all agree that the toll of death and destruction was enormous.

22 Eyewitnesses relate poignant stories of Algerians, especially women, positioning themselves between the tanks and armored cars of the sundry contending F.L.N. armed forces, shaming them to stop with cries of "enough."

23 In those early months of Algerian independence, all varieties of radical, from European Trotskyites to American Black nationalists such as Eldridge Cleaver, flocked to Algeria. It was deemed the country where revolutionary dreams would be realized. A foreign observer in Algeria at the time remarked wryly that there should be an eleventh commandment, "Thou shalt not steal thy neighbor's revolution."

24 This decision sparked considerable debate well beyond Algeria. Partisans of one side of the argument insisted that those in power can rightly stop a group intent on destroying the democratic system itself. The F.I.S., it was said, accepted only "one man, one vote, one time." On the other side was the bleak appraisal that the army never was and never would be supportive of democracy. Was there, however, a middle position between cancellation and the great unknown of an F.I.S. government? Could the army have negotiated an arrangement in which elections would proceed but the winning F.I.S. would agree not to change the constitution or the command structure of the army (whose officers knew what had happened to the shah's army leaders following the Islamic revolution in Iran)? If the F.I.S. had declined such a deal, public knowledge of that would have strengthened support for the army's cancellation of the elections.

Conclusion

L. Carl Brown

This book has sought to accomplish two goals: to reveal the working assumptions guiding the foreign relations of the states of the Middle East and of four of the outside powers most involved in Middle Eastern diplomacy, and to illuminate the multipolar nature of that diplomacy.

Ours has been a state-centered study. We do not claim that such an approach is definitive or exhaustive. Clearly, many institutions, individuals, and ideas beyond the state (any state or all states together) have their impact on Middle Eastern diplomacy. These include such a mixed bag as the United Nations, nongovernmental organizations in all their variety, multinational businesses, organized religions, and all kinds of ideologies, not to mention the increasingly pervasive media beyond the control of any state. Still, the institutionalized entities we call states, with their instruments of domestic control and a panoply of control mechanisms for dealing with the world beyond their borders (from alliances and armies to trade and immigration), are of primary importance in international relations. Given this primacy, "Bringing the State Back In"[1] for a study of Middle Eastern diplomacy needs no further argument. And since the Middle Eastern state has at times been viewed somewhat skeptically (to mention, yet again, the "tribes with flags" taunt), all the more reason to have a hard look at these states, one after another.

Another goal of this book, mentioned in the Introduction, was to "bring out the underlying pattern of international relations in the Middle East." This book has, we trust, contributed to that goal. Still, we have offered only one of several ways to address that important larger issue. A sports metaphor may clarify what we have done in this book and what we have not done: we have concentrated on the game plans and overall records of the several states.[2] We have not offered, except sporadically, a chronological account of the unending series of the games themselves. In other words, the organization of this book differs from that of conventional diplomatic histories such as William L. Langer's classic studies of late-nineteenth- and early-twentieth-century European diplomacy[3] or, for the Middle East, M. S. Anderson's *The Eastern Question*.

Our book also differs from books that treat the foreign policy of a single state in its relations with other states. Yet that is, perhaps, a distinction without substantive difference. Ours is, in fact, a collection of single-state studies. It offers the reader the opportunity to have readily at hand the information and interpretation needed to

303

compare different foreign policies and integrate them into the larger Middle Eastern whole.

We have not, however, directly addressed the issue of "the underlying pattern of international relations in the Middle East." Our approach has been from the perspective of the several discrete parts (the states) rather than from that of the whole (the system). Put differently, we have not sought explicitly to gauge our separate studies of Middle Eastern foreign policies according to the several prevailing theories about international relations, nor have we attempted to advance our own theory. We offer, instead, a series of case studies that can be used, individually and together, to probe how Middle Eastern diplomacy works.[4]

And yet we do presuppose several important points concerning the Middle East as an international relations subsystem: It is a distinctive region, characterized by a shared history and culture, that has been intensively penetrated by the Western state system for at least the past two centuries. It is, and has long been, composed of polities differing greatly in size, wealth, and power. These many polities interact among themselves and with outside powers in a complex pattern of multipolar diplomacy. No single regional power plays the hegemon. Usually, there has been no outside hegemon either, not even Britain during its "moment"[5] and probably not the United States today. Although at present the United States enjoys (if that is the right word) preemptive power as compared with other outside powers, it is not clear that this will endure, or even that it is in America's interest to play a hegemon's role in the Middle East.

These characteristics of Middle Eastern diplomacy may perhaps best be classified as a distinctive balance-of-power system. As such, it is not totally unlike other balance-of-power systems in other regions or at other times. Even so, those playing in this Middle Eastern diplomatic game, having done so for so long period of time, have developed their own rules that do produce a distinctive Middle Eastern diplomatic style.

A few findings that emerge from our separate country studies may shed some light on both the style and the system. Many of the twenty-one (or twenty-two if we add the Palestinian authority as a state-to-be) Middle Eastern states are vulnerably weak in their size or strength or poor domestic legitimacy. Yet over the past half century, border changes and the disappearance of states have been rare. The unity of Egypt and Syria lasted a mere three years, from 1958 to 1961. Libya under Qadhafi could not pull off a merger after at least a half-dozen attempts. An international coalition reversed Iraq's coup against Kuwait. Neither the brief border war between Morocco and Algeria nor the Saudi dispute with several of its Gulf neighbors over the Buraimi oasis changed borders significantly. The one successful and peaceful merger has been that uniting the two Yemens.

Moreover, significant border changes that do occur remain matters of contention and are sometimes later reversed. Iraq and Iran have, for example, experienced several different border changes along the Shatt al-`Arab, keyed to whichever had the upper hand at the time. The chances are that this process will continue. The Moroccan seizure of the Western Sahara continues to be resisted by the Polisario from within as well as Algeria from without.

The most dramatic territorial change was the Israeli conquest in June 1967 of Sinai, the Golan Heights, Gaza, and the West Bank. Interestingly, Sinai has been returned to Egypt, Gaza and parts of the West Bank seem destined to become the core of a Palestinian state, and all observers agree that an Israeli-Syrian peace is unthinkable without an Israeli return of the Golan to Syria.

Every example of would-be territorial changes has, of course, its own special circumstances. Even so, one can interpret the immediate and, where necessary, sustained resistance to such moves as demonstrating a multipolar balance-of-power system heavily weighted toward maintenance of the status quo. That members of the international coalition who ejected Saddam Husayn's Iraq from Kuwait were disinclined even to consider a partition of Iraq (feasible by Wilsonian standards of nationalism to accommodate Kurds or Shi`i Arabs) is another case in point.

This, in turn, helps to explain why states that are demonstrably weak or saddled with unpopular governments manage to survive. Even states that have (as do most Arab states) explicit statements in their constitutions about being merely a part of the larger entity (the Arab world), with the implication that absorption into that larger unity is the ultimate goal, manage their day-to-day politics and diplomacy very much like other states. Does this mean that ideologies positing a larger unity above and beyond the existing state are politically unimportant? There is no need to go that far. Indeed, observers have too often presented Arabism or Islamism in exaggerated terms—as either clearly the wave of the future or mere rhetoric lacking impact in a world of realist politics. What can be suggested is that the homeostatic nature of the system militates against merging or eliminating the existing state units. The reductio ad absurdum is the bitter power struggle between the two Ba`thist regimes of Syria and Iraq, with the former, "the beating heart of Arabism," even aligning with non-Arab Iran against Iraq.

States everywhere join in bilateral and multilateral alliances, and the latter at times create interstate institutions, such as the United Nations on a world scale or the Organization of American States regionally. Here the Middle East offers a rich history with interesting variations. As for the three non-Arab states, Turkey is a member of NATO. The shah's Iran was a founding member of the Western-supported Baghdad Pact, but since 1979 the Islamic Republic has taken an adamantly anti-Western orientation. It did not, however, adopt the common balancing tactics of seeking friendly ties with the Soviet bloc. Indeed, in the early years of the revolution, Ayatollah Khomeini labeled the Soviet Union the "lesser Satan" alongside the American "great Satan."

Israel has been throughout most of its existence a pariah state in the midst of the Arab world (the United Nations, bowing to early Arab pressure, grouped Israel among the European states). Israel is still very much in the process of overcoming that exclusion. It has had relatively good relations with Turkey (of late, military cooperation as well) and a sharp flip-flop in its relations with Iran—friendly until the 1979 Islamic Revolution, aggressively unfriendly since. Israel has relied on strong if informal ties with the West, and from roughly the 1960s overwhelmingly with the United States. Relations with the United States, often called an alliance, are not, in fact, based on any formal treaty.

The many Arab states offer the greatest variety of interstate groupings. First the Cold War dimension: Western efforts during the early years of the Cold War to line up Arab states in a Middle Eastern equivalent of NATO in Europe or SEATO in Asia failed. Egypt, both before and after Nasir, rejected two such Western efforts, and the alternative Baghdad Pact, bypassing Egypt, was able to bring in only Iraq along with Britain, Iran, Pakistan, and Turkey. When Iraq broke ranks with the Egyptian-orchestrated insistence on Arab unity, this contributed to the violent overthrow of the Hashimite regime there in 1958.

The Soviet Union, from the time of the 1955 arms deal with Egypt until the U.S.S.R. itself fell apart, developed strong relations with several states at different times, including Egypt, Syria, Iraq, and South Yemen. Yet the Soviet Union was unable to bring together its several different regional clients, and wisely never really tried. Soviet misinformation to Egypt about Israeli mobilization against Syria in 1967 was an ill-fated effort to line up two disputing clients, Egypt and Syria. The June War resulted.

The most extensive and long-lived regional organization is the League of Arab States, created in 1945. Yet it is by design a league of states, not the armature for the development of a single greater state. It was for long dominated by one state, Egypt, until the other Arab states ejected that country for having signed a treaty with Israel in 1979. Brought back into the League in 1990, Egypt again exercises a dominant influence in the service of Egyptian interests. Perhaps somewhat more meaningful since the 1970s have been the periodic summit meetings of Arab heads of state.

Other Arab interstate organizations include the Arab Maghrib Union (created in 1989) and the Gulf Cooperation Council (created in 1981).

In addition, two interstate organizations that transcend the Middle East are the Organization of Petroleum Exporting Countries (OPEC, established in 1960 with Venezuela as a founding member and several other non-Middle Eastern states now members) and the Organization of the Islamic Conference, founded in 1970. Interestingly, Iran is a member of both.

A great number of other bilateral and multilateral alliances could be recorded. Many have been short-lived and of little significance. Indeed, quite a number have been more ploys to control the signatory ally or allies than defensive measures against an outside enemy. The Egypt-Iraqi-Syrian unity discussions of the early 1960s offer a classic example of such behavior.

These many different alliances and interstate institutions appear, on balance, to confirm the continued viability, for all their weaknesses, of the existing cluster of Middle Eastern states. None of them seems to be evolving toward a greater union embracing all or some significant part of the Middle East. The alliances and interstate institutions are no less important as a subject of study for anyone who would understand the modalities of Middle Eastern diplomacy. They shed light on the style and texture of Middle Eastern multipolar diplomacy. But the situation may change, and may be changing even now, more than we are aware. Nothing is more to be avoided than the tendency to see the Middle East as locked into unalterable behavior patterns. Still, watching the changing scene from the perspective of these many different existing states may well be an especially effective approach. That, in short, was the plan of this book.

Notes

1　Thus the title of the book edited by Peter B. Evans, Dietrich Rueschemeyer, and Theda Skocpol.

2　Some object to the very idea of describing international relations—which involve such grave matters as war and peace—in terms of games. This is done with no intention of trivializing serious human activity but simply because such a metaphor does help to explain what is taking place. Games, it is often said, are sublimated conflict. Diplomacy and war are deadly games.

3　William L. Langer, *European Alliances and Alignments, 1871–1899,* and *The Diplomacy of Imperialism, 1890–1912.*

4　The bibliographical essay lists works using the opposite approach of proceeding from the system to the several states.

5　This evokes the title of Elizabeth Monroe's classic *Britain's Moment in the Middle East, 1914–1956.*

Bibliographic Essay

L. Carl Brown

This book has addressed a broad subject, in fact over two dozen subjects—the foreign policies of each of the Middle Eastern states plus the four outside powers that have been most involved in Middle Eastern diplomacy. Moreover, these many separate country studies have sought to shed light on the distinctive nature—the "rules of the game"—of Middle Eastern diplomacy.

Given this breadth of coverage, selecting recommendations for further reading poses a problem. Almost everything written on the modern Middle East has some relevance either to the foreign policy of one or another state caught up in Middle Eastern diplomacy or to the larger issue of how states in this area interact. Casting the bibliographical net that widely would produce a book-length essay. Presented here, instead, is a very scaled-down and wide-ranging selection. All together, the books and articles listed should illustrate the rich variety of sources available for the study of foreign policy and diplomacy in the Middle East and also point the way to further research.

For the study of a highly organized institution such as the state in its relations with other states, the official papers are clearly of fundamental importance. Access to these state papers, which are gathered in official archives and sometimes made available in selective published collections, is always subject to certain restrictions. States may make official documents available to researchers just a few years after they were written, or they may impose time limits of fifty years or more. Not all the records of the same period are released at same time. Some are never released. Many of the most secret papers—virtually all the records of intelligence agencies, it may be assumed—never become available. Sometimes the incomplete nature or poor organization of the public archives may frustrate access to their use. All in all, learning about the various public archives of the many different states is best achieved in a graduate seminar or by consulting specialized studies, or even through informal networking (where state policies governing access to archives are vague). This important subject will be addressed here only by referring to the very useful short statement on "Primary Sources" in the Bibliographical Guide to be found in M. E. Yapp, *The Near East since the First World War: A History to 1995,* 2nd ed. (1996), pp. 443–48.

It is important, however, to keep in mind the great difference in availability of public records in the Middle Eastern states, on the one hand, and the outside powers, on the other. And there are considerable differences of availability among the Middle

Eastern states. This produces an unfortunate imbalance. The diplomatic history of the modern Middle East has been written and continues to be written largely on the basis of the public records of only one side—that of the Western powers.

Second, even the archival record, although a fundamental source, should not be considered as preemptively determinative. As an eminent British diplomatic historian dismissively put it, the official document may be only "what one clerk wrote to another clerk." Just like any other source, whether memoir, media report, interview, or scholarly reconstruction, the official record must be scrutinized and contextualized.

An important limitation of the listing below is that it does not include works in the Middle Eastern languages. A more expansive annotated bibliography, including especially the works on Middle Eastern foreign policies and international relations in the Arabic, Hebrew, Persian, and Turkish languages, is badly needed, but that is a project for another time and place.

General Historical Studies: Eastern Question and Great Game

A standard study of Eastern Question diplomacy is M. S. Anderson, *The Eastern Question, 1774–1923: A Study in International Relations* (1966). Very much oriented to international relations as seen from Europe, the book does, however, give more attention to the Middle Eastern side of the story than did earlier accounts. It also includes a thorough bibliographical essay.

Efraim Karsh and Inari Karsh, in *Empires of the Sand: The Struggle for Mastery in the Middle East, 1789–1923* (1999), give more attention to the actions and attitudes of the Middle Eastern players. They argue, convincingly, that the diplomatic initiative during those years was much more in the hands of Middle Easterners than has usually been represented. They do, however, come close to suggesting, at times, that Middle Easterners brought their losses (such as the piecemeal breakup of the Ottoman Empire and European colonial rule over most of the sundered parts) upon themselves. Many scholars, while applauding the more balanced attention given to both Europe and the Middle East in *Empires of the Sand*, would question this interpretation. Most of the book treats the twentieth-century period until the end of the Otttoman Empire.

My *International Politics and the Middle East: Old Rules, Dangerous Game* (1984) advances the interpretation that a complex multipolar interrelationship between the Middle East and Europe grew up in the period of the Eastern Question. This distinctive pattern, I argue, continued to characterize Middle Eastern international relations well beyond the end of the Ottoman Empire.

None of these books includes Iran, however, since that country was not part of the Eastern Question, or of what the European state system was to do with the Ottoman Empire. Fortunately *The Middle East in World Affairs* by George Lenczowski makes up for this exclusion. This book has dominated the field since the first edition in 1952. It is now in its fourth edition (1980). The book opens with a historical section treating events from the rise of the Eastern Question through World War I and the peace settlement. This is followed by individual country studies of all of the Mashriq plus Afghanistan, but excluding the Maghrib and Sudan. Then come chapters on World War II, strategic waterways of the Middle East, inter-Arab relations, and the foreign powers in the Middle East—the four treated in our book plus Germany. The organization and coverage of Lenczowski's book with its individual country studies thus parallels in large measure that of our book. Lenczowski is also the author of *Russia and the West in Iran, 1918–1948: A Study in Big Power Rivalry* (1949), which offers additional historical coverage of the Great Game, Iran's equivalent of the Eastern Question.

Howard M. Sachar's *Europe Leaves the Middle East, 1936–1954* (1972) is a good and readable narrative history. His earlier book, *The Emergence of the Middle East, 1914–1924* (1969), is equally good, but has perhaps now been nudged out by David Fromkin's excellent *A Peace to End All Peace: Creating the Modern Middle East, 1914–1924* (1989).

What amounts to a general handbook on the modern Middle East is Ritchie Ovendale, *The Middle East since 1914* (1992), with chronologies, biographies, treaties, and other official documents, lists of rulers, foreign ministers, and political parties, plus a long bibliographical section (pp. 307–34).

General Country Studies

A well-established genre in scholarly writing is the study of a single state, and there is no lack of such overviews devoted to the Middle Eastern states. Indeed, several such works have been written by contributors to this book. Books of this sort do give some attention to the particular country's foreign policy, and they have the advantage of situating the country's diplomatic dimension within the larger context of that country's political structure, economy and culture.

For example, the series "Profiles: Nations of the Contemporary Middle East" edited by Bernard Reich and David E. Long offers studies on the following countries: Algeria, by John P. Entelis (1986); Bahrain, by Fred Lawson (1989); Iran, by John W. Limbert (1987); Israel, by Bernard Reich (1985); Lebanon, by David C. Gordon (1983); Libya, by Lillian Craig Harris (1986); Jordan, by Peter Gubser (1983); North Yemen, by Manfred W. Wenner (1991); Oman, by Calvin H. Allen, Jr. (1987); South Yemen, by Robert W. Stookey (1982); Tunisia, by Kenneth J. Perkins (1986); Syria, by John F. Devlin (1983); Sudan, by John Obert Voll and Sarah Potts Voll (1985); Turkey, by George S. Harris (1985); and United Arab Emirates, by Malcolm C. Peck (1986).

Other solid country studies in different series or produced separately include Phebe Marr, *The Modern History of Iraq* (1985); John Ruedy, *Modern Algeria: The Origins and Development of a Nation* (1992); Kamal S. Salibi, *The Modern History of Lebanon* (1965); Dirk Vandewalle, *Libya since Independence: Oil and State-Building* (1998); and P. J. Vatikiotis, *The Modern History of Egypt: From Muhammad Ali to Mubarak*, 3rd. ed. (1985).

Just as individual country studies provide considerable information on foreign relations while situating the diplomatic dimension within a larger context, so too do general histories of the modern Middle East. Two can be recommended: William L. Cleveland, *A History of the Modern Middle East*, 2nd ed. (2000), and Malcolm E. Yapp, *The Near East since the First World War*, noted above. Both have excellent annotated bibliographies. Neither, however, deals with the Maghrib, for which one can consult Jamil M. Abun-Nasr, *A History of the Maghrib*, 3rd ed. (1987). More on Maghrib diplomacy can be gleaned from the following: I. William Zartman, "North African Foreign Policy," in L. Carl Brown, ed., *State and Society in Independent North Africa* (1966); Werner

K. Ruf, "La Politique étrangère des états maghrebins," in W. K. Ruf et al., *Introduction à l'Afrique du Nord contemporaine* (1975), and a fascinating balance-of-power account of Maghrib diplomacy by Mary-Jane Deeb, "Inter-Maghribi Relations since 1969: A Study of the Modalities of Unions and Mergers" (1989).

Foreign Policy Studies of Individual Countries

Bahgat Korany and Ali E. Hillal Dessouki, eds., *The Foreign Policies of Arab States: The Challenge of Change*, 2nd rev. ed. (1991) deserves to lead the list. In many ways this fine book serves as a model for our own book, the major organizational difference being that we include the non-Arab states of Iran, Israel, and Turkey plus four outside powers. Separate chapters cover Algeria, Egypt, Jordan, Libya, Saudi Arabia, Syria, and Sudan, plus the P.L.O. The book also addresses the Arab system in general. The chapter on "The Global System and Arab Foreign Policies: The Primacy of Constraints" by Korany and Dessouki, and Paul Noble's "The Arab System: Pressures, Constraints, and Opportunities" are first-rate accounts. On the Arab state system, see also the several chapters in Ghassan Salame, ed., *The Foundations of the Arab State* (1987), especially Iliya Harik, "The Origins of the Arab State System," and Bahgat Korany, "Alien and Besieged Yet Here to Stay: The Contradictions of the Arab Territorial State."

An earlier work that concentrates on the foreign policies of several Middle Eastern states is R. D. McLaurin, Mohammed Mughisuddin, and Abraham R. Wagner, *Foreign Policy Making in the Middle East: Domestic Influence on Policy in Egypt, Iraq, Israel and Syria* (1977).

As for foreign-policy studies of a single Middle Eastern state, the coverage is uneven. For some countries there is an abundance, for others hardly anything at all, and the history of the foreign relations of these latter states must be extracted from many different sources.

Israel is by far the best studied. Michael Brecher has written three books that examine in careful detail the actual decision-making process in specific cases of Israeli foreign policy. They are *The Foreign Policy System of Israel: Setting, Images, Processs* (1972), *Decisions in Israel's Foreign Policy* (1976), and *Decisions in Crisis, 1967 and 1973* (1980). Uri Bialer examines an early period in *Between East and West: Israel's Foreign Policy Orientation, 1948–1956* (1990). In a sense, Nadav Safran's large (over 600 pages) *Israel, the Embattled Ally* (1978) may be seen as a foreign-policy study. Although this work began as a country study in the venerable Harvard American Foreign Policy Library series, published in 1963 as *The United States and Israel*, fully two-thirds of the book as revised and expanded treats Israel's foreign relations in organized chronological fashion.

The writing of Israel's diplomatic history has become a matter of intense debate within the state itself. Challenging older interpretations are the Israeli "new historians", who cast a much less benign eye on both Israel's role in the events leading up to the creation of the state in 1948 and the absence of peace with the Arabs thereafter. This scholarly confrontation is Israel's equivalent of American historians who contend over responsibility for the Cold War. My "State of Grace? Rethinking Israel's Founding Myths" (1998) provides a brief introduction to this heated debate with citations of the principal writings.

As for the Palestinians, it can be argued with considerable justice that tracing the history of a nationalist movement is necessarily largely a foreign-policy study. Much has been written on the Palestinians, the P.L.O., and the Palestinian Authority now evolving into a state, but for our purposes one source, encyclopedic in size and scope, can be cited. This is Yezid Sayigh, *Armed Struggle and the Search for State: The Palestinian National Movement, 1949–1993* (1997) This massive book (953 pages) is very detailed, but is well organized into a chronological narrative. Readers can thus read it through or consult it for specific times and incidents. The comprehensive and conveniently arranged bibliography (a full 69 pages), which includes official documents, periodicals, and books in Arabic, English, and Hebrew, is a treasure trove.

Rouhallah K. Ramazani has written a number of solid foreign-policy studies on Iran. His *The Foreign Policy of Iran, 1500–1941: A Developing Nation in World Affairs* (1966), *Iran's Foreign Policy, 1941–1973: A Study of Foreign Policy in Modernizing Nations* (1975), and *Revolutionary Iran: Challenge and Response in the Middle East* (1986) provide comprehensive coverage. Ramazani's later article on the split within Islamic Iran on foreign policy "Iran's Foreign Policy: Contending Orientations" (1989) is also recommended.

A good selection of works exists on Turkish foreign policy. An interesting little book that traces, in a scant 115 pages, Turkish foreign policy from its Ottoman roots to the present is Simon Mayall, *Turkey: Thwarted Ambition* (1997). Selim Deringil in his *Turkish Foreign Policy during the Second World War* (1989) traces Turkey's tortuous efforts to remain neutral during the Second World War, an approach very different from, and much more successful than, that of the Ottoman Empire during the First World War. Other good and up-to-date works include Heinz Kramer, *A Changing Turkey: The Challenge to Europe and the United States* (2000), especially all of Part Two entitled "Turkish Foreign and Security Policy after the Cold War"; Yesemin Celik, *Contemporary Turkish Foreign Policy* (1999); and several articles in two recent collected works—Mustafa Aydin, *Turkey at the Threshold of the 21st Century: Global Encounters and/vs Regional Alternatives* (1998), and *Turkey between East and West: New Challenges for a Rising Regional Power* (1996), edited by Vojtech Mastny and R. Craig Nation. Mustafa Aydin and M. Nail Alkan have also edited *An Extensive Bibliography of Studies in English, German and French on Turkish Foreign Policy (1923–1997)* (1997).

Other studies that concentrate on the foreign policy of individual countries include Abdul-Reda Assiri, *Kuwait's Foreign Policy: City-State in World Politics* (1990); Michael Doran, *Pan-Arabism before Nasser: Egyptian Power Politics and the Palestine Question* (1999); Alasdair Drysdale and Raymond A. Hinnebusch, *Syria and the Middle East Peace Process* (1991); Fred Halliday, *Revolution and Foreign Policy: The Case of South Yemen, 1967–1987* (1990); Jacob Goldberg, *The Foreign Policy of Saudi Arabia: The Formative Years, 1902–1918* (1986); Nicole Grimaud, *La Politique exterieure de l'Algerie* (1984) and *La Tunisie à la recherche de sa securité* (1995).

Middle Eastern diplomatic history has been largely written in terms of the great powers and the Middle East, with a resulting imbalance in coverage. Still, the importance of that interaction between the West and the Middle East over at least the last two centuries cannot be denied, and a copious literature exists on the relations of each of the major powers with the Middle East—except, surprisingly, for France.

Britain and the Middle East

A splendid book with which to begin any study of this subject is Elizabeth Monroe's *Britain's Moment in the Middle East, 1914–1956* (1963). This fine overview conveys with great insight the broad lines of British policies during that roughly half century of Britain's imperial presence in the Middle East.

Another excellent study of different scope is an interpretation of British policy in that critical half decade near the end of Britain's "moment." This is the narrative diplomatic history by Wm. Roger Louis, *The British Empire in the Middle East, 1945–1951: Arab Nationalism, the United States and Postwar Imperialism* (1984).

Three very detailed studies by Briton Cooper Busch carry the story of Britain's Middle Eastern policy from the late nineteenth century to 1923. They are *Britain and the Persian Gulf, 1894–1914* (1967), *Britain, India and the Arabs, 1914–1921* (1971), and *Mudros to Lausanne, 1918–1923* (1976). The second book covers the period of Britain's Middle Eastern diplomacy during the First World War, a subject on which there are scores of works, often strongly polemical, covering what wits long ago dubbed "the twice promised land" (that is, the British commitments to both Arabs and Zionists). On this subject, Elie Kedourie's strongly argued book that challenges the Arab case against Britain must be mentioned: *In the Anglo-Arab Labyrinth* (1976) is a thorough reworking of his *England and the Middle East*, which appeared twenty years earlier. An incisive scholar who attacked what he saw as misguided British thinking concerning the Middle East, Kedourie produced as well a number of hard-hitting articles that can provoke thought even now as these issues fade into history. For example, his "The Chatham House Version" asserts that a certain British image of the Arabs fostered by the likes of Arnold Toynbee and H. A. R. Gibb distorted British policy in the area. One might read also Kedourie's "Pan-Arabism and British Policy." Both of these articles are collected in his book *The Chatham House Version and other Middle Eastern Studies* (1970, reissued 1984). Several articles collected in two other books of his—*Arabic Political Memoirs and Other Studies* (1974), and *Islam in the Modern World and Other Studies* (1980)—deal as well, always forcefully, with Britain and the Middle East. For example, he takes on T. E. Lawrence, attacks Britain's Suez debacle in 1956 not for having entered into collusion to overthrow Nasir but for having failed, and compares British and American roles in the Middle East. One can best appreciate Kedourie's interpretations when one knows the interpretations of those he attacked, and they were not straw men—or women; Elizabeth Monroe, for example, represents a different interpretation. Kedourie's bête noir, Arnold Toynbee, wrote almost eighty years ago a study that still merits reading, *The Islamic World since the Peace Settlement* (1927). A readable book by John Marlowe is *Arab Nationalism and British Imperialism* (1961). Another useful book is M. A. Fitzsimmons's *Empire by Treaty: Britain and the Middle East in the Twentieth Century* (1964).

Among the more recent studies of Britain's Middle Eastern policy are Peter Sluglett, "Formal and Informal Empire in the Middle East," in Robin Winks, ed., *The Oxford History of the British Empire*, Vol. 5, *Historiography* (1999); Rosemary Hollis, "Great Britain," in Bernard Reich, ed., *The Powers in the Middle East: The Ultimate Strategic Arena* (1987); Frank Brenchley, *Britain and the Middle East: An Economic History* (1989); and

Michael J. Cohen and Martin Kolinsky, eds., *Demise of the British Empire in the Middle East: Britain's Responses to Nationalist Movements, 1943–1955* (1998).

John Darwin, *Britain and Decolonisation: The Retreat from Empire in the Post-War World* (1988), places British Middle Eastern diplomacy in the larger context of a declining world empire. Phillip Darby, *British Defence Policy East of Suez, 1947–1968* (1973) concentrates attention on military strategy, which is often strikingly downplayed in diplomatic history. To give the role of military planning and military planners their due, another good book is Michael J. Cohen, *Fighting World War Three from the Middle East: Allied Contingency Plans, 1945–1954* (1997). This book, as the title indicates, treats both British and American strategic planning during those years. The view of the Middle East as seen by these military planners is, in several respects, quite different from that conveyed by our sources that concentrate on Foreign Office and cabinet (or State Department and president). Among other matters, it places British thinking about Egypt during those years in a different light.

France and the Middle East

Given the long-standing French interest in the Middle East (which, in our definition, includes the Maghrib), the number of works directly or even largely concerned with delineating French foreign policy there is strangely limited. One can mention Christopher M. Andrew and A. S. Kanya-Forstner, *The Climax of French Imperial Expansion, 1914–1924* (1981), which gives considerable attention to the Middle East, or William Shorrock's *French Imperialism in the Middle East: The Failure of Policy in Syria and Lebanon, 1900–1914* (1976), or, for an even earlier period, *France and Ottoman Lebanon, 1861–1914* (1977) by John Spagnolo. World War I diplomacy as viewed and implemented by France is well set out in Jan Karl Tanenbaum, "France and the Arab Middle East, 1914–1920" (1978), with a good bibliography. Covering a later period is *A Tacit Alliance: France and Israel from Suez to the Six-Day War* (1974) by Sylvia Kowitt Crosbie. All of these are, however, rather narrow in focus.

For a broader view of France's Middle Eastern policy, one can now consult Henry Laurens's *Le Royaume impossible: La France et la genèse du monde arabe* (1990) or, for the period of decolonization, Remy Leveau, "Le Moyen Orient" in Françoise de la Serre, Jacques Leruez, and Helen Wallace, eds., *Les Politiques étrangères de la France et de la Grande-Bretagne depuis 1945: L'Inevitable ajustement* (1990), as well as Leveau's "La Mediterranée dans la politique française," (1987). The earlier *La Politique arabe de la France: De de Gaulle à Pompidou* (1973) by Paul Balta and Claudine Rulleau remains useful for that time period.

There is, of course, an important corpus of material on the painful period of French decolonization in the Maghrib, and especially in Algeria, where the brutal war for Algerian independence (1954–1962) almost produced a military putsch in France and did usher in the French Fifth Republic and de Gaulle. It must be recalled that Algeria was juridically a part of France. In this case, separating foreign policy from domestic concerns becomes elusive. From the many books that might be mentioned, perhaps the best for our purposes would be John Talbott, *The War without a Name: France in Algeria, 1954–1962* (1980). For the decolonization in Algeria's neighbors there are the very detailed study by Stephane Bernard, *The Franco-Moroccan Conflict, 1943–1956* (1968, French original 1963), and Charles-André Julien, *Et la Tunisie devint independent, 1951–1957* (1985). Julien, a scholar-activist and early French supporter of the Maghribi nationalists—his earlier *L'Afrique du Nord en marche: Nationalismes musulmans et souveraineté française* (1952, 4th ed. 1972) greatly influenced French and Maghribi public opinion—offers a well-researched study that benefits as well from his intimate knowledge of the principal participants on both the French and the Tunisian side.

The Soviet Union/Russia and the Middle East

Good coverage of Soviet involvement in the Middle East exits. As long ago as 1959, Walter Laqueur wrote *The Soviet Union and the Middle East*. Later studies include Michael Confino and Shimon Shamir, eds., *The USSR and the Middle East* (1973); Oles M. Smolansky, *The Soviet Union and the Arab East under Khrushchev* (1974), and *The USSR and Iraq: The Quest for Influence*, (1991); Hélène Carrère d'Encausse, *La Politique sovietique au Moyen-Orient, 1955–1975* (1975); Robert O. Freedman, *Soviet Policy toward the Middle East since 1970*, 2nd ed. (1978); Adeed Dawisha and Karen Dawisha, eds., *The Soviet Union in the Middle East* (1982); and Alexei Vassiliev, *Russian Policy in the Middle East: From Messianism to Pragmatism* (1993).

Studies of Soviet-Egyptian policy include Alvin Z. Rubinstein, *Red Star on the Nile: The Soviet-Egyptian Influence Relationship since the June War* (1977); Karen Dawisha, *Soviet Foreign Policy toward Egypt* (1979); and Mahrez Mahmoud El Husseini, *Soviet-Egyptian Relations, 1945–1985* (1987).

Galia Golan, an Israeli specialist on Soviet Middle Eastern relations, has written a number of fine works, including *Yom Kippur and After: The Soviet Union and the Middle East Crisis* (1977); *Soviet Middle East Policy under Gorbachev* (1990); and *Soviet Policies in the Middle East from World War Two to Gorbachev* (1990). She even has a post-Soviet book, *Moscow and the Middle East: New Thinking on Regional Conflict* (1992).

Efraim Karsh in his *The Soviet Union and Syria: The Asad Years* (1988) depicts the Soviet-Syrian relationship as being neither a case of the Soviet Union as patron dominating its regional client nor one of Syria manipulating its outside patron. It was what he dubbed "a matter of strategic interdependence."

The United States and the Middle East

A cornucopia of sources is available in this category. Two very good general studies are H. W. Brands, *Into the Labyrinth: The United States and the Middle East, 1945–1993* (1994), and Burton I. Kaufman, *The Arab Middle East and the United States: Inter-Arab Rivalry and Superpower Diplomacy* (1996). Two earlier books on American relations with the Arabs are John S. Badeau, *The American Approach to the Arab World* (1968), and Robert W. Stookey, *America and the Arab States: An Uneasy Encounter* (1975). Badeau's perspective is that of someone who spent a lifetime concerned with the Middle East, first as a missionary, then in academic scholarship, and later as president of the American University in Cairo. President Kennedy then chose him to be U.S. ambassador to Egypt in the 1960s. Stookey also had a combined diplomatic and scholarly career. After some two decades in the U.S. Foreign Service, with postings mainly in the

Middle East, he carved out a second career as a research scholar. Of these four books, only Brands treats Iran and Turkey as well as the Arab states of the east (Mashriq), and none of these books covers the Arab states west of Egypt (the Maghrib) or, for that matter, Sudan to the south.

Seth P. Tillman, *The United States and the Middle East: Interests and Obstacles* (1982) is a good study by a scholar who long served on the staff of the Senate Foreign Relations Committee, and this expertise makes Tillman's chapter 2, "American Interests and the American Political System," especially insightful. Separate chapters concentrate on U.S. relations with Saudi Arabia, Israel, the Palestinians, and the Soviet Union. Written well before the end of the Cold War, the book argues for a less confrontational U.S. approach to the area, as the chapter title "The Soviet Union: Predator or Partner?" suggests.

David Lesch, ed., *The Middle East and the United States: A Historical and Political Reassessment* (1996), has twenty-two articles, all but two treating the period since 1945. Most deal with bilateral relations between the United States and a particular Middle Eastern state (plus two on U.S.-Soviet relations concerning the Middle East).

Robert J. Pranger, "The Dimensions of American Foreign Policy in the Middle East," in Peter J. Chelkowski and Robert J. Panger, eds., *Ideology and Power in the Middle East: Studies in Honor of George Lenczowski* (1988), is a thoughtful essay that weaves together domestic interests, foreign policy, and prevailing ideology to present what might be called the American approach to foreign affairs.

America's Middle East policy is closely tied to the Arab-Israeli confrontation. Two books that cover the domestic dimension of U.S. policy on this issue well are George Lenczowski, *American Presidents and the Middle East* (1990), and Steven L. Spiegel, *The Other Arab-Israeli Conflict: Making America's Middle Eastern Policy from Truman to Reagan* (1985). Both trace the continuity or change in American policy toward the Middle East (concentrating on the Arab-Israeli confrontation) according to the different presidential administrations; they offer different evaluations, with Lenczowski critical of the American "tilt" in favor of Israel.

Among the many other books and articles on the American role in the Arab-Israeli confrontation, two books by William B. Quandt can be recommended. One, *Camp David: Peacemaking and Politics* (1986), describes in great detail the American-brokered negotiations leading to Egypt-Israeli peace. The other, *Peace Process: American Diplomacy and the Arab-Israeli Conflict since 1967* (1993), covers the broad lines of developments since 1967.

That Israel is a major factor in the shaping of American relations with the Middle East—deplored by some, supported by others—must surely be accepted by all. Although some have sought to argue the case for Israel as a strategic asset, the prevailing case for American support of Israel rests on normative rather than realist foundations—support for a fellow democracy, redressing the wrongs of anti-Semitism and the horrors of the Holocaust, plus the religious imperative of Zionism as well as its variant among those who could be called Christian Zionists. Tracing the historical roots of American concern about Israel with empathy and objectivity is Peter Grose's *Israel in the Mind of America* (1984).

Bernard Reich has written extensively on American-Israeli relations. His books include *Quest for Peace: United States-Israel Relations and the Arab-Israeli Conflict* (1977), *The United States and Israel: Influence in the Special Relationship* (1984) and, more recently, *Securing the Covenant: United States-Israel Relations after the Cold War* (1995). Another book that deserves mention is David Schoenbaum, *The United States and the State of Israel* (1993).

Many more works concerning U.S.-Israeli relations could be listed, but for present purposes only one more source need be added. This is "Fifty Years of U.S.-Israeli Relations: A Round Table" in the journal *Diplomatic History* 22/1 (Spring 1998). The articles by Yaacov Simon-Bar-Tov, Peter Hahn, and David Schoenbaum offer sound interpretations with, as well, many references that provide a historiographic review.

A selection of books that treat U.S. relations with other individual Middle Eastern states include, for Iran, Richard W. Cottam, *Iran and the United States: A Cold War Case Study* (1988), and James Bill, *The Eagle and the Lion: The Tragedy of American-Iranian Relations* (1988), both severely critical of American policy toward Iran. Barry Rubin's *Paved with Good Intentions: The American Experience and Iran* (1980), as the title suggests, is only slightly less so.

On U.S. relations with Turkey, one can consult George S. Harris, *Troubled Alliance: Turkish-American Problems in Historical Perspective, 1945–1971* (1972), and Dankwart A. Rustow's more recent *Turkey: America's Forgotten Ally* (1987), which contains a useful bibliographical essay.

An interesting monograph on American-Egyptian relations that illustrates the use of economic aid as a diplomatic instrument is William J. Burns, *Economic Aid and American Policy toward Egypt, 1955–1981* (1985). The Egyptian scholar Muhammad Abd-el-Wahab Sayed-Ahmed has exploited both Egyptian and American sources to present a balanced account of *Nasser and American Foreign Policy, 1952–1956* (1989).

A good study of American-Tunisian relations is Samya el-Machat, *Les Etats-Unis et la Tunisie: De l'ambiguïté à l'entente, 1945–1959* (1996). Alan Dowty has adopted the approach used by Michael Brecher in his studies of Israeli decision making in times of crisis by studying American responses at such times. His *Middle East Crisis: U.S. Decision-Making in 1958, 1970, and 1973* (1984) examines the American diplomatic responses to the 1958 Lebanese civil war, the 1970 crisis in Jordan that pitted the Hashimite regime against the P.L.O., and the 1973 Ramadan/Yom Kippur War.

Finally, on this subject of American involvement in the Middle East, attention is called to a first-rate historiographic essay on just this subject, "Gideon's Band: America and the Middle East since 1945" by Douglas Little (1994). The book compiled by Sanford R. Silverburg and Bernard Reich, *U.S. Foreign Relations with the Middle East and North Africa: A Bibliography* (1994) is also recommended. Fortunately, this book includes the Maghrib in its coverage.

The Arab-Israeli Confrontation

Even though more works on this subject than on any other have already been listed above under several different rubrics, this issue in Middle Eastern international relations deserves its own listing, if only to call attention to the four-volume study called *Futile Diplomacy* by Neil Caplan: Vol. 1, *Early Arab-Zionist Negotiation Attempts, 1913–1931* (1983);

Vol. 2, *Arab-Zionists and the End of the Mandate* (1986); Vol. 3, *The United Nations, the Great Powers, and Middle East Peacemaking, 1948–1954* (1997); and Vol. 4, *Operation Alpha and the Failure of Anglo-American Coercive Diplomacy in the Arab-Israeli Conflict* (1997). The Arab-Israeli confrontation is the Middle Eastern diplomatic issue that, more than any other, has persistently embroiled virtually all states of the region and engaged the outside great powers. Indeed, in many ways the diplomatic history of the Middle East can be organized around multipolar, long-lived Arab-Israeli confrontation, just as that area's history in the nineteenth century can be discussed in terms of the Eastern Question. It is, accordingly, useful to have an in-depth narrative of these diplomatic developments from the earliest days through 1956. Caplan and Laura Zittrain Eisenberg have added another volume that provides briefer treatments of Arab-Israeli diplomacy from the 1970s to the 1990s, *Negotiating Arab-Israeli Peace: Patterns, Problems, Possibilities* (1998).

Oil and the Middle East

The international politics of oil is of such importance for the study of the modern Middle East that we perhaps need to be reminded that European diplomatic jousting over control of the area predated by over a century the development of the Middle Eastern oil industry. Still, the importance of fossil fuels clearly intensifies and also changes the nature of Middle Eastern diplomacy. A good if somewhat sensational overview is Leonard Mosley, *Power Play: Oil in the Middle East* (1973). Weightier in every sense of the word (876 pages) is Daniel Yergin, *The Prize: The Epic Quest for Oil, Money and Power* (1991), an eminently informed and perceptive work that has the advantage of being a real page turner. The adjective "epic" in the title is well justified. Yergin's extensive bibliography can lead the reader to other works on this general subject.

One of the grand old men of international oil studies, Walter Levy, has a general work, *Oil Strategy and Politics, 1941–1981* (1982), and the even earlier work by George Stocking, *Middle East Oil: A Study in Political and Economic Controversy* (1970) offers a thoughtful and readily accessible guide to, as the title indicates, the mix of political and economic issues.

Oil was directly involved in the run-up to the American-British sponsored coup that overthrew Muhammad Musaddiq and restored the shah to his throne in 1953. See for this issue certain of the chapters and the many references cited in James A. Bill and Wm. Roger Louis, eds., *Musaddiq, Iranian Nationalism, and Oil* (1988).

For American oil policy in the decade of the 1940s, there are two monographs: Aaron David Miller, *Search for Security: Saudi Arabian Oil and American Foreign Policy, 1939–1949* (1980), and Michael B. Stoff, *Oil, War and American Security: The Search for a National Policy on Foreign Oil, 1941–1947* (1980). Covering a longer time span is Irving H. Anderson, *Aramco, the United States and Saudi Arabia: A Study in the Dynamics of Foreign Oil Policy, 1933–1950* (1981).

The Organization of Petroleum Exporting Countries (OPEC) represents one of the most influential interstate organizations to be created in the Middle East, indeed in the entire third world. For the story of OPEC there are many sources. It is, of course, given due attention in Yergin's *The Prize*. A good short account that deftly places OPEC in the larger context of Middle East oil in general is chapter 10, "Petroleum:

The Control of a Natural Resource," in Alasdair Drysdale and Gerald H. Blake, *The Middle East and North Africa: A Political Geography* (1985).

Middle Eastern Wars

If, as Clausewitz teaches us, war is the continuation of politics by other means, then this is the case, a fortiori, for wars as the continuation of foreign policies. Wars may be seen as sharply etched case studies that reveal what the contending countries regard as their basic interests. Wars, also, with their winners and losers, force upon states a reconsideration of their strategies and policies. For the Middle East, alas, we have all too many cases to be studied.

There are, first and foremost, the six different Arab-Israeli wars—1948, the Suez War of 1956, the Six-Day War of June 1967, the 1969–1970 Egyptian-Israeli War of Attrition, the October 1973 (Ramadan or Yom Kippur) War, and the 1982 Israeli invasion of Lebanon. All of these wars involved not only Israel and its neighbors but to a considerable extent the entire Middle East and certainly the great powers, especially the two Cold War contenders, the United States and the Soviet Union. The history of these wars (as of the other Middle Eastern wars to be noted) figures in many of the works already cited. Here will be added a few additional titles that concentrate more directly on one or another of these six wars.

For 1948, one can consult the several articles in Wm. Roger Louis and Robert W. Stookey, eds., *The End of the Palestine Mandate* (1986), and Avi Shlaim, *The Politics of Partition: King Abdullah, the Zionists and Palestine, 1921–1951* (1990, earlier published in 1988 as *Collusion across the Jordan*).

For the Suez War there are two good collected works: Wm. Roger Louis and Roger Owen, eds., *Suez 1956: The Crisis and Its Consequences* (1989), and *The Suez-Sinai Crisis: A Retrospective* (1990), edited by Ilan Troen and Moshe Shemesh. Among the many single-author studies of this war, that by Keith Kyle, *The Suez Conflict: Thirty Years After* (1989), is the most recent and, many would agree, the best.

The Six-Day War: A Retrospective (1996), edited by Richard B. Parker, brought together several people who had held official positions in their countries before and during that war to meet with academic scholars who specialize on this subject. The result is a many-sided overview with considerable agreement on many of the points, but remaining differences as well. A useful annotated bibliography can direct the reader to additional readings and varying interpretations. Before we move on to the wars after 1967, the now over thirty-year-old work by Nadav Safran, *From War to War: The Arab-Israeli Confrontation, 1948–1967* (1969) should be mentioned. We now know much more about these wars of 1948, 1956, and 1967, but Safran's work stands up very well as a serious, hard-eyed appraisal in the realist mode of international relations studies.

Two strong monographs on the Egyptian-Israeli War of Attrition are Yaacov Bar-Siman-Tov, *The Israeli-Egyptian War of Attrition, 1969–1970: A Case Study of Limited Local War* (1980), and David Korn, *Stalemate: The War of Attrition and Great Power Diplomacy in the Middle East, 1967–1970* (1992).

Richard B. Parker has also edited a follow-up study on the October War that is now in press: *The October War: A Retrospective.* Kenneth W. Stein, *Heroic Diplomacy: Sadat,*

Kissinger, Carter, Begin and the Quest for Arab-Israeli Peace (1999) concentrates on the period of the October War and the following years leading up to the 1979 Egyptian-Israeli peace treaty. Stein has, as well, a rich, up-to-date bibliographical listing.

Studies on the 1982 Israeli invasion of Lebanon include Ze'ev Schiff and Ehud Ya'ari, *Israel's Lebanon War* (1984); Geoffrey Kemp, "Lessons of Lebanon: A Guideline for Future U.S. Policy" (1988); and the entire issue of the *Middle East Journal* 8/2 (Spring 1984), with articles by Jim Muir, Ze'ev Schiff, Adeed Dawisha, William B. Quandt, Rashid Khalidi, and Marius K. Deeb.

On the Iran-Iraq war there is Majid Khadduri, *The Gulf War: The Origins and Implications of the Iraq-Iran Conflict* (1988), which may be balanced by Farhang Rajaee, ed., *The Iran-Iraq War: The Politics of Aggression* (1993). Other studies are Anthony H. Cordesman, *The Iran-Iraq War and Western Security, 1984–1987: Strategic Implications and Policy Options* (1987); Stephen C. Pelletiere, *The Iran-Iraq War: Chaos in a Vacuum* (1992); and Efraim Karsh, ed., *The Iran-Iraq War: Impact and Implications* (1989).

For the Gulf War resulting from Iraq's invasion of Kuwait, a splendid analysis and narrative history is *The Gulf Conflict 1990–1991: Diplomacy and War in the New World Order* (1993) by Lawrence Freedman and Efraim Karsh. Useful articles are also contained in *The Iraqi Aggression against Kuwait: Strategic Lessons and Implications for Europe* (1996), edited by Wolfgang Danspeckgruber and Charles R. H. Tripp. My review article "Shield and Sword in the Desert" (1994) discusses a wide variety of other sources.

There have been other Middle Eastern conflicts, including civil wars—in Algeria in early 1990s; in the Sudan off and on since before independence in 1956; in Lebanon from a decade and a half after 1975; and in Yemen from 1962 to 1970. Moreover, decolonization brought in its wake one long-lived and bitter war, in Algeria from 1954 to 1962. These struggles—as always in the Middle East—attracted the attention of foreign powers. For example, the Lebanese war set in motion the series of events leading to the Israeli invasion in 1982, not to mention earlier Syrian intervention. The Yemen civil war involved Egypt, which intervened on the side of the Republicans against the imam's forces supported by Saudi Arabia. The United States and Britain were, as well, hovering in the background. For the diplomatic dimension of one such case—the Yemeni conflict—a former Saudi official, Saeed M. Badeeb, has written a useful appraisal in his *The Saudi-Egyptian Conflict over North Yemen, 1962–1970* (1986).

The important, overarching war for the years after the Second World War was, of course, the Cold War (which happily for all never became hot). Many of the books already cited, especially the works on United States and Soviet policies in the Middle East, devote considerable attention to the Cold War dimension, but a few not yet noted can be added. One might begin with Bruce R. Kuniholm's *The Origins of the Cold War in the Near East: Great Power Conflict and Diplomacy in Iran, Turkey and Greece* (1980), a solid and detailed study of those immediate post-World War II years. See also Barry Rubin, *The Great Powers in the Middle East, 1941–1947: The Road to the Cold War* (1980), which sets the roots of the Cold War even further back in time.

John C. Campbell, *Defense of the Middle East: Problems of American Policy*, first published in 1958 with a second edition in 1960, stands out as a good example of establishment

U.S. thinking on the Middle East in the middle period of the Cold War. The book stems from a Council on Foreign Relations study group set up in 1954. Campbell's later article "The Soviet Union in the Middle East" (1978) is in the same vein. Another representative book is J. C. Hurewitz, ed., *Soviet-American Rivalry in the Middle East* (1969). Most such studies, and many others that could be mentioned, embraced the notion that containment as buttressed by deterrence was the appropriate American policy toward the Soviet Union in the Middle East, as elsewhere.

Now, after the end of the Cold War, some revisionist thinking concerning the United States and the Soviet Union in the Middle East is emerging. Richard Ned Lebow and Janice Gross Stein, in their *We All Lost the Cold War* (1994), use the 1962 Cuban missile crisis and the October 1973 Arab-Israeli war as case studies. "Deterrence and its twin strategy of compellence," they write, "have been given credit for restraining Soviet aggression, for convincing Khrushchev to withdraw Soviet missiles from Cuba, for preventing Soviet military intervention in the Middle East in 1973, and for the collapse of the Soviet empire. This book challenges all of these claims" (p. ix).

Charles A. Kupchan, in "American Globalism in the Middle East: The Roots of Regional Security Policy" (1988–1989), suggests an American exaggeration of the Soviet threat in the Middle East. Graham E. Fuller, in "The Middle East in US-Soviet Relations" (1990), offers an interesting review just at the time when, as he archly put it, "Washington has been deprived of the trusty analytical tool that served policymakers so well for decades: *cherchez les Russes*" (p. 418). Fawaz Gerges, in *The Superpowers and the Middle East: Regional and International Politics, 1955–1967* (1994), firmly anchors the superpower rivalry in the regional context and shows, inter alia, that the superpowers assumed that patrons often could not control their would-be clients in the Middle East.

In short, the debate on the Cold War in the Middle East, just like the debate on the Cold War in general, revolves around the question of which side was more responsible for starting the Cold War and for keeping it going. A corollary question Americans pose is whether their Middle Eastern policy paid too much attention to their Soviet rival and not enough to the situation in the Middle East itself. Now, with the Soviet material becoming available and the Cold War itself having faded into history, such questions can be reviewed to good effect.

Middle Eastern Diplomacy: A Distinctive Pattern?

A persistent theme underlying this book with its description of so many different states, Middle Eastern and otherwise, is that Middle East diplomacy is distinctive. Whether this justifies labeling the interaction of states in this region as an international relations subsystem can be argued, but it is believed that the separate studies of states presented in this book serve, among other purposes, to describe the special approach to international relations—the diplomatic culture—found in the Middle East. Among the works that address this issue more directly the following may be suggested: Leonard Binder, "The Middle East as a Subordinate International System," *World Politics* (April 1958), later included in his book *The Ideological Revolution in the Middle East* (1964); and Tariq Y. Ismael, "The Middle East: A Subordinate System in Global Politics" (1974). Fouad

Ajami wrote a strong rebuttal of the latter in "The Middle East: Important for the Wrong Reasons" (1975).

Other studies that address the Middle East as an international relations system are several articles in Moshe Efrat and Jacob Bercovitch, eds., *Superpowers and Client States in the Middle East: The Imbalance of Influence* (1991), and Michael Brecher, "The Middle Eastern Subordinate System and Its Impact on Israel's Foreign Policy" (1969).

Especially useful in demonstrating the kaleidoscopic nature of Middle Eastern diplomacy, with its many different states and contending forces within states, forming changing alliances but all within a certain rather fixed structure of possible patterns or combinations, are two books that have become classics in this field. They are Malcolm Kerr, *The Arab Cold War: Gamal `Abd al-Nasir and His Rivals, 1958–1970*, 3rd ed. (1971), and Patrick Seale, *The Struggle for Syria: A Study in Post-War Arab Politics, 1945–1959* (1965, reissued 1986). Stephen Walt in his *The Origins of Alliances* (1987) deals with the pattern of alliances and alignments in the Middle East from 1955 to 1979, and Michael N. Barnett, *Dialogues in Arab Politics: Negotiations in Regional Order* (1998), seeks to determine the systemic pattern of inter-Arab politics.

Memoirs of Statesmen

Alexis de Tocqueville, with his flair for studied ambiguity, once wrote, "I have come across men of letters who have written history without taking part in public affairs, and politicians who have concerned themselves with producing events without thinking about them. I have observed that the first are always inclined to find general causes, whereas the second, living in the midst of disconnected daily facts, are prone to imagine that everything is attributable to particular incidents, and that the wires they pull are the same as those that move the world. It is to be presumed that both are equally deceived."

At least those of us not "producing events" must not be deceived about the importance of the individual political player, whether king, president or prime minister, diplomat or warrior, cabinet minister or clerk. There are special problems in relying on the memoirs of those involved, of course, especially the memoirs of the great, and even more those who write while still politically active. For example, it is almost certain that Golda Meir's autobiography was ghostwritten, and the same may be said of Nasir's *Philosophy of the Revolution*. Yet presumably those individuals read what someone else wrote, and signed off on the work as representing the public statement they wanted to present. Memoirs, plus public archival records, for all their difficulties, add up to the best available substitute for "being there." Moreover, many of them are really quite readable, recreating the drama of involvement in stirring events. A weary cynic might add that they read like good fiction because… . That, however, would be going too far.

The available memoirs of those who have played the diplomatic game in the modern Middle East are too many to list. For the United States alone, almost every president and secretary of state has left memoirs that, while varying greatly in detail, offer useful insights on Middle Eastern diplomacy. Indeed, they can be "deconstructed" to reveal much more than the authors had in mind. For example, President

Nixon, in writing of the 1970 crisis in Jordan that pitted King Husayn against the P.L.O. supported by Syria, avers, "We could not allow Hussein to be overthrown by a Soviet-inspired insurrection," but there is no evidence that Syrian intervention was Soviet inspired. It seems established that the crisis was sparked by a dissident element within the P.L.O., and that the Syrians acted on their own. Or one might read Dean Acheson's depiction of Muhammad Musaddiq in his *Present at the Creation* to sense that U.S. officials deemed him an unreliable interlocutor.

Memoirs of participants in modern Middle Eastern diplomacy exist in great number, including not only those of Western leaders involved in Middle Eastern diplomacy but those of many Middle Easterners as well. The latter are, of course, not always available in English translations. Here then is a deserved research bonus for native speakers of Arabic, Hebrew, Persian, or Turkish, or for those non-native speakers who have toiled to learn these languages.

The memoirs of such figures as Anwar Sadat, David Ben-Gurion, King Abdullah of Jordan and his grandson King Husayn, Muhammd Riza Shah, Anthony Eden, Winston Churchill, and Charles de Gaulle, plus the different American presidents and secretaries of state, are well known and often cited, but let a random sampling of memoirs—not just of heads of states and foreign ministers but of other important players in the diplomatic game just a step or so down the pyramid of power—suggest the possibilities.

Parker T. Hart, whose distinguished diplomatic career in the Middle East included postings in Saudi Arabia from 1944 to 1946, from 1949 to 1951, and then as American ambassador to Saudi Arabia from 1961 to 1965, has written an account based on his personal experience in *Saudi Arabia and the United States: Birth of a Security Partnership* (1998).

Two senior Israeli diplomats who held top positions in their foreign service have written accounts drawing on their own personal experience. These books, by Walter Eytan—*The First Ten Years: A Diplomatic History of Israel* (1958)—and Gideon Rafael—*Destination Peace: Three Decades of Israeli Foreign Policy* (1981)—together provide an intimate, from-the-top description of Israeli diplomacy during that country's first several decades.

Evelyn Shuckburgh was principal private secretary to the British foreign minister beginning in 1951 and from 1954 to 1956, and was the minister responsible for Middle Eastern policies in the Foreign Office. His *Descent to Suez: Foreign Office Diaries, 1951–1956* (1986) offers a thoughtful insider's account of those years leading up to the Suez War.

Another very interesting book based on diary entries, available only in Arabic, is *Mudhakkirat `Abd al-Latif al-Baghdadi* (Memoirs of `Abd al-Latif al-Baghdadi) (1977). An original member of the Free Officers who seized power in 1952, Baghdadi was later eased out of office but remained in close touch with Nasir. The diary format he uses enhances the reconstruction of the thinking that went into Egyptian diplomacy during those years. Another of the early Free Officers who has written a useful memoir, again only available in Arabic, is Khalid Muhyi al-Din, *Wa al-an atakallim* (Now I Speak) (1992). There are also a number of memoirs of top Egyptian diplomats available in

English, such as Mahmoud Riad's *The Struggle for Peace in the Middle East* (1981), or Ismail Fahmy's *Negotiating for Peace in the Middle East* (1983), which is interesting for its criticism of Sadat's negotiating strategy after the October 1973 war.

Lawrence Grafftey-Smith was a British diplomat who served in parts of the Middle East during the first half of the twentieth century. He writes in *Bright Levant* (1970) about his experiences in the Arabia of Sharif Husayn, Egypt in the 1920s, and much more, with a puckish wit that veils important insights.

Finally, a word about Henry Kissinger's two-volume memoirs. *White House Years* (1979) and *Years of Upheaval* (1982) contain many chapters directly concerned with America's Middle Eastern diplomacy during the 1970s, and Kissinger interlaces his accounts of his diplomacy with ruminations on the conduct of diplomacy in general—what works and what does not. One can agree or disagree with his policies or his interpretation of the craft of diplomacy, but what amounts to an informed diplomatic memoir and textbook on diplomacy can never be uninteresting.

Bibliography

Abd al-Jabar, Faleh. "The Reconstruction and Deconstruction of Iraq's Tribes: Tribalism under Patrimonial Totalitarianism." Unpublished paper, School of Oriental and African Studies, London, 1999.

Abdel-Malek, Anouar. *Idéologie et renaissance nationale: L'Egypte moderne*. Paris: Editions Anthropos, 1969.

Abun-Nasr, Jamil M. *A History of the Maghrib*. 3rd ed. Cambridge and New York: Cambridge University Press, 1987.

Ahmad, Ahmad Yousef. "The Dialectics of Domestic Environment and Role Performance; in the Foreign Policy of Iraq." In Korany and Dessouki, *Foreign Policies*, pp. 186–215.

Ajami, Fouad. "The End of Pan-Arabism." *Foreign Affairs* 57/2 (1978–1979): 355–73.

———. "The Middle East: Important for the Wrong Reasons." *Journal of International Affairs* 29/1 (Spring 1975): 84–86.

Alani, Mustafa M. *Operation Vantage: British Military Intervention in Kuwait 1961*. Surbiton, Surrey, England: LAAM, 1990.

al-Alawi, Hassan. *al-Shi`ah wal-Dawlah-l-Qawmiyyah fi-l-Iraq* (Shi`ism and the National State in Iraq) *1914–1990*. 2nd ed. London: Dar al-Zawra', 1990.

Allen, Calvin H., Jr. *Oman*. Boulder, CO: Westview, 1987.

Anderson, Irving H. *Aramco, the United States and Saudi Arabia: A Study in the Dynamics of Foreign Oil Policy, 1933–1950*. Princeton, NJ: Princeton University Press, 1981.

Anderson, M. S. *The Eastern Question, 1774–1923: A Study in International Relations*. London: Macmillan, 1966.

Andrew, Christopher M., and A. S. Kanya-Forstner. *The Climax of French Imperial Expansion, 1914–1924*. Stanford, CA: Stanford University Press, 1981.

327

Anthony, John Duke. *Arab States of the Lower Gulf: People, Politics, Petroleum*. Washington, D.C: Middle East Institute, 1975.

Arcayürek, Cüneyt, *Cüneyt Arcayürek Açıklıyor—4: Yeni Demokrasi Yeni Arayışlar: 1960–1965* (Cüneyt Arcayürek Explains—4: New Democracy, New Directions, 1960–1965). 2nd ed. Ankara: Bilgi Yayınevi, 1985.

———. *Cüneyt Arcayürek Açıklıyor—5: Demirel Dönemi: 12 Mart Darbesi: 1965–1971* (The Demirel Era: The March 12 Intervention, 1965–1971). 3rd ed. Ankara: Bilgi Yayınevi, 1992.

———. *Cüneyt Arcayürek Açıklıyor—10: Demokrasi Dur, 12 Eylül 1980* (The Halt to Democracy: April–September 1980). Ankara: Bilgi Yayınevi, 1986.

Arnold, Guy. *The Maverick State: Gaddafi and the New World Order*. London: Cassell, 1996.

Assiri, Abdul-Reda. *Kuwait's Foreign Policy: City-State in World Politics*. Boulder, CO: Westview, 1990.

Aydin, Mustafa. *Turkey at the Threshold of the 21st Century: Global Encounters and/vs Regional Alternatives*. Ankara: International Relations Foundation, 1998.

Aydin, Mustafa, and M. Nail Alkan, eds. *An Extensive Bibliography of Studies in English, German and French on Turkish Foreign Policy (1923–1997)*. Ankara: Center for Strategic Research, Ministry of Foreign Affairs, August 1997.

Aykan, Mahmut Bali. *Türkiye'nin Kuveyt Krizi (1990–1991) Politikası: 1998 Yılından Geriye Yönelik Bir Yeniden Değerlendirme* (Turkey's Kuwait Crisis Politics [1990–1991]: A Reexamination Looking Back from 1998). Ankara: Dış Politika Enstitusu, 1998.

Badeau, John S. *The American Approach to the Arab World*. New York: Harper & Row, 1968.

Badeeb, Saeed M. *The Saudi-Egyptian Conflict over North Yemen, 1962–1970*. Boulder, CO: Westview Press, 1986.

al-Baghdadi, `Abd al-Latif. *Mudhakkirat `Abd al-Latif al-Baghdadi* (Memoirs of `Abd al-Latif al-Baghdadi). 2 vols. Cairo: al-Maktab al-Masri al-Hadith, 1977.

Baker, James A. III, with Thomas M. DeFrank. *The Politics of Diplomacy: Revolution, War and Peace, 1989–1992*. New York: G. P. Putnam's Sons, 1995.

Ball, George W. *The Past Has Another Pattern: Memoirs*. New York: W. W. Norton, 1982.

Ball, Nicole. *Security and Economy in the Third World*. Princeton, NJ: Princeton University Press, 1988.

Balta, Paul, and Claudine Rulleau. *La Politique arabe de la France: De de Gaulle à Pompidou*. Paris: Sindbad, 1973.

Bamberg, J. H. *The History of the British Petroleum Company*. Vol. 2, *The Anglo-Iranian Years, 1928–1954*. Cambridge and New York: Cambridge University Press, 1994.

Baram, Amatzia. *Building toward Crisis: Saddam Husayn's Strategy for Survival*. Washington, DC: Washington Institute for Near East Policy, 1998.

———. *Culture, History and Ideology in the Formation of Ba`thist Iraq, 1968–1989*. New York: St. Martin's Press, 1991.

———. "Neo-Tribalism in Iraq: Saddam Husayn's Tribal Policies, 1991–1995." *International Journal of Middle East Studies* 29/1 (February 1997), 1–31.

Bard, Mitchell. *The Water's Edge and Beyond: Defining the Limits to Domestic Influence on United States Middle East Policy*. New Brunswick, NJ: Transaction Publishers, 1991.

Barnett, Michael N. *Dialogues in Arab Politics: Negotiations in Regional Order*. New York: Columbia University Press, 1998.

Bar-Siman-Tov, Yaacov. *The Israeli-Egyptian War of Attrition, 1969–1970: A Case Study of Limited Local War*. New York: Columbia University Press, 1980.

Batatu, Hanna. *The Old Social Classes and Revolutionary Movements of Iraq*. Princeton, NJ: Princeton University Press, 1978.

al-Bazzaz, Sa`d. *Harb Talidu Ukhra* (One War Gives Birth to Another). Amman: al-Ahliyah lil-Nashr wa-al-Tawzi, 1993.

Belen, Fahri. *Demokrasinden Diktatörlüğe: On Senelik Siyasi Hayatımıza Dair Tenkit ve Tahliller* (From Democracy to Dictatorship: Ten Years of Our Political Life, Criticism and Analysis). Istanbul, 1960.

Bernard, Stephane. *The Franco-Moroccan Conflict, 1943–1956*. New Haven, CT: Yale University Press, 1968. French original 1963.

Bialer, Uri. *Between East and West: Israel's Foreign Policy Orientation, 1948–1956*. Cambridge and New York: Cambridge University Press, 1990.

Bidwell, Robin. *The Two Yemens*. Harlow, Essex: Longman; Boulder, CO: Westview Press, 1983.

Bill, James. *The Eagle and the Lion: The Tragedy of American-Iranian Relations*. New Haven, CT: Yale University Press, 1988.

Bill, James A., and Wm. Roger Louis, eds. *Musaddiq, Iranian Nationalism, and Oil*. Austin, TX: University of Texas Press, 1988.

bin Sultan, General Khaled, with Patrick Seale. *Desert Warrior*. New York: HarperCollins, 1995.

Binder, Leonard. "The Middle East as a Subordinate International System." *World Politics* (April 1958); also in his *The Ideological Revolution in the Middle East*. New York: John Wiley & Sons, 1964, pp. 254–78.

Birand, Mehmet Ali. *The Generals' Coup in Turkey: An Inside Story of 12 September 1980*. Translated by M. A. Dikerdem. London: Brassey's Defence Publishers, 1987.

———. *30 Sıcak Gün* (30 Hot Days). 10th ed. Istanbul: Milliyet Yayınları, 1987.

Bovill, E. W. *The Golden Trade of the Moors*. Oxford University Press, 1958.

Brand, Laurie A. "In the Beginning Was the State: The Quest for Civil Society in Jordan." In Augustus Richard Norton, ed., *Civil Society in the Middle East*. Vol. 1. Leiden & New York: Brill, 1995, pp. 148–85.

———. *Jordan's Inter-Arab Relations: The Political Economy of Alliance Making*. New York: Columbia University Press, 1994.

———. "Liberalization and Changing Political Coalitions: The Bases of Jordan's 1990–91 Gulf Crisis Policy." *Jerusalem Journal of International Relations* 13/4 (1991): 1–46.

Brands, H. W. *Into the Labyrinth: The United States and the Middle East, 1945–1993*. New York: McGraw Hill, 1994.

Brecher, Michael. *Decisions in Crisis, 1967 and 1973*. Berkeley and Los Angeles, CA: University of California Press, 1980.

———. *Decisions in Israel's Foreign Policy*. New Haven, CT: Yale University Press, 1976.

———. *The Foreign Policy System of Israel: Setting, Images, Process*. New Haven, CT: Yale University Press, 1972.

———. "The Middle Eastern Subordinate System and Its Impact on Israel's Foreign Policy." *International Studies Quarterly* 13 (June 1969): 117–89.

Brenchley, Frank. *Britain and the Middle East: An Economic History*. London: Lester Crook Academic Pub., 1989.

Britannica Book of the Year 1992, 1999, and 2000.

Brown, L. Carl. *International Politics and the Middle East: Old Rules, Dangerous Game*. Princeton, NJ: Princeton University Press, 1984.

———. "Nasser and the June 1967 War: Plan or Improvisation?" In S. Seikaly, R. Baalbaki, and P. Dodd, eds., *Quest for Understanding*. Beirut: American University of Beirut Press, 1991, pp. 119–37.

———. "Shield and Sword in the Desert." *International History Review* 16/1 (February 1994): 92–113.

———. "State of Grace? Rethinking Israel's Founding Myths." *Foreign Affairs* 77/4 (July/August 1998): 90–95.

Bulloch, John. *The Gulf: A Portrait of Kuwait, Qatar, Bahrain and the UAE*. London: Century Pub., 1984.

Bullock, Alan, *Ernest Bevin: Foreign Secretary, 1945–1951*. New York: Norton, 1983.

Burke, Edmund III. "Two Critics of French Rule in Algeria: Ismail Urbain and Frantz Fanon." In L. Carl Brown and Matthew S. Gordon, eds., *Franco-Arab Encounters*. Beirut: American University of Beirut Press, 1996, pp. 329–44.

Burns, William J. *Economic Aid and American Policy toward Egypt, 1955–1981*. Albany, NY: State University of New York Press, 1985.

Burrowes, Robert D. "The Republic of Yemen." In Michael C. Hudson, ed., *Middle East Dilemma: The Politics and Economics of Arab Integration*. New York: Columbia University Press, 1999, pp. 187–213.

Burrows, Bernard. *Footnotes in the Sand: The Gulf in Transition, 1953–1958*. Salisbury, Wiltshire: Michael Russell, 1990.

Busch, Briton Cooper. *Britain and the Persian Gulf, 1894–1914*. Berkeley and Los Angeles, CA: University of California Press, 1967.

——. *Britain, India and the Arabs, 1914–1921*. Berkeley and Los Angeles, CA: University of California Press, 1971.

——. *Mudros to Lausanne, 1918–1923*. Albany, NY: State University of New York Press, 1976.

Callahan, Raymond A. *Churchill: Retreat from Empire*. Wilmington, DE: Scholarly Resources, 1984.

Campbell, John C. *Defense of the Middle East: Problems of American Policy*. New York: Harper & Bros., 1958; 2nd ed., 1960.

——. "The Soviet Union in the Middle East." *Middle East Journal* 32/1 (Winter 1978): 1–12.

Caplan, Neil. *Futile Diplomacy*, Vol. 1, *Early Arab-Zionist Negotiation Attempts, 1913–1931*. London: Frank Cass, 1983.

——. *Futile Diplomacy*, Vol. 2, *Arab-Zionist Negotiations and the End of the Mandate*. London: Frank Cass, 1986.

——. *Futile Diplomacy*, Vol. 3, *The United Nations, the Great Powers, and Middle East Peacemaking, 1948–1954*. London: Frank Cass, 1997.

——. *Futile Diplomacy*, Vol. 4, *Operation Alpha and the Failure of Anglo-American Coercive Diplomacy in the Arab-Israeli Conflict*. London: Frank Cass, 1997.

Caplan, Neil, and Laura Zittrain Eisenberg. *Negotiating Arab-Israeli Peace: Patterns, Problems, Possibilities*. Bloomington, IN: Indiana University Press, 1998.

Carrère d'Encausse, Hélène. *La Politique sovietique au Moyen-Orient, 1955–1975*. Paris: Presses de la Fondation nationale des sciences politiques, 1975.

Celik, Yesemin. *Contemporary Turkish Foreign Policy*. London: Praeger, 1999.

Centre for Global Energy Studies. "Oil Production Capacity in the Gulf," Vol. 4, "Iraq," Section 3, "Politics, Economics and Oil Policy." Unpublished paper. London, 1997.

Chang, King-yuh. "The United Nations and Decolonization: The Case of Southern Yemen." *International Organization* 26/1 (Winter 1972): 171–204.

Chaudhry, Kiren Aziz. "On the Way to Market: Economic Liberalization and Iraq's Invasion of Kuwait." *Middle East Report* 170 (May–June, 1991).

Chubin, Shahram, and Charles Tripp. *Iran and Iraq at War*. Boulder, CO: Westview, 1988.

Cleveland, William L. *A History of the Modern Middle East*. 2nd ed. Boulder, CO: Westview, 2000.

Clover, Charles. "Dreams of the Eurasian Heartland: The Reemergence of Geopolitics." *Foreign Affairs* 78/2 (March/April 1999): 9–13.

Cobban, Helena. *The Superpowers and the Syrian-Israeli Conflict: Beyond Crisis Management?* New York: Praeger, 1991.

Cohen, Avner. *Israel and the Bomb*. New York: Columbia University Press, 1998.

Cohen, Michael J. *Fighting World War Three from the Middle East: Allied Contingency Plans, 1945–1954*. London: Frank Cass, 1997.

Cohen, Michael J., and Martin Kolinsky, eds. *Demise of the British Empire in the Middle East: Britain's Response to Nationalist Movements, 1943–1955*. London: Frank Cass, 1998.

Confino, Michael, and Shimon Shamir, eds. *The USSR and the Middle East*. New York: J. Wiley, 1973.

Cordesman, Anthony H. *Bahrain, Oman, Qatar, and the UAE: Challenges of Security*. Boulder, CO: Westview, 1997.

——. *The Iran-Iraq War and Western Security, 1984–1987: Strategic Implications and Policy Options*. London: Jane's, 1987.

Cottam, Richard W. *Iran and the United States: A Cold War Case Study*. Pittsburgh, PA: University of Pittsburgh Press, 1988.

Criss, Nur Bilge. "Strategic Nuclear Missiles in Turkey: The Jupiter Affair, 1959–1963." *Journal of Strategic Studies* 20/3 (1997): 97–122.

Crosbie, Sylvia Kowitt *A Tacit Alliance: France and Israel from Suez to the Six-Day War*. Princeton, NJ: Princeton University Press, 1974.

Crossman, Richard. *The Diaries of a Cabinet Minister*. Vol. 2. London: Hamilton: Cape, 1976.

Crystal, Jill. *Oil and Politics in the Gulf*. Cambridge University Press, 1990.

Daly, M. W. *Empire on the Nile: The Anglo-Egyptian Sudan, 1898–1934*. Cambridge and New York: Cambridge University Press, 1986.

Damis, John. "Morocco's 1995 Association Agreement with the European Union." *Journal of North African Studies* 4 (Winter 1998): 391–412.

Danspeckgruber, Wolfgang, and Charles R. H. Tripp, eds. *The Iraqi Aggression against Kuwait: Strategic Lessons and Implications for Europe*. Boulder, CO: Westview, 1996.

Darby, Phillip. *British Defence Policy East of Suez, 1947–1968*. London: Oxford University Press, 1973.

Darwin, John. *Britain and Decolonisation: The Retreat from Empire in the Post-War World*. Houndmills, Basingstoke: Macmillan, 1988.

David, Stephen R. "Explaining Third World Alliances." *World Politics* 43/2 (1991): 233–56.

Davison, Roderic. "Where Is the Middle East?" *Foreign Affairs* 38/4 (July 1960): 665–75.

Dawisha, Adeed, and Karen Dawisha, eds. *The Soviet Union in the Middle East*. New York: Published by Holmes & Meier Publishers for the Royal Institute of International Affairs, 1982.

Dawisha, Karen. *Soviet Foreign Policy toward Egypt*. London: Macmillan, 1979.

Dawn, C. Ernest. "The Egyptian Remilitarization of the Sinai, May 1967." *Journal of Contemporary History* 3 (July 1968): 201–44.

Deeb, Mary-Jane. "Inter-Maghribi Relations since 1969: A Study of the Modalities of Unions and Mergers." *Middle East Journal* 43/1 (Winter 1989): 20–33.

Deringil, Selim. *Turkish Foreign Policy during the Second World War*. Cambridge: Cambridge University Press, 1989.

Dessouki, Ali E. Hillal. "The Primacy of Economics: The Foreign Policy of Egypt." In Korany and Dessouki (1991), pp. 156–87.

Devlin, John F. *Syria: Modern State in an Ancient Land*. Boulder, CO: Westview, 1983.

Doran, Michael. *Pan-Arabism before Nasser: Egyptian Power Politics and the Palestine Question*. New York and Oxford: Oxford University Press, 1999.

Dowty, Alan. *Middle East Crisis: U.S. Decision-Making in 1958, 1970, and 1973*. Berkeley and Los Angeles, CA: University of California Press, 1984.

Drysdale, Alasdair, and Gerald H. Blake. *The Middle East and North Africa: A Political Geography.* New York: Oxford University Press, 1985.

Drysdale, Alasdair, and Raymond A. Hinnebusch. *Syria and the Middle East Peace Process.* New York: Council on Foreign Relations Press, 1991.

Dutton, David. *Anthony Eden: A Life and Reputation.* New York: Arnold, 1996.

Economist Intelligence Unit. *Quarterly Economic Report, Syria and Jordan.* No. 3 (1983).

Efrat, Moshe, and Jacob Bercovitch, eds. *Superpowers and Client States in the Middle East: The Imbalance of Influence.* London: Routledge, 1991.

El Husseini, Mahrez Mahmoud. *Soviet-Egyptian Relations, 1945–1985.* Houndsmills, Basingstoke, Hampshire: Macmillan, 1987.

Entelis, John P. *Algeria: The Revolution Institutionalized.* Boulder, CO: Westview, 1986.

Evans, Peter B., Dietrich Rueschemeyer, and Theda Skocpol, eds. *Bringing the State Back In.* Cambridge and New York: Cambridge University Press, 1985.

Eytan, Walter. *The First Ten Years: A Diplomatic History of Israel.* New York: Simon and Schuster, 1958.

Fahmy, Ismail. *Negotiating for Peace in the Middle East.* London: Croom Helm, 1983.

Farouk-Sluglett, Marion, and Peter Sluglett. *Iraq since 1958: From Revolution to Dictatorship.* London: KPI, 1987.

al-Farsy, Fouad. *Modernity and Tradition: The Saudi Equation.* London and New York: Kegan Paul International, 1990.

Federation of Jordanian Chambers of Commerce. Annual reports, selected years.

Fitzsimmons, M. A. *Empire by Treaty: Britain and the Middle East in the Twentieth Century.* Notre Dame, IN: University of Notre Dame Press, 1964.

Freedman, Lawrence, and Efraim Karsh. *The Gulf Conflict 1990–1991: Diplomacy and War in the New World Order.* Princeton, NJ: Princeton University Press, 1993.

Freedman, Robert O. *Soviet Policy toward the Middle East since 1970.* 2nd. ed. New York: Praeger, 1978.

Freiberger, Steven Z. *Dawn over Suez: The Rise of American Power in the Middle East, 1955–1981.* Chicago: I.R. Dee, 1992.

Fromkin, David. *A Peace to End All Peace: Creating the Modern Middle East, 1914–1924.* New York: Henry Holt, 1989.

al-Fukaiki, Hani. *Awkar al-Hazimah* (The Nests of Defeat). 2nd ed. Beirut, Lebanon: Riad El-Rayyes Books, 1997.

Fuller, Graham E. "The Middle East in US-Soviet Relations." *Middle East Journal* 44/3 (Summer 1990): 417–30.

Fuller, William C., Jr. *Strategy and Power in Russia 1600–1914.* New York: Free Press, 1992.

Gandy, Christopher. "A Mission to Yemen: August 1962–January 1963." *British Journal of Middle Eastern Studies* 25/2 (1998): 247–74.

Gareyev, General M. A. "Some Questions of Military Organizational Development." *Vooruzheniye, politika, konversiya.* Translated in Foreign Broadcast Information Service, FBIS-UMA-96-198-S, pp. 39–46.

Gause, F. Gregory III. *Saudi-Yemeni Relations, Domestic Structures and Foreign Influence.* New York: Columbia University Press, 1990.

Gendzier, Irene L. *Notes from the Minefield: United States Intervention in Lebanon and the Middle East, 1945–1958.* New York: Columbia University Press, 1997.

George, Stephen. *An Awkward Partner: Britain in the European Community.* New York and Oxford: Oxford University Press, 1990.

Gerges, Fawaz. *The Superpowers and the Middle East: Regional and International Politics, 1955–1967.* Boulder, CO: Westview, 1994.

Gillespie, Kate, and Clement Moore Henry, eds. *Oil in the New World Order.* Gainesville, FL: University Press of Florida, 1995.

Ginat, Rami, "British Concoction or Bilateral Decision? Revisiting the Genesis of Soviet-Egyptian Diplomatic Relations," *International Journal of Middle Eastern Studies*, 31/1 (February 1999): 39–60.

———. *The Soviet Union and Egypt, 1945–1955.* London: Frank Cass, 1993.

Golan, Galia. *Moscow and the Middle East: New Thinking on Regional Conflict.* London: Pinter Publishers for the Royal Institute of International Affairs, 1992.

———. *Soviet Middle East Policy under Gorbachev.* Santa Monica, CA: Rand/UCLA Center for Soviet Studies, 1990.

———. *Soviet Policies in the Middle East from World War Two to Gorbachev.* Cambridge and New York: Cambridge University Press, 1990.

———. *Yom Kippur and After: The Soviet Union and the Middle East Crisis.* Cambridge and New York: Cambridge University Press, 1977.

Goldberg, Jacob. *The Foreign Policy of Saudi Arabia: The Formative Years, 1902–1918.* Cambridge, MA: Harvard University Press, 1986.

Gordon, David C. *The Republic of Lebanon: Nation in Jeopardy*. Boulder, CO: Westview, 1983.

Gordon, Michael R., and Bernard E. Trainor. *The Generals' War: The Inside Story of the Conflict in the Gulf*. Boston: Little, Brown and Company, 1995.

Goriainov, S. *Bosfor I Dardenelly*. St. Petersburg, Russia: Tip. I. N. Skorokhodova, 1907.

Grafftey-Smith, Laurence. *Bright Levant*. London: John Murray, 1970.

Graham-Brown, Sarah. *Sanctioning Saddam: The Politics of Intervention in Iraq*. London: I. B. Tauris, 1999.

Grimaud, Nicole. *La Politique exterieure de l'Algerie*. Paris: Editions Karthala, 1984.

———. *La Tunisie à la recherche de sa securité*. Paris: Presses universitaires de France, 1995.

Grose, Peter. *Gentleman Spy: The Life of Allen Dulles*. Boston: Houghton Mifflin, 1994.

———. *Israel in the Mind of America*. New York: Schocken Books, 1984.

Gubser, Peter. *Jordan: Crossroads of Middle Eastern Events*. Boulder, CO: Westview 1983.

Hahn, Peter L. *The United States, Great Britain, and Egypt, 1945–1956*. Chapel Hill, NC: University of North Carolina Press, 1991.

al-Hakim, Tawfiq. *The Return of Consciousness*. Translated by R. Bayly Winder. New York: New York University Press, 1985.

Halliday, Fred. *Revolution and Foreign Policy: The Case of South Yemen, 1967–1987*. Cambridge and New York: Cambridge University Press, 1990.

Hamrush, Ahmad. *Mujtama` Jamal `Abd al-Nasir*. Cairo: Madbuli, 1983.

Harik, Iliya. "The Origins of the Arab State System." In Salamé, *The Foundations of the Arab State*, pp. 19–46.

Harkabi, Yehoshafat. *Fedayeen Action and Arab Strategy*. Adelphi Papers No. 53. London, 1968.

Harris, George S. *Troubled Alliance: Turkish-American Problems in Historical Perspective, 1945–1971*. Washington, D.C: American Enterprise Institute, 1972.

———. *Turkey: Coping with Crisis*. Boulder, CO: Westview, 1985.

Harris, Kenneth. *Attlee*. London: Weidenfeld and Nicolson, 1982.

Harris, Lillian Craig. *Libya: Qadhafi and the Green Revolution*. Boulder, CO: Westview 1986.

Hart, Parker T. *Two NATO Allies at the Threshold of War: Cyprus, a Firsthand Account of Crisis Management, 1965–1968*. Durham, NC: Duke University Press, 1990.

——. *The United States and Saudi Arabia: Birth of a Security Partnership*. Bloomington, IN: University Press, 1998.

al-Hashimi, Taha. *Mudhakkirat Taha al-Hashimi* (Memoirs of Taha al-Hashimi). Vol. 2 Beirut: Dar al-Tali`ah, 1967–1978.

Hashimite Kingdom of Jordan. Ministry of Trade. *Majmu`at al-Ittifaqiyyat al-Iqtisadiyyah w-al-Tijar-iyyah bayna al-Mamlakah al-Urdunniyyah al-Hashimiyyah w-al-Duwal al-`Arabiyyah* (Compilation of Economic and Trade Agreements between the Hashimite Kingdom of Jordan and the Arab States). Vol. 1. Amman, 1985.

Hashimite Kingdom of Jordan. Statistical abstract, selected years.

Hassan II. *Discours et interviews 3 mars 1978–3 mars 1979*. Rabat: Ministère de l'Information, Royaume du Maroc, 1980.

Haykal, Muhammad Hasanayn. *1967-al-Infijar* (The Explosion of 1967). Cairo: Al Ahram Press, 1990.

Helms, Christine Moss. *The Cohesion of Saudi Arabia*. Baltimore, MD: Johns Hopkins University Press, 1981.

Herzl, Theodor. *The Jewish State*. In Bernard Reich, ed., *Arab-Israeli Conflict and Conciliation: A Documentary History*. Westport, CT, and London: Greenwood Press, 1995.

Holland, Robert F. *Britain and the Revolt in Cyprus, 1954–1959*. New York and Oxford: Oxford University Press, 1998.

Hollis, Rosemary. "Great Britain." In Bernard Reich, ed., *The Powers in the Middle East: The Ultimate Strategic Arena*. New York: Praeger, 1987, pp. 179–225.

Horne, Alistair. *Macmillan*. 2 vols. London: Macmillan, 1988–1989.

Hurewitz, J. C., ed., *The Middle East and North Africa in World Politics: A Documentary Record*. Vol. 2, *British-French Supremacy, 1914–1945*. New Haven: Yale University Press, 1979.

——, ed., *Soviet-American Rivalry in the Middle East*. New York: Published for the Academy of Political Science, Columbia University, by Praeger, 1969.

Hurriyet. "Filistin'i Taniyan Ilk NATO Ülkesiyiz" (We Are the First Country to Recognize Palestine). November 16, 1988.

Ikenberry, John G., David A. Lake, and Michael Mastanduno. "Introduction: Approaches to Explaining American Foreign Economic Policy." *International Organization* 42/1 (1988):1–14.

Ionides, Michael. *Divide and Lose: The Arab Revolt of 1955–1958*. London: G. Bles, 1960.

Iraq. General Statistical Organization. *Annual Abstract of Statistics*, various years.

Ismael, Tariq Y. *International Relations of the Contemporary Middle East: A Study in World Politics*. Syracuse, NY: Syracuse University Press, 1986.

———. "The Middle East: A Subordinate System in Global Politics." In Tariq Y. Ismael, ed., *The Middle East in World Politics*. Syracuse, NY: Syracuse University Press, 1974, pp. 240–56.

Izady, Mehrdad R. *The Kurds*. Washington, D.C: Crane Russak, 1992.

Jentleson, Bruce. *With Friends Like These: Reagan, Bush, and Saddam, 1982–1990*. New York: W. W. Norton and Company, 1994.

Jones, Clive. "Saudi Arabia after the Gulf War: The Internal-External Security Dilemma." *International Relations* 12/6 (December 1995): 31–52.

———. "The Security of Arab Gulf States and the End of the Cold War." In M. Jane Davis, ed., *Security Issues in the Post-Cold War World*. Brookfield, VT: Edward Elgar, 1996, pp. 73–98.

Jones, Clive, and John Stone. "Britain and the Arabian Gulf: New Perspectives on Strategic Influence." *International Relations* 13/4 (April 1997): 1–24.

Joyce, Miriam. "Preserving the Sheikhdom: London, Washington, Iraq and Kuwait, 1958–61." *Middle Eastern Studies* 31/2 (April 1995): 281–92.

Julien, Charles-André. *L'Afrique du Nord en marche: Nationalismes musulmans et souveraineté française*. Paris: R. Julliard, 1952; 4th ed., 1972.

———. *Et la Tunisie devint independent, 1951–1957*. Paris: Editions Jeune Afrique, 1985.

Kandemir, Feridun. *Siyasi Dargınlıklar: Atatük-İnönü, İnönü-Mareğal Dargınlığı* (Political Disputations: Disputes between Ataturk and Inonu, between Inonu and the Marshal). Vol. 6. Istanbul, 1955.

Karsh, Efraim, ed. *The Iran-Iraq War: Impact and Implications*. London: Macmillan in association with the Jaffee Center for Strategic Studies, Tel Aviv University, 1989.

———. *The Soviet Union and Syria: The Asad Years*. London: Royal Institute of International Affairs; New York: Routledge, 1988.

Karsh, Efraim, and Inari Karsh. *Empires of the Sand: The Struggle for Mastery in the Middle East, 1789–1923*. Cambridge, MA: Harvard University Press, 1999.

Kaufman, Burton I. *The Arab Middle East and the United States: Inter-Arab Rivalry and Superpower Diplomacy*. New York: Twayne Publishers, 1996.

Kautilya. *Arthasastra*. Translated by R. Shamasastry. Mysore, 1960.

Kazemzadeh, Firuz. "Russia and the Middle East." In Ivo J. Lederer, ed., *Russian Foreign Policy*. New Haven, CT: Yale University Press, 1962, pp. 489–530.

Kechichian, Joseph. "Trends in Saudi National Security." *Middle East Journal* 53/2 (Spring 1999): 232–53.

Kedourie, Elie. *Arabic Political Memoirs and Other Studies*. London: Frank Cass, 1974.

———. *The Chatham House Version and Other Middle Eastern Studies*. London: Weidenfeld and Nicolson, 1970; reissued University Press of New England, 1984.

———. *England and the Middle East*. London: Bowes and Bowes, 1956.

———. *In the Anglo-Arab Labyrinth*. Cambridge and New York: Cambridge University Press, 1976.

———. *Islam in the Modern World and Other Studies*. New York: Holt, Rinehart & Winston, 1980.

Kelling, George Horton. *Countdown to Rebellion: British Policy in Cyprus, 1939–1955*. New York: Greenwood Press, 1990.

Kelly, J. B. *Arabia, the Gulf, and the West*. London: Weidenfeld and Nicolson, 1980.

———. *Eastern Arabian Frontiers*. New York: Praeger, 1964.

Kemp, Geoffrey. "Lessons of Lebanon: A Guideline for Future U.S. Policy." *Middle East Insight* 6 (Summer 1988): 57–68.

Kemp, Geoffrey, and Robert E. Harkavy. *Strategic Geography and the Changing Middle East*. Washington, DC: Brookings Institution Press, 1997.

Kent, John, ed. *Egypt and the Defence of the Middle East*. 3 vols. London: Stationery Office, 1998.

Kerr, Malcolm. *The Arab Cold War: Gamal `Abd al-Nasir and His Rivals, 1958–1970*. 3rd ed. New York and Oxford: Oxford University Press, 1971.

Khadduri, Majid. *The Gulf War: The Origins and Implications of the Iraq-Iran Conflict*. New York: Oxford University Press, 1988.

al-Khafaji, Isam "War as a Vehicle for the Rise and Demise of a State Controlled Society." Middle East Paper 4. University of Amsterdam Research Centre for International Political Economy and Foreign Policy Analysis, 1995.

Kissinger, Henry. *White House Years*. Boston: Little, Brown & Co., 1979.

———. *Years of Upheaval*. Boston: Little, Brown & Co., 1982.

Korany, Bahgat. "Alien and Besieged but Here to Stay: The Contradictions of the Arab Territorial State." In Salamé, *Foundations of the Arab State* (1987), pp. 47–74.

Korany, Bahgat, and Ali E. Hillal Dessouki. *The Foreign Policies of Arab States: The Challenge of Change*. 2nd rev. ed. Boulder, CO: Westview, 1991.

Korn, David. "Don't Deal with Dictators." *Christian Science Monitor* January 25, 1990.

——. *Stalemate: The War of Attrition and Great Power Diplomacy in the Middle East, 1967–1970.* Boulder, CO: Westview, 1992.

Kostiner, Joseph. *The Making of Saudi Arabia.* New York: Oxford University Press, 1993.

Kramer, Heinz. *A Changing Turkey: The Challenge to Europe and the United States.* Washington, DC.: Brookings Institution Press, 2000.

Kuniholm, Bruce R. *The Origins of the Cold War in the Near East: Great Power Conflict and Diplomacy in Iran, Turkey, and Greece.* Princeton, NJ: Princeton University Press, 1980.

Kupchan, Charles A. "American Globalism in the Middle East: The Roots of Regional Security Policy." *Political Science Quarterly* 103 (Winter 1988–1989): 586–611.

Kyle, Keith. *Suez.* London: Weidenfeld and Nicolson, 1991.

Langer, William L. *The Diplomacy of Imperialism, 1890–1912.* New York: Knopf, 1951.

——. *European Alliances and Alignments, 1871–1899.* New York: A. A. Knopf, 1956.

Laqueur, Walter. *The Soviet Union and the Middle East.* New York: Praeger, 1959.

Laurens, Henry. *Les Origines intellectuelles de l'expédition d'Egypte: L'Orientalisme islamisant en France (1698–1798).* Istanbul and Paris: Editions Isis, 1987.

——. *Le Royaume impossible: La France et la genèse du monde arabe.* Paris: A. Colin, 1990.

Lawson, Fred. *Bahrain: The Modernization of Autocracy.* Boulder, CO: Westview, 1989.

Leatherdale, Clive. *Britain and Saudi Arabia, 1925–1939.* London: Frank Cass, 1983.

Lebow, Richard Ned, and Janice Gross Stein. *We All Lost the Cold War.* Princeton, NJ: Princeton University Press, 1994.

Lenczowski, George. *American Presidents and the Middle East.* Durham, NC: Duke University Press, 1990.

——. *The Middle East in World Affairs.* 4th ed. Ithaca, NY: Cornell University Press, 1980.

——. *Russia and the West in Iran, 1918–1948: A Study in Big Power Rivalry.* Ithaca, NY: Cornell University Press, 1949.

Lesch, David, ed. *The Middle East and the United States: A Historical and Political Reassessment.* Boulder, CO: Westview, 1996.

Leveau, Rémy. "La Mediterranée dans la politique française." *Etudes* 367/3 (September 1987): 149–62.

——. "Le Moyen Orient." In Françoise de la Serre, Jacques Leruez, and Helen Wallace, eds. *Les Politiques étrangères de la France et de la Grande-Bretagne depuis 1945: L'Inevitable ajustement*. Paris: Centre d'Etudes et de Recherches Internationales, 1990.

Levey, Zach. *Israel and the Western Powers, 1952–1960*. Chapel Hill, NC: University of North Carolina Press, 1997.

Levy, Walter. *Oil Strategy and Politics, 1941–1981*. Boulder, CO: Westview, 1982.

Limbert, John. *Iran: At War with History*. Boulder, CO: Westview, 1987.

Lippman, Walter. *U.S. Foreign Policy: Shield of the Republic*. Boston: Little, Brown & Co., 1943.

Little, Douglas. "Gideon's Band: America and the Middle East since 1945." *Diplomatic History* 18/4 (Fall 1994): 513–40.

Long, David, E. *The Hajj Today*. Albany, NY: State University of New York Press, 1979.

——. *The United States and Saudi Arabia: Ambivalent Allies*. Boulder, CO: Westview, 1985.

Louis, Wm. Roger, *The British Empire in the Middle East, 1945–1951: Arab Nationalism, the United States and Postwar Imperialism*. Oxford: Oxford University Press, 1984.

——. "Churchill and Egypt." In Robert Blake and Wm. Roger Louis, eds., *Churchill*. New York: W. W. Norton, 1993, pp. 473–90.

——. "Libyan Independence, 1951: The Creation of a Client State." In Prosser Gifford and Wm. Roger Louis, eds., *Decolonization and African Independence: The Transfers of Power, 1960–1980*. New Haven, CT: Yale University Press, 1988, pp. 159–84.

Louis, Wm. Roger, and Roger Owen, eds. *Suez 1956: The Crisis and Its Consequences*. Oxford: Oxford University Press, 1989.

Louis, Wm. Roger, and Robert W. Stookey, eds. *The End of the Palestine Mandate*. Austin, TX: University of Texas Press, 1986.

Lucas, W. Scott. *Divided We Stand: Britain, the US and the Suez Crisis*. London: Hodder & Stoughton, 1991.

Luciani, Giacomo, "Allocation vs. Production States." In Luciani, ed., *The Arab State*. Berkeley and Los Angeles, CA: University of California Press, 1990, pp. 65–84.

Lutfi al-Sayyid-Marsot, Afaf. *Egypt and Cromer: A Study in Anglo-Egyptian Relations*. London: John Murray, 1968.

Luttwak, Edward N. "Cubans in Arabia?" *Commentary* 68/6 (December 1979): 62–68.

el-Machat, Samya. *Les Etats-Unis et la Tunisie: De l'ambiguïté à l'entente, 1945–1959*. Paris: L'Harmattan, 1996.

Maclean, Fitzroy. *A Person from England, and Other Travellers*. New York: Harper, 1958.

Macmillan, Harold. *At the End of the Day, 1961–1963*. London: Macmillan, 1973.

———. *Riding the Storm, 1956–1959*. London: Macmillan, 1971.

Mahan, Captain Alfred Thayer. "The Persian Gulf and International Relations." *National Review* (London), September 1902, pp. 26–45.

Makiya, Kanan. *Cruelty and Silence*. New York: W. W. Norton, 1993.

———. (Samir al-Khalil). *The Republic of Fear*. Berkeley and Los Angeles, CA: University of California Press, 1989.

Marlowe, John. *Arab Nationalism and British Imperialism*. London: Cresset Press, 1961.

Marr, Phebe. "Iraq in the 90s: Oil Revenues, Debt Management, Spending Priorities." *Middle East Executive Reports*. Washington, DC., June 1990.

———. "Iraq's Leadership Dilemma." *Middle East Journal* 24/3 (Summer 1970): 283–301.

———. "Iraq's Uncertain Future." *Current History* 90 (January 1991): 1–4.

———. *The Modern History of Iraq*. Boulder, CO: Westview, 1985.

———. "Turkey and Iraq." In Henri Barkey, ed., *Reluctant Neighbor: Turkey's Role in the Middle East*. Washington, DC: United States Institute of Peace Press, 1996.

Mastny, Vojtech, and R. Craig Nation, eds. *Turkey between East and West: New Challenges for a Rising Regional Power*. Boulder, CO: Westview, 1996.

Matar, Fuad. *Saddam Husain, the Man, the Cause, the Future*. London: Third World Centre, 1981.

Mayall, Simon. *Turkey: Thwarted Ambition*. Washington, DC: Institute for National Strategic Studies, National Defense University, 1997.

McDonald, Iverach. *The History of The Times*. Vol. 5, *Struggles in War and Peace, 1939–66*. London: The Times, 1984.

McDowall, David. "The Kurds: A Historical Background." Special Report. *Britannica Book of the Year* 1992, pp. 375–76.

———. *A Modern History of the Kurds*. London: I.B.Tauris; New York: St. Martin's Press, 1996.

McLaurin, R. D., Mohammed Mughisuddin, and Abraham R. Wagner. *Foreign Policy Making in the Middle East: Domestic Influence on Policy in Egypt, Iraq, Israel and Syria*. New York: Praeger, 1977.

Meital, Yoram. *Egypt's Struggle for Peace*. Gainesville, FL: University Press of Florida, 1997.

Menashri, David, ed. *Central Asia Meets the Middle East*. London: Frank Cass, 1998.

Miller, Aaron David. *Search for Security: Saudi Arabian Oil and American Foreign Policy, 1939–1949*. Chapel Hill, NC: University of North Carolina Press, 1980.

Milner, Helen. "International Theories of Cooperation among Nations: Strengths and Weaknesses." *World Politics* 44/3 (1992): 466–96.

Mitchell, Timothy. *Colonising Egypt*. Cambridge and New York: Cambridge University Press, 1988.

Mohsen-Finan, Khadija. *Sahara Occidental: Les enjeux d'un Conflit Régional*. Paris: CNRS Editions, 1997.

Monroe, Elizabeth. *Britain's Moment in the Middle East, 1914–1956*. Baltimore, MD: Johns Hopkins University Press, 1963.

Moore, Clement Henry. *Tunisia since Independence: The Dynamics of One-Party Government*. Berkeley and Los Angeles, CA: University of California Press, 1965.

Morris, Benny. *Israel's Border Wars 1949–1956*. Oxford and New York: Oxford University Press, 1993.

——. *Righteous Victims: A History of the Zionist-Arab Conflict, 1881–1999*. London: John Murray, 2000.

Mosley, Leonard. *Power Play: Oil in the Middle East*. London: Weidenfeld and Nicolson, 1973.

Mufti, Malik. *Sovereign Creations*. Ithaca, NY: Cornell University Press, 1996.

Muhyi al-Din, Khalid. *Wa al-an atakallim* (Now I Speak). Cairo: Markaz al-Ahram lil-Tarjamah wa-al-Nashr, Muassasat al-Ahram, 1992.

Mütercimler, Erol. *21. Yüzyıl ve Türkiye "Yüksek Strateji"* (Turkey and the 21st Century: "The Grand Strategy"). Istanbul: Erciyas Yayınları, 1997.

——. "Erbakan'dan Gizli Diplomasiye Devam" (Continuation of Secret Diplomacy since Erbakan). *Milliyet*, August 9, 1996.

Naff, Thomas, and Ruth C. Matson. *Water in the Middle East: Conflict or Cooperation*. Boulder, CO: Westview, 1984.

Noble, Paul. "The Arab System: Pressures, Constraints, and Opportunities." In Korany and Dessouki, *Foreign Policies* (1991), pp. 49–102.

Ovendale, Ritchie. *British Defence Policy since 1945*. Manchester: Manchester University Press, 1994.

——. *The Middle East since 1914*. London: Longman, 1992.

Parker, Richard B., ed. *The October War: A Retrospective*. Gainesville, FL: University Press of Florida, forthcoming winter 2001.

——, ed. *The Six-Day War: A Restropective*. Gainesville, FL: University Press of Florida, 1996.

Peck, Malcolm C. *The United Arab Emirates: A Venture in Unity*. Boulder, CO: Westview, 1986.

Pelcovits, Nathan A. *The Long Armistice: UN Peacekeeping and the Arab-Israeli Conflict, 1948–1960*. Boulder, CO: Westview, 1993.

Pelletiere, Stephen C. *The Iran-Iraq War: Chaos in a Vacuum*. New York: Praeger, 1992.

Penrose, Edith, and E. F. Penrose. *Iraq: International Relations and National Development*. London: Ernest Benn, 1978.

Perkins, Kenneth J. *Tunisia: Crossroads of the Islamic and European Worlds*. Boulder, CO: Westview, 1986.

Peterson, J. E. *Defending Arabia*. London: Croom Helm, 1986.

Podeh, Elie. *The Quest for Hegemony in the Arab World: The Struggle over the Baghdad Pact*. Leiden and New York: E. J. Brill, 1995.

Porath, Yehoshua. *In Search of Arab Unity*. London: Frank Cass, 1986.

Pranger, Robert J. "The Dimensions of American Foreign Policy in the Middle East." In Peter J. Chelkowski and Robert J. Pranger, eds., *Ideology and Power in the Middle East: Studies in Honor of George Lenczowski*. Durham, NC: Duke University Press, 1988, pp. 433–54.

Primakov, E. M. "200 Years of A.M. Gorchakov: Russia in World Politics." *Mezhdunarodnaya Zhizn'* No. 6 (June 1998): 3–9.

Quandt, William B. *Camp David: Peacemaking and Politics*. Washington, DC: Brookings Institution Press, 1986.

——. *Peace Process: American Diplomacy and the Arab-Israeli Conflict since 1967*. Washington, DC: Brookings Institution Press, 1993.

——. *Saudi Arabia in the 1980s: Foreign Policy, Security and Oil*. Washington, DC: Brookings Institution Press, 1981.

Rafael, Gideon. *Destination Peace: Three Decades of Israeli Foreign Policy*. New York: Stein and Day, 1981.

Rajaee, Farhang, ed. *The Iran-Iraq War: The Politics of Aggression.* Gainesville, FL: University Press of Florida, 1993.

Ramazani, Rouhallah K. *The Foreign Policy of Iran, 1500–1941: A Developing Nation in World Affairs.* Charlottesville, VA: University of Virginia Press, 1966.

———. *Iran's Foreign Policy, 1941–1973: A Study of Foreign Policy in Modernizing Nations.* Charlottesville, VA: University of Virginia Press, 1975.

———. "Iran's Foreign Policy: Contending Orientations." *Middle East Journal* 43/2 (Spring 1989): 202–17.

———. *Revolutionary Iran: Challenge and Response in the Middle East.* Baltimore, MD: Johns Hopkins University Press, 1986.

Reddaway, John. *Burdened with Cyprus: The British Connection.* London: Weidenfeld and Nicolson, 1986.

Reich, Bernard, ed. *Arab-Israeli Conflict and Conciliation: A Documentary History.* Westport, CT: Greenwood Press, 1995.

———. *Israel: Land of Tradition and Conflict.* Boulder, CO: Westview, 1985.

———. *Quest for Peace: United States-Israel Relations and the Arab-Israeli Conflict.* New Brunswick, NJ: Transaction Books, 1977.

———. *Securing the Covenant: United States-Israel Relations after the Cold War.* Westport, CT: Greenwood Press, 1995.

———. *The United States and Israel: Influence in the Special Relationship.* New York: Praeger, 1984.

Riad, Mahmoud. *The Struggle for Peace in the Middle East.* New York: Quartet Books, 1981.

Rieber, Alfred J. *The Politics of Autocracy: Letters of Alexander II to Prince A. I. Bariatinskii 1857–1864.* Paris: Mouton, 1966.

Roosevelt, Kermit. *Countercoup: The Struggle for Control of Iran.* New York: McGraw-Hill, 1979.

Rubin, Barry. *The Great Powers in the Middle East, 1941–1947: The Road to the Cold War.* London: Frank Cass, 1980.

———. *Paved with Good Intentions: The American Experience and Iran.* New York and Oxford: Oxford University Press, 1980.

Rubinstein, Alvin Z. *Moscow's Third World Strategy.* Princeton, NJ: Princeton University Press, 1988.

———. *Red Star on the Nile: The Soviet-Egyptian Influence Relationship since the June War.* Princeton, NJ: Princeton University Press, 1977.

Ruedy, John. *Modern Algeria: The Origins and Development of a Nation.* Bloomington, IN: Indiana University Press, 1992.

Ruf, Werner K. "La Politique étrangère des états maghrebins." In W. K. Ruf et al., *Introduction à l'Afrique du Nord contemporaine.* Paris: Centre National de la Recherche Scientifique, 1975.

Rustow, Dankwart A. *Turkey: America's Forgotten Ally.* New York: Council on Foreign Relations, 1987.

Sachar, Howard M. *The Emergence of the Middle East, 1914–1924.* New York: Alfred A. Knopf, 1969.

———. *Europe Leaves the Middle East, 1936–1954.* New York: Alfred A. Knopf, 1972.

Sa'd, Jamal. *The Problem of Mauritania.* Arab Information Center, Information paper no. 4. New York, 1960.

Safran, Nadav. *From War to War: The Arab-Israeli Confrontation, 1948–1967.* New York: Pegasus, 1969.

———. *Israel: the Embattled Ally.* Cambridge, MA: Harvard University Press, 1978.

———. *Saudi Arabia: The Ceaseless Quest for Security.* Cambridge, MA: Harvard University Press, 1985.

Sa`id, Ali Karim, *'Iraq 8 Shabat 1963* (The Iraq of February 8, 1963). Adabiyya, 1999.

Salamé, Ghassan, ed. *The Foundations of the Arab State.* London: Croom Helm, 1987.

Salibi, Kamal S. *The Modern History of Jordan.* London: I. B. Tauris; New York: St. Martin's Press, 1993.

———. *The Modern History of Lebanon.* London: Weidenfeld and Nicolson, 1965.

al-Samarra'i, Wafiq. *Hatam al-Bawabah-l-Sharqiyyah* (Wreckage of the Eastern Gate). Kuwait: Dar al-Qabas lil-Sahafah wal-Nashr, 1997.

Sayari, Sabri. "Turkey: The Changing European Security Environment and the Gulf Crisis." *Middle East Journal* 48/1 (Winter 1992): 9–21.

Sayed-Ahmed, Muhammad Abd el-Wahab. *Nasser and American Foreign Policy, 1952–1956.* Cairo: American University in Cairo Press, 1989.

Sayigh, Yezid. *Armed Struggle and the Search for State: The Palestinian National Movement, 1949–1993.* New York and Oxford: Oxford University Press, 1997.

Schiff, Ze'ev, and Ehud Ya'ari. *Israel's Lebanon War.* New York: Simon & Schuster, 1984.

Schoenbaum, David. *The United States and the State of Israel.* New York and Oxford: Oxford University Press, 1993.

Schwarzkopf, General H. Norman, with Peter Petre. *The Autobiography: It Doesn't Take a Hero*. New York: Bantam Books, 1992.

Seale, Patrick. *Asad of Syria: The Struggle for the Middle East*. Berkeley and Los Angeles, CA: University of California Press, 1988.

——. *The Struggle for Syria: A Study in Post-War Arab Politics, 1945–1959*. Oxford University Press, 1965; reissued New Haven: Yale University Press, 1986.

Sela, Avraham. *The Decline of the Arab-Israeli Conflict: Middle East Politics and the Quest for Regional Order*. Albany, NY: State University of New York Press, 1998.

Shamir, Shimon. "Basic Dilemmas of the Mubarak Regime." *Orbis* 30/1 (Spring 1986): 169–92.

——. "The Collapse of Project Alpha." In Wm. Roger Louis and Roger Owen, eds., *Suez 1956*. New York and Oxford: Oxford University Press, 1989, pp. 73–100.

Sheehan, Edward R. F. *The Arabs, Israelis, and Kissinger: A Secret History of American Diplomacy in the Middle East*. New York: Reader's Digest Press, 1976.

Shimoni, Yaacov. "Israel in the Pattern of Middle East Politics." *Middle East Journal* 4/3 (July 1950): 277–95.

Shlaim, Avi. *Collusion across the Jordan*. New York and Oxford: Oxford University Press, 1988.

——. *The Iron Wall: Israel and the Arab World since 1948*. New York: W. W. Norton, 2000.

——. *The Politics of Partition: King Abdullah, the Zionists and Palestine, 1921–1951*. New York: Columbia University Press, 1990.

——. *War and Peace in the Middle East: A Concise History*. New York: Whittle Books in association with Viking, 1994.

Shorrock, William. *French Imperialism in the Middle East: The Failure of Policy in Syria and Lebanon, 1900–1914*. Madison, WI: University of Wisconsin Press, 1976.

Shuckburgh, Evelyn. *Descent to Suez: Foreign Office Diaries, 1951–1956*. London; New York: W. W. Norton, 1986.

Sick, Gary. *All Fall Down: America's Tragic Encounter with Iran*. New York: Viking/Penguin, 1985.

Silverburg, Sanford R., and Bernard Reich. *U.S. Foreign Relations with the Middle East and North Africa: A Bibliography*. Metuchen, NJ: Scarecrow Press, 1994.

Skeet, Ian. *Muscat and Oman: The End of an Era*. London: Faber and Faber, 1974.

Sluglett, Peter. "Formal and Informal Empire in the Middle East." In Robin Winks, ed., *The Oxford History of the British Empire*. Vol. 5, *Historiography*. New York and Oxford: Oxford University Press, 1999.

———. "Progress Postponed: Iraqi Oil Policy, Past, Present and Future." In Gillespie and Henry, eds., *Oil in the New World Order*, pp. 227–56.

Smolansky, Oles M. "Russia and the Asia-Pacific Region: Policies and Polemics." In Stephen J. Blank and Alvin Z. Rubinstein, eds., *Imperial Decline: Russia's Changing Role in Asia*. Durham, NC: Duke University Press, 1997, pp. 7–39.

———. *The Soviet Union and the Arab East under Khrushchev*. Lewisburg, PA: Bucknell University Press, 1974.

———. *The USSR and Iraq: The Quest for Influence*. Durham, NC: Duke University Press, 1991.

Snyder, Jack. *Myths of Empire: Domestic Politics and International Ambition*. Ithaca, NY: Cornell University Press, 1991.

Soysal, Mümtaz. *Dış Politika ve Parlamento* (Foreign Policy and Parliament). Ankara, 1964.

Spagnolo, John. *France and Ottoman Lebanon, 1861–1914*. London: Ithaca Press for the Middle East Centre, St. Antony's College, Oxford, 1977.

Speiser, E. A. *The United States and the Near East*. Cambridge, MA: Harvard University Press, 1947.

Spiegel, Steven L. *The Other Arab-Israeli Conflict: Making America's Middle Eastern Policy from Truman to Reagan*. Chicago: University of Chicago Press, 1985.

Stein, Kenneth. *Heroic Diplomacy: Sadat, Kissinger, Carter, Begin and the Quest for Arab-Israeli Peace*. New York: Routledge, 1999.

Stocking, George. *Middle East Oil: A Study in Political and Economic Controversy*. Nashville, TN: Vanderbilt University Press, 1970.

Stoff, Michael B. *Oil, War and American Security: The Search for a National Policy on Foreign Oil, 1941–1947*. New Haven, CT: Yale University Press, 1980.

Stookey, Robert W. *America and the Arab States: An Uneasy Encounter*. New York: John Wiley & Sons, 1975.

———. *South Yemen: A Marxist Republic in Arabia*. Boulder, CO: Westview, 1982.

Swearingen, Will, and Abdellatif Bencherifa, eds. *The North African Environment at Risk*. Boulder, CO: Westview, 1996.

Syrian Arab News Agency and Jordanian News Agency. *Masirat al-Takamul bayna Suriya wa-al-Urdunn: 'Ala Darb al-Wahdah* (The March of Integration between Syria and Jordan: On the Path of Unity). Damascus, 1977.

Talbott, John. *The War without a Name: France in Algeria, 1954–1962*. New York: Alfred A. Knopf, 1980.

Talbott, Strobe. "Status Quo Ante: The US and Its Allies." In Joseph S. Nye, Jr., and Roger Smith, eds., *After the Storm: Lessons from the Gulf War*. Queenstown, MD: Aspen Strategy Group; Lanham, MD: Madison Books, 1992, pp. 3–30.

Tanenbaum, Jan Karl. "France and the Arab Middle East, 1914–1920." *Transactions of the American Philosophical Society* 68/7 (October 1978): 1–50.

Taylor, Alan. *The Arab Balance of Power*. Syracuse, NY: Syracuse University Press, 1981.

Tessler, Mark. *A History of the Israeli-Palestinian Conflict*. Bloomington, IN: Indiana University Press, 1994.

———."Moroccan-Israeli Relations and the Reasons for Moroccan Receptivity to Contact with Israel." *Jerusalem Journal of International Relations* 10/2 (1988): 76–108.

Thatcher, Margaret. *The Downing Street Years*. London: HarperCollins, 1993.

Tillman, Seth P. *The United States and the Middle East: Interests and Obstacles*. Bloomington, IN: Indiana University Press, 1982.

Toker, Metin. *Demokrasimizin İsmet Paşa'lı Yılları 1944–1973* (Our Democracy in the Ismet Pasha Years, 1944–1973). 2nd rev. ed. Ankara: Bilgi Yay□nevi, 1992.

Torumtay, Necip. *Orgeneral Torumtay'm Anıları* (Memoirs of General Torumtay). 2nd ed. Istanbul, 1994.

Toynbee, Arnold J. *The Islamic World since the Peace Settlement*. London: Oxford University Press, 1927.

Tripp, Charles. "Iraq." In Yezid Sayigh and Avi Shlaim, eds., *The Cold War and the Middle East*. New York and Oxford: Oxford University Press, 1997, pp. 186–215.

———. "Symbol and Strategy: Iraq and the War for Kuwait." In Wolfgang Danspeckgruber and Charles R. H. Tripp, eds., *The Iraqi Aggression against Kuwait: Strategic Lessons and Implications for Europe*. Boulder, CO: Westview, 1996, pp. 21–38.

Troen, Ilan, and Moshe Shemesh, eds. *The Suez-Sinai Crisis: A Retrospective*. London: F. Cass, 1990.

Twinam, Joseph Wright. *The Gulf, Cooperation, and the Council*. Washington, DC: Middle East Policy Council, 1992.

United States Department of State. *The Foreign Relations of the United States, 1933, Diplomatic Papers*. Vol. 2. Washington, D.C., 1933.

Urquhart, Brian. *Ralph Bunche: An American Life*. New York: W. W. Norton, 1993.

van Dam, Nikolaos. "Middle Eastern Political Clichés: Takriti and Sunni Rule in Iraq: Alawi Rule in Syria." *Orient* (German Journal for Politics and the Middle East) 21/1 (January 1980): 42–57.

Vandewalle, Dirk. *Libya since Independence: Oil and State-Building*. Ithaca, NY: Cornell University Press, 1998.

Vassiliev, Alexei. *Russian Policy in the Middle East: From Messianism to Pragmatism*. Reading: Ithaca Press, 1993.

Vatikiotis, P. J. *The Modern History of Egypt: From Muhammad Ali to Mubarak*. 3rd ed. Baltimore, MD: Johns Hopkins University Press, 1985.

Voll, John Obert, and Sarah Potts Voll. *The Sudan: Unity and Diversity in a Multicultural State*. Boulder, CO: Westview, 1985

Walt, Stephen. *The Origins of Alliances*. Ithaca, NY: Cornell University Press, 1987.

Warburg, Gabriel R. "The Sudan's Path to Independence: Continuity and Change in Egypt's Policy toward the Sudan." In Shimon Shamir, ed., *Egypt from Monarchy to Republic*, Boulder, CO: Westview, 1995, pp. 309–24.

Watt, D. C. "Britain and the Indian Ocean." *Political Quarterly* 42/3 (July–September 1971): 306–15.

———. "The Decision to Withdraw from the Gulf." *Political Quarterly* 39/3 (July–September 1968): 310–21.

Wenner, Manfred. *The Yemen Arab Republic: Development and Change in an Ancient Land*. Boulder, CO: Westview, 1991.

Winder, R. Bayly. *Saudi Arabia in the Nineteenth Century*. London: Macmillan, 1965.

Woodhouse, C. M. *Something Ventured*. London: Granada, 1982.

Wright, Denis. "The Changed Balance of Power in the Persian Gulf." *Asian Affairs* 60/3 (October 1973): 255–62.

Yamani, Shaikh Ahmed Zaki. "Saudi Arabia—Consumer-Producer Understanding." In Paul Tempest, ed., *The Politics of Middle East Oil—The Royaumont Group*. London, Graham & Trotman, 1993, pp. 175–80.

Yapp, Malcolm E. *The Near East since the First World War: A History to 1995*. 2nd ed. London: Longman, 1996.

———, ed. *Politics and Diplomacy in Egypt: The Diaries of Sir Miles Lampson, 1935–1937*. New York and Oxford: Oxford University Press, 1997.

Yergin, Daniel. *The Prize: The Epic Quest for Oil, Money, and Power*. New York: Simon & Schuster, 1991.

Zahlan, Rosemarie Said. *The Making of the Modern Gulf States: Kuwait, Bahrain, Qatar, the United Arab Emirates, and Oman*. London: Ithaca Press, 1998.

Zartman, I. William. "Explaining the Nearly Inexplicable: The Absence of Islam in Moroccan Foreign Policy." In Adeed Dawisha, ed., *Islam in Foreign Policy*. Cambridge and New York: Cambridge University Press, 1983, pp. 97–111.

———. "North African Foreign Policy." In L. Carl Brown, ed., *State and Society in Independent North Africa*. Washington, DC: Middle East Institute, 1966, pp. 41–72.

———. *Ripe for Resolution: Conflict and Intervention in Africa*. New York: Oxford University Press, 1989.

———. "Superpower Cooperation in North Africa and the Horn of Africa." In Roger Kanet and Edward Kolodziej, eds., *The Cold War as Cooperation*. Houndmills; London: Macmillan, 1991.

———. "The Ups and Downs of Maghrib Unity." In Michael Hudson, ed., *Middle East Dilemma: The Politics and Economics of Arab Integration*. New York: Columbia University Press, 1999, pp. 171–86.

Index

353